THE RESURGENT YEARS

1911-1927

Prepared under the Auspices of the
BUSINESS HISTORY FOUNDATION, INC.

w York Times.

THE WEATHER.
Fair to-day; probably fair to-morrow; moderate west winds.
For full weather report see Page 11.

TUESDAY, MAY 16, 1911.—TWENTY-TWO PAGES. ONE CENT In Greater New York, Jersey City, and Newark. | Elsewhere, TWO CENTS.

ANT
RAID
Cap-
king
lls.

TOWN
lans to
Bad

STANDARD OIL COMPANY MUST DISSOLVE IN 6 MONTHS; ONLY UNREASONABLE RESTRAINT OF TRADE FORBIDDEN

HALL CAINE ON THE GREAT AMERICAN NOVEL

Our writers, he says, have only been pioneering so far, and have a big field to draw from. Read it in

Next Sunday's Times

MRS. TAFT BETTER; NO ALARM FELT NOW

President Returns to Washington, Gets Reassuring Telegram, and Goes to Theatre.

WIFE LEAVES THURSDAY

Daughter Will Act in Her Place at White House Social Events for a Time.

Mrs. Taft, whose illness caused the President to return to New York Sunday night to see her at his brother's house, 36 West Forty-eighth Street, was so much improved yesterday morning that the President took an early train for Washington. In the evening, when he received a reassuring telegram, he went to the theatre. The telegram said that Mrs. Taft would return to Washington on Thursday afternoon.

Announcement was made at the White House that the programme which Mrs. Taft has mapped out for the Spring will be adhered to. The dinner to the Fur Seal Commissioners on Thursday night and the garden party Friday evening will be given. Miss Helen Taft, who is now with her mother, will act as mistress of the White House on both occasions.

Dr. Evan W. Evans, Henry W. Taft's family physician, called at the house yesterday morning to see the wife of the President, and remained about half an hour. Mrs. Taft was getting along so nicely that it was not thought necessary to issue a formal bulletin. She is rapidly recovering from her nervous attack.

The President had two callers before he left his brother's house yesterday morning. Henry L. Stimson, who is to join the President's Cabinet as Secretary of War, came to talk over matters connected with his appointment. Mr. Stimson was to have been sworn in as Secretary of War this week, but it was announced yesterday that he would not take the oath until next Monday.

The other caller was Postmaster General Hitchcock, who had been spending the week-end in New York. When he read of Mrs. Taft's illness he drove to the house to inquire about her.

The President, accompanied by Major Butt and Henry W. Taft, came out of the house at 9:40, and entered a waiting automobile. The presence of a squad of police and secret service men outside the door served to attract a small crowd, who cheered when the President came down the steps, smiling broadly as he raised his grey Fedora hat.

The President's automobile was preceded down Fifth Avenue by two bicycle policemen and followed by two automobiles containing detectives and secret service men. The President sat with his brother. At the Pennsylvania station he boarded the private car Ideal, which was attached to the 10:08 train.

PRIEST ARRESTS A BOY.

Crap Player Tried to Strike Father Brann, the Latter Declares.

Father Henry A. Brann of St. Agnes's Church, at 143 East Forty-third Street, was seated at a front window of the rectory yesterday afternoon when he noticed a group of boys playing dice on the sidewalk opposite. He quietly left the building, but five of the lads saw him and ran. Isadore Berkowitz, 15 years old, a telegraph messenger living

And of Such Unreasonable Restraint the Supreme Court Finds the Standard Guilty.

DECISION PLEASES TAFT

Decision Reads "Unreasonable" Into Law and Is What Trusts Wanted, Says La Follette.

LOWER DECISION MODIFIED

More Time Given and Injunction Against Doing Business Meanwhile Is Removed.

JUSTICE HARLAN DISSENTS

Objects to Limiting the Sherman Law by the Use of the Term "Unreasonable."

WHAT STANDARD WILL DO

Chicago Counsel Says It Will Go On as Usual After Changes Are Made.

Special to The New York Times.

WASHINGTON, May 15.—Final decision was returned late this afternoon by the Supreme Court of the United States in one of the two great trust cases which have been before it for so long—that of the Standard Oil Company. The decree of the Circuit Court for the Eighth Circuit directing the dissolution of the Oil Trust was affirmed, with minor modifications in two particulars. So far as the judgment of the court is concerned the action was unanimous, but Justice Harlan dissented from the argument on which the judgment was based.

The two modifications of the decree of the Circuit Court are that the period for execution of the decree is extended from thirty days to six months, and the injunction against engaging in inter-State commerce on petroleum and its products pending the execution of the decree is vacated. This latter modification is made distinctly in consideration of the serious injury to the public which might result from the absolute cessation of that business for such a time.

Broadly speaking, the court determines against the Standard Oil Company on the ground that it is a combination in unreasonable restraint of inter-State commerce. For the first time since it has been construing the Sherman Anti-Trust act the court takes that position, and thus definitely reads the word "unreasonable" into the law. It was on this ground that Justice Harlan dissented. This decision, therefore, is a practical reversal of the position taken by the court in the trans-Missouri case, one of the first cases under the Sherman law.

In that case Justice White joined with the late Justice Brewer in a dissenting opinion, while Justice Harlan was with the majority of the court. That decision held, as Justice Harlan now holds regarding the Standard Oil Company, that

President Taft himself, in messages to Congress and in public speeches, has declared himself earnestly in favor of retaining the economy and efficiency of combinations and of destroying merely those practices which unduly restrained inter-State commerce and stifled competition. There was a time when the President was in favor of some amendment to the Sherman law in the effort to reach this situation. But he finally came to the conclusion that it was impracticable to write the word "unreasonable" into the law, and pointed out that more and more the Supreme Court was tending toward the point where its decisions in trust cases would be based on that construction of the statute.

Way Out for Corporations.

Now it seems to have been done, and the forceful personality of Chief Justice White has so impressed itself upon the court that he has carried seven of the other Justices with him. Representatives of "big business" who heard him this afternoon did not hesitate to declare emphatically that the decision was all that the big corporations could ask. They regarded with especial favor the establishment of the proposition that a combination must be in "unreasonable" restraint of commerce to be unlawful.

This they believe points out the way by which the big corporations in the country can continue to exist. They recalled with satisfaction the fact that President Taft has specifically declared that it is not mere size which puts a corporation or combination under the ban of the law; it is not the breadth or scope of its operations, or the amount of its capitalization, but whether or not it does two things; fixes prices and controls output.

The representatives of corporations here to-day find in Chief Justice White's decision a practical agreement with the position of President Taft. They have been satisfied with that position and have realized for a long time that business must conform to such standard. Now they find relief in the decision of the highest court in the country, and some of them expressed the opinion this evening that the effect on the general business situation would be good.

There is very little difference in the views of the progressives and those of big business men here as to the effect of the decision. But whereas the corporation representatives regard it with favor, the progressives find in it cause for distrust and dissatisfaction. This view was especialy emphasized by Senators La Follette and Kenyon.

La Follette Not Satisfied.

"In the light of what Justice Harlan in his dissenting opinion said of the Chief Justice's decision," said Senator La Follette, "I think that if it is true that the court holds that the law applies only to unreasonable restraint of trade it is a very dangerous decision. In that view of it I should say it is precisely what the trusts want, and they, more than any others, will be pleased with the decision. The court has amended the Sherman anti-trust law just as it was attempted over and over in the Senate to do it. What they did not get in the Senate they have now got from the court.

"If Justice Harlan interprets the decision correctly we shall have a plenty to do now with the law so amended. Every trust will now come into court and claim justification on a special set of facts going to support the claim that it is not restraining trade unreasonably, and it is to be expected that courts will make use of a sliding scale of reasonableness to apply to each case. I fear that the court has done just what the trusts have wanted it to do and what Congress has refused steadfastly to do."

Senator Kenyon of Iowa took a view similar to that of Senator La Follette. He said:

"I think the court has amended the anti-trust law, and it will lead to trouble. The courts will now be obliged to consider the reasonableness or unreasonableness of trust operations, and to-day's decision will prove to be only the beginning of a long and hard fight. It suggests that legislation will be demanded by the

OPINIONS ON THE DECISION.

Attorney General Wickersham: "Substantially every proposition contended for by the Government is affirmed."

Frank B. Kellogg, counsel for Government: "It is a complete victory for the Government."

Senator Kenyon, formerly Assistant Attorney General: "I think the court has amended the anti-trust law, and it will lead to trouble."

Senator La Follette: "I fear that the court has done what the trusts wanted it to do, and what Congress has steadily refused to do."

Alfred D. Eddy, Standard Oil counsel in Chicago: "The business of the Standard Oil Company will go on as usual, although changes will be made."

affirmed by the Supreme Court. In the reasoning by which the Chief Justice reaches the conclusion in which the whole court concurs he expresses the view that only contracts, combinations, &c., which in any way unreasonably or unduly restrain inter-State trade and commerce or which are unreasonably restrictive of competitive conditions are within the prohibition of the first section of the Sherman act. Justice Harlan, on the other hand, dissents from this view and contends that every contract, &c., which does restrain trade and commerce is within the inhibition of the statute, but he concurs with the whole court in the decree of affirmance.

"The Chief Justice further holds that the second section of the act seeks, if possible, to make the prohibitions of the act all the more complete and perfect by embracing all attempts to reach the ends prohibited by the first section that is, restraint of trade by any attempt to monopolize or monopolization thereof, even although the acts by which such results are attempted to be brought about, or are brought about, be not embraced within the general enumeration of the first section. He further hold that the criterion by which it is to be determined in all cases, whether a contract, combination, &c., is a restraint of trade within the meaning of the law, is the direct or indirect effect of the acts involved."

Courtroom Crowded.

It has been a long time since there was such a scene in the Supreme Court as that of this afternoon. With the House not in session at all, and the Senate engaged in interesting controversy for only a few minutes, the court was the chief attraction for the ordinary visitors to the Capitol. And of course there were many more persons interested in the two trust cases than could possibly find room in the restricted quarters of the great court.

Long before noon there was a long line of waiting men and women in the corridor before the door of the courtroom, a line that extended clear across the rotunda of the Capitol. And despite the oppressive atmosphere of the courtroom very few of those who managed to get in left and made room for others.

As the afternoon waned there were many significant nods about the room and gestures at the big clock over the head of the Chief Justice, showing how the audience took note of the fact that it had got beyond the hour of closing for the Stock Exchanges. Every Justice on the bench had at least one opinion to deliver, and they prosed along through them until it began to look as if there would be no trust case to-day.

At length it came the turn of the Chief Justice. The aged Justice Harlan had lingered a weary time over a number of railroad cases, and when Chief Justice White began to read, and it was seen that he was delivering not an opinion, but the orders of the court on certain motions, it began to look as if the trust cases would

The Resurgent Years

1911-1927

by GEORGE SWEET GIBB
and EVELYN H. KNOWLTON

HARPER & BROTHERS NEW YORK

THE RESURGENT YEARS, 1911-1927

Library of Congress catalog card number: 55-8055

Contents

Appendices

Illustrations

These illustrations come from Standard Oil Company (New Jersey) and its affiliates, Esso Standard Oil Company, Esso Research and Engineering Company, The Carter Oil Company, Interstate Oil Pipe Line Company, International Petroleum Company, Limited, Creole Petroleum Corporation, Esso Standard do Brasil Inc., Esso Sociedad Anonima Petrolera Argentina, Esso Standard (Belgium), Esso-Nederland N.V., Esso A.G., Dansk Esso A/S, Svenska Esso A/B, and Standard-Vacuum Oil Company; from W. C. Teagle, H. Riedemann, R. G. Heard, and Mrs. R. V. Whitman; from Underwood & Underwood, Brown Brothers, and Blank & Stoller; and from the *New York Times*, *New York Tribune*, New York *Call*, and *New York Evening Journal*.

Charts and Maps

Tables

Foreword

IN EVERY branch of the physical sciences groups of scholars have learned how to work together toward a common end. The preparation of the *History of Standard Oil Company (New Jersey)* is the first instance in which a similar group of scholars in the social studies have attempted to co-operate in a major project in a relatively new field, that of business history. In her introduction Associate Professor Henrietta M. Larson, Editorial Director of the Business History Foundation, on leave from the Graduate School of Business Administration of Harvard University, has explained the relationship among trustees, editors, authors, and other members of the staff and between them and the officers of the Standard Oil Company (New Jersey).

Although the Business History Foundation originated in the necessity of finding a medium that would provide a framework for the history which had been under consideration for some time, the trustees hoped that it would be merely the first of a series of comparable studies in what is known as "Big Business." That hope is already being realized. The Business History Foundation is now engaged in two other undertakings which promise to be highly significant. The trustees hope that eventually the series, begun with Volume I of the history of the Standard Oil Company (New Jersey), *Pioneering in Big Business*, will include a study of at least one major corporation in each segment of industry, thus providing a basis for a new approach to many economic and social problems.

The Board of Trustees of the Business History Foundation consists of Ray Palmer Baker, Vice-President Emeritus of Rensselaer Polytechnic Institute, Chairman; Charles W. Moore, Business Consultant, President; Ralph M. Hower, Professor of Business Administration in the Graduate School of Business Administration of Harvard University, Secretary; Herbert Heaton, Professor of Economic History in the University of Minnesota; Ralph W. Hidy, Professor of History in New York University; John

G. B. Hutchins, Professor of Business History and Transportation in Cornell University; and Associate Professor Henrietta M. Larson. They owe much to the counsel of N. S. B. Gras, Straus Professor of Business History, Emeritus, in the Graduate School of Business Administration of Harvard University, the late Joseph H. Appel, biographer and executive, Thomas R. Navin, then Assistant Professor of Business History in the Graduate School of Business Administration of Harvard University, and Philip Young formerly Dean of the School of Business of Columbia University, who served as trustees in the early years when the Board of Trustees was wrestling with complex and difficult problems of organization and policy. Professor Gras, who conceived the idea of an independent institution devoted to research and publication in the field of business history, and who became its first president and first editorial director, was largely responsible for the form finally assumed by the Business History Foundation and for the background for this *History of Standard Oil Company (New Jersey)*.

RAY PALMER BAKER
Chairman of the Board

April 30, 1956

Editorial Director's Introduction

EVERY age has its own problems, and each generation turns to history for light upon them. Nearly two hundred years ago the authors of our federal Constitution studied ancient and modern governments and the history of political thought to learn how a people might govern itself. So it has been with other institutions of society when crises have faced them. Today the institution of private business is straining to meet challenges of the times, and again we turn to history. Now, however, what is needed is the enlightenment not only of a James Madison, who so diligently studied the history of government in the 1780's, but of Everyman, who manages business or who casts the vote that will have much to do with determining its fate.

What can history reveal about this great and all-pervading institution of our times? How has business come to be what it is today? What were the factors that over the centuries influenced its development, and how did business administrators of the past bend the circumstances of their times toward the objectives of their enterprises? How well and by what policies and practices have the drives of business and the welfare of society been joined? What has been the effect on business of cultural change and of new concepts and techniques of government regulation or control?

Today the central question is: How can this basic institution of modern life be made to serve society, while maintaining the freedom necessary to work efficiently and the flexibility to adapt to changing needs and opportunities? This is, essentially, the problem of maintaining a dynamic society, which involves the old issue of a workable balance between freedom and authority and the question of where controls to effect that relationship should be lodged. A generation ago many outside business believed control should lie in government. Men in business believed that the only checks required were those inherent in business itself, in what eighteenth-century philosophers called natural law. The issue today merges with the larger one of what best contributes toward the attainment of the individual and social values that we have come to cherish.

This volume is a case study of how one particular company, representing a type of private enterprise that Americans popularly call big business, operated in a certain span of years. Here is revealed something of the struggle for balance between government control and the need for freedom of action, of the nature and effect of increasing world-wide competition, of the potentialities of business in wartime, of the application of science and engineering toward achieving a greater mastery and utilization of the resources of nature, of American business pioneering in underdeveloped countries, of the problems and methods of co-ordinating the operations of scattered units, of new ways of effecting better co-operation between management and employees, of providing more and better products at decreasing costs, and of making the profits necessary for continued operation and growth.

The preparation of the series of studies of which this volume is a part has been based on certain general principles originally defined by Professor N. S. B. Gras, now Straus Professor of Business History, Emeritus, Graduate School of Business Administration, Harvard University. First of all, the Standard Oil Company (New Jersey) agreed to give the authors and their assistants unrestricted access to the records of the company and freedom to publish from them as appeared to be advisable; it also agreed to recommend that its affiliates do likewise. The officers of the holding company fulfilled this agreement, as also did those of the affiliates participating in the project. It was further agreed that the manuscripts would be read by company representatives, that they might submit suggestions for corrections or changes, but that the final decision as to the acceptance of such suggestions should be the authors'. These reviews, by present and retired directors, technological specialists, and others, have proved invaluable to the authors. Again, however, the company meticulously observed the original understanding that decision should rest with the authors.

One principle followed within the project itself shall be noted: that authors must have full responsibility for their work. Here arose the universal problem of organizations in which those who bear the ultimate responsibility—in this case the trustees of the Business History Foundation—must delegate authority in order to stimulate the best efforts of those doing the work itself. The primary safeguard in such instances is to select for authorship persons of both trained ability and integrity. It was the function of the Editorial Director, with the advice of others who read the manuscripts, to challenge and to encourage, but never to dictate. Final decisions as to factual content, organization, generalization, and interpretation were made by the authors, who wrote as they understood and interpreted what they found in the records.

The problems met in the progress of this undertaking were many and varied. The question as to where one volume should end and the next begin had to be answered. The dissolution of the Standard Oil group by decision of the United States Supreme Court in 1911 provided a logical ending for the first volume, *Pioneering in Big Business,* and the beginning of this, the second. The ending of *The Resurgent Years* is somewhat arbitrary. The period chosen, however, has a distinct unity in that during those years the Standard Oil Company (New Jersey) recovered its strength and laid the foundations for the recent phase of its history, which will be covered by a third volume now in preparation.

The historian's dream of adequate records was in this project realized as an embarrassment of riches. There were tons of documents within the offices and vaults of the holding company alone. Even after eliminating most of those which seemed to be merely routine, there was still a staggering number to be examined carefully. Extensive research was also necessary in the records of the major affiliates operating in the Americas. In addition, a considerable amount of work had to be done in newspapers, trade journals, government publications, and other printed materials in various libraries.

The greatest challenge lay in the scope and complexity of the organization and operations of the Standard Oil Company (New Jersey) and its affiliates and in the great diversity of conditions in which they operated in time and place. The legal structure was infinitely complex; the reality was the functional organization. How could something approaching unity be found in this diversity of companies, men, operations, and products in a dynamic industry and world?

Certain general guiding decisions were made at the beginning of the research. The primary focus of interest was to be on administration by the holding company, that is, on executive personnel and policy, as far as possible dealing with the general implementation of policy in the operations of holding company and affiliates. A logical result of this decision was to emphasize men and functions rather than structure. The subordination of details of operations was easier to accomplish in the present volume than in the first one, the authors of which had to assume that readers would have little knowledge of the oil industry. Especially difficult to handle was the problem of background—the ever-changing social, political, and economic environment in which operations were carried on. Space devoted to both operations and background had to be severely limited, but an attempt was made to give some feeling of the work of countless employees in the many nooks and crannies of the operations of holding company and affiliates and to note and evaluate the main developments in external conditions that bore heavily on central administration and on far-flung operations.

Because several corporations use Standard Oil as part of their names, it is important to know what is meant by Standard Oil Company (New Jersey). This company has not since 1911 been affiliated with Standard Oil Company (California), Standard Oil Company (Indiana), Standard Oil Company (Kentucky), or The Standard Oil Company (Ohio); it has never had any corporate relation with the Standard Oil Company of Texas. Major domestic affiliates of Standard Oil Company (New Jersey) at this time are The Carter Oil Company, Esso Export Corporation, Esso Research and Engineering Company, Esso Shipping Company, Esso Standard Oil Company, Humble Oil & Refining Company, and Interstate Oil Pipe Line Company.

To make adequate acknowledgment of the many contributions to this project is impossible. Recognition must go first of all to the Board of Directors of the Standard Oil Company (New Jersey) for making possible this venture into a nearly unexplored field of historical research and to the directors of affiliates who gave permission for research in their companies' records. As the first Editorial Director, Professor Gras set a standard of independence for scholars and of relations with the company that is based on time-honored principles of historical scholarship, and that provides a workable pattern for other similar studies to follow. For continuing support of the project over the years, credit is due Mr. George H. Freyermuth, former head of the Public Relations Department of Standard Oil Company (New Jersey); to Mr. Stewart Schackne, the present head; and to Dr. Frank M. Surface, Consultant to the Executive Officers, who is the official channel for our relations with the company. Acknowledgment is also due to Dean Stanley F. Teele and to his predecessor, Donald K. David, of the Graduate School of Business Administration of Harvard University, who in many ways helped to make possible this *History of Standard Oil Company (New Jersey)*.

HENRIETTA M. LARSON
Editorial Director

November, 1955

Authors' Preface

THE ACT of facilitating the writing of such a history as this would not and perhaps could not have been considered by the Standard Oil Company (New Jersey) at any time in the years from 1911 to 1927. A truly profound difference between that epoch and the present is suggested by this circumstance alone.

There are, of course, many differences. Already the world of the 1920's has begun to inspire nostalgic reminiscences, while the Standard Oil Company (New Jersey) of 1918 now appears, in perspective, to have been closer to Rockefeller's organization of the 1880's than to the company of today. In tracing the evolutionary pattern of the 1911-1927 period we attempt to bridge a gap that is wider than years only. Our story concerns a business environment that has since been altered in many fundamental aspects, but without a knowledge of which we cannot understand our own. An appreciation of this fact is implicit in the desire of the Standard Oil Company (New Jersey) of today to lay its past upon the pages of history.

The reader must constantly remember that the present volume is an integral part of a broader study. The facts we report and the conclusions we state not only have limited implications but may even be seriously misleading unless they are viewed in conjunction with that part of the history recorded in the volumes of this series dealing with events preceding 1911 and following 1927.

Much of the story recorded in this volume is known to relatively few people, even among the ranks of those who were active participants in the middle years of the company's history. This is because our volume attempts to record the history of administration and management at the highest company level. The Jersey Company in all its parts was and is a vast and fluid organism. Even by thus restricting our objectives we have found it impossible to be complete.

In selecting the historical episodes that seemed to warrant emphasis we have been guided by three major considerations: first, the importance to the company (and to the business world) of the tangible or intangible results achieved; second, the value of the particular incident as an illustration of methods employed or conditions existing; and finally, the importance attached by company executives to the episode at the time.

In order to present clearly those phases of the history which we have deemed important, the opportunity for examining routine operations in many branches of the business has been reluctantly but deliberately sacrificed. Failure to study carefully those events which gave the 1911-1927 period its unique flavor would have been inexcusable, whereas failure to deal exhaustively with operating routines and personnel is merely, in this particular set of circumstances, regrettable.

Any such exercise of choice at once invites criticism, but our hope is that even the reader who disagrees with the emphasis of the volume may catch from it some feeling for the larger developments and issues in every branch of the business. At appropriate places and for illustrative purposes we have abandoned the broad treatment in favor of minute description in an endeavor to show in detail how certain issues were created and resolved by the men on the firing line of operations.

The mechanical aspects of the history present problems of a particularly vexing nature. We have endeavored to confine all information about company operations to the text, in order that only those readers who are particularly interested in source materials will find it necessary to consult the footnotes. An awareness of possible diversity in the interest and training of readers also conditions our treatment of technical subjects. The authors have assumed that the task of providing a highly technical account of oil industry operations was not one which should be attempted in a predominantly administrative history. Such information is available elsewhere. We have endeavored to simplify this side of the story so that it may be readily understood by those who have never been inside a refinery or seen a drilling rig. Yet, at the same time, we have also tried to avoid that irritation which oversimplification can stir in the scientifically trained reader. Such a delicate compromise is not possible in all instances, but a recognition of the authors' problem may be of assistance to those who scan these pages. We have endeavored to employ nontechnical terminology throughout, though petroleum industry usage has been followed where such terminology is self-explanatory.

Any company in which the Standard Oil Company (New Jersey) owned an interest—minority or controlling—we refer to as an "affiliate." This broad label was adopted because of the near impossibility of working out terminology that would clearly indicate the varying degrees of parent company ownership and control. The term "subsidiary" has been avoided, since it carries with it inappropriate and misleading connotations and would be a literally and legally correct designation of only certain of the companies that were integral segments of the operating organization.

One further explanation is necessary to assist the reader to an understanding of the objectives of this volume and of the methods employed in compiling it. The authors were employed by the Business History Foundation, Incorporated. They were instructed to write an objective history with the understanding that their findings would be published whatever they might be. To this end the Standard Oil Company (New Jersey) agreed to permit the authors free access to all its records. These agreements have been scrupulously observed.

The completed manuscript was subjected to a conscientious review by the Editorial Director and was submitted, in whole or in part, to a large number of persons in the company for comments on facts and conclusions. Many of these comments were of great value, and much additional information was elicited which was incorporated in the final draft of the manuscript. In a history of this scope unanimity is not to be expected. The authors found themselves unable to accept as valid some information and interpretations which were volunteered. Our conclusions are our own, and we have arrived at them under a single compulsion only—to record the history as we found it to be.

So numerous are those who assisted us in our work and so indispensable did that assistance prove to be that proper acknowledgments are difficult.

Elizabeth Bricker Currier participated in most of the research and in much of the preparation of the manuscript, which reflects her lively interest and clear critical perspective. The research and editorial processes were measurably shortened by the efforts of Priscilla Wilson, Elizabeth Bacon, Mrs. Hélène M. Dunn, Herbert Kip, Robert E. Ferris, A. John Fair, and Helen I. Cowan, all of whom, as members of the staff of the Business History Foundation, worked at various times with the authors. Charles Sterling Popple assisted in establishing profitable contacts in the company and provided information about post-1927 operations. Kenneth Wiggins Porter and Henrietta M. Larson furnished essential information about the Humble Oil & Refining Company in general and about the conservation movement in particular. John S. Ewing compiled the material on Canadian operations, reviewed those sections of the manuscript devoted to Imperial Oil, Limited, and helped the authors in many other ways. Ralph W. and Muriel E. Hidy read the manuscript carefully, devoted many hours to comments which were of great value, and stood constantly ready to assist the authors in understanding the pre-1911 period of Jersey Standard history.

A high level of editorial assistance was provided by Elsie Hight Bishop, formerly of the Harvard Graduate School of Business Administration, who edited the chapters and prepared the index. Josepha M. Perry corrected and styled parts of the manuscript, and Hilma B. Holton performed many editorial tasks. Frances Carpenter Holbrook did much of the preliminary typing, and Florence Glynn typed the final draft of the manuscript and assisted in its assembly.

Particular sections of the manuscript have benefited greatly from comments by Allan R. Nevins of Columbia University, Richard S. Meriam, Robert W. Austin, and John G. McLean of the Harvard Business School, Paul Giddens of Hamline University, John A. DeNovo of the Pennsylvania State University, and Howard Cline of the Library of Congress. Thomas R. Navin, formerly of the Harvard Business School, read the manuscript, provided extremely helpful criticisms, and assisted the authors constantly and effectively over the entire span of the project.

To N. S. B. Gras, Straus Professor of Business History, Emeritus, and Henrietta M. Larson, Associate Professor of Business History of the Harvard Business School, the authors owe a heavy debt of gratitude. Both, as trustees and executive officers of the Business History Foundation, followed the preparation of the manuscript attentively, while at the same time allowing the authors complete freedom in arriving at and recording their conclusions. Both were exceedingly generous in sharing their wisdom and experience in the field of business history and both discharged their heavy responsibilities in connection with this volume with distinction. Personally, as well as professionally, both have been sympathetic and inspiring.

In their work the authors were granted every convenience and courtesy by the executives and employees of the company, many of whom at times were extraordinarily inconvenienced by the demands of the history project. It is not possible to list by name all those persons in New York, Bayonne, Bayway, Tulsa, Baton Rouge, Shreveport, Toronto, and elsewhere who assisted, but the authors are grateful to them for their help and interest. George H. Freyermuth and N. D'Arcy Drake helped to lay open the storehouse of Jersey records and made possible the liaison between the research team and company people. Without such effective mediation no history could have been written. The authors also wish to thank Dr. Frank M. Surface and all those persons connected with the company who read some or all of the finished manuscript and supplied helpful comments based on their personal recollections of the events recorded. Especially do we wish to acknowledge the effort and time devoted to the manuscript by the late Edwin S. Hall. The advice and assistance of C. E. Springhorn played a large part in the preparation of charts and illustrations and in the layout of the volume.

The trustees of the Business History Foundation extended every consideration to the authors in their work, and in the final stages of the project the Harvard Graduate School of Business Administration allotted time to one of the authors from other tasks in order that the manuscript might not suffer from divided attention. We wish to thank both the trustees of the Foundation and Dean Stanley F. Teele for their appreciation of the problems involved in bringing the manuscript to satisfactory completion.

The husband and the wife of the authors deserve a particular acknowledgment of gratitude, for theirs was more than an average burden. Both participated actively in the preparation of the history—assisting in the performance of many chores, offering helpful comments, and providing, by their patience and understanding, the atmosphere prerequisite for research and writing over a prolonged period.

GEORGE SWEET GIBB
Assistant Professor of Business History
Harvard Graduate School of Business Administration
EVELYN H. KNOWLTON
Associate of the
Business History Foundation, Inc.

November, 1955

THE RESURGENT YEARS

1911-1927

Chapter 1

Dismemberment

PROLOGUE

ON MAY 15, 1911, the Supreme Court of the United States found Standard Oil guilty of violating the Sherman Antitrust Act. The so-called dissolution decree entered by the court directed the dismemberment of the Standard combination and divested the parent holding company of major corporate affiliates.

This event terminated the first broad phase of Standard Oil history. It was also a significant step in the synthesis of our business civilization. Succeeding generations, each in its own way, have insisted upon attempting a fruitful blending of big business, active competition, private initiative, and social responsibility. Out of that insistence a unique economic system has grown. The evolutionary process has involved the clash and tempering and conciliation of many opposing concepts.

Standard Oil executives believed and contended that theirs was an organization of conscientious men who through great abilities and opportunities had made a success by legitimate means in a legitimate business.[1] Some sincere and reputable observers tended to agree with these sentiments but held, nevertheless, that the action of the Supreme Court was both equitable and necessary. Enemies of the organization—and these were many, for the political winds were blowing from an unfriendly quarter—took a different view. The more impassioned detractors proclaimed that the people had triumphed and that a crafty public enemy, driven from subterfuge to subterfuge by a dedicated band of statesmen, editors, businessmen, and journalists, had at last been run to ground.

These intense and diverse contemporary reactions to the dissolution decree involved larger issues than the business philosophies and the behavior of the Standard Oil group. A new chapter was about to unfold in that struggle to develop, preserve, and control large business units which has been so conspicuous a part of American history. An understanding of

1

the evolution of the Standard Oil enterprise up to 1911 and of the disaffiliated components of that enterprise thereafter contributes much to
an understanding of the motivations and circumstances underlying the
broad movement.

The Standard Oil history is also a story of one of the organizational
giants of all time, comparable in importance to any of the vast commercial
enterprises of the past. This broad panorama of administrative evolution
has its own significance, but in addition it provides an opportunity for
examining the magnified strengths and weaknesses of free private enterprise at work not only in America but in a thousand places and in an
infinite variety of circumstances all over the world. A more cosmopolitan
company could scarcely be found in the annals of history, or a wider and
more colorful background of operations discerned in all the records of
man's quest for gain.

The scope and complexities of this history demand a clear delimitation
of the field in which the recording effort is to be made. What, corporate-
wise, *was* the Standard Oil Company (New Jersey) in the years from
1911 to that time in 1927 when internal problems (many arising directly
out of the dismemberment) forced a major managerial reorganization?
This New Jersey corporation—interchangeably referred to hereafter as
"Jersey Standard" or "the Jersey Company"—had been the holding
company at the top of a sprawling pyramid of some seventy directly
held and thirty indirectly held companies. It was the heart of the industrial combination that the dissolution decree of 1911 sought to split
apart. After 1911 it was no longer *the* Standard Oil Company, but rather
only the largest of several companies which bore the name of Standard
Oil, most of which thenceforth were completely independent of Jersey
Standard and increasingly competitive. It was also, even after dismemberment, the largest oil company in the world.

The Standard Oil Company (New Jersey) was, however, both before
and after 1911, much more than a holding company. It was also an operating company, owning and managing in its own name an imposing array
of refineries, tank wagons, storage tanks, and marketing stations. The
history must, then, differentiate between the activities of the company
as an operator and its functions as a holding company into which were
channeled the profits and losses of a large number of affiliated and more
or less specialized corporations. At some points reference is made to
Jersey Standard as an operating company, while elsewhere the title is

used in an all-embracing sense and refers to the entire network of operating affiliates.

The ensuing chapters attempt to picture the primary functions of producing, refining, transporting, and marketing—as they were performed by the Jersey Standard group of companies; as these functions evolved in the years from 1911 through 1927; and as they were reintegrated and coordinated and made to fit into a new master scheme of world-wide industrial organization. The historical reality is sought in an account of policy and operations, viewed in relation to the environment in which Jersey Standard lived.

To understand both the company and the world which shaped it and was, to a degree, shaped by it in the decade and a half after 1911, the events of that year must be outlined briefly. A glance backward still further into history is necessary, too, for Standard Oil traditions which were to play a great part in subsequent development had already been established by 1911. The fact must never be lost from sight that this volume grows out of the history of the earlier years and, in turn, paves the way for the history of a later period. Trends that originated long before 1911 came to fruition in the sixteen years that followed; many developments instituted in these years did not mature until after 1927. Certain broad themes run through the entire course of Standard Oil history from 1882 to the present. The dates that separate the volumes in this Standard Oil history series are necessarily arbitrary in many respects, though not without particular significance. The essential continuity of the Jersey Standard story demands both a careful introduction and a careful conclusion to the story of the middle years.

PIONEERING IN BIG BUSINESS

Behind the public attitudes toward Standard Oil that culminated in the dissolution decree of 1911 lay the boisterous years of an infant industry. Out of the chaos and indiscriminate warfare of pioneering days some degree of order had emerged. A remarkable business organization had taken form, and a growing range of oil products of increasingly high quality moved to markets in ever-increasing regularity and volume.

In the confused times of the early producing and refining industry in the Appalachian oil regions, John D. Rockefeller and his associates saw the profit that stability in this recklessly competitive industry could bring. They began to reach out to integrate the various functions and bring them into some semblance of economic balance. Refineries were constructed in strategic locations from which petroleum products could be carried away by water as well as by rail, and efforts were directed at achieving a degree of control over rail, pipeline, and water transportation.

The expanding Standard Oil organization aggressively cultivated the markets upon which the prosperity of the refineries and the utility of the transportation system depended. Kerosene was by far the most important though by no means the only product; the huge market potential encouraged the building of a formidable distributing organization. The group began to market to wholesalers and then, in due course, to retailers and ultimate consumers. Standard spread out to most of the world, particularly to those markets which could easily be reached by water transportation, and became the principal distributor of oil products. Extension of the marketing network was accompanied by determined efforts to obtain assured sources of crude oil supply, both at home and abroad. From the viewpoint of size, scope of operations, consideration of long-range objectives, devotion to technological advance, utilization of financial resources, control of administrative complexities, and consciousness of public issues, Standard Oil was pioneering in big business—not alone, but conspicuous among the precursors of a new form of enterprise.

Long before 1911, however, Standard Oil had begun to encounter increasing opposition. In Europe the movement toward integration was well under way. Small, specialized companies began to pull together into group alignments with the object of increasing their competitive power. In the Nobel and the French Rothschild petroleum groups Standard encountered formidable adversaries with marked expansionist proclivities. The building of a pipeline across the mountains separating Baku on the Caspian Sea from Batum on the Black Sea brought increased competition in European markets from the Russian oil in which the Nobels and the Rothschilds were interested. The opening of the Suez Canal to petroleum cargoes facilitated the movement of Russian oil to the Far East and encouraged the shipment of oil from the Dutch East Indies into Europe, increasing the competitive pressures in those market areas. British economic imperialism was on the march, and powerful British interests were reaching out into Europe, the Middle East, Mexico, and South America. The Royal Dutch-Shell combine, though of comparatively recent origin (1907), had already, by 1911, successfully challenged the international might of Standard Oil.

There was competition at home as well, for, despite Standard's domination of the American industry, there had always been "independents" doing business in the United States. This group of smaller operators had been expanding greatly with the opening of rich oil fields in the Mid-Continent area, on the Gulf Coast, and in California. In many of these regions the independents needed comparatively little capital to produce oil, transport it to tidewater, and refine it there. Their cumulative and often co-operative efforts had begun to sting their mighty adversary long before the time of the dissolution decree. An estimate by a Jersey Standard man held that, whereas in 1906 Standard Oil had accounted for 86 per cent of the oil refined in the country, by 1911, prior to the dissolution, Standard was refining only 70 per cent of the domestic total.[2] Clearly, even before the decree, economic factors at home and abroad had already begun to undermine Standard's domination of the petroleum industry of the world.

Equally important, the Standard Oil group was beset by increasing political and judicial opposition. For a generation, the struggle between Standard and its variously motivated opponents was one of the more spectacular features of the American business scene. A succession of important legal actions, one of which dissolved the Standard Oil Trust and most of which were punctuated by antagonistic publicity, bore testimony to the efficacy of particular attacks upon the organization. Quite apart from the specific merits or failings of the Standard Oil group, however, the fact of a broad swing in public sentiment was becoming evident. The spectacular rise of big business was generating uneasiness in a nation traditionally and often indiscriminately fearful of concentrations of power.

In 1906 in the Federal Circuit Court of the Eastern District of Missouri the case of *United States* v. *Standard Oil Co. of N. J. et al.* was instituted. Throughout 1907, 1908, and most of 1909 the court gathered evidence and data from individuals inside and outside the company. Journalists followed the hearings closely and pounced upon particularly newsworthy bits of evidence. The public became intimately acquainted with the things that were being said about Standard, but usually it was the unfavorable which were reported soonest and most fully.

In the fall of 1909 the court ruled that Jersey Standard, the parent company, and thirty-seven of its affiliates were guilty of violating the Sherman Antitrust Act.[3] Charges against thirty-two other Standard companies were dismissed. The court directed that the stocks of the convicted companies should be transferred from the possession of Jersey Standard on a ratable basis back to the individual Jersey Standard stockholders. A shareholder owning 1 per cent of Jersey Standard's stock, for example, was to receive 1 per cent of the stock hitherto held by Jersey in each of the companies to be disaffiliated.

At this time prorata stock distribution seemed to be the most practicable method by which the court could order a dissolution to be effected; many observers were quick to point out that such a plan would not result in a basic change in ownership. This charge was true. The effect of the decree was merely to make the individual Jersey stockholders the direct rather than the indirect owners of the disaffiliated subsidiaries. The decree, however, was pointed not at the ownership of those companies, but at the unified control which the officers, acting through the holding company, had exercised over them. The intent of the court was to destroy the concert of command, casting the specified affiliates loose not only from the parent company, but from each other as well.[4] The Missouri decision was to take effect thirty days after its entry, provided that no appeal was sought.

An appeal, however, was immediately made to the Supreme Court of the United States, which returned its opinion in May of 1911, after nearly two years of deliberation. This opinion upheld the Missouri decision, but with modifications. An extension of time was granted for complying with the dissolution decree from thirty days to at least six months after June 21, 1911, the filing date of the mandate. During the liquidation period business could be carried on as usual. Most important of all, the Supreme Court ruling departed from earlier interpretations by holding that only *unreasonable* restraint of trade rather than *all* restraint of trade was illegal. The legality of particular actions was not to be circumscribed by precise definitions, but rather was to be judged in accordance with the "light of reason, guided by the principles of law." This was a significant point, for, although no person could hope to predict what specific corporate actions the courts would subsequently view as "reasonable restraint of trade," it did hold forth a promise that the procedures normal and essential to the conduct of large-scale business operations might be tolerated.[5]

The companies marked for severance from Jersey Standard included sixteen out of the twenty largest affiliates. Aggregate net value (total assets minus current liabilities) of the thirty-three disaffiliated corporations totaled $375,000,000, or 57 per cent of Jersey's predissolution total net value.[6] Even so, after the dissolution the Jersey Company, with a total net value of $285,400,000, was surpassed in size by only one other industrial company in the country (United States Steel) and still towered above all the other oil companies. In terms of net value, Jersey was five times as large as the Standard Oil Company of New York; five and one-half times as large as the National Transit Company; six and one-half times as large as The Ohio Oil Company; and seven and one-quarter times as large as the Standard Oil Company (California). These four companies were the greatest of those which were disaffiliated, and each in turn far surpassed in size any of the so-called independent oil companies in the country.[7]

These rough quantitative comparisons provide a graphic but by no means comprehensive measure of the impact of the decree. Much more important than the changes which the dissolution wrote into Jersey's balance sheet were the functional dislocations threatened by the various corporate separations. Tables 1 and 2 indicate those companies severed and those retained, together with the primary functions performed by each. The actual organizational maladjustments are considered in some detail in subsequent chapters. In terms of 1911 figures, Jersey Standard, having lost 57 per cent of its net value, suffered a shrinkage of 91 per cent ($86,774,-000) in its annual earning power.[8] This shrinkage was spread over the operating functions of the business in a highly erratic and completely haphazard fashion.

Among the companies disaffiliated in 1911 were those which performed for the Standard Oil organization virtually all of the pipeline transportation of crude oil from the fields to the refineries. The largest tanker fleet in the organization also passed from Jersey Standard's ownership. The company was severed from its principal domestic crude oil producing and purchasing organizations, retaining through two affiliates only a tenuous grasp of production in the Appalachian and Gulf Coast areas. Jersey Standard was also left with refining capacity far in excess of markets provided by its own organization and that of retained affiliates, which together distributed petroleum products in only one-sixth of the states that comprised Standard Oil's predissolution territories. On the other hand, such disaffiliated companies as the Standard Oil Company of New York and the Standard Oil Company (Kentucky) were legally separated both from sources of finished products adequate to supply their existing markets and from crude oil sources from which such products could be manufactured. The foreign business was similarly afflicted. Jersey Standard retained most of its European and South American marketing affiliates, as well as the only affiliate which was engaged in crude oil producing operations outside the United States, but the dissolution ripped from the parent those com-

Table 1: COMPANIES DISAFFILIATED
from Jersey Standard in 1911[a]

PRIMARY FUNCTIONS:

1. Producing
2. Refining
3. Domestic marketing
4. Foreign marketing
5. Domestic manufacturing and/or distribution of specialty products
6. Pipeline transportation and storage
7. Tanker transportation

COMPANY	1	2	3	4	5	6	7
Anglo-American Oil Company, Limited				X			X
Atlantic Refining Company, The		X	X				
Borne, Scrymser Company				X	X		
Buckeye Pipe Line Company, The						X	
Chesebrough Manufacturing Company, Consolidated				X	X		
Colonial Oil Company				X			
Continental Oil Company			X				
Crescent Pipe Line Company, The						X	
Cumberland Pipe Line Company, Inc.						X	
Eureka Pipe Line Company, The						X	
Galena-Signal Oil Company			X	X	X		
Indiana Pipe Line Company						X	
National Transit Company						X	
New York Transit Company						X	
Northern Pipe Line Company						X	
Ohio Oil Company, The	X					X	
Prairie Oil & Gas Company, The	X					X	
Solar Refining Company, The		X					
Southern Pipe Line Company						X	
South Penn Oil Company	X						
South-West Pennsylvania Pipe Lines						X	
Standard Oil Company (California)	X	X	X			X	X
Standard Oil Company (Indiana)		X	X				
Standard Oil Company (Kansas), The		X					
Standard Oil Company (Kentucky)			X				
Standard Oil Company (Nebraska)			X				
Standard Oil Company of New York		X	X	X			X
Standard Oil Company (Ohio), The		X	X				
Swan & Finch Company			X		X		
Union Tank Line Company[b]					b	b	
Vacuum Oil Company		X	X	X	X		
Washington Oil Company	X						
Waters-Pierce Oil Company		X	X	X			

[a] The following companies were listed in the 1909 (Missouri) ruling, but not in the 1911 (U. S. Supreme Court) decree, having been liquidated, disaffiliated, or become dormant in the interval: Corsicana Refining Company, Security Oil Company, The Manhattan Oil Company, and Standard Oil Company (Iowa).

[b] The Union Tank Line Company owned and operated railroad tank cars.
Source: SONJ, Fin. Recs.; Corp. Recs. U. S. v. Standard Oil Co. of N. J. et al., 173 Fed. 177 (Nov. 20, 1909). Standard Oil Co. of N. J. et al. v. U. S., 221 U. S. 1 (May 15, 1911).

Table 2: **THE JERSEY STANDARD CORPORATE GROUP**
after Dissolution (1912)[a]

PRIMARY FUNCTIONS:

1. Producing
2. Refining
3. Domestic marketing
4. Foreign marketing
5. Natural gas
6. Domestic manufacture and/or distribution of specialty products
7. Pipeline transportation and storage
8. Tanker transportation

COMPANY	1	2	3	4	5	6	7	8
Standard Oil Company (New Jersey) [parent company]		X	X					
Aktien Gesellschaft Atlantic								X
American Petroleum Company (Holland)				X				X
Bedford Petroleum Company, S.A.F.				X				
California Natural Gas Company					X			
Carter Oil Company, The	X							
Clarksburg Light and Heat Company					X			
Connecting Gas Company, The					X			
Det Danske Petroleums-Aktieselskab				X				
Deutsch-Amerikanische Petroleum-Gesellschaft				X				X
East Ohio Gas Company, The					X			
Gilbert & Barker Manufacturing Company						X		
Hope Natural Gas Company					X			
Imperial Oil Company, Limited, The		X		X				
Interstate Cooperage Company, The						X		
Marion Oil Company	X							
Oklahoma Pipe Line Company							X	
Pennsylvania Lubricating Company, Incorporated						X		
Peoples Natural Gas Company, The					X			
Raffinerie Française[b]		X						
Reserve Gas Company					X			
River Gas Company, The					X			
Societate Anonimă pentru Industria, Comerciul și Exportul Petrolului (Româno-Americana)	X	X		X				
Società Italo-Americana pel Petrolio				X				
Standard Oil Company of Brazil				X				
Standard Oil Company of Louisiana	X	X	X				X	
Taylorstown Natural Gas Company					X			
Tuscarora Oil Company, Limited							X	
Underhay Oil Co.						X		
United Fuel Gas Company					X			
West Coast Oil Fuel Company, Limited				X				
West India Oil Company				X				
West India Oil Refining Company, The		X						

[a] The Jersey Standard affiliates included in this list are (with one exception) those in which the parent company held at least a majority of stock. For information about other holdings see Appendix 1. Functions of several of the companies listed changed shortly after 1912. Some of the affiliates also were holding companies, as indicated in Appendix 1.
[b] Company inactive, but facilities utilized for storage of petroleum stocks.
Source: SONJ, Fin. Recs.; Corp. Recs.

panies which were charged with selling Standard Oil products in the United Kingdom, the Far East, and in many other foreign areas.

Thus the decree tore into shreds the carefully integrated and far-flung corporate network which the Standard Oil group had built up over four decades. Jersey Standard retained some foreign footholds, but it was no longer a nationwide organization. The system of achieving eminence in many areas by means of subsidiaries had revealed its serious political weakness. The complexity and decentralized nature of the organization had failed to conceal the real unity from the enemies of bigness.

Despite the drastic corporate changes, however, immediate economic realities had not been altered by the action of the Supreme Court. In 1911 Jersey Standard faced a dynamic business situation. The real efficacy of the dissolution decree was a point at issue. Cynics regarded the court decision as a sop to democratic public sentiment, without any true potency. If, on the contrary, the objectives of the court were really to be achieved, the basic question was whether Jersey Standard would survive as an industrial cripple or prove the validity of old organizational concepts under new conditions and once again aspire to a position of world-wide power in the petroleum industry.

SURVEY OF THE MIDDLE YEARS

The history of Jersey Standard from 1911 through 1927 is essentially the story of a tremendous task of reconstruction, for, despite public suspicion to the contrary, the dissolution decree of 1911 did in time effect a devastatingly real dismemberment. These years witnessed a determined drive to preserve and strengthen the integrated nature of the business. Jersey Standard executives did not entertain integration as a conscious goal—the word itself was rarely heard—and yet it was to that end that their major policy decisions were pointed. Among the leaders of the organization determination and ability to pursue sound business tactics went, after a period of cautious readjustment, hand in hand with strong confidence in the future of the Jersey Company. Expansion is the keynote of the 1911-1927 period: expansion of specific parts to achieve once again that organizational effectiveness which existed before the dissolution; expansion of the whole to keep pace with an expanding industry and economy.

On December 31, 1912, total assets of the Jersey Company stood at $369,300,000. By December 31, 1927, assets had grown to the enormous total of $1,426,600,000, and Jersey continued to occupy a position of preeminence among the industrial organizations of the world.[9] This fourfold expansion, however, was not to be a measured, level growth in all branches of the business, nor was the growth process to be spread evenly over the span of years.

In this sixteen-year period the world became increasingly oil-conscious, and markets for petroleum products changed greatly. The dissolution suit came during a period of transition which saw kerosene begin to relinquish its position as the industry's most important refined product. Natural gas and gas oil (used in the manufacture of gas), as well as electricity, were taking the place of kerosene in many areas in the United States and abroad. Demand for gasoline and lubricants was increasing with the growing use of the automobile. There was an increasing demand for fuel oil for vessels.

These shifts in markets tended to favor the independent operators, who, despite their progress before 1911, had been handicapped by Standard Oil's hold on the kerosene market and by the narrow opportunities that had hitherto existed in any other product field. The already existing trend toward increasing competition was accentuated by the dissolution decree itself. The independent operators were no longer subject, after 1911, to the pressure of one dominating group. These companies exploited their new freedom gradually, however. In the few years between the decree and World War I they made some progress, but it was the tremendous acceleration in demand for petroleum products brought about in the war and postwar years which furthered that growth of the independents for which the decree had helped to pave the way.

Some of these independent organizations, such as the Gulf Oil Corporation, The Pure Oil Company, Limited, and The Texas Company, expanded greatly, reaching out in the direction of more nearly complete integration and becoming formidable competitors of the Jersey Company, which, at the same time, was handicapped by the political climate in which it sought to carry on its business. The smaller independents made up for their size and were growing stronger by uniting into associations. H. C. Folger, Jr., formerly a director of Jersey Standard, wryly observed to Judge John G. Milburn, who had conducted Standard's defense in the dissolution suit, that it looked to him as though the only "independent" oil people after 1911 were those formerly in the Standard group![10]

The eventual effect of the dissolution decree was also to foster competition between former members of the Standard Oil family. The situation arising out of the decree imposed upon Jersey Standard's one-time affiliates the same necessities for integration that the Jersey Company itself faced after 1911. Standard of New York, Standard of California, and Standard of Indiana, together with The Atlantic Refining Company, the Vacuum Oil Company, and other disaffiliated members of the old trust, branched out and began to compete with their former parent with whom they once had amicably served. This change, too, was slow in coming and did not assume its greatest momentum until the war years and after.

Competition abroad, which had already been keenly felt before 1911, was accentuated in the years that followed. As Jersey Standard became more and more deeply involved in foreign spheres of operation, the activities of Royal Dutch-Shell, the Anglo-Persian Oil Company, the French Refiners, the Nobel and Rothschild interests, the Deutsche Bank, and other great commercial organizations came to have increasing influence upon company policies. Tremendous international conflicts and potent international alliances characterized Jersey Standard's struggle for business, molded the form of the entire world petroleum industry, and influenced the course of world politics.

The growth of competition and markets, clearly a major facet of Jersey's history in the middle years, went hand in hand with the Jersey Company's relations with the government and the public. These relations were characterized throughout by queer crosscurrents. Various efforts were made to surmount the terrible handicap of prejudice that existed and to ease the stigma attached to the name Standard Oil. Many, though not all, of these efforts had both sincerity and reality. The chapters that follow show in some detail how virtually every phase of Jersey Standard operations was influenced not just by the normal factors of competition, supply, demand, and technology, but also by a fear of public censure which not infrequently was paralyzing and with which Jersey management at times seemed almost powerless to cope.

Across the period, too, fell the long shadows of a world war. To a company engaged in the producing and marketing of fuel and lubricants on an international scale this fact could not have other than revolutionary implications. These will be examined with special care and in some detail.

Almost hidden in those shadows, however, lay fully as potent, if less dramatic, external forces which were molding company policy and the form and size of the company itself. American business was growing up. As markets expanded and productive facilities expanded with them, new marketing techniques were born and new skills in merchandising were called into play. Just as the American businessman had at his disposal new tools, new materials, and new sources of power, so, too, was he given new managerial techniques. Labor movements of some intensity forced upon makers of business policy the necessity for formulating labor policies. In many cases this involved merely the formalization or modification of existing and effective paternalistic relationships, but in a few trouble spots wholesale changes were in order.

But beyond such specific evolutionary tendencies, large segments of the business world began to note the deficiencies which rapid growth and increasing competition were exposing in the system of free enterprise. Business moved to oil the squeaking joints in the interest of private gain. At the same time, the intense preoccupation of federal and state governments in remedying those same deficiencies in the interest of the public welfare waned somewhat under the pressure of war and long-term prosperity. In fact, the demarcation between private profit and public gain that was so clearly enunciated in political circles between 1890 and 1914 became strangely confused for a time, as American business successfully met the demands placed upon it by war and by the surging quest of the American public for a more bountiful life.

As Jersey Standard's history is unfolded, topic by topic, in succeeding pages, normal business development must be recognized and traced. Yet, at many points in the company's growth normal trends were warped and bore the imprint of forces that few other American corporations have ever felt with equal might. The multilateral character of the evolutionary process must never be lost from view. The plurality of influences—legal, social, political, economic, technical—which entered into the making of even the simplest policy decisions must be recognized. No history of the Jersey Company can hope to detail all or, sometimes, even the most important motivations which underlay the pattern of Jersey's business behavior, but no history of these eventful years would be adequate that did not search for causation outside the company in the broad background of the times in which Jersey Standard fought for life and strength.

What key unlocks the riddle of this unfamiliar span of time from 1911 to 1927? We may assume that it was an eventful period, even without the assurance that the Standard Oil Company, said to have been "established . . . as an outlaw, and wound up, abated, and dissolved," was still, as Jersey's chief attorney put it, a "pretty lively corpse."[11] Why and how did Jersey Standard in this 1911-1927 period survive decrees, panics, depressions, wars, political intrigue and persecution, changes in business systems, policy errors of omission and commission, and the occasional hot glare of public suspicion? What did the dissolution decree of 1911 mean for Jersey

Standard, for the oil industry, and for the public? How did the Jersey Company employ its rich legacy of business skills and experience in an environment which was both propitious and frustrating? What were the problems and privileges of almost unparalleled size and financial power? What did Standard take from, and what did it give to, the economy and society of which it was so conspicuous a part? These are only a few of the pertinent questions that launch the history of these resurgent years.

Answers were to be provided by a handful of men, working informally together to design and carry out those modifications of administrative mechanisms demanded by expansion and alteration of the operating branches of the business. These members of the top administrative echelon bore heavy responsibilities which a generation of grueling experience had equipped them to discharge effectively. Their efforts to apply that experience to problems of mounting complexity in a world of stress and transition constitute the essence of Jersey Standard's history from 1911 to 1927.

Chapter 2

Reactions and Vistas
1912-1917

CARRYING OUT THE DECREE

THE ACTION of the United States Supreme Court in upholding the earlier findings of the Circuit Court in Missouri was not unanticipated by high-ranking Standard Oil officials. There was, indeed, momentary satisfaction in the Jersey Company with the terms of the 1911 decree, though a complaint was voiced that the company had been given no opportunity to propose changes before the decree was entered. This satisfaction probably derived from a sense of relief that the Missouri ruling had been liberalized somewhat. Jersey's imperturbable chief counsel informed a correspondent, "I can assure you that we will be able to continue business as before, except that officers of the different companies will control the business, instead of the Standard Oil Company of New Jersey. As I stated for publication two or three days after the decision the different companies will continue to do the same business as heretofore, under the management of their officers."[1]

The first and most routine response of the Jersey Company to the decree was to determine the amount of stock of disaffiliated companies to which each stockholder was entitled. In 1911 parent company stockholders numbered 6,078, and there were 983,383 shares of Jersey Company stock outstanding. To complicate matters further, Jersey Standard's stock holdings in the various affiliates were not evenly divisible. Jersey stockholders, for example, were entitled to receive 0.054 share of The Eureka Pipe Line Company stock for each share of Jersey Standard stock held. In a few months, however, the formidable problems of arithmetic were worked out, scrip certificates being issued for fractional shares. The stock register of the Jersey Company was closed on September 1, and by December 1, 1911, distribution of the stock of the disaffiliated companies was virtually completed. Plaintive appeals from bewildered stockholders continued to be forwarded to Jersey's Legal Department for some months afterward.

At the same time that the stock in the coffers of the parent company was being parceled out, the Herculean task was undertaken of selecting new officers and directors for the companies affected by the decree. In the old Standard Oil organization directors of the parent company had also held top executive positions in a number of affiliates. The terms of the decree prohibited such relationships between the separated companies and established the necessity for widescale resignations and new appointments. To add to the difficulty, certain directors who had been in office for many years wished to retire completely. John D. Rockefeller, Sr., William Rockefeller, H. M. Flagler, and O. H. Payne had already ceased to be active in management and availed themselves of the opportunity afforded by the 1911 reorganization to sever their formal executive connections with the organization.

The Jersey board of directors was reduced in size from fifteen members to nine, all of whom, in the old Standard Oil tradition, were executives of or large investors in the company. John D. Archbold, in whom virtually complete responsibility for directing Standard Oil operations had been vested for a decade and a half, stepped from a vice-presidency to the presidency of Jersey Standard, the position which Rockefeller had nominally occupied since 1899. James A. Moffett, Sr., retained a vice-presidency held since 1909, and directors A. Cotton Bedford and Walter Clark Teagle were promoted to vice-presidencies.

In the disaffiliated companies similar steps were taken. Local vice-presidents were promoted to presidencies, and men in responsible operating posts were made directors. At the expiration of the six months of grace allowed by the Supreme Court for carrying out the dissolution decree, most of the disaffiliated companies had their own separate and distinct directorates and executive officers.[2]

These changes were reported and distorted by certain metropolitan newspapers. Under the headline "Oil Trust Lamp Beat Aladdin's With Its Magic," the New York *World* exclaimed, "Humble Clerks, Agents and Mechanics 'Called Upstairs' in No. 26 Broadway, and Lo! They Were Directors!"[3] The essence of these recriminations was that the old Trust members were still dictating the policies of the disaffiliated companies, and that these companies had been staffed with dummy officers endowed with phantom responsibilities, while real control was still centered at 26 Broadway. The facts were that in the dissolution process many subordinate officials were elevated to high positions overnight, frequently without substantial immediate change in their duties. Intent to evade or vitiate the terms of the decree can scarcely be inferred therefrom. The managerial reorganization inevitably was slow-moving and confused, and it seems reasonable to assume that the new executives were forced for a time to work closely with their predecessors.

These managerial shifts had both good aspects and bad. The process of replacing older men by younger had been going on before 1911, but it was greatly expedited by the events of that year. Executives who had, through age or straying interests, become virtual figureheads yielded their offices to the subordinates who had been doing the work. On the other hand, the committee system by which Standard Oil affairs had been managed was smashed and key men were lost to the Jersey Company.

Functional as well as personnel adjustments were undertaken by the new Jersey Standard board. The basic problem was to preserve the operating organization while observing the legal limitations imposed by the decree. New clerical staffs were set up, particularly by the Jersey Company, which had relied upon Standard of New York for the performance of much routine administrative work. Space at 26 Broadway was reallocated, since both Jersey Standard and Standard of New York continued to use this building as their headquarters. The Atlantic Refining Company packed up its records in huge crates and moved out to new offices in Philadelphia.

There was considerable uncertainty as to the business dealings that might legally be entered into between the Jersey Company and its castoff affiliates. The essence of the decree, of course, was that there should be no secret or special arrangements between Jersey Standard and its former affiliates that might be construed, under the 1911 ruling, as illegal restraint of trade. For example, supply contracts with the disaffiliated Anglo-American Oil Company, Limited, which were exclusive in their terms, had to be canceled. By the same token, the exclusive use of the private telegraph network which had been built along pipeline rights of way was denied the Jersey Company when the pipeline companies were separated. Business with former affiliates was to be at arm's length, and instructions to this effect were issued in the organization.

A great deal of business after 1911, however, was transacted in much the same channels as before. Standard of New York continued to purchase large quantities of refined products from Jersey Standard and crude oil from some of the disaffiliated companies. The Union Tank Line Company received permission from the court to continue to supply tank cars for the transportation of petroleum to the companies from which it had been severed. Jersey Standard's Bayonne and Bayway refineries continued to receive crude oil through the pipelines of former affiliates, and former Jersey Standard companies that had purchased crude oil at the wells continued to buy for resale to their former parent after 1911.

Small wonder, then, that protests almost immediately began to be voiced that Jersey Standard was not living up to the terms of the decree. The public did not understand that the decree permitted normal business transactions between the Jersey Company and its former affiliates. On the surface there were few changes. Men and departments performing certain duties for one company before the dissolution now found themselves performing identical functions under a new letterhead and, possibly, in a new office. Unfortunate incidents were publicized which seemed to point to a continuation of control by 26 Broadway. D. S. Bushnell, for example, was forced on the witness stand to admit that, when the Northern, Indiana, and Buckeye pipeline companies and the New York Transit Company were disaffiliated from Jersey Standard and he was made president of these companies, he was moved, not even to another floor at 26 Broadway, but merely to another office on the same floor.[4] To an undiscriminating and suspicious public such a trivial episode was evidence enough of the artificiality of the dissolution process.

Some of the outcry in postdissolution months came from those newspapers which had long delighted in baiting Standard Oil. The New York *World* reported how "deadly rivals of oil" sat in "sweet peace" at luncheons on the fifteenth floor of 26 Broadway.[5] Doubts as to the efficacy of the decree were also expressed in more reputable, though not necessarily much more cognizant or impartial, quarters. In 1912 Theodore Roosevelt asserted that the dissolution decree had not checked the Standard Oil monopoly. This allegation was promptly denied by Attorney General Wickersham, whose investigators had not found sufficient evidence of noncompliance to press further charges against the Jersey Company.[6] Sensationally bad publicity for both Jersey Standard and its former affiliates, however, was generated by events growing directly out of the forced distribution of stock of the separated companies.

Early in 1912 both the *New York Times* and the New York *Financial World* indignantly reported that the Colonial Oil Company refused information to stockholders who had purchased fractional lots of stock at $500 in order to bring the allotments they had received in the dissolution up to full shares. Events within the company soon thereafter sent the price of Colonial stock plunging 400 points and immediately raised cries of manipulation.[7]

At almost the same time, Standard of Indiana declared a $29,000,000 stock dividend, and the price of Indiana shares shot up from $1,400 to $4,100 "after insiders," the *Financial World* declared, "had got all they could get."[8] This episode was still being discussed when The Prairie Oil & Gas Company, another disaffiliated company, declared a dividend substantially higher than the usual rate. Eastern stockholders were not informed of the declaration until five days later; when the news broke, Prairie stock jumped 85 points almost overnight. Once again "insiders" were accused of manipulation; Prairie's announcement that the delay in making known the new dividend rate was the result of "oversight of a Kansas official" only added to the indignation of the stockholders.[9]

These three incidents prompted the *Financial World* to voice the suspicions that such actions so richly nourished. "The evident aim of the old Standard Oil party is to gain and retain a majority interest in all the subsidiary companies of the old Trust, thereby exercising quite as much power as formerly when the merger was intact."[10] A Jersey Company representative replied that, in the past, dividends on stock of wholly owned companies had always been paid only to the Jersey Company and that outsiders did not have to be considered. Hence, the men at the head of these companies had not realized the necessity for new procedures now that the stock was publicly held. The Jersey Company added to this flimsy-sounding but quite possibly correct explanation a strong denial that Jersey Standard stock was being manipulated, but dodged responsibility for the actions of former affiliates with the unquestionably correct statement that the stock of these companies was "very hard to trace."[11] The *Financial World* advised its subscribers that purchase of the stocks of disaffiliated companies was blind speculation. The New York Curb Association refused for a time to list the stocks of those companies which did not furnish the information requested.[12]

Meanwhile, fuel was being poured on the fires of suspicion by the action of Henry Clay Pierce, head of the Waters-Pierce Oil Company. Even when Jersey Standard had owned a large interest in this company, the independent actions of its uncontrollable chief executive were a thorn in the side of 26 Broadway. Pierce seized upon the dissolution as an opportunity to acquire complete control of the stock of his company. In the dissolution process John D. Rockefeller personally had received a large number of

Waters-Pierce shares, formerly held by the Jersey Company. At an annual meeting of the Waters-Pierce Company shortly after the dissolution Pierce adamantly refused to count the votes which these shares entitled Rockefeller to cast. In the ensuing lawsuit Pierce cleverly played upon public suspicion and leveled the damaging charge that here lay evidence of the intent of the old Trust members, acting now as individuals, to regain control of the former affiliates. Rockefeller finally settled with Pierce and sold him his shares, but the damage wrought by the episode was incalculable. Pierce's charges, originating as they did within the very bosom of the Standard family, were hailed as conclusive evidence that efforts were under way to circumvent the decree.[13]

The public also seized upon contemporary events in Texas as further indication that Jersey Standard and certain alleged affiliates were flaunting the spirit if not the letter of the law. Earlier, when the Navarro Refining Company and the Security Oil Company were convicted on charges of violating Texas antitrust laws and forced to liquidate, a substantial portion of what were believed to have been Standard Oil interests in Texas had passed into the hands of Jersey Standard directors. In 1911 the Magnolia Petroleum Company was formed to take over these interests, and by 1912 about 90 per cent of the Magnolia stock was held in approximately equal blocks by H. C. Folger, then president of Standard of New York, and John D. Archbold, president of Jersey Standard. Almost immediately Magnolia, Standard of New York, Jersey Standard, and several officers of these companies were attacked in the courts.[14]

In 1913 a compromise settlement was effected with the state of Texas. The court directed that the Magnolia stock held by Archbold and Folger be placed in trust, in order to ensure that in the future Magnolia would operate independently of Standard Oil control. Jersey Standard agreed to accept a finding of guilt covering certain phases of its operations in Texas up to 1909, and submitted to a fine of $500,000. All other charges were dismissed.[15]

The damaging aspect of the Magnolia incident was that both the Jersey Company and Standard of New York had stoutly denied ownership or control of Magnolia. This claim was based on the legal distinction that it was not these two companies but Archbold and Folger who actually owned the stock. Both men vigorously maintained that they were acting in a private capacity when they took the Magnolia stock, but what was claimed as legal fact the public hailed as palpable subterfuge.

The chorus of recrimination, which had diminished somewhat during the months when the dissolution case was before the Supreme Court, again began to mount. Once more the antitrust mania in the United States attained a fever peak. In New Jersey the administration of Governor Woodrow Wilson was openly hostile to big business, as were those of many other states and the federal government as well. A wave of antitrust legislation, both proposed and enacted, swept the country. The "Seven Sisters" acts passed in New Jersey in 1913 set up restrictions on corporations holding the stock of other companies; other legislation attempted to control discriminatory pricing. Wilson evidenced a critical attitude toward big business practices on the national as well as the state level, and he moved to the White House committed to antitrust action. Within six months after the new administration had taken office early in 1913, twelve antitrust bills were introduced into the Senate and sixteen such bills were placed before the House. The Clayton Act of 1914 contemplated on a federal basis some of the objectives that the Seven Sisters acts had sought in the state of New Jersey. The Federal Trade Commission was created in this same year. The pipeline companies were under attack in a federal effort to make them subject to regulation as common carriers under the terms of the Hepburn Act of 1906; a new investigation of the Standard Oil dissolution was launched by the Attorney General's office; and two Congressional resolutions called for investigations of phases of the oil industry's operations.

A few efforts were made by Jersey Standard to answer the public outcry, and a very considerable effort was expended to avoid further legal attack. Company lawyers went to the greatest pains to avoid trespass on questionable legal grounds. The United States Attorney General's office was frequently consulted and consistently advised of proposed moves. The instructions which were issued throughout the organization in 1911 appear to have been followed by the operating department heads with faithful intent of conforming to the laws of the land. The Legal Department continually urged upon top management the necessity for living within the law, and the Jersey Company management on several occasions insisted publicly that it was doing just this. These efforts in the direction of compliance, however, were neither widely publicized nor convincing to the public. There is, indeed, no clear evidence that Jersey Standard executives appreciated the necessity for giving the public information of any significance concerning the company and its operations. All attention was focused on avoiding illegality, as defined by the 1911 decree and by subsequent federal opinions.

Efforts to counter the thrusts of an aroused press were ineffective.

Formal and usually accurate, if not always complete, replies were made to some of the charges that were being aired on every side. These carefully phrased statements appear to have had little effect, being released at a time when a deliberate policy of secrecy was being pursued and requests for information were being denied even accredited stockholders both by Jersey Standard and by its former affiliates. In 1912 the president of The Ohio Oil Company wrote as follows to Jersey's chief counsel:[16]

Inquiries are being made by stockholders in reference to our annual financial statement. We have given all kinds of excuses and evaded sending out a statement, which I hope we may be able to continue, but it is possible that we may get hold of some disgruntled fellow who will compel us to do it under the laws of the State of Ohio.

A Standard Oil official was reported, in 1913, as having offered the following explanation for the prevailing secrecy:[17]

Technically, the public has not the right to inquire even whether retiring directors of this company have been re-elected at an annual meeting. If we give the information, it is only as a matter of courtesy; and we don't believe in public financial statements because we consider an important feature of competition is to prevent information concerning us getting into the hands of rivals.

John D. Archbold himself was opposed to revealing stockholder lists, and access even to information of this sort was denied until it became apparent that such refusal constituted an absolute breach of the law. Having been victimized by inflamed journalism for so many years, Jersey Standard management seemed convinced that nothing it might say would be fairly reported; therefore, the less said about anything, the better. The reticence in imparting financial information probably derived in part from this cautious philosophy and in part from the hitherto closely held nature of the Standard Oil interests.

Both the *New York Times* and the *Financial World* lashed out at the secrecy which shrouded Jersey Standard affairs. The *New York Herald* complained, "It is as difficult . . . to get any real information from No. 26 Broadway as it was ten years ago, and, as in those days, rubber heels are worn by everybody. Nobody speaks above a whisper, and the press bureau is as full of real information as an almanac of 1876."[18]

The press bureau upon which the *Herald* heaped this abuse in reality consisted of one individual, J. I. C. Clarke, poet and man of letters, who had been effectively employed by Jersey Standard as a publicist since before the dissolution. Clarke's work consisted of releasing prepared statements to the press, writing publicity releases, and parrying requests for additional information. Few companies of the day had been doing this much. In the highly charged postdissolution environment, however, methods which once had been deemed adequate were no longer so. There was no precedent at this time for a large-scale publicity counterattack, and even such a program probably would have proved of little avail. Such efforts as were actually made had virtually no hope of producing an alteration in public attitudes toward the company. A defeatist attitude appears to have taken root which was in marked contrast to the determined and by no means inconsequential efforts that the organization had made between 1906 and 1911 to carry its cause to the public.

The issues of the day were not, however, finally to be decided by words. In the years that followed 1911 "business as heretofore" was marked for eventual alteration. However inconspicuous the outer physical manifestations of the dissolution appeared to the public, the truth is clear in retrospect that a revolution had been started within the operating branches of the Jersey Standard organization that promised to spread and embrace the oil industry and oil operations all over the world.

THE OPERATING ENTITY

There were few persons indeed in the vast Jersey organization who had a true perspective of the entity which they served, but to a handful of men at 26 Broadway the infinite complexities of that organization were scarcely mysterious. The operating details, to be sure, were appalling in their number and complexity, but all fitted into an operational pattern which was comprehensible in total and susceptible of logical manipulation in a single purpose. The nine men in the boardroom at 26 Broadway manipulated immense and diverse groups of resources like chessmen. A move here necessitated a move there. Every move had meaning: some moves were critical, and all could be expected to produce counterplays from skilled opponents.

The Jersey Standard organization revolved around markets for petroleum products—in 1911, chiefly kerosene. Markets lay everywhere, and it was the task of the directors to decide which to pick for exploitation. Perhaps a competitor was too strongly entrenched in one promising area for forthright entry; another region might be closed by government monopoly or tariffs; still another by prohibitive transportation rates or lack of an adequate transportation system. Jersey critics claimed, too, that there was obvious disinclination to enter the marketing territories of former affiliates. All these factors must be weighed, and all were subject to constant change. A policy decision in 1912 might profitably be reversed in 1913; a competitor might suddenly force a change in a carefully worked-out price schedule; a new refinery might be constructed here or a new oil reserve tapped there to open virgin markets.

Subsidiary questions were faced, once a weighing of economic factors had yielded the decision to enter a market. Alternate means of transportation might be considered. A choice might be necessary as to which affiliate should be employed to go into the proposed area. Often there was the problem of deciding which of several refineries should supply the product, and always there was the question of price, sensitive not only to market conditions but also to abrupt and unpredictable changes in the crude oil supply situation and to the equally unpredictable vagaries of public opinion and legislative regulation.

Behind the marketing organization—concentrated in 1912 in the Middle Atlantic states and the lower Mississippi basin, with numerous outposts scattered across Canada and South America and a cluster of important offices in Europe—lay the great refineries at Bayonne and Linden, New Jersey. There were smaller plants at Baton Rouge, at Teleajen in Romania, at Sarnia in Ontario, and in Maryland, West Virginia, Cuba, and Argentina. Market demand directed the activity which went on there, but the relationship was reciprocal. A new combination of tubes and tanks; a higher pressure here or a lower temperature there; a different chemical employed in a different place—and an entire market might be revolutionized. This was one of the exciting "X" factors in the petroleum industry. What would Louis Link, that notably skillful, rule-of-thumb refinery superintendent, bring out of his practical laboratory at Baton Rouge? Could "Doc" Robinson at Bayonne get the sulphur out of this crude or the wax out of that? Every new oil discovery set off a flurry of activity. No two crudes were alike. The value of the discovery depended in large measure on the success of the refinery men in evolving an economical manufacturing process. Always there existed the critical question of cuts. Should a crude be skimmed and sold as fuel oil, or would greater returns accrue from running it to kerosene and lubricating oils? The nature of the crude was a determining factor, together with the relative and constantly shifting strength of gasoline, kerosene, lubricating oil, fuel oil, and by-product markets. Perhaps, too, a competitor had gained the edge with a new process. Should it be leased at any cost? Would it be cheaper and worth the risk to try to develop a competing process?

From scores of fields and thousands of wells streams of crude oil poured into the arterial maze of refinery tanks and pipes. Here, too, lay ponderous economic forces to be directed. No Jersey Standard director knew where oil would next be found, but none expected that it would be discovered at the back door of an existing refinery, or within stone's throw of an existing pipeline, or adjacent to a large metropolitan market. In postdissolution months the question of crude supplies was largely one of purchase rather than of production or discovery. A whole group of Jersey Standard's economic chessmen was blocked. Could the organization depend on its nominally independent former affiliates? Would antitrust sentiment permit the founding of new producing and transportation companies? What crudes should be purchased from whom, in what amounts, and at what prices? And what was the long-term supply situation? Did an uncharted sea of petroleum lie under the Oklahoma prairie, or should greater effort be put forth in the hills of West Virginia and Ohio? Should money be poured into subsidiary producing ventures abroad, or was Henri Deterding of the Royal Dutch-Shell already too strong and the State Department still too indifferent?

These questions were considered daily at 26 Broadway. At the fingertips of the directors lay a tremendous fund of information, swollen and freshened hourly by new facts which poured into headquarters from outlying offices in many parts of the world. Often these men journeyed out to view operations at first hand, and in an almost uninterrupted stream the field lieutenants reported to the main offices. In the boardroom the pace of one segment of the organization was geared to that of the others, and the tempo of all phases of operation adjusted to the general movement of business. Only here, at 26 Broadway, could the common denominator be found; only here was the operating entity and the purposeful unity evident. Here the nine directors, each with his specific responsibilities and interests, gathered to blend their broad understanding and their command of far-flung resources into courses of action that spelled profit and security for the company.

THE "BIG BOARD" AND ITS FUNCTIONINGS

The policies formulated at 26 Broadway for Jersey Standard and its remaining affiliates bore the imprint of strong personalities. To an enormously important extent company progress was simply a reflection of the individual abilities of the men on the directorate, and of their success or failure in getting along with one another. As in earlier years, not all these men were endowed with active managerial responsibilities in the company. The Jersey board had strong men and weak men; active directors and inactive directors as well. In substance, important company policy was determined by fewer than nine men—on some occasions by many fewer.[19]

The part played by Orville T. Waring on the Jersey directorate, for example, was scarcely a critical one. Waring's connection with Standard Oil went back to 1876. For many years he had been in charge of the Lubricating Oil Department, but after 1911 Waring's chief function was to supervise the management of company offices at 26 Broadway. His presence on the Big Board in this minor capacity is explained both by his distinguished past and by the requirement that the company have at least one resident of New Jersey as a director. Walter Jennings, who served as director from 1903 through 1927, came up through the marketing side of the business and was for a time in charge of Jersey Standard's domestic marketing business. A rich man in his own right, Jennings' greatest interest in later life was not in management but in his philanthropies. Charles W. Harkness, like Jennings, was a carry-over from the predissolution board, but poor health virtually eliminated him from active participation in management long before 1911. In 1913 he resigned. Charles M. Pratt, the handsome, cultivated, and public-spirited director who had formerly headed Standard Oil of Kentucky, was old in the service of the company, and in 1913 declining physical capacities forced his retirement also.[20]

James A. Moffett had been a director since 1901. His early experience, which included the presidency of Indiana Standard and many other one-time affiliates, was exceptionally well rounded and particularly strong on the manufacturing side. Moffett was impetuous, positive, and quick to voice an opinion. "The Old Devil" his contemporaries called him. His entry into the boardroom was often the precursor to debate, and his wide experience rendered him capable of useful participation in the discussion of almost any phase of operations. From 1911 until his death in 1913 Moffett exerted a strong influence on the Jersey board.[21]

In 1911 Frederick H. Bedford was made a director. His association with Standard Oil went back three decades, and most of his experience had been concentrated in the lubricating oil business. Bedford was both competent and energetic in his administration, as a director, of Jersey Standard's lubricating oil business, but his participation in company affairs tended to be limited to the area of his designated responsibility.

John D. Archbold, Jersey's president from 1911 to 1916, was the mellowed veteran of a turbulent oil generation. His capacities were not specialized but general, for his service with Standard Oil from 1879 to 1911 had been rich and varied. For years his keen business acumen and his skill in parrying political attacks had made Archbold's services of greatest value; Rockefeller had made him the effective head of the Standard Oil enterprise with complete faith in his ability. While age and hard work had failed to impair the capacity for leadership of this buoyant, well-loved, and influential man, the postdissolution months saw Archbold, who had always believed in a multitude of good counselors, increasingly willing to delegate the responsibilities for active management to his fellow directors. The aging Archbold continued to be a good committeeman and a superb presiding officer. This was perhaps his most valuable contribution to the company's well-being between 1911 and 1916. In board meetings he liked to lean back in his chair and listen while his directors argued back and forth. When tempers flared and tension in the boardroom mounted to a dangerous pitch, Archbold, with a fine sense of crisis, would abruptly intrude a humorous remark or a joke into the debate. Invariably his infectious humor cleared the atmosphere and enabled discussion to continue on a calmer plane. Archbold was no figurehead. He knew the oil business and he was a man of great moral strength. Few dared to cross him when he was aroused, for, when he exploded in one of his infrequent white flashes of temper, his power of retort and invective was withering.[22]

All these seven men named—Waring, Jennings, Harkness, Pratt, Moffett, F. H. Bedford, and Archbold—had seen long service. Five of these directors were very near the end of their company careers; one was serving in a subordinate role; two of the younger of the group were specialists rather than general administrators. It was clear that here in the Jersey Company, as elsewhere among the affiliated organizations, an exceptional opportunity was at hand for promising and qualified young men to assume wide general administrative responsibilities. The junior vice-presidents and directors, A. Cotton Bedford and Walter Clark Teagle, appeared to be in direct line for rapid accession to leadership.

In 1912 A. Cotton Bedford, the cousin of F. H. Bedford and a protégé of the Pratts and Rogers of earlier Standard Oil fame, was fifty years of age. His career had commenced thirty-two years earlier and evolved through a succession of positions which included management of The Bergenport Chemical Company, participation in the affairs of several natural gas companies, and supervision of certain outside interests of his sponsors. Bedford's appointment as a Jersey director in 1907 caused widespread comment, for he admittedly was no oilman. Bedford himself professed surprise that he should have been thus honored.[23]

A. C. Bedford liked to explain his rise to success in terms of the homespun virtues—hard work, honesty, eagerness to learn, and willingness to obey. This man, however, was no homespun office drudge. A background of wide travel and much social intercourse in the service of the company had given Bedford polish. He was handsome, self-possessed, and naturally eloquent—an effective organizer and an exceptionally competent contact man. He was the complete antithesis of the rough-and-ready oilman of cherished tradition, and, indeed, he was regarded by some men of that type as cool and pompous. His fellow directors, however, liked and respected Bedford. His backing among the older directors was particularly strong, for Bedford was stable, openhanded, and essentially conservative.

Walter Clark Teagle, in quite marked contrast to his fellow junior vice-president, was an oilman's oilman, though his career scarcely constituted a rags-to-riches chronicle. Teagle graduated from Cornell University in 1899 and went to work in his father's oil firm in Cleveland. When Standard Oil interests acquired and reorganized the firm, the younger Teagle was made vice-president and general manager. In 1903 he was transferred from Cleveland to the export trade group. Thereafter, on the basis of his own exceptional merits, he was rapidly promoted over the heads of various other executives who had been much longer in the company's service. In 1908 Teagle became head of European marketing. In the following year he was named to the Jersey Standard directorate.

While working for his father in Cleveland, Teagle had learned much about the oil business. He had warmth and a fine sense of humor and was a good listener. In appearance Teagle was a solid oak of a man—6 feet 3 inches tall and 240 pounds in weight—but with a boyish, almost cherubic, countenance. Endowed with prodigious energy, Teagle turned naturally to the outdoors for relaxation. Hunting and fishing were passions in which he indulged at every opportunity, and the time spent in the field was not idle. Here Teagle cemented many an important friendship and laid many a vital plan. The real genius which drove this man who was to dominate Jersey Standard history for a full generation, however, is hard to define. There are innumerable testimonials to Teagle's unstrained democracy and ready sympathies, but there also existed a hard core of practicality which enabled him to subjugate personal considerations to the necessities of business situations as he saw them. To this must be added the ambition of this young man both for himself and for his company, as well as his uncanny flair for resolving or circumventing obstacles that stood in his path. In 1912 Walter Teagle was thirty-four years of age and already a major force on the Jersey board.

As time passed, the make-up of that board was substantially altered by death and retirements. The replacement of old and inactive directors by younger and more energetic men was, of course, salutary. Perhaps the most noteworthy addition to the directorate in the 1912-1917 period was that of Frederic D. Asche, in 1914. Like so many of the Jersey Standard directors, Asche was a seasoned marketing man. Starting work for Standard Oil in 1891 as an office boy, he soon had become secretary and then a member of the Export Trade Committee, where he worked with Teagle. By 1911 Asche, who was then thirty-eight years of age, was second only to Teagle in this branch of the business. He was extremely hard-working and habitually stayed at his desk long after the company offices had closed for the day, often laboring over tasks that should have been entrusted to subordinates. Asche lacked Teagle's sociability, hated speechmaking, shunned public notice, and indulged in no hobbies until Teagle himself persuaded him to try fishing. The two men thought highly of each other, and in the strenuous trials that lay ahead Asche proved to be a trustworthy and capable lieutenant.[24]

George H. Jones, elected to the directorate in 1917, had scarcely known anything but grueling work. His career was an incredible chronicle of self-inflicted disciplines as in succession he mastered typing, shorthand, bookkeeping, accountancy, law, and finance. His penchant for painstaking care in the preparation of reports finally prompted James Moffett to exclaim to the other directors, "How much are we paying this man?" Moffett insisted that Jones' salary be increased by 50 per cent. After Jones had been made a director, he served as the walking encyclopedia of the board. His ability to recite from memory the statistical details of thousands of transactions made him invaluable. At board meetings he would lean back and cite exact figures on tons, barrels, cubic feet, gallons, dollars, and cents, to the never-ending amazement of his associates and sometimes, apparently, mainly for his own amusement. It is said that, had the Jersey record books of the day been destroyed, Jones could almost have re-created them out of the depths of his marvelously retentive mind. Jones, who was also credited by some observers with being one of the clearest thinkers on the board, was notably loath to defend his own viewpoints against those of the more forceful members of the directorate, and therefore participated less than he might have in the formulation of top policy.[25]

Other specialists were added to the board. In 1913 Frederick W. Weller became a director, representing refining interests in general and the Standard Oil Company of Louisiana in particular. Seth B. Hunt, whose background was also in refining, joined the directorate a year later. Both men had come up through the ranks. Hunt in particular, while lacking the grasp of the business possessed by Asche and Jones, contributed to the directorate a strong sympathy for the human problems of the business. In 1915 William H. Libby, who had served as Standard's genial and competent foreign ambassador-at-large, became a director. By this time Libby's brilliant career was almost at an end, and he was not an important figure on the board. This was true also of H. M. Tilford, another prominent pre-dissolution executive, who served as a director in charge of the domestic trade department for a few months in 1917.

The general pattern of the postdissolution directorate was thus a clear and familiar one. Strength and knowledge of operating details were provided by the traditional policy of developing leadership in the ranks, either in the Jersey Company itself or in affiliated organizations. Age tempered youth, but many of the older men perhaps served longer than they should have, and the abilities of some of the board members were confined to a relatively narrow operational plane. The recommendations of these specialists were subjected to the scrutiny of others, like Archbold, Moffett, Teagle, and A. C. Bedford, who through their broad perspective and great personal prestige influenced company policy in an important way.

Quite apart from the wide variations in strength, in training, and in personality to be found here, this directorate, upon which fell the task of rebuilding the Jersey Standard organization, was no ordinary group. Faced with problems that seemed to require the ultimate in dynamic direction and centralized authority, the board of directors was actually neither dynamic nor autocratic. Long before 1911 Standard Oil management had worked out its highly effective committee system of administration, the essence of which was the more or less free give-and-take of men in the company of peers. This strong and very real democratic managerial tradition survived the dissolution decree and even outlived many of the committees themselves. The boardroom continued after 1911 to be a meeting place for the exchange of ideas, not the fountainhead of arbitrary orders. Though certain board members became more influential than others, discussion remained the foundation stone of management; if Jersey Standard occasionally failed to move rapidly, the explanation more often than not was that the directors were still pondering.

This, of course, is not to say that harmony and co-operation characterized all contemplation by the directors of company policy. There were arguments and there were enmities, but for the most part the exchanges in the boardroom seem to have been well under control. Even strong individualism was chastened by tradition, and the pattern of co-operative administration remained in evidence even while administrative devices and practices were undergoing profound changes.

DIVISION OF BUSINESS IN THE CORPORATE FAMILY

Only when viewed as a group did the Jersey Standard companies present a picture of integrated operations. For the most part the affiliates performed specialized functions and often conducted the operational details of their business with a large measure of independence. The total pattern of Jersey Standard's business, therefore, is most advantageously described in functional terms, and proper places for the corporate children on the family tree are best assigned by reference to the duties they were called upon to perform.

The true importance of the network of affiliated companies is at once established by the fact that over the 1912-1917 period 61 per cent of the Jersey Company's earnings came from affiliates, the balance representing income from the company's own operations.[26] Of the income accruing to Jersey Standard from activities carried on in its own name, 54 per cent came from refining and general manufacturing activities and 25 per cent from interest, chiefly on loans to affiliates. Thus the specialized nature of the parent company and its essential functional dependence upon affiliated organizations stand clear.[27]

Even with the business of the affiliates added to that of the parent company, however, the total operational pattern still presents evidence of the disruptive implications of the dissolution decree. An informative set of figures for the year 1911 has been preserved, demonstrating the changes that took place. Table 3 compares earnings of the whole Standard Oil group in that year, by functions, with earnings computed for the same period of the companies that remained in the Jersey Standard group after the dissolution.

By the end of 1917 the unbalanced nature of operations had scarcely been remedied, and the immense revenue losses inflicted by the dissolution in the fields of production, transportation, and domestic marketing had not been restored in kind. The Jersey Standard group was still top-heavy with refining capacity and could carry on its operations only through critical dependence on disaffiliated companies. Table 21 suggests the relationship between major areas of Jersey's business; it also depicts the trends that form the subject matter for the chapters which follow.

Table 3: **NET EARNINGS**
     Classified by Operating Functions, for the Calendar Year Ending December 31, 1911

	(Parentheses indicate net loss)	
	All Standard Oil Companies	Post-dissolution Jersey Standard Group
Domestic refining and manufacturing[a]	$ (2,662,000)	$ (6,711,000)
Domestic marketing[b]	12,774,000	1,769,000
Domestic producing	28,329,000	1,159,000[c]
Natural gas business	5,193,000	5,184,000
Domestic transportation business	37,006,000	[d]
Crude oil purchasing	(302,000)	[e]
European business[f]	3,102,000	2,695,000
South American business[f]	(183,000)	(262,000)
Australian business[f]	815,000	none
Asiatic business[f]	3,180,000	none
African business[f]	529,000	none
Miscellaneous[g]	7,645,000	4,818,000
Total	**$95,426,000**	**$8,652,000**

a Includes returns from The Imperial Oil Company, Ltd., and The West India Oil Refining Company.
b Includes marketing returns from The Imperial Oil Company, Ltd., West India Oil Company, and Waters-Pierce Oil Company's business in Mexico.
c Includes earnings from domestic transportation.
d Included under Producing.
e Included in Miscellaneous.
f Includes net earnings from all phases of operations in these areas not included in classifications above.
g Largely composed of interest received on loans to affiliated companies by Standard Oil Company (New Jersey).
NOTE: In addition to the classification variations pointed out in notes a through f, certain items of overhead were not allocated on a functional basis. The figures as stated, however, were compiled and used in this form by the company and are valid for general comparative purposes. For explanations of the individual functional earnings and losses, see Hidy and Hidy, *Pioneering in Big Business.*
Source: SONJ, Fin. Recs.

To describe the Jersey group only in terms of functions, however, would be to lose the whole gusty flavor of the enterprise, for, as in all large families, the interplay of personalities had much to do with the course of events. Certainly there were colorful corporate personalities among the principal organizations which channeled streams of revenue into 26 Broadway. Aside from the Jersey Company itself, four European, one South American, and six North American companies constituted the principal breadwinners of the Jersey Standard family in the representative year

1913.[28] Together, the earnings of these eleven affiliates—out of the thirty-two directly owned and retained by Jersey Standard after the dissolution—constituted 85 per cent of the profit which the Jersey Company recorded from affiliated operations in that year, and 62 per cent of the total earnings of the Jersey Standard group. Table 4 records these companies and lists their absolute and relative earnings at one point in the constantly shifting pattern of Jersey's history.

Table 4: **NET EARNINGS**
Standard Oil Company (New Jersey) and Affiliates, 1913

Company	Location	Principal Functions	Amount	Per Cent of Total
Standard Oil Company of Louisiana	U. S.	Producing, refining, marketing, transporting	$ 7,443,000	16
Imperial Oil Company, Limited, The	Canada	Refining, marketing	4,748,000	10
Deutsch-Amerikanische Petroleum-Gesellschaft	Germany	Marketing, transporting	4,083,000	9
Hope Natural Gas Company	U. S.	Natural gas business	2,677,000	6
Romãno-Americana	Romania	Producing, refining, marketing	2,296,000	5
East Ohio Gas Company, The	U. S.	Natural gas business	1,651,000	4
Peoples Natural Gas Company, The	U. S.	Natural gas business	1,453,000	3
American Petroleum Company	Holland	Marketing	1,267,000	3
West India Oil Company	S. A.	Marketing	1,126,000	3
Carter Oil Company, The	U. S.	Producing	1,121,000	2
Società Italo-Americana pel Petrolio	Italy	Marketing	1,041,000	2
All other affiliates	Various locations and functions		4,963,000	11
Standard Oil Company (New Jersey)	U. S.	Marketing, refining, holding company	12,010,000	26
Total			$45,879,000	100

Source: SONJ, Fin. Recs.

CONTROL AT TWO LEVELS

In scores of offices all over the world where the outriders of the Jersey Standard organization were encamped, provincial independence and local autonomy were the rule rather than the exception. This situation was a clear reflection of the democratic governing principles that prevailed in the boardroom at 26 Broadway.

The incorporation of the Standard Oil Company of Louisiana in 1909 had been a characteristic Standard Oil stratagem, a skillful and far-thinking adaptation to the shifting relationship between crude oil supplies and

markets for refined products. It was a group of men from Standard's refinery at Beaumont, Texas, who chose the refinery site among the weevil-
ridden cotton fields at Baton Rouge, on a sandy bluff overlooking the
Mississippi. Almost from the first day that Frederick W. Weller, his
brother Daniel R., and A. K. Gordon set up their office in the run-down
little river town, the Louisiana organization began to acquire a provincial
flavor. Set in a rural atmosphere far removed from the clamor of industry,
even the influx of technicians from the New Jersey refineries failed to disturb the homogeneity of this compact group. The Wellers presided over
the affairs of company and town alike with an easy, personal touch. The
memories of men still living recall the Old South social caste system which
took root and flourished in an atmosphere of small-town rivalries. Company affairs furnished grist for the social mill, and table talk revolved
around rumors of promotions, discharges, and the state of Louisiana's
business and politics. At times it seemed to these people that 26 Broadway was far away indeed.

This same attitude was also to be found, though to a less pronounced
degree, in The Carter Oil Company, Jersey Standard's only important
domestic producing company. The corporate psyche of this organization
derived from that of Colonel John Carter himself, a fiercely individual-
istic old man of great capacity and wide influence, who had seen the
early boom days in the Pennsylvania fields. In the Carter Company the
feeling ran high that the Jersey Standard directorate of postdissolution
months was scarcely qualified to pass judgment on production matters—
an opinion that was shared by some of the men at 26 Broadway. When
the center of Carter producing operations was moved, in 1915, from
Sistersville, West Virginia, to Tulsa, Oklahoma, the administrative tie with
Jersey grew weaker with the miles.

Local independence flourished in Ontario, too, as well as in Baton
Rouge and in Tulsa. Solid Canadian nationalism in The Imperial Oil
Company, Limited, however, began to break down under the impact of
a thoroughgoing reorganization of the company between 1914 and 1918.
A change of management kindled new fires and established a somewhat
more sympathetic relationship between parent company and affiliate,
while at the same time building up the self-respect and self-sufficiency of
the Canadian organization. Strong reluctance to admit Imperial's subservi-
ence to an American company, nevertheless, was to be found among most
of the Canadians in Imperial's employ.

In Germany the affairs of the Deutsch-Amerikanische Petroleum-Gesellschaft, one of Jersey Standard's most important foreign marketing affiliates, were literally conducted in a world apart from 26 Broadway. Experience had long since proved that most European operations could not be managed without Europeans. Certainly DAPG, as it was called, was thriving in the rattlesnake's lair of the Continental oil industry. The cool Prussian efficiency and polished Old World diplomacy of Heinrich Riedemann were piling up profits. A ripening friendship between Teagle, head of Jersey Standard's export business, and the brilliant and cosmopolitan Riedemann prophesied interesting developments on the international stage. Riedemann's opinions on European affairs were accorded great weight in co-ordinating American and European operations, and he was allowed maximum freedom to operate in his own way.

In Romania, too, affiliated operations were conducted under circumstances not always comprehensible to American managers or subject to close control from the Broadway offices. A promising start had been made there in 1904, but managerial difficulties had multiplied. In 1909 Everit J. Sadler, an energetic young engineer who had graduated from Annapolis in 1899 and entered the employ of The Prairie Oil & Gas Company, was dispatched to take charge of Jersey Standard's principal venture into foreign production and refining. The output of Româno-Americana's refinery at Teleajen was strategically essential if the Jersey Company was to compete successfully with Russian and Galician oil in Continental markets; the refinery in turn was geared to production from company wells in the nearby Ploesti and Moreni fields. In the immediate prewar years the aggressive and virtually unhampered work of "Sad" and his lieutenants in applying American technology and managerial methods in Romania was beginning to show results.

In each of these important companies, then, as in all the affiliates, a large measure of independence flourished. The "Big Board" at 26 Broadway formulated general policies, which were turned over to the various board members for execution. These men worked more or less closely with the responsible operating committees and with the managers in the field. Results were reported back to 26 Broadway, where the directorate sat in judgment. As long as satisfactory results were reported and no critical problems arose, the directorate as a whole maintained a hands-off policy, and the individually responsible directors did not press themselves upon their subordinates unnecessarily. In the Jersey Standard organization integration was in no sense synonymous with domination. Few affiliated offices were acutely conscious of the pull of the invisible reins that led back to 26 Broadway. Parent company control was at an administrative level far from the sight and comprehension of most men in the field, and the presence of one or more Jersey Standard directors in executive positions or as members of the boards of some affiliated companies was scarcely noticeable. Far from constituting a source of weakness, this relative freedom of local management tended to encourage strength, initiative, and local pride.

The mechanics of operating control in the organization were essentially simple and appear to have undergone little evolution throughout the 1912-1917 period. There was considerable personal intercourse, both in the field and at 26 Broadway. Jersey Company auditors continued, as they had done before 1911, to make periodic examinations of the books of affiliates. The routine financial reports that were forwarded at regular intervals to the parent company were standardized in form and adequate for the needs of the time, but accounting uniformity throughout the organization was a hope that had not been realized. The accounting system of the Jersey Company gathered and sifted an immense amount of information, though at this time there was less dependence on figures and greater reliance on the personal knowledge and experience of the men who read them than was to be the case later.

In predissolution years the committee system of management, which cut across corporate lines of organization, had worked effectively both in controlling affiliated operations and in dovetailing those operations into an over-all plan. The potentialities of control through such groups of specialists, however, were diminished by the dissolution decree, less on any theoretical grounds than for the eminently practical reason that the services of some key men on all committees were lost to the Jersey Company. Between 1911 and 1917 the committee system probably was most effective as a means of administering the internal affairs of the Jersey Company itself, but available evidence suggests that even at this restricted level administrative difficulties were encountered. In the confused months of 1912 most of the initiative and responsibilities formerly vested in the various committees passed to the directorate or to certain strong individuals in the top echelons of management. This was a natural consequence of the blow that the dissolution decree dealt the administrative organization.

Control by Jersey Standard of its corporate dependencies and of the functions that they performed was a critical operating problem, as was the internal management of the parent company's own affairs, but control at this level held far less interest for the public and for federal agencies in charge of enforcing antitrust legislation than the question of *who controlled the Jersey Company*. The plain implication imparted by newspapers and by the reports of some investigating committees in the period was that Rockefeller and the other members of the old Trust— Flagler, Pratt, Payne, Folger, and the rest—not only held the Jersey reins but were hauling on them vigorously.

Stockholder lists indicate that a large majority of the Jersey Company stock was closely held. In 1911, 1.5 per cent of the stockholders owned 72 per cent of the company stock. Approximately 38 per cent of the stock stood in the names of the directors. Another 10 per cent was owned by identified members of their families. Institutions endowed by these men or families owned an additional 2 per cent. By 1917 only a barely detectable dispersion of stock ownership had taken place.[29]

The controlling power over the Jersey Company in 1911 resided with directors and former directors and Trust members and remained in the same hands throughout the years to 1918. These potent stockholders,

Table 5: **STOCK INTERESTS OF DIRECTORS**
Standard Oil Company (New Jersey), August, 1911

Director	Number of Shares Held	Percentage of Total Shares Outstanding
Rockefeller, J. D.	244,345	24.9
Harkness, C. W.	43,400	4.4
Payne, O. H.	40,000	4.1
Flagler, H. M.	15,000	1.5
Rockefeller, William	8,000	0.8
Archbold, J. D.	6,000	0.6
Pratt, C. M.	5,005	0.5
Jennings, W.	3,500	0.4
Bedford, E. T.	3,000	0.3
Folger, H. C., Jr.	1,616	0.2
Moffett, J. A.	400	a
Waring, O. T.	367	a
Bedford, A. C.	100	a
Drake, L. J.	37	a
Teagle, W. C.	15	a
Total Holdings	370,785[b]	37.7[b]
Total Shares Outstanding	983,383	100.0

a Less than 0.1 per cent.
b In addition to these interests, 94,375 shares were owned by persons bearing the family names of directors and by Rockefeller's two daughters and their families. Four institutions, endowed by directors, held stock as follows: Flagler Hospital, 118 shares; General Education Board, 14,514 shares; Pratt Institute, 150 shares; University of Chicago, 5,000 shares.

Source: SONJ, stock list of August 31, 1911.

moreover, in 1911 were also handed the opportunity to control the disaffiliated companies, for by the terms of the dissolution decree they received an equivalent percentage of these stocks as well.

This ostensible importance of the old Standard Oil group gave rise to public misunderstanding and hence to suspicion, but, in fact, it was more apparent than real. The ownership of even a clear majority of stock did not inevitably mean that the owners exercised the control to which such ownership nominally entitled them. The Jersey Company after 1911 was not dominated by the men who held the controlling blocks of stock. Neither, apparently, did these men dictate the policies of the disaffiliated companies. Postdissolution policies of the Jersey Company were formulated by the postdissolution board of directors, the nine members of which together owned only 6 per cent of the company stock in December of 1911 and less than 2 per cent two years later. In 1913 Jersey's chief counsel informed a confidant in the Indiana Company:[30]

There has never been a time since I have been connected with the Standard Oil Company (of New Jersey) that the directors have owned so little of the stock as at the present time. Within a very short time, Harkness and Pratt resign and their places will be filled by people who own very little of the stock. As you know, the Rockefellers, who as large holders of the stock controlled the company as directors for more than thirty years, have absolutely retired, and are simply receiving their dividends and voting at the annual meetings.

The votes of a very large majority of the stockholders proved, in practice, to be the tools rather than the fetters of the directorate. The directorate itself was virtually self-perpetuating. After 1911 it was only on exceptional and infrequent occasions that the Rockefellers (notably John D., Jr.) were to participate actively in the affairs of any of the Standard Oil companies in which they held such formidable blocks of stock. The Trust was certainly dead, though its ghost haunted Broadway and moaned in legislative halls throughout the country.

JERSEY FINANCE AND THE COURSE OF BUSINESS

Jersey Standard's varied, complex, and numerous operating activities, traced in some detail in chapters following, are best discerned against the broad background of general trends and summary results. Growth in the demand for petroleum products and steady increase in competitive pressures were the basic external factors that channelized company development in the 1912–1917 period.

From 1911 to 1914 the oil business showed an over-all tendency to decline as American business in general tottered on the brink of a depression and the world moved toward war. A long-term increase in the use of petroleum products, however, served to cushion the impact of less favorable economic factors. In 1915 the petroleum industry began to respond to the stimulus of war. The year 1916 brought a further boost in activity, and by 1917 an obvious boom was under way. Business of the Jersey Company followed this general pattern of expansion. In 1917 world consumption of petroleum products was 34 per cent higher than in 1912. Annual crude oil runs in Jersey Standard refineries over this same period leaped 16,000,000 barrels, a gain over 1912 runs of 44 per cent.[31] Competition, however, was increasing. Despite absolute increases in sales, the Jersey Company had increasing difficulty in holding its own against rising rivals in volume of business done.

Earnings over this six-year period, however, exhibited spectacular characteristics. A small decline between 1912 and 1914 was followed by a brilliant recovery in the three war years following. Earnings were 130 per cent higher in 1917 than in 1912. Over the period Jersey Standard and its affiliates piled up total earnings of $324,600,000, an amount equivalent to an annual average return of 19 per cent on invested capital.[32] The fact that earnings increased roughly four times as rapidly as refinery activity may be explained in general terms by the economies of capacity refinery operations and by the significant increase that occurred in prices of all types of petroleum products. So drastic was the rise in gasoline prices in 1915 that widespread public protest was stirred and the Federal Trade Commission launched a vigorous anti-Standard investigation. Crude oil prices, too, had advanced sharply, and to a large refiner like the Jersey Company this advance in the price of a basic raw material (the supply of which now had to be purchased largely from others) might well have canceled out gains from rising gasoline, lube oil, and kerosene prices. Jersey Standard, however, providentially had caused the Carter Company to purchase 15,000,000 barrels of crude early in 1915, when the crude price structure in the Mid-Continent field was collapsing under the impact of flush production in the Cushing and Healdton districts. This cheap crude, together with other large stocks which apparently were being carried elsewhere in the organization, was converted into high-priced products. The timing was superb, the tremendous competitive advantage of Jersey's capacity to finance large-scale purchase and storage programs was demonstrated, and the profits proved politically embarrassing.[33]

This is not to say, however, that the great profits of 1915, 1916, and

1917 were exclusively a product of inventory speculation—a term that was anathema at 26 Broadway. Operating results in all phases of the business reflected rising demand at good prices for products that were being manufactured and marketed with a fair degree of efficiency. The grimy refineries on the Jersey marshes piped a fragrant distillate of profit across the Hudson—almost $56,000,000 from Bayonne and Bayway in the 1912-1917 period. Interest charges on loans to affiliates by the parent company brought in $34,500,000 more, and sale and lease of tankers showed profits of close to $13,000,000. Earnings of affiliated companies continued in total to surpass those of the parent company, with Standard of Louisiana, the Hope Natural Gas Company, the West India Oil Company, and Imperial leading the way. In 1917 these four companies alone accounted for over $24,000,000, or almost one-third, of total Jersey Standard earnings. Louisiana Standard was at the top of the list with a fat $8,500,000 contribution to the family hoard. This was a golden era in a golden trade.[34]

Like the cautious parent that it was, Jersey Standard carefully invested a substantial share of its own earnings and those of the corporate children. Approximately 52 per cent ($167,300,000) of total net earnings of the organization over the 1912-1917 period was plowed back into the business. About $34,800,000 was put into the Jersey Company's own plant; some $62,400,000 went into plant and equipment of affiliated companies. The earnings plowed back into subsidiary operations were channeled chiefly into existing organizations, for the political climate was unhealthy for the creation of new affiliates, though the need was great. Of the $62,000,000 put into fixed assets of affiliated companies, approximately $22,000,000 went to finance expansion of producing facilities of The Carter Oil Company, more than $11,000,000 went into general expansion of the Standard Oil Company of Louisiana, and about $7,000,000 went to assist The Imperial Oil Company, Limited, to launch a producing venture in South America and enlarge its refining and marketing organizations in Canada.

Of the $157,300,000 in dividends distributed by the Jersey Company in this period, the sum of $39,335,000 represented an extra, declared in 1913 and paid out of funds returned to the parent by disaffiliated companies in the dissolution process. In effect, therefore, this dividend represented a distribution of capital. Regular dividends over the period were paid at an unchanged rate of 20 per cent on the par value of stock, a total of 34 per cent of net earnings.

To these probings of Jersey's fiscal policy must be added the consideration of one last and vastly important phase of operations. The fact that interest revenues for the period totaled about 25 per cent of the Jersey Company's own earnings is proof enough of the importance of the parent company's function as banker for the group. References to the Jersey Company's private banking activities as such, however, were carefully guarded by company men, for they did not wish to emphasize the financial dependence of the affiliates upon the parent. On one occasion when news of this activity spilled out upon the witness stand, a newspaper caption exclaimed, "*So Easy to Get Cash!*" and the account went on to build the simple and normal transaction of an interorganization loan into a crime against society.[35]

A steady flow of funds streamed back and forth between Broadway and the offices of affiliated companies. This stream had its origin in a tremendous reservoir of liquid funds at 26 Broadway, the residue of unexpended past profits, and the proceeds from liquidation of debts during the dissolution. Cash reserves, however, were never allowed to accumulate, nor does there appear to have been any substantial movement of Jersey Standard funds in this period into the call loan market. Excess funds went almost exclusively into working-capital loans. As of December 31, 1912, Jersey's ledgers recorded outstanding credits, principally to affiliated companies, of $110,800,000. This balance was not exceeded in the five years following, but at no time did it fall below $50,000,000. Between 1912 and 1917 the heaviest borrowers were Carter, Imperial, and Louisiana Standard, all engaged in one area or another in attempting to expand producing operations.[36] In 1912 Louisiana Standard owed the parent company about $11,500,000, but this sum was surpassed by Carter, which at one time in 1916 was indebted to the extent of $23,000,000. Imperial also used Jersey Standard funds extensively, but repaid them rapidly and did not allow its debt to accumulate.

Terms of these working-capital loans were not standardized as to time. To some affiliates and at some times, funds were advanced in regular weekly amounts and repaid at regular intervals. At certain times very large sums were advanced for particular needs, such as for one of Carter's great lease-plays in the Mid-Continent field. The larger transactions involving nonroutine transfer of funds were recorded in so-called Loan Accounts, set up on the books of the parent company in the name of each affiliate. These accounts were charged with advances by Jersey and credited with payments to Jersey, both of loans and of dividends. Interest on the balance of the accounts was paid semiannually, and complaints were voiced in the organization that, while the Jersey Company itself paid only 2.5 per cent interest on amounts it owed, the affiliated companies were charged 5 per cent interest on balances due the parent company. This instance of petty financial tyranny was by no means typical of the general tenor of intraorganizational relations.

Often the Loan Account balances indicated that because of the inclusion of dividends and miscellaneous transactions the affiliates had paid in more to the Jersey Company than was owed. This reflected the policy of gathering in funds which were temporarily in excess of needs in one place and employing them elsewhere in the organization. Number 26 Broadway was, in effect, a gigantic clearinghouse, directing the movement of millions of dollars daily here and there throughout the world wherever required by the shifting necessities of the oil business. Jersey Standard's command of immense amounts of ready capital was to be a factor of dominant importance at many times and in many places in the years which followed 1911, as, indeed, had been the case before that time.

For an organization which had disposed of more than half its corporate assets and lost the services of many of its key executives, Jersey Standard was exhibiting surprisingly lively symptoms. Measured in financial terms, recovery from the dissolution had been amazingly rapid, though the favorable trend of business in the oil industry had played as great a part in this recovery as had the abilities and efforts of the company's leaders. The Jersey Company was able to profit from this trend primarily because it persisted in continuing its business relationships with disaffiliated companies, thereby avoiding the disrupting effects that an absolute decree of divorcement would have wreaked upon the pattern of integrated operations. In these years, however, Jersey Standard had already begun to employ its great wealth to raise bulwarks where it was potentially weakest. The next six chapters tell how the organization was able to stay abreast of a growing and changing and increasingly competitive industry.

Chapter 3

Domestic Supplies of Crude Oil and Gas
1912-1917

POSTDISSOLUTION SUPPLY PROBLEMS

T HE QUEST for oil has captured the imagination of men, and justly so. In the closing decades of the nineteenth century the probing of the earth's subsurface had become an exciting treasure hunt on a scale unprecedented in commercial history, spurred on by great rewards for the successful.

But, like most fabulous quests, the search for hidden petroleum riches involved huge risks. The fascination of the drill had scant allure for Standard Oil leaders as long as a dependable supply of crude oil could be purchased at satisfactory prices. Such conditions, however, proved transitory. Competition for supplies increased as the petroleum industry grew. More important, the existing and anticipated needs of the Standard Oil group had at times threatened to outpace production from existing fields. By the late 1880's outright control of a portion of the sources of supply had become a strategic necessity. Rockefeller and his associates undertook the risks and began to learn the skills involved in locating and extracting the raw material of which they were the principal users.

The dissolution decree of 1911 raised vital questions for the Jersey Company directors to ponder. Had the decree in point of fact imperiled Jersey Standard's crude oil supplies? If so, of what avail was a huge refining and marketing organization? What could be done within the limitations imposed by law, public opinion, and organizational realities to remedy the situation? One observer, reminiscing in recent years, summed up the situation with the typical gusto of the oilman. "The dissolution," he declared, "left Standard with so little crude production that a good man could have drunk it all!"[1]

The Jersey Company itself had never been a producing company. In

43

the years before 1911 the functions of finding and producing adequate supplies of crude oil for the greedy refineries on the Atlantic seaboard had been performed by affiliates. Through The Prairie Oil & Gas Company, The Ohio Oil Company, and the South Penn Oil Company, Jersey Standard had tapped the crude of the Mid-Continent, the Illinois and Ohio, and the Appalachian fields, respectively. All three of these companies were separated from the parent organization by the decree. This was a structural blow which could well have the most serious repercussions.

Offsetting factors in the domestic crude oil supply situation were not obviously encouraging. The Jersey Company in 1912 retained its stock in The Carter Oil Company and in the Standard Oil Company of Louisiana, both of which were already engaged in producing operations. Carter, however, was operating only in the Appalachian fields. This company's output was small, and even before 1912 it was clear that far greater potentialities for crude production lay in the Middle West and Southwest. Louisiana Standard had originally been conceived as a refining and marketing company and had built the Baton Rouge plant with the intention of running Mid-Continent crude. By a fantastic stroke of luck this refinery was located on the very edge of the great Sabine Uplift, but in 1912 the potentialities of the Louisiana oil sands had only begun to be probed. Moreover, the organization was not equipped for large-scale producing activities even should the newly discovered fields prove to be extensive. It was quite obvious, therefore, that Jersey Standard could not look to these affiliates for substantial immediate increases in crude oil production.

The extent of the problem was clearly reflected in production and refining figures for the year 1912. Against a refinery consumption of approximately 96,000 barrels of crude daily in the United States and Canada, the Jersey organization showed daily net crude oil production of only 7,500 barrels (2,500 barrels from Carter, 4,700 from Louisiana, and the remainder from affiliated gas companies). By way of comparison, South Penn, Ohio Oil, and Prairie had channeled to the parent company in the year 1911 a total average daily supply of 68,000 barrels.[2]

A clear determination of the meaning of these figures was essential to the formulation of Jersey Company policy in 1912. Basically, the difficulty was one of an almost overnight transition from an integrated to a specialized organization, from a company that exerted control through ownership over suppliers who furnished a large percentage of its raw material to a company that processed and marketed raw materials which it must now purchase from independent organizations. The immediate question—one which was of pressing concern to Jersey Standard and of great interest to the courts of the land—was, how independent would these independent organizations prove to be?

For the years between 1911 and 1918 the over-all supply picture is that of crude oil moving in vast quantities over great distances in accordance with an intricate planned pattern. Always the objective was preservation of a precarious balance between crude production and refinery consumption, with a maximum of three or four months' supply available in storage as the narrow margin of safety. No amount of foresight could assure complete control over the economic factors involved; periods of plenitude and scarcity alternated with disconcerting rapidity. Newly discovered pools glutted crude oil markets and depreciated the value of existing inventories of manufactured products. On other occasions the exhaustion of old pools, the temporary failure to locate new reserves, and surging new demands for oil products combined to create eras of famine, which continued until resultant high prices stimulated the discovery and development of new fields.

These old but recurring phenomena of the oil business were fundamental determinants of the crude oil market in which Jersey Standard operated, but other factors as well were at work. The following paragraphs take as their starting point the question of the real efficacy of the dissolution decree in the field of crude oil procurement and show the methods by which Jersey Standard was able to appease the almost insatiable appetite of its refineries for oil. The supply story then traces the gradual breaking down of those methods over the years to 1918, by which time the directors, led by two prophets among them, had come to appreciate the fallacy of the "business as usual" philosophy and had begun to adopt those new courses of action that constitute the main theme of Jersey Standard history in the years from 1919 to 1927.

PURCHASING IN ACCUSTOMED CHANNELS

The dissolution decree did not initially deprive Jersey Standard of access to a single barrel of crude oil; neither did it require that the company adopt unfamiliar methods of raw-material procurement. An experienced crude oil purchasing division was already in existence in 1911. Upon this group fell the burden of supplying the needs of refineries still operated by the Jersey organization.

The problem of crude supply was more apparent than real as long as former affiliates were willing to sell their oil and continue their shipments to Jersey Standard as in the past. Legally independent though they were, the disaffiliated producing companies were under the strongest economic compulsion to continue to supply Jersey's refineries. If Jersey Standard had "lost" its crude suppliers, those suppliers, it must be remembered, had also "lost" their principal market. Obvious economic interdependence could not be dissolved by legal incantations, however solemn, and oil supplies actually continued to flow in predissolution channels. It is said, in fact, that the dissolution decree did not even substantially alter clerical procurement routines in the Jersey Company offices at 26 Broadway.[3] In immediate postdissolution years the murmur of Jersey-destined crude through the pipelines of "separated" companies was a comforting—even soporific—sound.

Jersey continued, as in the past, to supply its refineries in New Jersey, Maryland, West Virginia, and Canada in large part with oil obtained from South Penn, Ohio Oil, and Prairie. Prairie also shipped crude to the Baton Rouge refinery. In 1912 these companies, bound to their former parent by economic interest and tradition but not by ownership, supplied Jersey Standard's refineries in North America with an amount of crude equivalent to 90 per cent of the crude run in those refineries in that year.[4]

Crude oil for these refineries was also purchased outside the United States. Cost of transportation was a limiting factor here, however. Romanian, Russian, or Dutch East Indian crude, for example, could not be shipped to Bayonne or Bayway and refined for local or export trade at a cost that would permit competition with products refined from American crude. Mexican crude, however, was a different story. Since 1908 Jersey men had been watching developments south of the border with intensified interest.

Shortly after 1900, both California oilman Edward L. Doheny and an English group headed by Sir Weetman Pearson had commenced operations in Mexico. In 1908 the Pearson interests brought in their Dos Bocas well, which, though destroyed by a tremendous conflagration, was believed to have been the largest gusher ever seen. In 1909 the Doheny group brought in the famed Juan Casiano No. 7, which recorded an initial daily production in excess of 50,000 barrels. News of these Mexican gushers stirred the oil industry. But local refining facilities in Mexico were

primitive, and the wells were far removed from large markets for petroleum products. In 1911 Jersey Standard directors were informed that 10
cents per barrel at the wells was considered a liberal and profitable price
to the producer.[5] At such prices the company found it advantageous to
increase its purchasing activity. Commencing in 1911, large purchase contracts were made with several independent producers in Mexico.

Much of the Mexican crude oil was well suited for fuel oil. As the market for that product expanded, Jersey Standard in 1913 started construction of a refinery at Tampico to top the heavy Pánuco crude and supply
fuel oil and light distillates to the company and its customers. By 1918,
despite an acute wartime shortage of tankers, Jersey Standard was purchasing an average of 40,000 barrels daily of Mexican crude, as compared
with a daily average of 78,300 barrels obtained by the company from its
old suppliers, South Penn, Ohio Oil, and Prairie.

Between 1912 and 1918 the Jersey Company obtained a high percentage
of its crude oil supplies from former affiliates. In these postdissolution
years the amount of purchased crude run in Jersey Standard's domestic
refineries averaged 87 per cent of the company's total crude oil consumption, and there was no pronounced lessening of the gap between
production and consumption by the organization. Prairie, South Penn, and
Ohio Oil all sold to Jersey substantial amounts of crude oil that they
themselves produced and even larger amounts that they had purchased
from others. In addition, several of Jersey Standard's affiliates purchased
crude for their own account and also obtained crude for the Jersey refineries on the East Coast. The Jersey Company itself purchased crude
for the eastern refineries, for the account of certain affiliates, for resale to
nonaffiliated companies, for storage, and for export.

The chart on page 49 illustrates in a general way the crude oil supply
lines as they existed in 1918. The chart is at best, however, an oversimplification of the procurement structure. Oil supplies moved in a complex pattern dictated by prices, quantities, and types of crude oil produced and
demanded, and by the accessibility of crude oil to refining centers. Supplies might and often did move in opposite directions at the same time, in
answer to demands for different types of crude oil at widely separated
points. Transportation costs, pipeline and tanker capacity and availability,
tariffs, legal restrictions, and competitive circumstances all were involved.
Crude oil purchasing, in short, was far from being a routine operation,
and it commanded the detailed attention of the highest executives in the
organization.

PROCEDURES AND PRICES IN TROUBLED MARKETS

The purchasing methods by which Jersey Standard's large supplies of crude oil were obtained present further evidence of the operating bond which necessarily existed between the parent company and its former affiliates after 1911. As in predissolution years, the procurement routines were influenced not alone by economic and geographic considerations, but by fluctuating, important, and often unpredictable political factors generated by the size and potential power of the Jersey organization.

The negotiation of large procurement contracts was entrusted to one or more of the Jersey directors, but the burden of routine crude oil purchasing fell largely on George W. McKnight, secretary of the important Manufacturing Committee, which supervised all refinery activities. The dual nature of McKnight's responsibilities was indicative of the necessity for close co-ordination of refining and purchasing schedules. Too much crude would clog the supply lines; too little would close down the manufacturing establishment. The co-ordinator had a precarious margin of safety, for Jersey Standard refineries had only enough storage capacity for from two to three days' operations.

McKnight dealt with officials in the New York office of the South Penn Oil Company and with representatives of The Ohio Oil Company and of The Prairie Oil & Gas Company in their offices at Findlay, Ohio, and Independence, Kansas, respectively. Because of the need for careful scheduling of deliveries, a co-ordinator of traffic was appointed in the joint employ of the three supplying companies. His task was to route and time crude shipments from points of purchase at the fields or storage depots through the network of pipelines that fed the major refining centers.[6] It seems clear that these three important crude oil producers and purchasers, by that time legally independent not only of Jersey Standard but also of one another, found effective ways within the law to preserve the administrative organization and perpetuate the close co-ordination of activities that had prevailed in predissolution years.

The Jersey Company procured its crude oil by spot purchase and by long-term contracts, both methods widely utilized in the petroleum industry. Almost all purchases involved the risk of loss through sudden price declines, and often the company was forced by urgent refinery needs to place orders when prices were high. The extent of Jersey Standard's crude oil requirements, as well as the highly unpredictable nature of the market, virtually precluded calculated and extensive hedging operations. In so far-

WESTERN HEMISPHERE CRUDE OIL SUPPLY LINES IN 1918
Standard Oil Company (New Jersey) and Affiliates

Figures in barrels per day

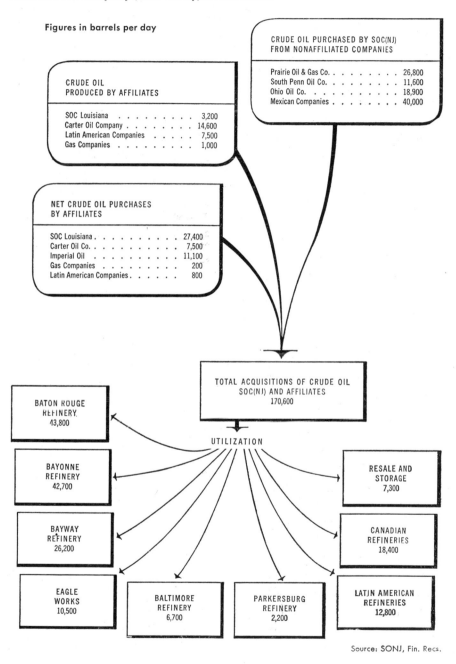

CRUDE OIL PURCHASED BY SOC(NJ) FROM NONAFFILIATED COMPANIES

Prairie Oil & Gas Co.	26,800
South Penn Oil Co.	11,600
Ohio Oil Co.	18,900
Mexican Companies	40,000

CRUDE OIL PRODUCED BY AFFILIATES

SOC Louisiana	3,200
Carter Oil Company	14,600
Latin American Companies	7,500
Gas Companies	1,000

NET CRUDE OIL PURCHASES BY AFFILIATES

SOC Louisiana	27,400
Carter Oil Co.	7,500
Imperial Oil	11,100
Gas Companies	200
Latin American Companies	800

TOTAL ACQUISITIONS OF CRUDE OIL SOC(NJ) AND AFFILIATES
170,600

UTILIZATION

BATON ROUGE REFINERY
43,800

BAYONNE REFINERY
42,700

BAYWAY REFINERY
26,200

EAGLE WORKS
10,500

BALTIMORE REFINERY
6,700

PARKERSBURG REFINERY
2,200

RESALE AND STORAGE
7,300

CANADIAN REFINERIES
18,400

LATIN AMERICAN REFINERIES
12,800

Source: SONJ, Fin. Recs.

flung an organization, to be sure, the losses incurred in one branch of operations often were counterbalanced by gains elsewhere. The wish to optimize these internal compensatory adjustments was to be a basic determinant of long-range company policy after 1911, as it had been in the days when the old Standard Oil organization was being integrated.

Spot purchases were arranged at prices posted by the major purchasing companies in the various fields and were paid for in cash. For many years the prices paid for crude oil by the Jersey Company and its affiliates were those prevailing on the day of delivery by the suppliers; in 1914 prices were changed to those prevailing on the day the order was given. By thus eliminating the uncertainty as to what prices would do in the interval between the order and the delivery, the new procedure greatly facilitated the planning and financing of purchases. To the posted price for crude were added the commission of the supplying company (in this period usually 2 to 5 cents a barrel) and the pipeline and storage charges to lines participating in the transportation of the crude. Allowances were credited to the purchaser for various types of losses in transit. These charges and allowances were to some extent fixed by experience, custom, and law; the Jersey Company, as in the years before 1911, dealt with affiliates in the same manner and on the same terms as with its nonaffiliated suppliers.

The price and supply uncertainties involved in day-to-day purchasing of crude supplies made heavy reliance upon the spot market hazardous to an organization that was consuming close to fifty million barrels of crude oil annually. Many of Jersey Standard's purchases were made by long-term contract for large amounts. In such purchases price reflected general supply and demand factors far less than it did the relative bargaining position of the contracting parties.

The long-term trend in crude oil prices was strongly influenced by demand factors, which exerted substantial inflationary pressure throughout most of the 1912-1918 period. On the supply side of the price equation, alternate periods of plenty and scarcity worked their influence. Short-range price movements of some violence followed in the wake of flush production from new fields, such as Healdton and Cushing in Oklahoma. In 1914 these fields boomed into peak production, poured crude oil into hastily improvised storage, and glutted the market. Prices declined precipitously. Cushing crude fell from $1.00 per barrel to 55 cents, and Healdton crude went from $1.05 per barrel to 50 cents.[7] The local oversupply, moreover, was aggravated by generally unsettled conditions throughout the industry, which saw falling prices even in the older fields.

Situations such as these created exceptional opportunities for companies with large capital and substantial storage facilities to purchase advantageously. The Jersey Standard organization, possessing both storage capacity and capital and rapidly adding to each, purchased tremendous quantities of crude oil in areas of flush production and often at distress prices, storing the excess over immediate refinery needs in tank farms at the fields and along the pipelines. In no other area of operations did size and wealth appear to be such pronounced blessings. In its ability to benefit from such conditions the Jersey Company enjoyed a distinct advantage over smaller refiners. Here lay a source of potential profit for the big companies which the small could scarcely tap. In practice, nevertheless, offsetting factors were continually at work. The risks of inventory accumulation were formidable, if intangible, and storage costs incessantly nibbled away at inventory gains. It seems reasonably certain, moreover, that the maximum utilization of Jersey Standard's powerful market position was never realized.

The abrupt decline in prices in the newly opened fields raised a political storm which swept across state boundaries and into Washington. In the Cushing field in 1914 The Prairie Oil & Gas Company, purchasing crude oil destined in part for Jersey refineries, announced a cut from 75 cents to 55 cents in the price which it would pay. The producers in the field launched violent protests, and the Corporation Commissioner of Oklahoma issued an order that no oil was to be taken from the wells and sold for less than 65 cents. Prairie thereupon halted all purchases. This may have been good economic practice but it proved to be poor political strategy. Within a week the Commissioner was forced to withdraw his ruling; the bitterness of independent producers against the large purchasers who controlled the supply lines from fields to refineries knew no bounds.[8]

In the Healdton district physical violence flared. The Magnolia Petroleum Company, which was believed by many, including the District Attorney of Oklahoma, still to be controlled by Jersey Standard, was accused of cutting purchases abruptly, after having promised to increase its commitments in the field. To be sure, Magnolia was able to present very strong evidence to support its action and was cleared by a federal investigation of charges of restraint of trade, but suspicion lingered on. In Texas small independent producers, who naturally desired to obtain the highest possible prices for their crude oil, were almost continually antagonistic toward Magnolia, The Texas Company, and the Gulf Oil Corporation, the three large companies that owned and controlled most of the pipeline network in the state. These companies were charged with controlling the market to keep prices low and with discrimination against the independents in the running of oil.[9] Virtually every major purchaser and pipeline company, including Jersey Standard, was attacked in the political arena as a result of economic conditions in the oil fields. Scant attention was given to the fact that by purchasing and storing excess supplies these companies had often helped to stabilize market conditions.

Most unfortunately, gasoline prices were being raised at the very time that independent producers were protesting against the ruinous prices they were receiving for crude oil. Few of these producers, even had they had the disposition to study the total situation objectively, were in a position to grasp the over-all industry picture. Again and again normal supply and demand relationships were shattered as flush production in particular areas brought the local price structure crashing, while the world at the other end of the pipelines was clamoring for oil products. Charges of monopoly, collusion, intimidation, and restraint of trade flew about promiscuously. Jersey Standard was accused (informally) of acting in concert with the pipeline companies and former affiliates to reduce prices, and there were ample witnesses to the "observed practices" of the "oil monopoly" to chop down the price of oil in periods of flush production or to refuse to take oil except to a minimum specified degree. The old hue and cry about the long arm and sticky fingers of the Standard Oil Trust was raised again and again and was echoed in high state and national political circles. The Attorney General of the United States was reportedly convinced at this time that the dissolution decree was not strong enough to bring about actual competition between former Standard affiliates.[10] Resolutions were introduced in the United States Senate calling for sweeping investigations of the oil industry in general and Standard Oil companies in particular. The purchasing policies and practices, both of Jersey Standard and of its principal suppliers, were under constant assault in the political disturbances which grew out of the unstable conditions in the oil industry in 1914 and 1915.

Records of the Jersey Company throw little direct light upon the facts behind the charge that there was conspiracy between the company and former affiliates to depress prices in the fields or to accomplish other illegal or unethical practices. In view of the frequency with which such charges were voiced, it seems well both to analyze the term "collusion" as it was used at that time and to probe further into the nature of the Jersey Company's relations with former affiliates.

There was obvious mutuality of interest between Jersey Standard and its suppliers. In view of the often-demonstrated anxiety of the Legal Department not to violate the letter of the law, however, it seems difficult to believe that the company committed intentional and outright violations of state and federal antitrust statutes. Contracts which reflected the exercise of influence, which occasionally were secret, and which promised exclusive mutual advantages to the contracting parties were being made without challenge by hundreds of other companies in all lines of business. This was and is one of the most normal situations in business. Most large business contracts, in fact, tend to a certain extent to restrain trade and create a monopolistic situation in which parties outside the contract may find themselves at a temporary disadvantage. So deeply under suspicion was the Jersey Company, however, that it was widely and instantaneously condemned for almost every move it made, even though other companies might and did make similar moves with impunity. The fact that Jersey Standard entered into contracts with former affiliates was construed by the company's industrial and political enemies as prima-facie evidence of restraint of trade. These contracts appear, however, to have been such as might have been and actually were made between the Jersey Company and any other independent supplier. Insofar as can be ascertained from the most intimate records of the Jersey Company, former affiliates were completely divorced from control by their former parent, though they were obviously not immune to the economic influence of the nation's largest purchaser of crude oil. No company was compelled to sell to Jersey Standard, though many found it to their interest to do so and some were forced to do so for economic reasons quite beyond the control of either themselves or the Jersey Company.

The conditions that gave rise to the widespread unrest among independent producers stemmed primarily not from conspiracy among the major companies but from physical restrictions and the normal exercise of business judgment by the purchasers of crude. The traditional law of capture was working its evils; producers operated their leases desperately in order to "get their share" before the pools were exhausted. At times there simply was too much oil at the fields. Few impartial contemporary observers would have said that purchasing companies were under any legal or moral compulsion to absorb the excess at prices higher than the economic circumstances of market glut required, and the fact could not be denied that on many occasions field production far exceeded existing pipeline and storage capacity of the crude oil buyers. The large oil companies were, in substance, blamed for conditions which were to their advantage, but which would have existed, irrespective of their action or lack of action, just as long as oil producers were forced by existing conditions to tap the prolific new pay horizons without restraint. Jersey Standard and other purchasing and refining companies obviously benefited from such circumstances, but could be held responsible for them only in a vague, accessory-after-the-fact sort of way.

Conditions such as these were finally to impart strength to programs of conservation and prorationing. In the general absence of effective voluntary or compulsory regulation in the years before 1918, however, the small operators seized upon vociferous protest as their chief weapon in the economic struggle in which they were involved. This weapon they used with deadly effect, and much of the time they used it unscrupulously and without discrimination. Their cry was that of the politically popular underprivileged. Frequently taking the name of the consumer in vain, they attacked a system of distribution which was deeply rooted in the prevalent practices and conditions of the industry and for which no effective substitute had as yet been worked out. Their bitter protests hastened the time when solutions offering mutual advantages to producers, purchasers, and public alike were widely instituted.

The point, however, in outlining the disturbed market conditions of 1914 and 1915 is less to assess the validity of charges and countercharges than to indicate the most important conclusion that there was no such thing as a "normal" market for crude petroleum, if, indeed, there ever had been. Demand exerted, at best, only a long-term influence on local supply situations, which were continually being disrupted by the questing drills of adventurous wildcatters. Roaring gushers, blasting tool strings and derrick tops sky high, blew the top off many a stabilized market as well. Price, that classic barometer of market conditions, fluctuated wildly from time to time and from place to place as sudden oil strikes cut across existing trend lines. And finally, superimposed on this naturally complicated market structure, was the potent weight of public opinion and political action, often directed not by intelligent and studied considerations of consumer interest but by the dog-eat-dog attitudes that flourished in the mêlée of booming new oil fields.

Purchasing policies might be predicated on the assumption that large capital could be employed to advantage in a competitive and fluctuating market, but bitter experience proved this to be only partially true. Political action was the limiting factor, and that action tended to be intensified by those very circumstances which normally worked to enhance the position of the large companies. Here was a serious restriction to the formulation and execution of advantageous operational plans. It was not, however, a new restriction; neither was it to become less onerous with the passing of years. Had Jersey Standard been even less efficient in utilizing its great wealth and power, the company might well have avoided much condemnation and abuse.

OLD TIES WEAKEN

For reasons quite aside from the difficulties attendant upon heavy reliance on purchased crude and upon the political ramifications of Jersey Standard's purchasing policies, certain key men in the organization were becoming dissatisfied with procurement policies and methods. The fact was that the one-time affiliates upon which the Jersey Company relied so heavily for crude supplies were increasing their traffic with Jersey's competitors, as they, like the Jersey Company itself, began to get the feel of independence. In 1912, the South Penn, Ohio Oil, and Prairie companies were supplying nine-tenths of Jersey Standard's purchased crude oil requirements; by 1918, they were furnishing less than one-half.

A set of figures has survived which illustrates roughly how the crude oil market was divided at a point of time midway in the 1912-1918 period. In 1915, South Penn, which was then producing or purchasing three-quarters of the output of the Appalachian field, was selling not only to Jersey but also to The Atlantic Refining Company, the Vacuum Oil Company, and the Standard Oil Company of New York. The Jersey Company received less than half of South Penn's crude in that year. In the Illinois field, Ohio Oil was taking slightly less than three-quarters of the field's production, but sold Jersey Standard only about one-half of its takings. In the Mid-Continent, Prairie was taking about one-third of the crude oil run to pipelines, and approximately four-fifths of these takings were being sold to Atlantic, Standard of New York, Standard of Indiana, and companies other than Jersey Standard.[11] To be sure, South Penn, Prairie, and Ohio Oil had for many years shipped a portion of their takings to these and other one-time Jersey affiliates. Before 1911, however, when there had been a question of important shortage, telegraph lines from 26 Broadway had crackled out instructions on allocation. After 1911 the directing voices were silent, and suppliers dealt with companies offering the best terms. Co-ordination gave way to competition in the scramble for crude oil supplies.

By 1917 the dependability of the Jersey Company's existing sources of crude oil had already begun to be questioned; some complaint was even voiced that at times suppliers had taken advantage of Jersey's dependence upon them. The leading critic of company procurement policies was Everit J. Sadler, who, following his return from Romania in 1917, was dispatched to Mexico, where he labored for a year to build up Jersey Standard producing interests. In a letter dated March 5, 1917, addressed to S. B. Hunt, treasurer and director in charge of producing activities, Sadler made the statement, "In the United States possibly we [the Jersey Company] have some protection in the production and transportation facilities controlled by friendly concerns."[12] This comment tells much about the short-term impact of the dissolution decree upon existing supply lines. Sadler, however, appended a significant expression of doubt: "This may or may not be sufficient for our protection."

Two years later Sadler was more explicit in his concern. "Prior to the dissolution," he stated, "the production of such companies as the South Penn, Ohio Oil, and Prairie Oil & Gas . . . protected the refinery investments of this Company, while today we have no claim on them nor influence in shaping their policies."[13] This statement when placed beside Sadler's earlier comment expresses as well as may be, and in authoritative words, the difficult definition of Jersey Standard's relations with former affiliates—friendship without control.

Sadler went on to elaborate upon the dissatisfaction with which he regarded the existing state of affairs. These three important suppliers, he stated, had not since 1911 been obliged to wildcat or take any risks such as would have been justifiable and necessary if they had had refinery investments to cover. Since the dissolution they had had no compelling interest in taking chances to obtain oil for other companies. The respective managements evidently felt that the interest of their stockholders was best served by following that policy which promised the greatest immediate profit. As a result, Sadler concluded, none of the three had been aggressive in expanding production during the years between 1912 and 1918. Consequently their production did not increase in proportion to total American production and lagged even further behind the increase in Jersey Standard's refinery capacity.[14]

These comments echoed in tone those which had been heard in 1887 and 1888, when somewhat similar circumstances had first led Standard

Oil men to venture into producing activities. The fulfillment of Sadler's desire for a pronounced change in procurement policies was not to be achieved until after 1918, but the forces that made such a change increasingly imperative were at work in varying degree throughout the 1912-1918 period.

The importance of Jersey Standard's purchasing activities is paramount in these years, but a start was also being made in expanding the production of affiliated companies. These beginnings merit attention not just for the interest that attaches to all such early efforts, but because developments in domestic and foreign producing were soon to overshadow almost all other aspects of the Jersey Company's operations.

BACKGROUND OF A PRODUCING POLICY

In 1911, as on a number of earlier occasions, some petroleum men feared that America was running out of oil. Certainly the oil strikes in California were encouraging, but foreboding statisticians pointed to the pronounced downward trend of production that characterized the important Appalachian, Lima, Illinois, and Gulf fields.

The search for new fields was eager. Some prospectors used divining rods. Grizzled veterans of the oil game claimed they could smell an oil formation, or spot a good location by the contour of the countryside. All knew by now, of course, that petroleum could exist only in certain geologic formations. The trick was to find the formations, and real knowledge was meager. Seepages, where oil escaped through natural fissures to gather on the earth's surface in telltale pools, were avidly sought. Surface outcroppings of petroliferous formations were also guides for the prospectors. By 1911 there were not many men, even among the ranks of the reactionary, who still doubted that petroleum gathered on and around anticlines and domes. These subsurface hills, formed by structural folding in the dim epochs of geologic time, sometimes revealed their subterranean presence by surface indications. The twentieth-century prospector, however, was not so naïve as to think any longer that every hill encased an oil-saturated anticline, like the shell on a pecan. Then, too, it was well known that oil was often encountered where no such structures existed. These obscure underground reservoirs, which in later years came to be known as "stratigraphic traps," were virtually unpredictable in location, and very early in the history of the petroleum industry they gave rise to the saying, "Oil is where you find it."

As the more obvious surface indications were rapidly tracked down, the quest for oil became almost blind. Chance as well as knowledge guided the successful. Knowledge, however, was slowly accumulating. Commencing in 1907, important reports of the United States Geological Survey began to convince even the skeptics that the science of geology was of basic value in prospecting. These reports supplemented even earlier investigations by certain state geological departments. Armed with Brunton compass and plane table, the geologists took their place beside the veteran prospectors and studied the earth's surface scientifically for signs of what lay beneath. Scores of these men began to desert the government service and the universities to capitalize on their scientific training. Lack of practical experience in some instances made them favorite objects of ridicule in the field, but the ridicule of field-trained oil prospectors was no doubt tinged with uneasy envy.

Still, science and divining rods notwithstanding, the only sure prospecting device was the drill. American wildcatters combed the countryside of a score of states, seeking to bolster their purses by bolstering the nation's reserves of oil and drilling one dry hole after another in their quest.

Early in March of 1912 one of these wildcat operators was "making hole" on the Wheeler farm, near Cushing, a tiny hamlet some fifty miles west of Tulsa, in north central Oklahoma. The weather was wretched and the surroundings were bleak. At 2,000 feet the Wheeler well was beginning to look like just another dry hole, and the drilling crew was impatient to get back into town to spend its pay. On March 10 the cable-tool bit punched into a new sand at 2,300 feet, and the first well of the famous Cushing oil field came in.[15]

By November one of the wildest oil booms in American history was under way. Of the first 46 wells driven, only one was a dry hole. The quiet prairie became a shambles and the town a seething, wide-open frontier settlement. Oil gushed into improvised earthen storage reservoirs, where losses from leakage and evaporation sometimes exceeded 25 per cent. Mud, blood, money, oil, and liquor were blended into scenes of blazing violence.

Then anxious speculators in the crowded lobbies of Tulsa hotels began to ask whether Cushing had blown its head off. Production was falling. By June of 1913 field output was down to 16,000 barrels daily, a figure that one good well alone could easily surpass. The boom-and-bust pattern so familiar to the American mining scene seemed to be again appearing. Roustabouts were already drifting off to greener pastures when, on the eventful last day of November, 1913, Prairie Oil & Gas drilled into the Bartlesville sand at 2,600 feet and literally blew the top off the Mid-Continent development. The discovery of this spectacularly rich formation marked the beginning of a new chapter in the history of The Carter Oil Company and in the efforts of Jersey Standard to increase its oil reserves.

CARTER GOES WEST

In 1915 The Carter Oil Company began to assume a position of enlarged importance in the Jersey Standard organization. This company, organized in 1893, had for many years maintained offices in West Virginia and was managed by its colorful founder and president, Colonel John J. Carter.

Carter's producing properties in West Virginia, Ohio, and Kentucky were in the older oil-producing regions of the United States. Old wells were cleaned, deepened, or plugged back to shallower formations and some new wells were drilled in an effort to maintain the production so essential for the Jersey refineries, but by 1912 the 2,500 Carter wells were averaging little better than one barrel each in daily output.[16]

Business in 1913 was conducted at a pace that must have been considered leisurely by the frenzied Mid-Continent operators. No vast sums were being poured into operations in Carter's territory, and the 150 employees did what they could within the limitations of modest budgets to maintain the status quo. The brick farm buildings on the old Wells estate in Sistersville, West Virginia, housed the field offices and provided sleeping accommodations for the clerical staff. Carter personnel talked as much about their splendid cuisine at Sistersville as they did about their oil wells. Field superintendents saddled their horses for weekly inspection trips of the wells, secure in the knowledge that no wild-flowing gushers were likely to disturb the equanimity of their life. An occasional lease-play caused the tempo of business to quicken momentarily, but in only one of the 31 fields in which the company operated leases in the 1912-1918 period had Carter drilled the discovery well. In only the Junction City District field, in Perry County, Ohio, was production increasing substantially, though the Bremen and Middaugh fields, in Ohio, were modestly active.[17]

Junction City operations were typical of Carter oil-field methodology. The first lease was acquired here by Carter seventeen years after the discovery well had been drilled, and six years after the Bremen Oil & Gas Company had really opened up the field. Most of Carter's leases were obtained from other oil companies, for, by the time that Carter came in, there were few original landowners who had not signed leases. In one instance Carter paid a bonus of $7,000 for an unusually promising bit of acreage, in addition to the customary one-eighth royalty interest in production which most leases specified be paid the lessor. This bonus was considered substantial—only 7 of the 57 leases which Carter eventually took in the field involved bonus payments of more than $1,000, and for 30 of the 57 leases no bonus whatsoever was paid.

On these properties 70 wells had already been drilled preceding acquisition by Carter, and Carter drilled 145 more. Of the 215 wells drilled or acquired, 37, or 17 per cent, were dry holes or had been abandoned by December 31, 1919, while 12 other holes showed inconsequential production. Still, Carter production was on the increase here, and the Junction City pool provided a pleasant contrast to the played-out properties in other areas. Even the once famous Sistersville district was on the wane, and Bear Run, in West Virginia, had fallen off from 203,000 barrels in 1913 to 63,000 in 1914 and to 34,000 in 1915.

If Carter did not, at the moment, possess the physical resources required to meet Jersey Standard's increased demands, still this company was one of the few places in the Jersey organization where men experienced in producing operations could be found. The decline of Carter's eastern fields indicated that the time to employ this talent to better advantage was at hand. Carter had no great capital resources, but the Jersey Company was rich in liquid funds. The drilling of the Bartlesville sand confirmed earlier promises held forth by developments on the prairies of Oklahoma and indicated the direction of the Jersey-Carter move.

Carter followed the vanguard of an industrial migration reminiscent of much earlier waves of emigration from settled and exploited regions in the East. This company was drawn to the oil frontiers of America by precisely those same forces which had lured hunters, trappers, miners, farmers, and lumbermen westward, but Carter was far from being the Daniel Boone of this latter-day economic tide. The belated decision to enter the Mid-Continent was made only after careful calculation of the costs involved, and every effort was made to eliminate the element of speculation from the move. The employment of an already existing affiliate was a necessity, since public suspicion effectively denied to Jersey Standard the alternative of forming new companies to undertake the burden of expansion in any field of operation. The pressing question of the day was whether Carter would be able to compete effectively with those who had already shouldered the risks and reaped the first benefits of exploration.

For this conservative little company the move west was of near-cataclysmic dimensions; sweeping organizational changes were required. Colonel Carter resigned, and to ease the transition from the firing line for this battle-scarred old warrior the Jersey board found new tasks for him elsewhere. On August 1, 1915, Arthur F. Corwin was named president of the Carter Company to succeed the Colonel. Corwin had come up through South Penn, the Forest Oil Company, Carter, and Penn-Mex. His production experience was well rounded.

The entire administrative organization was shifted. Having fulfilled in 1913 the necessary legal qualifications to do business in Oklahoma, Carter split into two divisions—eastern and western. Offices for the latter were established in Tulsa in 1915, and permission to do business in Kansas, Wyoming, Arkansas, Colorado, and New Mexico was sought and obtained. Corwin established his office at 26 Broadway, for his duties were to include supervision of all Jersey domestic producing operations. A forceful, energetic, and reliable man was sought to take charge of the western division.

These qualifications were amply fulfilled by J. Edgar Pew, a member of the family that organized and directed the Sun Oil Company. Accounts vary as to how Pew was enticed away from the family oil business in Pennsylvania. High compensation probably was the lure, but the belief was also expressed that the young scion of oil had been turned loose to make his own way in the world. Pew's impact on Tulsa was resounding, the more so for the fact that, figuratively speaking, he came fortified with a pocketful of Jersey Standard blank checks.

Early in 1915 activity at Cushing was at an all-time peak. Lease brokers, landowners, and representatives of every major oil-producing company were engaged in frenzied exchanges of property rights. Lawyers luxuriated in a profusion of claims and counterclaims. The fever-pitch of speculation was raised still higher by the rediscovery of rich formations at Healdton, just north of the Texas border, and by new strikes at Muskogee and other points in the Tulsa area. Late in the year the El Dorado field in Butler County, Kansas, came in. Oilmen poured into the Mid-Continent district, abandoning less spectacular territories elsewhere without bothering to complete their exploratory efforts. Tulsa became a frantic clearinghouse for land and oil deals. Arriving late upon the scene, Pew's task of buying Carter into the Mid-Continent was no easy one.

Pew moved with decision to organize for the venture. An office staff was set up. Drillers and other field personnel were drawn from the eastern division; some eventually came direct from Jersey Standard's Romanian fields, where war had struck and the invading Germans had shattered Româno-Americana's operating organization. A young Bartlesville lawyer named James A. Veasey was engaged to supervise the imposing array of lease work, and in 1916 a geological staff was set up under L. Murray Neuman. The number of Carter employees leaped from 181 in 1915 to 2,277 in 1918.

All this was aside from the main task of acquiring properties and was accomplished over a period of many months. Pew's first efforts were directed at scouting the fields and at organizing the lease-plays which at a given signal were to sweep into action and pluck promising acreage out from under the noses of alert, aggressive, and sometimes not too scrupulous competitors. Money was Pew's great weapon, and he wielded it freely, but Pew's inner strength was a bold and aggressive nature. He was quite willing to fight fire with fire.

A contract was signed with Prairie covering the purchase by Carter of 2,000,000 barrels of Cushing crude oil and a large number of new storage tanks. The contract was a carefully guarded secret, for in this market it was economic suicide to show one's hand. News that Carter had taken over huge tankage facilities would have put every operator and lease-holder on guard against the lease-plays that would follow in the wake of such a move. The relatively high price of $1.25 per barrel specified in the contract, moreover, was a bad precedent for Carter to set for itself, and the Jersey directors did not wish it to be known that Carter was in the market for crude.[18]

On February 7, 1915, Carter signed its first two leases in the Cushing field. The Yahola lease covered 165 acres of developed territory on which 13 producing wells were already located. For this property Carter paid a bonus of approximately $400,000, the lease being subject to the customary one-eighth royalty interest in production. The Manuel lease, in Township 18 North, Range 7 East, covered 160 acres, an L-shaped tract wedged in between the Bessie Offut lease of C. B. Shaffer, who had drilled the discovery well at Cushing, and Prairie's lush Sam Lucas leases. For this undeveloped but highly promising acreage Carter paid a cash bonus of $460,000 outright and agreed to pay an additional compensation, over and above the usual royalty, of 25 cents per barrel until the sum of $1,000,000 had been reached. These sums were unprecedented in Carter's earlier operations in the East, but the flow of oil at Cushing was unlike anything the company had ever experienced.

In the eleven months remaining in 1915 Carter obtained more oil from the Yahola property alone than the combined output for the entire year from all its properties in Ohio and West Virginia. On March 22, 1915, Carter's first well on the Manuel lease came in, and before the year was out this property had surpassed the Yahola in productivity. The value of oil taken from the Manuel lease in ten months ($951,700, net after one-eighth royalty) nearly covered the entire capital outlay on the lease in that year ($604,300) and the equipment, development, and operating costs ($390,100). Of the 40 wells which were eventually drilled there only 2 proved to be dry holes.[19] For the year 1915 total production from the Yahola and Manuel properties was four times as large (2,810,000 barrels) as that obtained from Carter's entire eastern division properties in 31 fields.

The pattern of operations in the Mid-Continent field as a whole differed in dramatic fashion from that in the eastern fields insofar as productivity and acquisition costs were concerned; but in the Mid-Continent, as in the East, Carter confined itself to developing pools discovered by others. Carter's preference appeared to be for promising but unproved properties adjacent to proved acreage. Between March, 1915, and December, 1917, Carter acquired nine properties in the Cushing field. Of these, only one (the Yahola lease) actually constituted proved acreage, but all the other properties eventually yielded oil and only one lease was abandoned. Of the 71 wells drilled here from 1915 through 1919, only 6, or 8 per cent, proved to be dry holes. By way of comparison, dry holes drilled in the United States in 1918 comprised 22 per cent of all wells drilled.[20] Carter's expansion, though ambitious in scope, was clearly conducted along the most conservative possible lines. Oil operations being what they were, however, the element of risk could not be reduced by a consequential degree, much less be eliminated.

Cushing was only the beginning. Pew, described as a hard driver by men who in the same breath swore that he was honest and infallibly ready to back his men to the limit, plunged Carter into dozens of lease-plays all over Oklahoma and in Kansas. In every potential producing area, Pew retained trustworthy key men, each of whom had at his fingertips the names of from 25 to 50 available lease men. It required only a signal from headquarters to swing any segment of this poised organization into action and to send the lease men scurrying through the countryside in

MID-CONTINENT—GULF COAST PIPELINES AND PRINCIPAL OIL FIELDS, 1924

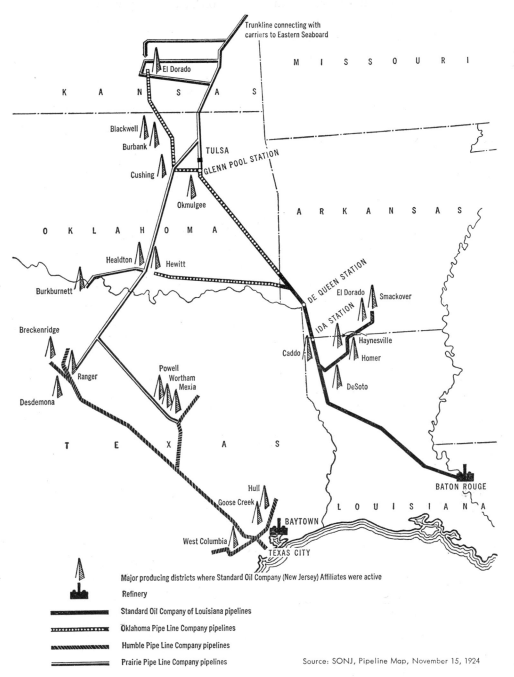

Trunkline connecting with carriers to Eastern Seaboard

MISSOURI

El Dorado

KANSAS

Blackwell
Burbank

TULSA
GLENN POOL STATION

Cushing

Okmulgee

ARKANSAS

OKLAHOMA

Healdton   Hewitt

Burkburnett

DE QUEEN STATION

El Dorado   Smackover

IDA STATION

Breckenridge

Haynesville

Caddo   Homer

Ranger

Powell
Wortham
Mexia

DeSoto

Desdemona

TEXAS

Hull
Goose Creek

BATON ROUGE

BAYTOWN

LOUISIANA

West Columbia

TEXAS CITY

Major producing districts where Standard Oil Company (New Jersey) Affiliates were active

Refinery

Standard Oil Company of Louisiana pipelines

Oklahoma Pipe Line Company pipelines

Humble Pipe Line Company pipelines

Prairie Pipe Line Company pipelines

Source: SONJ, Pipeline Map, November 15, 1924

search of options. Carter scouts ranged the prairies, building up friend-ships with farmers and with drillers in the employ of rival oil companies. These friendships yielded vital information about what was going on in the fields, where secrecy about drilling and leasing was considered a *sine qua non* of successful operation.

Under Pew and the Tulsa management, Carter's reputation for integ-rity was firmly established in the Mid-Continent. Many an unfavorable agreement between Carter and its lessors was adhered to where other participants took advantage of legal loopholes to escape. Pew, too, built Carter's first modern oil-field camp, did constructive work in standard-izing oil-field equipment, and encouraged scientifically trained men to enter the employ of the company.[21]

In 1915, 1916, and 1917 Pew checkerboarded all of western Oklahoma with leases. By the end of the year 1915 Carter, pursuing acquisition methods similar in kind to those employed in the Cushing field, had ob-tained producing properties in the Boynton, Healdton, Okmulgee, No-wata, and Blackwell fields in Oklahoma. Piles of leases, for which no storage space could be found, were stacked in the corridors of the Tulsa office building. In the following year, leases were taken in the Hewitt and Garber districts of Oklahoma and in the Porter–El Dorado and Pea-body fields in Kansas. In 1917 Carter acquired properties in the Osage district of Oklahoma, thus virtually completing the company's infiltration of the then-known producing territories in the Mid-Continent. In that year, too, producing properties were acquired in the Maverick Springs district of Wyoming. Production from all these fields from 1915 through 1917 totaled 9,850,400 barrels, as compared with 2,157,400 barrels realized from eastern division districts in West Virginia, Ohio, and Kentucky. In all these fields, as at Cushing, high bonuses were paid for developed or very promising acreage. Carter showed no disposition to engage in wild-cat searches for new fields.

Costs of expansion were tremendous. From 1915 to 1918 Carter spent over $34,000,000 for new property, well drilling, and development in the western division, of which some $6,000,000 was charged to operations and the remainder capitalized. The capital necessary to finance Carter's expansion was obtained from the Jersey Company without recourse to banks or to the general investment market. In the years 1915, 1916, and 1917 Jersey advanced a total of $57,785,000 in working-capital loans. Carter repaid $25,841,000 in cash in these years and in 1917 expanded its capital stock from $2,000,000 to $25,000,000, issuing the increase to the

Jersey Company as an offset to outstanding debt. By December of 1917 the indebtedness had been reduced to the nominal figure of $8,139,000.[22]

During these three years of growth, Carter declared no dividends, but net income rose from $450,000 in 1915 to $5,700,000 in 1917. Net value (total assets less current liabilities, including Carter's indebtedness to Jersey) shot up from $2,129,000 in 1912 to $37,828,000 in 1917.[23]

In the process of moving into the Mid-Continent, Carter encountered difficulties that extended far beyond the purely technical and administrative. Carter, like Jersey Standard itself, was hedged about by restrictions. Not the least of these was the prejudice that attached itself to any company known as a Standard Oil affiliate. Carter's corporate connection was never advertised, and often it was categorically denied by lease men endeavoring to acquire property rights at a fair price from suspicious landowners who would have been only too glad to avail themselves of an opportunity to get a fat price from Standard Oil.

In addition to the restrictive influence of the various federal and state antitrust acts, which as then interpreted seriously restricted large-scale contractual relationships between major companies in the field, Carter faced other hindrances in its westward expansion. In Oklahoma, for example, some of the most promising oil lands were owned by Indian tribes and were under federal supervision. Since Carter's greatest troubles with tribal leases did not come until after 1918, discussion of this difficulty is reserved for a later chapter. Regulations were also in force which specified the number of acres which a company might lease, and there were prohibitions against leasing school lands to any company that was directly or indirectly interested in pipelines.[24] In many instances legal obstacles of one kind or another forced Carter to stand aside while promising territories were developed by smaller independent producers, from whom Carter then purchased crude oil. Carter's purchases in the Mid-Continent, in fact, were heavy in these years, at times exceeding the company's own production.

Despite these difficulties, the western move had proved, as early as 1918, to be successful in achieving the primary objective of obtaining more oil. It had also been accomplished with considerable profit, notwithstanding the heavy prices paid for leases in developed districts. Prospects for the future seemed promising, provided that the risky operations of the wildcatters continued to open up new fields for Carter to develop. Carter had succeeded, too, in establishing for itself a reputation for reliability in a new area and in a surprisingly short space of time had been accepted as a "native" company.

For these accomplishments Carter and Jersey Standard were indebted to J. Edgar Pew, but Pew's stay in Tulsa was short. In 1917 he resigned as general manager of the western division. Some said that Pew turned out to be too dynamic for the conservative Jersey directors back East. Certainly Pew, an extreme individualist, was not a man who was easily controlled. His disposition was such that he scorned to deal with second-line management. He took his problems directly to Teagle, Bedford, and other top men at 26 Broadway, often entirely bypassing Corwin, Carter's president and Pew's immediate superior. Be this as it may, Pew left behind him a remarkable record, and his activities over the short span of three years substantially influenced the course of Carter and Jersey Standard history.

OIL IN THE BAYOUS FOR LOUISIANA STANDARD

By the time Carter had signed its first western leases, the Standard Oil Company of Louisiana had come to occupy a position in the Jersey Standard organization somewhat different from that which had been conceived for it when the company was incorporated. The fact became apparent that, though the Baton Rouge refinery was favorably located to draw crude oil from Mexico and the Mid-Continent, the company also was in an extraordinarily good position to profit from the development of the Louisiana fields.

The Savage brothers had made their oil strike in Caddo Parish, in the northwest corner of Louisiana, in 1906. Three years later, at the very time that the Baton Rouge refinery was rising above the cotton fields, the Trees well Number 4 on Jeems Bayou erupted in a roar of escaping gas and oil. An oily slick which was never to disappear spread over the black waters of Caddo Lake. Derricks reared up on pilings in the bayous and along the cypress-lined shores of this swampy wilderness.[25] Louisiana Standard executives at once organized a producing department. Since the company was predominantly staffed by marketing and refining men, field personnel and supervisors for the new department were imported from The Ohio Oil Company.

On November 3, 1910, the company acquired six leases from the J. C. Trees Oil Company, all on proved property in Caddo Parish. These negotiations were carried on by A C. Bedford and John D. Archbold, who are said to have expanded their initial bid of $2,000,000 into a final purchase price of $6,000,000 (plus one-eighth royalty)—an amount double that which the owners had previously agreed among themselves would be satisfactory. One of these leases alone (the W. P. Stiles lease, comprising 3,254 acres) commanded a bonus of $4,261,717, but this property already had 26 producing wells on it and from 1911 through 1917 produced 6,244,000 barrels of oil.[26]

The J. C. Trees Oil Company itself seems to have played a significant, if somewhat indirect and ill-defined, part in Standard Oil's history. This energetic wildcatting organization was led by two colorful men, J. C. Trees and M. L. Benedum, former Standard Oil employees who had joined forces and struck out on their own.[27] The economic service performed by this and other such companies in shouldering the heavy risks of exploration was an important one and often led to great rewards. Trees and Benedum, financed in part by Jersey Standard loans, were among the most successful wildcatters in the industry. They found the oil, sold out to development companies such as Louisiana Standard and Carter, and moved on to new territories. The bonuses they received were modest when compared with the value of the oil eventually taken from the fields they discovered, but the high cash payments and early withdrawal from the proved fields appear to have been more to their liking than the routine tasks of producing, refining, and marketing.

Between 1910 and 1918 Louisiana Standard's producing operations spread out geographically in much the same way as did Carter's in the Mid-Continent. It became apparent, as wildcat operations of independent producers became more extensive, that the gentle dome of the Sabine Uplift covered an extensive area in northwestern Louisiana. Oil was discovered in 1913 in De Soto Parish and in 1914 in Red River Parish. These discoveries south of the Caddo field squarely straddled the pipeline that Louisiana Standard had built to connect Baton Rouge with the Mid-Continent lines of Prairie Oil & Gas and the Oklahoma Pipe Line Company. As successive strikes were recorded closer and closer to the Baton Rouge refinery, the Louisiana people could not help but be struck by the fact that nature, so often the foe of the oil operator, in this instance was co-operating handsomely with man's best-laid plans.

In 1915 Louisiana Standard acquired properties in the Crichton-Red River district, paying close to a million dollars in royalties to Trees, the Atlas Oil Company, the Pennock Oil Company, and other independent operators. Leases were also taken in the Bossier Parish field and at scattered points elsewhere in northern Louisiana. Between 1910 and 1920 the company drilled 389 wells in the Caddo district, most of which were on properties purchased from Trees and Atlas Oil. Of these wells only 31, or 9 per cent, were dry holes. Production at Caddo reached a peak of 2,935,000 barrels in 1913, a figure that was exceeded only by Carter's Mid-Continent production after 1916. Expansion into Bossier, De Soto, and Red River parishes after 1912, however, did not succeed in offsetting the declining output of the older fields in the Caddo district. Total crude production of the Louisiana Company declined from a peak of 2,960,000 barrels in 1913 to 1,287,000 in 1917.[28]

Louisiana Standard itself did comparatively little wildcatting. The producing staff was not large. Since crude oil was plentiful and cheap, the refinery and marketing men who dominated the company did not push exploration and producing operations so hard as they might have done had the market been less favorable. In the Louisiana area, too, geology had turned out to be none too useful an ally. It seemed safer and more economical in the long run to acquire producing properties near new discoveries and to purchase crude oil produced by other operators than to attempt to locate new fields and produce all the oil required at Baton Rouge. Louisiana purchases for the years 1912 through 1917 far exceeded the company's own crude production.

The cost of buying into established fields was as high in Louisiana as it was in Oklahoma. Working capital to finance Louisiana Standard's expansion came exclusively from earnings and from the Jersey Company, which extended large loans, some of which were canceled by the issuance of additional Louisiana stock to the Jersey Company. Louisiana's indebtedness to the parent company, which stood at $11,467,000 in December, 1912, had been reduced to less than a million dollars by December, 1917.[29]

Net value of the Louisiana Company increased from $6,692,000 in 1912 to $42,485,000 in 1917, an increase of 535 per cent, as compared with Carter's increase over the same period of 1,090 per cent. No dividends were paid in these years, but total net earnings from all branches of operation ranged from a low of $1,662,000 in 1912 to a high of $8,512,000 in 1917. These earnings, however, were derived largely from refining activities; Louisiana's producing department yielded far more modest returns. Highest net earnings from producing for the period were $2,423,-000 in 1913. In 1914 and 1915 Louisiana producing operations registered a net loss, in 1916 showed a return of only $297,700, and in 1917 a return of $649,000.[30]

A comparison of Carter and Louisiana operations at once reveals similarities that reflected common direction from 26 Broadway. Both companies financed their expansion programs in identical fashion. Both pursued the conservative, if expensive, policy of expanding into proved producing areas. Carter, however, had been bolder and more successful. For the years 1912 through 1917 Carter's profits totaled $11,434,000, as against Louisiana's producing-department profits of $2,809,000; Carter produced 13,742,000 barrels of oil, while Louisiana Standard produced 10,880,000 barrels. In 1917 Carter operations, moreover, were expanding, while production and interest in production in Louisiana were beginning to sag.

The difference in performance in the two companies, of course, is only partially explicable in terms of respective managerial attitudes. Rich though the bayous were, the prairies were richer. Louisiana Standard was extensively engaged in a wide range of activities, too, while Carter was a producing company only. The important point, so well demonstrated both in Louisiana and in Oklahoma, was that both companies realized the tremendous advantages that the use of Jersey Standard's great financial strength made possible in certain segments of the expanding oil economy.

THE NATURAL GAS COMPANIES

Although Jersey Standard was known primarily as an oil company, it had long been interested in the production and marketing of natural gas as well. The history of Jersey's natural gas companies between 1912 and 1918 was dynamic in terms of profits—if stable, substantial profits through good times and bad can be said to be dynamic. In this period, their earnings held to a solid range of from 9 to 21 per cent of Jersey's total net earnings. The natural gas affiliates merit consideration as a small and certainly neglected, but not inconsequential, part of the total domestic producing picture.

The natural gas affiliates had not been affected by the dissolution decree, since the gas companies were not proved to be part of the combination found by the courts to be unlawful. At the end of 1912 the Jersey Company owned directly a majority of the stock of nine such companies and held substantial stock interests in three others. By 1918 the Jersey Company had narrowed its holdings by disposing of four companies to outside interests and one company to another affiliate. Appendix 1 lists the gas companies owned at various dates after 1912.

In the early years of the petroleum industry, natural gas, like gasoline, was an unwanted child except in fields near large consuming centers. Wells that proved to be gas producers were disappointments only slightly less acute than dry holes. In many areas gas continued to be blown off and burned. The waste of gas resources was appalling, but science had not yet shown producers what might be done with this unwelcome by-product, and most gas wells were not accessible to markets. Inadequate storage and transportation facilities left little alternative but to apply the torch. By the 1890's, however, the Standard Oil group was making money from gas wells owned in West Virginia, discovered when drilling for oil. Gas pipelines were built to communities where private and industrial consumers could be reached. As time passed, Standard Oil expanded its natural gas operations; there was a steady drive to find markets for the West Virginia production. Profits came principally from transporting and marketing of gas. As distribution lines and markets grew, an effort was made to obtain additional producing facilities.

In the years following the dissolution decree the natural gas companies, like the Jersey Company itself, faced government investigations and were circumscribed by government restrictions. In 1913 the state of West Virginia declared such companies to be public utilities. Pennsylvania and Ohio followed this precedent soon afterward. Company managers reluctantly submitted to the necessity for filing reports, for obtaining permission to change rates, and for submitting to various other public utility regulations. In Ohio the natural gas companies were required to deal in matters concerned with rates and practices with local supervisory commissions rather than a state board, the latter having only appeal jurisdiction. Efforts were made in West Virginia to extend government control still further by declaring the gas companies to be common carriers. The natural gas affiliates of the Jersey Company fought these efforts vigorously, and, by demonstrating that the nature of the commodity necessitated its production, transmission, and distribution by a single company, operating as a public utility, were able to prove the common carrier theory to be impractical and inapplicable.[31]

In this same postdissolution period a federal investigation of Jersey Standard's natural gas operations was launched; considerable anxiety was felt in New York lest another antitrust suit might be instituted. The point at issue was the relationship between operations in West Virginia of two affiliates, the Hope Natural Gas Company and the United Fuel Gas Company. As a result of the investigation, connections between the two organizations were severed. Hope transferred its gas leases in southern West

Virginia to United Fuel, and in 1915 Jersey disposed of its stock interest in United. The investigator then gave a clean federal bill of health to Jersey Standard's natural gas interests.[32]

Though political obstacles may have impeded the expansion of the gas network into new marketing territories and decidedly increased the difficulties of doing business in existing markets, Jersey Standard's natural gas operations were still of formidable dimensions. In 1918 the seven gas affiliates were producing and distributing over 100,000,000,000 cubic feet of natural gas. The largest gas producer was the Hope Natural Gas Company, of West Virginia. The largest marketer was The East Ohio Gas Company, which was selling 48,000,000,000 cubic feet of natural gas to 350,000 customers in 49 cities and towns in Ohio and nearly 400,000,000 feet of artificial gas to 3,300 consumers in Cleveland. Not far behind East Ohio was The Peoples Natural Gas Company, serving Pittsburgh and cities as far east in Pennsylvania as Altoona.

To only a very small degree did the natural gas companies help to fill Jersey Standard's great need for expansion of crude oil production. Crude oil produced from their wells averaged only slightly less than 5 per cent of the Jersey Standard organization's total domestic crude production in the 1912-1918 period. The operations of these companies did, however, assist directly and more substantially in meeting the unprecedented demand for gasoline.

For years the gasoline content of natural gas had been considered a hazard rather than an asset. Research efforts were directed at elimination rather than recovery, for gasoline had a limited market. By the turn of the century, however, market conditions were already changing, and before 1911 the change had progressed to the point where the efforts of two Standard chemists, George M. Saybolt and Roger Chew, to find efficient ways to remove and recover the gasoline had come to have a very practical meaning. In 1913 a gasoline absorption plant was built in Hastings, West Virginia, by the Hope Natural Gas Company. Other plants were subsequently constructed; by 1918 most of the gas produced in the Appalachian fields by Jersey Standard affiliates was being treated to remove the gasoline content. In 1915 the treatment of gas from the Caddo field was also commenced by Louisiana Standard. In 1917 and 1918 six processing plants were set up by Carter in the Cushing, Nowata, and Boynton fields in Oklahoma. Production of gasoline by the natural gas companies increased from an insignificant figure in 1913 to over 13,000,000 gallons in 1918, equivalent to 2 per cent of all gasoline delivered to home and export trade by Jersey Standard's domestic refineries.[33]

In 1918 organizational changes were effected to separate the natural gas operations from the oil-producing and refining business of the affiliated gas companies. The oil-producing and refining properties were transferred to the newly formed Hope Construction & Refining Company, probably for the primary purpose of removing such properties from the jurisdiction of public utility commissions in the various states.

Viewed in perspective, the activities of Jersey Standard's natural gas affiliates can scarcely be said to have formed a part of that drive for greater control over raw-material production at home and abroad which by 1918 had come to be a major facet of company policy. Neither can these companies be disregarded in any examination of producing operations in these years. They produced little crude oil, but their gas produced both gasoline and high profits, and in the offices of these little-known companies men were trained who became influential in the affairs of the parent company.

SUMMARY ASPECTS OF
POSTDISSOLUTION PROCUREMENT POLICIES

Efforts by Jersey Standard to expand domestic producing activities had met with considerable success, measured either in absolute or in relative terms. Over the 1912-1917 period domestic crude oil production by the organization leaped 169 per cent, as compared with an increase in domestic refinery crude oil consumption of 25 per cent. In 1912 production by the Jersey Standard group in the United States had been equivalent to 8 per cent of the organization's domestic refinery consumption; by 1917 production equaled 17 per cent of consumption.[34] Even these figures fell short of measuring the achievement; in many areas efforts to increase production had not come to full fruition, for it took time to lease acreage and bring in wells.

Nevertheless, it was apparent that Jersey Standard had yet to duplicate the performance of certain predissolution years, when the old Standard Oil group had produced more than one-third of all crude oil in the United States and had supplied up to 40 per cent of its own crude oil needs.[35] Even more important, the Jersey Standard group in 1918 (the first year for which reliable comparative statistics are available) was far removed from the pattern of integration then widely prevalent in the oil industry.

Several integrated competitors were more firmly entrenched than was Jersey Standard in producing territories that supplied crude oil for refineries in the United States. The Jersey Company, with a domestic refinery capacity larger than that of any other oil company in the country, produced less crude oil in 1918 than the Standard Oil Company (California), the Gulf Oil Corporation, The Texas Company, or the Shell Oil Company interests. In ratio of crude oil produced to refining capacity, Jersey Standard fell behind a number of other companies. In 1918 production by the Jersey Standard group in the United States and Mexico was equal to 17 per cent of the organization's domestic refining capacity. Production in these same areas by Shell, Standard of California, Texas, and Sinclair was equivalent to about 50 per cent of the refining capacities of those companies, while Gulf was producing at the rate of almost 90 per cent of refining capacity.[36]

Foremost among the forces preventing still greater expansion of Jersey Standard's production were the political obstacles that stood in the way of conspicuous growth by any of the corporate segments of the old Standard Oil combination. At the same time, the ability of the Jersey Company to purchase oil in accustomed channels and, by and large, on advantageous terms unquestionably had a large effect upon procurement policy. Since the dissolution decree precipitated no immediate and crucial supply problem, the decidedly ambitious plans for Carter and Louisiana Standard seemed for a time to be all that were required. Possibly the greatest accomplishment in the years from 1912 to 1918 was not the undeniably impressive production increases which were recorded, but the growth and sifting upward through the ranks of management of the realization that even greater effort must be put forth. Predissolution years had witnessed the conception and birth of policies looking toward greatly increased domestic and foreign production. Now the necessity was upon the company again in all its urgency and was hedged about with greater complications than ever before.

Attempts to translate a renascent producing policy into action encountered at many points the active public suspicion that Jersey Standard could not achieve a state of integration comparable to that which existed before the dissolution decree without employing methods that had been judged by the courts to be illegal. Nevertheless, the economic advantages of an integrated organization had not become less with the passing of years. Jersey Standard's postdissolution management soon demonstrated its appreciation of those advantages and worked as best it could within the letter of the law to achieve them. The Jersey Company, in effect, re-fused to accept the mandate of 1911 as a denial of its right to expand and reintegrate. This attitude was legally justifiable and absolutely neces-sary for survival in the increasingly competitive environment the company faced. Caution, however, dominated company policy and operations.

The acquisition by existing affiliates of established producing properties was a conservative, legal, and relatively sure way of expanding produc-tion. Jersey Standard policy in this respect, nevertheless, could be and was criticized from a business viewpoint. Proved or promising acreage was purchased at high prices, after calculation of the amount of oil that such properties might be expected to yield per acre or per annum. This procedure amounted to buying storage oil in the ground, and the total investment required was heavy. It is hard to find a single instance in the years from 1912 to 1918 where a real field discovery was made by a pro-ducing affiliate of the Jersey Company. This fact was disturbing to some members of the organization, who pointed out that important producing territories, such as the Cushing, the Glenn Pool, and the El Dorado, yielded tremendous returns to aggressive operators, while Jersey Stand-ard had entered late into small areas where the cream had rightfully been skimmed by the discoverers.[37] This critical viewpoint had much logic behind it and was easily entertained by men in the organization who were close to field operations.

Even before these domestic producing activities had progressed to the point where they could decisively be appraised in terms of costs and re-turns, a realization was developing in the Jersey Company that aggressive tactics must be employed in expanding existing production abroad and in acquiring additional foreign reserve territories for future production. The first stirrings of a new interest in foreign producing operations were contemporary with, though less conspicuous than, the events detailed in the present chapter. Jersey Standard's efforts abroad, however, rapidly assumed a large importance, overshadowing not only the domestic pro-ducing operations but all other branches of the business as well and exerting much influence upon the course of Jersey Standard history to the present day. Dealing with lease brokers and small-town politicians and Oklahoma farmers was quite a different matter from attempting to acquire producing territory from the Dutch Colonial Administration, Mexican revolutionaries, and the wily descendants of South American *conquistadores*. The rewards that glistened abroad, nonetheless, could scarcely be ignored by a company beset by formidable difficulties at home.

Chapter 4

Looking Abroad for Oil
1912-1917

FOREIGN POLICY AND
INTERNATIONAL COMPETITORS

I N POSTDISSOLUTION months the specific directions that Jersey Standard's foreign producing policy was to take were far from clear. Despite frequent efforts which the old Standard Oil group had made at widely scattered points throughout the world to acquire producing properties, foreign crude oil production by Jersey Standard affiliates was small. In 1912 such production, concentrated entirely in Romania, amounted to less than half the crude oil consumed by affiliated foreign refineries. Compared with the volume of products refined from North American crude and shipped to foreign markets, Jersey Standard's foreign production was very small indeed—about 6 per cent.[1]

The long-felt need to build up holdings of foreign producing properties was directly influenced by considerations affecting all branches of Jersey Standard's operations. Many broad problems, some of which grew out of the size and complexity of the foreign business, were chronic and had been encountered repeatedly in the years before 1911. The dissolution decree and the unfriendly political climate in the United States accentuated some of these old difficulties and posed new ones. Before efforts to obtain greater production abroad could be resumed, the company was forced to consider how its collective foreign operations could most advantageously be managed and controlled. A tentative answer to this basic question was soon worked out.

In 1914 Jersey Standard, oppressed by legislative restrictions at home and fearful that its remaining investments abroad might be brought under federal attack, took the first steps to remove the management and control of its foreign operations from under the zealous scrutiny of United States government agencies and centralize the direction of those operations in

London. Walter Teagle, who had been in charge of European marketing since before the dissolution, was the logical man to establish and direct such a foreign headquarters.

In an atmosphere of considerable suspicion and political hostility it was perhaps inevitable that the company's plans should be shrouded in secrecy. That secrecy, in turn, appears to have generated further suspicion. When Teagle arrived in London, in February of 1914, a warning was forwarded to him that government investigators were disgruntled that he had taken with him certain correspondence files containing information on foreign operations. He was also told that a federal agent was shadowing him, seeking information about Jersey Standard plans. Government sleuths were said to be negotiating with an informer within the Jersey Company and to have offered bribes or "retainers" for information about what was taking place there.[2] Whether these particular reports were true or false, it seems entirely possible that premature disclosure of Jersey Standard's intent would have generated legislative or judicial action to thwart the establishment of a foreign base of operations. Such action did not materialize, apparently because of the difficulty of proving the real purpose behind the changes that were taking place.

Teagle's stay in London was short. With the outbreak of war in Europe in the summer of 1914, he went to Canada and set up offices in Toronto, serving thenceforth as the president and active head of The Imperial Oil Company, Limited. While this move had the appearance of a routine managerial shake-up, far more was involved than the appointment of a new leader for Jersey Standard's Canadian affiliate. Teagle had actually begun to participate in Imperial's internal affairs in 1913. When he assumed the title of president in the following year, he plunged energetically into a reorganization of all branches of the Canadian company. This was a trying task and one to which Teagle devoted meticulous attention. It is scarcely conceivable that even the most competent of executives could have had the time and strength for any other mission. Nevertheless, from 1914 to 1918, while he served as Imperial's chief executive, Teagle served on the directorates of several foreign affiliates and continued—though without official title as such—to act as the head of Jersey Standard's European business.[3] This outwardly obscure and seemingly awkward administrative overlapping made sense only as the first step in removing control of the foreign business from the United States and was possible only because of the astonishing administrative capacity of Walter Teagle himself.

Meanwhile, the international petroleum industry had become inextricably entwined in broad questions of nationalism and world politics, and the large operators had spun a tangled skein of competitive alignments. In this situation no factors were static, and few agreements were inviolable. In the conduct of its foreign operations Jersey Standard was doing business in a world outside the pale of the Sherman Antitrust Act and the mores of American business life. At home, operations were circumscribed by legislative restrictions and public attitudes and were geared to the pace of competition with a large number of small and medium-sized companies, all on a substantially equal footing. Abroad, the restrictions and attitudes were of a markedly different nature, and rivalry was largely between great organizations enjoying strong protection from their respective governments. Survival in the foreign business was necessarily and directly contingent upon the use of power politics and commercial combination—by the employment of many measures that were illegal in the United States and, by and large, repugnant to the American public. There was no alternative, short of refusing to do business in this alien environment.

On every side powerful pressure groups were moving in directions which had ominous implications for American oil interests abroad. Britain's ocean-nourished empire was threatened by the substitution of American-controlled fuel oil for British-controlled coal. With strong though not obvious government backing, groups of British financiers had begun, in the first decade of the twentieth century, to move to secure a British lion's share of the world's known petroleum-producing regions. The particular episodes that marked the evolution of this significant movement are best reserved for study in later chapters. At the same time, a young and vigorous organization in the Far East was fast becoming a major power in the oil industry. The Royal Dutch Company, founded in 1890, was a monument to tenacity, aggressiveness, and commercial brilliance.[4]

This company controlled rich producing properties in northern Sumatra and operated a small refinery there. Under the leadership of J. B. A. Kessler, the Royal Dutch had survived a precarious decade, fighting Standard Oil and several small local Dutch and British competitors for markets in Java, Sumatra, Borneo, and Singapore. When Kessler died, in 1900, management of the company passed to the hands of Henri Deterding, who had started work in Holland as an obscure and penniless bank clerk and had risen fast in the organization.

The almost legendary career of Deterding occupies a commanding place in the history of the international oil industry. This man was called "Napoleonic in audacity and Cromwellian in thoroughness."[5] He detested wasteful competition with a fine Dutch fervor and promptly set about combining with his smaller rivals to stabilize the markets in which he wished to operate. In 1903 a brilliant stroke of strategy, conceived by Deterding and executed by another legendary figure, Frederick Lane, combined the three largest international competitors of Standard Oil into a single marketing group. These three were the Royal Dutch, the Rothschild interests which were prominent in the Russian oil industry, and The Shell Transport & Trading Company, Limited, an English petroleum organization of growing power. Each group agreed to stop fighting the others in the East and to set up The Asiatic Petroleum Company to market their products. In 1907 Deterding and Lane effected an outright combination of the Royal Dutch and the Shell groups to form the Royal Dutch-Shell. The next year Deterding was sufficiently powerful to negotiate an agreement with Standard Oil dividing the market for kerosene in China.

Deterding, however, was not satisfied. He saw no reason why a much broader agreement with Standard would not entirely rid the oil trade of its incessant price troubles. Walter Teagle agreed completely, and the two men, suffused with enthusiasm, called upon John D. Archbold. Deterding, in his emphatic and blunt way, hotly argued his point. Archbold appeared amused rather than resentful that the intrepid Deterding should seek to show one of the most successful commercial organizations in the world how to be more successful. Deterding came away empty-handed.

In 1910 Standard Oil demands for a revision of existing marketing agreements with the Royal Dutch-Shell were unacceptable to Deterding, and an oil war commenced between the two great rivals in many of the markets of the world. Deterding shrewdly realized that until he started trading in the American market Standard Oil might be able to make up at home any losses it suffered in fighting the Royal Dutch-Shell abroad. In 1911 he was laying plans to commence both producing and marketing operations in the United States, seeking to form an anti-Standard bloc there under cover of the confusion created by the dissolution decree.

Elsewhere in the world Deterding continued to move boldly and had obtained or was about to obtain producing interests in Romania, Egypt, Russia, and Latin America. By 1911 Royal Dutch infiltration of the rich European market had already taken place. Here other organizations also were stirring. In 1906 the Nobel and Rothschild petroleum groups had combined with expansionist German interests vested in the Deutsche Bank. This tripartite agreement resulted in the formation of the European Petroleum Union, a marketing organization which handled Romanian, Galician, and Russian products and with which Standard Oil affiliates had agreed to share certain European markets. Deterding, on his part, had visions of a much broader European petroleum trust which would embrace producing, refining, transporting, and marketing functions and which would force Standard Oil to come to terms. At the same time, crafty Arthur von Gwinner, head of the powerful Deutsche Bank, was seeking in the fluid situation that existed in 1911 to advance Deutsche Bank interests in Europe, the Middle East, and elsewhere.

With these currents and crosscurrents Standard Oil men were well acquainted. For years, however, effective efforts to build a producing organization abroad had been thwarted by the Closed Door policy of the colonial powers—and perhaps by the fear of moving too aggressively abroad at a time when the organization was under severe public attack at home. After the dissolution, moreover, Jersey Standard, the great refiner and marketer, was handicapped by inexperience in foreign producing operations and by lack of skilled producing personnel. Leaders in the Taft and Wilson administrations and career men in the federal agencies seemed, with only a few exceptions, to be unaware that a revolutionary new factor—oil—had been added to the international political situation and were intent on hamstringing the one company which at the time could successfully oppose foreign economic aggression in the petroleum industry.

FIERY SKIES IN ROMANIA

By 1911 Româno-Americana, Jersey Standard's Romanian affiliate, was reporting good news to 26 Broadway, and good news from this source had been noticeably meager since this first important venture by Standard Oil into foreign producing had been undertaken in 1904.

E. J. Sadler, dispatched to Romania in 1909 with instructions to revitalize the venture, was hopeful that his optimistic estimate of the situation would prove correct and that his application of American drilling methods in the Romanian sands would be successful. By 1911 events had begun to vindicate both Sadler's estimates and his methods.

These oil fields on the eastern spur of the Carpathians had been mentioned in old travelers' tales as early as the seventeenth century. Oil from seepages and primitive hand-dug wells had lighted the lamps and greased the cartwheels of the Boyars for generations. By the time that Standard Oil commenced operations, Romanian production had grown apace and come to be surpassed in Europe only by that of Russia. By 1910 all Standard's large international competitors had acquired producing or refining interests there, with the Deutsche Bank in control of much of the producing acreage. Development had been expedited by the fact that, as in America, individual landowners controlled the subsurface rights to their properties and were free to lease to the oil companies. On the other hand, the Romanian government had refused to grant many exploration rights on the extensive and promising state lands.

Romanian operations presented the most trying technical obstacles, to say nothing of political uncertainties and the difficulty of attempting to do business with a staff of native workmen, most of whom spoke no English and some of whom had proved none too honest. Production was obtained from shallow sands, the average well being less than 1,650 feet deep. Many of the older wells were hand-dug, measuring up to 39 inches square, their sides boarded up to prevent cave-ins of the soft sands in which the oil was found. These soft formations imposed serious difficulties in drilling, and low gas pressures made it necessary to recover the oil from many wells by a laborious bailing operation.

Sadler took these obstacles in stride and spent an energetic two years reorganizing Romāno's producing facilities. The condition of Romāno Americana producing properties at Bustenari, Tescani, Moreni, and Pacureti was vastly improved.[6] In the years from 1912 through 1914, the reorganization and extension of producing properties continued. Funds to carry out the program were supplied by Jersey Standard. The difficulties were many, but there were compensating encouragements.

Field operations were undertaken at Banesti and at Baicoi, though Romāno-Americana was most active at Moreni. Here the wells were big producers, though short-lived. Sadler found that recovery of oil by bailing caused the well casings to wear out at an alarming rate. External events also hampered production. The Balkan War, foreshadowing more serious troubles to come, impaired transportation. Electrical service was so unreliable and expensive that Romāno was forced to rely upon other sources of power. In midsummer of 1912 a serious fire swept the Moreni field, destroying five Romāno wells. Company operations were curtailed somewhat, pending the outcome of political disturbances, and Sadler commented that the year had been a most trying one. His ambitions were not fully realized, but some substantial improvements had been made. During

1912 the use of wooden drilling rigs was virtually abandoned; Sadler began to build his derricks with heavy four-inch pipe filled with concrete. For the first time, Sadler stated, Romåno's rigs were in thoroughly satisfactory condition, and wells could be drilled without stopping to effect derrick repairs. In 1912, too, Sadler drilled past the 3,000-foot mark, a depth hitherto not reached by Romanian drillers.

Through 1913 and 1914 activity picked up and production continued to increase. Sadler pushed his crews hard and steadily expanded drilling operations. In the first six months of 1914 the number of tool strings was increased from 20 to 36. The drilling force was augmented until by June Sadler was employing 6 superintendents, 3 assistant superintendents, and 40 drillers. Progress was made in the difficult but significant process of training Romanian nationals, hitherto largely inexperienced in modern industrial skills and unused to modern industrial disciplines. In 1911 Sadler had reported that most of the drillers were Americans, who came to Romania on two-, three-, or five-year contracts. Three years later he wrote, "Many of the strings of tools are running with Romanians, under the supervision of Americans . . . , and these Romanians are steadily improving as they become more accustomed to the responsibility of drilling."

In 1913 Sadler introduced rotary drilling at Baicoi. This relatively new technique, which had proved particularly useful in soft formations, worked to advantage even in the difficult Moreni field. Wells drilled by the Galician system, which was widely used in Romania at the time, required from 18 months to 3 years for completion. Sadler cut the drilling time to as little as 40 days.[7] Producing operations in 1913 and 1914 showed a profit, in contrast to the losses incurred in the three preceding years.

The year 1915 was a hopeful one for Romåno, though production was down somewhat from the preceding year. A total of 47 wells were producing, and 80 more were in the process of completion. Almost 60,000 feet of hole were drilled in that year, as compared with 30,500 feet in 1913 and 25,700 feet in 1912. Total investment in the producing department had grown to $3,715,000—a jump of 75 per cent from 1912. Sadler and Romåno-Americana, it seemed, were well on their way toward the goal of meeting Jersey Standard's Balkan and Mediterranean market requirements with Jersey-controlled crude. Romåno's producing and refining activities also compared favorably with those of its principal competitors. The company's crude oil output in 1915 comprised 23 per cent of total Romanian production, while Astra-Romåna, the Royal Dutch-Shell subsidiary, produced 20 per cent and Steaua-Romåna, the Deutsche Bank subsidiary, produced 22 per cent of the total. The remaining 35 per cent was split among smaller operators.[8]

But now the rumble of war was growing louder. Romania was being subjected to terrific political pressures, and neutrality was daily becoming more difficult. German diplomacy was directed at forcing Romania's hand, for Romania had laid an embargo on oil shipments and huge stocks were piling up. With Romania on the side of the Central Powers, this oil could be requisitioned for German use; with Romania as an enemy, the oil might be captured, together with the extensive producing and refining facilities in the oil regions. Britain, at the same time, was exerting strong diplomatic pressure to bring Romania into the war on the side of the Allies. By early 1916 a crisis was building up, and the effects of the war began to be felt increasingly in the fields. The only sea route by which company products and supplies could pass was shut off by the closing of the Dardanelles. Storage facilities became jammed as transportation difficulties multiplied. Many company employees were called into military service. Company operations began to slow down.

On August 27, 1916, Romania yielded to forceful British demands and declared war on Austria-Hungary. Initial Romanian military gains were turned into reverses, and the Prussian war machine rolled across the Romanian border. By October the key port of Constanta had fallen, company offices at Bucharest were shaken by German aerial bombing attacks, and Sadler began to evacuate some of the men, women, and children who comprised Româno's American colony. On December 2, 1916, the Anglo-Romanian Destruction Commission notified oil operators that all installations must be destroyed to prevent them from falling into the hands of the Germans. At half-past eight on the morning of December 5 the torch was applied to Româno's refinery and field installations.

Against a fiery sky Sadler and the group of 34 men, 24 women, and 31 children who still remained fled Romania and commenced a harrowing journey across Russia to embarkation points in Sweden. On December 26 Sadler cabled from Petrograd to 26 Broadway his final report on Româno-Americana operations:

All Americans except Seidel and Andrews arrived Petrograd. Going America unless otherwise instructed. Fields and refinery totally destroyed. Compensation guaranteed by allied powers. All important books saved.

The exploding orange flames at Teleajen and Moreni, however, could not destroy all that Jersey Standard had gained from its Romanian producing experience. The most important product of this operation was probably Sadler himself. If he had not gone to Romania in 1909, he might have remained with The Prairie Oil & Gas Company and been lost to Jersey Standard in the dissolution process. Sadler returned to America in time to take charge of important operations elsewhere and to lend his support to those who wished to urge a more decisive producing policy on the Jersey Standard board.

The political and managerial experience gained in Romania up to 1916 was unquestionably one of the more valuable, if intangible, results of operations there. The necessity for allowing field lieutenants flexibility in adapting to local conditions was well demonstrated, and Jersey had learned anew the difficulties of dealing with men of a different nationality.

Yet, viewed in relation to total operations, the Romanian producing venture had not, despite Sadler's brilliant reorganization, been impressive. His effort represented, at best, only the perpetuation, improvement, and enlargement of existing facilities in a long-exploited area, rather than the creation of substantial new capacity in regions that held real promise of meeting Jersey Standard's still unfulfilled need for crude oil production. The new task assigned Sadler in 1917, however, was to seek in Mexico those very goals which were unattainable in the intensively developed Romanian fields.

MEXICAN OIL AND REVOLUTIONARIES

Oil and Mexican politics were closely intermixed. Sir Weetman Pearson (later Lord Cowdray) was an English railroad builder who in 1909, in company with Mexicans of the ruling Díaz group, had formed the Aguila Company and obtained unusually favorable oil concessions on state lands. When Díaz was deposed in the Madero revolution of 1910, the Aguila Company found itself in a precarious situation. It may have been this temporary reversal in the fortunes of the English which sent Arthur F. Corwin, soon to head Carter and the producing operations of the Jersey Standard organization, to Mexico late in 1911 to report on the prospects for entry into producing operations there.[9]

Economic as well as political factors indicated that Jersey Standard must make its move quickly or not at all. Potential producing properties in Mexico, then among the most promising oil territories in the world, were fast disappearing from the market. It was apparent that Mexican oil production was going into the hands of large independent producing interests which already had established market affiliations of their own and

that Jersey Standard might soon find relatively little Mexican oil to purchase. The Doheny group (chiefly the Huasteca Petroleum Company and
the Mexican Petroleum Company) was beginning to set up its own market outlets; Aguila's oil was earmarked for British use; the Anglo-Mexican
Petroleum Company, Limited, another British-controlled group, had its
own markets outside Mexico. The Royal Dutch-Shell entered upon an
aggressive career in Mexico in 1912 and had its own market outlets, as did
Mexican Gulf of the Mellon group, and The Texas Company. Corwin's
report recommended purchase of an established company, provided that
the price was right—otherwise he suggested continued exclusive reliance
on crude oil purchases.

In March, 1912, Teagle and A. C. Bedford dined at the University Club
in New York with Lord Cowdray and his son, Clive Pearson, and discussed the possibilities of purchase by the Jersey Company of the rich but
politically unstable Pearson interests. These negotiations, however, came
to nothing. The possibility cannot be discounted that Madero, the foe of
the British, was equally opposed to the entry of a large American company. Apparently, too, the cautious Jersey board balked at the price demanded. Neither was the time propitious for expansion, for the company
was wrestling with the problem of dissolution and was under closest public and governmental surveillance. Jersey's chief counsel remarked, "Every
move that is made by any of the companies, looking toward any substantial change, is viewed with suspicion by the public at large." Teagle's
belief that a bargain could be driven received scant support, and what
may well have been an exceptional opportunity to expand oil reserves
abroad was lost.[10]

Nine months later, however, the undaunted Teagle was negotiating
with M. L. Benedum and J. C. Trees for the purchase of a controlling interest in their Penn-Mex Fuel Company, which held 160,000 acres of
leased land in the Mexican fields. This venture, too, failed to materialize,
although agreement was reached on price and terms. In March of 1913
Jersey's chief counsel stated that the passage of New Jersey's new corporation laws had made it too dangerous for the company to acquire the
stock of another, such as Penn-Mex. The possibility was examined, too, of
sending The Carter Oil Company into Mexico. This alternative was not
adopted, probably because Jersey Standard was more successful than had
been expected in signing long-term purchase contracts with a number of
suppliers for large amounts of Mexican oil at low prices.[11]

Political events in Mexico took a turn for the worse and imposed serious

obstacles upon any American company seeking entry there. The fall of
Madero in 1913 was followed by the regime of Victoriano Huerta, who
gave some promise of restoring order if not democracy, and whose downfall came in July of 1914 largely because of the active opposition of the
Wilson administration to his government. Between 1914 and 1917 the
tragic land was in a state of utter confusion. Huerta's fall initiated a
period of strife between revolutionary leaders that lasted until October,
1915, when the United States extended *de facto* recognition to the government of Carranza, which was marked by revolutionary reforms, confusion, corruption, and violence, and which finally ended in Carranza's
overthrow and murder in 1920. During those years government largely
broke down in Mexico, and ambitious revolutionary leaders tried to win
support by extravagant promises of social and economic reform. Radicals
and reformers from abroad, chiefly the United States, rushed in to capitalize on the opportunities for self-advancement or the furthering of
reform opened by the revolution. Conditions were further aggravated by
the activities of German nationals, who saw military advantage to Germany in fomenting strife and impairing oil production that was vitally
needed by the Allies.

It was under such conditions that representatives of the Jersey Company continued to investigate opportunities for acquiring Mexican producing properties. Armed with introductions to important men in the
various political groups, James W. Flanagan entered Mexico in June of
1914 to see what he could find out for the man he addressed in his correspondence as "Dear Boss"—Walter C. Teagle. His employment had
routine rather than sinister connotations in an environment in which effective business action would often have been impossible without initial
recourse to secrecy, and Flanagan's counterpart was found in other oil
companies of the day. His adventures made a relatively small impact
upon Jersey Standard history, but they shed much light on the conditions
under which the company was forced at times to operate.

James Flanagan was not a regular employee of the Jersey Company but
was engaged to perform special tasks for Teagle, to whom he reported
directly. Few in the Jersey Company knew about Teagle's trusted retainer,
and probably even fewer knew exactly what he did or how he operated.
To Flanagan were entrusted foreign missions of a confidential nature. His
company affiliation a carefully guarded secret, Flanagan roved the Latin
Americas gathering information, making contacts with important political
figures, and operating behind the scenes to smooth the path for Jersey

Standard expansion abroad. It was he who had warned Teagle in 1914 that federal investigators were ferreting out the company's foreign plans and that there appeared to be a leak at 26 Broadway through which vital information was escaping.

Flanagan's search for oil properties took him by foot and dugout canoe into the very heart of the Gulf Coast jungles. "It is impossible to convey to you in an intelligent manner the extreme chaotic conditions that exist in this country . . . ," Flanagan reported to Teagle. The rebels were assessing forced loans and fines on everyone who had money to pay them. Because of the insecurity of the currency, many persons would not discuss sales or leases. One of the greatest problems was the exorbitant price demanded for property from anyone known to have substantial financial backing. Graft flourished in the government offices that regulated land transactions. One engineering firm informed Flanagan, "We believe that a deed to the property can be gotten through at the present time for some fifteen or twenty thousand pesos of graft money and expenses." Flanagan's comment to the company's chief counsel in Mexico was that "to date we had not contributed one dollar in any kind of graft or political features, and that I felt that it was the policy of my friends to so continue."[12]

Flanagan worked to obtain parcels of land within or near proved territory, mostly in the vicinity of the Tuxpan River in Veracruz. He was especially interested in getting a lease near the Potrero del Llano well, which had a phenomenal production. Sometimes he pretended that what he wanted was mahogany; in all cases his contracts were in his own name. Before the full results of his work could be realized, however, Flanagan was recalled by Teagle and dispatched on an even more urgent mission to Peru. He was succeeded by John Kee, of Carter, who by April of 1917 had obtained 33 leases of 15 to 37 *hectares* in several promising areas.[13]

Late in 1917 the Jersey Company at last commenced producing operations in Mexico. This entry, the culmination of nearly a decade of investigation, procrastination, and failure, was effected by the purchase, for $2,475,000 in gold, of the Compañía Transcontinental de Petróleo, S.A. This organization, backed by a combination of English, American, and Mexican interests, had acquired leases in Mexico and had drilled one successful well before the time of sale. The purchase gave to Jersey Standard a Mexican charter, a going organization, valuable concessions, and a beginning in virtually all lines of the business except refining. Jersey, however, already had a small refinery at Tampico, completed in 1914.

In February of 1918 E. J. Sadler was made president of Transcontinental, thus bringing into Latin American operations a vigorous and experienced producing man. On the very day of his election, Sadler recommended in a fifteen-page letter consideration by the Jersey board of a policy of aggressive expansion in Mexico.[14]

It was important, wrote Sadler, to become active at once. Transcontinental had only one well producing, at Pánuco, while all principal competitors, who had made earlier entries and purchased their properties under more advantageous conditions, were strongly entrenched and ready to make deliveries the moment war-engaged tankers should become available. Properties might be obtained, Sadler reported, from many small companies which were hard pressed for money in consequence of being unable to export oil.

Sadler pointed to many encouraging facts. In the six months ending in July of 1918, the figures for Mexico's potential production had been increased to a point where they exceeded those of actual production in the United States. Transcontinental's own daily potential had increased from 12,000 to 50,000 barrels, all in the Pánuco field, while a production of 75,000 barrels of the more valuable light crude in the Tuxpan fields to the south was a probability for the company in the following year. Transcontinental's producing and transporting facilities were increasing, Jersey Standard's investment in Mexico had grown from $730,000 to $5,230,000, and loans from the parent company to Transcontinental increased from $1,408,000 outstanding at the end of 1917 to $5,547,600 by the end of 1918.

Sadler reported, however, that political conditions had deteriorated still further and that attacks by bandits had become frequent and bold. Only intervention by the United States, he felt, would end the troubles.[15] In a payroll robbery Sadler himself was severely beaten by bandits and narrowly escaped with his life. Thereafter he made it a practice never to carry more than twenty-five dollars on his person, and he habitually wore a cheap watch which could be used to placate frustrated outlaws.

Sporadic banditry, however, paled to insignificance before the threat of official spoliation of foreign property rights enunciated by the Carranzista government in the newly framed constitution of 1917. Sadler wrote:[16]

The desire of the Mexican Government to enforce article 27 of the constitution, practically confiscating the subsoil rights, has been demonstrated during the last six months by the promulgation of a decree on February 19th [1918] and the subsequent efforts to nationalize the industry, including a radical increase of the export tax on crude and its products. You may be interested in hearing, if you have not already done so, that the English Government made a very strong protest against the decree of February 19th, which I had an opportunity to read. It was along similar lines to the American note but briefer and less courteous in tone. It stated that the British Government would hold the Mexican Government responsible for any loss sustained by British interests due to the enforcement of the decree.

Thus Jersey Standard commenced producing operations in Mexico under the dark threat of political storm. That Sadler and the Jersey board did not foresee how destructive were the forces soon to be unleashed may be inferred from the way Jersey Standard increased its investment in Transcontinental. The promise implicit in Sadler's reports in 1918 was not to be fulfilled, nor was the Jersey Company to achieve the measure of control it sought over the production of crude oil from the fabulous pools of Pánuco and the Golden Lane.

DRY HOLES IN CANADA

In Canada yet another failure was recorded in the attempts of the Jersey organization to expand its control over crude oil production. The effort here, to be sure, was halfhearted. Jersey directors simply did not believe there was much oil in Canada, and Jersey geologists were inclined to agree.

Before the dissolution The Imperial Oil Company, Limited, had shown little interest in production. Refining operations were on a modest scale, and nearly all the crude to feed those operations was purchased. Imperial saw no necessity or excuse for supporting expensive oil-prospecting ventures and did not even have exploration and producing staffs.

This indifference was jolted somewhat in 1913 when an oil strike was made in the Black Diamond district, near Calgary, Alberta. This crude proved to be almost pure gasoline, and by May of 1914 a promotional boom had been launched in the area. Walter C. Teagle, then president of Imperial, and Seth B. Hunt, Jersey's director in charge of producing operations, agreed that events warranted an investigation.

In the fall of 1914 two geologists were dispatched to Alberta by the Jersey Company, but their report was not encouraging.[17] Jersey's chief geologist had little confidence in the Alberta oil fields, although he did advise Imperial to pick up some leases in the gas fields there. In May of 1915 two experienced oilmen from West Virginia were hired to go to Alberta, without revealing their connections, to look further into producing prospects and to examine the possibility of laying a gas pipeline into Edmonton. They found that such a pipeline project had already been established, and they submitted reports on oil prospects that were not encouraging. They did, however, recommend that Imperial carry on lease work as a measure of protection in case commercial production was discovered in Alberta.[18]

Teagle wished to form a separate company to carry on leasing activities and to purchase crude for Imperial. It was felt at Imperial headquarters that as a matter of expediency Imperial's control over such a company should not be made known. To this plan there was some objection from 26 Broadway. A. C. Bedford considered that such a step was out of line with the spirit and tendency of the times, and he advised Teagle that Imperial ought to purchase on its own account.[19] Teagle, however, stood his ground and pointed out that, were Imperial to enter a producing area openly, another boom would be started and effective leasing and purchasing would be impossible. Teagle also refused to accept the dictum of Jersey geologists that oil prospecting in Canada was not likely to prove fruitful.

Late in 1915 an experienced oil buyer and refiner was employed to become Imperial's field man in the West, and a geologist was engaged.[20] An engineer and an assistant were hired to manage field operations, and in 1917 the Northwest Company, Limited, which very soon became a wholly owned Imperial affiliate, was organized to engage in exploration in western Canada.

Behind Teagle's determination to organize a Canadian producing operation lay not only increasing crude prices and the ever more obvious need for Jersey Standard to assure itself of oil supplies, but also the fact that the Royal Dutch-Shell had become interested in Canadian oil reserves. Henri Deterding had gone so far as to offer the Canadian government a half interest in producing profits in return for exclusive exploration rights in northern Alberta.

By 1918 the fact had been well demonstrated in Canada that the finding of oil in new territories was a long-drawn-out and costly process. About all that could be said at that time about Imperial's producing operations was that Teagle, combating an apparent lack of enthusiasm at 26 Broadway, had made a defensive counterplay to an aggressive move by the Royal Dutch. Since Imperial lacked even a good guess as to the extent of Canadian oil reserves, the efficacy of Deterding's move and of Teagle's counter could scarcely be appraised. Teagle simply refused to run the risk that someone else might exclude Imperial from Canadian oil reserves. In six years of very sporadic effort the company had succeeded in developing no important production of its own, and the embryonic producing organization faced a nebulous future.

STALEMATE IN THE DUTCH EAST INDIES

Both in Mexico and in Canada the growing boldness of the Royal Dutch-Shell had indirectly influenced Jersey Standard policy and operations. The oil fields of the Dutch East Indies, however, were Deterding's bastions of strength, and there his company stood, in all its regal might, squarely in the path of rivaling ambitions. There Jersey Standard and the Royal Dutch-Shell matched wits anew in the mighty contest which shook and shaped the international petroleum industry for a full generation.

Long before the dissolution decree, Standard Oil had acquired an Orient-wide market, though it had no production of its own in the Orient. From the middle 1890's to 1911, Standard tried again and again to acquire concessions to explore and produce in British and Dutch colonial territories and to develop production of its own in the East to serve the Eastern markets. These efforts, related in detail in *Pioneering in Big Business*, were thwarted by the determined opposition of British and Dutch interests, which feared the all-powerful Standard Oil and which were strongly backed in their opposition by their respective governments.

In the spring of 1912 Jersey Standard made another attempt. At that time the oil war that had followed in the wake of the breaking of the 1910 agreements between Standard and the Royal Dutch-Shell was in full swing, and Deterding was attacking on many fronts. The renewal of efforts in Deterding's "home" territory, therefore, partook of the nature not only of a quest for crude oil reserves, but of a very well-timed and threatening counterattack upon Jersey's chief international competitor. In this attempt the Jersey Company organized a Dutch affiliate to carry on exploring and producing operations in Dutch colonial territory. The new company was incorporated in the spring of 1912 as the Naamlooze Vennootschap Nederlandsche Koloniale Petroleum Mattschappij, N.V., and was owned not by the Jersey Company directly but by the American Petroleum Company, Jersey's marketing affiliate in the Netherlands. The incorporation in Holland was necessary in order to conform with the requirements of the Dutch Mining Law of 1899; indirect ownership of the new company may have been meant to appease the militant nationalistic spirit of the Dutch and to make the Standard Oil connection less obvious. Deterding greeted the new move with indignation and redoubled his efforts to extend the activities of his company into the United States.

Even before NKPM (as the new company was called) had been formed, however, the American Petroleum Company had quietly been acquiring concessions in the Indies which the Royal Dutch and others had given up. NKPM took over these concessions from its Dutch parent, and in the next few years applied to the Dutch government for nearly five thousand prospecting permits, of which under a hundred were granted.[21]

This precarious toehold in the Indies was scarcely satisfactory. The NKPM had been formed not to develop the scattered and unpromising concessions that Jersey Standard's affiliate was able to wangle from the Dutch government, but with the hope of getting into the Djambi, a Sumatran field that was considered to hold great promise. The Royal Dutch-Shell, however, also wanted the Djambi and opposed Jersey Standard's efforts to gain concessions there.

Here was an impasse for the Dutch colonial administration. If it granted the Djambi to the Royal Dutch, the administration was in danger of attack for furthering a monopoly which was beginning to become unpopular in Holland because of its large British participation. Neither, on the other hand, could the Dutch government go directly counter to the wishes of Deterding and his great concern. The government saved itself by suspending, as of May 1, 1913, the Mining Law under which concessions were granted in the Indies. With new leases denied to all parties, the stalemate was absolute and would remain so until the political winds veered, or until the NKPM managed to find oil on the properties that it already controlled.

This last-named prospect was not encouraging. For ten years NKPM continued with negligible success to drill on its concessions, hoping somewhere or somehow to find oil in remunerative quantities. Wells were drilled in north and south Sumatra, Java, Dutch East Borneo, and in British North Borneo. A field report submitted to 26 Broadway in 1918 by a Jersey Standard investigator contains succinct statements about results already achieved and conditions then prevalent.[22]

In all, 66 wells had been drilled, at depths ranging from 89 to 2,941 feet. Of these wells 39 had been abandoned, and from the remainder a total average production of 135 barrels per day was being realized. This small yield was from the Petak and Tremboal concessions in Java, where wells ranged from 2,350 to 2,650 feet in depth and were costing about $60,000 per well. To understand how disappointing were these results after six years of development work and the expenditure of some $6,000,-

000, the fact need only be noted that Deterding's interests in the Dutch East Indies produced 12,500,000 barrels of oil in the year 1917 alone.[23]

Problems encountered here made European operations seem simple by comparison. Transportation of machinery and field supplies, always difficult in undeveloped countries, was doubly so in jungle areas. Materials for the south Sumatra fields were shipped to Palembang, freighted up a river, and then brought in by oxcarts to the wells. Roads were hacked out of the jungle at high cost, but in rainy seasons they became nearly impassable. Coolie backs sometimes provided the only means of transportation on the last lap of journeys to the fields.

The labor situation, too, was difficult. In 1918 NKPM was employing about 150 Europeans and 2,500 native laborers. Skilled labor, of course, was not obtainable locally. In Java unskilled labor was available at very low rates, but in other areas such labor was imported on an expensive contractual basis. The supply of workmen from Macassar was good, and Chinese and Javanese labor was heavily relied upon for unskilled work. Eurasians, Poles, and Germans were employed in the less difficult drilling operations, though they proved to be poor drillers. On rotary and cable-tool drilling operations Americans and Canadians were employed.

Health conditions were bad in the fields, although the company employed doctors and set up field hospitals of a kind in territories under development. In some areas even coolie contract laborers refused to stay on after the expiration of their first contract. In 1918, 10 to 20 per cent of the workers were reported to be continuously incapacitated because of sickness—chiefly malaria. Americans and Europeans found the climate particularly trying, and a serious managerial problem was encountered in maintaining a competent supervisory staff in the Indies. Executive skill and technical ability were perhaps lesser qualifications for employment in responsible positions there than men's ability and willingness to undergo the rigors of prolonged employment in the tropics. In 1918, for example, an American manager, who was reported to have shown a lack of appreciation of the fundamentals of the business and who got along with the local authorities only by giving in to them, was retained because he was honest, knew the Dutch language, and was willing to stay.[24] The difficulty in obtaining competent resident managers was complicated by the fact that there were few places in the Jersey Standard organization from which men skilled in production could be drawn. There was virtually no reservoir of men with experience in operations such as those which were progressing in the Javanese and Sumatran jungles. Lack of a well-defined producing department in the Jersey Company may also have impeded the parent company's efforts to assist its producing subsidiary to comprehend and solve the problems of tropical field-development work.

The field investigator sent from New York to report on conditions in the Dutch East Indies found it difficult to recommend a policy for Jersey Standard and NKPM to follow, and his observations were pessimistic. If wells continued to be drilled without good results and if a new concession law passed in 1916 was not improved, he felt that the whole development should be abandoned. From the way the Dutch government was then administering its colonial resources, there seemed little chance of obtaining more promising areas to develop. The American State Department had shown little inclination to take a firm stand in support of American nationals. "Generally speaking," the 1918 report concluded, "the situation is not very hopeful."

This inauspicious beginning, however, had an importance which transcended actual operating results. It was a pioneering effort in tropical areas—a type of operation which was then of a most difficult nature but which later became routine. As in Romania, the operating experience gained was probably the most important return realized from the venture. The political experience, too, had been valuable; the more so for the failures recorded in these years. Deterding had been challenged on his home ground. If Dutch nationalism and the great power of the Royal Dutch-Shell had combined to block Jersey ambitions, Jersey Standard had at least served notice that it intended to fight for a larger share of the world's crude oil reserves. The fact that the company stayed on in the face of seemingly hopeless odds indicated a keen awareness that political and economic odds alike might abruptly and drastically be altered.

STRUGGLING TOWARD COMPROMISE IN PERU

In the first decade of the twentieth century Peru was the only Latin American country outside Mexico that could boast of oil production in commercial quantities. In 1889 British mercantile interests had organized the London & Pacific Company, which by 1913 had become the oldest producing company in Latin America. London & Pacific operations were centered on the barren, desert-like *tablazo* of the La Brea y Pariñas Estate, near the northern tip of Peru and on the westernmost hump of the South American Continent.[25]

Here, on this desolate and broken terrain hemmed against the ocean

by a low range of Andean hills, were the pitch pits which from time beyond record had been worked by the Incas and later by the *conquistadores*
and their descendants. When oilmen first came to this 600-square-mile
tract of land in 1869, they found scattered villages, inhabited not by the
Creoles of civilized Peru or the sturdy Indians of the Sierra country but
by *mestizos*—diseased, illiterate, and completely inexperienced in modern
industrial skills and routines. There were no roads, and all cargo transport
was by water.

For twenty-five years William Keswick, a partner in the British mercantile houses, Jardine, Mattheson & Company and Balfour, Williamson &
Company, Limited, poured money into London & Pacific operations. After
his death his heirs showed little disposition to continue the venture, and
Walter Teagle learned that the London & Pacific could be purchased.
Jersey Standard's president, John D. Archbold, was not enthusiastic about
acquiring what to that time had been only a graveyard of oilmen's hopes,
but in 1913 he agreed to Teagle's proposition that a party consisting of
Colonel Carter and five other experts be sent to inspect the properties.[26]

Colonel Carter's reports were extremely enthusiastic, in striking contrast to the dour statements of John Worthington, who had inspected
Peruvian producing properties in 1910. Had this property fallen into the
hands of experienced oilmen, Carter wrote, the results would have been
different. "But the experienced men were not in evidence, hence the
delay in getting results; hence the expenditure of capital and labor for
so many years, and the disappointments and heartaches which made the
sale of the property necessary—and possible."[27]

Jersey Standard moved swiftly, apparently determined to avoid the delays which had impeded efforts in the East Indies in 1911. Carter's report
appears to have reassured Archbold and the directorate. The option to
purchase a controlling interest in the London & Pacific was quickly exercised.[28] In August of 1913 three representatives of Jersey Standard interests were elected to the board of the British company.

The London & Pacific stock, however, was purchased not by Jersey
Standard but by The Imperial Oil Company, Limited, notwithstanding
the fact that Imperial had no producing staff at the time. Purchase by the
Canadian company was a necessary procedure in the circumstances. The
London & Pacific minute books make clear that the British owners pre-
ferred to sell to a Canadian rather than an American company. No doubt
the British government also favored this course. Moreover, British and
Dominion subjects enjoyed far more prestige in Peru than did American

businessmen, and Britain, in contrast to the United States, was known for the support and protection it extended to interests under the Empire flags.

The purchase of the Keswick interests in the London & Pacific was but the first step in the acquisition of producing properties in Peru. In addition to the minority interests in the London & Pacific still outstanding, Teagle in November of 1913 proposed the purchase of certain other Peruvian properties which Colonel Carter had recommended. The prices asked were high, Carter reported, but the oil was good, the geographic location was of the best, and the shipping facilities were superb. Carter also urged the importance of Peruvian production in competing for markets on the west coast of South America.[29]

The additional properties which Teagle proposed to purchase were the Lagunitos Oil Company, operating under a sublease from the London & Pacific and owned by Herbert Hoover and his associates; the Lobitos Oilfields, Limited, which had a production almost equal to that of the London & Pacific; and the West Coast Oil Fuel Company, Limited, of which 70 per cent was owned by Jersey Standard and 30 per cent by Balfour, Williamson & Company, Limited. The business of these companies was closely connected. Teagle held that it could more economically be handled by one organization.[30]

These proposals were adopted, and Teagle himself conducted the negotiations in London for purchasing the properties. There apparently was no difficulty in acquiring the outstanding minority shares in the West Coast Oil Fuel Company. High prices were asked for the London & Pacific minority shares, but these, too, were all finally obtained. Large blocks of common and preferred stock of the Lagunitos were bought from Hoover and his associates, the remaining shares being purchased in a long operation on the London stock market. It proved impossible, however, to obtain more than a small minority interest in Lobitos, which was largely owned by the Balfour, Williamson group.

On September 10, 1914, a new subsidiary was called into existence to take over ownership of those Peruvian properties which had been purchased outright and the lease of the La Brea y Pariñas Estate held by London & Pacific. The incorporation of the International Petroleum Company Limited in Canada marked the fruition of more than a year of discussion as to where in the Jersey organization ownership of the Peruvian acquisitions should be lodged. International was set up as an affiliate of Imperial, as Teagle had urged and International's counsel had advised.[31]

There is some evidence that the incorporation of International in

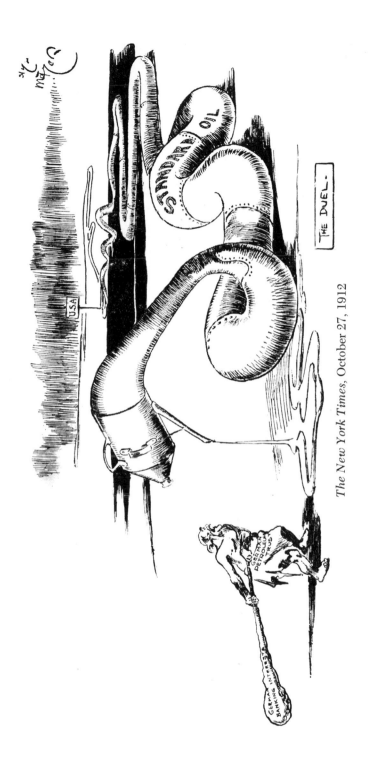

The New York Times, October 27, 1912

NOW ORGANIZE !

By ROBERT MINOR

New York *Call,* July 28, 1915

Canada was looked upon as a first step in the direction of consolidating foreign operations of Jersey Standard in one foreign holding company. Behind the formation of International lay the old fear that to Jersey Standard itself the paths to expansion were closed by the hostility of federal agencies and the American public, as well as by such legal impediments as New Jersey's "Seven Sisters" laws.

Immediately after Imperial had acquired a major interest in the London & Pacific, administrative control was shifted from London to Toronto and New York. The taking over of a going concern did not prove to be a simple matter. The Jersey and Imperial executives knew from Colonel Carter's reports that much money would have to be spent on the La Brea Estate and many difficulties ironed out before the operation could be brought into good order. Equipment, management, and skilled personnel were all in a bad way.

Steps were at once initiated to improve London & Pacific operations. A new manager was put in charge, chosen especially because of his experience with foreign labor. Late in 1913 an Imperial director made a careful inspection of Peruvian operations and recommended changes. As a result, it was decided that $1,500,000 be spent at once in geologic work, providing adequate power, and improving and expanding equipment for producing, refining, storing, and transporting oil in order to bring production and refinery throughput up to 5,000 barrels a day. The improvement of operating facilities was forthwith undertaken, as were extensive geologic surveys. At the same time, British and American engineers and skilled workers were added to the operating staffs, and Canadian and American drillers were brought in.[32]

By 1915 Peruvian crude oil production (Appendix 2, Table VII) had actually reached the established goal of 5,000 barrels daily—as contrasted with approximately 400 barrels daily in 1913, the highest production achieved under the former owners. This was a formidable achievement, but Teagle still was not satisfied with operating conditions, and there was scant assurance that the future would yield either oil or profits.[33]

There were the usual troubles of that time arising out of conflicts between geologists and field-trained men. The new manager disregarded the advice of the geologist in selecting drilling sites. There were difficulties growing out of putting a new man, and an American, at the head of operations; the employees antedating the new manager looked, in the case of conflicts, to the old British managers, still in residence. New engineers and skilled workers brought still further troubles: the Americans commanded higher salaries than the British; California drillers complained of the 12-hour shift; the new men in the field were lonely and restless.[34]

International also felt the impact of widespread labor unrest in Latin America. Strikes occurred in 1916 and 1917. In 1916 the workers requested, among other things, the removal of the new manager. This request was granted, and separate managements were set up for producing and refining. Large wage increases were also demanded and granted. In a strike late in 1917, precipitated by the demands of workers for a 50 per cent wage increase, government troops were sent in to protect property. Fortunately International escaped the clashes between civilians and soldiers which in a strike against the Lobitos had resulted in the death of several strikers and onlookers.[35] Finally, there was difficulty with housing and the company colony, a perennial problem even in well-established foreign operations. To the credit of the earlier managers of the London & Pacific, the housing, hospital, and other facilities for supervisory personnel at Negritos (producing) and at Talara (refining) were said to have been as good as, or superior to, those of other company towns in South America. The workers' colony, however, was under the supervision of a Peruvian, and it suffered from freedom to run its own affairs. Here there was much discontent and poor morale.[36]

All these impediments to efficient operations were amendable in time by the efforts of the new managers, but relations with the Peruvian government were of a different nature. For several years the rights and obligations involved in International's control of the La Brea y Pariñas Estate (which was purchased outright in 1916) were in such a condition of uncertainty that there was even doubt that International could continue to operate in Peru. Circumstances arose which confused the real issues between government and company and made understanding and agreement difficult.

Since 1888 the Estate had been subject to a mining tax of £3 per *pertenencia* (about 10 acres) actually worked. The court having jurisdiction in the matter had determined the size of the area to be taxed, which was recorded on the tax register as 10 *pertenencias*. On March 15, 1915, the Peruvian government, though it confirmed the property rights of the owner, decreed that all land held by International should be subject to a mining tax, whether developed or not. Since the Estate included over 41,000 *pertenencias*, the effect of the decree was to increase the annual tax from £30 to £124,000. Teagle and his legal advisers claimed that this action was unconstitutional and that it amounted to virtual confiscation of the property.[37]

The company did not press the question of constitutionality, but tried to effect a compromise settlement with the government. International believed that on the basis of the original grant by the government in 1826 of ownership of La Brea subsoil minerals, confirmed by subsequent official pronouncements, the government had no right virtually to confiscate the La Brea property by taxation. Recognizing, on the other hand, that a tax of £30 was obviously not a fair tax but holding that a tax of £124,000 was too heavy a burden for the property to sustain, International requested that the enforcement of the decree be postponed while the company had sufficient opportunity to submit facts and arguments for the government's consideration.[38]

The result of the company's presentation was an agreement, drawn up in December of 1915 by representatives of the government and the company, which was submitted to the Peruvian Congress for ratification. The provisions of this agreement acknowledged the ownership by the La Brea Estate of the minerals underlying it, declared that the Estate should for fifty years be subject to an annual tax of £3 for each *pertenencia* worked for petroleum and 75 centavos for each *pertenencia* not worked, and permitted the abandonment of such parts of the land as the owners did not wish to retain.[39] These terms seemed to represent an equitable compromise of the issues involved, but almost immediately strong political opposition to ratification developed in the Peruvian Congress. It soon became clear that difficult negotiations lay ahead and that International's Peruvian venture was facing a major crisis.

Primary responsibility for working out the 1915 proposals and for carrying through subsequent negotiations with the government over title and tax matters rested on the shoulders of two men. Dr. Garcia Irigoyen, a distinguished Peruvian attorney, had charge of developing the legal background of the La Brea question. The major role, however, was played by R. V. LeSueur, International's Canadian legal counsel, who went to Peru in 1915 to represent the company. LeSueur was a fortunate choice, for he appreciated the high quality of the Peruvian bar, conducted his relations with the government with dignity and sincerity, and was personally acceptable to Peruvians. He tried to stay aloof from Peruvian politics. On one occasion, when asked during an election campaign to provide facilities for campaigning among the workmen at Talara for a candidate believed to favor the company, he expressed his approval with the comment, "We would, of course, have to extend the same courtesies to other candidates if they demanded it."[40] In reply to some violent attacks against the company in the press, LeSueur caused a series of straightforward, factual articles about London & Pacific to be printed in Lima newspapers and in a small booklet. Since these appeared over the company's name, the source was clear.[41]

The Peruvian Congress, meanwhile, was considering another means of augmenting its revenues from the oil industry. It proposed in 1916 to increase the tax on petroleum exports from one *sole* per ton to four *sole* on crude and eight on refined oil. LeSueur and Teagle believed that such an increase was an unjustifiable burden on the oil companies and suggested instead that a general income tax be levied. Their proposal did not appeal to the Peruvians, and no final action on the mining tax was taken in the Congress at that time.[42]

Meanwhile, the La Brea tax controversy had become entangled in Peru's efforts to bolster its weak financial condition by obtaining a foreign loan of £3,000,000. The Peruvian government pressed International and its affiliates to make a loan to Peru or to join a group in subscribing to such a loan. The company took the position that it could not as a commercial concern participate in a transaction of this kind, but in the summer of 1916 Jersey Standard executives were instrumental in bringing together the Peruvian financial agent and a New York banking group headed by the National City Bank. The bankers indicated their willingness to participate, but only if tobacco, copper, and petroleum taxes were pledged for a period of time. This condition could scarcely be satisfied, however, until the La Brea Estate and export tax issues were settled. Negotiations for the loan were suspended. Some Peruvians believed—notwithstanding the company's earlier mediation—that Jersey Standard was actually opposing the loan and intended to threaten Peru with financial ruin unless the La Brea tax issue was settled.[43]

Efforts by International throughout 1916 to reach a settlement of the La Brea and export tax controversies showed few signs of success, as basic issues became engulfed in the Latin American ramifications of World War I. Hope of favorable action in Congress faded in the summer of 1916, and International—following established precedent in such cases —petitioned the British government to propose arbitration or referral of the dispute to the International Court of Justice at The Hague.[44]

The subsequent report of a Committee of the Privy Council in London mentioned evidence submitted by International to the effect that German interests were offering Peru £6,000,000 for the La Brea y Pariñas properties and observed that "if the project of virtual confiscation which is involved . . . is carried into effect, with a view to making the property of the owners available for German interests, the occasion for prompt and energetic action on the part of His Majesty's Government to defeat this end is very manifest."[45] This was wartime; the two principal contenders were Britain and Germany, and a vital resource in the struggle was oil. His Majesty's Government took the position, however, that no appeal could be made to The Hague until remedies provided by the Peruvian courts had been exhausted.[46]

Teagle discussed the situation with President Pardo of Peru in November, 1916, shortly after Congress had adjourned. He then informed Pardo that, in view of the uncertainties of the tax questions, "future operations here could not be continued on a profitable basis" and that it would be necessary to curtail operations. Teagle also explained the necessity of making further investments in International's Peruvian operations, but held that such a course could hardly be recommended to the stockholders under prevailing uncertainties. Pardo explained the difficulties that Peru faced in its tax problems and indicated his strong belief in the advantages to be derived by Peru from encouraging foreign capital. With reference to La Brea he told Teagle that he recognized that International "had made the investment in good faith and that inasmuch as the previous owners had been in practically undisputed possession for a period of 26 years, there was a moral obligation for the Peruvian Government now to come to some amicable arrangement with the Company."[47] Meanwhile, Teagle had supplied information for editorials on the Peruvian situation in the *New York Times*, the *Philadelphia Ledger*, and certain other United States publications.[48]

At this time Teagle had a personal representative in Peru. This man was James W. Flanagan, who had been buying oil land leases in Mexico and was proving useful in obtaining information about oil developments elsewhere in Latin America. In 1914 Flanagan had inquired about the possibility of obtaining oil concessions in Peru; in 1915 he had visited that country to see a former manager of the London & Pacific, who was believed to have information about certain legal papers having to do with the La Brea y Pariñas Estate. In 1916 he returned to Peru, this time to direct his efforts particularly toward obtaining a concession to build a railroad in territory that Jersey Company geologists believed might have oil. This railroad was projected to run from the coast to the Marañon River, in the Amazon watershed. Following the common practice of the time in seeking concessions abroad—as, indeed, in obtaining oil leases at home—Flanagan's real affiliations were not made known. To win support for his project and to establish contacts by which to obtain information, Flanagan entertained lavishly and developed close relations with newspapermen and a few others, including a representative in the Peruvian Congress from the region of the proposed concession. He also channeled a steady stream of information to Teagle on Peruvian economic and political matters. Although Flanagan had no official connection with International, he used the Marañon project to win support for that company in Congress, expressing the belief that United States capital would probably not be interested in investing in Peru until a reasonable solution was arrived at in the La Brea matter.[49]

Flanagan left Peru in the autumn of 1917, after it had become clear that a workable concession could not be obtained for the Marañon railroad. Some measure of the attitude of the Peruvians toward his mission may be found in comments in the Lima press: *La Crónica* alluded to his connections with Jersey Standard interests in a sarcastically critical article, while *El Tiempo* expressed deep regret that so beneficent a public work as the Marañon project had been opposed by certain factions in Peru.[50]

The year 1917 brought little progresss in the La Brea situation, but the company continued to improve its producing and refining operations in the belief that a settlement would eventually be effected. Its British connection, however, which had originally been regarded as advantageous, now made the company liable to British wartime restrictions on product sales to German interests in Peru and, in consequence, brought the company into conflict with the Peruvian government.

"I have not as good news as I gave you in a previous letter," Teagle wrote his company's legal counsel in London in August of 1917. "It seems that the British Government has ordained that the L. & P. Co. shall not provide any German firm that is on the blacklist with Petroleum and this the Peruvian Government does not seem disposed to tolerate—that its own productions should be dispossessed of on its proper soil by a foreign power." This was a serious matter, for Germans and German interests were influential in Peru, not only in business, but also socially and politically. The issue was finally resolved by an adjustment that allowed the company to continue to supply its Peruvian customers, but the effect on International's relations in Peru was most unfavorable.[51]

Late in 1917 affairs took a still more decided turn for the worse. In November the Senate passed the La Brea land tax measure, but in doing so raised a new issue of major importance. To the President's proposals of December, 1915, were added the stipulations that the company be subject to the national courts' decisions under Peruvian law and that the company renounce all recourse to diplomatic intervention.[52]

At this critical point in the La Brea controversy the impact of the emerging Latin American doctrine of nonintervention was clearly to be discerned. There were precedents in many countries—in Latin America and elsewhere—for foreigners to seek the intervention of their home governments or of international agencies in settling disputes, particularly in controversies with the foreign state in which they were domiciled or with which they had relations. The La Brea issue, however, rose at the very time when several Latin American countries were beginning to reach for freedom from all such external pressures or controls. The principle of nonintervention was to be accepted in practice by the United States in the 1920's in its relations with Mexico and was to be formally agreed upon by a convention of American states in 1936.[53] In 1917, however, the doctrine of nonintervention was in its early developmental stage and its application was an inexpedient course for the Allied Nations to pursue consistently, seeking as they were to neutralize German influence in the Western Hemisphere and protect vital Latin American sources of supply.

The La Brea issue continued to lag in Congress in 1918. LeSueur worked throughout the spring and summer to forward the matter with the government, aided by staunch support among Peruvians. Indeed, the stalemate was evidence of the fact that the affair was not just a case of Peru against International but also of a division within Peru itself on the many issues involved. In April President Pardo was informed by the company that, if progress was not made before Congress adjourned, operations would have to be curtailed. When Congress adjourned in June, the question had not yet been placed before the Chamber of Deputies. On Pardo's assurance that it would be considered at the earliest possible moment after the convening of the regular session in July, operations at Negritos and Talara were continued as before.[54]

In the meantime, however, the Canadian headquarters of the company had been making plans for curtailing operations. LeSueur advised strongly against such action. Teagle, by this time president of Jersey Standard and nominally only in a position to advise International, urged patience. When G. Harrison Smith, then president of International, proposed a complete shutdown at Negritos, a partial closing at Talara, and the dismissal of workers with a small severance allowance, Teagle advised that pumping be continued lest the wells be injured. He further urged that workers be employed on cleanup jobs around the plant or be paid a half or a third of their current wages if laid off. In Teagle's attitude at that time is demonstrated the germination of a policy within Jersey Standard that was to grow to great significance later.[55]

For several months it appeared that the hoped-for compromise might be reached, but unfortunately the differences over title and tax matters, which were amenable to compromise, had ceased to be the chief points at issue. A revision of the original proposal submitted to the Chamber of Deputies in October of 1918 was even more unfavorable to the company than the one adopted by the Senate in 1917. To the company this measure —the so-called Barreda Dictamen—could only mean eventual loss of its investment in Peru.[56]

By this time, therefore, even LeSueur was ready to concede the necessity for curtailment of operations. When he admitted in a newspaper interview that a shutdown was impending at Talara and Negritos, something of a crisis followed in commercial and political circles in Peru. Prominent Lima newspapers took the position that this action constituted a direct economic attack on Peru, and suggestions were voiced that the government take over the producing properties. LeSueur asked that the British government be requested to propose arbitration.[57]

At this point an action which had been broached as a possibility in the report of the Committee of the Privy Council in London in September, 1916, was actually taken by the Canadian government. Canada requisitioned the two remaining tankers engaged in International's operations in Peru—two others having previously been lost by enemy action. This, to be sure, was a critical point in the war, and drastic action was being taken elsewhere as well to keep strategic supplies moving in the face of serious shipping shortages. The result was that, lacking tankers, the shipment of oil from Talara to Callao—the port that supplied Lima—was discontinued; operations at the Talara refinery were curtailed, as was production at Negritos.[58]

Matters then reached a crisis. Lima had a month's supply of oil; the operations of railroads and other large fuel oil consumers were threatened; labor on the La Brea Estate was restive. Both the Peruvian administration and the company appealed to Washington, and International began to press even more firmly for arbitration. Yielding at length to demands from the government of Peru, however, Canada released one tanker, which early in November began to carry oil to Peru. By that time the critical phase of the war had ended. The victory of the Allies was apparent and soon was to be formalized in the Armistice of November 11. On December 4 the Chamber of Deputies, by a vote of 52 for and 32 against, adopted an arbitration resolution; on the following day the Senate, by a vote of 25 for and 5 against, also passed the measure. The resolution specifically authorized the President of Peru to enter into an agreement with the British government to submit the controversy to an international court of arbitration.[59]

This action of the Peruvian Congress forms a convenient historical division point and presents an opportunity to reflect upon the events of preceding years. Though the factors that shaped the long controversy are so numerous and complex as to make evaluation all but impossible, some general considerations can be ventured. On the one side stood the company, fearful of losing its large investment and committed to the side of the Allies in the war; on the other stood Peru, concerned that it would not receive its just share of the financial harvest reaped from the working of the Negritos field and driven by an awakening desire for complete control of its internal affairs to oppose any recourse to external agencies for the settlement of disputes. Both sides appear at times to have followed the counsel of expediency rather than to have attempted to appraise the realities of the situation in terms of justice and mutual gain. Clearly, a rational, equitable solution to such a problem could come only with mutual confidence and mutual understanding of the issues, both of which were probably impossible to achieve in those confused times.

But this was not the end. Adoption of the arbitration resolution late in 1918 was a first step in the growth of a relationship that in the decades ahead was to be of benefit both to the company and to the people of Peru. From this struggle over title and tax matters in the years from 1915 to 1918 the company derived an understanding of the problems and the aspirations of one Latin American nation that was to contribute to the development of a broader concept of its responsibilities to all those countries within which it operated.

CRYSTALLIZATION OF A PRODUCING POLICY

As World War I moved into its final bloody stages, Jersey Standard faced expropriation, confiscation, or possible ruin in three of its five foreign producing ventures, while the remaining two held little more than the promise of dry holes.

These disturbing circumstances were modified by several considerations. In the first place, the development of profitable producing ventures abroad was a slow process; in the span of five or six years it was unlikely that without unusual good fortune decisive results could be expected. Black though the political situations in Mexico, Peru, and the Dutch East Indies appeared, moreover, Jersey directors had long since learned that such situations could change overnight—perhaps for the worse, but possibly for the better. Tangible producing results, too, were in some respects favorable. Total net foreign production (Appendix 2, Table VII) reached a peak of 11,770 barrels daily in 1915—up 225 per cent from 1912. This level was equivalent to 22 per cent of the volume of refined products shipped by Jersey Standard out of the United States, as compared with 6 per cent in 1912. Total net world production by the Jersey Standard group reached a peak of 28,853 barrels daily in 1915—up 160 per cent from 1912 levels. In terms of world-wide refinery runs of the organization, production had grown from 11 per cent in 1912 to 23 per cent in 1915.[60] Because of war dislocations, production figures for 1916 and 1917 were less impressive, but 1915 had demonstrated an encouraging potential.

On the other hand, the Jersey Standard organization, yet to produce as much as one-quarter of the crude oil it processed, was still dangerously dependent upon purchased crude—dangerously, because old suppliers were making new alliances and competition for crude oil reserves was growing, even as the petroleum industry itself was growing. Moreover, in the international struggle for petroleum reserves, the Royal Dutch-Shell had taken a decisive lead over all competitors and was still aggressively expanding. In 1918 Deterding's group of companies was producing at the rate of 83,800 barrels daily (6.1 per cent of total world production) as compared with Jersey Standard's 26,568 barrels daily (2.3 per cent of world production). The Royal Dutch-Shell's greatest production was in the Dutch East Indies—33,600 barrels daily, or 96 per cent of the total production in that area. In Russia, second only to the United States in crude oil output and where Jersey Standard had no production, the Royal Dutch was producing 11 per cent of the total. In Egypt, Venezuela, and British Borneo, Deterding's organization enjoyed a virtual monopoly; total production was small in those areas, but the degree of control was significant. Alarmingly enough, even in the United States the Royal Dutch, producing 27,500 barrels daily (almost 3 per cent of the total), had surpassed Jersey Standard's output of 18,783 barrels daily (2 per cent of the total).[61]

Between 1912 and 1918, Jersey Standard had improved its position as a producer, but not to the extent demanded by competitive conditions and by the exhortations of such men as Teagle and Sadler. For the producing results obtained in the period one could point by way of explanation to factors quite beyond the control of 26 Broadway—the Mexican revolutions, for example, or the German invasion which cost Jersey Standard its Romanian fields. The Jersey board, however, itself bore a measure of responsibility. Among the board members, no one of whom was a full-fledged producing man and several of whom were well along in years, there appears to have been no pronounced enthusiasm for launching ambitious new ventures. The fact that this hesitance was overcome on occasion does not minimize its importance. Costly slowness in getting into Mexico was probably due as much to the caution and reluctance of these men as to external deterrent circumstances.

Some of the blame for the company's foreign difficulties could be laid on the doorstep of the White House. In October of 1913 President Wilson had stated that businessmen had hampered the development of Latin American countries and that the foreign policies of nations had been based on material, sordid interests. He intimated that it was the mission of the United States government to free those countries of foreign domination.[62] This strong pronouncement seems to have had little effect upon Jersey Standard's international competitors, who were active in Colombia, Mexico, and Venezuela, but it did serve to deny to American companies even token diplomatic support. A modification of Wilson's opposition to "economic imperialism" was made imperative by the war, but at no time in the 1912-1917 period was effective diplomatic action taken to back Jersey Standard in its efforts to acquire oil reserves in the face of determined resistance from strong competitors and strong foreign governments.

The Jersey directorate, however, was more interested in what was to be than in what was or had been. Nor were barrels of crude oil the only, or even the best, measure of Jersey Standard's position. Recognition of the necessity for a strong producing policy had at last taken root, nourished by the perceptive insistence of Teagle and Sadler. Teagle was forced to devote much energy to other branches of the business, but Sadler hammered away unceasingly on the one theme.

"It appears to me," Sadler wrote, "that the future of the Standard Oil Company, particularly the New Jersey Company, lies outside of the United States, rather than in it."[63] Continuing in a remarkably clear and simple summary of the company's position, Sadler stated, "This is due primarily to the fact that the New Jersey Company's business is largely outside of the United States, its principal refineries are on tidewater, and it seems naturally designated for expansion in foreign fields. It is also true that the trust laws of the United States and their present trend seem to preclude continued expansion in this country."

Sadler pointed out that more than a third of the world's production of petroleum was being obtained from sources outside the United States and that foreign production was almost entirely in the hands of competitors. The British, French, Dutch, and German governments all were working effectively in diplomatic channels to advance the ambitions of their nationals, and only the greatest effort could hope to meet such competition successfully.[64]

Sadler's recommendations were forceful and lucid:[65]

In protecting our foreign investment, we protect ourselves and our friends by controlling a greater percentage of the foreign business which comes directly into competition with American products. By owning it, we can influence its activity at times when production is too great or too small in America and maintain more regular conditions.

If the policy of foreign expansion is admitted in principle, it seems to me that the Jersey Company is by all means the one indicated to handle it and that we should be efficiently organized with three principal ideas in view. We should know what is going on in all foreign fields as to development work and transfers of property, and we should be before the eyes of all owners of property who might sell or lease. While in America we are well known as purchasers of producing property, abroad this is only so in a very limited sense. Lastly, we should collect data as to the future possible producing areas in the world and interest ourselves in the most promising. We are not protected by getting only what is most handy today if other people lease for very long periods what at the present moment is perhaps accessible only with difficulty. Neither is it sufficient to be limited to a few localities, as political events, government monopolies, freight rates, or many other causes can shut particular sections out from competition.

The growing sympathy of the Jersey board with these sentiments was bolstered by the realization that refining and marketing expansion was increasing the pressure on the crude oil procurement program and that opportunities for obtaining adequate blocks of territory in the United States were limited by the great number of landowners and the small size of their holdings. That sympathy also derived in part from changes which had taken place since 1912 in the board itself. Moffett, Archbold, Pratt, and Harkness were gone, and their places had been filled by younger men more likely to be in sympathy with expansionist plans. Teagle himself had greatly enhanced his power and prestige.

As circumstances became more and more favorable for the institution of more vigorous producing policies and as the necessity for such policies became clearer, the efforts that had been made in the years before 1918 came to have more meaning. The precarious foreign toeholds that insistence and wealth had enabled Jersey Standard to retain, despite difficulties and high cost, assumed an importance quite out of proportion to the crude oil these properties had yielded. Producing operations were still suffering from organizational deficiencies and from lack of means for the scientific evaluation of producing prospects. Still, the rudiments of a producing department had appeared. In the years between 1914 and 1917 geological staffs had been established in each of Jersey Standard's producing operations, and the number of experienced field personnel had grown. An impressive background of rich and varied producing experience had already been acquired. If the future was, in fact, to bring a great expansion in producing activities, then the statistics measuring past effort were not an adequate indication of what had been accomplished.

Chapter 5

Refining: A Bulwark of Jersey Strength
1912-1917

PRELUDE TO BOOM

T‌O MANY Jersey Standard employees and executives the greasy refinery pipes and stills represented the heart of the organization. This was as true of the Jersey Company in 1912 as it had been of John D. Rockefeller's enterprises forty years earlier, when the Cleveland refineries had comprised the core of the business. Over the intervening generation the feeling had scarcely diminished that it was refining that demanded the real skill and nerve; refining that really was "the oil business." Perhaps this was because the refineries themselves were tangible and obvious. The blazing flares which lit the night skies over the New Jersey marshes and the acrid odors which drifted to leeward advertised Standard Oil more graphically than thousands of words. This *was* "Standard Oil" to thousands of employees who had never seen a pipeline or an oil well and who scarcely were aware of the vast and intricate organization that filled the tanks of those refineries with crude oil and directed the disposition of millions of barrels of refined products throughout the world. In 1912, moreover, the obvious came very close to being the real. The decree of the Supreme Court of the United States, in effect, left Jersey Standard predominantly an oil refining company, and a somewhat localized one at that.

The Bayonne refinery, running 35,000 barrels of crude daily in 1912, was reputed to be the largest in the world; the output of all Jersey Standard's domestic refineries in that year approximated the potent total of 18 per cent of all crude refined by the petroleum industry of the United States.[1] More than 94 per cent of the fixed assets shown on Jersey Company balance sheets in 1912 represented investments in refining facilities.

Of all Jersey's major refineries Bayonne, commenced in 1875 and acquired by Jersey in 1882, was the most venerable, as well as the largest. Here for many years Standard Oil had manufactured most of the products known to the growing industry. Like most other refineries, Bayonne had long devoted its principal attention to kerosene. The Eagle Works, in Jersey City, New Jersey, was devoted to the manufacture of lubricants, running 13,000 barrels of crude daily in 1912. The Bayway refinery, at Linden, New Jersey, and the Baton Rouge refinery in Louisiana were Jersey's pride. Both were less than five years old at the time of the dissolution and both were being equipped with the latest refinery facilities to turn out a range of petroleum products. Bayway's 1912 crude throughput was 24,600 barrels daily, while Baton Rouge, expanding rapidly, was running 11,600 barrels. A smaller refinery at Baltimore refined a general line of products for local and Caribbean markets, and another installation at Parkersburg, West Virginia, specialized in lubricants. The combined runs of these two plants in 1912 totaled 8,200 barrels daily.

Jersey Standard refineries abroad fell short of the domestic plants in point of size. At Sarnia, Ontario, The Imperial Oil Company, Limited, was running 3,100 barrels of crude daily. At Teleajen, Romania, Româno-Americana was running 4,400 barrels. Plants at Havana, Cuba, and Campana, Argentina, ran a combined total of only 670 barrels daily.

These comprised Jersey Standard's major refinery facilities in postdissolution months—six domestic refineries, which accounted for nine-tenths of all crude run by the organization in 1912, and four foreign refineries, whose importance was yet to be demonstrated. Altogether, the crude run in these ten refineries totaled 37,126,000 barrels in 1912, or 12½ per cent of all crude run in the world in that year. In Germany and Norway seven small specialty plants manufactured a line of products for local markets.

Impressive and unsurpassed by any other single company as these output totals were, Jersey Standard in 1911 had lost major segments of its refining organization. Gone with the decree were the splendid facilities of Indiana Standard at Whiting, Indiana, Sugar Creek, Missouri, and Wood River, Illinois. The loss of the Whiting capacity, which was nearly as great as Bayonne's, was to prove less significant than the loss of the men who were directing Whiting's technical destinies. Gone, too, were the Point Breeze (Pennsylvania) Works of The Atlantic Refining Company, at that time the second largest refinery in the country, and the two refineries of the Standard Oil Company (California), which tapped the West Coast fields and served the West Coast markets. Altogether, the 19 refineries scattered from coast to coast that Jersey Standard lost in 1911 had a combined output about twice as large as that of the domestic refineries that the Jersey Company retained.

The size of the disaffiliated segments was only a partial measure of the effects of the decree. Each refinery of the old Standard Oil organization had fitted into a carefully worked-out plan for the distribution of petroleum products. The loss of certain refineries created an acute organizational unbalance which could immediately be remedied only by dependence upon companies that Jersey Standard no longer controlled. Thus, the loss of the Whiting and Wood River refineries cut Imperial off from a controlled supply of refined products. Similarly, Jersey Standard lost control of important specialty plants such as those of Vacuum (lubricants) and Galena-Signal (railway signal oils), the output of which had been taken into consideration in planning the type of products to be run at Bayonne, Bayway, and other retained refineries. Despite the fact that in 1912 refining constituted a bulwark of Jersey strength, much of the history of the refining organization in the six years after the decree is explicable in terms of the magnitude and nature of the blow which had fallen on this department of the business.

The 1912-1917 period forms a transitional segment in a pattern of development which must be looked at as a whole. The organizational break in 1911 had relatively little significance insofar as technological progress in the Jersey Company and its one-time affiliates was concerned. Scientific improvement was rooted deep in the past and continued in its familiar cumulative, adaptive, and imitative pattern. The critical points of technical progress bear no relation to those corporate changes which serve as the most convenient markers on the paths of business history. Coincidentally enough, however, these years witnessed not only the organizational transitions imposed on Jersey Standard by the dissolution decree, but a great technological transition as well.

As automobile and oil-fueled steamship traffic increased, much of the interest, a great deal of the emphasis, and many of the facilities of the refining organization began to swing more and more from the manufacture of kerosene to that of gasoline and fuel oil. Further qualitative changes in refinery facilities were called forth by geographic alterations in markets and by continued and occasionally abrupt changes in the nature of available crude oils. Pressure for flexibility of refining facilities was increased by the rapidity with which markets and sources of crude supply were changing. Quantitative alterations were made necessary by a surging over-all increase in the use of petroleum products—an increase that demanded not only larger refineries but also higher yields of the more valuable refined products per barrel of crude. These various stresses and strains inevitably gave rise to serious operational and administrative problems which at the end of 1917 were still unsolved.

The period from 1912 to 1917, though characterized by many substantial achievements, was predominantly one of preparation. Retrenchment and expansion of the organization prepared the way for profound administrative changes in 1918 and for tremendous growth thereafter; suffusion of the organization with new technological ideas prepared the way for Jersey Standard to play a more active role in the advancement of skill and knowledge in the world petroleum industry. For the Jersey Company these years were prelude to a period of greater fulfillment yet to come.

U. S. PATENT NUMBER 1,049,667

Petroleum technology in the United States was being substantially altered. The changes that took place from 1911 to 1918 foreshadowed but faintly the great scientific strides that were to come, but contemporary observers held that a new spirit was stirring in the industry. This, indeed, seems to have been the case, though scientific advances after 1911 clearly derived from progress made on a wide scale before that time.

In the year 1911 refining was probably more accurately described as a skill than as a science. With a few notable exceptions, "practical" men ruled the refineries. They would have resented the allegation of a later writer that petroleum refining was scarcely more exact than making bathtub gin and that the sum of their technique was to dump crude oil into a vat and build a fire under it.[2] By 1911, in fact, rather close control had been obtained over the physical separation, by distillation, of the complex mixture of hydrocarbons that constituted crude petroleum. To be sure, this control depended more on the stillman's art than on complex apparatus and instrumentation, but it was only a later generation that belittled the competency of men who had never read a chemistry text.

Scientific laboratory testing of petroleum products was well established, but petroleum chemistry was in its infancy. The rate of technological progress was closely circumscribed not only by the nature of market demands but by the technical advance required of other industries to make available the better instruments, better tank iron, better pipe, and the host of other mechanical necessities upon which chemical scientists were crucially dependent. There were no specially trained petroleum chemists or petroleum engineers, though a number of practical and scientifically trained men had by experience achieved an advanced comprehension of theoretical possibilities. Even the largest refineries did little to foster creative research; small staffs were maintained, or possibly a part-time consultant was retained to work on specific problems that cropped up. Education in chemical engineering was in its infancy, too, and there were few specialized scientific courses aimed particularly to fit men for a career in the petroleum industry. At the operating level trade secrecy, the archenemy of general scientific progress, flourished. Even within companies the interchange of information was sometimes guarded. Many of the practical refiners were as mysterious about their professed skills as the alchemists of old, and many of those very skills were predicated upon hand-me-down traditions of earlier days.

Commonly, the equipment of the 1911 refinery consisted of batteries of horizontal shell stills set in brickwork and connected at their domes with vapor pipes which led to condensers. Successive cuts were drawn off as the still temperatures were increased: first gasoline, or refinery naphtha, as the Jersey account books called it; then kerosene, the major product; then gas oil, used in the manufacture of illuminating gas; and finally the wax distillates and heavy lubricating and fuel oils. When the batch of crude had been run, the stills were allowed to cool. Then the coke residues—up to a foot in thickness—were removed from the still bottoms, and a new batch of crude was charged in. Basic progress before 1911 had been directed along the lines of closer control of fractionation and quality of products obtained.

Improved techniques had also been evolved for operating continuous batteries of stills. This system represented an attempt to reduce the intermittent shutdowns that characterized batch-type operations. The stills were connected and operated in a continuous manner by slowly charging the first still in the battery and transferring the partially reduced oil from still to still by means of overflow pipes. By firing each successive still more strongly than the one immediately preceding, fractions of different boiling points were obtained simultaneously from all the stills in the battery. Actually the heavy-end stills in these "continuous" batteries could be operated for only about two days before being shut down for cleaning. Experiments were under way to find ways of extending the time of the operating cycle.

By 1911, too, the use of a series of air-cooled condensing towers between the still and the final condenser, which permitted closer control of the refining process, had become widespread. On the West Coast considerable progress was being made in vaporizing the crude oil in heated pipes, rather than in shell stills, for still-refining had proved its deficiencies in skimming the heavy California crudes to produce gasoline, kerosene, and fuel oil. Several processes had also been worked out for eliminating sulphur and other undesirable components of the various crudes. A host of other improvements had been made, too, many of them unpatented and localized but all directed at the common goals of cheaper and better and more diversified refined products.

Behind the relatively simple refining processes that existed in 1911 lay the complex matter of by-product utilization. The cumulative ingenuity of the oil refiners had long since adapted once-discarded distillates to more and more uses, and in so doing not only had provided the world with new products of great commercial value but had exerted a downward pressure on the prices of the old products.

After the turn of the century, market pressure on the refineries for increased gasoline output mounted steadily, but the usual distillation methods were capable of recovering only the gasoline present as such in any given amount of crude. Of course, more gasoline could be turned out by running more crude; but even if adequate plant facilities had existed and crude had been obtainable in sufficient amounts at reasonable prices, this remedy would have presented difficult problems in disposing of by-products, few of which were being demanded at such an accelerating rate as was gasoline. Since the proportions of the various distillates naturally present in the crudes did not match the relative market need for each of those distillates, the industry began to focus its attention on altering the old ratio of cuts to yield a higher percentage of the valuable light fractions.

Experimental scientists and practical men alike had known for a great many years that under certain conditions of heat and pressure the heavier hydrocarbons decomposed chemically, or "cracked," to form lighter fractions. Cracking processes, in fact, had long been in use as a means of increasing kerosene yields. It was Dr. William M. Burton's famous patent Number 1,049,667, however, which in 1913 forecast the first commercially profitable means of cracking relatively low-value gas oil and other middle distillates into the valuable light fractions. Gasoline could now be manufactured, literally, as well as merely recovered.

The story of the decade or more of scientific endeavor that laid the groundwork for patent Number 1,049,667 is not properly a part of Jersey

Standard's history, yet no history of Jersey refining could be written without reference to Burton and his work. In immediate predissolution years the Standard Oil Company (Indiana) was among the most progressive of the various Standard affiliates in pushing scientific research. Earlier Standard Oil management had seen the need for scientifically minded or trained experts in the refineries and had obtained the services of such men as Herman Frasch, Dr. W. M. Burton, Dr. Clarence I. Robinson, George M. Saybolt, and a few others to work on specific problems. These men were scattered throughout the organization; the dissolution decree served effectively to freeze them in the places where they happened to be working at the time. Indiana's chief chemist, Burton, had been trained at Johns Hopkins University and had gathered together a group of highly competent young Johns Hopkins men to work under his direction at the Whiting refinery.[3] As the demand for gasoline grew, Burton turned his attention to research on cracking. His laboratory organization, headed by Dr. R. E. Humphreys, solved many of the basic problems, and by 1912 a workable process had been devised.

The Burton-Humphreys process consisted of distillation under such conditions that chemical decomposition of the base stock took place without the excessive carbon formation that had hindered earlier attempts at cracking. The first Burton unit was started at Whiting in the summer of 1912. On January 7, 1913, the first of the Burton patents was issued, and on March 1, 1913, the Standard Oil Company (Indiana) announced a new "motor spirit." It was to cost the consumer three cents a gallon, or about one-fifth less than straight-run gasoline. A laboratory inspection report stated that the "new motor spirit resembled gasoline in distillation range, was yellow in color, and had a pungent odor." Some experienced refiners doubted that such a product could be marketed, and a general belief persisted that the gasoline produced by nature could not be equaled by the "artificial" variety produced by man.[4] It was some time before the industry came to appreciate the fact that cracked gasoline was actually superior to the straight-run product in its ability to reduce or eliminate "knocking" in automobile engines.

The gasoline market proved to be less discriminating than the experts who wrinkled their noses at the new fuel. When marketable blends of cracked and straight-run gasoline were worked out, other companies became interested. The whole field of experimental petroleum chemistry was stimulated to activity along old lines and new, and the many patents on cracking processes that had been issued earlier took on new importance in the light of Burton's successful work. Indiana Standard believed, nevertheless, that through the Burton patent and a series of later patents covering aspects of the operation it held a lawful monopoly on the cracking process and proceeded thenceforth on the basis of that assumption.

The statement has been made by a qualified observer that had Indiana not at that time been confined within its existing marketing territory it probably would not have licensed others to use the Burton-Humphreys process.[5] As a result of the dissolution decree and the restrictions of state and federal trade-mark and corporation law under which it then operated, Indiana Standard found it economically impractical to expand the geographic scope of its refining organization. Consequently, the company set the policy of giving the industry the "greatest possible liberty" in using the process. Seeing no point in fostering competition at home, however, Indiana refused to grant licenses to others in its own territory.[6] This restriction was no deterrent to Jersey Standard, which operated no refineries in Indiana's territory.

Less than a month after Indiana had announced its new "motor spirit," letters began flying back and forth between Teagle and Frederick W. Weller, of Jersey Standard, and W. P. Cowan, president of the Indiana Company. Teagle, who had taken over the management, though not as yet the presidency, of The Imperial Oil Company, Limited, was anxious to push through an agreement at once to permit Imperial to incorporate the new cracking process in construction then under way at the Sarnia, Ontario, refinery. He was interested, too, in probing European possibilities and dispatched a hasty memorandum to the directors of DAPG, Jersey's German affiliate, informing them of Indiana's cheap new fuel. Weller, who at that time was a director of the Jersey Company and president of Standard of Louisiana, was interested primarily in working out terms under which Jersey Standard's refineries in the United States might install the Burton-Humphreys process.

Negotiations dragged on. Some felt that Indiana's policy of allowing competitors the "greatest possible liberty" really meant "greatest possible liberty at the highest possible price." Between May and December of 1913 Teagle and Cowan tried without success to arrive at a mutually satisfactory price. At one point in the negotiations Cowan informed Teagle that the Indiana Company would do better to build its own stills in Canada than to accept the figure Teagle had named. It also became apparent that Imperial would not be able to obtain the exclusive rights in Canada that Teagle had sought. Meanwhile, extensive transoceanic correspondence and much figure work by George McKnight and others on Jersey's Manufacturing Committee seemed to indicate that DAPG could not install the new process to advantage in Germany. The Burton-Humphreys gasoline was not acceptable in that market, McKnight reported succinctly, primarily because of its odor.[7]

Cowan finally wrote Teagle that he did not think they could get anywhere by correspondence and suggested a conference. Shortly after this, on January 30, 1914, Indiana Standard signed an agreement granting Imperial the right to manufacture under the Burton-Humphreys patents. This was the first license covering the new cracking process. Teagle's persistence and persuasiveness were successful in obtaining some reduction in the price Indiana had first offered, but in the last analysis the trump card was patent Number 1,049,667, and Cowan held it. Imperial agreed to pay Indiana the sum of $15,000 for the right to manufacture up to 50,000 barrels of gasoline annually, plus 30 cents per barrel for all amounts in excess of 50,000.[8]

More dickering followed before Weller was able to come to terms with Cowan for a license for Jersey Standard's domestic refineries. Finally, on August 15, 1915, Jersey and Indiana signed an agreement permitting the Jersey Company to use the Burton patents in New Jersey, Maryland, and West Virginia.[9] Men from Indiana's Wood River refinery were dispatched to Bayway, where by October of that year 10 new stills were in operation. Plans called for the installation of 160 stills, all of which were in operation by the spring of 1917. On March 15, 1917, an agreement was signed between Indiana and Standard of Louisiana, and the installation of 60 stills was started at Baton Rouge.[10] Jersey Standard derived both satisfaction and advantage from being the first large refining organization outside Indiana Standard to adopt the new improvements on a wide scale.

Both these agreements called for the payment to the Indiana Company of a flat 25 per cent of profits realized from the sale of the cracked gasoline. Weller had asked Cowan for exclusive rights in the various Jersey territories, but Cowan had refused. A proviso, later to become significant, was included in both agreements whereby Jersey Standard was prohibited from selling in Indiana's territory the products manufactured under the Burton patents. These terms were substantially the same as those which Indiana Standard extended to others in the industry: to Standard of Kansas (February, 1914), Solar Refining (June, 1914), Magnolia (December, 1915), Tide Water (July, 1916), Standard of Kentucky (July,

1916), Standard of Ohio (October, 1916), Standard of California (July, 1918), and to others.

Further agreements followed the signing of the primary licenses. Despite the discouraging reports that McKnight had given Teagle about the German market, an opportunity for profit was discerned in handling the Indiana cracking-process rights abroad. Jersey Standard had good contacts there, and in certain European areas its marketing position was strong. The Indiana Company, on the contrary, had few contacts with the petroleum industry outside the United States and no established foreign affiliate through which it could hope to sell the cracking-process rights, patents for which had been granted by many European and South American countries. Teagle expressed the belief that the cheaper price of the Burton gasoline would overcome prejudice against the odoriferous new product.[11]

In 1914 a contract was signed that made Teagle Indiana Standard's representative abroad in the sale of the cracking-process rights.[12] Where the initiative lay in this transaction is not clear. Although Teagle's agreement with Indiana seemed by its terms to be a private one, Teagle actually was acting as Jersey Standard's agent in the negotiations.[13] It seems probable that the reason for handling the foreign rights in this way was the Jersey Company's fear of negotiating a contract with a former affiliate covering such broad and exclusive rights. Though the transaction was entirely normal, such a contract between two of the most prominent members of the old Standard Oil group would certainly have been seized upon as evidence in support of the charges of collusion which were being voiced so vociferously at that particular time.

There is little information as to how the Teagle-Indiana Standard contract worked out in practice. In 1915 a controversy arose when it became apparent that Indiana Standard was under obligation to pay Teagle for patent rights sold in Latin America. Cowan held that the intent of the contract, whatever its wording, was to cover sales in European countries only, and he suggested that it would be a gracious act for Teagle to waive his claims to the Latin American business. Conflicting patent claims and the outbreak and spread of World War I, however, placed serious obstacles in the way of doing business under the contract. Jersey Company records fail to show whether Cowan gained his point or whether Teagle held Cowan to the letter of the contract. Teagle himself returned from abroad and thenceforth was in no position to act as Indiana's agent. By

this time the political atmosphere in the United States had cleared somewhat. Teagle now negotiated an agreement, dated April 15, 1915, that
granted the Jersey Company sole foreign licensing rights to the Indiana
cracking patents. For these rights Jersey Standard agreed to pay the Indiana Company 10 cents per barrel on all gasoline manufactured under
such sublicensing contracts as might be made.[14] Little could be done
abroad, however, until political conditions there had become stabilized.

Meanwhile, production of gasoline in Jersey Standard's refineries increased steadily. The Burton process was a providential answer to war-
swollen demands for gasoline. In 1916 about 10 per cent of Jersey's
domestic output of gasoline was cracked in Burton stills. In 1917 the output was more than doubled, and the percentage of cracked gasoline rose
to 15 per cent of Jersey's total domestic gasoline output.[15]

The Burton-Humphreys process itself was greatly improved by Indiana's engineers in the months following its introduction. Old-timers,
however, looked at the new units with considerable apprehension. In
order to obtain the best results the stills, which measured 8 feet in
diameter and 20 feet in length and were charged with 6,000 gallons of
stock, had to be operated at a temperature of about 750 degrees Fahren-
heit. Pressures ranged up to 95 pounds per square inch. The softening
point of the steel then used in the stills was 900 degrees, and the firebox
temperatures ranged from 1,100 to 1,200 degrees. Even a very thin layer
of carbon deposited on the still bottom so insulated the steel from the
relatively cooler oil that the still rapidly heated up, or developed a "hot
bottom." With pressure in the still, dire consequences might follow if the
stillman should fail to gauge the danger point correctly. The fires must be
drawn, the still cooled and emptied, and the carbon deposit scraped off.
Despite the hazards, the temptation to push a run to the limit was hard
for some of these rough-and-ready oilmen to resist. Always the pressure
was for more production, and stillmen were known to keep batteries in
operation at peril to life and limb of self and fellow workers rather than
be thought squeamish.[16]

The first pressure stills operated on a cycle of about 24 hours, in which
approximately one-third of the stock was distilled. They were then shut
down, to permit the carbon to be removed. When the still temperature
dropped to about 250 degrees, a workman crawled inside, heavily padded
against the heat, and began with all possible dispatch to chip the car-
bonaceous residue from the still bottom. Every effort was bent and no

physical discomfort spared to reduce the shutdown time of the batteries. Gradually these primitive and hazardous conditions were improved. In 1914 movable false-bottom plates were installed in the stills to catch some of the carbon deposit. These plates enabled the operating cycle to be increased to 48 hours, in which time about two-thirds of the charging stock was distilled. A young Indiana Standard refiner named E. M. Clark in that same year devised a means of preheating the charging stock in tubes, through which it circulated in and out of the stills, thereby eliminating direct firing on the stills.[17] These improvements and others made on the Burton process produced a steady increase in the percentage of gasoline obtained from the charging stock and were part of a widespread surge of effort in all technical branches of the industry.

This advance in almost all instances was market-inspired, for there was virtually no "pure" refining research. Progress in petroleum refining continued to illustrate the essential continuity of technological evolution. Improvements on existing methods and devices were the order of the day, and major new developments were not numerous. Neither, by the same token, did much of the work under way in this period begin to show tangible results until after 1918.

The manufacture of lubricating oils was affected, in this period, by the same demand factors that were stimulating research effort on cracking processes. Whereas the gasoline cracking research was directed along lines of high-temperature and high-pressure operations, some progress was being made in perfecting processes of distilling lubricating oils under vacuum and at comparatively low temperatures. At the same time, techniques were being worked out for controlling the solidifying point of lube oils through reducing the wax content by dilution with naphtha, artificial refrigeration, and high-speed centrifuging. Refining methods were also being evolved to produce superior transformer and turbine oils and the so-called "white oils," used mainly for medicinal purposes. Increases in paved-road mileage and in the demand for tires called forth improvements in the manufacture of asphaltic compounds and of carbon black, and the oil-absorption process for recovering the gasoline content of natural gas was worked out and adopted widely. Considerable improvement was effected in reducing losses through evaporation of stored oil by the construction of better steel tankage, and the old wooden tanks and wood-covered steel tanks of an earlier day were well on the way to becoming curiosities which old oilmen could point out to neophytes. Important though some of these advances were, it was gasoline cracking that constituted the prime interest of refiners in the years immediately following the issuance of the first Burton patent.

Work was under way in different parts of the country on several alternate methods of cracking. These developments were watched by Jersey men as closely as possible, and there was much correspondence about them among Teagle, Bedford, Weller, McKnight, and other interested men in the Jersey Standard organization, as well as with Cowan of the Indiana Company. By 1917 none of these experiments had matured into a commercial process capable of competing seriously with that owned by Indiana Standard and licensed by that company to Jersey and others. Other improvements, nevertheless, were made and widely adopted. Still sizes were increased. As means were perfected for welding stronger tank seams, refiners began to work with higher pressures. In 1917, too, Jersey Standard became interested in the bubble towers at the Whiting refinery, which increased yields and saved on the cost of steam-treating the refined distillates. In that same year comments began to pass back and forth in the manufacturing organization on the respective merits of shell stills of the Burton type and an alternate method, yet in the experimental stage, of cracking in tube-type stills. This discussion was the prelude to technological events of greatest importance which were later to unfold to the vast advantage of the Jersey Company.[18]

JERSEY RESEARCH AND REFINING ADMINISTRATION

Of the many and diversified product and process developments that were taking place the Jersey Company was well informed. To the question of how much creative research effort the organization was expending to keep ahead of current trends, however, only one answer could be given —very little. To the more particular question of which of the major improvements effected in petroleum refining in this period had come out of Jersey Standard laboratories, the unequivocal answer had to be—none. But still, there was advance and, more important, a growing realization of the need for basic research.

In a section of one of the buildings at the Bayonne refinery there was located what was called a research department. Here a chief chemist, C. I. Robinson, and two assistant chemists carried on testing and experimental work. Robinson labored unsuccessfully to develop a method of increasing gasoline yields by treating the crude with aluminum chloride.

In 1913, after some five years of effort, the laboratory succeeded in producing a satisfactory medicinal oil, which was released to the trade under the brand name of Nujol. Little creative research of an important nature, however, was undertaken. The functions of this laboratory were limited chiefly to crude oil evaluation, complaint investigation, and advice on chemical treating.

No branch of the organization felt any special responsibility for making technical progress. On the contrary, the efficiency of each department or affiliated company was being judged solely by the extent to which it could hold down current operating costs. This left no opportunity for anything more than minor types of process development work, and even these efforts were often clandestine, to avoid criticism. It is said that Robinson on one occasion was unable to obtain funds for so slight a piece of equipment as a small test agitator, costing about $50. There was, moreover, a grave organizational deficiency in the Jersey Company's handling of patents. No person in the company possessed extensive experience with patents an an instrument of economic offense and defense, and the outside patent attorneys who were consulted from time to time were, by the limitation of their employment, unable to do anything constructive or to participate in any integrated planning.[19] Reports of new technical developments that came to the attention of the various Jersey executives were forwarded to the superintendents of the different refineries for lack of a central research organization capable of processing such material and recommending appropriate action.

This is not to say that Jersey Standard was unusually backward in all matters relating to mechanical and chemical progress. It seems probable that most companies in the industry were at a comparable stage of development, though some—like Indiana Standard—were further advanced. In the various Jersey Standard refineries good work was done in effecting improvements in existing processes. At Baton Rouge, for example, Superintendent Louis Link was directing refinery affairs in the interest of increasing efficiency. This old-school refiner was working by cut-and-try methods on his tower distillation units. In him the Louisiana Company possessed a gifted, if stubborn, technician, and Link, with his short, rotund figure, a thatch of amazingly red hair, and a German accent that made his excited directions almost unintelligible at times, was well on his way toward becoming a company tradition. Here at Baton Rouge, too, progress was being made in other fields than cracking. It is said that in the Baton Rouge refinery of pre-World War I days the mixing of lubricating oils was more a matter of artistry and judgment than of precise chemical synthesis. Nevertheless, success was being reported in developing additives to make the lower grades of lubricating oils flow smoothly and give them body and in working up special oils to meet particular needs. In this relatively young plant the spark of research was alive, though glowing only faintly and tended sparingly by the men at 26 Broadway.

Considerable progress was also recorded in these years along purely mechanical lines and in setting up an organization to plan and supervise construction. In 1913 Charles H. Haupt, chief engineer at the Bayway refinery, was placed in charge of a newly created General Engineering Department, which employed about ten men. This organizational change reflected the heavy dependence of affiliates upon the Jersey Company for help in designing and supervising the construction of new plants and for support of the small engineering departments scattered throughout the world. There were obvious economy and efficiency in this service which the parent performed, since no one of these affiliates had a high enough load factor for work of this kind to permit it to maintain a separate organization of adequate size. The specific functions of the General Engineering Department were to design and supervise special refinery construction; to perform the same service for the various installations of the Marketing Department; to recommend improvements in apparatus; and to carry on needed tests and experiments.[20] Haupt and his men played a part in refinery changes in Canada, South America, Mexico, Romania, and Louisiana—wherever, in fact, Jersey Standard or its affiliated companies were expanding. Haupt himself, though trained as a civil engineer, had much in common with the group of old-school German refining men who early in the decade had come to Bayonne from The Atlantic Refining Company and the Standard refineries on Long Island. This group included Link, of Baton Rouge, and W. C. Koehler, who was later to become general manager of Bayonne. All were gifted men, but not all were flexible in their thinking or subject to easy control. Haupt had great confidence in the work of his department and was not easily won over to new ideas. Conservative though Haupt's leanings were, however, the fact remains that here in his department lay one of the areas of closest co-ordination between 26 Broadway and the outlying offices of the organization. Haupt planned well, built enduringly, and was an outstanding teacher of young men.

The performance of the General Engineering Department was more than equaled by that of the Standard Inspection Laboratory. Even if Jersey Standard's research effort in the years from 1911 to 1918 can scarcely be called dynamic, it seems clear that the inspection laboratory was unsurpassed in the industry. This was because of the brilliant work of George M. Saybolt, who first set up his equipment to test the products of Standard Oil in the 1880's and at once launched a vigorous program of both routine and creative work. By 1912 his department had grown to include twenty employees.

Saybolt's was a control laboratory, its primary functions being to establish quality specifications and devise testing methods for petroleum products. The day had not yet come when testing had ceased to rely heavily on fallible human judgment. At Baton Rouge a bent old German could still be seen puttering along a line of 500 lamps, peering at the flame in each and jotting down his opinion of the quality of the kerosenes being tested. Nevertheless, Saybolt, with his electric fire tester, melting-point testers, universal viscosimeter and chronometer, testing lamp, and many other devices, had gone far toward making a science out of testing. Under his direction control laboratories were set up in many branches of the refining organization. So valuable were some of the devices that Saybolt perfected for measuring the physical qualities of petroleum that the United States Bureau of Mines urged they be made available for general use, as they eventually were. He was easily the foremost authority in his field in the country, and his influence ranged far beyond the confines of the Jersey Standard organization.[21]

The work of the Standard Inspection Laboratory and the General Engineering Department was part of a broader movement to obtain uniformity and co-ordination among the various branches of Jersey Standard's rambling refining organization. This movement, set in motion by the dislocations growing out of the dissolution decree, progressed little in the 1912-1917 period. In those years, however, the Jersey Company and its affiliates were able to profit from organizational techniques and mechanisms that had been worked out much earlier. In the confused months following the dissolution, the once-powerful Manufacturing Committee almost passed out of existence. Seth B. Hunt, at the time general manager of the Eagle Works and New York representative of the Parkersburg and Baltimore refineries, was one of those who insisted that it be kept, and this counsel prevailed. Frederick W. Weller was named committee chairman and was succeeded in this post by Hunt when Weller was made a Jersey director in 1913.

As it had in the years before 1911, the Manufacturing Committee served to co-ordinate diverse functions. Its members were charged not only with the meshing of refining activities at the various plants into one master manufacturing plan, but also with the procurement of crude oil and some supplies and with the transportation of crude. The committee also appraised probable demand for petroleum products, seeking thus to maintain a balance between refining and marketing activities. Through Hunt the committee also reached out to influence producing policies of the Jersey Company and its affiliates and to try to key crude oil production to existing refinery demands. The exercise of these far-flung responsibilities varied from time to time and with changes in the nature of operations and in the make-up of the committee. Executive routines were subject to endless exceptions, and in these years administrative controls were often confused and overlapping. The Manufacturing Committee was amorphous in form, and many of its responsibilities were ill defined. Its basic function of obtaining a measure of co-ordination of refining operations all over the world was probably achieved, but the existence of this central administrative group failed to eliminate the local inefficiencies and the inter-refinery rivalries that impeded technical advance and multiplied the difficulties of master planning.

It is rather remarkable that despite these transitional administrative difficulties growing out of the dissolution the Jersey directors were able to do as well as they did in this period of growth and change. The fact is that, despite the vague and often conflicting lines of authority in the Manufacturing Committee, somehow things did get done—not always promptly or in the most efficient manner, to be sure, but well enough, for the time at least. Possibly this was because certain men shouldered tremendous burdens of responsibility. Perhaps, too, the rapid expansion of the oil business after 1914 permitted a certain amount of leeway in the administration of company affairs.

GROWTH AND SCOPE OF THE MANUFACTURING ESTABLISHMENT

Change in the Jersey Standard refineries was clothed in many garbs, and the intensity of the evolutionary forces at work varied considerably throughout the organization. Some of these forces cannot be or have not been traced out in the paragraphs that follow. In this period, for example, reductions in the cost of refining were effected through the medium of the process improvements already detailed. There was, moreover, a wide and fluctuating variation in refining costs as between the different Jersey refineries, which was a matter of much concern to the respective managers and to the men on the Manufacturing Committee. Surviving statistics on these important cost trends and variations are too fragmentary to form a satisfactory basis for detailed conclusions.

A deficiency must also be noted in the record of changes in crude oil supplies for the refineries, though some suggestive trends have been noted in Table 6. In this period crude from the Ohio, Indiana, Illinois, West Virginia, and Pennsylvania fields was being replaced at an accelerating pace by that from the Mid-Continent and Louisiana fields. This transition was of considerable significance, for, since no two crudes are alike, continual processing alterations were required in the different refineries. Even more important was the increased influx of heavy Mexican crude after 1911. This oil differed very greatly in properties from the domestic crudes that the New Jersey and Louisiana refineries had been set up to run and required correspondingly greater changes in equipment and methods. Though the impact of these alterations in the character of the crudes that were being run cannot be accurately measured, the conclusion may safely be advanced that the shifting supply situation, exerting as it did a continual challenge to the refiners, tended to prohibit the rooting of technological stagnation and the growth of complacency.

Not all phases of Jersey Standard's refining history, however, exhibited such obvious alterations as took place in the crude oil supply situation. Between 1912 and 1917 relatively few conspicuous changes were made in the physical facilities of the New Jersey refineries.[22] At Bayonne the management purchased 133 additional acres of land. A specialty plant was erected for the manufacture of Nujol, the new medicinal oil, and 40 stills were converted to process the Mexican crude that was being purchased. Additional facilities were installed for manufacturing steel barrels; Bayonne's picturesque wood-barrel factory, where for a generation almost a quarter of all the Bayonne refinery workmen had been employed, was doomed to go the way of many other landmarks of the nineteenth-century oil business. Improvements were also made in machine packaging of refined products in Bayonne's Case and Can Department, an important annex of the refining operation which employed 1,200 workmen and processed as many as 20,000,000 five-gallon cans per year. At the same time, some increases were made in Bayonne's general refining capacity, and total investment in plant in 1917 was 25 per cent higher than it had been in 1912. In 1917 Bayonne had 102 stills in operation, with

Table 6: **INDICATIONS OF SHIFTING CRUDE OIL SUPPLIES
1912 and 1918**

	Per Cent of Total	
	1912	1918
Crude oil run in all SONJ refineries in the U. S.ᵃ:		
Domestic	99	86
Foreign (principally Mexican)	1	14
	100	100
Domestic crude oil purchased by SONJ from non-affiliated suppliers for eastern refineriesᵇ:		
Pennsylvania	19	13
Illinois, Indiana, Ohio	56	23
Mid-Continent	25	64
	100	100
Crude oil purchases by SOC of La.:		
Louisiana	50	20
Mid-Continent	35	65
Foreign (principally Mexican)	15	15
	100	100

ᵃ Includes Baton Rouge refinery.

ᵇ Consists of purchases from The Prairie Oil & Gas Co., The Ohio Oil Co., and South Penn Oil Co., which together constituted about 90 per cent of total domestic purchases by Standard Oil Co. (N. J.).

Source: SONJ, report by C. H. Whitman entitled "The Louisiana Division Crude Oil Situation," dated May, 1949; Stat., two statements: Purchases of Crude Oil and Crude Run at Jersey Standard's U. S. Refineries.

storage facilities consisting of 450 steel tanks which were capable of holding 4,000,000 barrels of oil. The number of employees totaled 4,600.

Physical expansion at Bayway was relatively greater than at Bayonne. Here the principal addition was that of the Burton cracking units. Refinery investment in 1917 was 48 per cent higher than it had been in 1912. Although in 1917 Bayway could boast of only 2,200 employees and was running a quarter less crude than Bayonne, Bayway was on its way toward challenging Bayonne's long-held supremacy in the refining organization.

In both refineries the basic operational pattern was slowly being altered to supply an active demand from old markets for kerosene and to serve dynamic newer demands, such as gasoline for automobiles and fuel oil for factories and vessels. The 1912-1917 period was not a uniformly prosperous one for Bayonne and Bayway. The years 1913 and 1914 were less active than 1912; it appeared that, while the domestic kerosene market was suffering from the increased use of electricity and illuminating gas, the gasoline and fuel oil markets were not as yet effectively taking up the slack. An important part of the business of both refineries, however, lay in supplying the export trade with kerosene. Foreign demand for this product had not begun to feel seriously the inroads of competing fuels and illuminants and held up well in the interval when the domestic market was depressed. In 1915, 1916, and 1917 the situation changed greatly. Both refineries had increased the percentage of their facilities devoted to gasoline and fuel oil, the demand for which became very heavy, both at home and abroad. At the same time, the foreign kerosene market, disrupted by war conditions, declined precipitously. As a result of the compensatory effect of these shifts in markets, total crude throughput of the two refineries (Appendix 2, Table VIII) was virtually the same in 1917 as it had been in 1912, although the components of the product lines in both refineries were considerably altered. The change in product emphasis itself tended to slow down the volume of throughput, since longer running times were required to step up the proportion of the lighter distillates.[23]

Qualitative differences between Bayonne and Bayway were pronounced. Gasoline became an increasingly important product at Bayonne, but at Bayway the trend was still more pronounced. By 1917 Bayway's gasoline production, in fact, nearly equaled that of Bayonne, despite the larger amount of crude run at the latter plant. Bayway's kerosene sales actually surpassed those of Bayonne. The Bayway refinery, then, though smaller, concentrated on a more restricted line than did Bayonne, which spread its large capacity over a greater range of refined products. A breakdown of product sales by the Bayonne and Bayway refineries is presented in Table 7 in order to demonstrate variations between the two plants and the changes that took place in each between 1912 and 1917.

At Parkersburg, the Eagle Works, and Baltimore, the other three refineries owned and operated directly by the Jersey Company, the Manufacturing Committee made few changes. Parkersburg, which specialized in the manufacture of lubricating oils, was situated close to producing fields, but these fields were now declining in importance. Eastern markets could be better served from the Eagle Works in New Jersey, and the southern markets from the new Baton Rouge refinery. The Baltimore refinery, turning out a general line of products, was well served by pipelines from major producing areas and was near marketing territories in the southern coastal states and in the Caribbean. Experience showed, however, that many of these markets could more economically be supplied from Bayonne and Bayway. Neither Parkersburg nor Baltimore, therefore, was in a position that favored dynamic growth.

At Baton Rouge, on the contrary, a vigorous program of expansion and diversification was in progress. In 1911 a paraffin plant had been estab-

Table 7: **DELIVERIES OF PRODUCTS**
from the Bayonne and Bayway Refineries
June-December, 1912 and 1917

| | B A Y O N N E | | | | B A Y W A Y | | | |
| | 1912 | | 1917 | | 1912 | | 1917 | |
Products	Value (000 omitted)	Per Cent of Total	Value (000 omitted)	Per Cent of Total	Value (000 omitted)	Per Cent of Total	Value (000 omitted)	Per Cent of Total
Kerosene	$ 4,636	29.8	$ 3,537	9.3	$ 3,690	41.6	$ 3,625	13.4
Gasoline	3,681	23.7	15,761	41.2	2,631	29.7	15,344	56.8
Paraffin oil	1,958	12.6	6,022	15.7	1,735	19.6	3,918	14.5
Fuel oil	1,929	12.4	7,278	19.1	none	none	3,355	12.4
Gas oil	1,883	12.1	2,924	7.7	249	2.8	none	none
Crude scale wax	986	6.3	1,317	3.4	479	5.4	762	2.8
Road oil	298	1.9	469	1.2	none	none	none	none
Asphaltum	107	0.7	279	0.7	none	none	none	none
Refined wax	none	none	526	1.4	none	none	none	none
Nujol	none	none	89	0.2	none	none	none	none
Other products	81	0.5	53	0.1	83	0.9	36	0.1
Total	$15,559	100.0	$38,255	100.0	$ 8,867	100.0	$27,040	100.0

Source: SONJ, Fin. Recs.

lished. This was followed, in 1913, by a lubricating oil plant. A year later an asphalt plant was built. Crude stills were added, increasing refinery throughput from 10,000 barrels daily at the beginning of 1912 to about 40,000 in 1918. Cracking stills were installed in 1917, at which time total refinery plant investment was 117 per cent higher than in 1912. Here in Louisiana virtually untouched markets combined with splendid sources of cheap crude to provide opportunities for growth that did not exist in the East, and the Baton Rouge refinery was hastening to round out its product line.

In Canada, too, there was a robust stirring as Imperial moved decisively to make itself less dependent upon American supplies of refined products. Here in Canada could clearly be seen at work the economic factors that dictated when and where and why a company should build a refinery and what type of refinery should be built. Execution of the expansion program was entrusted by Teagle, Imperial's president, to the capable C. O. Stillman, who had served as the first superintendent of the Sarnia refinery.[24]

A market study in 1913 estimated that the markets served by the Sarnia refinery could absorb a far greater amount of refined oil than Sarnia's existing capacity. Expansion of those facilities was at once undertaken, and, as previously noted, the Burton-Humphreys process was installed there. Throughput increased from 3,000 barrels daily in 1912 to 10,000 in 1918. Teagle, moreover, was particularly concerned with the quality of Imperial products, for the company had fallen below the standards set by Jersey's refineries in the United States. A program was therefore undertaken to replace obsolete equipment.

On January 25, 1915, the first still was fired in the new Ioco refinery at Vancouver, British Columbia. This refinery, with an initial capacity of 2,000 barrels daily, was constructed in order to lessen Imperial's dependence upon Standard Oil of California for refined products for Imperial's markets on the west coast of Canada. The Ioco refinery, moreover, could handle crude shipped by tanker from Peruvian fields, where Imperial's affiliate, the International Petroleum Company Limited had commenced producing operations.

A plant at Regina, Alberta, formed the second link in the new refinery chain. This refinery served the prairie farming market, a market that could not be exploited fully until crude supplies could be obtained within a reasonable distance. This essential condition had been fulfilled when the northern Wyoming fields came into production. Teagle's connections with the major producers who were developing the Wyoming field were excellent, and he was able to make advantageous purchase contracts for supplying Regina, which commenced operations in September of 1916 with an initial capacity of 2,000 barrels daily.

At the same time, a refinery was commenced at Montreal. Many factors were involved in this strategic move. A good market existed for kerosene and gasoline, and ships could be fueled here as well. Crude from Mexico and Louisiana could be shipped to Montreal by tanker at economical rates. The market for asphalt which was being created by a decided drive to improve roads in the Province could also be served, for Mexican crude with its asphalt base was especially suitable for the manufacture of road surfacing compounds. By 1918 the Montreal plant was running about 3,000 barrels daily.

By the end of 1917 no one of these three new Imperial refineries was turning out a large volume of products, but Sarnia's output had more than tripled since 1912. The total amount of crude run in all Imperial refineries had increased from 3,000 barrels daily in 1912 to 13,700 in 1917. Teagle's aggressive expansion had maintained Imperial's virtually complete domination of Canadian refining. By 1917 the company had made substantial progress in adjusting its refining facilities to increased and diversified market needs—both civilian and military. The organizational disruption threatened by the dissolution decree appeared to be a threat no longer. The way was prepared for even more rapid expansion of output, should market conditions demand it.

Elsewhere in the Western Hemisphere the scale of Jersey Standard's refining activities varied widely. The refineries in Cuba and Argentina, which had been established because of tariff situations to serve local needs, continued to turn out insignificant amounts of refined products. Neither underwent appreciable expansion in this period. Jersey Standard was much more vitally concerned with its important refineries in Tampico, Mexico, and Talara, Peru, both of which were situated adjacent to abundant crude supplies. Tampico, completed in 1914 as a topping plant, was rapidly expanding its throughput; Talara, an older unit, was being modernized. Both Tampico and Talara reported full-scale operations in 1915. In 1917 Tampico was running 8,600 barrels daily—Talara, 4,600. In both places the potentialities of future expansion were being weighed by the Jersey board against the threat of local political interference.

Refining operations by affiliated companies in the Eastern Hemisphere differed in many more respects than size from those under way in the United States. Româno-Americana's refinery at Teleajen, which had started operating in 1905, felt the guiding hand of E. J. Sadler, just as had Romanian producing operations. Originally, the Teleajen refinery had followed the European system of small distilling units run by highly skilled men. While the batch-type stills were not replaced, Sadler endeavored to apply American refining methods and coax a larger output from his facilities. In 1915 Teleajen was refining 6,300 barrels daily—20 per cent of total Romanian output. Its two principal competitors, Steaua-Română (Deutsche Bank) and Astra-Română (Royal Dutch-Shell), refined 20 per cent and 22 per cent respectively of the total.[25] Despite the expenditure of considerable sums of money on plant over the 1912–1916 period, refinery output did not increase greatly. Possibly this was the result not so much of failure to effect improvements as of the Balkan political disturbances which intermittently interfered with operations. Here in Romania Jersey Standard faced nearly unprecedented operating handicaps and had to content itself with the lessons learned rather than the tangible results achieved.

In other countries in Europe Jersey Standard affiliates did little refining. In France there were two inactive refineries, one belonging to the Bedford Petroleum Company and the other to the Raffinerie Française. In

Germany, the DAPG operated five small benzine works. These had been set up for the purpose of manufacturing various light-gravity gasolines for industrial use and as fuel for Continental automotive engines. DAPG also owned a substantial interest in the small Korff refinery in Bremen, where a high grade of lamp oil was manufactured for the German trade. Another small unit was operated at Vallö, Norway. The operations of these plants, none of which was comparable in size to the refineries in the United States, were co-ordinated with foreign marketing activities, and the Manufacturing Committee had no direct jurisdiction over them.[26]

Aside from these refining interests, Jersey Standard conducted certain manufacturing operations—either directly or through affiliates—which were closely allied to the refining function. The Bergenport Chemical Works imported and processed chemicals and actually served as a department of the New Jersey refineries. The Interstate Cooperage Company, a separate but closely co-ordinated organization, provided oak staves for the barrel factory at Bayonne. In Pittsburgh, the Pennsylvania Lubricating Company, Incorporated, prepared and sold lubricating oils and greases to iron and steel mills. The Gilbert & Barker Manufacturing Company in West Springfield, Massachusetts, manufactured burners, tanks, dispensing pumps, and various other devices for the combustion or handling of petroleum products. Jersey's manufacturing and marketing divisions were vitally dependent on Gilbert & Barker equipment and profited from the appreciable improvement in that equipment in these years and later.

Measures of the over-all growth of this vast Jersey Standard manufacturing establishment, with all its facets and its increasing geographical dispersion, are difficult to arrive at, particularly when the attempt is made to measure growth of the refining function against quantitative changes in other branches of the business. Expansion in the refining department, of course, reflected expansion in markets for petroleum products and in marketing activities of the Jersey Company and its affiliates. The fact that crude oil production by the organization had grown at a relatively faster rate than had refinery throughput, however, still did not mean that in 1917 Jersey Standard had succeeded in repairing completely the structural damage inflicted by the dismembering blows of 1911, or that in 1917 it could be characterized as a fully integrated company.

Indeed, if net earnings rather than physical volume of activity were considered, the unbalance appeared to have increased further. In 1917 net income from refining activities, which in 1912 had equaled 24 per cent of all net income reported by the Jersey Standard organization, now totaled 47 per cent.[27] These earnings figures, however, reflected external forces quite distinct from the efforts to bring the organization into better functional balance. By 1915 demand for refined products began to stimulate an accelerating rise in the prices of those products. Some of the increase was channeled into marketing profits, but some was also reflected back into the prices received by the manufacturing division. This growing demand was supplied largely by products refined from crude that had been purchased in areas of flush production at advantageous prices. Thus, the disproportionate increase in refinery earnings reflected a cost-price situation that temporarily favored the refiners and by no means indicated a lack of progress toward the goal of organizational equilibrium. Jersey management knew well that growth in one branch of the business could not safely be permitted without compensating gains in the others.

Considerations of internal balance were not all that a new hierarchy of Jersey Standard executives had to ponder in the transitional year of 1918. Crude runs in all Jersey Standard refineries everywhere were 60 per cent higher in that year than they had been in 1912, and Jersey Standard's share of the refining business of the world had increased from 12½ per cent in 1912 to 14 per cent in 1918. At home, however, the organization had lost ground, in 1918 accounting for only 15 per cent of the crude run in the American industry—a loss of 3 per cent from 1912. The refining business in the United States was growing fast. Absolute figures were no safe measure of progress. Whether in size or technology, it was not what Jersey Standard itself accomplished that was important, but rather what it accomplished in relation to increasingly active business rivals.

From a competitive viewpoint, the best that could be said about refining operations in the period was that Jersey Standard was just about holding its own. This in itself, perhaps, was an achievement of no small dimensions, and the organization had not fallen so far behind as to make hopeless the task of an aggressive new management. It remained to be seen whether that management could successfully come to grips with one further problem. At the close of 1917 labor relations, like most other phases of the business, were in a critical and delicate state of transition.

Chapter 6

Crisis in Labor Relations

THE JERSEY TRADITION OF LABOR RELATIONS

THE RUDIMENTS of a Jersey Standard labor policy had been forged in the top echelon of company command, and probably at a very early date. Both Rockefeller and Archbold had insisted upon good wages and kindly treatment for the employees. In the lower levels of management as well, the idea appears to have been widespread that Standard Oil men should be entitled to pay and working conditions at least equivalent to, and preferably a little better than, those extended by competitors. This, in substance, was Jersey Standard's labor policy.

Subject to varied interpretations throughout the branches of the organization and never formalized in a set of rules binding on all divisions, this policy was so amorphous in form as to make a definition in other than platitudinous terms quite impossible. "We have no fixed regulations or rules, as between the company and its employees," wrote Jersey's chief counsel in 1912.[1] Few American businessmen, indeed, felt any necessity for attempting to enunciate and study their labor practices as such. Detailed labor policy was made to meet particular situations. Usually it was formulated by the foremen; rarely by any representative of management higher than the superintendent level.

The time was rapidly approaching, however, when matters of labor policy could no longer be ignored or delegated to subordinates by the leaders of business. In the years from 1912 to 1918 the character and thinking of the workers were undergoing as profound changes as were the machines and products upon which these people labored. It lies outside the province of these pages to examine the nature and roots of the significant alteration that was taking place. It is pertinent to Jersey Standard history, nevertheless, that in 1907 the flow of immigrants into the United States reached an all-time peak. This one-way human traffic was also heavy in the years immediately preceding and succeeding 1907.

135

A large percentage of these immigrants, who were from central, southern, and eastern Europe, experienced great transitional difficulties in fitting into the American pattern of economic and social life. Recruiting ragged but virile armies from these ranks, trade-unionism, crushed to earth countless times and in many places, seemed to spring up with renewed vitality after each defeat. Implacable opposition to collective bargaining continued to be found even among those businessmen who preached and practiced fair play and fair pay. Professional agitators, representing both genuine reformist movements and subversive influences in the commonwealth, found a ready market for their shiny wares.

Far too many vestiges still remained of those primitive and inhuman working conditions that had characterized large segments of the newly industrialized nineteenth-century American economy. Much of American business had outgrown the stage when personal intercourse between employer and employed made possible the good will and confidence between individuals that is the basis for good labor relations. No effective substitute had been found for this most grievous severance, though paternalistic welfare work had been tried in large doses. A surging interest in scientific management, becoming widespread about 1911 or 1912, had called the attention of management to the need for a careful study of man power, but this study was launched on an engineering rather than on a human basis.[2] The movement rapidly became a cause of, rather than a cure for, labor dissatisfaction. There were present, in short, the component ingredients for severe explosions in many places on the American business scene.

The explosion that occurred in Ludlow, Colorado, in September of 1913 was a reverberating one and was to echo in Jersey Standard history. Striking members of the United Mine Workers of America clashed with armed guards hired by the Colorado Fuel & Iron Company and other local mining corporations. When the smoke cleared, six miners, two women, and eleven children were dead. The entire nation was aroused by the so-called Ludlow Massacre, and much abuse was heaped upon the Rockefellers, who owned 40 per cent of the Colorado Fuel & Iron stock and had at times been represented on the directorate of that company.[3] The publicity focused attention upon the labor relations of all companies in which the Rockefellers were known to be large investors—most notably the various corporate segments of the old Standard Oil combination.

Jersey Standard's labor relations had long been characterized by general tranquillity, though labor attitudes varied considerably throughout the organization. Although there had been at least three strikes in various sections of the Bayonne refinery, no widespread strikes—and very few disturbances of any sort—had occurred among the 25,000 persons who were employed in 1912 by the Jersey Company and its domestic affiliates. In the investigation that grew out of the Ludlow Massacre John D. Rockefeller, Jr., had testified that he felt it proper and advantageous for labor to associate itself into organized groups for the advancement of its legitimate interests.[4] There is evidence, however, that those sentiments were not entertained throughout the Jersey Standard organization; here and there strong antiunion attitudes prevailed. Actually, although the boilermakers at Baton Rouge were members of a national union organization, there had been few difficulties with unions in any segment of the Jersey Company or its affiliates. Up to 1915 the issue of collective bargaining had yet to precipitate a major disturbance; neither had wages, hours, and working conditions furnished ammunition for serious public criticism of the company.

Scattered evidence indicates that in the manufacturing divisions, where approximately three-quarters of the Jersey Company's employees were to be found, working conditions varied widely.[5] In 1912, refinery mechanics and maintenance workers labored 54 hours and salaried employees 44 hours a week. Employment was steady, and considerable attention was paid in some places to the health and contentment of the employees. Difficult working conditions and long hours, however, characterized some jobs in continuous-process operation of the distilling units. Before 1914 a working week averaging 84 hours in length was widespread for process workers. The 84-hour average week for such work was computed on a two-week cycle. One week consisted of six 10-hour days and one 24-hour day; the other was made up of six 14-hour days and one 24-hour period off. There were a day and a night shift for each job, and at the end of the two-week cycle the men who had been working days changed places with the night shift. The meshing of the two shifts was as follows:

Hours Worked	*Mon.*	*Tues.*	*Wed.*	*Thur.*	*Fri.*	*Sat.*	*Sun.*	
FIRST WEEK								
Day shift	10	10	10	10	10	10	24	on
Night shift	14	14	14	14	14	14	24	off
SECOND WEEK								
Day shift	14	14	14	14	14	14	24	off
Night shift	10	10	10	10	10	10	24	on

These long shifts were also to be found in drilling, oil lifting, and pipeline pumping—wherever the nature of the job necessitated around-the-clock operations.

There was considerable and increasing criticism of these process-shift hours, as well as of the nearly inhuman task of still-cleaning. Industry spokesmen in the 1912-1913 period, however, stressed the necessity for the unpleasant jobs and for continuous operations. They claimed that some of the complaints were exaggerated and pointed to the fact that relatively few employees were engaged in these trying occupations.[6] The workmen themselves, comparatively few in number and faced with practices that were universal and traditional throughout the oil industry, found themselves in a poor bargaining position. There can be no denial that Jersey Standard and the rest of the industry were guilty of allowing primitive labor conditions to persist in some branches of the business.

In other industries comparable conditions prevailed. In the iron and steel industry in 1911, blast-furnace workers were on two shifts of 12 hours each, 7 days a week. Most other iron and steel mill laborers worked on a 6-day schedule, either 10 or 12 hours per day. In 1914 the weekly average worked by all occupations in this industry was 64.9 hours. The average for all manufacturing industry in the United States was 55.2 hours. In that year all Jersey Standard employees at Bayonne, which may be taken as representative of the other company refineries, averaged 55.8 hours weekly.[7]

Jersey Standard pay rates compared favorably with those for similar work in other companies and industries. Among the Jersey Company process workers in 1914, utility men received 22.25 cents per hour, firemen 24.1 cents, and stillmen 31.6 cents. Among the non-process workers, mechanical helpers received 22.67 cents and first-class fitters 34 cents. Average annual earnings at Bayonne in 1914 were $783.34, compared with $765.00 in all American petroleum refineries and $580.00 in all manufacturing industries.[8] Tables XIV and XV, in Appendix 2, present more wage data. The purpose here is not to attempt a definitive comparison, but merely to emphasize that this was the year 1914 in America.

Already there was stirring a realization that something more should be done for employees, and some forward-looking steps had actually been taken. In 1903 Jersey Standard had inaugurated and in 1909 had liberalized a noncontributory old-age pension plan for its officers and employees. Several other concessions were made to employees. Some of these, to be sure, were purely local in scope. When Seth B. Hunt was head of the

Eagle Works in 1910, he and Superintendent C. E. Graff devoted much thought to the hard life of the process men and finally threw in an extra shift in order to give them a day off after they had worked six shifts. By 1912 the practice of breaking the long shifts every seventh day had begun to spread to the other works, and in 1914 process men in all Jersey Standard refineries were cut from the 84-hour week to one averaging 76 hours. This was computed on a six-week cycle consisting of six 10-hour days, six 14-hour nights, seven 10-hour days, six 14-hour nights, six 10-hour days, and seven 14-hour nights. Shift breakers were employed to fill the average 8-hour weekly gap left by the reduction in working time. Some mechanics and laborers in field and pipeline work stayed on the seven-day 84-hour week, but in 1914 many of these had been cut to a 76-hour week.[9]

The company had gone beyond compliance with the requirements of the various state workmen's accident compensation laws that had been passed, and in most cases had extended benefits substantially in excess of its legal liability. In 1915 Walter Teagle followed precedents set by companies such as Swift and United States Steel when he instituted a stock-acquisition plan for Imperial employees. This plan was well received in Canada, though its success was on a limited scale.

Employment practices generally were marked by lack of standardization and centralization. Foremen did their own hiring, usually by the simple process of going to the company gates and calling out to the hopeful group of job hunters which gathered there, "Any of you men boilermakers?" They would then weed out the prospects with such questions as, "What experience have you had? What tools can you use?" In Louisiana, General Labor Foreman Callahan, who had charge of all Negro employees, is said to have inspected the hands of job applicants. If they were callused, the man was probably a farmer and accustomed to hard work; if not, the chances were that he was a city man and hence (in Callahan's esteem) a poor prospect. Callahan had one further test. "Where do you buy your groceries?" he asked the applicants. Callahan owned an interest in a grocery store.[10]

In the New Jersey refineries nationality, rather than experience, often was the prime qualification for a job. Here the working force, which in the 1890's had been predominantly Irish and German, had by 1915 swung to a heavy preponderance of central and eastern Europeans.[11] Many of these men came straight from Ellis Island to the Bayonne and Bayway yards, newly arrived immigrants being preferred because they were docile and not inclined to strike. Slavs were regarded as particularly tractable and efficient in the performance of unskilled tasks. In October of 1915 about 30 per cent of the Bayonne employees could neither read, write, nor speak English. Most of the foremen (predominantly Irish) preferred to mix nationalities in their working gangs in order to prevent clannishness.

The refinery working force was brawny, and there was some justification for the widely held managerial attitude that such men could be ruled only by strong-arm methods. At Bayonne, in particular, foremen's decisions were backed by the threat of physical violence to dissenters. Here there were no company bowling teams or baseball leagues for the men. The corner saloon was their recreation. The "boilermaker and his helper"—a potent gulp of straight whiskey with a beer chaser—was the proverbial acme of relaxation after a hard day's work.[12] At Baton Rouge conditions were better, and a fine *esprit de corps* is said to have existed. The foremen there were tough and heavy-handed, but, by and large, they were fair. The working force itself was nationally more homogeneous than at Bayonne, and the urban setting, though far from perfect, was infinitely more wholesome than the grimy New Jersey slums. Whatever the Wellers may have lacked as operating managers they made up in kindliness and tolerance. The gentle hand of Dan Weller was felt from the top to the bottom of the organization. Efforts were made to improve living conditions and to provide out-of-hours recreation. The refinery band, for example, was the Louisiana Company's pride, though some observers relate that it was also the head accountant's despair. If the attention of management was called to an unusually promising musician anywhere in the state, he was promptly offered a job, irrespective of his business qualifications. If he accepted the offer, he was usually placed in the Accounting Department.

The only generalization applicable to Jersey Standard labor relations in the years from 1912 to 1918 would appear to be that such relations were what the individual superintendents of the various operating divisions made them. Between the best and the worst spots in the organization were to be found as many different attitudes toward labor as there were local managers. Each plant and department had its own rules and methods, all of which represented the local interpretation of the Jersey tradition of fair wages and reasonable working conditions. It seems clear that, though some segments of the organization were outstandingly progressive and the company numbered many fair-minded and liberal men among its top executives, labor policy had seldom become an issue at the top level of management. To the directorate of postdissolution years labor was akin to the stretch of pipeline from Moore Station to Bunkie, Louisiana—a matter which was properly and satisfactorily entrusted to managers, superintendents, assistant superintendents, and foremen. The only way in which labor relations could be impressed on the directorate as worthy of regular contemplation was for something extremely serious to happen. The Bayonne strikes of 1915 and 1916 were the explosions that were needed.

THE BAYONNE STRIKES

The bloody episodes at Bayonne clearly constitute a dark page in Jersey Standard labor history, but condemnations must be restricted with some care and tempered with understanding. Here was one unswept corner in the Jersey house—a house which in the main was well kept and reasonably tidy, viewed from inside or out. The Bayonne strikes were tragedies of local supervisory ineptitude, mutual misapprehension on the part of both labor and management, intolerance, stubbornness in high places, and low, political chicanery, subversive agitation, and mob hysteria.[13]

The first strike commenced on July 15, 1915, but underlying causes were rooted deep in the past. To those sources of dissatisfaction already present—national animosities, lack of mutual understanding between management and workers, unwholesome civic surroundings, and austere foremanship—must be added the appointment of G. B. Hennessey as general refinery superintendent in 1913. Hennessey had come from The Atlantic Refining Company in 1903 and was a good friend of George B. Gifford, general manager of the refinery. His task in 1913 was to unite the four hitherto independent divisions of the refinery (the refinery proper, the cooperage works, the barrel factory, and the Case and Can Department) into a more effective operating entity. With the heavy influx of non-English-speaking workers, these units had all experienced minor labor troubles under their separate supervisors. The unification appeared to stimulate disharmony in the yard. Under Hennessey the abuses perpetrated by foremen in the divisions were not corrected. At 26 Broadway, General Manager Gifford appears to have been out of touch with actual conditions under his command, or at least seems to have underestimated the seriousness of the situation. Rising living costs, the knowledge that the company was making high profits, and the general feeling of labor unrest so prevalent throughout America at the time were important contributory factors in bringing matters to a state of crisis.

On July 15, 1915, the still-cleaners went out on strike. One cause of the walkout was the rumor (which was false) of a cut in wages. The still-cleaners' demands were for a 15 per cent increase. They also claimed grievances against their foremen, who, they said, made unruly men stay longer than necessary inside the stills, where temperatures ranged from 135 to 200 degrees. The viciousness of this discipline scarcely needs to be pointed out. It was far from an uncommon event for cleaners to be carried unconscious from the stills even after normal exposure to the heat and gases.

The strike commenced, and the strikers displayed an aggressive spirit. General Manager Gifford appealed to Chief Reilly of the Bayonne police for protection of company property and nonstriking employees. Unrest spread throughout the plant and into the neighboring Tide Water Oil Company refinery. On July 19 some 900 men in the cooperage and barrel factory went out after a demand for an 11 per cent increase in wages, which carried with it a time ultimatum, had been ignored by Hennessey and Gifford. These men had been earning from $1.75 to $3.00 per day. They complained that, though many of them worked in a fine new building with concrete walls and a glass ventilating roof, the foremen refused to open the skylights to alleviate the summer heat. Complaints to the superintendent elicited the retort that such conditions were good enough for them. Only one piece of ice was put into the drinking barrel, and this melted by 10:00 A.M. so that only warm water was available thereafter. The charge was also leveled that Jersey Standard could afford to pay wage increases out of war profits, which were believed to be 50 per cent higher than those of the preceding year. (Earnings of the Bayonne plant actually were $332,000 in 1914 and $6,552,000 in 1915.)

Working conditions certainly offered grounds for complaint, but the strikers were less justified in their contention that wages were unduly low. There may well have been specific wage inequities in the plant, but the compilation of statistics in Appendix 2, Tables XIV and XV, suggests that Jersey Standard wages in general were at a level that compared favorably with those in other industries. Although those wages had not been increased at anything like the rate at which profits were piling up, the wage rises had exceeded the increases in living costs. No detailed figures of any sort were publicized by the company at this time to negate the strikers' claims.

From the strikers' viewpoint the timing of the walkout was propitious: the company had orders for thousands of barrels of oil for the Allies which should be sent out at all costs. Six tankers destined for Britain were tied up at the wharves. Because of the labor shortage, moreover, strikebreakers were not obtainable in large numbers.

A statement which the company had prepared in several languages was distributed. This notice warned the men not to be influenced or misled by the importunings of professional agitators and stated that the company would only deal directly with the men. Management, the statement continued, stood ready to consider any complaint, but would not recognize an ultimatum demanding an answer within 24 hours, such as the one delivered by the coopers.

On the morning of July 20 many workers were prevented by the strikers from entering the plant. There were angry denunciations and fisticuffs. Seeing the increasingly ugly mood of the strikers and the spreading effect of the strike, Gifford ordered the plant closed down. At that point approximately 5,000 men were said to be out. The Tide Water plant, employing 1,600 men, also closed down as a precautionary measure.

On the night of July 20 the rioting and destruction began—the worst the East Coast had seen in many years. Both sides had armed themselves. Hennessey and Gifford hired scores of armed guards from the detective and strikebreaking firm of P. J. Bergoff, of Liberty Street, New York. Some 150 armed men were stationed along the strategic pipelines from Bayonne to Bayway. The Bayonne police and fire departments were out in force, but serious fires broke out among the railroad cars and at the pump house in the Bayonne yard. Schools were closed and cross-town streetcar traffic was suspended. The city of Bayonne became a battle camp and the refinery a fortress under siege.

The morning of July 21 brought a continuance and intensification of the struggles between strikers, police, and armed company guards. One man was killed and six others were wounded by police fire. Mayor Garven of Bayonne and the local Chamber of Commerce both appealed to Governor Fielder of New Jersey for troops, but Fielder refused to take so decisive a step as to declare martial law. Sheriff Kincaid, of Hudson County, appeared on the scene and promptly swore in 100 deputies.

On the following day the battle surged around the Bayonne and Tide Water plants. Fire broke out at the latter place, and the firemen were hampered by broken water mains. Crowds attempted to rush the barricades of the Bayonne yard and were driven off by the gunfire of the guards. Two more strikers were shot dead and a score were injured. Sheriff Kincaid appealed again to Governor Fielder for troops, but Fielder was unwilling to order out the National Guard unless the company agreed to arbitrate the dispute.

Now the strike was beginning to attract widespread attention. On July 22 it was splashed across the New York papers. The *Financial American* stated that it was strange indeed to hear of a strike in a Standard Oil plant, for labor relations had been uniformly harmonious. This paper pointed an accusing finger at professional agitators and condemned the ultimatum delivered to the company by the strikers. The Socialist *New York Call* let loose fiery blasts at the company. The *New York Times* saw fit to print a letter from a striker which accused Standard Oil of living up to its past policy of "absolute terrorism." The *New York Journal of Commerce* confined itself to straight reporting, but the *New York American* condemned management and pointed by way of comparison to the success of Major Penfield in effecting a peaceful settlement of labor troubles at the Remington Arms plant in Bridgeport.

Jersey directors enlisted the influence of Lieutenant Governor Walter E. Edge, a friend of Teagle and a member of an advertising firm that handled Jersey and Imperial advertising, in an unsuccessful effort to persuade the Governor to declare martial law.[14] Taking complete initiative into his own hands, Sheriff Kincaid appealed to W. B. Wilson, United States Secretary of Labor, to send federal mediators.

On July 23 the turmoil subsided as the mediators met with company officials to discuss relief measures. The next day, the tenth of the strike, the federal mediators met with the strikers and assisted them in framing a petition to the company. This statement of requests was moderate in tone and omitted the demand of an earlier petition that the foreman of the still-cleaners be discharged and that in the future the men be given "decent treatment." Many of the strikers felt that they were asking too little in the new petition. They requested a 15 per cent increase throughout the Bayonne plant or, if the company could not agree to this, that the wage issue be submitted to arbitration. Other requests included a 50-hour week; time-and-a-half pay for work over 9 hours a day, Saturday afternoons, Sundays, and holidays; and assurances that no men would be discharged because of their strike activities. The petition was signed by Anton Dworzanskinsey, Jeremiah Baly, Jan Bazan, Zygmund Litinaki, Albert J. Tzeliezy, and Alexander Trozdzienuski. Of these signatories, Baly, by his own initiative and aggressive advocacy of the workmen's cause, had come to occupy the position of leader and spokesman of the struck forces.

The strikers' demands were delivered to Hennessey at 3:00 P.M. and were forwarded to 26 Broadway, where a tense group of Jersey directors were gathered. At 4:45 P.M. Adjutant General W. F. Sadler of the New Jersey National Guard troop called A. C. Bedford from Bayonne and said he hoped the company would see its way clear to arbitrate. Bedford replied, "General, you certainly do not expect us to do that!"[15]

Fifteen minutes later Bedford's telephone buzzed again. Governor Fielder was on the line. He hoped, he told Bedford, that the company would agree to arbitration. Bedford replied that he would do everything the Governor might wish but that arbitration was quite out of the question; there was nothing to arbitrate. The situation, Bedford continued, had been brought about through the effort of a labor agitator working on a few men, who had struck and intimidated the others. Neither the company nor its men, Bedford went on, had received adequate protection. The company stood ready to discuss all grievances when the violence had subsided and the men returned to work. Fielder then told Bedford flatly that, if the company did not agree to arbitrate the dispute, it would get no more protection than it then had.

"Governor, you certainly are not forcing us to accept arbitration by threatening us!" Bedford retorted.

Fielder then said he understood that the Jersey management had refused to talk with the federal mediators. Bedford answered that this was not true. They had received them and given them all the information asked for. The conversation terminated; Fielder, apparently annoyed by Bedford's stand, released to the press his end of the talk.[16]

At 9:00 P.M. on July 24 the company's reply to the strikers' demands was received. This was written by Seth B. Hunt and forwarded to Hennessey to deliver to the federal mediators. It read as follows:

You may say to Messrs. Moffitt and Smythe, Commissioners of Conciliation of the Dept. of Labor, that we appreciate their kind offer of mediation and will furnish them with all the information concerning the situation that they desire.

We regret, however, that the situation is such that we cannot avail ourselves at this time of their kind offer. Our position is that order and peace in the community must first be restored and when this is accomplished we are willing to take back all of our employees and fairly to consider any reasonable demands. . . . The Company has only the kindest feelings for its employees and hopes that they will return to work.

Hennessey presented this reply to the strikers and added that the only conditions which the company would agree to were that, if order was restored and the men returned to work, they might then send a committee to management to present their grievances.

On July 25 the strike moved toward a climax marked by an incongruous blending of bloodshed and comic-opera antics. The *New York Times* brought its stout editorial ruler down across the knuckles of Governor Fielder with a resounding whack. The Governor, the *Times* felt, had dealt weakly and foolishly with the situation, had left Sheriff Kincaid to his own devices, and had gone to bed. This, the paper soliloquized, was the way politicians in office acted when afraid of the labor vote.

Sheriff Kincaid now became the chief actor on a busy stage. That he was a very brave man no person, friend or foe, could deny. His fervor showed a fine impartiality as well. As the Sheriff's forces marched to take up their battle posts for the day, they were stoned and fired upon by the strikers. This was said to be the first assault by strikers on the police in which the company armed guards were not the precipitating cause. Father Sigismund Schwiger, who had asked the strikers to return to work, was also shot at. Kincaid sent for two additional priests and with their help was able to contain the threatening mob. He then marched boldly to the refinery gates, accompanied by only two aides, and entered. After a company guard had set upon the Sheriff and beaten him severely, Kincaid demanded that Bergoff, the head of the armed-guard agency, deliver all the guards into custody. Bergoff refused, whereupon the intrepid Sheriff and his two aides arrested Bergoff and 30 guards and smuggled them out on a tugboat after the men begged not to be taken outside the gates. News of Kincaid's arrests and the Sheriff's own statement that he would not stand for the employment of guards to shoot down citizens were widely circulated. Kincaid gained the confidence and respect of the strikers. He then left the refinery and proceeded to town, where he arrested seven saloon keepers charged with disobeying the ban on liquor sales. He also forbade the sale in Bayonne of the radical *New York Call.*

Meanwhile, the strikers met again in Bayonne's Mydosh Hall. Reformists and labor union organizers were moving in. Labor sympathizers Amos Pinchot and Mrs. J. Sergeant Cram arrived in a New York taxi and were warmly greeted by Jeremiah Baly, the strike leader. Pinchot gave Baly $200 for the strikers' fund and said there was more if needed. (One newspaper charged that the money collected to aid strikers' families was being spent for arms.) J. J. Dowd, vice-president of the International Boilermakers and Iron Shipbuilders Union, had been on the scene since the 20th, attempting to sign up men. Frank Tannenbaum, a representative of the Industrial Workers of the World, had shown up early, too, and received a peremptory warning from Kincaid. Representatives of the Central Labor Union of New Jersey and the AFL Machinists Union appeared on the scene, established headquarters, began organizing activities, and announced they would support the strike against Standard. Frequent and long conferences took place between the federal mediators, Hennessey, Gifford, Baly, and state and county representatives. The City Commissioners of Bayonne went ahead with their own efforts to mediate the strikers' grievances.

On the following day the Sheriff suddenly turned his fists upon Jeremiah Baly and dramatically placed him under arrest. Investigation had disclosed that Baly was not even in the company's employ, but actually worked for the Singer Sewing Machine Company! Baly said that in mingling with the strikers and gaining their ear he had been carried away by the excitement of his role. Federal investigators took charge of this particular situation, and Baly was seen no more in Bayonne.

That evening, when the strikers met again, the Sheriff was on the rostrum. Kincaid opened the meeting by asking if there were any Socialists present. There were three—one a reporter for the *New York Call.* The Sheriff ejected them. He then addressed the workers in a scene replete with melodrama.

The Sheriff had two of his men unfurl the American flag and started the strikers cheering it. In moving terms he urged the men, in the name of the sovereign authority of the United States of America as represented by the flag before them, and of the Sheriff of Hudson County, to return to work. He read a message from Hennessey pledging that as soon as the men returned Hennessey would recommend to his people that a wage increase be granted.

"I have risked my life and been wounded protecting you," cried Kincaid. "Unless this proposal is accepted by you I propose to have the Standard open its plant and they can refuse or accept you as they wish!"

The American citizens and English-speaking men thereupon voted to return to work. On the following morning, July 27, many of them straggled back to the refinery and entered the yard. By the end of the next day the strike was over. Sheriff Kincaid collapsed at his desk and was sent to the country for a rest. There was talk of running him for governor, and the foreign people addressed him as *Kresni Ocec*—godfather.

The most serious strike in the thirty-three years of Jersey Standard's history was over, but it was not soon forgotten. Both sides licked their wounds and groped for an explanation of the sudden blaze of violence. Two more strikers succumbed to wounds, bringing the total fatalities to five. Bitter press attacks on the company continued. The directors discussed the episode with some feeling among themselves and pondered what now should be done.

On July 29 the company released an official statement. Management's viewpoint was that the strike had not grown out of wages or working conditions, which were "at least equal to or in advance of conditions of other men doing a similar class of work." From time to time the company had voluntarily made general advances in wages and given careful attention to local conditions in the plants. The trouble had been started by professional agitators. Rioters had shot at men in the yard, and the company had been forced to protect its property. The guards had obeyed strict instructions and at no time were guilty of acts of violence. At the time of the strike the company had under consideration another general wage increase in recognition of the increasing cost of living. Now that peace had been restored, Jersey Standard would deal with the matter along lines of its general policy.

Private opinions of the Jersey directors went beyond these public utterances. Bedford was annoyed at Governor Fielder's attempts to force arbitration by refusing protection. He felt certain that a strong show of force at the beginning would have prevented all the bloodshed, and that it was most unfair of the Governor, who knew very well the "utter irresponsibility" of the people with whom the company was dealing, to insist upon arbitration. The feeling persisted that the matter had been "all politics."[17]

Bedford and the other directors possessed confidential information which convinced them that the strike had been instigated by professional agitators.[18] The nature and source of this information, unfortunately, are not disclosed in their correspondence, but it evidently was sufficiently reliable to serve as the whole foundation for the company's attitude. The directors believed that in view of all facts their anger over the strike and its political undertones was eminently justified.

There were other angry voices as well. Two employees of the United States Commission on Industrial Relations investigated the strike. One of these was George P. West, who earlier had put his name to a damaging report on the Ludlow Massacre. Their report on the Bayonne strike constituted a sharp attack on the Jersey Company and attempted to drag the Rockefeller name into the controversy. Frank P. Walsh, chairman of the Commission and a critic of the Standard Oil Company, was bitter in his denunciations. Both Gifford and Hennessey were accused of entertaining reactionary industrial theories and of having little sympathy for the foreign workers in their employ. Immediately on publication of these findings, Commissioner Harris Weinstock, apparently acting as chairman of the Commission while Walsh was busy with duties on the War Labor Board, denied that this was an official report. He stated that the "investigation" actually had been motivated by the *New York Call.* Newspaper editorials criticized the farcical antics of the Commission and complained of the waste of taxpayers' money.[19]

The dangerous aspect of all this was that in the mêlée of charges and countercharges old war cries were sounding forth again. Rockefeller and the Standard were once more accused of grinding the faces of the poor. Whatever else it may have been, the Bayonne strike of 1915 constituted as damaging a breach of good public relations as could possibly have been committed. Nevertheless, Jersey management held firm to its conviction of righteousness and ignored the shower of blows which fell upon it.

An objective estimate of the strength of the company's position in the highly controversial Bayonne affair is not easy to arrive at. No official excuses could hide the fact that working conditions in some departments at Bayonne were very bad. In later years Teagle declared that the strike should never have occurred and unequivocally laid the blame upon the local management.[20] This appears to be a fair judgment insofar as it went, but the Big Board had also to accept a share of the responsibility. The men at 26 Broadway had not realized the essential facts in time. The failure of top management to check upon delegated authority had backfired with terrible consequences. No doubt the company statement was true: in time wages would have been raised still more and working conditions improved. But on this occasion, as had happened before and was to happen again, the conservatism of company management had been disastrous. Jersey Standard had been too lethargic in recognizing the increasing restiveness of labor; too blind in its complacent belief that Jersey workmen were better off than the workmen of other companies; too certain that the men realized their own good fortune; too naïve regarding the men's susceptibility to outside influences; too indifferent to the racial animosities among immigrant workers which contributed so materially to the difficulties.

In judging the company's handling of the strike once it had started, the fact must at once be recognized that the directors, like other businessmen of that day and later, were imbued with the fervent belief in their right to protect their property at any cost. They were bitterly opposed to any collective action by the men that had its origins in leadership from outside the company. They firmly believed that the Bayonne strike originally had involved the complaints of only a very small percentage of the men. They were convinced that the men who had provoked and prolonged the violence were not only radical reformers but enemies of the United States. With such agitators there could be no arbitration and no compromise. The directors had acted on these premises with a firmness calculated to crush the existing threat and to establish beyond question their determination to fight all such threats in the future. All these factors are essential to an understanding of the events of July, 1915.

In the following months it became obvious that the directors, blinded by their conviction that the strike had been instigated by outside influences, had failed to grasp the greatest issue involved in the disturbance. Nevertheless, the sentiment was strong among them that concessions were in order. On July 31, 1915, a general increase in wages was announced for the Bayonne, Bayway, and Eagle Works. All men, except common laborers, receiving up to $2.50 per day were to get a 10 per cent increase. Men earning over $2.50 per day were granted a 25 cent per day increase. Common laborers, then receiving $1.75 per day, were to get $1.98, or about a 13 per cent raise. These changes were eventually to apply also at Baltimore and at Parkersburg, as well as at Baton Rouge, where there had been no changes in the wage scale since 1910.[21]

On September 3 the directors voted a reduction in the working week from six 9-hour days to six 8-hour days for all employees, including those in the process departments. Workers were to receive the same pay for the shorter hours that they had had before the change was made. This action was of greatest significance in view of the fact that the clamor for an 8-hour day had not yet been heeded in a great many industries. It was also precedent for the substitution of the three-shift for the two-shift system and for the establishment of the 8-hour day in most of the affiliates.

Standard of Louisiana introduced these reductions almost immediately, but Imperial did not follow until 1918. "You cannot work three shifts to advantage," Teagle commented to a correspondent. "As you know, at the Sarnia and Vancouver refineries we have been obliged to refuse to recognize the request for an 8-hour day and this is even more impossible in the operation of a producing property."[22] In the Carter Company, where working conditions were different than in the refining organizations, some of the employees were granted the 8-hour day, but many of the field men continued until 1925 to work much longer hours.[23]

In June of 1916 the Jersey Company also announced, in connection with the current troubles between the United States and Mexico, a plan for generous bonus payments to employees who were called to active duty in the armed forces. Married men were paid a sum equivalent to a full year's salary; single men with no dependents, half their salary. Company management was careful to designate all these concessions as being along the lines of established company policy and in no way the result of the recent labor disturbances.

These were the answers that management in America had to give to the resurgent forces of labor. The very wording of Jersey's public statements was that employed by other businessmen faced with identical situations in other companies and in other industries. It is indeed remarkable how homogeneous were American managerial attitudes toward labor situations at this time. The answers usually involved minimum concessions in regard to wages and such improvement of working conditions as, in the opinion of management, would suffice to keep the men from taking strike action. The Jersey Company's response, to be sure, appeared at the time to have surpassed that minimum level. These concessions were welcomed at the moment, but they were not enough, possibly because they were concessions and probably because they were granted in the wake of strikes or threats of strikes. On the other hand, it must be recognized that Jersey management, like that of most other companies that faced labor difficulties in the period, was confronted not by a mature group of labor leaders but by a disorganized, unruly, impetuous, and unskilled group of bargainers whose very right to speak for all the struck forces was questionable.

The anxiety and frustration implicit in the labor situation of the time were forcibly brought home to the Jersey directors once more. On the evening of October 7, 1916, mass meetings were held at Bayonne to discuss the possibilities of another general strike. The very liberality of management seemed to have been a cause for the new agitation, for at the meeting of pro-strike advocates the thesis was advanced that, since a strike had been successful in obtaining pay increases before, it would be equally successful again.

In this new disturbance the principal issue was that of wage levels, though in 1916, as in 1915, figures showed that the Jersey Company wage advances had exceeded the rise in costs of living and a 10 per cent increase had been granted only five months before. Some of the old complaints of abusive treatment by the foremen were also heard. There was a strong faction, however, opposing a general strike. The mass meeting of strike opponents was said to be fully twice as large as, far better organized, and much more orderly than the concurrent meeting of would-be strikers. The line of cleavage seems, in general, to have been racial. English-speaking workmen opposed strike action, while the foreign-speaking element favored it. With majority sentiment opposed, the possibility that a strike would occur seemed somewhat remote.[24] Gifford and Hennessey, nevertheless, prepared to fight. A large number of armed guards were ready. Gifford stated that strikebreakers would not be employed, but the plant would be closed if a strike commenced.

On October 9 the pro-strike faction, numbering somewhat less than a third of the 5,400 Bayonne employees, voted to strike. The following day they walked out; those who wished to work were prevented from entering the plant. Once again the strike spread to neighboring establishments, and by October 12 it was said that 10,000 men were out.[25]

There is little need to follow closely the course of the 1916 strike. It was 1915 all over again, without the dynamic handling of Sheriff Kincaid, who was now campaigning for Congress on the basis of his earlier exploits. Again there were strong racial and political undertones. Social reformers appeared once more on the scene, as did P. J. Bergoff, the purveyor of brawn and firearms. Federal mediators were sent for by the civil authorities. Fires and rioting broke out. Three persons were slain and thirty more were wounded seriously. Hennessey and Gifford, backed by the directorate, stood firm in their refusal to discuss the issues until order had been restored and the men had returned to work. On October 19, 1916, the strikers, sickened by the violence and angry with the agitators in their midst for the pay losses incurred, seized upon a somewhat indefinite company promise to adjust wages and agreed to return to work. On October 21, 1916, the strike was over.

Here, at last, was the point of transition from one age to another. These terrible difficulties shocked the directors into new action and called forth the enunciation of a Jersey Standard labor policy.

Chapter 7

Expansion of the Transportation Network
1912-1917

I N THE middle years of Jersey Standard's history the evolution of transportation facilities was prodded by the same forces which were working to change the shape and size of other segments of the organization. Chief among these were growth of the business and the pressing necessity for ensuring that the threat to integrated operations posed by the dissolution decree did not materialize. No one of the primary functions of the business had an independent genesis or an isolated growth. The relationship between refining and marketing had always been close, and, as we have seen, efforts were under way to shape producing policies more effectively to manufacturing needs and market demands. Each of these three primary activities—producing, refining, marketing—in turn was serviced by transportation facilities of various kinds. These facilities formed a visible link not only between units performing different primary functions but also between like units within each of the primary spheres of activity. As producing, refining, and marketing facilities expanded after 1911, so, in consequence, did the transportation network grow.

This expansion, far-flung though it was and touching many branches of the business, is best looked at as a whole. In a general way the spreading web of Jersey Standard pipelines principally answered the need for moving the increasing supplies of crude oil to the refineries, while the growth of the tanker fleet is linked both with the expansion of crude output and with the enlargement of markets for refined petroleum products.

THE JERSEY COMPANY ACQUIRES A FLEET

As had been the case with refining and production, the postdissolution years were transitional in the history of Jersey marine transportation. The ocean-going tank steamer began to complement in an increasingly important way the pipeline movement of crude oil to refineries. This trend was suggestive of the earlier shift from railroad tank cars to pipelines. The tanker, however, augmented rather than replaced the established transportation system. Tankers themselves underwent changes to render them more adaptable to the tasks required, and an administrative group was trained to handle what, for the Jersey Company, was a new branch of operations. But most important of all in these years was the transition in policy which the growth of the tanker fleet signalized. The dissolution decree of 1911 showed only too well how vulnerable to political and economic forces were the corporate ties that provided Jersey Standard with the services of subsidiary assets. In 1914 this lesson was hammered home again, and from this time forward the company moved to integrate more fully into the parent organization the resources of water-borne transportation.

In the early months of 1912 Jersey directors faced a situation that threatened to become acute. The five ships and six barges which before the dissolution had helped to service the East Coast refineries and marketing organization belonged to Standard of New York; after 1911 they were no longer owned or controlled by Jersey Standard. Much more important was the loss to Jersey of the Anglo-American fleet of twenty-six steamers, two barges, and eight sailing vessels—at that time the largest single petroleum-carrying fleet in the world. Though many of these ships had been used in the Far Eastern trade, others had formed an important transatlantic link between Jersey Standard and its European markets. These losses came at a time when the shortage of water transport was already acute and widespread. In 1912 operations everywhere were expanding. A growing flood of cheap Mexican crude was waiting for shipment to refineries in the United States.

To this need the Jersey Company fortunately could apply substantial marine transportation facilities owned by retained foreign affiliates. This circumstance of foreign ownership of the bulk of the Standard Oil tanker fleet was neither curious nor obscure. The American merchant marine had long been unable to compete with that of European nations. German, English, Dutch, and Scandinavian vessels could be built and operated far more cheaply than American ships; in postdissolution months it was the fleet owned and operated by the DAPG upon which Jersey Standard relied most heavily for moving petroleum cargoes by water. In 1911 the German affiliate had twenty-three tankers in operation. Twenty more were on the ways in various stages of completion.[1] The fact that DAPG possessed the second largest tanker fleet afloat was scarcely surprising, for Wilhelm Riedemann, one of the founders of the firm and the father of Heinrich, the active head of the company, had played a substantial role in the development of the modern tanker. The DAPG had been employing transatlantic tankers since 1885.[2]

The DAPG fleet, together with eight tankers owned by the American Petroleum Company, Jersey's Dutch affiliate, and three tankers acquired in 1913 by Italo-Americana, the Italian affiliate, comprised a formidable total of tonnage. These vessels, however, were being used chiefly to supply the Continental market with refined products. They could be converted to carry fuel oil and crude, "dirty cargoes," by the addition of heating coils, but if they were subsequently needed for refined cargoes they had to be thoroughly steamed out and cleaned. This circumstance tended to discourage the facile shifting from one type of trade to the other, but even had this obstacle to mobility not existed, the tonnage at Jersey Standard's command was still insufficient to fill all needs.

This deficiency of controlled tonnage was a more or less chronic condition; in predissolution years the Jersey Company at times had relied to a considerable extent on tonnage chartered by the Standard Oil Company of New York. In 1911 a total of 43 charter agreements had been concluded. Commencing in December of 1911, Jersey systematically began to charter tankers wherever and whenever they could be found. In 1912 the Jersey Company signed 171 charter contracts.[3] Those DAPG vessels that could be spared from the Continental trade were chartered by the German company to its parent, but Jersey obtained many more ships from nonaffiliated shipowners.

The charters themselves were of the three types common in foreign trade. On time charters the Jersey Company paid the owners for the use of the vessel for a designated period, usually a year or more. Rates normally were 16 per cent of the vessel's book value, plus 5 shillings per deadweight tonnage, plus all expenses of operation. Voyage charters were drawn for the use of a vessel on one voyage, the rate being determined primarily by the destination. Freight charters stipulated that the owners be paid a fixed sum per barrel or case or gallon, according to the cargo carried and the destination intended.[4]

A relatively small volume of the traffic handled by these charter transactions was for the account of the Jersey Company itself. The Bayonne refinery, for example, was supplied with about 90 per cent of its crude oil requirements by pipeline; only a small amount of Mexican crude, which was beginning to move in such volume to Baton Rouge and to the Imperial refineries in Canada, was shipped to the East Coast refineries. Neither were many of the charter contracts covering shipment of refined products made by the Jersey Company for its own account. The company acted, in effect, as a shipping agent or middleman. Jersey's Foreign Shipping Department at 26 Broadway served as a clearinghouse and co-ordinating agency for the movement of crude and refined products among the affiliates and between the affiliates and unaffiliated oil companies.

The Foreign Shipping Department was called into existence in the wake of the dissolution decree, this work having previously been done for the Standard Oil organization by Standard Oil of New York. Teagle was made responsible for the new division, being succeeded in 1914 by F. D. Asche. This was a logical step, for each had been for a time in charge of foreign marketing, to which foreign shipping activities were closely tied, and both men had assisted in purchasing foreign crude supplies. The operating management of the new department was entrusted to David T. Warden, who had come to work for Standard Oil in 1901 after an appren-ticeship in a British shipping firm. In 1911 Warden's department num-bered twenty employees and no ships, but it was one of the most active offices at Jersey headquarters.

Orders for crude oil and refined product cargoes were forwarded to Warden's office by the various foreign affiliates lacking tankers of their own. The office routed the orders to the proper places, arranged for ship-ping space, prepared bills of lading and cargo-inspection certificates, and supplied the Treasurer's Department with the necessary information from which proper charges could be made against the accounts of the affiliates, or, in cases of outright payment, from which drafts on the proper foreign banks could be prepared.[5]

In substance, the Foreign Shipping Department performed in the field of marine transportation somewhat the same function as Haupt's General Engineering Department in matters of refinery construction and as the Manufacturing Committee in refinery affairs. It placed at the disposal of widely scattered affiliates a centralized administrative body—a body pow-erful in the command of resources and informed as to general develop-ments, specific requirements, and particular situations all over the world. The 0.5 per cent brokerage which the Jersey Company assessed upon most of these transactions was small enough, in view of the services rendered. It is of more than passing interest, too, that Warden's office was a co-ordinating agency rather than a high command post. Occasion-ally there was disagreement, and not infrequently Warden bowed against his will to the wishes of the foreign affiliates and entered into transactions that were disadvantageous to the parent company. Serious difficulties sporadically were encountered, and in these years from 1912 to 1918 the Foreign Shipping Department probably failed to achieve as high a degree of co-ordinating efficiency as was desirable. The earlier experience of many Shipping Department employees in the New York Company office was of limited usefulness under rapidly changing conditions. Only further experience could point the way to optimum utilization of the vast facilities that were being created.

An analysis of Jersey-negotiated charter contracts for the first six months of 1912 gives a fair indication of the scope and nature of Warden's work, although it must be remembered that these charters represented only a part of the foreign shipping operation and did not include the voyages of those vessels which DAPG and others operated for their own account. Table 8 suggests the far-flung international character of the marine busi-

Table 8: TANK-STEAMER VOYAGE CHARTERS
Initiated by Standard Oil Company (New Jersey)
First six months, 1912

Total charter contracts for the period—76

Point of Origin of Shipment		Point of Destination		Tanker Registry	
New York	57	New York	1	British	45
Norfolk	1	U. S. Gulf ports	3	German	8
San Francisco	1	U. S. West Coast	2	American	4
Baton Rouge	4	Argentina	7	Italian	1
Sabine, Texas	3	Peru	1	Danish	1
Tampico, Mexico	4	Brazil	8	Norwegian	1
Lobitos, Peru	2	Uruguay	5	Dutch	1
European ports	2	Cuba	6	Belgian	1
Unspecified	2	Italy	8	Unspecified	14
		United Kingdom	8		
		Iceland	2	**Chartered for account of**	
		Scandinavia	8		
		Holland-Belgium	2	West India Oil Co.	16
Cargo carried		Germany	2	SONJ	12
		France	1	Italo-Americana	9
Refined products	62	Spain	1	DAPG	8
Crude	12	Unspecified European	5	S. O. of Brazil	7
Unspecified	2	Africa-Egypt	4	Other Jersey affiliates	14
		Unspecified	2	Non-Jersey companies	10

Source: SONJ, Tanker Charter Files.

ness, the importance of Jersey's trade in refined products, the relatively small amount of charter tonnage devoted to carrying crude, and the dominant position occupied by the English merchant marine in the charter trades.

However active Jersey was in chartering tonnage, the demand for shipping space continued to exceed the available supply. The tanker shortage became acute through the summer of 1912. During 1911 tank-steamer rates for voyage charters to European ports had ranged around twelve shillings and sixpence to fifteen shillings per ton, but late in the year the scarcity of shipping forced these rates up to as high as seventy shillings.[6]

The combination of these high rates, the general scarcity of needed bottoms, and the particular need for tankers for the Gulf trade finally prompted Jersey Standard to abandon its exclusive reliance on chartered vessels and on the DAPG fleet. In 1913 the building of two tankers for the company was commenced at the Newport News shipyards. This move coincided with a general acceleration of shipbuilding in the United States, Britain, Germany, and elsewhere, and it is clear that commercial considerations were thus unwittingly preparing the civilized world for war. The two new vessels were christened the *John D. Rockefeller* and the *John D. Archbold.* These were twin ships of about 11,000 deadweight tons, the *Rockefeller* burning coal and the *Archbold* burning oil. Both went into service in 1914, a year that is memorable in the history of Jersey's Foreign Shipping Department.

On the other side of the Atlantic the DAPG fleet was rapidly expanding its 1911 tonnage. In 1912 three new tankers were launched and two vessels were converted to burn fuel oil. In 1913 the tanker shortage all over the world was alleviated somewhat, and shipping rates declined considerably. This, perhaps, was less the result of new construction than of the decline in business which characterized that year. Nevertheless, the tankers that DAPG had contracted for in the earlier months of stringency continued to slide down the ways. In 1913 thirteen new tankers were put in operation. In the first half of 1914 three more new vessels were added to the fleet, but five ships were transferred to other affiliates or sold— perhaps an indication that Jersey executives were becoming uneasy about the safety of their German marine assets. By August of 1914 the DAPG fleet consisted of thirty-five tankers with a total carrying capacity of over 200,000 tons. This fleet comprised approximately 95 per cent of the total existing German tanker tonnage and 12 per cent of the total number of non-United States tankers in operation in that year.[7]

Though the possibility of war had been foreseen at 26 Broadway, the actual commencement of hostilities burst upon Jersey Standard and DAPG with disrupting suddenness; Warden's office sent frantic messages to all the DAPG tankers that could be reached. Incoming ships were instructed by Warden's office by wireless to try to intercept vessels which had left the United States for Continental ports. Tankers proceeding from Gulf ports were warned to seek refuge within the three-mile limit. Many vessels were unaccounted for, and great anxiety was felt for the safety of the *Leda,* which was known to be in British waters off Bermuda.

The war history of the Jersey–DAPG fleet is a story in itself. Suffice it to say at this point that of the thirty-five tankers owned by DAPG only nine were berthed in German ports when war was declared. The bulk of the fleet was operating in United States or adjacent waters, a highly fortunate circumstance that derived from the nature of the trade in which these vessels were engaged at the time rather than from lack of proper devotion to the Fatherland by the German managers of the DAPG.

Of the suddenly expatriated German tankers, eleven were transferred to American registry and Jersey Standard ownership in 1914. In 1915 fifteen more DAPG vessels were added to the Jersey flag. These transfers were not easily accomplished. Before 1912 there had been no statutory provisions authorizing the admission of foreign-built vessels to American registry. The Panama Canal Act of 1912 provided some relief, but it still excluded all foreign-built ships which were more than five years old at the time of application for registry. On August 18, 1914, however, the President of the United States approved a bill repealing the five-year clause and certain other restrictive shipping statutes. On the American side, the way was then clear for the registry of foreign-built tonnage.[8] Teagle, in London when war was declared, hastened to The Hague for a conference with his German associates and with the American Minister to The Hague. Teagle explained to the Minister how essential it was that the Jersey Company should, if possible, secure control of the DAPG tankers so that they could be retained in the neutral trade in which they were then employed. Acting upon advice obtained through the Minister, Teagle obtained a power of attorney for the transfer of the DAPG vessels to American registry.[9] The Jersey Company simultaneously sought through diplomatic channels the assurance from Britain and France that the legality of the tanker transfers would be recognized by those governments. Both Britain and France affirmed the company's interest in the assets of its German affiliate and sanctioned the transfers. These diplomatic assurances were to be of extraordinary interest and importance in later years.[10]

Thus the war produced a most important change in Jersey's marine transportation policies. Almost overnight the company fleet expanded in size from two to twenty-eight tankers. The Foreign Shipping Department was abruptly transformed from a co-ordinating to an operating agency, though the company's former practice of chartering for its own account and for that of others was not abandoned. Altogether, the years from the dissolution to America's entry into the war were eventful and trying ones. Some picture of the operational problems that were faced is preserved in voluminous correspondence between Warden, the captains and mates of the various vessels, and Riedemann, head of the DAPG.

Heinrich Riedemann, like his father before him, was intensely interested in improving the performance of tankers. His ideas were criticized severely by New York men, but in the end Riedemann proved to be right on many points. Conservative viewpoints prevailed at 26 Broadway. In 1911 the marine Diesel engine was acknowledged to offer great promise, but the New York experts felt that further work needed to be done before Diesels were installed in company ships. There was also a well-entrenched school of thought at 26 Broadway which held that small vessels towing barges were the most economical form of transportation. Riedemann scoffed at this idea and was eager to install Diesel engines in his ships. He took a vigorous stand for tankers as large as 14,000 tons, but New York countered that anything larger than 8,000 tons could be berthed in but one or two ports, and that such capacity was not adapted to the shipping of lubricating oil, fuel oil, and other products which the company transported in relatively small volume. In 1911 Riedemann also advocated that the company should build new vessels for the Gulf trade rather than try to convert existing tonnage. New York men opposed this and recommended that old tankers be made to do the job. In his advocacy of improved dockage at Bayonne and Bayway, Riedemann was joined by several New York men. Bayway, where most of the naphtha storage capacity was located, could not be reached by ocean-going tankers.[11]

Late in 1911 Riedemann had a 7,400-ton Diesel tanker in operation, and soon her performance was beginning to change New York attitudes. A hope was expressed at 26 Broadway that by some means a "real basis for scientifically working out a transportation scheme" could be evolved. There was great technical confusion, no two experts agreed, hours were consumed in discussing merits or demerits of equipment, and Riedemann was finally asked to have his experts prepare standardized specifications for three classes of tankers. This did not mean, however, that the New York office had at last accepted Riedemann as the supreme authority on tanker construction. A fairly acrimonious exchange of correspondence took place between New York and Germany over the question of tanker speeds. Riedemann's idea that a slow tanker (9½ knots) was most economical was challenged by the New York men, who held out for speeds up to 11 knots. Teagle, who as head of foreign marketing figured largely in all these controversies, was convinced by Riedemann's figures that his German friend was right in this matter. Teagle also agreed with Riedemann's characterization of the Standard Oil and DAPG vessels as a "mongrel fleet." Ships had been built at random, without a fixed policy. Thus, while good, strong vessels had been obtained, costs of construction and operation were higher than they should have been and the building program of the past ten years had not, Teagle thought, been a success.

In 1912 operational difficulties attended the transfer of German tankers to the Gulf trade. The crews objected strenuously to the uncomfortable working conditions and the longer time spent away from home ports. The captains objected to the conversion of their vessels from coal to oil burners, since, among other reasons, they had been accustomed to receiving from the dealers a surreptitious gratuity on coal and other supplies taken on board. As a result of the changed traffic pattern, the officers and crews were given a bonus of 25 per cent for time served in the Gulf.

In 1913 three more Diesel vessels were added to the fleet, and more troubles brewed with the European captains and crews serving in American waters. A basic difficulty was the differential existing between the wages of European and American seamen. On the *Hesperus,* for example, a third of the crew had been hired in Hamburg at German wage rates. The remainder consisted of American seamen who, despite their lesser experience, had been taken on at the higher rates prevailing in the United States. Both Warden and Teagle hammered away at Riedemann to increase the wages of the DAPG crews, but Riedemann was stubborn. He pointed to the fact that DAPG carried old-age and liability insurance, which, he held, was better than a salary increase. Riedemann apparently felt that the New York men were being taken in by the DAPG captains, and he wrote Warden a fatherly letter advising him to be firm. Warden replied that he did not believe the prevailing bonus and wage levels were sufficiently high to maintain morale.

Warden's prediction of trouble was prophetic. Agitation for higher pay continued and was fed by the scarcity of ships' officers and engineers. Administrative difficulties were multiplied by the policy of attempting to establish differential bonus and wage rates for service in the Gulf, the Atlantic, and the West Coast trades. Complaints, moreover, were handled on an individual ship basis, and in many controversial matters no over-all policy was established. Up to the time when the DAPG fleet was transferred to Jersey ownership the tanker captains were serving two masters—Warden and Riedemann—and this, too, caused difficulty. Appeals were directed to Warden over the heads of the DAPG managers. Outstanding in all the give and take between 26 Broadway and the DAPG offices, however, is the evidence of free consultation between Jersey Standard and its affiliates, without pressure or coercion by the parent company. All matters of discussion were fully aired, and decisions were made on the basis of carefully reasoned arguments. Wily protagonist that he was, Riedemann carried many points.

The years 1913, 1914, and 1915 brought virtually continuous agitation for higher wages for the crews of the Jersey–DAPG tankers. There is a suggestion in company correspondence of organized opposition on the west coast of South America to the demands of the crews there. Representatives of two Jersey Standard affiliates (the West Coast Oil Fuel Company, Limited, and the London & Pacific Petroleum Company), together with Lobitos Oilfields, Limited, and the Union Oil Company concluded that they should, without any binding agreement, try as far as possible to have more or less uniform rates on their respective steamers and postpone the question of wage increases as long as possible. This effort came to nothing and wages continued upward.

On March 1, 1914, the Jersey Company agreed to pay a bonus of from 40 to 45 per cent to officers and crews of vessels engaged in the Gulf trade. This increase helped to erase the differential that had existed between German and American crews. Further difficulties of this nature were eliminated by the outbreak of war. All German nationals, both officers and men, were removed from Jersey tankers, paid a discharge allowance, and provided with funds for their return to Germany. Their places were filled with American officers and seamen. Wage increases, however, continued to be demanded by the crews as war conditions introduced new hazards and precipitated a shortage of officers and men.

In the spring of 1915 the salary scale of deck officers and engineers was raised. Just before this advance the Neptune Association, a trade association for ships' officers, had complained about company wage rates. Warden had informed the Association that the company would not recognize the Association as a bargaining group, nor feel obliged to employ Association members. The salary increase was stated to have been made independently of outside pressure, and Jersey's new rates actually were very close to what the Association had demanded. At this time Jersey captains were receiving $190 per month, chief officers $115, second officers

$95, and third officers $85. In addition, a yearly gratuity was paid, the amount dependent upon the years of an officer's service with the company.

In 1916 and again in 1917 there were further increases in wages in response to the general agitation on the American waterfront and to an increasingly critical shortage of experienced ships' officers. In its wage negotiations the Jersey Company incurred the wrath of the Marine Engineers Beneficial Association, but this was on the particular point of war bonuses rather than on general wage levels. In 1916 the company was paying a war bonus of 25 per cent of salary or wages to the officers and crews of all vessels in the transatlantic trade. On April 18, 1917, however, the company yielded to pressure for additional increases in wages and benefits. Bonuses of 50 per cent were granted to officers and crews on transatlantic tankers and of 25 per cent to officers and crews on all other vessels. Free life insurance was provided in amounts which ranged from $1,000 for crewmen to $5,000 for captains. The crews promptly rejected the bonus and insurance offers, asking instead for a flat $15 per month pay increase. On April 27 this increase was granted to the men, in lieu of the bonus. The company decided to continue the insurance and also to extend the increase to the officers, who had accepted the bonus. Five days later the further decision was made to grant to crewmen both the wage raise and the bonus, and in addition to pay all crewmen $100 and all officers one month's salary in event of loss of their personal effects through loss of the vessel. Officers and crews of vessels lost in foreign service were to receive full wages for the period it took them to return to the United States.[12]

A glance about the industry indicated that on one vessel of the Sun Oil Company and on one of the Vacuum Oil Company war bonuses of 100 per cent had recently been paid for transatlantic voyages. The Atlantic Refining Company had increased the wages of its crews on Gulf voyages to about the level of the new Jersey Company scale, but paid no bonuses to its officers or men. The Huasteca Petroleum Company, also operating tankers in the Gulf trade, paid a 25 per cent bonus to officers and engineers but not to the crews. The Standard Transportation Company, affiliate of the Standard Oil Company of New York, had granted the same $15 increase as had Jersey and paid a 25 per cent bonus to officers and engineers but not to the crews. The Texas Company, operating tankers only in the Gulf, had also increased crew wages $15 monthly but paid no bonuses whatever. The Gulf Refining Company had increased wages on one vessel but paid no bonuses.[13]

It thus appeared that Warden at last had pegged marine wages at a level that compared favorably with that of other American employers—a long battle which probably could not have been won if the management of the DAPG fleet had not passed at the outbreak of war in 1914 from the DAPG offices to 26 Broadway. Wages and salaries on Jersey Standard tankers equaled or exceeded the rates specified by the Marine Engineers Beneficial Association, and in all classifications company wages were either equal to or slightly higher than the average of those of all shipping companies that were members of the American Steamship Owners' Association. By the end of 1917 the pay of captains had gone as high as $250 per month; first mates received up to $155; second mates $145; and third mates $130.

Meanwhile, the fleet was growing. The twenty-eight vessels which had comprised the Jersey Company fleet in 1915 were inadequate to meet the normal annual requirements of slightly more than one million tons of petroleum products for the European market plus the need for four more tankers on the West Coast, though the South American and Mexican trades appeared to be provided for at the moment. The surge of war demand was beginning to be felt. An extensive shipbuilding program was therefore authorized. Despite the high cost of American construction, the contracts were let to American yards, principally to the Newport News Shipbuilding and Dry Dock Company. At this time there was little choice but to place orders there, for the war had necessarily forced abandonment of the traditional policy of having ships built abroad. The company also continued to charter as many vessels as possible, though at no time in the years from 1913 through 1917 was the 1912 peak of 171 charters surpassed.

In 1916 the fleet was augmented by three new American-built tankers, and the Jersey Company stepped far ahead of its competitors in authorizing new construction. In May of 1916 fifteen new vessels were being built for the Jersey Company in American yards; whereas three tankers were on order for Atlantic Refining, two for Gulf, five for Huasteca, four for Sun Oil, four for Texas, and three for Vacuum Oil. In 1917 ten new Jersey tankers were placed in operation. The company then had forty-one ships on the seas, slightly more than a quarter of all American-registered tankers afloat at the time. Fifteen more tankers were on order. In addition to these vessels belonging to the Jersey Company itself, there was a fleet of ten tankers sailing under the flags of Imperial and International. The American Petroleum Company (Holland) owned four ships (four others having been sunk), Italo-Americana three, a Norwegian affiliate two, and a South American affiliate one.

Five of Jersey's forty-one vessels were on the West Coast, fourteen were in the Atlantic trade, and twenty-two were engaged in the coastwise, West Indies, Mexican, and South American business. Of these ships twenty-three were engaged in transporting naphtha, an indication of the then great importance of the gasoline market. The increasing recourse to tanker transport in the fuel and crude oil trade was reflected by the fact that about half of the fleet was equipped with heating coils to handle these products. Riedemann's determined stand in favor of large vessels had been vindicated; most of the new contracts authorized in 1915 and 1916 called for ships of from 10,000 to 14,900 tons.

This record of growth indicates that, whatever the internal strengths or weaknesses of the Foreign Shipping Department, company policy had been boldly and effectively shaped to continue down the altered path that political events of 1914 had opened. That command of transportation facilities which had played so vital a part in the early development of the Standard Oil organization in the United States had lost none of its high strategic importance in bargaining for business at home and abroad. In its command of the largest tanker fleet in the Western Hemisphere Jersey Standard possessed an unquestioned advantage over domestic competitors. This fleet, ensuring to the company the availability of shipping tonnage at all times and making possible the increased mobility of petroleum supplies, also constituted an indispensable weapon of offense and defense in the contest with the Royal Dutch-Shell and other foreign commercial powers for world petroleum supplies and markets. The fact that the principal marine assets of the organization were held in the Jersey Company's own name and operated directly from 26 Broadway seems to indicate that in some areas of operation, and for the time being at least, Jersey Standard was now able to formulate and administer essential policies with a certain degree of freedom from government interference. This, of course, did not mean that the company had suddenly been freed from surveillance by the Federal Trade Commission or the Department of Justice, but rather that the condition of the American merchant marine had at last begun to cause anxiety in Washington. Quite undesignedly, the Jersey Company in its efforts to survive and profit had taken steps in the management of its Foreign Shipping Department that were to prove of inestimable value to the cause of the Allied Nations and to the military security of the United States.

THE PIPELINES

The reliance of Jersey Standard and its affiliates on the pipeline system that already existed in 1911 was heavy, and the demands made upon that system thereafter expanded rapidly under the pressure of a growing business. New field discoveries and increased refining capacity after 1911 caused new lines to be constructed and the capacity of old lines to be increased. Like mammoth roots, the pipeline system spread into fertile areas, sending out hundreds of branch feeders in quest of nourishment and continually altering its shape and size in accordance with the sustenance it received.

Before the dissolution, Standard Oil had spanned half the continent with a network of lines which brought the crude oil from the fields to the Standard refineries. Though many companies participated in the pipeline movement of crude oil, this network had been a carefully integrated system with headquarters in New York. The dissolution decree destroyed the administrative unity of the whole with one judicial blow, and the major corporate parts, now legally independent of one another, were left to find some legal substitute for centralized ownership and control. Since the decree had not forbidden the disaffiliated fragments to deal with one another as independent corporate bodies, however, there was no disruption of service.

The cleavage of corporate pipeline affiliates from the Jersey Standard organization was initially more nominal than real. The pipelines winding across the plains and mountains to the eastern refineries were the reality, and they were unmoved by the words of the Supreme Court justices. Initial difficulties arising out of the breaking-up of the centralized communications system which regulated the flow of oil were soon ironed out, and contractual relationships were established to replace the centralized controls of predissolution days. New contracts were drawn up, letterheads and order forms were changed, and personnel were shifted and assigned new titles. The flow from fields to refineries continued, and it was not until new lines began to be projected, both by former Jersey affiliates and by large independents like Texas and Gulf, that the effect of the decree began to alter long-established transportation ties.

By 1911 an intricate pipeline system (map on page 411 of *Pioneering in Big Business*) had been established to connect the producing fields as then constituted with the various Standard Oil refineries. The Prairie Oil & Gas Company initiated the flow of crude oil in the Mid-Continent, making connections with lines that carried the oil northeast and east across Illinois, Indiana, and Ohio. From the eastern boundary of Ohio the so-called northern system of lines offered a combination of routes to terminal points at Centerbridge, on the eastern boundary of Pennsylvania, and at Saddle River, near the New York–New Jersey boundary. Jersey's

Table 9: NET EARNINGS FROM TRANSPORTATION
Standard Oil Company (New Jersey) and Affiliates[a]
1912-1918

Earnings

Dollar figures in thousands (Parentheses indicate net loss)

	1912	1913	1914	1915	1916	1917	1918
PIPELINES							
Domestic							
Jersey Standard Pipeline Dept.	—	—	$ 79	$ 492	—	—	—
Oklahoma Pipe Line Co.	$ 157	$ 388	625	275	$ 773	$ 1,056	$ 1,081
Tuscarora Oil Co., Ltd.	925	941	946	1,495	1,739	1,518	1,098
Louisiana Standard Pipeline Dept.	—	—	—	(11)	168	822	1,202
Tide-Water Pipe Co., Ltd., The[b]	1	1	2	1	1	1	1
Total domestic	$1,083	$1,330	$1,652	$2,252	$2,681	$ 3,397	$ 3,382
Foreign							
Româno-Americana, Romania	—	12	15	16	12	c	c
Total world	$1,083	$1,342	$1,667	$2,268	$2,693	$ 3,397	$ 3,382
MARINE							
Jersey Standard tankers	$ 445	$ 481	$ 492	$2,329	$3,174	$ 8,261	$10,101
DAPG tankers	3,275	121	340	649	—	—	—
Other	29	25	c	c	c	c	c
Total	$3,749	$ 627	$ 832	$2,978	$3,174	$ 8,261	$10,101
Unsegregated transportation earnings							
Imperial Oil, Canada[d]	—	$ 216	$ 133	$ 97	$ 63	$ (183)	$ 397
Total transportation earnings	$4,832	$2,185	$2,632	$5,343	$5,930	$11,475	$13,880

Earnings as percentage of total transportation earnings[e]

	1912	1913	1914	1915	1916	1917	1918
Pipelines	22.4	61.4	63.3	42.5	45.4	29.6	24.4
Marine	77.6	28.7	31.6	55.7	53.5	72.0	72.8
Unsegregated	—	9.9	5.1	1.8	1.1	(1.6)	2.8
Total	100.0	100.0	100.0	100.0	100.0	100.0	100.0
Total transportation earnings as percentage of total Jersey earnings[e]	13.7	4.8	8.4	8.8	8.3	11.0	17.9

[a] Several of the affiliated companies included some revenue from transporting in other functional earnings classifications. This table indicates only the main sources of transportation revenue.
[b] Dividends paid to Standard Oil Company (New Jersey).
[c] Comparable data not available because of war conditions.
[d] Includes earnings from tankers, tank cars, and pipelines.
[e] Since the percentage figure for any one earnings classification is determined not only by the actual earnings recorded in that classification but also by earnings and losses in each of the others, no attempt should be made to trace year-to-year variations in one classification without careful reference both to other percentage classifications and to the pertinent dollar figures. All functional earnings figures given in SONJ, Fin. Recs., for the years 1912 through 1924 have been adjusted by the authors to match, insofar as possible, the account classifications employed in those records in the years 1925 through 1927.
Source: SONJ, Fin. Recs.

own Tuscarora Oil Company, Limited, organized in 1910, ran lines from western Pennsylvania across to Centerbridge. Crude oil shipments that originated in the Ohio, Kentucky, and West Virginia fields traveled over the southern system across southern Pennsylvania and Maryland to Centerbridge and other key terminals in the Middle Atlantic area.[14]

From Saddle River the Jersey Company itself ran three lines of about 45,000 barrels total daily capacity to Bayonne. The company also ran three lines of 48,500 barrels total capacity from Centerbridge across New Jersey to the Bayway refinery. One of these continued on to Bayonne and the Eagle Works at Jersey City. In addition, the Jersey Company owned and operated eight interrefinery lines between Bayonne and Bayway, as well as two lines between Bayonne and the Eagle Works. The Baltimore refinery was supplied with about 6,000 barrels daily through a link with the southern system, the Maryland segment of which was owned by the Jersey Company. The Parkersburg refinery in West Virginia was supplied with about 2,500 barrels daily by southern system lines.

The new refinery at Baton Rouge was receiving Mid-Continent crude through a 402-mile pipeline that had its origin at Council Hill in north central Oklahoma. The Oklahoma Pipe Line Company, a Jersey Standard affiliate which had been organized in 1909, owned that segment of the line which lay in Oklahoma. The 90 miles of the line that traversed the southwest corner of Arkansas were owned by Prairie, and the remaining 268 miles of line from the northern Louisiana border south to Baton Rouge were owned by Standard of Louisiana. Despite the tripartite ownership, this line was operated as a unified whole, carrying crude only to Louisiana Standard. The Imperial Oil Company, Limited, in 1913 constructed an important pipeline from Cygnet, Ohio, to the international border near the Sarnia refinery, but it was on the Mid-Continent–Baton Rouge axis of the Jersey Standard overland transportation system that most changes occurred after 1911. Pipeline operations in the old Appalachian fields had become well stabilized, and the movement of crude oil eastward through the lines of former Jersey affiliates had become an established routine which varied principally in respect to types and quantities of crude shipped.[15]

Not routine, but most important nevertheless to an understanding of pipeline operations after 1911, was the legal background against which policy decisions were made. In 1911 it was still uncertain whether the pipelines were subject to regulation as common carriers by the Interstate Commerce Commission under the terms of the Hepburn Act of 1906. Late in 1911, when Jersey's Legal Department was swamped with the task of carrying out the dissolution decree, the Commission commenced an investigation aimed at bringing the pipelines under its own jurisdiction. Behind this move lay the agitation of the small independent producers and refiners, who claimed that the "public" (i.e., themselves) were deprived of the use and benefit of the lines, which only the larger companies could afford to construct and maintain. The pipeline companies rose promptly to the defense, for if the lines were declared common carriers they would be required to furnish detailed operating information to the Commission and might also be forced to carry oil for producers and refiners who competed with the companies that controlled the lines or, like Jersey Standard, were the best customers. The counterargument advanced by the pipeline companies was that their lines were parts of integrated, private systems and had never been designed to serve public needs. The Commission inquiry named Jersey Standard and sixty-one other companies as corespondents. Hearings were scheduled and held in several cities. In the course of these hearings the so-called Standard Oil pipeline companies were branded as "unjust, unreasonable, unjustly discriminatory, unduly preferential and prejudicial" in their conduct of business. Jersey's counsel tartly responded that the Interstate Commerce Commission had been organized to supervise common carriers, not to create them.[16]

As the hearings progressed, it became apparent that political considerations were involved and that the pipeline companies were by no means united in their fight against government regulation. In November of 1912 W. S. Fitzpatrick, general counsel of Jersey's former affiliate, The Prairie Oil & Gas Company, reported to Jersey's counsel a conversation he had held with President Taft:[17]

The President was in excellent humor and spirits, and after discussing politics generally at some length, listened very attentively to what I had to say and asked several questions. There is no question but that he understands the attitude of the Secretary [Walter L. Fisher, Secretary of the Interior] in regard to the oil business and realizes that the Secretary is trying to hit upon some line of action which will make him famous. The President said: "I understand Mr. Fisher. He wants to do something that will make a record, which may be brought forth at some future time when he may be a candidate for President of the United States, and I have no objection to his doing it so long as he does not do it in a way to make my administration appear ridiculous."

Fitzpatrick presented to Taft the basic arguments of the pipelines:

I went over, to quite an extent, the production in the Mid-Continent field and the manner of its development, called his attention to the fact that the oil was only valuable as it could be marketed; that we had done everything we could to find markets for Mid-Continent oil and dispose of this oil in those markets; that there were a number of years when we had no help, and that even in those years we did not monopolize the business there because there was more oil offered than we could take and much of it was wasted because nobody wanted to or could use or take care of it. The best evidence in the world that our business was not creating a monopoly in the Mid-Continent field was that the other two pipe lines had built into the field since we came, and that more than twenty-five independent refineries were operating in or near to the field, all of which had been built since our pipe lines were established and put in operation; that they were getting all the oil they needed and all claimed to be prosperous; that most of them showed prosperity by continued enlargement of their plants in the field of their activities.

Prairie's counsel concluded his talk with the President with a protest which was being echoed in many places:

I explained to him that while the other people were incorporated under laws which made them common carriers and held themselves out to the public as willing to engage in such business, that in fact they had never transacted any business of that character, but had bought and sold oil, transported by their own pipe lines very much the same as we had done. That we hesitated and refused to represent to the public that we were willing to do that which we did not expect and intend to do, and therefore had refused to assume the obligations of a common carrier in order to obtain from the Department permits to build pipe lines.

I told him that we had complied with the decree of the United States Court in the dissolution suit; that we believed that we were complying with the letter and spirit of every law everywhere; that such was our ambition and our aim. We did not ask any favors that our competitors could not enjoy, and all we did ask was that we be protected in such rights as the law did give us as a corporation, on an equality with any other corporation. That we contributed in taxes and all manner of support to our Government as other people did, and did not think it right that the American Government in any of its departments should deny us our legal rights and equal protection and equal privilege with any other corporation or syndicate, foreign or domestic.

These arguments were unavailing. On June 13, 1912, the Interstate Commerce Commission announced its decision declaring interstate pipelines to be common carriers, and the defendants at once obtained a delaying order pending appeal to the United States Commerce Court. In 1913 this court overruled the Commission and declared the Hepburn Act to be unconstitutional, since it deprived companies of the use of their own property without just compensation. This victory for the pipelines was short-lived. The pipeline cases were carried to the Supreme Court, which on June 22, 1914, reversed the lower-court decision and declared pipelines to be common carriers. Jersey's chief counsel, M. F. Elliott, confided his opinion to a colleague that the courts were running wild and upholding almost any radical provision intended to cripple corporations.

Feeling in Washington against the defendants ran high. The pipeline companies alleged that the independent producers, who were granted a Congressional hearing and an interview with the President, had misrepresented the situation. Nevertheless, agitation for severance of pipelines from refineries was strong, and demands for a sweeping investigation of pipeline operations led to the launching of an inquiry by the Federal Trade Commission into operating conditions and practices.[18]

The dissolution had thus failed to modify the anti-Standard viewpoints of the Interstate Commerce Commission or to soften the attitudes of the independent operators, who declared that oil flowed through the same pipelines, in the same way, to the same points of delivery, and from the same fields as before the dissolution, and that the public still had no access to the lines. These charges, which have been studied by others and need not be reported in detail here, clearly grew out of the tremendously weak position in which the small operators found themselves.[19] Stripped of its legal superfluities, the profound basic issue was whether the large companies, which had painstakingly built up their competitive puissance over the years, were under obligation to help their smaller rivals to survive. The Supreme Court decision theoretically affirmed this point of view, greeted by the pipeline companies as radical but actually well precedented in American railroad history. The independent producers watched with interest to see what would happen next.

The immediate effect of the 1914 ruling was to cause a scramble among the oil companies to divest themselves of pipeline departments. The Ohio Oil Company, for example, set up the Illinois Pipe Line Company to take over its pipeline operations. Prairie Oil & Gas organized the Prairie Pipe Line Company. The Jersey Company, too, decided to take itself "out from under" and on July 1, 1915, sold its lines in New Jersey to its affiliate, Tuscarora, and to the independent New York Transit Company. The lines in Maryland were sold to the Maryland Pipe Line Company. Jersey's

Legal Department forwarded a terse note to the Federal Trade Commission stating that the company had sold all its common-carrier pipeline systems, "thus severing itself completely from the business of transporting crude petroleum by pipe line in which, indeed, it had never voluntarily engaged."[20]

This statement was typical of the Legal Department of the day and, indeed, of the public attitudes and utterances of Jersey management as a whole. The cautiously phrased sentences were legally impeccable, and the company's allegation that it was no longer in the pipeline business was technically unassailable. Yet everyone concerned, and particularly those to whom the statement had been addressed, knew very well that Jersey Standard—through its three affiliates, Standard of Louisiana, Oklahoma Pipe Line, and Tuscarora—was heavily involved and keenly interested in the transportation of crude oil by pipeline. Statements like this unquestionably fanned the smoldering flames of public suspicion and roused the ire of federal regulatory bodies.

In practice the management of the pipeline affiliates was necessarily scattered. In the Louisiana Company the producing department had first managed the pipelines there, but in 1914 a separate pipeline department was set up with offices in Shreveport. The main office of the Oklahoma Pipe Line Company was at Muskogee, Oklahoma, and Tuscarora's was at Pittsburgh. The principal officers and several of the directors of these companies had their offices in New York, however, and top policy was formulated there, where the essential co-ordination with other operations could be most readily worked out. Far from having severed itself from the pipeline business, Jersey management had worked out a system of central planning which actually was superior, in point of effective control, to that which characterized producing operations of the day.

Characteristic of pipeline operations in these years was the necessity for expansion to accommodate the peak output of the new fields to which the lines were run. In the absence of any effective sort of control over production from the new-found pools, the pipeline companies expanded their facilities rapidly in order to take full advantage of the floods of cheap crude which followed in the wake of discovery wells. Indeed, failure by these companies to expand their capacity to match flush production resulted, on more occasions than one, in the most severe government and public condemnation. When the pools blew themselves out and production precipitously declined, the excess pipeline capacity in many instances represented economic waste—an additional cost which more careful regulation of production might, and later did, reduce. Standard of Louisiana followed this practice of expanding to take full advantage of flush production, but the strategic location of Louisiana's lines was such that at no time between 1911 and 1918 was there excess capacity for any substantial amount of pipeline mileage. As old pools declined, new pools were found, all within easy range of the trunk line from Council Hill down to Baton Rouge. As the years went by, it became increasingly apparent that this line had threaded a golden course through the very heart of the Mid-Continent–Louisiana oil regions. Expansion of the Baton Rouge refinery placed heavy demands upon this line and dictated virtually continuous expansion of pipeline mileage and capacity.

The map on page 64 indicates the main pipeline route over which Mid-Continent and North Louisiana crude moved to Baton Rouge. That portion of the line owned by Louisiana Standard which ran from Ida, Louisiana, to Baton Rouge had been designed, in 1909, to handle 10,000 barrels daily. Four pumping stations were originally installed between the two points, and steel tankage was constructed at each station to take care of incoming crude whenever repairs necessitated closing sections of the line. From 1910 to 1918 the history of this line was one of continuing growth as Caddo production increased, the De Soto–Crichton fields came in, and increased supplies of Mid-Continent crude were demanded at Baton Rouge.

Investment in pipeline net assets by the Louisiana Company increased from $2,633,000 in 1912 to $6,066,000 in 1917. This increase of 130 per cent compared with an increase of 117 per cent in the refining assets of the company. At the same time, Prairie and the Oklahoma Pipe Line Company had increased the capacity of their connecting lines to 30,000 barrels daily. Oklahoma built a line from Council Hill to Glenn Pool and Drumright and increased its investment in fixed assets to $2,723,000 in 1917, a gain of 64 per cent over the 1912 figure. Tuscarora, by way of contrast, had increased its fixed assets to $5,424,000 by 1917, a gain of only 24 per cent.[21]

Techniques of line laying, maintenance, and operation underwent small changes from 1911 to 1918, though, as in refining, many developments which were later to become important were then in the experimental stage. The process of laying a line was essentially a manual one, although here and there ditching machines had made their appearance. The Louisiana Company, for example, employed gangs of 120 whites and about a like number of Negroes. These men coupled the lengths of pipe which had been strung along the route, dug the 18″-deep ditch, let the pipe in, and covered it—all without benefit of mechanical assistance. The men worked an 84-hour week and lived in company-provided camps. These camps and the food the company furnished were necessarily of high quality, for in no other way could labor be held to the difficult task at wages the company thought it could afford to pay.[22]

In the Louisiana swamps unusually difficult conditions were encountered, and costs were high. The line from Ida to Baton Rouge averaged $6,409.22 per mile to construct, while the highest average cost reported by any of the Mid-Continent and Gulf Coast pipeline companies had been $6,970.88 and the lowest $5,733.05. Maintenance costs commenced virtually on the day the pipe was laid, for pipe construction and design were far from perfect. The pipe itself was of lap-weld construction, joined by thread and coupling. Diameters of 6″ and 8″ were used on the high-pressure ends of the lines, since the lap-weld pipe did not have sufficient strength in larger sizes. On the low-pressure ends of the lines some 10″ and 12″ pipe was used. Line walkers patrolled the pipe route in a never-ending search for leaking joints or pitted pipe. When leaks were found, repair crews placed a saddle gasket over the pitholes. If the damage was extensive, the flow of oil was shut off and corroded pipe sections removed. Late in 1913 it was discovered, to the dismay of the Louisiana men, that a large section of the company line laid in 1909 had been seriously affected by soil acids. After considerable investigation, the decision was made to renew the damaged sections and encase the pipe in cement. In 1914 and 1915 some 250 miles of pipe were given cement protection, at a cost of $725,000.[23] This, of course, was not a usual operating condition, but pipeline men, like refiners and drillers, soon became hardened to the common occurrence of the improbable.

Despite high construction expenditures and such occasional difficulties as Louisiana Standard had encountered with its lines, the cost of transportation by pipeline was low in comparison with rail rates. So great was the differential, in fact, that the small operators who did not possess pipeline facilities and to whom access to such facilities had been effectively denied were at a serious disadvantage in being forced to ship by rail. Herein lay one of the specific grounds for the agitation that accompanied the common carrier dispute of 1911-1914. In 1915, for example, the railroad rate per barrel from Cushing, Oklahoma, to Bayonne, New Jersey, was $1.40, while the trunk pipeline rate was 70 cents. To be sure, even the large companies sometimes shipped by rail for special reasons—for instance, when a sudden increase in production from a given pool over-burdened storage and pipeline capacity. This happened at Cushing in 1914, where at one time 40,000 barrels per day were being shipped by railway tank cars. Then, too, refiners sometimes wished to preserve the identity of a particularly high grade of crude. In 1913, for example, Standard of Louisiana took 626,694 barrels of Muskogee crude by tank car in order to avoid mixing this fine lube stock with other crude in the pipeline. Generally speaking, however, railroads and pipelines were al-most noncompetitive.[24]

The pipeline ruling of 1914 by the Supreme Court forced all the desig-nated common carrier lines to file the tariffs at which they would ship oil for others. These published tariffs were subsequently criticized by the Federal Trade Commission in its 1916 investigation. In 1913 combined trunk- and gathering-line costs from Glenn Pool to Baton Rouge were 26.02 cents per barrel, while the tariff rate published in 1914 was 49.50 cents. On the basis of posted tariffs, the Commission concluded, the five Mid-Continent and Gulf Coast systems under investigation would have earned in 1913 an average return on their net investment of 41.5 per cent. The Commission noted the serious implication of these high tariffs, calling attention to the fact that transportation costs formed a very large percentage of the total delivered price of crude oil at the refinery.[25]

Both rates and profits of the Jersey pipeline affiliates, however, had little real meaning as long as these companies continued to serve only the parent company or other Jersey affiliates. Jersey could charge itself whatever it pleased and shift its profits from one pocket to another at will. The real issue was whether the published rates were actually working a hardship on the customers whom the newly christened common carriers were supposed to be serving. The Federal Trade Commission answered this question in its own report. In 1915, a full year after the Supreme Court decision, no one of these pipeline companies had shipped other than its own oil or that of closely affiliated companies. High posted rates had worked no hardship on the "public," because no one outside these companies was getting a chance to pay them. The common carrier desig-nation was purely fictional, and little could be done about it.

The device whereby the pipeline companies avoided the necessity for transporting the oil of unaffiliated companies and acting as real common carriers was simple and legal. While expressing their complete willingness to perform the common carrier function, many of the lines established large minimum shipment requirements—so large as to make it impracticable for small producers or refiners to ship their crude by pipeline. Over the Oklahoma–Baton Rouge line the minimum shipment required was 100,000 barrels, an amount that most small producers would have taken months or years to accumulate and which would have flooded the small independent refineries, few of which handled more than 200,000 barrels of crude a year. Neither, in practice, could the small operators pool their resources to meet the minimum requirements, though posted regulations stated that such lump shipments would be accepted. The additional stipulation was attached that such shipments must be con-signed to the same point of delivery. Thus, while there was a possibility that small producers might combine their shipments for delivery to one common customer, it was obviously impossible for a scattered group of refineries to avail themselves of the provision.[26] On the Oklahoma–Baton Rouge line, moreover, there was a rule that shippers must provide their own storage at the terminus of the line. Since Louisiana Standard owned the only terminal storage facilities, it was obvious that no other company could at the time meet this condition. The smaller producers and refiners in any case could ill afford the required investment in tankage.

The Commission attacked these and similar regulations of other com-panies in its report and pointed out that, since oil was running through the lines almost continuously and no attempt was made to preserve the exact identity of specific shipments, there was no real reason why small shipments could not be accepted. The pipeline companies regularly made small shipments for their own account and delivered small quantities of crude at scattered points. The Oklahoma–Baton Rouge system received crude into its line from the producers' settling tanks, which usually had a capacity of 250 to 500 barrels, and made numerous small shipments for Prairie, some as small as 91 barrels. Shipments on this line and on others, the Commission reported, were regularly made to suit the convenience of the companies concerned, without the slightest regard to minimum quantities. The pipeline companies ran into real difficulty only when ship-ments offered exceeded the capacity of the lines. On these occasions, the Commission felt, the pipeline companies should, as common carriers, work out an equitable rule for apportioning shipments and give no prefer-ence to crude belonging to themselves or affiliated concerns. In 1915 this Utopian situation was far from realization, attitudes of the line operators being what they were.

Those attitudes have high historical significance, and the pipeline com-panies offered arguments that were strong indeed in those years when the struggle for mastery between federal agencies and private enterprise was in its youth. One very apparent reason for the failure of the lines to accept the shipments of others was that in 1914, 1915, and 1916, as well as in the ensuing years of the war, the capacity of those lines was severely taxed. Expansion of the pipeline network in itself showed the continuing heavy demand for transport. In 1913 the five systems serving Mid-Continent fields had a rated capacity of only 80 per cent of the marketed production of those fields. The pipeline companies felt strongly that, since they could scarcely meet their own requirements, there certainly was no valid reason for them to come to the rescue of others, who had borne none of the risks, the managerial burdens, or the costs of laying the lines. In some instances, moreover, it seems clear that there were real physical limitations upon the ability of the pipelines to function effectively as common carriers.[27]

The nineteenth-century concept of private property rights was deeply rooted, and federal and state attempts to force even minor concessions to a new economic and political age were stubbornly resisted. If, in fact, the pipelines *were* common carriers, they obviously were operating in violation of the spirit if not the letter of the law. The Supreme Court had said that they were common carriers, but the word of law was not enough to command immediate conformity to federal views. The lines had been built not to serve as common carriers, but as essential parts of carefully integrated private business systems. This much was historical fact. When many of the lines were laid down there had, indeed, been no demand that they perform such carrier functions. But meanwhile, conditions had changed. The number of small operators multiplied prolifically, both because of general economic conditions in the petroleum industry and because of the dissolution decree of 1911. The pipelines then found themselves surrounded by a clamorous market for which most of them had scant liking and little desire to serve and strengthen. The 1914 decision of the Supreme Court simply was not accepted, and the lines did all in their power within the law to avoid its practical application. Before 1911 much of the pipeline network in the United States had been controlled from 26 Broadway in the interest of a single giant organization. After that time the transportation system was dominated, instead, by a group of large companies, which included both former Jersey Standard affiliates and growing independents like Gulf and Texas. Most small operators appeared to be little better off under the new alignment than under the old.

Here was an interesting and illuminating parallel to the dissolution decree itself. In the case of both the dissolution and the common carrier decrees legal conformance by the parties involved had followed. While Jersey Standard was tenaciously working to regain the strength, the balance, and the security which some federal agencies and many commercial rivals of the day wished to deny it, Jersey's pipeline affiliates, like other pipeline operators, were emphasizing the physical limitations on their ability to perform the common carrier function and were clinging to the legal toeholds which had prevented the threatened plunge into the abyss of public business. These various manifestations of passive resistance clearly derived from the unshaken conviction of the businessman of the day that his business, like his home, was his castle.

Chapter 8

Mending the Market Fences
1912-1917

MARKETING IN TWO WORLDS

THE DISTRIBUTION system that Standard Oil had built up before 1911 was remarkably efficient for the times. In postdissolution months it was continued by Jersey Standard, in principle though not in geographic form, with few changes. Domestic and foreign markets were organized in a pattern long familiar to executives of the organization.

Each refinery served a particular market area and originated shipments of refined products to bulk stations at home and abroad for ultimate delivery to the retail and wholesale trade, or even directly to household consumers. Jersey Standard also contracted for bulk deliveries from its refineries to large domestic and foreign companies, such as the Standard Oil Company of New York and the Anglo-American Oil Company, Limited. Lubricants and fuel oil were supplied directly to industrial users scattered throughout the cities in which the company did business. The Jersey Company and its affiliates did a large direct business in fuel oil with shipping concerns and supplied gas oil to municipal and industrial customers for use in enriching coal gas destined for household consumers. The natural gas affiliates supplied heating and illuminating gas directly to many household and industrial and wholesale customers in Ohio, West Virginia, Pennsylvania, and New York communities. The petroleum business, indeed, was characterized by a great variety of consumer demands, but so remarkably flexible were the manufacturing and selling organizations that no market was too great and no market too small for Jersey Standard to serve.

One facet of marketing is revealed by the contracts which supplied great companies and cities with millions of barrels of petroleum products. Elsewhere in the marketing organization of 1912 operations were simultaneously being conducted on a far different scale. In Romania the peasant peddler distributed kerosene from cans suspended on a yoke across his

179

shoulders. In the United States salesmen were seeking out the general-store proprietors and garage owners in back-country towns, taking orders for Aladdin Security Oil and specialty products. Here and there an enterprising merchant had installed a 50-gallon drum equipped with a hand-pump, from which he filled a long-snouted oilcan with Standard Motor Gasoline to carry to the automobilist waiting at the curb outside his garage or store. In most rural and suburban areas there were few paved roads to facilitate solicitation and bulk deliveries. In Louisiana mule-drawn tank wagons carrying from 200- to 500-gallon loads plied their routes through the parish towns. In Baton Rouge and New Orleans, it is said, the mules knew the trade as well as did the driver and made the regular stops without a word of command. The driver hopped from his seat, loaded a wheelbarrow with gallon cans, and rattled up the side streets crying, "Oil! Oil!"[1]

Measures of both the volume and the vast range of business which Jersey Standard and its affiliates transacted are not easy to find. Statistical records, the most useful of which are presented in Table 10 and in Appendix 2, fall far short of providing perfect indices of company activity and give no complete measures of the dollar volume of business done. The years from 1911 through 1917 brought several qualitative changes in the Jersey Standard marketing divisions. There was considerable expansion, together with some modification of administrative techniques. The Jersey Company's own investment in marketing facilities increased about 90 per cent from 1911 to the end of 1917, while the Louisiana Company recorded an increase of slightly more than 200 per cent. Marketing profits were high, the result of Jersey Standard's ability to purchase, transport, store, and utilize large quantities of low-priced Mid-Continent and Mexican crude oil over a period when the direction of demand and prices for petroleum products was generally upward.

In foreign marketing the 1912-1917 period witnessed important, though in some cases temporary, adjustments. The swing in export demands for particular products has already been examined in Chapter 5. Even more important than the need for modifying the product line, however, was the necessity for adapting marketing methods to a competitive environment that knew few restraints. In its foreign marketing, as in its attempts to acquire foreign producing territories, Jersey Standard was faced with two alternatives—to withdraw entirely or to play the game according to rules that were not of its making. As in its foreign producing efforts, the Jersey Standard organization fought alone, deriving little encouragement or assistance from the federal government.

Nevertheless, the foreign business continued to be of very great importance and was pursued in most areas with singular success. Long before 1911 the great potentialities of export sales had been recognized, and foreign markets had vigorously been sought by the men at 26 Broadway. In 1912 foreign shipments constituted 54 per cent of total deliveries from Jersey's refineries in the United States. By 1917 the export trade of these refineries had, despite war dislocations, fallen only to 44 per cent of the total. Both figures, failing to include the deliveries of affiliated refineries in Canada, Romania, and Latin America, almost all of which went to markets outside the United States, understate the amount of foreign business actually done.[2] Though some activities were curtailed as a result of the war, the expansion of investments in foreign marketing facilities—particularly in Canada and South America—was substantial. Thus, after a perusal of the domestic situation, it becomes essential to look abroad at a vital segment of Jersey Standard's marketing development.

Earnings figures provide one measure of the relative importance of the various branches of domestic and foreign marketing activity. Table 10 indicates the geographic marketing pattern and sets forth the fluctuations that are considered in detail in the paragraphs following.

SHARING THE DOMESTIC MARKET

The dissolution decree dealt the domestic marketing organization of the Jersey Company a heavy blow. In 1912, in fact, there was not enough of an organization left to justify the existence of a marketing committee. On the Jersey directorate both Charles M. Pratt and Walter Jennings had a marketing background, while several other directors at one time or another had gained some experience in the field. Active management of domestic marketing continued to be vested in the hands of T. J. Williams, who had been in charge of the Domestic Trade Department since 1908. No domestic marketing committee as such was re-established until 1919.

Williams directed Jersey's own domestic marketing, which was centered in two main district offices, one in Newark and the other in Baltimore. The Newark office marketed company products in the state of New Jersey, while the Baltimore office and four branch offices took care of distribution in Maryland, Virginia, West Virginia, North and South Carolina, and the District of Columbia. By the end of 1917 there were 80 bulk stations in the

Table 10: **NET EARNINGS FROM MARKETING**
Standard Oil Company (New Jersey) and Affiliates
1912-1918

Earnings	Dollar figures in thousands (Parentheses indicate net loss)						
DOMESTIC	1912	1913	1914	1915	1916	1917	1918
Jersey Standard	$ 1,307	$ 1,302	$ 821	$ 2,081	$ 2,545	$ 2,909	$ 3,561
Louisiana Standard	123	116	(150)	138	236	498	207
Other	15	24	9	24	16	20	23
Total domestic	$ 1,445	$ 1,442	$ 680	$ 2,243	$ 2,797	$ 3,427	$ 3,791
FOREIGN							
Canadian							
Imperial Oil	$ 1,562	$ 1,768	$ 1,249	$ 2,132	$ 1,944	$ 3,019	$ 2,865
Latin American							
West India Oil Co.	$ 934	$ 1,126	$ 837	$ 2,003	$ 4,130	$ 6,272	$ 6,613
Standard Oil of Brazil	451	484	426	987	2,131	3,805	1,302
Other	89	97	(16)	9	(37)	—	—
Total Latin American	$ 1,474	$ 1,707	$ 1,247	$ 2,999	$ 6,224	$10,077	$ 7,915
European							
American Petroleum Co.	$ 1,310	$ 1,267	$ 844	$ 1,228	$ 1,292	$ 494	a
Bedford Petroleum Co.	67	15	18	52	96	192	$ (43)
Det Danske	766	818	710	1,202	1,554	911	404
DAPG	1,243	3,962	2,887	2,205	a	a	a
Italo-Americana	935	1,041	891	1,499	1,770	933	1,323
Româno-Americana	2	2	2	2	a	a	a
Other	35	346	(156)	(73)	579[b]	1,294[b]	2,165[b]
Total European	$ 4,358	$ 7,451	$ 5,196	$ 6,115	$ 5,291	$ 3,824	$ 3,849
Total domestic and foreign	$ 8,839	$12,368	$ 8,372	$13,489	$16,256	$20,347	$18,420

Earnings as percentage of total marketing earnings[c]

	1912	1913	1914	1915	1916	1917	1918
Domestic	16.3	11.7	8.1	16.6	17.2	16.9	20.6
Canadian	17.7	14.3	14.9	15.8	12.0	14.8	15.5
Latin American	16.7	13.8	14.9	22.2	38.3	49.5	43.0
European	49.3	60.2	62.1	45.4	32.5	18.8	20.9
Total	100.0	100.0	100.0	100.0	100.0	100.0	100.0
Total marketing earnings as percentage of total Jersey earnings[c]	25.0	27.0	26.7	22.1	22.6	19.5	23.7

[a] Comparable data not available because of war conditions.

[b] Profits from consignments of lubricating oil to Continental markets.

[c] Since the percentage figure for any one earnings classification is determined not only by the actual earnings recorded in that classification but also by earnings and losses in each of the others, no attempt should be made to trace year-to-year variations in one classification without careful reference both to other percentage classifications and to the pertinent dollar figures. All functional earnings figures given in SONJ, Fin. Recs., for the years 1912 through 1924, have been adjusted by the authors to match, insofar as possible, the account classifications employed in those records in the years 1925 through 1927.

Source: SONJ, Fin. Recs.

Newark division, together with 688 horses, more than 400 tank wagons, 107 motor trucks, 79 automobiles, and a force of about a thousand employees. The Baltimore division, which also supervised the work of the Baltimore refinery, was somewhat larger, having 1,259 employees, 439 bulk stations, 1,163 horses, 691 tank wagons, 70 motor trucks, and 40 automobiles, together with a small fleet of barges, motor boats, and lighters.[3]

A similar marketing organization had been set up in Louisiana, under the local direction of C. O. Scholder, who had been trained in the selling division of Kentucky Standard. James A. Moffett, Jr., who had commenced work for Standard in 1906 and gained experience in several of the affiliated companies, was made New York representative of the Louisiana sales division. Louisiana marketing operations were thus co-ordinated with the activities of the parent company and of the other affiliates in much the same way as were refining operations. The Louisiana Company did business from 71 bulk stations and branch offices in Louisiana and 72 in Tennessee, the latter representing territory taken over in 1910 from Kentucky Standard. In 1914 marketing operations were extended into Arkansas, where by 1916 the company had opened 37 bulk stations and offices. This last-named move was important for more than its immediate objectives and results. As the first venture by a Jersey affiliate into territory not served at the time of the dissolution decree, the expansion into Arkansas was, in fact, a significant omen of things to come, though not at the time recognized as such.

From the branch offices in all the divisions Louisiana Company salesmen went out to call on retail outlets for refined products. These men were regular employees of the company, paid on a straight salary basis. The tank-wagon drivers made deliveries from the bulk stations and in some instances solicited business directly from the ultimate consumers, being paid either a straight salary or a commission for orders obtained. Since the radius of the tank wagon was only about twelve miles, however, Jersey Standard could dispense with middlemen only in areas where roads were good and the population fairly concentrated. In more sparsely populated regions company products were placed in the hands of local wholesalers or commission agents, many of whom handled products other than refined oil. Some of these agents drove a tank wagon themselves, being supplied with their equipment by the company.

The day of the company-owned service station had not arrived. There were, in fact, very few service stations as such to be found, for gasoline and motor oil in this period were dispensed to the consumer mainly by garages, livery stables, and stores. One experimental service station was opened by the Louisiana Company in Memphis as early as 1912. This harbinger of things to come remained unique in the company's distribution system until 1916, when another company-owned station was opened in Baltimore. By 1919 there were only five Jersey-owned retail service stations in Baltimore, three in North Carolina, and three in South Carolina.[4]

The way for the rapid spread of the filling station was being prepared, however, by improvements in facilities for the safe and accurate dispensing of gasoline at roadside. By 1918 the use of barrels for storage and dispensing purposes had virtually been eliminated, and the trade was being educated to the advantages of Gilbert & Barker tanks and pumps, sales of which in 1917 were nearly 200 per cent above those in 1912. The 1-gallon, self-measure sidewalk pump with a 550-gallon storage tank began to replace the old method of carrying gasoline by hand to the curb. The Standard Motor Gasoline illuminated globes which were part of these outfits became a familiar landmark to automobile drivers.[5] In this period steel barrels completely supplanted wooden ones, and bulk deliveries of lubricating oils replaced to an increasing degree the relatively expensive barrel, half-barrel, and can packaging of earlier days.

A considerable degree of specialization had already appeared by 1911 among the sales forces operating out of the branch offices. Between 1912 and 1917 the group of salesmen who handled the big contractual accounts were the elite of the organization. Many of these representatives were quite independent and liked to feel that they "carried their customers in their pocket." A separate sales force—the "smokestack salesmen"—handled some thirty industrial oils and greases, such as Capitol Cylinder Oil and Renown Engine Oil. These men were chosen, as far as possible, for their practical mechanical knowledge and were assigned districts where intensive direct solicitation of the ultimate industrial consumer was possible. The marketing of Polarine Oil, the company's automobile lubricant which had been introduced in 1910, was handled by the regular sales force in the same manner as kerosene and gasoline. Motor trucks were equipped to deliver Polarine, and some were compartmented to handle both Polarine and Standard Motor Gasoline. Between 1914 and 1918 four different grades of Polarine were placed on the market—ample testimony to the increasing diversification of the motor trade. Each sales district was staffed with an expert mechanic to advise on particular problems and to assist the salesmen. A course of instruction was inaugurated for the salesmen. Free road markers, danger signs, and school warnings, all bearing the Polarine trade-mark, were distributed to communities in Jersey sales territories.

The Jersey Company line of branded specialty products included Marking Crayons, Handy Ironing Wax, Parowax, Mica Axle Grease, Eureka Harness Oil, Compound Harness Oil, Standard Carriage Axle Oil, Visco Axle Oil, Household Lubricant, Matchless Liquid Glass, Ruddy Harvester Oil, Eureka Belt Dressing, and Plumbers' Thread Cutting Oil. These, like Nujol, the medicinal oil which had been placed on the market in 1914, were handled by a special force of salesmen who solicited orders directly from department, drug, hardware, and general stores. Other products included hoof oil, railroad signal oil, valve and journal oils, candles, wicks, and burners. Jersey branch offices also sold Perfection cookstoves and heaters and Rayo oil lamps to retail outlets. This class of products had been introduced before 1911 to bolster the sale of kerosene, and sales were far from inconsequential. In 1917 the Baltimore district offices sold 27,000 stoves (as compared with 9,000 in 1908), while Newark sold 11,000 (as against 4,000 in 1908). Over this same period sales of heaters by the Newark division increased from 6,000 to 54,000.

In retrospect, domestic marketing in the years from 1912 to 1917 seems to have been characterized by careful and continuous attention to methods of increasing sales in existing territories, with great care being taken to abide by the letter and spirit of the law. Possibly as a result of that caution, advertising expenditures were small, brand policy was indecisive, and no widescale effort was made to associate existing or new products with the company's name.

There was, indeed, the greatest reluctance to employ the world-famous "Standard Oil" mark, since in these postdissolution years the question as to the legal rights of the various Standard Oil companies to this and allied marks had not been put to a test. There had been complex difficulties, particularly abroad, in disentangling the brand marks when the dissolution decree was put into effect, and the whole question of competition with disaffiliated companies was a perplexing one. Subsequent events indicate clearly that in the process of dissolving the old Standard Oil group far too little attention had been paid to brand policy and to the subsequent right of the several companies to use their corporate names. The oversight was to prove costly in years to come.

The Jersey Company undertook nationwide advertising and distribution for Nujol, and sales of such products as did not bear the trade-mark

"Standard" or other conflicting brand names were made in territories of former affiliates. In general, however, there was no competition among the various Standard Oil companies in major branded products, for each company confined its business in such products to its own territory. Federal investigating committees were quick to hail this practice as a conscious restraint of trade, to which charge A. C. Bedford replied in the following words:[6]

In what directions there shall be change, expansion or development of the business of any company is in every instance a matter for the determination of its own officers, and one governed purely by business considerations. Every such problem has its own conditions. Whether there shall be an extension of marketing stations into new territories must of necessity in every instance be a problem with its own factors. For instance, to make such an extension into any particular territory may jeopardize and curtail a large and profitable wholesale trade without any compensating gain. Again, a territory may be so fully supplied by existing marketing plants that to add another would be a relatively unprofitable investment. These are merely examples of the questions that have to be taken into consideration in determining the nature of a company's operation in any particular region.

Even had the Standard companies found it necessary to compete with one another in these years, a competitive campaign could not easily have been launched. The whole predissolution marketing system had been carefully worked out on a geographic basis, each refinery serving an adjacent marketing area. In a great many instances transportation rates alone would have placed Jersey Standard and each of its former affiliates at an economic disadvantage in attempting to market their products in areas originally serviced by the others. This situation could be altered only by laborious, costly, and time-consuming alterations in the existing marketing structure of pipelines, storage depots, bulk stations, wholesale and retail dealers, and sales forces—and, in some cases, by the construction of supplementary refining facilities. Many of the now independent Standard Oil companies, moreover, were effectively bound to their own territories. No company with "Standard Oil" in its title could itself comply with corporation laws in states where there already was a corporation of substantially the same name doing business. Neither could brand names incorporating the words "Standard Oil" be employed by any company in other than its home territory, for to do so would have been to infringe the rights of other Standard Oil companies to the use of such marks in their home states.

Thus Jersey Standard and its former affiliates were criticized by federal agencies for failing to do that which in many instances federal and state corporation and trade-mark laws effectively helped to prevent. To invade the territory of disaffiliated companies bearing the Standard Oil name, the Jersey Company would have had to abandon its "Standard Oil" brands and engage in business there under some other corporate designation. In the years from 1912 to 1917 such expansion was politically dangerous, if not virtually impossible. Moreover, such a course, entailing as it did a large-scale promotional effort, was quite unnecessary. With minor exceptions, it was not until pressure for orders became acute and distinctive new brand names had been developed in the years following World War I that the various Standard companies began to come into substantial competition with one another. The absence of competition in branded products before 1918 appears to have represented not calculated collusion but the bowing to business and legal realities of the day. Jersey Standard found the alternative of selling bulk products to former affiliates vastly more attractive at that time than attempting to sell branded products to the customers of those affiliates.

Much of this bulk business grew indirectly from the terms of the dissolution decree. Like Jersey Standard itself, certain of the disaffiliated companies had been left in badly unbalanced condition. The Jersey Company, so heavily endowed with refining capacity that it lacked sufficient trade outlets within its own marketing territory, was able and only too willing to continue to remedy the deficiencies of companies such as Standard of New York, which possessed highly developed marketing facilities and inadequate refining capacity to serve them.

Between 1912 and 1918 the Jersey Company supplied from 33 to 53 per cent of New York Standard's gasoline requirements. In 1917 these orders amounted to slightly less than 2,000,000 barrels, which represented 42 per cent of New York's gasoline sales and 40 per cent of Jersey's gasoline sales. By way of comparison, gasoline sales by Jersey's Newark division for that year were 1,200,000 barrels and by the Baltimore division 1,000,000 barrels.[7]

These New York Standard orders, of course, were not the only bulk sales made by the company. Between 1911 and 1916 arrangements were made for bulk deliveries to Standard of Kentucky, Anglo-American Oil, and Atlantic Refining, all former affiliates, and to the Magnolia Company. Many of these sales were of Mexican crude or reduced crude, which Jersey Standard's exceptionally well-developed tanker fleet enabled the company to handle to advantage. There were also large supply contracts covering the requirements of many Jersey affiliates at home and abroad.

The quest for large orders was diligently pursued in many quarters. In 1912, for example, Walter Teagle was writing to A. P. Coombe, of Ohio Standard, and pointing out that at Bayonne the Jersey Company was manufacturing a very superior grade of road oil from Mexican crude. "I wonder if it would be possible for us to sell you these products in considerable quantities," Teagle asked, noting that the Jersey Company could deliver this oil at different points in Ohio at a price less than the actual cost of similar products manufactured from western crudes. Teagle, D. T. Warden, and F. D. Asche all took a hand in placing contracts and arranging deliveries of fuel oil—a business which before the dissolution had been handled by Standard of New York and which, in consequence, had to be thoroughly reorganized. As this market expanded, the number of bunkering stations throughout the world multiplied. By 1919 the Jersey Company was maintaining supplies of fuel oil at New York, Bayonne, Norfolk, Baltimore, and Baton Rouge, from which points other nearby ports were serviced. Abroad, these facilities were extended to ships by arrangement with affiliates or former affiliates. Bunkering stations were maintained in many ports on both coasts of Canada and South America, in Central America, the West Indies, England, Norway, Sweden, Denmark, Italy, and North Africa.[8]

Within domestic sales territories competition both for the bulk trade and for the small-order business was on the increase. This was probably the most important characteristic of company marketing history in these years. Total domestic deliveries, both to other marketers and through owned outlets, by Jersey Standard and its affiliates in 1918 approximated 7.63 per cent of sales by the entire industry, as compared with 7.76 per cent in 1912. This relative equilibrium, however, was not characteristic of all company marketing divisions. Along the Atlantic seaboard, for example, Jersey Company sales through owned outlets declined from 73 per cent of industry total in 1912 to 60 per cent in 1917.[9] In the Newark and Baltimore divisions the number of bulk stations owned by the company declined from 76 per cent of all such stations in 1911 to 58 per cent in 1917.[10] The Texas Company, Gulf, and other independent companies, unfettered by the dissolution, stimulated by favorable economic trends, and able to expand in states where Jersey Standard and its affiliates did not or could not market, were gathering momentum in their competitive drives. Jersey was being forced to an increasing extent to share its domestic markets.

REFINERY DELIVERIES TO HOME TRADE AND EXPORT
Standard Oil Company (New Jersey)
and Standard Oil Company of Louisiana, 1912-1927

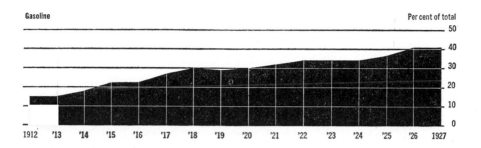

Gasoline — Per cent of total

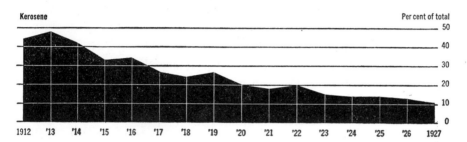

Kerosene — Per cent of total

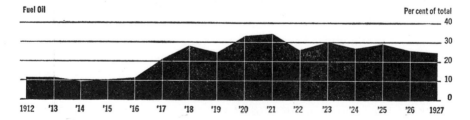

Gas Oil — Per cent of total

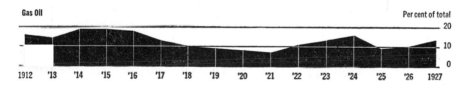

Fuel Oil — Per cent of total

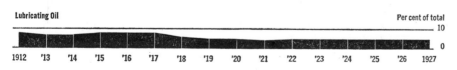

Lubricating Oil — Per cent of total

Source: SONJ, Stat.

Agitation over prices characterized the growth of competition, and continued legal attacks or fear of legal attacks restricted the company's market aggressiveness. The federal Clayton Act of 1914 and various laws enacted in states in which Jersey Standard operated attempted to control price discrimination in the interest of greater competition. Under the provisions of these laws the company was usually able, if it so desired, to discriminate in its prices between different localities in order to meet reductions initiated by local dealers. In certain states, however, the one-price laws effectively prohibited Jersey from initiating price reductions on anything less than a state-wide basis. Thus, in these states the company's full power could not legally be brought to bear in competing with the large number of local dealers whose operations were sufficiently restricted to escape regulation under the one-price laws. Even in periods of active business and generally rising prices, such competitors sought and were able to gain advantages by slightly underbidding their giant rival. The company did not believe in most instances that the advantages of meeting localized competition in one-price states were sufficiently large to justify a general territory-wide lowering of prices. Even when outright violations of the price laws were encountered or where localized price cutting was legally possible, Jersey Standard—possibly fearing political repercussions—was not aggressive in pressing charges or meeting reductions.[11]

The net effect of state and federal one-price and antitrust legislation, aimed at the goal of more vigorous competition in the interest of the consumer, may at times in this period have defeated the very purpose contemplated. Jersey Standard's inability to initiate localized price reductions and its unwillingness to effect broad reductions acted as an umbrella over smaller operators in the company's marketing territories; it was these operators and not Jersey Standard which set the price floors. From the business it retained the company pocketed high profits, as, it may safely be surmised, did the more efficient of the independent marketers. Competition increased, but prices did not fall so low as the Jersey Company could have driven them in an unrestrained effort to maintain or better its position. The one-price laws functioned, insofar as the public was concerned, as high-price laws. "Practically the only way the Standard can get in trouble," wrote one Legal Department correspondent, "is by reducing the price of oil."[12]

A similar situation prevailed in the steel industry. In both petroleum and steel the highly effective utilization of huge sums of capital by the large producing and distributing units appears to have been channeled by government regulation in this period not into lower prices for consumers but into higher profits for both the large and the small companies. Some would have said that in this particular situation the public unwittingly was being cheated by its elected representatives. Others might have replied that the higher prices to the consumer represented the cost of keeping small operators in business—thus preserving, over the long range, a reasonably competitive environment. Certainly, however, the paralyzing fear of monopoly was fostering some of the very evils that monopoly was traditionally supposed to bring. The blame for this paradoxical situation of high prices in an era of strict regulation was generally laid at the door of Big Business.

While unwilling to act as price leader in declining markets from 1912 to 1914, the Jersey Company definitely took the lead in the increases in prices of refined products that followed each other after 1914.[13] The only penalty that might seem to follow from raising prices was loss of business to competitors, and by 1915 Jersey management appeared to feel that there was going to be plenty of business for all. The fact was, however, that the company was in trouble no matter what happened to prices. The trend of the times, which produced such profits for the organization, almost inevitably spelled public hostility. On the few occasions when prices were cut, some competitor was certain to cry that Standard Oil was out to force independent operators to the wall. Yet every rise in the price of petroleum products brought howls of protest from consumers.

Complaints against Standard companies originated from many quarters within the industry. Some producers alleged that unduly low prices were paid them for crude oil and that many of the pipeline rates for transportation were too high. Many independent refiners claimed, at the same time, that the prices they were obliged to pay for crude oil were too high and subject to monopolistic control, while the prices at which they had to sell their refined products were too low because of alleged unfair practices of competitors. When crude prices rose, the complaint was voiced that a Standard Oil conspiracy was being hatched to drive independent refiners out of business.

Federal Trade Commission investigators made little sense out of the welter of conflicting claims, and extensive federal investigations launched in 1914 in response to various Senate resolutions showed a marked propensity to bog down. In some cases the hand of politics was to be discerned. One commissioner of the Federal Trade Commission was accused of capitalizing his activities in the investigation of Standard Oil operations in connection with his campaign for a state governorship.[14] Few issues could be assured of enlisting votes more certainly than a vigorous antitrust attitude. When the Federal Trade Commission in 1915 launched an investigation of gasoline price increases, Jersey Company officials were faced with a situation which, from their viewpoint, was intensely provocative. Hampered by state legislation in initiating or even meeting price cuts, the company now was confronted with federal condemnation of its efforts to raise them.[15]

In its report the Commission severely criticized the whole price structure of the industry. The thesis advanced was that the big companies, having the resources to purchase and store crude in periods of flush production, enjoyed a vast market advantage over small operators, who were dependent on the current market for their supplies. Gasoline prices, the Commission noted, bore scant relation to prices paid for crude at the well. The Commission further reported that accumulation of crude stocks in 1915, both by Standard Oil companies and by others, was excessive; that increases in gasoline prices were excessive; and that profits from gasoline sales were excessive.

The Federal Trade Commission's conclusion that big companies enjoyed certain advantages over small companies was scarcely a startling revelation. To other charges, however, Jersey Standard made strong replies. The essence of the company's defense was that the crude stocks accumulated in 1915 as a result of Mid-Continent purchases from The Prairie Oil & Gas Company and others had been equivalent to only six months' supply and were currently being exhausted at a rapid rate, while gasoline prices reflected an unforeseen demand in 1915 which could not possibly have been met by existing refinery facilities. A. C. Bedford, the spokesman for Jersey Standard in matters relating to the government, assailed the Commission's charge that prices and markets were being manipulated by agreement among the corporate members of the old Standard Oil group. He pointed to the Commission's own figures showing that the percentage of gasoline business controlled by the various Standard Oil companies had declined from 87 per cent of industry total in 1911 to 65 per cent in 1916. Bedford also noted that the Commission had not been able to accuse former Standard Oil companies of unfair competition with the great number of new oil companies which had been organized since 1911. Neither, Bedford stated, had the Commission in its report of an exhaustive inquiry into Jersey's business proved that any practice or policy of the company was at variance with the terms of the dissolution decree. To the

A. COTTON BEDFORD

WALTER C. TEAGLE

The Cushing field

A view of part of the El Dorado pool in Kansas in 1919

Spudding in a well

Oil wells in Romania

Coating a pipeline in Louisiana with cement in 1919

Baton Rouge refinery in 1918

Row of cracking stills at Baton Rouge

Tubes of a cracking still at Baton Rouge

Strike scene at Bayonne, New Jersey, in 1915

Launching of *John D. Archbold,* January 28, 1914

Negritos field in Peru about 1915

Lobitos field in Peru, 1925

Ancient pitch pits in Peru

Talara, Peru, about 1915

New trestle in Peru

Railroad construction gang in Peru

Dog cart in The Netherlands

Tank trucks in Argentina in 1912

Street scene in Belgium about 1920

Barreling in The Netherlands

The tanker *John D. Rockefeller* in 1914

Bulk plant at Savona, Italy, in 1914

charge of high profits, however, Jersey Standard could offer no effective defense. Once again the company stood accused of originating and perpetuating conditions which obviously derived in substantial part from uncontrollable economic trends—trends from which the Jersey Company had not proved reluctant to profit.

With some bitterness Bedford protested against the investigation, both in public and in private utterances. One memorandum, addressed to the Federal Trade Commission but unsigned and apparently never sent, provides a lucid commentary on company attitudes of the day:[16]

I beg to say that this Company gave its assurance to the Department of Justice, when the decree was handed down, that it would be scrupulously obeyed, and that assurance has been carried out to the fullest extent. We have been constantly under the supervision of the Department of Justice, to which all information asked for has been furnished. That Department has investigated complaints which have been made to it without finding that any charges against us are well grounded. Under these circumstances, it is discouraging and disheartening to be met with an attitude of distrust and suspicion on the part of the Federal Trade Commission. For years now, there has scarcely been a time when representatives of some department of the Government have not been in our offices examining our records and calling for information of every nature and description. All this, we believe, has served very little useful purpose and at the same time has naturally had very serious adverse effect upon the morale of our organization. I can only say that I hope the time may come when there will be an end to all this so that the Company may devote its energies to the proper conduct of its business.

The most discouraging aspect of the entire investigation was the determined persistence of the Commission in grouping all Standard Oil interests together, as though the dissolution decree had never been. Bedford attacked this attitude as follows:[17]

To perpetuate and to emphasize, as does the memorandum, the designation and segregation of "Standard Oil interests," in contradistinction to the so-called "Independents" is unjust and really misleading, in view of the decree of the court under which these companies have lived and must live, under the constant supervision of the Department of Justice, and which, speaking for this Company, we say has been conscientiously executed and observed. To generalize respecting these companies, in an investigation such as this, involves misconceptions and inaccuracies when any statement is sought to be applied to a single company—a result which, we have no doubt, the Commission is anxious to avoid. To assume that there is a comprehensive control or policy covering all the so-called Standard Companies, making any statement or conclusion applicable equally to all of them, when there is no such control or policy, is both unwarranted and prejudicial.

In attempting to defend itself against the charge of failing to compete with former affiliates, however, the Jersey Company found itself in a most difficult situation. As it was doing with its purchasing contracts (see Chapter 3), the company endeavored to keep its supply contracts with former affiliates as secret as possible in order to minimize the danger of public criticism that the terms of the dissolution decree were being violated. Like the purchase contracts, however, Jersey's agreements with companies such as Standard of New York were quite normal business transactions and unquestionably would not have been attacked had they not been made by and between two companies bearing the Standard name. Here was an ironical situation—a situation in which the Jersey Company could seemingly do no right. Had the company dared to emphasize the extent of its trade with former affiliates—trade which by every definition was legal, natural, and as undiscriminatory as any business contract can be—there would have been little basis for the charge that the company was refraining, to the detriment of the public, from entering the territory of former affiliates. These contracts represented by far the most economical manner of supplying the needs of the public until such time as the organizational balance of the companies involved could be restored. Yet federal pressure was steadily being applied to force the adoption of competitive measures which the respective companies were ill equipped to undertake and for which the times were not yet propitious. It was, on the other hand, impossible for the federal regulatory and investigatory agencies to foresee that the competition they sought was on the way and that the dissolution decree could not be made immediately and completely effective without imposing a tremendous penalty on the ultimate consumer of petroleum products. Those agencies, it should be recalled, were deep in the task of developing new policies and methods for regulating Big Business in the interest of maintaining effective competition. Precedents were few, complexities were many, and political pressures—as always—were acute. The conflicts and the mistakes were part of the trial-and-error process of evolutionary politico-economic development.

THRUST AND PARRY IN FOREIGN MARKETS

Marketing effort abroad was marked by an aggressiveness almost totally lacking at home. In foreign markets Walter Teagle's propensity for bold and broad and brilliantly calculated negotiations was eminently appropriate and useful, for many foreign countries, particularly in Europe, had long since come to accept as a *fait accompli* the existence of the giant company, the monopoly, and the cartel. At home, as we have seen, the power of contract deriving from the power of great wealth and influence had accomplished much that Jersey Standard's enemies sought to prevent, but had failed, even so, to hold increasing competition in check. In certain foreign areas, however, that power could be and was unleashed. By skillful negotiation and astute competitive moves Teagle and his associates began to repair the damage which the dissolution had wrought and to parry the attacks which competitors, made bolder by the decree, were launching upon Jersey Standard's position in many parts of the world. In no two areas were marketing problems precisely similar, but in virtually all areas state regulation and control was becoming an increasingly difficult obstacle to surmount successfully. The very diversity of regulations and the divergent attitudes of the various foreign nations toward American capital were problems in themselves. Jersey Company men, however, seemed confident that the proved efficacy of their marketing methods coupled with a firm brand of diplomacy would prove equal to any challenge.

Teagle, serving during the 1912-1917 period as active leader of The Imperial Oil Company, Limited, and as dominant molder of foreign policy in the whole Jersey Standard organization, devoted much of his attention to the European market. In this area lay the most pressing problems, for the important Far Eastern markets were lost when Standard of New York was disaffiliated. The dissolution decree had also taken from Jersey the United Kingdom markets served by the Anglo-American Oil Company, as well as the virtually world-wide lubricating oil business of Vacuum Oil. Anglo-American continued to purchase petroleum products from its former parent, however, and, notwithstanding the loss of Vacuum's business, Jersey's European trade was still formidable, accounting in 1912 for 12 per cent of total earnings and 49 per cent of marketing earnings. The Canadian market was much smaller (18 per cent of Jersey's marketing earnings in 1912) and had not been disturbed by the dissolution. The South American business, roughly equivalent in size of earnings to the Canadian, was expanding fairly rapidly and, except in Peru, was threatened by no immediate formidable challenges.

Marketing policy in Europe, Canada, and South America was closely allied with producing and refining objectives; so much so, in fact, that policy changes often involved all three functions. At home, the Jersey Company was consciously striving to achieve more complete integration of these basic functions. The efficiency with which the company supplied its foreign markets by tanker with American products, however, tended to delay the drive for integration abroad. Gradually, as world-wide competition grew, as shipping costs increased, and as tanker shortages developed in the years after 1911, Jersey Standard accelerated its efforts to acquire and expand foreign producing and refining facilities to serve the foreign markets more effectively. South American and Canadian operations in particular bore the imprint of a new pattern, which was to become of paramount importance in the years after 1917. Here and there in Jersey's foreign enterprises lay evidence that even before 1917 the advantage or even the necessity of integrating foreign producing, marketing, and refining functions more closely had at least been seen, though efforts in this direction had nowhere matured.

In Canada vigorous efforts were expended to adapt the marketing structure of The Imperial Oil Company, Limited, to rapidly changing conditions of demand and competition.[18] The organization was expanded, new divisions were set up, the number of bulk stations was increased, and new branch managers were trained. Despite the appointment of experienced and hardworking G. W. Mayer to head the Canadian marketing program, Teagle himself exercised minute supervision of operational detail and carefully scrutinized the reports which he had caused to be compiled. In 1914 the services of an advertising agency were obtained, and in 1915 the first major advertising campaign was launched. The market for gasoline began to boom. Mayer took steps to meet the demand growing out of what he characterized as the "jitney craze."

Imperial's nearly complete domination of the Canadian market, however, began to be challenged. Teagle and Mayer fought increasing competition with decisive tactics. Seeking to market the Burton-Humphreys process gasoline of the Sarnia refinery, Mayer encountered serious opposition to company-operated service stations from the garage owners in Ontario and Quebec. A new company was forthwith organized to operate such stations, its connection with Imperial being concealed. When some of the jobbers through whom a part of Imperial's product line was marketed became too strong, the company purchased an interest in their business. Some rival marketers were bought out entirely, and, when this was not possible, conciliation and co-operation were sought.

Persistent detailed attention to marketing possibilities and a willingness to invest in new distribution facilities proved especially rewarding as the Canadian economy expanded and demand for petroleum products grew. Between 1913 and 1917 the volume of products sold by Imperial increased 89 per cent—an increase of considerably greater proportions than that recorded by the Jersey Company in the United States over the same period. Relative freedom from restrictive legislation, lack of legal impediments to geographic expansion, less acute competition, and a less conservative philosophy of marketing management went far toward explaining the more rapid acceleration of sales volume in Canada.

In South American markets, too, dynamic expansion characterized the postdissolution years. Ultimate responsibility for this business was vested in Joseph H. Senior, head of the West India Oil Company, and the executives of the Standard Oil Company of Brazil and of the International Petroleum Company Limited. Few leaders of the organization recorded at the time a more brilliant operating performance than these men. As in Canada, local marketing efforts were aided by general economic trends.

Most Latin American countries, because of their relatively undeveloped economic state and low planes of living, had been slow to generate a large market even for kerosene. The absence of coal production, however, put fuel oil on a stronger competitive basis than it was in Europe and the United States, where coal was plentiful. In the early 1880's Latin American sales of Standard Oil had, with certain exceptions, been handled through merchants in Atlantic ports. Later, resident South American agents were utilized, to whom Jersey Standard shipped products on consignment. The consignment agency business was a costly form of distribution which the company found it profitable to short-circuit when volume grew sufficiently large to justify direct outlets. The trend of the 1912-1917 period, therefore, was toward establishment of Jersey-controlled branch marketing stations to augment the agency channels of distribution established earlier. By 1918 the shift to such stations was well under way.

The Brazilian market had first been tapped through the Empreza Industrial de Petróleo, a Standard Oil affiliate organized in 1896. In 1911 the name of this company was changed to the Standard Oil Company of Brazil, and an office was set up to replace the earlier consignment agency through which Empreza had distributed its products. The familiar organization of substations, jobbers, and agents was established. Oil products were shipped in cases from Jersey refineries in the United States to Rio de Janeiro, and as the business developed after 1915 bulk shipments began to a slight extent to replace the packaged-goods business.[19] Brazil, unfortunately, did not have a good system of inland communications, and business was limited largely to the coastal markets.

On the west coast of South America, the West Coast Oil Fuel Company, Limited, organized in 1911, was building up a trade in fuel oil with the nitrate and copper companies and other industrial customers. Bulk stations were established, but the business obtained was small from 1911 to 1914, when the company was taken over by Imperial and made an integral part of the South American group of companies which were subsequently consolidated under the management of the International Petroleum Company Limited. For some time the West Coast Oil Fuel Company, Limited, drew its stocks principally from the Talara refinery in Peru.

Additional outlets for products refined from Peruvian crude were obtained by extending the contracts which a group of British mercantile firms doing business on the west coast had entered into with the old London & Pacific group. International also shipped products from Talara to New York, Continental Europe, and the United Kingdom. Upon expiration of contracts whereby Standard Oil of California supplied Imperial's light-distillate needs on the west coast of Canada, the California stocks were replaced by Peruvian. To permit more of the Peruvian crude to be run to gasoline, fuel oil supplies for the South American trade were augmented by purchases of California stocks. In 1917, of course, this intricate distribution system was being threatened by the political difficulties in Peru and by the wartime shortage of tankers.[20]

The West India Oil Company, organized in 1902, greatly increased the scope of its business in postdissolution years. To existing markets in the Caribbean Islands and on the north and east coasts of Central and South America the company added those in southern sections of South America previously handled by the Colonial Oil Company. These various market requirements were met largely by shipments from refineries in the United States. Because of tariff regulations the Cuban market was served by The West India Oil Refining Company's small Havana refinery. The Argentinean refinery at Campana also owed its existence directly to local tariff restrictions, and it helped to supply the local market. After 1914 both the Havana and the Campana refineries, which had relied upon crude supplies from the United States, began to draw upon the developing Peruvian fields.

West India Oil sold both through its own stations and through consignment agencies, the latter type of business being handled from the

West India office in New York. Traveling representatives from this office checked on the work of the agencies in an effort to help them realize the full potential of the market, for many of the consignees were general merchants who were not familiar with the oil business. As these agencies came to be displaced by company stations, many became jobber customers for company products.

Although West India Oil faced competition from established European agencies and independent importers in Latin America, its introduction of the tank-wagon system of distribution gave the company an important competitive advantage. Merchandising policies were adapted to the South American markets, and simple but effective promotional methods were practiced. Additional market outlets were acquired in the Carribean area; a new branch office opened in Buenos Aires served as the base for extension of the distribution system throughout southern Latin America. By 1918, following a half decade of remarkable expansion, West India Oil controlled a network of sales stations and substations covering the Caribbean Islands and parts of Dutch and British Guiana, Bolivia, Colombia, Ecuador, Venezuela, Chile, Panama, Nicaragua, Guatemala, Argentina, Paraguay, and Uruguay. These stations were almost exclusively wholesale organizations which distributed to jobbers and commission agents. Some direct business was done with manufacturers and with the United States Navy. From 1912 to 1918 the largest business came from the stations at Buenos Aires, Montevideo, San Juan, Havana, and Valparaiso, but business everywhere, both for West India Oil and for Standard of Brazil, was rapidly growing.

The sale of illuminating oil in South America suffered few of the inroads made in the United States by electricity, while lubricants and fuel oil became increasingly in demand for railroads, mining, and manufacturing. The tremendous growth from 1911 to 1918, when assets of the West India Oil Company increased thirteenfold and earnings from all South American marketing leaped from 16 to 40 per cent of total Jersey marketing earnings, reflected the general increase in all South American business that characterized those years. The market boom reflected the more particular influence of the war-induced elimination of British coal from the South American market, the conversion of shipping to fuel oil, and the increased mobility of oil and other industrial supplies that resulted from the opening of the Panama Canal.

Thus did Jersey Standard and its affiliates assist in promoting the industrial revolution in Latin America. An efficient mass-distribution system was created to supply the petroleum needs growing out of that revolution, and Jersey Standard reaped the benefits from an early entry and a strongly entrenched position there. The success of this marketing effort—success that accrued both from fortuitous circumstance and from careful planning and expensive investment in distribution facilities—made it imperative to develop additional local production to serve the markets which still were clamoring for oil. In 1918 the Jersey directors could look at South American operations with satisfaction but not with complacency, for changes in markets inevitably spelled out a need for adjustment in other branches of the business.

In Europe the outbreak of war necessarily meant not expanded business for the Jersey Company, but loss, managerial difficulties, and great uncertainty. Even before 1914, however, a dramatic marketing story had been recorded, and important parts of the carefully negotiated system of competitive checks and balances in the Continental oil business had been threatened with drastic upheaval. The strong position of Standard Oil in Europe prior to 1911 had derived from early entry in the market, possession of abundant supplies of oil for export, and ownership of the all-important transportation facilities for supplying the market. Competition, however, had increased in the three decades preceding the dissolution, and Standard's reign was threatened. The threats were met by price wars, by purchase of competitors, or by agreements dividing the markets with the more formidable opponents. These stringent measures continued to be invoked by the company whenever necessary in the years following the dissolution. A degree of boldness was imparted to foreign negotiations after 1911 which reflected not only Teagle's direction but also the need for more forceful handling of international competitors, who now were vastly more powerful than in the old days when the Standard trust had overawed the world industry.[21]

Operations in the Lowland and Scandinavian countries after 1911 were marked by no major crises until 1915, after which time increasingly acute war shortages of refined products and of tankers in which to ship them produced a notable falling off in the tempo of operations. Before the war the business in these countries, as elsewhere in Europe, was characterized by that same growth in marketing stations and in the tank-wagon system of distribution which was to be found in operations at home and in South America.

Requirements of the American Petroleum Company, which marketed through two branches and a half-dozen affiliates in Holland, Belgium, and on the west bank of the Rhine, were supplied from Jersey refineries in the United States and carried from there by American Petroleum's own small fleet of tankers. This organization remained under the guidance of local managers W. T. Klaare, A. O. and Frederick Horstmann, Albert and Yvan Maquinay, and Maurice and Frederic Speth, all of whom were Belgian or Dutch. Those men knew the trade intimately and were allowed great freedom in managing the business.

Of lesser importance to Jersey Standard, insofar as earnings were concerned, was Det Danske Petroleums-Aktieselskab, which marketed, also through a group of affiliates, in Denmark, Norway, Sweden, Iceland, Greenland, and Finland. At the head of this company was aggressive, ambitious Christian Holm, who had been fighting to increase Det Danske business since 1901, when he had been appointed managing director. In the Scandinavian countries, as in Holland, Belgium, and Germany, a kerosene marketing agreement concluded in 1907 with the European Petroleum Union remained in effect after the dissolution.

This agreement and others concluded about that time had marked a truce in the battle between Standard Oil and powerful European interests for domination of the Continental kerosene market. The European Petroleum Union—owned jointly by the Deutsche Bank, the Rothschilds, and the Nobels, and controlled by the Deutsche Bank—had signed long-term contracts with various Jersey Standard affiliates for a division of markets. In 1910 the European kerosene business had fallen roughly 75 per cent to Standard Oil, 20 per cent to the Petroleum Union, and 5 per cent to others.[22] These agreements represented at best a flimsy and leaking dam against increasing competitive pressures which threatened at any moment to burst all bounds and drench the European market in a flood of oil.

Having failed, in 1910, to renew the marketing truce with Standard covering kerosene sales in the Far East and benzine sales in Europe, Henri Deterding was ambitious to obtain for the Royal Dutch-Shell a larger participation in European business. Deterding's Asiatic Petroleum Company was already raiding the European market of Standard and the European Petroleum Union, despite protests from the Petroleum Union and from Jersey Standard's American Petroleum Company. Skillfully this consummate master of economic strategy manipulated his forces to build a great producing, refining, and marketing combination with which to attack Jersey in its European strongholds. With a man like Deterding involved, this threat was not to be taken lightly, and the broad shadow of the Royal Dutch leader fell across many of Jersey's undertakings in Europe in these prewar years.[23]

In Italy, too, agreements were in effect with the European Petroleum Union which protected Società Italo-Americana pel Petrolio, Jersey's Italian affiliate, against competition from that marketing group. Italo-Americana continued after 1911 under the direction of August von Hartz, an American citizen of German birth who had built up a system of marketing in Italy, in part of Switzerland, and in Sicily, Malta, Tunis, and Algeria. Italo's three tankers, acquired between 1911 and 1913, were employed in bringing refined products from the United States, while oil supplies were also moved overland by rail from Romania. Business in Italy was disturbed by the Balkan Wars, but von Hartz was successful in expanding Italo's fuel oil business, which, it was hoped, would eventually take care of the major part of the fuel oil output of Jersey Standard's Romanian refinery. Markets in Switzerland were tapped through an affiliate owned 40 per cent by Italo and 60 per cent by DAPG.

In Romania the Jersey men had come face to face in 1908 with severe governmental regulation of marketing activities. To meet the restrictions imposed in this area, where supplies far exceeded local demand, the principal competing oil companies had established a joint marketing company, the Societate Anonimă pentru Distribuirea Produlselor Petrolului. The stock of Distributia, as this company was called, was subscribed by the participants in proportion to their refining capacity, and all profits realized from Distributia's commissions on sales were divided among its owners. By 1913 Româno-Americana held only 14 per cent of the stock of Distributia, while Deutsche Bank interests owned 58 per cent and Royal Dutch-Shell interests 28 per cent. Since the Romanian market was thus restricted by law, outlets for Româno-Americana production and refining were sought elsewhere. Some oil was shipped from Teleajen to Jersey Standard affiliates elsewhere in Europe, many Balkan and Mediterranean customers were supplied, and contracts were filled for Standard of New York and the Vacuum Oil Company.[24]

In France and Spain marketing conditions were quite different from those in neighboring countries. With the relatively minor exception of lubricating oils sold by the Bedford Petroleum Company, a French affiliate, Jersey Standard did not market directly in either country. This situation grew out of marketing agreements concluded in predissolution years between Standard Oil affiliates and the French and Spanish Refiners.[25]

In the 1880's competition for the French market had been bitter, and as a result the various local refiners had concluded arrangements among themselves to pool and share the market, thereby creating a virtual monopoly of the existing business. The 1910 agreement with the French Refiners, which remained in force until the late months of World War I, called for Jersey Standard to supply a minimum of 2,000,000 barrels of petroleum products annually. The French Refiners on their part agreed not to purchase American oil from others. Two refineries in France owned by Jersey affiliates were used only as storage depots or were run for the account of the French Refiners. The perpetuation of Jersey Standard ownership of these plants apparently served as a reminder to the Refiners, when the time came for negotiating new supply contracts, that the company had in its hands the wherewithal to threaten their position.

Profits realized from this business cannot be ascertained, and the supply agreements were most carefully guarded secrets. Partnerships in France were not required to open their books to inspection by French government officials. Since the component firms in the French refining combination were partnerships, they objected, for fear of investigation, to dealing with a corporation. Purchases and contracts, therefore, were not made directly with the Jersey Company or its affiliates, but through an intermediary, John J. Hoff, head of the Bedford Petroleum Company. Hoff performed the same function in dealings with the Spanish Refiners, for in Spain, a much smaller market, approximately the same situation existed as in France.

While the iron grip of the French Refiners on the French market had been loosened somewhat by competing units, this group still dominated the market in 1917. Profits for the Refiners are said to have been high, the distribution system none too efficient, and the French public the losers from the near-monopoly. It is a most interesting and far from coincidental fact, in view of developments then occurring in Germany, that here in France where the much-maligned Standard Oil interests were discouraged by French legislative restrictions from competing, the consumer was so poorly served.

THE PETROLEUM MONOPOLY AFFAIR IN GERMANY

The local marketing situations in France, the Scandinavian countries, Romania, and Italy were mainly a reflection and an extension of pre-1911 conditions. The outbreak of war in 1914 posed difficult questions of supply, to be sure, but with this exception the story was largely one of continuing efforts in established patterns. Not so in Germany. Here, in Jersey Standard's most prosperous Eastern Hemisphere market, an explosive episode sent reverberating echoes around the world. A narrative account of the petroleum monopoly affair is warranted not only by its importance but also for the insight it provides into Jersey Standard's foreign operations and those of some of its chief competitors.

Heinrich Riedemann, carrying on where his able father Wilhelm had left off, was unsurpassed by any of the managers of the foreign marketing affiliates in establishing an efficient distribution system. The Deutsch-Amerikanische Petroleum-Gesellschaft brought in its oil supplies from America, unloaded them at the mouths of the principal rivers, and barged them to main distributing stations for transshipment. Tank wagons carried oil to retail outlets, and in some cities DAPG peddlers solicited the final consumers directly. A competitor ruefully commented that one constantly came across Standard gallon kerosene cans in the most remote country districts! DAPG also handled the distribution of a line of lubricants, greases, and waxes in North Central Europe. In 1912 company representatives were established in 21 cities in Germany, Scandinavia, Holland, Austria-Hungary, and Russia; in 8 cities DAPG operated gas plants. By 1914 some 750 stations and substations had been set up to serve the trade, and over $2,000,000 in kerosene storage and dispensing equipment had been loaned to small retail outlets, a program which had been tried earlier in the United States but abandoned.[26]

In Germany, as elsewhere in Europe, the 1907 agreement to divide the kerosene market with the European Petroleum Union was in effect. By the terms of this agreement DAPG allotted 20 per cent of its market to the German Petroleum Selling Company (Deutsche Petroleum Verkaufs-Gesellschaft), a Petroleum Union subsidiary. The marketing of the Romanian and Galician oil with which the German Petroleum Selling Company supplied the trade was administered by DAPG. Actual or potential competitors of this combine in Germany were the Pure Oil Company, a German subsidiary which had been organized by The Pure Oil Company, Limited, in the United States, and OLEX (Oesterreichische-Ungarischen Petroleum Produkte), an organization of Austrian refiners controlled by the Deutsche-Erdol Aktiengesellschaft, which in turn was owned by the German banking firm of Disconto Gesellschaft. For these companies there was scant sustenance in the German trade. In 1912 it was estimated that the DAPG–European Petroleum Union group controlled 80 per cent of the German market, and the prospects were not hopeful that this hold would be loosened.

Riedemann, a tall, ruddy-complexioned German, was soft spoken but as hard as steel. His marketing tactics were in the best aggressive German tradition; his organization was suffused with energy and regulated with efficiency. There were probably few marketing groups in all Europe that could match the hard-hitting effectiveness with which DAPG served the German consumer with Jersey Standard products. The Riedemann family itself stood high in the councils of the Church and of the Imperial State. In 1911 Heinrich Riedemann was already respected and feared for his brilliant and agile statesmanship.

Profits of the DAPG were high, but here once again, as in so many other chapters of Standard Oil history, great success proved to be a danger. Envy, enmity, and desire for a share of the wealth were stirring.

In the spring of 1911 Teagle, as the responsible Jersey director, was informed that a movement was under way to form a government monopoly in Germany to take over the marketing of kerosene.[27] A flood of alarming correspondence confirming the early rumors poured into 26 Broadway. Popular support of the proposal grew in the months that followed. Five of the six political parties in Germany were reported in favor of such a monopoly, and it became clear that a serious threat to the lucrative German business was materializing.

There was ample precedent for a government monopoly. For centuries European countries had fostered such measures as a means of obtaining revenue. At least twice before 1911 plans to nationalize segments of the petroleum industry had been broached in Germany, and at this very time the Austrian government was successfully harassing foreign petroleum interests in that country. Jersey Standard was in a particularly vulnerable position abroad. The dissolution decree had been widely publicized in Europe, and much of the public, at least, believed that the Standard Oil empire was now crashing in ruins. The action of the Austrian government in closing the refinery of the Vacuum Oil Company had provoked a diplomatic protest but no decisive action from the American State Department. Was the American government willing to have Standard Oil brought to its knees abroad by foreign governments? In 1911 all facts pointed to an affirmative answer to this important question.

Official denials of the monopoly plans were issued by the German government, but through 1911 and early 1912 the movement gathered momentum and the terms of the proposal began to crystallize. In substance, the protagonists of the monopoly planned to submit to the Reichstag a bill calling for establishment of a government-financed company to take over existing private wholesale kerosene distribution facilities in Germany, paying indemnity to the old owners and operating those facilities or causing them to be operated for the benefit of the state. Oil supplies were to be drawn chiefly from Continental rather than American supply sources. Such a scheme, the sponsors claimed, would enable kerosene to be provided at a moderate price and at the same time obtain for the government an annual income of about $15,000,000, which could be employed in useful welfare work.[28]

Behind the monopoly bill lay strong forces and complex motivations, few of which were known to the German public. At the time not even Teagle or Riedemann knew for certain all the factors involved. That the DAPG had enemies was obvious. A whole economic group and social class in Germany had been offended when DAPG established a bulk distribution system which virtually eliminated the wholesalers. Notwithstanding Riedemann's efforts to take some of the wholesalers into the organization and to ease the loss for the others in various ways, these solid, middle-class merchants had enlisted the support of the powerful German Merchants Guild in their cause and were staunchly aligned in support of the monopoly. In some quarters this group of disgruntled oil distributors was believed to have originated the monopoly idea.

On February 8, 1912, Jersey Vice-President A. C. Bedford, who had hastened to Europe to obtain firsthand information, reported that the instigator of the whole affair was the Deutsche Bank, possibly in alliance with Austrian refining interests. Motivations were not hard to discern. The bank, encouraged by the general European opinion that the American government would not extend diplomatic support to Jersey Standard, saw not only an opportunity to increase its participation in German marketing, but also the chance to oust entirely the DAPG from power.[29]

Teagle surmised that Arthur von Gwinner, head of the Deutsche Bank, had not been successful in making the bank's large investments in Romanian properties profitable and that he was seeking a greater market for his Romanian oil in Germany in order to retrieve something from the venture. Extensive Deutsche Bank investments in Galician fields, too, would be benefited. Since both Romanian and Galician products were poorer in quality than the American and since DAPG had built so efficient a distribution system, the successful marketing of substantial quantities of these oils in unrestrained competition with DAPG was virtually impossible. If the monopoly bill passed, the DAPG marketing facilities would be taken over on confiscatory terms, Jersey Standard would have to come on its knees to the monopoly to get contracts, and in any case complete control of the market would be in German (Deutsche Bank) hands. Von Gwinner could then unload his Romanian and Galician oil. At worst, the threat of monopoly might force DAPG and Jersey Standard to concede better terms than those contained in the 1907 agreement with the European Petroleum Union, the bank's petroleum marketing affiliate. Beyond these advantages the Deutsche Bank also planned, once the monopoly bill had passed, to take over on a fee basis the administration of the government distributing company which was to be set up.

Teagle and Riedemann speculated as to whether von Gwinner was secretly working hand in glove with the Royal Dutch-Shell. Riedemann reported that Deterding was in Berlin, ostensibly to promote his plan for a general European petroleum trust. "An imaginative mind," Riedemann wrote grimly to Teagle, "can form all sorts of opinions as to the attitude taken by von Gwinner and Deterding toward a monopoly and what plans they may be scheming over and discussing."[30] Undismayed, however, by the formidable power of the opposition, Riedemann calmly advised his American superior that somehow this storm, like earlier ones, would be weathered. Early in 1912 Riedemann launched a clever counterattack. For the next eighteen months the German nation and the world petroleum industry followed with keen interest the progress of the Riedemann–von Gwinner battle. Behind the scenes moved the figure of Walter Teagle— counseling, cautioning, and slowly marshaling powerful forces in the United States to the aid of the beleaguered German company.

In his February, 1912, report on the German situation A. C. Bedford had suggested some of the defensive tactics which should be employed. The German government, he reported somewhat naïvely, probably would never consider the monopoly proposal if the selfish motives behind it were known. Thus, the public should be enlightened and the inadequacy of non-Jersey supply sources should be pointed out. Shortly after this Riedemann caused a pamphlet to be prepared and published setting forth a critical exposition of the monopoly plans. Where, specifically, was the government to get an adequate supply of oil? The pamphlet presented figures which clearly demonstrated the vital dependence of the German nation on Jersey-controlled supplies. The pamphlet then went on to attack in damagingly factual terms the allegation that the German government would make a profit from the monopoly. Not lower but higher prices would follow, the pamphlet declared, because of the expensive machinery the government proposed to employ. This broadside by Riedemann caused a stir. So able and sound was the reasoning that advocates of the monopoly were thrown on the defensive. Never, thereafter, was the claim advanced that substantial profits would accrue to the government. Instead, Riedemann's foes shifted their tactics to a violent attack upon the "Standard Oil monopoly."[31]

All this, however, was smoke for the public eye. While the German press and the Reichstag membership were lining up either for or against von Gwinner, a grim and secret struggle was going on for petroleum supplies. Here lay the crucial issue. If von Gwinner could assure the nation of adequate supplies, the bill would pass. If he failed, so, too, would the monopoly bill fail. Teagle and Riedemann moved to checkmate their German adversary.

Early in 1911—as soon, in fact, as the rumors of the monopoly were heard—Teagle had concluded negotiations to purchase the Pure Oil Company (German), one of the two important independent suppliers outside the DAPG–Petroleum Union combine. Although this move was backed by sound commercial considerations, it was in direct anticipation of the monopoly attempt and was concluded in order to keep out of von Gwinner's hands marketing assets that would have enhanced his claim of being able to supply the German market. Neither Jersey Standard nor the DAPG participated directly in the purchase. Stock of the German Pure Oil Company was acquired by a Swiss corporation—the Schweizerische Handels-und Beteiligungs-Aktiengesellschaft, later changed to Standard Petroleum Co. (Glarus)—which was personally controlled in Jersey Standard's interest by Teagle and other trusted individuals.[32] At the same time, the Jersey Company concluded a contract with The Pure Oil Company, Limited, in the United States for the purchase of 100,000 tons of export oil—the first step in a carefully planned campaign to corner the American export oil market.

Two, however, could play at this game, and the Deutsche Bank was simultaneously negotiating to purchase outright the Gulf Oil Corporation and The Pure Oil Company, Limited (American). These efforts were watched anxiously throughout 1912 by Teagle, who finally reported with relief to Riedemann that the Balkan political situation had so upset the Berlin money market that the Gulf–Deutsche Bank deal would probably not be put through.[33] Teagle opened negotiations with Gulf for its entire supply of refined oil for export.

Gulf, however, was not overeager to be drawn into the Teagle camp, and held out its strategic oil supplies to the highest bidder. It became apparent that the Jersey Company would not be able to get a contract for all of Gulf's export supply, but negotiations were continued in the hope and with the solace that prices which the Deutsche Bank would have to pay were being bid up. The belief was expressed that, as long as the Mellons controlled Gulf, a comprehensive deal could not be made. Jersey Standard, wrote Riedemann to Teagle, would have to be prepared to pay handsomely if it wanted to achieve anything.[34] Meanwhile, both Jersey and the Deutsche Bank bid against each other for uncommitted Romanian petroleum supplies and forced prices there to very high levels —to the vast advantage of Astra-Română, Henri Deterding's Romanian subsidiary.

As the fight for oil supplies progressed through these preliminary stages, Teagle and Riedemann did not neglect other defensive tactics. An appeal was addressed to Ambassador Leishman, in Berlin, stressing the danger implicit in discriminatory attacks on United States interests abroad. To further press the Jersey case, John D. Archbold, a personal friend of Leishman, himself departed for Berlin. Unofficial remonstrances by the American Embassy, however, were ineffective. William H. Libby, who had served Jersey abroad for many years, endeavored to enlist Congressional support for the pending Curtis bill, which provided greater powers for the Executive Department in safeguarding American investments abroad. Libby also addressed a formal appeal to the State Department, asking that the Secretary invoke the retaliatory provisions of the Payne-Aldrich tariff act. In November of 1912 the State Department cabled Leishman to ascertain the facts about the attack on American interests, but no official protests were made, on the excuse that the German government had not yet acted.[35] Altogether, the Jersey Company received scant encouragement or help from the United States government. The failure of strong diplomatic support at this stage of the monopoly question inevitably encouraged Jersey's antagonists to go forward.

Both in Germany and in America increased effort was expended to generate opposition to the monopoly movement. Teagle was anxious to receive a copy of the DAPG pamphlet, which he planned to use at home to stir up popular sentiment, particularly among the crude oil producers.

This sentiment, Teagle told Riedemann, could not but have a good effect in influencing the position of the American government. Teagle also urged Bedford to employ a new publicist to launch a campaign in the American press. In Teagle's opinion it was useless to entrust this matter to J. I. C. Clarke, the publicist already employed by the Jersey Company, for Clarke was too closely identified with Standard Oil. In Germany two new DAPG pamphlets attacking the Deutsche Bank were issued in the fall of 1912. Riedemann called attention to the effects the monopoly bill would have on DAPG employees. The German Petroleum Selling Company returned caustic answers.[36]

Now, clearly, the monopoly conflict was moving into a decisive stage. Action by the Reichstag was imminent, and many believed that the monopoly bill would pass easily. Teagle and Riedemann began to play high trump cards.

Despite initial reports that independent Galician producers and Austrian refiners were behind the monopoly bill, the fact became apparent that one important group of these suppliers had made no commitments. Like the Gulf Company, the Disconto Bank–Deutsche-Erdol–OLEX combine waited for the highest bid. As early as July of 1911, Noellenburg, a director of Deutsche-Erdol, approached Riedemann and offered to negotiate. This opportunity to acquire control of the only remaining independent supplier of the German market (now that Pure Oil had been purchased by Jersey) came prematurely. Riedemann and Teagle at this stage of developments apparently felt no need for guaranteeing Noellenburg a large chunk of the DAPG market in return for his support. By the fall of 1912, however, the situation had changed. Teagle was reluctant, but Riedemann desperately wanted to keep Noellenburg from allying himself with von Gwinner.

On September 10 a general meeting was held in the offices of the Anglo-American Oil Company, Limited, in England. In attendance were Bedford and Archbold of the Jersey Company, Maquinay and Klaare of the American Petroleum Company, Riedemann, and other representatives of Jersey Standard marketing interests in Europe. Noellenburg presented his case, and the Jersey men offered to allow him to sell 35,000 tons of refined products annually in Germany and 5,000 tons in Switzerland. This, wrote Riedemann to Teagle, was not so bad as it appeared, for the Noellenburg agreement really would replace that with the European Petroleum Union and the difference could be figured as the net cost of keeping Noellenburg out of the von Gwinner camp. The end, Riedemann wrote, justified the means. Riedemann believed that Noellenburg would go to the Deutsche Bank, if Jersey Standard did not come to terms with him, and then a systematic and slanderous campaign against DAPG could be expected.[37] To the strenuous objections of both Teagle and F. D. Asche over particular features of the agreement, Riedemann replied that, if the Deutsche-Erdol deal was not closed, he would take no responsibility for ultimate consequences. In the face of the strong and virtually unanimous stand of his foreign managers, Teagle gave in. On November 19, 1912, Riedemann cabled that the contract had been concluded. Riedemann admitted his regret that concessions had to be offered, but concluded philosophically, "We accept this for the sake of the situation."

An unexpected bonus from the Deutsche-Erdol alliance came in the form of information which Noellenburg had gathered as a result of his close connection with the Disconto Bank. The restless promoter of the monopoly, Noellenburg told Riedemann, was, in fact, Henri Deterding himself, who hoped to gain from the monopoly an outlet for his Romanian oil. Through Deterding's wide European banking connections, Noellenburg reported, he was quietly but unceasingly pursuing his plans with the German government. This, of course, was rumor, and there was some conflicting evidence on the point of Deterding's participation in the monopoly affair. More important still, there was evidently a movement afoot late in 1912 to bring the open warfare to an end. Independent hints to this effect emanated from the Jersey Standard camp, from Deterding, and from von Gwinner.

On October 8, 1912, Teagle wrote to Riedemann that just before Archbold had left London, Sir Marcus Samuel (the directing genius of the English Shell interests) had called to hold out the olive branch and suggest a friendly alliance both in Europe and in the Far East between Jersey Standard and the Royal Dutch-Shell interests. Samuel had been anxious for Archbold to meet Deterding and negotiate, but Archbold had refused, saying he did not know enough nor have the time. Sir Marcus had then stated that the monopoly threat was not of a serious nature— a hint, Teagle thought, that the Royal Dutch-Shell was not allied with the Deutsche Bank in its efforts with the German government.[38]

On October 30, Teagle informed Riedemann that he had seen an "important gentleman," who had shown him a cable from von Gwinner. This cable stated that von Gwinner had nothing personally against Standard Oil but that business practices of DAPG had antagonized tens of thousands of wholesalers and retailers. If Jersey Standard was interested in obtaining contracts to supply the monopoly, it should send over a representative. It appeared, Teagle commented, that von Gwinner hoped for an alliance and was looking for a place in Jersey's cellar. After the Teagle conference the "important gentleman," significantly enough, cabled von Gwinner that the Jersey Company was not interested in supplying the monopoly and would probably withdraw from the German market entirely if the monopoly bill passed.[39]

Shortly after this Teagle sailed for Germany, crossing, whether by design or accident, on the same ship with Deterding. Deterding told Teagle that he felt the monopoly bill had an even chance of passing and that he had been approached for a supply contract. This, Deterding stated, he had refused in the belief that after the bill had passed he could dictate his own terms. Deterding asserted that he had seen this whole affair coming five or six years before. The DAPG had been too successful. It was a grave mistake for one company to control so large a percentage of the business. Riedemann, Deterding continued, was one of the cleverest marketers and most efficient managers in the petroleum business, but he had overlooked the sentimental side of the question and now should not be surprised that disgruntled competitors like von Gwinner were trying to appropriate what had been created. Deterding then sounded out Teagle with the remark that it would be for the best interests of both their companies to control competition in Europe and the Far East by some friendly understanding. Teagle was noncommittal and commented later to Bedford that apparently Deterding was trying to give the impression that he held the trump card for monopoly: if he made a supply contract, the bill would pass; if not, the bill would fail.[40]

That Teagle failed to swallow the tempting bait held out both by von Gwinner and by the Royal Dutch-Shell was probably attributable to the fact that he already had conceived an idea along the same lines and possibly wished to preserve the initiative in any grand combine of all conflicting interests. His specific suggestion was to form a European holding company, nonvoting shares in which should be widely distributed where they would do the most good among influential Europeans and Jersey customers. The voting control, vested in a small issue of preferred stock, would be retained by a small and friendly group. This, Teagle pointed out, was the way Royal Dutch did it. The holding company would take over the stock of all Jersey companies in Europe, and then offer to take over all the Deutsche Bank interests, and perhaps the Deutsche-Erdol as well.[41]

None of these grand plans, however, came to pass. It may be that each of the parties involved thought that it could win a victory without compromise. The battle went on.

Riedemann, in order to consolidate still further Jersey Standard's advantage in having tied up by contract or purchase much of the oil von Gwinner needed to win his fight, now wished to accept a German government offer whereby the company would guarantee to supply a percentage of the nation's demands at a fixed price for ten years. This, Teagle exploded, was going too far! In a masterly analysis he pointed out to the directors of the DAPG the dangers of such a long-range contract in the dynamic petroleum industry. Teagle's exposition was sheer prophecy, as paragraph by paragraph he suggested what might be expected to happen in the future to world demand for refined products. His concluding phrases expressed the danger of allowing local situations to befog the total operational plan:[42]

Suppose therefore the worst happens, and the proposed Bill is passed. While we will probably suffer a not inconsiderable loss in our German investment, does it necessarily follow that there will be a curtailment of the Refined Oil output of the Standard Oil Co. in New Jersey? This is the all-important question to be answered, and if it is answered in the negative, i.e., that the Refined Oil output of the Standard Oil Co., New Jersey, will not be materially affected by their forced withdrawal from the German market, then why should we now guarantee in view of all of the uncertainties in connection with the Petroleum business to supply the entire German demand for a period of 10 (ten) years at a fixed price of 7 cents a gal.?

In his great concern over this issue Teagle had, in point of fact, done his German associate a considerable injustice. In replying to Teagle's forceful memorandum Riedemann patiently explained that Teagle had misunderstood. Riedemann had not the slightest intention that such a contract would ever actually be concluded with the German government. He had included provisions which would make the contract completely unsatisfactory to the backers of the monopoly bill. The contract, therefore, would be opposed by them, and the government would be totally unable to accept the proffered terms. The whole proposal, in short, was merely intended for propaganda purposes. At that, Teagle wrote in an admiring note to Riedemann, it might have been accepted![43]

Meanwhile the monopoly bill was published, and the conflict neared a climax. Just before leaving America on a business trip to Europe, Teagle was advised by cable not to be seen in Berlin with Riedemann. He registered at his hotel under the name of W. A. Hoskins, but despite this precaution his movements and those of Riedemann appear to have been under surveillance. A last-minute plan was drawn up to form a company in England to which the DAPG tankers could be transferred, should the monopoly bill pass. Sentiment in Germany, however, seemed suddenly to have shifted, and it was rumored that the bill was doomed to failure. Evidence that von Gwinner was desperate lay in an offer he made through a member of the Reichstag to Riedemann. Von Gwinner offered Riedemann a contract for his services at 250,000 reichsmarks annually for life if Riedemann would withdraw from the DAPG. The German financial press began to taunt von Gwinner with having fatally underestimated the strength and fighting capacity of "Mr. Rockefeller's corporation."[44]

The action now moved entirely into the political arena, where no person could surely predict what might happen. The Centrum Party, representing the Catholic minority group in Germany, had strongly opposed the bill from the beginning. It was alleged that the elder Riedemann was a strong financial backer of the Centrum; whether this was true or not, the party was opposed to monopoly and anxious to avoid displeasing the United States. The Social Democratic Party, the National Liberal Party, the Conservative Party, and the Liberal Party were not firm in their stand, but in general tended to favor the monopoly proposal. Outwardly, the bill seemed to have a clear majority backing in the Reichstag. Jealousies and rival political ambitions, however, were intermeshed in the main issue to a completely inextricable extent.[45]

While the bill was in committee the Centrum Party skillfully exploited a divergence among the other parties over the details of the monopoly. Clauses were introduced which soon had the various interests supporting the bill at swords' points. It became apparent, too, that, though a majority of the Reichstag members had initially favored monopoly in some form, a majority also favored cutting out the none-too-popular Deutsche Bank as manager of the monopoly and using any profits the monopoly might make for the government to reduce the price of oil. This being the case, both the government and the Deutsche Bank could be expected to lose their incentive to press for passage.[46]

Riedemann was approached by representatives of the various parties and asked why, if the bill passed, Standard should refuse to sell and deliver to the monopoly. Riedemann avoided making a direct commitment, but stated his "opinion" that he could well understand that a concern like Standard Oil would make it a point of principle to fight a monopoly which had been introduced against its interest. The precedent thus set in Germany, Riedemann told his questioners, would be a bad one throughout the world. These informal statements of Riedemann's constituted, to all practical intents and purposes, a direct and timely warning that if the bill passed Jersey Standard would withhold its supplies from the German petroleum market. Contemporary sentiment in Berlin apparently did not underestimate the potency of these warnings. "We say here in Germany," one informed observer remarked at the time, "that the three greatest organizations in the world are our army, the Roman Catholic Church, and the Standard Oil Company."[47]

Riedemann's private opinion early in 1913 was that because of internal politics the monopoly bill had virtually ceased to be a threat. The Centrum continued its determined program of resistance, the backers of the bill continued to disagree among themselves, and on February 1, 1913, Riedemann informed Teagle that the bill in its original form had been defeated in the Reichstag and sent back into committee for redrafting.[48] Scarcely taking time to congratulate each other, Teagle and Riedemann rushed to consolidate their victory and to meet new threats.

Oil supply was still the crucial issue, and von Gwinner, after his initial defeat in the Reichstag, now redoubled his efforts to sign up suppliers. He directed his energies at concluding a contract for Gulf's export oil, and negotiations also continued for the outright purchase of Gulf by the Deutsche Bank, at a reputed price of $25,000,000 or more. Teagle learned that a Gulf man had sailed for Germany, and he advised Riedemann that if someone watched his movements, observed what parties called on him, and whom he visited, it might be learned whether the Gulf had disposed of its business to European capital. Evidently Gulf now favored the monopoly, feeling, like Deterding, that if the bill was finally passed the company could dictate its own prices. Von Gwinner offered Gulf a ten-year supply contract on favorable terms. Riedemann hoped, through the friendship with the Gulf representative of one of Jersey's European agents (John G. Lamont, formerly general European agent of Pure Oil), to prevent the deal. Three days after Riedemann had expressed this hope to Teagle, Lamont reported that he had closed a contract with Gulf for 100,000 tons of refined products annually.[49] Once again, it appeared, von Gwinner had been thwarted by Jersey's superior bargaining power and diplomacy.

By mid-1913, while the monopoly bill was in committee for redrafting, the Jersey Company was able to contract for the export oil of The Texas Company. Negotiations were also well along for the entire 1914 export supply of Magnolia. Contracts had already been signed tying up Tide Water's export supplies. "This," wrote Teagle to Lamont, "would seem to leave comparatively small quantities of oil available during 1914 to be bought up if the German monopoly should be created." The Gulf Oil Corporation, moreover, had fallen out with von Gwinner because the latter had made a small purchase in 1913 from its rival, Magnolia. This same purchase also caused Riedemann to express annoyance; but Teagle, in a statement which had a double interest in view of the charges being aired in the Magnolia suit in Texas, remarked that the Jersey Company had "no interest whatsoever in Magnolia and knew nothing about their export sales." Neither Folger nor Archbold, both large Magnolia stockholders, had ever mentioned the matter.[50]

Having been defeated in his effort to get substantial contracts with these important suppliers, von Gwinner, in a measure of desperation, turned to the small independent refiners in the United States. Late in 1912 Teagle had ridiculed the idea that the offers of these refiners could be taken seriously; yet, in order to arm Riedemann against the propaganda value of such claims, Teagle forwarded careful and conclusive figures showing that the total amount of oil available from these sources could not conceivably supply the German market.

C. D. Chamberlin, secretary of the National Petroleum Association, appeared to be the spokesman for some of these independents. He traveled to Germany, not in his capacity as secretary of the Association but as representative of three of the member companies. In Germany, Riedemann reported, Chamberlin assured proponents of the monopoly bill that undoubtedly the pipelines in the United States would be declared common carriers. He created among the Reichstag members (most of whom had only hazy ideas of pipelines anyhow) the opinion that when the common carrier decision was promulgated every inland refinery would be able to ship export kerosene through the lines. Chamberlin also sent a "letter of information" to the members of the National Petroleum Association strongly urging them to support the German monopoly bill. In 1914 Chamberlin was still lobbying for the bill. Teagle reported to Archbold that Chamberlin had been retained by the Union Petroleum Company, which purchased American crude for European markets and a majority interest in which was owned by the Deutsche Bank.[51]

Late in 1913 negotiations between the Deutsche Bank and the Western Refiners Association, a group of Kansas and Oklahoma refiners, were also under way. Von Gwinner had dispatched his representative, von Stauss, to talk with these independents. The Union Petroleum Company was actively endeavoring, at the same time, to show the Association and its individual members that large markets would be open if the monopoly bill passed. The Association was asked to write to German government officials, furnishing the most optimistic figures possible as to available export supplies.[52]

Once again Teagle, with a magnificent fund and command of statistical information, furnished Riedemann with facts which could be used to discredit completely any claim von Gwinner might make as a result of the transactions of his agent in America. Teagle also recommended that the Jersey Company conclude a purchase contract with members of the Association. This move was primarily inspired by a desire to wean this group of independents away from the Deutsche Bank camp, but Teagle was not unmindful of the need for strengthening Jersey's standing in the domestic industry. Conditions among the small refiners in Oklahoma and Kansas were very bad, Teagle reported. "If this oil is not purchased by the Standard Oil Company, New Jersey, a good many of these refiners will have to shut down."[53]

Through these months in 1913 and early 1914, while the monopoly bill was being thrashed about in committee and Teagle was successfully defeating von Gwinner's efforts to acquire supply contracts, Riedemann, too, was active, and further appeals had been addressed to Washington for diplomatic aid.

Riedemann left no stone unturned in his effort to convince influential Germans of the danger of a break with Standard Oil. Admiral Rampoldt, of the Kaiserlich Automobile Club, approached Riedemann and asked for a twelve-month contract to supply the club's needs. Riedemann told Rampoldt that this was impossible under existing conditions, and should the monopoly bill pass, DAPG's imports of benzine and naphtha would probably be cut off. On hearing this the Admiral exclaimed, "But that is terrible, because then we are at the mercy of Mr. Deterding!" Riedemann gave this same answer to a retired German Army general representing the Military Aero Club, confiding with some satisfaction to Teagle that this certainly would at once be reported to "headquarters" and would create a great impression there.[54]

In April, 1914, a formal and detailed memorandum was presented by Jersey to the United States State Department, setting forth the substance of the monopoly threat as then constituted.[55] This memorandum pointed out that total indemnities, which would be paid for DAPG's wholesale kerosene marketing facilities if the monopoly bill passed, would amount to only $3,556,000. Jersey Standard claimed its business in Germany was worth $48,000,000. Even valuing the assets on the most conservative possible basis, it was obvious that the monopoly bill represented virtual confiscation of Jersey Standard property.

The bill had actually been drawn in a highly adroit manner so as not only to cause the utter dismemberment of DAPG properties but also to exclude from any indemnification whatsoever substantial segments of those properties. DAPG was also penalized by the skillful wording of the bill for its minimization of the tax burden over the preceding years. Indemnification for loss of business (as contrasted to loss of physical properties) was to be made only to those firms which had earned a net profit of 4 per cent or more on their capital. Determination of earnings was to be arrived at by examination of the taxes paid on dividends. The capital structure of the DAPG consisted of 9,000,000 reichsmarks in shares, 21,000,000 reichsmarks in share warrants, and 30,000,000 reichsmarks in debenture bonds. Since dividends on share warrants and interest on bonds were not taxable in Germany, the DAPG could report only the three-twentieths of its dividends which was evidenced by the taxes paid on the 9,000,000 reichsmark issue of shares. The salt rubbed into this particular wound consisted of the fact that no protest to the German government could be made, for, in Teagle's own words, "a divulging of the amount of DAPG's profits would be dangerous."[56]

In Berlin Ambassador Leishman had been replaced by his Democratic successor, James W. Gerard. Teagle visited Gerard and found him "sympathetic." He was not at all surprised, Gerard told Teagle, at the lack of action by the Taft administration, but the new administration was made up of men of different caliber. Teagle confided to Riedemann that it appeared to him that the Democrats were willing to do more for Jersey Standard than their predecessors, "who were supposed to be our friends." Gerard suggested that Teagle should see President Wilson, explain Jersey's sincere desire to co-operate with the President in carrying out his current Mexican policy, and then ask him the pointed question whether, now that the Standard Oil had in every particular carried out the dissolution decree, he would not promise the company the entire support of his administration. Before seeing the President, Gerard recommended, Teagle should first approach Colonel House and obtain his influence.[57]

In this interview with Gerard, Teagle made one of his highly infrequent slips. Once more the legalistic distinctions in which Jersey men sometimes took refuge redounded to their embarrassment. Gerard asked Teagle point-blank whether Jersey Standard did not own the stock of the Pure Oil Company in Germany. Teagle replied that Jersey did not. A week later Teagle learned to his great surprise that the German government knew of the Pure Oil deal and had actually published a statement that the Pure Oil Company was owned by Jersey Standard. After consulting with his European managers, Teagle then wrote Gerard saying that, whereas his previous statement had been "correct in every particular," he felt it was desirable in confidence to advise him of the entire situation. He then related all the particulars of the indirect ownership of Pure Oil and concluded his note with the expressed desire to supply Gerard with any other information in the matter that Gerard might wish.[58]

Before Teagle could see what the Democratic administration in Washington was going to do for the company, however, the entire monopoly question took a new turn. An open break was reported to have occurred between Deterding and von Gwinner over the marketing of Romanian gasoline in Germany. Deterding, it appeared, had been using his influence to have the monopoly bill cover gasoline as well as kerosene.[59] Here was a fragmentary but tremendously interesting bit of evidence that Deterding had been supporting the bill the whole time. The real part played by the Royal Dutch-Shell leader in the German monopoly incident, however, remains a mystery to this day.

More important than the reported Deterding–von Gwinner rift, however, was a rather abrupt shift in the attitude of the German government. Gerard, in his autobiography, states that this shift was a result of a conference he held with the German Chancellor. At this conference Gerard indicated that the United States government would insist that Jersey Standard receive full indemnification for its properties, including a very large sum to cover "Goodwill." When he advanced this claim, the Chancellor said, in astonishment, "You don't mean to say that President Wilson and Secretary Bryan would do anything for the Standard Oil Company!" Gerard replied that his instructions as well as his principles dictated that he give all American citizens equal protection, whether or not they were supporters of the Wilson administration.[60]

Gerard's intervention may well have been a factor of large importance in the situation, but there were other decisive considerations. Evidence in Jersey Standard records indicates that it was in or about February of 1913 that the German War Ministry became sufficiently concerned with petroleum supplies for war to engage in the controversy. Heretofore military considerations, though mentioned, had not actually been a major issue. Party politics and domestic issues had been the dominant motives in the political background, but the bill which was redrafted after the February, 1913, defeat definitely reflected the concern of the War Ministry.[61] On April 10, 1913, Riedemann wrote to Teagle that now one of the principal factors involved in the monopoly controversy was that the German government wanted, in case of war, to be independent of outside petroleum supplies for at least a year. Therefore, if the monopoly bill was to be withdrawn, Riedemann stated, it was imperative that the Minister of War be satisfied that DAPG would keep a sufficient stock of petroleum supplies on hand. Riedemann explained to the War Ministry that the shortage of tankers prevented DAPG from making any such guarantee at the time, but that a large stock of gasoline might, with proper compensation from the government, be collected in about two years' time. Negotiations were opened between Riedemann and the German government which contemplated the annual maintenance by DAPG for a period of five years of a stock of from 33,000 to 58,000 tons of gasoline.[62]

This was the final blow to the monopoly bill. Apparently through fear that Jersey Standard would withhold its supplies if the monopoly bill passed, the German government unofficially withdrew its support. This action, coupled with the continued effective opposition of the Centrum Party and the general inability of the supporters of the monopoly proposal to agree on details, made it apparent that the bill could no longer hope to gain a majority in the Reichstag. Late in May of 1914 the government caused the Reichstag to be dissolved. Riedemann reported that this action had been taken in order to avoid the further embarrassing consideration of what obviously had become a lost and largely unlamented cause. Jersey Standard had triumphed over what may have been the most powerful coalition of international petroleum interests the world had seen to that date. The fallacy of the belief that the dissolution decree had impaired the company's great economic and political strength stood dramatically revealed.

Chapter 9

Jersey Standard at War

FOR ALMOST three years Jersey Standard officers and directors surveyed the conflagration in Europe—not with aloofness, but with a fervent hope that, while flames might blister the fringes, the heart and center of the Jersey enterprise would escape the searing. Moving, however, with a foresight and perspicuity not to be found everywhere in America, Jersey men prepared for the worst and were ready in a substantial degree when it came.

DESECRATION OF THE SEA LANES

The uncertainty of Jersey officials regarding the fate of the DAPG tanker *Leda,* reportedly en route through British waters when war was declared in 1914, was soon removed. Dispatches received from the United States Consulate at Bermuda related that this ship had been seized as a prize of war by the British cruiser *Suffolk* and was being held in the custody of the British government pending prize-court proceedings. To obtain the release of the vessel the Jersey Company promptly engaged the consulting services of John Bassett Moore, distinguished State Department adviser, member of the Permanent Court of The Hague, and professor of international law and diplomacy at Columbia University. There was high indignation at 26 Broadway. DAPG tankers were Jersey Standard property, and President Wilson had proclaimed American neutrality before the martial world. Britain and Germany had declared petroleum products to be conditional contraband of war, but the right of neutral ships to engage in commerce outside the periphery of blockade was clearly recognized in the annals of international law.

Concern over the *Leda* incident was almost immediately swallowed up in greater fears and uncertainties. Indeed, the whole foundation of the international legal structure trembled in the months that followed. The bulk of the DAPG fleet, of course, came safely under American registry, following the transfers in 1914 and 1915. In the fall of 1915 the German government had forbidden further transfers of merchant tonnage to non-German subjects, but by the time this law had become effective there were only eight serviceable DAPG tankers still in German ports. Since the British blockade had throttled German sea commerce, these vessels presumably would remain safely berthed for the duration of the war. The Jersey Company's new *John D. Rockefeller,* however, was shortly seized en route to Copenhagen by British cruisers and detained at Kirkwall, in the Orkney Islands.[1] Seven of the eight tankers belonging to the Dutch affiliate, the American Petroleum Company, also were seized by the British. All these Dutch tankers had been destined for Belgian or Dutch ports, and the detention precipitated acute petroleum shortages in the Low Countries. Many other Jersey Standard vessels, exclusively engaged in supplying neutral nations, were detained for varying periods or were halted and searched by British naval forces. These acts, Professor Moore stated, constituted an interference with the rights of neutral trade of a very substantial and in some respects unprecedented nature. "It is obvious," he concluded, "that the trade of the United States with Europe is placed in serious jeopardy."[2]

Meanwhile, the precious importance of petroleum fuel was being revealed on the battle lines. Marshal von Kluck's legions, transported and supplied by a strategic network of rail lines, were threatening Paris when General Galliani commandeered the taxicabs and lorries of the city to rush a fresh army to the front, smashing von Kluck's flank and enabling Marshal Joffre to halt the Germans at the Marne and save the city. British government attitudes toward the detained tankers changed as the Allied need for petroleum supplies became evident and increasingly desperate. The *Rockefeller* and the Dutch tankers were eventually released. In November of 1914 the Supreme Court in Bermuda had ruled that the *Leda* was enemy property and subject to confiscation, but a year later this ship, too, was released.[3] By 1916 it was clear that Jersey Standard's marine operations as then conducted had come to enjoy the tacit sanction of the British Admiralty. American aid and American oil were becoming vital to Allied victory.

The German War Ministry was not slow to grasp this fact. At seven o'clock on the morning of December 2, 1916, the S.S. *Palacine,* an Imperial Oil Company vessel, unarmed and loaded with Jersey products, was nosing into the approaches of the English Channel. The sea was moderate, but a haze prevented the uneasy skipper of the ship from identifying a low-lying craft which was hanging off in the mists on the port quarter. Just as the sun broke through the haze and the men on the *Palacine* were able to identify their stalker, the U-boat opened fire, heading across the bow of the *Palacine* and coming around in a sweep to starboard. The helpless ship was hastily abandoned, and the crew watched from their boats as men from the submarine carried bombs aboard the ship and sank it.[4]

Other Jersey Standard vessels had been accosted earlier in the war by German U-boats. The tanker *Cushing* had even been attacked by a German aircraft in the opening months of the war—one of the first instances of the dropping of bombs by aircraft on a vessel. These had been incidents of war, not part of a calculated campaign of destruction. In January of 1917, however, Germany unleashed its U-boat pack, and unrestricted submarine warfare became a planned reality. A month later the Jersey Company tanker *Healdton,* unarmed and loaded, was proceeding twenty-five miles north of Terschilding, Holland, when it was struck without warning by two torpedoes. The vessel took fire and sank with heavy casualties. American neutrality was now conjectural, and the Jersey Company felt that it was at war.[5]

As early as February of 1917 President Wilson had announced the right of merchant vessels to arm in self-defense, and on March 12 a bill to that effect had been passed by Congress. The Jersey Company promptly began to arm its vessels and make berthing alterations to accommodate 14-man Navy armed-guard crews. There was much correspondence with the Navy Department about camouflaging, smokeless fuel, and smoke-screen protection. Jersey captains received instructions about zigzagging and other precautionary navigational tactics to be pursued in dangerous waters. Wireless equipment was installed on those tankers which did not already have such facilities, and skilled operators were hired from the Marconi Company at a stipulated monthly rate. The declaration of war on Germany by the United States on April 6, 1917, was rumored in advance. A few days earlier Jersey's Foreign Shipping Department had dispatched instructions to vessels at sea, advising them of the imminence of open hostilities and instructing them to seek neutral ports. Despite all these precautions the Jersey Company lost six vessels between May and September, 1917: the *Petrolite, Platuria, Moreni, John D. Archbold, Motano,* and *Campana.* The *Archbold* was one of the largest tankers then in service. In these disasters thirty-three men were reported dead or missing. In this same period Imperial lost the *Retlaw* and the American Petroleum Company lost four of its eight tankers.[6]

PETROLEUM CRISIS

The U-boat campaign assumed disastrous proportions for the Allied cause. By the end of 1917, sinkings exceeded by some 2,500,000 tons the amount of new shipping launched. The convoy system inaugurated in 1917 reduced the submarine menace, but it increased the passage time of transatlantic tankers by five days. Romanian and Galician sources of petroleum supply were in German hands, and fuel oil stocks of the Allies in Europe were so low that it appeared that part of the British fleet must be demobilized. In France, the association of companies known as the French Refiners had guaranteed to supply the government's petroleum needs. The Refiners, however, had not been successful. The French war department began to push the Refiners, but there was difficulty in obtaining tankers. "We must have oil," declared Marshal Foch, "or we shall lose the war." A consortium at length was formed of the principal French distributors, who associated themselves in a limited liability company and, under strict regulation, entered into a new contract to supply the French government. Urgent appeals for help were directed by the British and French governments to Washington, and the United States government and the American oil industry moved together to meet the critical situation more effectively.[7]

In September of 1916 the United States Shipping Board had been established to assist in creating a naval auxiliary, a naval reserve, and a merchant marine adequate to meet the necessities of the day. The Board received complete authority to regulate the disposition of privately owned vessels and to place under direct government requisition such vessels as were needed.[8]

In answer to appeals for additional tanker tonnage, American oil companies, including Jersey Standard, volunteered a total of fifteen vessels, chartering them, under direction of the Shipping Board, to various Allied governments at about half the existing market rate. Three Jersey Company ships, one of which (the *John D. Archbold*) was, however, sunk on its first passage, provided the principal link between the French market and American supplies; in 1917 and 1918 approximately 47 per cent of all petroleum products imported into France came from Jersey Standard.

The Jersey organization marshaled its resources in a magnificent productive effort, and Jersey refineries began to pour forth the fuel oil and gasoline so urgently needed. As the flow of petroleum products grew, the strain upon the transportation network became increasingly acute. In addition to the tonnage required for the movement of crude oil to the refineries and refined products to the war zones, tankers had to be allocated for indirect war purposes. A large amount of tonnage was engaged in supplying fuel oil to the Chilean nitrate companies and in transporting molasses needed in the production of alcohol. Fuel oil requirements of the British Admiralty, which had at first been met by Gulf Coast refineries, including the Baton Rouge plant of Louisiana Standard, expanded so rapidly that the East Coast refineries were forced to change manufacturing procedures substantially in order to enlarge their limited output of this product. Tank-car shipments of fuel oil were made between points as widely separated as Oklahoma and Montreal, and the delivery of petroleum products at a great number of ports lacking adequate storage and handling facilities created difficulties and delay. Tank steamers were also placed in coastwise service to carry fuel oil from Gulf ports to more accessible points of supply at New York, Philadelphia, and Halifax. Jersey Standard's coastwise shipments of this nature tripled between 1917 and 1918. Total exports of gasoline from Jersey and Louisiana Standard refineries showed an increase over the preceding year of 14 per cent in 1917 and 33 per cent in 1918. Fuel oil exports leaped 221 per cent in 1917 and another 81 per cent in 1918. Fuel oil supplied by Jersey Standard to the United States Navy from Atlantic ports totaled 4,656 barrels in July of 1917. In May of 1918 the figure was 368,883 barrels.[9]

The rapid expansion in refined output, in turn, brought occasional complaints about the quality of products. The irate quartermaster of the transport *Yosemite* reported that the fuel oil supplied was dirty, poor-burning, and so smoky that it called the ship to the attention of all submarines within a twenty-mile radius. Such deficiencies were unfortunate, but they probably were unavoidable in the press for higher output. Inadequate cleaning of tankers was a common cause of excessive impurities in the fuel supplies. Complaints about American gasoline arose out of the fact that this fuel conformed to United States Navy specifications, and as such was not well suited for use in British motor lorries. Quality failings and specification difficulties were gradually corrected.[10]

The Jersey Company's tanker fleet continued to expand and to maintain its pre-eminent position among the tanker fleets of the world. Despite the fact that eight ships had been stricken from the register in this fateful year, the ten tankers launched in 1917 still left the company with a total of forty ocean-going vessels. In 1918 nine more vessels were lost by enemy action. Included among these were the *O. B. Jennings* and the

William Rockefeller. Both these American-built tankers were large (14,900 and 10,400 deadweight tons, respectively) and both were new. In 1918, however, nine tankers were launched. These vessels, constructed at high cost in American yards, were taken over by the War Shipping Board even before they had been completed.

FLEET REGULATION AND INSURANCE

The powers of the War Shipping Board had been steadily enlarged and clarified since its formation, and all Jersey Standard's marine operations came under strict regulation. Even before America's entry into the war, the company had been forced to abandon all efforts to supply its prewar markets in Switzerland, Algeria, Tunis, and Malta, for neither the German nor the British government could or would guarantee safe passage to these points. In April of 1917 the company was forbidden to charter any of its vessels to foreign persons or corporations without the prior approval of the Shipping Board. This interdict, while clearly in the best interests of a co-ordinated war effort, caused hardships among those affiliates in neutral countries which looked to the parent company for transportation aid. The British Admiralty, moreover, was adamant in its stand that neutral countries must supply their own needs only with vessels of their own flag. A plan to charter two Norwegian tankers to meet the critical needs of Det Danske, the Danish affiliate, was thereby thwarted.[11]

The requisitioning of private vessels by the War Shipping Board proceeded apace. By the middle of March, 1918, all of the Jersey Company's fleet except the *El Capitan* and six auxiliary motorships had been requisitioned by the government. By this process the Shipping Board assumed absolute control over the disposition of the vessels and took full responsibility for damage and loss. Some of these requisitioned tankers were returned to Jersey Standard at such times as they could be spared, and the company used them for such purposes as it saw fit, subject always to Shipping Board approval. Other ships were returned for the company to use for specific purposes, such as the coastwise transportation of fuel oil. With the approval of the Shipping Board, Jersey Standard also chartered tankers as the need arose to the Italian High Commission, the French High Commission, and the British Shipping Controller.[12]

All outstanding contracts for new construction which had been entered into by the Jersey Company with various American shipbuilding firms were also brought under the control of the War Shipping Board, which asserted and exercised its authority to modify the original terms. In February of 1918 the Shipping Board notified the Jersey Company that it proposed to put all contracts on a basis of cost plus $10 per ton, since the shipbuilders, because of rapidly rising building costs, stood to lose heavily on the original contractual terms. The Shipping Board also proposed to eliminate all penalties for delays in fulfilling the contracts. David T. Warden and F. D. Asche objected strenuously. If the shipbuilders were threatened with loss, that was all part of the game. Jersey Standard itself had always stood by its contracts, good or bad. The views of the Shipping Board, nevertheless, prevailed, and the company had to pay nearly double the original contract price. All things considered, this was only fair, though the reluctance of Asche and Warden to forfeit a favorable bargain was understandable.[13]

Much of this business with the government was characterized by confusion and uncertainty. Jersey Company officials, imbued with the typically intense patriotism of the day, showed patience and fortitude. The company stood willing to do its part and more than its part, but federal policy fluctuated from week to week and the loose threads of federal administration were tangled. The good intentions of government agencies frequently were submerged in the ignorance, inexperience, and confusion of the times. War-risk insurance was a case in point.

Early in 1914 the United States Bureau of War Risk Insurance was created to facilitate commerce by extending insurance protection beyond that offered by private underwriting firms. The contemplated purpose was a sound one. At the outbreak of the war the American insurance market was inadequate and unwilling to meet the demands placed upon it. Jersey Standard, for example, was totally unable, in 1914, to obtain adequate insurance coverage on tankers destined for European ports. It soon appeared, however, that in practice the War Risk Bureau, while going further than the private underwriters, was not willing to go far enough. Bureau rates quoted on a voyage of the *John D. Rockefeller* to Copenhagen in September of 1914 ranged up to 5 per cent for $250,000. Jersey men considered this rate prohibitive and the coverage inadequate. No private American underwriter, however, would extend more than $50,000 coverage, and this at 3 per cent. By 1917 the inadequacy of the insurance market had not been relieved. Private underwriters still would not extend satisfactory coverage, even at the prohibitive market rates prevailing. Because of the U-boat campaign the rates quoted by the War Risk Bureau were also very high. In this year, for example, government insurance on vessels destined for Mediterranean ports ranged up to 10 per cent per voyage, and up to 14 per cent on limited coverage for European ports. To cover the difference between the valuations accepted by the Bureau and the valuations Jersey Standard placed upon its vessels would have cost between 15 and 20 per cent. In July of 1917 the War Risk Bureau raised its coverage valuations to more satisfactory levels, but the company still deemed it conservative to establish a war-risk reserve account of its own to cover discrepancies between government valuation and company figures.[14]

With the high risks went high profits for those companies fortunate enough to own tanker fleets. Jersey Standard's marine transportation earnings burgeoned from $220,000 in 1914 to $10,637,000 in 1918 and were destined to go twice as high in post-Armistice months. A clue to the source of these earnings is contained in the Shipping Board rates on tankers, which in 1918 specified charges of $40 per ton from North Atlantic ports to the United Kingdom and $45 per ton from Gulf ports to the same destination. Jersey figures showed that operating costs were $17 and $23 per ton from Atlantic and Gulf ports, respectively. War-risk insurance added $9 more per ton from both points, leaving a profit per ton of $14 from Atlantic ports and $13 from Gulf ports.[15]

Because of the large profits that were being piled up in marine transportation at this time, all the Jersey Company's stricken-vessel accounts showed heavy credit balances when they were closed. The *Moreni*, for example, which was sunk on June 12, 1917, was valued at $1,200,000 on the books. The *Moreni's* account, charged with the cost of the ship and credited with the insurance collection and with past earnings, showed a credit balance of $1,781,496.81. Some of this profit, of course, would be consumed in procuring a new vessel at the high replacement costs prevailing. In certain instances, however, the settlements received made some provision for the inflated replacement market. For the *William Rockefeller,* sunk while being operated by the Navy, Jersey Standard received $3,308,000. The valuation placed on this ship by the company was $2,800,000. The *Walter Jennings*, which was under charter to the British Admiralty when sunk, was valued at $3,000,000; the company received from the Admiralty the total of $4,500,000.[16]

Despite such settlements, the company reported in 1919 that tanker losses had totaled $5,924,000.[17] This statement indicates that total insurance settlements were inadequate to cover inflated replacement valuations, but if consideration is also given to high war profits earned, Jersey's actual monetary losses on the sunken vessels were probably far from severe. The important point, however, is not the financial aspect of tanker operations, but rather the highly effective and possibly indispensable contribution made to the Allied cause by the Foreign Shipping Department and all its employees in these harrowing months.

HOME FRONT AND ENEMY AFFILIATES

The sea lanes were not, of course, the only battle fronts for Jersey Standard, nor did the multiple complexities of tanker operations under federal supervision provide the only anxieties. The gasoline season of 1917 closed with virtually no stocks on hand at the refineries. A coal shortage, precipitated by nationwide railroad strikes, threw a heavy burden upon petroleum fuels and illuminants just at the time when every other demand upon the petroleum industry was at its maximum. Then blizzards and frigid temperatures ushered in the terrible winter of 1917-1918. Average tank-car mileage decreased from 25 miles per day to 15, and when the blast of winter reached full force rail traffic virtually ceased to move at all. Canals, harbors, and internal waterways were locked in ice, bringing water-borne deliveries to a standstill. The Marketing Department tried desperately to supply a clamorous demand for oil heaters and for kerosene. For months company motor trucks and tank wagons carted oil day and night to relieve suffering communities. Upon the Jersey and Louisiana refineries fell not only the smothering burden of supplying a substantial share of the military petroleum requirements of the United States and its Allies at a time when such demands were at a peak, but also the acute necessity for serving greatly increased domestic demands for fuel and illuminants. These responsibilities largely were met, despite the fact that by July of 1918 the Jersey Company and its affiliates had lost to the armed forces a total of 3,047 employees.[18]

Since statistical measures of Jersey Standard's performance in the various areas of operation during the war years are presented in detail in other chapters, only illustrative figures need be noted here. Despite the loss of the Romāno-Americana installations, crude oil run in all refineries of the Jersey Company and its foreign and domestic affiliates was 28 per cent higher in 1918 than it had been in 1916. Export deliveries by Jersey Standard refineries in the United States (including the Baton Rouge plant) increased 15 per cent between 1916 and 1918, notwithstanding the loss of important foreign markets and the derangement of foreign trade generally. Deliveries of these same refineries to the home trade increased 48 per cent over the period.

These had not been merely quantitative increases, for demand had changed as well as grown. In 1916 about 22 per cent of deliveries by Jersey's refineries in the United States had consisted of gasoline; by 1918 the proportion had risen to 30 per cent. Fuel oil increased over the period from approximately 11 to 28 per cent of total deliveries, while kerosene declined in the face of new demands from 34 to 24 per cent of total. These alterations called forth substantial and far from facile shifts in refining techniques and installations. The relative and absolute increase in gasoline output was achieved primarily through the use of Indiana Standard's Burton-Humphreys cracking process. Facilities were also adapted to the manufacture of a more volatile gasoline to meet military specifications for aviation fuel, and additional stills were set up to run Mexican crude to fuel oil. By the end of 1918 these Jersey refineries were turning out a 50 per cent larger number of barrels of refined products than in 1914, though to achieve this result the investment in plant had been more than doubled.[19]

In Canada the new refineries built by Imperial came into operation, and the refined output of that company nearly quadrupled between 1914 and 1918. Ships of the Allied navies were fueled and lubricated at Halifax, St. John, Sidney, Glacé Bay, Quebec, and Montreal, and petroleum cargoes were dispatched to Europe and Britain from these ports. In France the inactive La Pallice refinery of the Bedford Petroleum Company was utilized by the French government in manufacturing explosives, while tankage there was placed at the disposal of the American Expeditionary Forces. Affiliated refineries in Peru, Argentina, and Havana were throttled by lack of transport facilities, but the Tampico plant expanded its output of precious fuel oil to the full extent of existing manufacturing facilities. Every segment of the wide-flung Jersey Standard organization responded to the great demands of the time, and patriotic fervor was much in evidence at all operating levels.

Meanwhile, Jersey directors anxiously sought news of the foreign affiliates in enemy territory. Through roundabout channels scraps of information about the DAPG and Româno-Americana found their way to 26 Broadway and there were pieced together to form a reasonably accurate picture of events behind the enemy lines. It was not until the cessation of hostilities that all the facts were ascertained. The attitude of Jersey men toward these two companies was philosophical but far from passive. Whatever could be done to safeguard the company's property in Germany and in Romania was done, but the directors were resigned to the possible complete loss of their investments in enemy lands or, at best, to the utilization of those assets in the war against the Allies. A long-range viewpoint was manifest at 26 Broadway. The American public generally and even many persons in informed government circles saw only the immediate necessities of war; leaders in the international oil industry, however, constantly and anxiously looked beyond the cessation of hostilities, closely following and attempting to influence wartime economic policies of the Allies and of the Central Powers which might have important repercussions on the postwar petroleum trade. The governments of Britain, Holland, and France all were conscious of the economic future and did not spurn such opportunities as presented themselves to advance the interests of their nationals. Rampant nationalism was held in check, however, as long as the Kaiser's armies remained in the field.

For two years after the outbreak of hostilities in 1914 Walter Teagle was able to follow closely the fate of the DAPG and keep the Jersey board in close touch with Continental affairs. The discipline in self-sufficiency through which all Jersey affiliates passed now stood both parent company and affiliates in good stead. Heinrich Riedemann was on his own, cut off from the material assistance of 26 Broadway and enmeshed in precarious circumstances. His 1913 proposal to provide a stipulated reserve of gasoline in Germany for a five-year period could not, of course, be fulfilled. The transfer of the DAPG tankers and the imposition of the British blockade relieved the Jersey Company of the embarrassment of such a traffic. Neither, despite official American suspicion to the contrary, did Jersey Standard exports to the Scandinavian countries, which might well have sifted through into Germany, increase substantially after 1915. In 1917 shipments declined sharply, and Christian Holm, head of the Danish affiliate, was frantically beseeching 26 Broadway for enough petroleum to meet minimum requirements of the Scandinavian market.[20]

With the abrupt cessation of imports into Germany following the outbreak of war in 1914, the various German oil companies were drawn together into an agreement with one another and with the government for supplying, as best they could from European sources, the military and domestic needs of the nation. Competition was declared to be at an end, and each company was allotted its share of the war market.[21]

By February of 1917 Riedemann realized clearly that war between Germany and the United States was inevitable. What could be done within the limitations of time and communications to strengthen the position of Jersey's German affiliate? Riedemann moved quickly and surely.

The Jersey board, on its part, responded with a swift decisiveness which was almost unprecedented in dealing with major issues in times of peace. Negotiating by cable and by radio, Riedemann proposed to purchase from the Jersey Company at par value all the parent company's stock shares in the DAPG, pledging as collateral all American securities and bank balances held by the Riedemann family. This was an astute plan. With complete ownership of the DAPG stock vested in German hands, the company's assets might, in case of war, escape sequestration as enemy alien property. By the same token, the Riedemann family funds and securities in the United States, which Riedemann directed the National City Bank of New York to turn over to A. C. Bedford, would presumably be given protection against sequestration by the American government.[22]

Riedemann's proposal was dispatched from Berlin on February 4, 1917, and received at 26 Broadway the following day. Bedford at once cabled Riedemann: "Proposition respecting sale of all shares of Deutsch-Amerikanische Petroleum-Gesellschaft on terms stated accepted and sale confirmed." This message apparently did not get through, for Riedemann continued to cable frantic requests for action. On February 27 communication channels between America and Central Europe began to close down. The Jersey Company's acceptance of the sale finally reached Riedemann via the Swiss Legation in Washington, which was able to get a message through to company representatives in Zurich. This transfer of the 9,000 shares of DAPG voting stock, having a par value of about $3,780,000, was recorded on the books of both companies as of February 21, 1917. The entire transaction was subsequently disallowed and the sale declared to be invalid by the United States Alien Property Custodian, but in Germany the desired purposes appear to have been realized.[23]

A detailed account of the DAPG at war lies outside the scope of these pages, but the fact should be noted that Riedemann fought fiercely to preserve the position of his company against attacks that were launched by the Deutsche Bank and by other competing German interests in an endeavor to receive larger allocations of the strictly regulated German business. In spite of these attacks, Riedemann was able to maintain his organization intact and preserve for the DAPG a relatively large share (about 70 per cent) of the restricted market. "This I managed," Riedemann later told Teagle, "by claiming first consideration for American interests which it would be unwise to hurt and then after the U. S. declared war claiming that DAPG was entirely German owned."[24] By spring of 1918, however, continued agitation by the old enemies of the DAPG had rendered the situation increasingly desperate for the German affiliate, and there was a threat that the company might be taken over by the government. This is scarcely surprising, for DAPG, far from having furthered the ambitions of the War Ministry, had virtually stripped Germany of tanker tonnage in the years 1914 and 1915 and had offended powerful German financial groups who apparently had hoped in the stress of war to accomplish that humbling of the company which they had failed to bring about in time of peace.

Once again, Riedemann proved himself capable of effective improvisation in the face of a difficult situation. On May 2, 1918, the Riedemann family disposed of half of the 9,000 shares of DAPG voting stock acquired in 1917 from the Jersey Company. The invalidation of the 1917 transaction by the United States government, of course, was no obstacle to the sale in 1918, for Germany regarded the Riedemanns as sole owners of the company. Of the 4,500 shares sold in 1918, half were purchased by the Hugo Stinnes combine and half by the Hamburg-American Line. Stinnes and Hamburg-American representatives were elected to the DAPG board. This sale was motivated by the urgent necessity for enlisting the support of these very influential groups for the company. Though this disposal by Riedemann of a half interest in the DAPG posed difficult legal questions for postwar settlement, the short-term objectives of the stratagem were achieved. The wide and solid backing of the company rendered it impervious to local attack. Riedemann was later able to report that, although profits quite understandably had declined from 1,728,-000 reichsmarks in 1915 to 346,000 in 1918, the DAPG came out of the war without the loss of a single storage tank or customer.[25]

It was not in Germany but in Romania that Jersey Standard felt the full impact of war's destructiveness. On October 31, 1916, E. J. Sadler wrote to director S. B. Hunt that many Romàno-Americana storage tanks at Constanta had fallen intact into German hands when that terminal port was occupied. It had been the intention to destroy all handling facilities and stored oil, but responsibility was delegated to one person and then to another, and in the confusion of evacuation very little property actually was destroyed.[26] A month later, at the refining center at Teleajen and in the oil fields, the story was different. Here, under the direction of the Anglo-Romanian destruction committee, a more systematic and apparently successful effort was made to cripple the refineries, auxiliary installations, and wells. Virgil Teremia, one of the native workmen, described the scene:[27]

After we fired up Teleajen on Tuesday, 5th December, I went myself again and put fire to the barrel house, carpenter shop, store house, and painting shop, which did not take fire, so that the whole works were under fire, excepting, of course, the buildings and offices. That was our last visit at the Works, which I left with the greatest regret, like any other man who has given there his best part of his life. Then we left in the evening. You could see from Balea Catugare-asca the whole district, looking like an ocean of fire, especially Ploesti was wonderful. In every moment you could hear the bum-bums of the tanks, boiler houses, etc., exploding. Hundreds of meters in height was the smoke. . . . Nobody, for more than five or six hours after our departure, couldn't say a word. Everybody was thinking of their homes, to their wives, to their children, to their sisters. It is something which I am unable to explain, even in my own language.

Harry G. Seidel, assistant general manager of the company, remained behind in Bucharest to look after Romåno's interests under German occupation. His reports, forwarded by circuitous routes to 26 Broadway, tell what happened after the fateful day of destruction.

Seidel was prevented by high water and the destruction of bridges from visiting the Teleajen refinery or the fields until the end of December. He reported that, while the destruction at Teleajen had been extensive, the distillation units and the office building had escaped, although preparations for their destruction had been made. It is entirely possible that the preservation of these important installations was an accident of oversight, such as occurred at Constanta. Virgil Teremia's casual reference that "of course" the main buildings were not fired, however, is suggestive. Sadler, acting on his own initiative, might well have felt that destruction of the wells and of the auxiliary properties was sufficient to deprive the Germans of any use of the installations. If this was, indeed, the prompting thought, a serious error in judgment was made, as subsequent events were to show. Sadler, moreover, had been reluctant to order the installations destroyed until signed assurances were given him by the British that restitution would be made. These assurances could not be obtained in a form which Sadler deemed adequate, and valuable time was lost. There was, indeed, a decided and very wide antipathy on the part of all the oil companies toward a policy of complete destruction, and only where the work was personally supervised by the Destruction Commission were thorough results achieved.[28]

Seidel reported that some looting had been perpetrated by former employees. Other companies also reported wholesale pillaging by resident workmen, who took advantage of the general confusion to break into offices and private dwellings. Seidel asked for and received a German military guard to protect what was left. A trip to the Ploesti fields showed Seidel that destruction there was widespread, though he was not able at the time to tell how effectively the wells had been plugged.[29]

From the end of January to the middle of March, heavy snows blanketed Romania and the Germans were unable to start rehabilitation operations. Seidel utilized this time to gather valuable papers together and secrete them in a safe in the American Legation in Bucharest. Austrian officers confiscated the Româno office space in Bucharest. Not to be outdone, high German officials demanded their pick of Româno's office furniture and rugs. A German Oil Authority (Erdol Kommando) was established, and in April work on the wells was begun. Româno and other oil companies were ordered to submit an operating plan.[30]

When war between Germany and the United States was declared, Seidel's position became a delicate and dangerous one. Româno was put under military administration. The administrators took over the keys to the cash deposits and seized all the records they could find. In April of 1917 a new administrator was appointed, who formerly had been in the employ of Steaua, the Deutsche Bank subsidiary. With great skill and patience the Germans were remarkably successful in fishing the debris out of Româno wells at Baicoi and Moreni, and oil began to flow again. The military administrator took great care to protect the German properties, but showed gross negligence in caring for Româno installations and those of Astra (Royal Dutch). Production at any cost was the aim, and expenses were charged to Româno-Americana.

Seidel had no voice in management, but he did what he could to take care of the families of former workmen who had fled or joined the Romanian Army. Regular payments, amounting to 25 per cent (later increased to 50 per cent) of the pay the men had been earning, were made to these dependents. At the same time Sadler, in America, was making every effort to see that Româno men who had returned to the United States, to England, or to Switzerland were employed elsewhere in the organization or paid part of their salary while they were seeking new jobs. Many of the American employees of Româno found work with The Carter Oil Company. Sadler urged that their pay for such work be raised to the level which they had been receiving in Romania. Altogether, a splendid record was achieved in caring for these displaced men and their families. The workmen retained in Romania to work under the Germans were given 30 to 50 per cent increases in wages to match the rise in living costs. Local feeling toward Româno-Americana consequently was more favorable than toward some of the other companies operating under the German administration. This was certainly astute policy in those times of peasant unrest and Bolshevik agitation.[31]

Under the ex-Steaua administrator matters went from bad to worse. Seidel charged that the administrator furnished no receipts for expenditures charged to Româno's account and that this man was utilizing seized equipment to enlarge the Steaua works. Materials charged to Româno were purchased recklessly and at high cost, and no action was taken to protect Româno's expiring leases. Only German companies were given permission to make new leases or to extend old ones. Lawsuits against Româno were defended with grievous laxity.[32] Seidel was annoyed, too, that the military administration had forced Româno to pay full rent for the offices from which they had been evicted, and that the Germans were using dynamos on the Româno wells and making the company pay the electric bill. This latter was a special affront, for in prewar days Româno had been unwilling to utilize electricity at the wells because of the cost involved!

In April of 1918 the German military administration ordered the liquidation of all companies in which Allied capital was invested. Româno's various lease concessions were sold to a German liquidating corporation, the Erdol-Industrie-Anglagen Gesellschaft, or Eiag, as it was called. The forced sale to Eiag at artificial prices of the Constanta properties, all materials on the leases, all furniture, and all tank cars followed. The liquidating commission then began the systematic dismantling of such of the Teleajen refinery installations as remained intact. The purpose of this action, obviously looking ahead to the return of peace, was said to be to cripple Româno to the greatest possible extent and to increase the capacity of the German refineries.[33] Seidel's action in keeping vital lease and operating records out of German hands fortunately thwarted spoliation of a more devastating nature.

The success of the Germans in obtaining production in damaged Romanian fields was remarkable. In 1917 production was obtained at a rate equivalent to about 40 per cent of the 1916 rate, and in 1918 the prewar level was nearly achieved. This amounted to virtually all the crude that could be refined and transported with facilities then existing. From Româno-Americana fields at Moreni, Baicoi, and Pacureti the Germans obtained 3,000,000 barrels of crude—or approximately two-thirds of the 1915 rated capacity.[34]

As the war drew to a close, Jersey Standard's Romanian venture appeared to be almost a total loss. The competent and devoted Seidel was in jail, charged with interference with the military administration. Company property was scattered or destroyed, and it seemed improbable that, even if the Germans moved out, they would do so without destroying the wells which they had put back into production. Only a nucleus of experienced workmen remained. Some records were safe but many were missing, and the accounts were in a tangle. A tremendous legal problem had accumulated, and the status of many important charter and leasehold rights was in doubt. No one at 26 Broadway could even hope at the time to assess the total damages in terms of dollars—or in terms of Româno-Americana's postwar competitive power.

MR. BEDFORD'S COMMITTEE

Coincidentally with these stirring operational developments in 1917 and 1918 an episode less spectacular in kind, but of considerable significance nevertheless, was being enacted on the home front by the leaders of the American petroleum industry. But first, a break must be made in the narrative of war events to note an important milestone in Jersey Standard's managerial history.

On December 5, 1916, John D. Archbold died. This was the passing of an Elder Statesman. The entire organization mourned for the diminutive, gay-hearted, courageous man onto whose resourceful shoulders John D. Rockefeller many years before had eased the burden of Standard Oil management. A. C. Bedford, the senior vice-president and the favorite of the Old Guard, succeeded Archbold as president of Jersey Standard.

Bedford, like Archbold before him, presided successfully over the Jersey board. Being a younger man, Bedford had a greater capacity than Archbold for active managerial endeavor, and his influence may be discerned at many points in company management through 1917. The charming and beautiful Mrs. Bedford did much to assist her husband in perpetuating cordial and effective relationships with fellow directors and business associates. Bedford, however, was not an oilman in the broad and popular sense of the term. It seems clear that he lacked Teagle's drive and detailed grasp of the business. Soon it became apparent that, though on several occasions the more cautious Bedford was to act as a check on his energetic and ambitious contemporary in the Toronto office, Bedford was not to employ his new position and power in an effort to dominate the operational phases of the company's business. His interests lay elsewhere, and he followed a path which he alone among the Jersey directors was able and willing to travel. Many men in business held at the time that this path led nowhere and that those who followed it did so in default of a clearer sense of direction. Not for a full generation was this viewpoint blasted in all its terrible shortsightedness. Bedford, instinctively perceiving the larger public responsibilities of great concerns like the one he headed, set his step upon the path of business statesmanship.

Late in 1917, after only twelve months in office, Bedford resigned the Jersey Standard presidency and was appointed to the newly created office of Chairman of the Board. The creation of this office at that particular time was of more than passing significance. Bedford was not an operating man, and as long as he occupied the office of president the Jersey Company could not obtain maximum utilization of the services of Walter Teagle, whose capacity and influence had expanded enormously in the war years. The widely divergent individual interests of Bedford and Teagle led them naturally and apparently without personal conflict into the respective paths they were to follow after 1917. The move was far-sighted, and the two Jersey leaders, markedly different in personality and outlook though they were, worked together thereafter in a mutually harmonious and complementary fashion. Bedford, relieved of responsibilities which Teagle was better able to bear, now was free to devote his chief efforts to work which had an immediate bearing upon Jersey Standard's relations with the public, the industry, and the government. Into that work he plunged with great vigor, and soon he was devoting almost his entire attention to the war effort of the petroleum industry.

As war struck home, the American petroleum industry in all its clashing factions began to draw together as never before in its history in a pattern of co-operative effort. In this constructive work of co-ordinating the industry's war effort A. C. Bedford played a large part, and he considered it the greatest work of his life. Although sincere patriotism was involved, the Co-operative Committee on Petroleum of the Council of National Defense also grew out of some shrewd and long-range thinking in the industry.

On March 24, 1917, Bernard M. Baruch, then a member of the Advisory Committee of the Council of National Defense, asked Bedford to form and head an advisory committee on petroleum, to function under the Council of National Defense. After consulting with his associates, Bedford agreed, and set about assembling the committee. Bedford's genius was for organization; soon he had enlisted E. L. Doheny, president of

Mexican Petroleum, G. S. Davison, vice-president of Gulf, J. W. Van Dyke, president of Atlantic Refining, C. F. Lufkin, president of The Texas Company, H. F. Sinclair, president of Sinclair Oil & Refining, and J. H. Markham, an independent producer. Walter Teagle and the heads of three petroleum trade associations were soon added.[35] James A. Moffett, Jr., was given leave from his position as head of the Louisiana Standard marketing division to serve as secretary; his hard work had much to do with the efficiency with which the committee subsequently functioned.

This body had a semiofficial standing, and almost immediately its work went beyond the advisory stage. The main effort at first was to ascertain the requirements of the armed forces and to arrange for the prompt and efficient supplying of those needs. Working from headquarters at 26 Broadway, Bedford established co-operative understandings with the United States Shipping Board and with the British, French, and Italian embassies relative to petroleum needs. Allocation plans had been worked out by May of 1917, and Allied purchase requests were routed through the Petroleum Committee.[36]

In July of 1917 the loosely organized Council of National Defense was dissolved, and its functions were taken over by the War Industries Board. There was fear that the Petroleum Committee would pass out of existence. Bedford campaigned vigorously against this possibility, obtaining widespread support in government and industry circles alike. The United States Chamber of Commerce, in which Bedford was a prominent figure, called a convention of American businessmen to work out plans for the perpetuation of such advisory industry committees. As a result of these efforts, the Petroleum Committee stayed alive, passing then under the jurisdiction of the War Industries Board. The title of the group was changed to the National Petroleum War Service Committee. A short time later Harry Garfield, chief of the newly created United States Fuel Administration, announced that his office would assume charge of the oil as well as the coal industry. On January 12, 1918, Garfield, M. L. Requa, chief of the Oil Division of the Fuel Administration, and Bedford held a meeting. Garfield asserted that although full responsibility for operations must be vested in the Fuel Administration, he was anxious to have the Petroleum Committee continue to function as before. Bedford, of course, consented and soon appointed several new members to the committee so that it came to represent virtually every major oil company in the United States. Dr. Van H. Manning, director of the Bureau of Mines, was also named to the committee. Sixteen geographic and functional advisory subcommittees were formed, and over-all responsibilities of the Petroleum War Service Committee were greatly expanded.[37]

The position of the committee was not an easy one. While the government was pressing for a stabilized price level, the oil industry was caught in a rising tide of costs. There was continual pressure for higher prices. Between 1916 and 1918 the Bureau of Labor Statistics index of all wholesale commodity prices advanced 54 per cent. Over this same period wholesale gasoline prices rose only 15 per cent. Fuel oil, however, the output of which was more than double that of gasoline in this period, increased 106 per cent in price. The average increase of these two major petroleum products, weighted in accordance with their respective importance, thus outran general commodity price trends. Crude oil, at the same time, advanced 77 per cent in price.[38]

Defenders of industry pricing could point to the fact that refinery output in the United States in these years had expanded nearly twice as fast as had domestic production of crude oil, while the shortage of tanker tonnage impeded efforts to import Mexican crude, which was the chief source of fuel oil. The smaller refiners, who lacked controlled sources of crude oil, were being forced to pay large premiums for their supplies. Producers, on their part, asserted that drilling costs in the fields had doubled, and it could be reasoned with much logic that only by the promise of high profits could the oil industry be induced to make the hazardous investments necessary to discover and produce the additional petroleum supplies which were needed. In August of 1918, when the accelerating price rise of crude and fuel oil began to cause alarm, Bedford's committee forestalled the imposition of government controls, such as had already been placed on wheat, iron and steel, copper, and coal, by working out a voluntary price-control system.[39]

In August of 1918 Oil Director Requa approved the prices that the Petroleum Committee recommended; this action strengthened the position of the committee in its efforts to set and hold an industry price line. Although crude and fuel oil price increases had already far outstripped the rise in prices of many commodities vital to the war effort, the voluntary restraints thus imposed during the remaining few months of the war were effective. Between August and December of 1918 increases in crude oil, fuel oil, and gasoline prices, like those in commodity groups which were under direct government control, were negligible. The opinion was entertained in industry circles that the Petroleum Committee's action had prevented petroleum prices from going as high as they might have gone without restraint and under prevalent market conditions.[40]

In many other ways the Petroleum War Service Committee assisted the industry while assisting the war effort. A subcommittee was organized under the chairmanship of Henry L. Doherty to study war excise and income-tax proposals then pending before Congress. This subcommittee presented its findings and recommendations before House and Senate committees and was able to incorporate in the Revenue Act of 1918 a more nearly adequate recognition of the uncertainties and hazards of the producing branch of the oil business. Since March 1, 1913, when a depletion allowance for the exhaustion of oil properties had first become effective for tax purposes, the valuation of newly discovered producing properties had been restricted to the historical cost of the individual property. The cost of unsuccessful drilling and other nonproductive exploration expenses could not be included in figuring the cost to the operator of his productive property. These tax provisions acted as a deterrent to investment in exploration—particularly by the small operators who lacked adequate capital resources. The Revenue Act of 1918 provided that new fields should be appraised thirty days after discovery; either cost or the appraised discovery value (whichever was higher) could be used as the basis for depletion charges on the property. The increased allowances and consequent reduced taxes on these properties permitted the operator to absorb expenditures incurred in unsuccessful efforts elsewhere and acted as a stimulant to exploration. This objective was particularly desirable in 1918, when the nation's oil reserves were being heavily drawn upon.[41]

It was clear that the Petroleum War Service Committee, with its many cordial government contacts, was an exceptionally useful vehicle for acquainting official Washington not only with particular domestic problems such as prices and depletion allowances, but with general conditions in the world industry as well. Industry leaders appeared to feel that it was high time for the government of the United States to be thus awakened. Even at the peak of the Allied co-operative war effort there were premonitory rumblings of the storms to come. In September of 1917 the Standard Oil Company of New York complained to the Shipping Board that the Royal Dutch-Shell had presented misleading figures in an effort to prejudice government departments against American oil companies. New York Standard men also charged that the British Admiralty, acting under pressure from The Asiatic Petroleum Company, their principal Far Eastern competitor, had requisitioned the nineteen tankers belonging to the Standard Transportation Company, Limited, of Hong Kong—the New York Company's shipping subsidiary. New York Standard, like Jersey Standard before it, felt that the ownership and not the flag of vessels was the true test of nationality. No other oil company, the New York Company men alleged, was treated by the Admiralty in such a cavalier fashion. The observation was then made that the government of Britain acted on the premise that wars were temporary, while the economic prosperity of a nation depended on permanent situations.[42]

Shell men, on their part, countered with the allegation that Standard Oil representatives in Washington were promoting propaganda that the Royal Dutch-Shell was pro-German. Deterding is supposed to have issued a directive to his employees instructing them not to address correspondents in the United States in Dutch, and the quick-tempered leader of the great organization was persuaded only with difficulty not to pursue further the quarrel with his erstwhile wartime allies.[43]

Bedford caused the charges to be investigated and concluded that the British demand for greater utilization of East Indian crude for war needs was quite unjustified, in view of the distances involved and because of the success with which American refineries were meeting European demands. The various allegations advanced by Standard of New York were aired before the Petroleum Committee, and a so-called Eastern Agreement was concluded between the British and American governments which regulated marine assignments. Though this agreement failed to satisfy American interests, at least it could be said that the matter had been brought in sympathetic fashion to the attention of high officials in Washington.[44] Instances of close liaison and of the advantageous exchange of viewpoints between Bedford's committee and the various bureaus of the federal government might be multiplied many times from the records of the Petroleum Committee's activities.

In total, the accomplishments of Bedford's group were impressive. The Petroleum Committee had introduced order and efficiency in allocating purchase requests and in directing the movement of oil. In the early months of the American war effort these endeavors had been of critical importance. A statistical department had been established which provided information essential for the intelligent direction of the war effort. Various special endeavors had been furthered by committee planning and support. The dire effects of tank-car and tank-steamer shortages had been overcome by central planning and industry-wide co-operation. Teagle's suggestion that voluntary gasolineless Sundays be instituted to relieve shortages in certain areas had been adopted and made effective. Bedford had co-operated with the War Fuel Administration in an effort to eliminate competitive premium bidding for crude oil. The committee kept the Allied governments and the petroleum industry informed about mutual needs and events affecting oil problems in many areas.[45] In return for these services the committee had, in effect, demanded for the oil industry the preservation of a substantial margin of profit and the institution of a tax concession of an important, though equitable, nature.

Both Jersey Standard and the petroleum industry had ample reason to extend their gratitude to A. C. Bedford. It was his genuine talent for organization, his skill as a presiding officer, his capacity for hard work, and his talent for making contacts which brought the committee to life and enabled bitter rivals in the petroleum trade to work side by side in a common cause. At a dinner given for Bedford at the Hotel Biltmore in New York, on March 14, 1919, Consul Général Gaston Liebert awarded him the title *Chevalier de la Légion d'Honneur* in recognition of his services and those of his committee in the Allied cause. Leaders of the American oil industry might appropriately have had another medal minted and awarded him in recognition of a different service. By his prompt and bold assumption of prerogatives, his able enlistment of all the industry leaders, and his smooth liaison with the men of the federal bureaus, A. C. Bedford had effectively blocked the inviting path which the war opened for government regulation of the American petroleum industry. For Jersey Standard his efforts probably constituted the most effective endeavor to improve relations between the company, the industry, and the government that had been made since John D. Rockefeller entered the oil business.

THE FLUSH OF VICTORY

Transitional difficulties attended the return of peace, but these were small indeed. The policy set by the Petroleum Committee of contracting for petroleum supplies on a thirty-day basis enabled the industry to unburden itself of war commitments in very short order. Some confusion resulted as the Shipping Control Committee of the War Shipping Board disintegrated prematurely, its members resigning and returning to private pursuits before all business had been cleared up. Jersey Standard tankers were gradually released from requisition, commencing in December of 1918. Company employees, guaranteed a postwar job, began to stream back to the refineries, field installations, and marketing offices.[46]

Bedford went about the thankless task of collecting from the oil companies their ratable share of the Petroleum Committee's outstanding indebtedness of $75,000. Larger companies represented on the committee were asked to contribute $5,000 each and the smaller companies half that amount. These assessments were responsibly met, though certain companies complained that their share appeared high. Henry L. Doherty was paid $20,000 for his services on the tax committee, a remuneration which, in view of the lasting benefits he had obtained for the industry, was nominal indeed.[47] Jersey Standard, in addition to paying its regular share of the committee's expenses, also had continued to pay Bedford's entire salary ($125,000 per annum), despite the fact that for two years Bedford had devoted virtually all his time and energy to the committee.

In the weeks following the signing of the Armistice a glow of satisfaction began to spread upon the countenance of the American petroleum industry as the total results of the war effort were surveyed. In the warm camaraderie of the victory hour, British and French statesmen heaped their laurels freely. "The Allies floated to victory on a sea of oil," exclaimed Lord Curzon, British Secretary of State for Foreign Affairs, who then pointed out that 80 per cent of Allied petroleum needs came from America. Captain Arthur Snagge, R.N., Naval Attaché of the British Embassy in Washington, confessed that 48 per cent of the fuel requirements of the British fleet were met by American companies. Consul Général Liebert, of the French Embassy, stated that of the 35,000 tons of gasoline being consumed monthly by the French Army in 1918, 30,000 came from the United States. Impressive statistics were invoked showing the vast increases in American output and exports.

Jersey men surveyed the figures and calculated that 25 per cent of the entire war requirements of the United States and of the Allied governments had been supplied by Jersey Standard—a gigantic achievement. American vessels had supplied roughly 51 per cent of the tanker tonnage employed in the Atlantic trade. Spokesmen of the American industry noted, with a touch of bitterness which in this particular instance was not entirely rational, that Britain, crucially dependent upon American oil, had supplied only enough tankers to carry 33 per cent of the tonnage transported in this perilous trade. Of the American tonnage, by far the largest share was transported in Jersey Standard ships. The company's contribution to the Allied cause had truly been a notable one.[48]

Viewing the fiscal results of the year 1918, the directors at 26 Broadway had ample cause for good feeling. Profits had been adequate, if not handsome, and the company was in excellent financial shape. Though deprived entirely of the earnings of Româno-Americana and DAPG, and taking into consideration all the disruption to normal trade that characterized the war years, the company showed earnings of $105,800,000 before taxes in 1917—a figure 46 per cent higher than in 1916. In 1918 earnings before taxes were 40 per cent above the 1916 figure and were equivalent to about 25 per cent of sales. The federal tax burden, however, had increased from approximately $1,600,000 in 1916 to $44,000,000 in 1918. As a result, combined earnings after taxes for 1917 and 1918 were only slightly larger than for the 1915-1916 period.[49]

Summary aspects of earnings and financial condition are presented in Table 21 in Chapter 19 and in Appendix 2. Even a casual survey of company balance sheets shows that fiscal policy remained conservative in the face of the great war activity. In 1918 the usual dividends of $19,668,000 were paid out—the disbursements representing a 20 per cent return on par value and about a 3½ per cent yield on the average market price of company stock, which had declined somewhat from 1917 highs. Total fixed assets of the Jersey Company were up 26 per cent from the 1916 level. By the end of December, 1918, the consolidated surplus account (Jersey Standard and affiliates) stood at close to half a billion dollars. Outstanding liabilities were nominal in amount, for the business of the Jersey Standard organization, parent and affiliates, had been financed almost exclusively out of Jersey Company funds.

With such figures as these before them and in the heady optimism of the day, the Jersey directors, like the directors of many another American company, great and small, began to lay plans for still further expansion of their business. The tide of prosperity was still flowing, and few businessmen indeed realized how near to the high-water mark their fortunes had approached. While the men at 26 Broadway could but faintly discern the shadowy form of things to come, the immediate past was immensely satisfying and the present was reassuring. Quite aside from financial success and certain internal changes which promised much for the future, Jersey Standard had, in the years 1917 and 1918, come a long way. For the company and its leaders the war experience, though trying in the extreme, had a tonic effect. It capped with recognized exploits a five-year era during which a harvest of public animosity had been reaped and great operational difficulties had been faced. Great results were promised from the public service of A. C. Bedford and from the truly remarkable operating achievements of the organization itself. The directors could reasonably hope that those achievements, by helping so measurably to make the world safe for democracy, might also have the effect of making the world comfortable for Jersey Standard.

Chapter 10

A Time of Transitions

BETWEEN TWO ERAS

IN THE history of any company some years stand out in dramatic importance, marking great endings or great beginnings. More often than not such pivotal points of evolution escape contemporary notice, but in the perspective of history the year 1918 emerges as just such a time for Jersey Standard. Even while the organization was straining its capacities to meet the emergencies of war, Jersey's leaders were looking beyond victory and anxiously instituting new policies and overhauling old. Imagination and verve were more abundantly in evidence at 26 Broadway than at any time since 1911. A spark from the supercharged environment had penetrated two badly worn insulators—tradition and conservatism—to electrify the organization. More than any other, this year marked the division point between the Jersey Company of the Rockefeller era and the company as we know it today. For Jersey Standard this was a time of great beginnings.

Transition was not, of course, confined to a single year nor was it confined to the Jersey Company. The return of world peace was accompanied by many hopes and widespread uncertainties. Numerous aspects of civilization either had themselves been altered or were viewed with altered perspectives. This was particularly true of the commercial environment. The independent elements of the American petroleum industry had achieved, at least for the moment, a cohesiveness unprecedented in its earlier history. Leaders of the industry had learned to work together on problems common to all companies and had gained a deeper understanding of the public ramifications of their business. Government attitudes toward the larger companies were less harsh than they had been earlier, possibly because the industry itself had evolved along lines calculated to allay fears over the development of undue restraints of trade. Many competitors of the Jersey Company were no longer small, the number of competitors had multiplied, and companies which in 1912 had

247

been regarded by Jersey men as virtually noncompetitive could no longer be so considered. The form of the international petroleum industry, too, had been greatly altered by the war, and the effect of the change seemed to promise more rather than less competition, both at home and abroad. As early as 1918 it was obvious that, although adjustments to the dissolution decree were still continuing, the period of direct reaction was at an end. The Jersey directors could reasonably expect that henceforth they would be free of drastic government interference in their pursuit of normal business objectives.

These were a few of the circumstances combining to make the world of 1918 a far different one from that which Jersey Standard had faced in postdissolution months and in which the company had operated for six years following the dissolution. In 1918 the company was poised between two eras. New policies were being charted to guide the course of postwar business. While those policies were predicated upon anticipated changes in operating conditions, they were also conditioned by what had been done or left undone in the immediately preceding period.

In the years from 1912 to 1917 Jersey Standard had held its defenses and made considerable progress in rebuilding an integrated organization. The frame of reference in which this reconstructive effort had been set consisted of a seemingly insatiable market for petroleum products—between 1912 and 1918 world consumption had increased 42 per cent and United States consumption 73 per cent; from 1914 to 1918 automobile registrations in the United States had nearly tripled. In response to this growth, Jersey Standard had expanded its facilities greatly. The company had also shifted those facilities about in order to take advantage of opportunities such as the boom in Mid-Continent crude oil production. Rich financial resources and wide operational experience had been accumulated, but particularly serious difficulties had been encountered in labor relations and in the acquisition of foreign producing properties.

These operational episodes—described in preceding chapters—constitute only the more tangible segments of Jersey Standard history. It is equally necessary, in order to understand the company as it existed in 1918 and to establish the background for events after that time, to interrupt the narrative flow in order to examine certain transitional developments in top administration and in public relations. Here lay many of the generating forces which were to distinguish the postwar decade from the era just ending.

MEN AND ATTITUDES

In the field of public relations there had been sporadic indications, from 1915 on, of a transition in Jersey's attitudes. By the end of 1917 these manifestations had multiplied to such an extent as to suggest to the casual contemporary observer that Jersey Standard was indeed about to embark upon a new and enlightened way.

Public relations, like labor relations, had received small recognition as an area requiring intense and specialized executive attention. "We have," wrote Jersey's chief counsel in 1912, "no fairly defined policy except to sell goods to as many people as we can, at a fair price."[1] This was the old Rockefeller philosophy of depending for judgment upon calm, detached public appraisals of company operations and objectives—to the grim fallacy of which the dissolution decree itself bore testimony.

To be sure, prevailing public attitudes had left their mark on company policy. Jersey's Legal Department, which in postdissolution months ruled over matters pertaining to public and government relations with undisputed authority, continually urged the necessity for living according to the strict letter of the law. Company management lost few opportunities for insisting that it was doing just this. Abandoning the original Standard Oil ambition of dominating the petroleum industry wherever and whenever possible, Jersey management made only conservative adjustments to the growth of domestic competitors. Throughout the 1912-1917 period great caution had been exercised in setting up new companies and buying into established ones, lest public wrath be stirred again. The Jersey Company and its responsible officials, moreover, continued, as they had before 1911, to be bound in their actions by a strict code of honor, the foundation of which was sanctity of the written and the oral contract. These measures and policies were not widely apparent outside the business, and the beneficial effects were swallowed up in public reaction to other and more obvious courses which Jersey Standard simultaneously pursued.

Legislative activities, both real and presumed, were a fertile breeding ground for public suspicion. Jersey's Legal Department kept the closest possible watch on legislative developments everywhere. James K. Jones was the permanent representative of the company in Washington, and William H. Libby and other men sometimes appeared there on special missions. Jones' duties included reporting on all pertinent legislative and judicial trends, with particular attention to the activities of Jersey's competitors and political opponents. Jones frequently appeared before legislative committees, had many friends in Congress, and served as the principal contact with government officials up to and including the Presidential level.

Jones' efforts covered many areas. In 1912 he joined with others to attempt the removal of the Commissioner of Indian Affairs, who had been opposed to the efforts of The Prairie Oil & Gas Company to acquire leases in the Osage Nation. In 1914 he endeavored unsuccessfully to stop passage of the Gore and Chilton resolutions, which called for sweeping investigations of the petroleum industry. He was also active in the pipeline common carrier dispute and probably had a hand in the passage of the bill authorizing the transfer of foreign-built shipping to American registry.[2]

A stream of correspondence poured out of the Legal Department at 26 Broadway to Jersey Standard representatives in various state capitals. Much of this correspondence was directed at enlisting influential party men to support or oppose bills in which the company was interested. In Louisiana, Hunter C. Leake, counsel for Standard of Louisiana, enjoyed the confidence of the Corporation Commission and in some instances was apparently able to influence legislation in the company's interest.[3]

Virtually all these legislative activities were defensive in scope, the answer to challenges from many quarters. They were legal and an accepted part of the routine of government. James K. Jones had scores of counterparts in the Washington representatives of farm groups, trade associations, labor organizations, and individual companies. There is no evidence in the Jersey records that bribery was employed, and there are many testimonials to the fact that in its legislative contacts the company endeavored to hold itself above reproach.

By far the most commonly employed technique in dealing with legislative issues was for the company to seek to present its case directly before Congressional committees, or even before the President—supplying from its own records and experience pertinent information not otherwise available. Jersey men testified often and openly before various special investigating groups. Jones reported that Archbold in particular made an excellent witness. His replies were prompt, direct, and emphatic. He made a good impression on the investigators, and the press representatives were enthusiastic about his frank manner of testifying.[4] The point deserves particular emphasis, too, that the tenor of the times being what it was, the Jersey Company absolutely could not sponsor measures in its own interest where its motives might be questioned by either the public or the petroleum industry.

Although it seems clear in retrospect that the company's domestic legislative activities were neither insidious nor unique, certain politicians believed, or professed to believe, that Standard Oil was corrupting the commonwealth. The statement "Standard Oil is the invisible government," which appeared in the *Congressional Record* in 1914, was an irresponsible utterance, but one to which many persons gave credence.[5] A damaging burst of publicity in 1912 over revelations of large campaign contributions, allegedly made in 1904 by Standard Oil leaders, helped to keep alive the public belief that such practices were common.

Public suspicions of the Jersey Company's lobbying activities, however exaggerated, were harmful, but other company activities (many of which have already been delineated) nourished still more damaging beliefs. The Magnolia episode in Texas, which suggested collusion between the Jersey Company and Standard of New York, had been poorly handled. Marketing operations in some areas outside the United States had been conducted in a forceful fashion. Jersey Standard had not been reluctant to utilize the services of individuals to perform business abroad which it could not attempt in its own name. Entry into producing territories, both at home and abroad, could not for legal and practical reasons be made directly by the Jersey Company, and circuitous means had been adopted. In Canada the affairs of The Imperial Oil Company, Limited, had been so closely guarded that not even minority stockholders knew all that was going on. Efforts were made to conceal the fact that Imperial was controlled by American capital, and in order to strengthen the company's position important Canadian political figures had been given an opportunity to purchase the scarce and valuable Imperial Oil stock.[6] Indeed, secrecy and even petty subterfuge had characterized Jersey Standard operations in several places.

Abundant evidence exists of the Jersey Company's determination to comply with the terms of the dissolution decree, but there is little to suggest that up to the time of America's entry into the war the company had persuaded the public, the government, or the industry that it was doing so. Notwithstanding the admitted failure of vigilant federal agencies to discover violations of the decree, government and public alike continued to regard Jersey Standard as in the past, and professed to see no indication of any great change in the Standard Oil organization or its methods.

In the public mind and, indeed, in the belief of many persons in the petroleum industry, the Trust lived on. Prejudice against Standard Oil men and Standard Oil companies remained strong at least until 1916.

This failure to win favorable public opinion stemmed in large measure from circumstances which Jersey Standard could have avoided only by going out of the petroleum business entirely. Every one of the postdissolution business policies and practices presents evidence of the company's unquenched will to expand and reintegrate. Basic business objectives simply could not have been attained in the unfavorable political climate of the time without recourse to secrecy. Hostility from many quarters had all but closed to Jersey Standard the normal paths to growth, profits, and security, and had condemned the company for practices that had long been an accepted part of business life in a competitive economy. For Jersey Standard to go forward and realize a measure of success inevitably meant conflict of the most bitter nature with determined adversaries.

Though Jersey men could muster strong arguments in support of those measures which by their very nature prolonged the political and social storm, company management itself had, as indicated in Chapter 2, been slow to adopt constructive policies and techniques for dealing with the public. Instead, the attention of the directors appears to have been focused chiefly upon avoiding even the most trivial violations of law and upon creating a favorable impression before Congressional committees. In 1912 John D. Archbold, who earlier had been active in obtaining the publication of informative articles about Standard Oil, proclaimed that the outcry against the corporations was not from the public at all, but from impractical yellow journals and political demagogues.[7]

This attitude—honest enough, but blind and stultifying in its limitations—appears to have been the foundation for Jersey Standard's public relations policies from 1912 to Archbold's death in 1916. For the most part the company simply stood on its record in the face of what it felt to be unjust accusations by irresponsible assailants. Often it failed to indicate adequately what that record was. In virtually no case was information volunteered or publicity sponsored except as a defensive measure. J. I. C. Clarke, Jersey's publicist, apparently accomplished less after 1911 than he had before; those in quest of information had come to feel that Clarke had little to tell them, for the executives told him little. In 1913 he resigned, and his duties were taken over by William H. Libby, whose efforts at this time seem to have been directed toward government rather than press relations. It is said that at 26 Broadway reporters were met with courteous rejections. Mr. Archbold and Mr. Moffett were usually "in conference." Notwithstanding the favorable impression Archbold made on the witness stand, in at least some quarters of the press the opinion prevailed that the postdissolution Jersey management consisted of "frosty, well-tailored gentlemen."[8]

A transition to new public attitudes was promised by the rise of the new generation of company leaders. When A. C. Bedford assumed the Jersey presidency in 1916, he at once manifested an interest in the public relations of the company which he now headed. "I mean to keep my door wide open to every person having a legitimate call upon my attention," he declared on taking office.[9] This was a newsworthy statement for a Jersey Standard president to make, but it did not necessarily mean that Bedford was to be any more accessible than Archbold before him. Bedford's activities were prodigious in scope, and he was often hard pressed to find time even for urgent company business. The nature of those activities, however, lent credence to the spirit of his inaugural utterance.

Bedford's work with the Petroleum War Service Committee was only one phase of the effort he expended on matters of public interest. His prolific speechmaking brought the company's name before diverse audiences in many places. His participation in the affairs of the United States Chamber of Commerce constituted a Jersey Company endorsement of such a well-regarded activity. Bedford also took an active part in the founding and early management of the American Petroleum Institute, the first truly national trade association in the United States petroleum industry.

The career of Elbert Gary in the United States Steel Corporation presents a significant analogy to that of Bedford in the Jersey Company. Gary, too, assumed a newly created board chairmanship and devoted his energies to building good will for his company and stability for the industry. This was the era when trade associations were being hailed as the great new force in business, and Gary was instrumental in forming the Iron and Steel Institute, which held its first meeting in 1910. Jersey Standard may well have been consciously following this pattern. Certainly such coincidence of policy in these two great organizations is interesting and suggests the thesis so patently overlooked by historians that businessmen are often influenced by fashions as compelling as those which dictate the garments of their wives. Behind the vogue, to be sure, very practical advantages could be discerned—trade associations provided a legal means for co-operative action not otherwise available to the companies concerned.

Bedford's new tasks as chairman of the Jersey board were not easy ones, nor were his endeavors always appreciated. Most old-time oilmen had scant reverence for the public affairs which Bedford regularly attended and still less reverence for men who talked rather than drilled wells or built refineries. Nor could it be said, in all impartiality, that Bedford's efforts had a strong, direct influence upon public attitudes toward the Jersey Company. The industry appreciated his achievements, but the plaudits of the industry were not the plaudits of the public. Nevertheless, Bedford's work was of very great importance—more important in retrospect, possibly, than appeared at the time.

Other evidences of transitional trends were to be seen. In the wake of the furor raised by the Ludlow Massacre in Colorado in 1913, John D. Rockefeller, Jr., had taken the decisive step of employing a publicist. Ivy L. Lee had served as a reporter for the *New York Journal,* the *New York Times,* and the New York *World* before assuming the position of publicity agent for the Pennsylvania Railroad. When he joined the personal staff of the Rockefellers in 1915 some observers felt that the appointment was unfortunate. Newspapermen felt that Lee was adept at making the worse appear the better reason, and they viewed his efforts with suspicion. Nevertheless, Lee was a man of great ability, who had worked out sound public relations principles. He possessed a keen appreciation of the need of the press for real news, and he indulged in no recriminations or debates.[10] Lee's philosophy was that publicity should be dynamic, not defensive. He felt that he could overcome attacks on his clients, not by the usual denials, but by publishing material of a substantial and authoritative nature calculated to swing public opinion to a favorable judgment. Lee conceived his position to be that of an adviser, not a representative, and he insisted that the press releases come directly from his employer, not from himself.[11]

In 1917 Bedford engaged Lee to serve on a consulting basis as publicist for the Jersey Company. If this move was not actually suggested by the younger Rockefeller, it clearly derived from the precedent set by him in the Ludlow affair. Shortly after Lee's services had been retained, Bedford plunged into war work, and in November of 1917 Teagle assumed the presidency of the company. Exactly what this meant for the new publicist and his work was not entirely clear. The fact was obvious, however, that company attitudes toward the public would henceforth derive in substantial measure from the forceful personality of the new president. The personal characteristics, past training, and business philosophies of Walter Clark Teagle now became of paramount importance not only to the course of Jersey Standard's public relations but to developments in all the operational branches of the organization.

In the years that followed the dissolution decree Teagle had recorded outstanding achievements in assigned tasks. He came to New York from Canada with the prestige and confidence imparted by a constructive and important managerial experience. To a marked degree Teagle possessed the capacity for making his services indispensable. By prodigious effort both in and out of office hours he had made himself one of the best-informed men in the organization. His grasp of operational details in every branch of the business was prodigious. When answers were needed, Teagle had them. What is more, an astonishing percentage of his answers proved to be correct. More and more, Teagle's associates came to rely on him, not just for facts but also for incisive decisions on large matters and small in every branch of the business. Though he nominally resigned his Jersey directorship in 1914 to accept the Imperial presidency, Teagle's influence continued to be felt at 26 Broadway, where, indeed, Teagle himself was not infrequently to be found. The Canadian interlude, far from being a block to further advancement, broadened Teagle's qualifications for a still higher position. His ebullience and phenomenal capacity for work were too great to be confined to any one segment of the operating organization. As president of Jersey Standard, Walter Teagle was in a position which gave full scope to his remarkable energies.

For all his unusual qualities, Jersey's new president was a man, not a legend.[12] He was a man who had conditioned his acceptance of the proffered presidency with the startling provision that he be granted a three months' vacation each year. The Jersey directors already knew, of course, that Teagle would sooner have considered making his annual quail-shooting trip to the Norias Plantation without his favorite pointer than without his brief case. Whether in Georgia, Maine, or New Brunswick, Teagle remained in close touch by telephone with affairs at 26 Broadway. He liked to slip away from the offices at times when major crises were threatening, and not infrequently important bits of company strategy were conceived on the salmon pools of the Restigouche.

For a time following his arrival in New York, Teagle lived in an apartment at 903 Park Avenue. In 1921 he purchased "Lee Shore," a charming estate on Long Island Sound, at Greenwich, Connecticut. This was named after Mrs. Teagle, the former Rowena Bayliss Lee, of Memphis, whom Teagle had married in 1911. A son, Walter, Jr., had been born in 1913. In Teagle's active years as Jersey's leader, Mrs. Teagle carried with grace and a remarkable memory for names and affairs that burden of social obligations which naturally went with her husband's new position. Since Teagle worked and traveled constantly, over long spans of time the Teagles' social life together necessarily was almost nonexistent.

The new president was quite unimpressed with his own importance, and reporters calling at his office were able to note few eccentricities. Of Teagle's personal characteristics, only his large size was unusual. On most occasions he spoke in moderate tones, occasionally with a noticeable twang. Despite daily familiarity with the correct pronunciation of foreign names, he retained Middle Western renditions which must have jarred the sensitive ears of his foreign managers; in the Teagle vernacular Det Danske, the Danish affiliate, was always "The Dansky." He swore judiciously, was a light drinker, and seldom was seen without a pipe or a cigar in the familiar amber holder clenched in his teeth. Teagle kept a box of pipes next to his desk and chewed through the bits by the dozen.

In addition to his hobbies of dogs, hunting, fishing, and an occasional golf game, Teagle also enjoyed cards and looked forward to the commuters' bridge game that enlivened the daily train rides to and from New York. Certain of the clubs to which he belonged were those largely patronized by successful New York businessmen: the University Club, The Links, the Cornell Club, the Greenwich Country Club, and the Blind Brook Country Club. Teagle's more particular interests were reflected by membership in The Anglers Club (New York), the Gatineau Fish & Game Club and the Magannassippi Fish & Game Club (Ontario), and the Restigouche Salmon Club (New Brunswick).

Teagle's office at 26 Broadway was large, but not ornate. He worked from a huge, leather-covered, flat-top desk, with an oversized chair that had to be made especially for his big frame. On one side of the room stood the high, roll-top desk once used by John D. Rockefeller. Pictures of hunting dogs adorned the walls. A personal secretary, a traveling secretary, two office secretaries, and three Negro messengers comprised the office staff.

Here the business day commenced promptly. Often an associate's phone would ring at 9:05 A.M., and a familiar voice would come over the wire: "Say, Bill, I was thinking about that matter while shaving this morning. . . ." Teagle left no letters unanswered and carried on a voluminous correspondence which kept two and sometimes three secretaries busy. It was characteristic of him that in the middle of one hectic morning he insisted on taking the time to write a letter to Nancy, an eight-year-old admirer who had asked for his autograph. He always dictated rapidly, but made frequent changes, even in unimportant passages, to get the exact wording he wanted. His letters, like his speech, were friendly and natural, but retained, nevertheless, stilted beginnings such as "Yours of the tenth instant received. . . ."

One of Teagle's most frequently used phrases—"I have read your letter with the greatest possible interest"—was no mere figure of speech, for Teagle was a prodigious reader and enthusiastically digested a staggering mass of reports, correspondence, and trade publications daily. In his passion for detail he often wore his assistants out with changes and refinements in projects that they had assumed were completed. Nothing was too minor to escape notice or provoke a comment. A typical Teagle letter (this one to his marketing division leader in Canada) might contain excerpts like the following:[13]

I drove out to Oakville on Saturday and looked over the plant there. Your sign writer has done a very good job—too bad he wasn't competent to paint the wagon at the same time. I noticed that there was a shingle stain company with quite a plant located just across the Railroad from your plant. . . . They must have had 200 or 300 empty barrels on hand and, I presume, use a considerable quantity of naphtha. Do we sell them their requirements?

In his relations with associates and assistants Teagle was demanding. These men came to know that he would subject their work to painstaking scrutiny and would reprimand them in no uncertain terms if that work was performed in slipshod fashion. Letters exist in the Jersey Company files recording Teagle's impatience with what he felt to be stupidity or shortsightedness. Teagle, however, was equally quick and conscientious with his praise. The heads of affiliated companies are known to have received notes from the president's office calling their attention to a particularly fine piece of work by some executive or workman. In arguments before the directorate Teagle was persuasive, reasonable, and objective. He could lose his temper and pound the table when aroused, yet leave the meeting in company with his erstwhile adversaries in greatest good humor. Teagle fought for or against ideas and liked most men whether they agreed with him or not.

These are a few clues to the man that Teagle was and the life he led as Jersey's leader. The general impression of a warm, spontaneous, and gregarious nature is not a false one, but the fact must not be obscured that in Canada Teagle had driven hard, bargained sharply, and rarely allowed profit maximization to be subjugated by other considerations. The total picture is thus by no means a simple one. Teagle's human as well as professional characteristics must not be forgotten as the story of his administration is unfolded in the paragraphs and chapters that follow.

The new president's influence was at once manifest at 26 Broadway. When Teagle moved into his office, he not only greeted reporters warmly but even invited them to call at any time or to telephone him at his hotel.[14] Representatives of the press were charmed by the boyish grin, the hearty handshake, and the informality of Bedford's successor.

Teagle's sincere friendliness, however, did not imply the adoption of a positive public relations program. Much operating information was made public in the company's first published annual report, covering the year 1918, but beyond this there is little evidence that Teagle had seen fit in the first year of his presidency to utilize the full capacities of Ivy Lee or adopt the philosophies of the company's new publicist.

On the other hand, the situation at the close of 1918 was one of expectancy. Transition was in the wind. In a few short months the precedent for sweeping change in virtually every department of the business had been firmly established by the new administration. The realization had dawned on many that a company might suffer cruel and even fatal blows while passively waiting for Truth to prevail. The mechanisms were at hand to launch a vigorous campaign of laying old ghosts; the time was at hand, as well. Jersey's war effort had lessened hostility in some important quarters. Jersey's relations within the industry appear to have been much improved. Despite criticism at the top levels of the Wilson administration that the petroleum industry was meddling in Mexican political affairs, the company's reputation in certain government circles had definitely been strengthened. These gains were very real, and they owed much to Teagle and, more particularly, to A. C. Bedford, one of the first men in the industry to turn his full attention to matters lying outside the confines of his own company. The general outcry against Jersey Standard had perceptibly diminished since 1916, probably as a result of preoccupation by the public and the Federal Trade Commission with the war. By force of circumstances more than as a result of company policy, the public attitude had evolved in the space of two years from rampant hostility to suspicious tolerance. Jersey men, on their part—proud of their splendid war record and taking the cue from Bedford and Teagle—were beginning to exhibit a more relaxed and casual relationship both with government officials and with the press.

There was, however, a broader issue than the scope of company efforts to win and perpetuate a favorable public attitude—an issue which the reader who has carefully followed the course of Jersey Standard's efforts to survive the dissolution decree would do well to ponder. Teagle, somewhat like Rockefeller before him, looked to the broader issue and passed over the narrower. A limitation to the benefits of even the most enlightened and aggressive public relations program existed. Jersey Standard could somewhat improve its public position by words, but only actions of a broad and clearly useful social nature could secure that position permanently and beyond reach of all attack. In placing ends ahead of means in many operating areas, Jersey management had already propounded a great historical question. Did the efficient, integrated empire which the Jersey Company sought to forge, in the face of all obstacles and suspicions, promise greater total gains for the American public than would accrue if the company's commercial and political opponents prevailed? As one era in Jersey Standard's rich history closed and another opened, dramatic events in Europe were beginning to indicate what might happen and who the losers could be when those opponents did prevail, even momentarily.

THE PATH AHEAD

With Teagle's appointment to the presidency of the Jersey Company, he assumed the leadership of a board of directors which, with the breaking up of many of the important committees in 1911, had come to assume great and detailed managerial responsibilities.[15] In 1918 the directorate was younger, more flexible, and probably bolder than had been the case for several years. Leaders cut in the broad pattern of John D. Archbold and James A. Moffett, Sr., had passed from the stage. The new men—men like Hunt, Weller, Asche—were specialists much as their predecessors had originally been, but in 1918 they lacked that richness of experience which transcended departmental lines. Because of their specialized aptitudes these men were the more easily guided by Teagle; he had their support and confidence from the very beginning of his administration as president. He did this not by being domineering, but by being magnetically logical and irrefutably convincing. The co-operative and democratic pattern of the directorate was preserved, for, in his abundantly friendly manner, Teagle was adept at working with and through others. As the undisputed leader of a board enjoying highly centralized prerogatives, Teagle gathered great powers into his own hands—though these were necessarily conditioned upon the continued confidence and co-operation of his fellow directors. The administrative road was clear for the transformation of company policies along lines that Teagle and a few of his closest associates had long held to be desirable and necessary.

Past achievements and difficulties, coupled with the assumption that both demand and competition would continue to increase at a rapid rate, dictated the specific courses of action to be pursued after 1918 in the various operating segments of the business. The refining organization must be raised to a new level of technological proficiency and an active research program instituted. Since the war had developed new markets and stimulated old ones, it appeared that both quantitative expansion and sweeping alterations in refining facilities would be required. Marketing mechanisms needed a thorough overhaul. Domestic producing territories demanded further expansion, and crude oil purchasing activities of affiliated companies needed to be intensified—both requirements pointing to the additional need for extension of the pipeline network. Long-term goals in the foreign trade indicated a pressing necessity, not only for renewed attempts to obtain foreign crude oil reserves, but also for a search for new market outlets and a solution to difficult marine transportation problems posed by the cessation of hostilities. Neither could the company progress far into the postwar future without a serious effort to eradicate actual and potential sources of labor difficulties.

Unquestionably, the most pressing of these operating objectives was that of replacing and augmenting those sources of crude oil supply which the dissolution decree of 1911 had robbed of their exceptional one-time expediency. For reasons which had been clearly demonstrated even before 1918, the Jersey Standard organization could not hope to supply its world-wide needs without enlarging its ownership of producing territory outside as well as within the continental limits of North America. Thus the course of action dictated by profits and security was precisely that one which would precipitate the company soonest and most completely into the international conflicts that were brewing. A direct clash between Jersey policy and renascent nationalism throughout the world was inevitable.

In the months following the Armistice of 1918 the flush of Allied victory faded rapidly. With peace came profound unrest in victorious and vanquished countries alike. World brotherhood seemed scarcely more imminent in 1919 than it had been in 1913. Nationalism became more pervasive, more insistent, and more intolerant. Former war allegiances were forgotten, and nations clawed at one another in their efforts to achieve economic security. By the end of the war it was evident that adequate petroleum supplies had become a necessity for the existence of civilized nations. Petroleum took its place among the basic natural resources for which diplomats bargained; the international struggle for oil assumed a new scope and intensity.

Jersey Standard's evolving role in the international petroleum industry after 1918 cannot be understood without reference to the diplomatic attitudes of the principal nations of the world in respect to petroleum supplies and to the broad ambitions of the company's chief competitors. The 1914 pattern of the world petroleum industry had been seriously disarranged by the war. Even before the Armistice, gigantic dickers were in progress between those who needed oil and those who possessed it. These negotiations paid scant homage to traditional economic alliances. The general postwar unsettlement nourished a conviction in many quarters that the time was ripe to oust "Standard Oil" from its European and Asiatic strongholds.

In 1914 many conservative English voices still taunted Admiralty Lord Fisher with the charge of being an "oil maniac" because of his insistence upon converting the British fleet from coal to oil. Nevertheless, Great Britain had by that time already acted decisively on the premise that petroleum possessed economic, political, and military significance of a high order. After 1914, Britain asserted by diplomatic and military action an increasingly strong faith in the counsel of its oil prophets—Fisher, Sir Marcus Samuel, and Winston Churchill. National oil policy was a two-edged sword. The commercial ambitions of British nationals were strongly supported, while the competing endeavors of foreign interests were blocked wherever possible.

The specific methods employed from time to time by Britain in seeking these ends included barring aliens from owning or operating oil properties in British territory, direct participation by the British government in ownership and control of oil companies, the prevention of property sales by British oil companies to foreign interests, and the prohibition of disposal of their stock by British oil companies to other than British subjects. Certain of these measures had been practiced by the Dutch government as well as by the British; in the war and postwar years both nations continued with remarkable vigor their policy of discrimination. In 1918, as for some years past, American oilmen faced severe restrictions or outright exclusion in large segments of the British Empire and in the Netherlands dependencies. Both British and Dutch nationals, on the other hand, had been permitted to exploit American oil fields with no greater restrictions than those which had been imposed by the federal and state governments on domestic companies.[16]

Other nations, some of which had hitherto lagged far behind the British and Dutch in commercial perceptiveness, also began in the months following the Armistice to make petroleum an instrument of national policy. The French, the Russians, and the Turks all showed, in varying degree, a tendency to look upon oil not so much as a commodity of intrinsic commercial worth to themselves as a lever with which to force concessions in the peace conferences which were then convening. In Russia the oil industry was being nationalized by the new Soviet regime, and foreign properties there were being confiscated. Steps toward nationalization of oil fields, oil markets, or both, had been proposed or taken in Mexico, Colombia, Argentina, Salvador, Santo Domingo, and Romania, while in both France and Poland the question of government control was the subject of heated debate. Severe taxes or other restrictions had been laid on petroleum exports by Mexico, Peru, Poland, Romania, and other nations. The drift toward regulation of oil in the national interest became pronounced in all parts of the world.[17]

The cumulative significance of these trends at last came to be widely appreciated in America. A British boast published in the United States in 1920 aroused American public sentiment.[18] Sir Edward Mackay Edgar, of the London banking house of Sperling & Company, announced that two-thirds of the improved oil fields of Central and South America were already in British hands and would be developed by British capital, while the Royal Dutch-Shell combine owned exclusively or controlled interests in every important oil field in the world, including the United States. Edgar's conclusion was a stinging classic of imperialism:

We shall have to wait a few years before the full advantages of the situation shall begin to be reaped, but that that harvest eventually will be a great one there can be no manner of doubt. To the tune of many millions of pounds a year, America before very long will have to purchase from British companies, and to pay for in dollar currency in progressively increasing proportion, the oil she cannot do without and is no longer able to furnish from her own states. . . .

With the exception of Mexico, and to a lesser extent of Central America, the outer world is securely barricaded against an American invasion in force. There may be small, isolated sallies, but there can never be a massed attack. The British position is impregnable.

Edgar was interested in the flotation of British oil securities and probably had no idea that his pointed press release would stir such repercussions. His statement was most awkwardly timed from the viewpoint of British foreign policy, and it elicited strong denials from representatives of the petroleum industry. In 1921 the British Foreign Office issued a long official memorandum minimizing the extent of British restrictions. Britain's eminent oil economist, Sir John Cadman, took pains to point out that Britain and British nationals controlled only 4 per cent of world production.[19] Nevertheless, a tremendous cry of indignation and alarm went up in America.

Edgar, it appeared, had been most indiscreet, but a highly authoritative statement issued from another quarter a few months later indicated that his utterances, though unquestionably exaggerated, were not without a factual basis. The annual report of the Royal Dutch-Shell for 1920 did not receive wide circulation in America until it was published in part by the Federal Trade Commission in 1923, but this report contained a trenchant summation of the world situation:[20]

As regards competition, the fight for new production deserves our special attention. This struggle became especially keen when the significance of fuel oil became generally manifest. . . . The advantage of having production not concentrated in only one country, but scattered all over the whole world, so that it may be distributed under favorable geographical conditions, has been clearly proven. It needs hardly to be mentioned that the American petroleum companies also realized, though too late, that it was not sufficient to have a large production in their own country. As regards our own group in this respect, its business has been built up primarily on the principle that each market must be supplied with products emanating from the fields which are most favorably situated geographically. It goes without saying that we are now reaping the benefits resulting from this advantageous position.

For American oilmen, who with little diplomatic support had fought the international battle for petroleum supplies for so many years, there must have been a kind of grim satisfaction in watching dismay over the world petroleum situation spread from legislator to legislator. Accusations of Congressional stupidity, blindness, and negligence began to fly about the country like shrapnel. An editorial appearing on May 24, 1920, in *The Annalist* succinctly voiced an opinion which was beginning to enjoy wide circulation: "England was engaged in placing a mortgage on the world supply of petroleum at the time when the United States was doing its best to wreck the possibilities of America being a factor in the world development." What had been believed by a few informed men in the petroleum industry now was proclaimed by many: even through the most critical years of the war, Britain had relentlessly pursued long-term commercial objectives in preparation for the peace to come. "The English," Aristide Briand told the French Chamber of Deputies, "are more subtle than some of us are willing to believe. I am inclined to say that they display a continuity of view which gives them strength."[21] This charge was almost identical with that leveled two years earlier by executives of the Standard Oil Company of New York, protesting against British confiscation of their tankers.

Though the outcry of the day was directed at British imperialism and at economic malpractice by Wilsonian and preceding administrations, leaders of the American petroleum industry did not escape a measure of condemnation for the position in which the United States found itself. Charges against these leaders, however, were heard chiefly within the industry itself. The implications of Royal Dutch-Shell's annual report of 1920 were echoed by a well-informed European petroleum leader, who charged that the "all-powerful and overbearing" Americans had become overconfident, unintelligently allowing competitors like the Royal Dutch to establish a foothold.[22] Certain Jersey men themselves lent credence to the charge that Jersey Standard had been inordinately conservative in developing foreign sources of supply. E. J. Sadler had voiced this opinion in 1917. In 1919 he declared, ". . . this Company up to the present has failed to get the share in the foreign producing business to which its world position and capacity entitle it." Writing from Paris in 1921, one of the leaders of Jersey's French marketing affiliate stated, "My own feeling is that we are a bit ultra-conservative as regards our policy of expansion over here. . . . It is very easy to magnify things when one lives in the middle of the present European excitement, but it is also very easy for you, who are on the other side, to minimize these questions." These sentiments had also long been expressed by Heinrich Riedemann, an astute analyst of petroleum industry conditions.[23]

All these comments minimized or ignored entirely the obstacles Jersey Standard had faced in its efforts to do business abroad in the 1912-1918 period, but some observers believed Jersey had done less than it might have. Worth noting, too, is the further fact that, amid the protests of foreign discrimination against the American oil industry, at least one commentator had the temerity to suggest that perhaps the American oil companies were not altogether hapless and impotent. This was the theme sounded by Harry D. Frueauff, of the Cities Service Oil Company, who asserted that internationally minded American companies still dominated the world industry and were obviously anxious to minimize the postwar negotiations they had entered into for the acquisition of additional foreign properties and markets.[24] In some countries, such as Canada, moreover, the so-called restrictions on American participation were easily surmounted by the chartering of resident corporations.

Frueauff's article was probably no more welcomed by leaders of the American industry than Edgar's boast had been by the British. Companies like Jersey Standard stood to gain largely from an aroused anti-British sentiment in America and from the growing concern over the nation's future petroleum supply. Both Walter Teagle and T. A. O'Donnell, president of the American Petroleum Institute, indirectly took issue with Frueauff. Addressing the 1920 convention of the American Petroleum Institute, Teagle asked that equal opportunity be given Americans to share in foreign economic development:[25]

Our British friends, in endeavoring to explain the position their Government has taken since the armistice, have argued that, as the United States is now supplying 70 per cent of the world's current production, we should be well content with things as they are. This is an entirely fallacious view. They should restate their deduction in this way: The United States is now spending its petroleum wealth for the world's benefit, in order to meet 70 per cent of the world's present demand.

Americans have done this primarily because they had the most accessible oil and the facilities for refining and distributing it. Is it reasonable, however, to ask that they go heedlessly on to the quick exhaustion of their supply and then retire from the oil business?

O'Donnell, in a speech before the International Chamber of Commerce on June 29, 1920, voiced a similar plea, and in an article written for *The Lamp* declared:[26]

The trend of international events renders it imperative that the Government and the people of the United States grasp the existing situation and act resolutely; they must abandon that indifference to the morrow which has hitherto characterized their attitude toward the petroleum industry and its problems at home and abroad. Co-operative and constructive action between the Government and the industry will satisfactorily solve the problem, and in doing this we shall but put ourselves upon an equality with British oil companies in their relation to their Government. . . . The American oil industry asks only the support of the nation in giving it an equal status, putting it upon an equal footing with the nationals of other countries in the development of the world's petroleum resources—and it asks this in the interest of the nation.

Both Teagle and O'Donnell appealed for help on the ground of national interest. Teagle in particular and O'Donnell to a lesser extent had an obvious commercial incentive, but the counsel of both men was echoed in many quarters. Government investigations of world conditions, together with a succession of political events in Europe, furnished strong evidence of the essential identity at this time of American public and private interest and of the existence of a genuine threat to both.

The restrictive policies pursued by the British and the Dutch had been damaging in themselves, but the real menace, only partially explicable in terms of those policies, had been the rise of great international competitors. At the end of the war, to be sure, the Deutsche Bank had been crushed and its petroleum interests appropriated by the Allies. Business of the Galician and the French refining groups had been severely upset. The European marketing interests of the Rothschilds and the Nobels had been thrown into confusion by expropriation of their Russian sources of supply. The Royal Dutch-Shell, however, emerged mightier than ever.

After Deterding had taken over the management in 1900, the Royal Dutch in several instances threw in its interests with the English. The 1907 alliance of the Royal Dutch and Shell companies (Chapter 4) had strengthened the co-operation by means of corporate ties, and the rejection by Standard men of the truce with Deterding in 1910 had welded the British and Dutch groups still more firmly together. Although the Royal Dutch leader had not been averse to acting independently of his English associates and had even been accused of harboring pro-German sentiments in the early stages of the war, the Armistice found the British and Dutch oil interests in effective, if somewhat uneasy, rapport. Royal Dutch-Shell geologists were permitted access to British-conquered territories where no Americans were allowed to set foot. In 1919 the Royal Dutch purchased the Pearson interests in Mexico, for which the Jersey Company had unsuccessfully negotiated in 1912. In 1919 this purchase could not have been made without the approval of the British Foreign Office, and it was said at the time that the British government did not wish these properties to fall into American hands. The purchase was believed to have increased the world production of the Royal Dutch-Shell by about 50 per cent. Royal Dutch agreements were also in effect to supply the Admiralty with much of its fuel oil and to permit certain English companies to refine and market petroleum products in the United Kingdom without competition from Royal Dutch marketers. These commercial treaties were strengthened by the forthright encouragement of the Admiralty and of the Foreign Office.[27]

The British-Dutch alliance had thus become a serious menace to Jersey Standard's world trade in postwar months. Deterding, though retaining his Dutch citizenship, was made a Knight of the British Empire. Allegedly to foster the appearance of identity between British and Royal Dutch-Shell interests, but also, no doubt, because of the greater commercial convenience, Sir Henri moved his headquarters from The Hague to London. Here, before the great semicircular desk in the offices at St. Helen's Court, Deterding worked until close to midnight almost every night—driving himself and his organization mercilessly. Under Sir Henri's blustery and determined leadership, the Royal Dutch-Shell had come, by 1921, to control 11.0 per cent of the world's crude oil production, as compared with Jersey Standard's production of 6.6 per cent of the total.[28]

Well established, too, was Deterding's ambitious and clever scheme of attacking the Standard on its home ground. An aggressive marketing campaign had been launched on the West Coast and producing properties had been acquired there. Domestic competitors began to speak of the "Yellow Peril" as the characteristically colored Shell signs blossomed across the California countryside. In the Mid-Continent, bad luck and the managerial rigidities deriving from absentee control hampered Shell operations. American oilmen contemptuously referred to the Roxana Petroleum Corporation, the Royal Dutch Mid-Continent producing affiliate, as "Water Well Shell." In 1921 total Royal Dutch production in the United States, while large, was somewhat less than it had been in 1917. Nevertheless, when all the United States interests of the organization were consolidated in 1922 and vested in the Shell-Union Oil Corporation, it appeared that Royal Dutch-Shell holdings ranked among the largest in the petroleum industry of the country, with a net value on June 30, 1922, of $205,000,000.[29] The threat of these holdings was obvious, though the full impact of Henri Deterding's American sally had not yet been felt by Jersey Standard.

Despite the undoubted increase in the power of Deterding's great company, however, it was not easy at first for the general American public to reconcile the alarmist statements which began to multiply in 1919 with statistics of the day. Had not the United States industry supplied 80 per cent of Allied war needs? Did Americans need to worry about British imperialism when two-thirds of the world's production came from fields in the United States? Was it a matter of slight consequence that in 1920 the Jersey Standard organization had increased its crude production 48 per cent over that of the preceding year? Emphatic answers to these questions were forthcoming. On May 2, 1920, the Bureau of Mines warned of a probable gasoline shortage by summer. The United States, it appeared, was using up its supplies sixteen times faster than the rest of the world—a direct result of the tremendous automobile boom. There were predictions of gasoline price increases to 40 cents per gallon by autumn.[30] The attention of public and oil industry alike turned anxiously from figures of present production to those of potential crude supplies.

It was not difficult to prove that, if consumption did not level off or production increase, America would soon be dependent on foreign supplies. A survey by the engineering firm of Arthur D. Little, Inc., of Cambridge, Massachusetts, voiced the apprehension of the times: "To infer that still other fields remain to be disclosed is almost as unreasonable as to assert that the country has not yet been fully pioneered."[31] The Little report then pointed to the probability that the mounting curve of Mid-Continent production would soon flatten and condemned the petroleum industry for leading the nation down a blind alley: "In making the most of its [the petroleum industry's] opportunities for expansion, especially in connection with the war, it has assumed economic responsibilities far in excess of what it can hope to meet." The conviction that production in the United States would soon begin to decline was also shared by Dr. Van H. Manning of the Bureau of Mines.[32]

News from Mexico augmented growing fears for the future. In December of 1918 the magnificent Portrero del Llano well Number 4, which in eight years had yielded more than 100,000,000 barrels of oil, began to flow salt water. Eleven months later the same fate overtook Doheny's famed Juan Casiano Number 7. Between December of 1918 and April of 1920, encroachment of salt water in the southern Mexican fields snuffed out one well after another and reduced the potential production of those fields by about 50 per cent. These misfortunes, coupled with political interference with the petroleum industry by the Carranza government, threatened to deprive the United States altogether of the large supplies it had been drawing from across the border.

Public agitation over the international aspects of the petroleum situation was accompanied by private concern in company and State Department circles as Jersey Standard's efforts to effect an equitable disposition of certain of the war-tangled affairs of its German and Romanian affiliates began to encounter the first chill blasts of hostile postwar diplomacy.

Compared with the vast operational stakes for which the Jersey Company elected to gamble in 1919, the matter of war damage and seizure claims was small indeed. Nevertheless, certain important principles were involved. It soon became apparent, too, that such claims could not be considered by the company as a problem distinct from that of obtaining an equitable participation in foreign markets and producing properties. These claims fell into two main classes: the validation of Jersey Standard's title to twelve DAPG tankers which had remained in German ports or shipyards during the war and the reimbursement for destruction of Româno-Americana property. In both cases the company believed that, legally and morally, its rights were established beyond question.

In 1914 and 1915 Britain and France had formally consented to the transfer of most of the DAPG fleet to the Jersey Company. Jersey men contended that this consent was tantamount to a direct acknowledgment of Jersey's beneficial interest in the properties of its German affiliate. Furthermore, invalidation by the United States Alien Property Custodian of the 1917 "sale" by the Jersey Company to the Riedemanns of its stock in the DAPG effectively negated any possible argument that because of that transfer the DAPG was no longer an American-owned company.

In Romania a part of Jersey Standard's loss had occurred as a direct result of the orders of the Anglo-Romanian Destruction Commission, which at the time had promised restitution. The remainder of the loss there was occasioned by German military occupation and clearly was redeemable within the reparations provisions of the Versailles Treaty. In both cases it seemed that the voluble expressions by high British and French officials of their indebtedness to American oil interests for supplying critical Allied war needs betokened a speedy and satisfactory settlement of losses incurred by such interests in meeting those needs.

The disillusionment was swift. Early in 1919 an astonishing rumor was heard that the twelve DAPG tankers, of which eight had been afloat and four under construction, were to be turned over by the Reparations Commission to France, in alleged conformance to provisions of the impending peace treaty.[33] The treaty provisions cited were those which stated that Germany should replace, ton for ton, the Allied shipping destroyed during the war. For this purpose all German vessels of 1,600 tons or larger were to be confiscated and turned over to the Reparations Commission for allotment to the Allies.

A Jersey Company effort to repossess the eight serviceable tankers was blocked by the Allied Supreme Economic Council. The company then launched a vigorous protest with the State Department. This protest and the voluminous arguments presented by Jersey's counsel, Chester O. Swain, and consultant, John Bassett Moore, failed to bring about a satisfactory settlement of the issue. A second attempt by the company to take possession of the DAPG ships was thwarted by the Allied Naval Court at Hamburg, and in August of 1919 the Shipping Section of the Supreme Council allocated the vessels on the following basis: to France, 23,000 tons; to Great Britain, 12,800 tons; to Belgium, 12,000 tons; to Italy, 10,-000 tons; to the United States, 3,200 tons. The eight serviceable tankers were placed in British custody and dispatched to British waters pending final settlement of the dispute. This action, coming at a time when the shipping shortage was acute, placed Jersey Standard at a disadvantage in the race for European markets. Behind the move Jersey men professed to discern the influence of its rivals for those markets.[34]

While the Jersey Company was making every effort through official channels to block the allocation of the eight tankers then in British custody, an ingenious plan was devised to prevent the four unfinished vessels in German shipyards from encountering a similar fate. Company records give no clue to the author of this plan, but the keen comprehension displayed of the fluid German political situation of the day strongly suggests that Heinrich Riedemann was responsible.

In September of 1919 Dr. Wilhelm Riedemann, a brother of Heinrich and a resident at that time of the German city of Danzig, organized a company known as the Baltisch-Amerikanische Petroleum-Import-Gesellschaft, mbH. To Bapico, as the new company was called, were then sold the four unfinished DAPG tankers. This sale was effected at a time when the Versailles Treaty had been drawn up but before the German ratification had become effective. It was known, then, that Danzig was to be made by the treaty a Free City, but until the effective date of the treaty (January 10, 1920) Danzig was still German and Danzigers were still Germans. Since there was no provision in the treaty which covered the sale of property by one German subject or company to another, the sale by DAPG to Bapico was perfectly valid. Yet, when Danzig formally

achieved the status of a Free City some weeks later, the property of
Danzig citizens became immune from seizure under the reparations provisions of the treaty.[35]

Faced with this neat coup, the Reparations Commission at first challenged the validity of the sale and then approved the transfer. In May of
1921 the four Bapico tankers were formally declared by the Reparations
Commission not deliverable to the Allies under the Versailles Treaty. All
shares of Bapico were subsequently acquired by the Standard Petroleum
Co. (Glarus), a wholly owned Jersey Standard affiliate.[36]

Meanwhile, the agitation over the eight British-confiscated tankers continued. Jersey's position was backed by the United States Shipping Board,
the Navy, and the State Department, but American diplomatic efforts
were impaired and American prestige abroad lowered by the refusal of
Congress, in November of 1919, to ratify the Versailles Treaty. Moreover,
France, which had long depended upon Jersey Standard for a major percentage of its petroleum supplies and which at that very time was actively
soliciting financial aid and political backing from the United States for its
treaty demands, demonstrated a perplexing reluctance to support the
Jersey cause before the Reparations Commission. Senator Berenger, head
of the French Petroleum Mission, launched a movement to convert the
wartime government controls into a permanent government monopoly
which threatened Jersey's marketing outlets in France. In March of 1920
Berenger publicly condemned the company's efforts to take over the
DAPG tankers and suggested to a Jersey representative that the company
should help the French obtain the tankers, for, among other reasons, this
gesture would emphasize the French victory over Germany. He also
hinted that the Jersey Company might have better success in dealing with
the Reparations Commission if it would offer better trading terms for
supplying the French market.[37]

Contemporary efforts by the Jersey Company to effect a settlement of
its Romanian war-damage claims also ran into difficulty, strengthening
still further the uneasy American conjectures as to what was happening in
the postwar world of oil.

After much research and consultation, Jersey Standard and Româno-
Americana executives had arrived at a figure of 284,000,000 *lei*, which
was taken to represent damages and lost profits resulting from the actions
of the Anglo-Romanian Destruction Commission. On January 21, 1919,
the Jersey Company instituted a claim for restitution in this amount from

the British government. An additional claim of 673,000,000 *lei* was filed with the Reparations Commission against Germany for losses, chiefly crude oil, suffered under German military occupation.[38]

Company records do not indicate at what conversion rate these claims were figured, and the constantly diminishing postwar value of the *lei* in terms of dollars makes comparisons difficult. It is known, however, that because of the depreciation of the *lei* the Jersey claims were computed at approximately five times the prewar values. On this basis the claim against Britain was approximately $28,400,000 and against Germany $67,300,000. In supporting these figures E. J. Sadler pointed out that, on the basis of prewar earnings and prospects, Româno was worth $100,000,000 rather than the meager $10,586,000 at which the properties had been carried on the Jersey books in 1917.[39]

The claim against Britain was based directly upon the sequence of political events in 1915 and 1916, which, Jersey Standard alleged, established British responsibility for the destruction, and upon the British promises made in those years and later. Romania's entry into the war, Jersey counsel asserted, had been the result of a virtual ultimatum delivered by Great Britain and Italy. The military reverses that led to the destruction of the fields had followed from Britain's policy of allowing the Romanians to fight alone against great odds. The British War Cabinet had initiated the mission to destroy the fields and refineries before German occupation, and a British officer had been given the task of administering the scorched-earth policy. This officer had declared that the Allies would pay and had given a letter to this effect to the Romanian government. On December 3, 1916, England had dispatched a letter of indemnification to Romania, promising that the Allied governments would pay for the damage. In the spring of 1917 the British government had invited all who had suffered to file claims for damages and allowed the claimants to believe that the Allies, or at least Great Britain, would make good on the promises of payment.[40]

From the time its claim was filed the Jersey Company worked closely with the State Department, which made several inquiries as to Britain's intent to pay. Lord Curzon, Minister of Foreign Affairs, replied to the American Ambassador that Britain and the Allies were responsible only to the Romanian government for destruction incurred. Soon thereafter the British Court of Appeals in London held that there had been no agreement on the part of the Crown to make restitution to private companies for property damaged in Romania. Britain asserted that responsibility for these damages lay with the Romanian government, since that government had assumed control of the oil fields shortly before the destruction of installations and had ratified the acts of the Destruction Commission.[41]

In 1920 it was difficult indeed to look upon such diplomatic and legal rebuffs in a dispassionate way. Irrespective of the legal arguments advanced, the initial course of both the Romanian and the tanker disputes lent credence to the suspicion that powerful international forces were aligned against American commercial interests. Jersey men viewed both episodes from an understandably partisan viewpoint and without benefit of historical perspective. It appeared to them that Britain—pinched, to be sure, by economic pressures and wounded in the war she had done so much to win—was not averse to the employment of forceful measures in the interest of national recovery. In the tanker controversy the French, too, were displaying a marked and adroit propensity for employing strong economic controls to advance national goals. Early in the course of both disputes the fact had been demonstrated that the war-born spirit of international co-operation had vanished with the coming of the peace. In an aggressively nationalistic postwar world it seemed clear that justice could best be obtained by the strong. But it was equally clear that commercial strength no longer sufficed to guarantee the achievement of international commercial ambitions. These pointed lessons were not lost upon the men at 26 Broadway who were directing Jersey Standard's quest for foreign oil resources.

The various public revelations of the actual or presumed course of nationalistic policy in foreign nations, coupled with facts, fears, and suppositions regarding the exhaustion of petroleum reserves in the United States and Mexico, generated the prerequisite heat and excitement for Congressional action. More important still, a profound change in American foreign policy was ushered in.

For years American businessmen had practiced their "dollar diplomacy" abroad in the face of indifference to their ventures on the part of the State Department. The year 1919 marked the end of this period. The swing of history's pendulum had reached one extremity and was beginning its ponderous reversal. The fact that the State Department commenced to extend its active support to American businessmen abroad is not only of utmost significance in this period of Jersey Standard's history, but is fundamental to an understanding of the Jersey Company today.[42] The complex reasons for this change in official attitude need not be examined in detail, for they have been exhaustively studied by others.

Fear for the future of America's petroleum supplies was only one element in the situation. As a result of the war effort, federal agencies had become more cognizant of and more sympathetic toward the problems of the domestic petroleum industry than ever before. A significant confidential report of the Bureau of Mines admitted, in 1918, that amalgamation of individual petroleum interests into strong, integrated units offered the greatest hope for efficiency in foreign producing operations.[43] The policy of critical surveillance which characterized the first years of the Federal Trade Commission activities had been somewhat modified; a Commission report in 1916 formed the basis for the Export Trade Act of 1918, which permitted business combinations in foreign trade.[44] The crushing defeat of the Democratic Party in the 1920 elections was reassuring to business, notwithstanding the facts that the second Wilson administration in mid-term had abandoned its harassing tactics and that the new State Department attitude had been initiated by Democrats. On a broader scale, the leaven of nationalism, it must be remembered, was working in the United States as well as elsewhere in the world. The country had emerged from the war a mighty world power, with all the pride, the responsibilities, and the necessities that went with such a position of eminence. This was an intangible factor, but one of considerable importance. Congress, therefore, spurred by private interests, armed with professional prognostications, and supported by a reasonable unanimity of official executive, administrative, and diplomatic viewpoints, was able and willing to act.

In April of 1920 Congress, urged on by aroused legislators, authorized the Secretary of the Navy to apply leasing restrictions to certain oil-bearing areas. These naval reserves were established ostensibly to assure an adequate supply of naval fuel, but the provisions of the act allowed the government to exclude from these regions such companies as it wished. The United States, faced with the Closed Door policy abroad, thus closed its own door slightly. In May, President Wilson transmitted to the Senate a report authorized earlier in response to a resolution by Senator Gore. The so-called Polk Report severely denounced British policy and showed that Americans were excluded from many important oil-producing regions of the world. On the same day that the Polk Report was transmitted, the Phelan bill was introduced into Congress, authorizing the formation of the United States Oil Corporation—a government company devoted to the purpose of exploiting oil in foreign countries. This bill was not enacted into law, but the fact that it was drafted and in-

troduced was a sign of the prevalent agitation. Another Phelan bill introduced in January of 1921 was designed to cut off American petroleum
supplies to countries that discriminated against American nationals.
In March of 1922, Secretary of the Interior Fall amended regulations
about leasing Indian lands to prohibit alien intrusion on these properties. The Open Door was closed a little more. In March of 1923 the
Federal Trade Commission reported the detailed results of an investigation, authorized in 1922, of foreign ownership and national restrictions
in the world petroleum industry. This investigation confirmed the earlier
findings of the Polk Report and pointed in some detail to the menacing
growth of the Royal Dutch-Shell. Though these general measures had
only a limited effect upon the existing situation, they did serve to publicize the facts and issues involved, thereby paving the way for the particular and decisive diplomatic actions which are considered in the pages
that follow.

Against this general politico-economic background Jersey Standard
enunciated what was termed at the time a new policy and began to take
the organizational steps to make that policy effective.

ADMINISTRATIVE FOUNDATION FOR
A "NEW POLICY"

In January of 1920 Walter Teagle announced that henceforth Jersey
Standard intended to show an interest in every producing area in the
world, no matter where situated. This, of course, was not a new policy at
all. Teagle's statement signified that the existing policy of foreign expansion which he and Sadler had been advocating and which the company
had been practicing on a restricted scale for at least six years would be
broadened. Some such formal public statement of company plans was
essential, however, as a basis for subsequent efforts to enlist active government support for Jersey Standard abroad.

Within the company administrative changes were already under way.
The reader will recall from Chapter 4 that E. J. Sadler had forcefully outlined the necessity for Jersey Standard to expand its foreign producing
activities. In 1917 he recommended that the work then being done in
foreign fields be consolidated in a single department. In 1919 Sadler attacked company procedures again, reiterating and amplifying his earlier
recommendations:[45]

Our attitude toward producing proposals is not such as would improve our
chances to take advantage of them. We have no special department or channel

through which to look for such opportunities, or even to receive them. There is hardly a desk in the building to which foreign proposals do not come as a side issue, and I might almost say as an inconvenience, if not a nuisance. We are so little disposed to take on foreign production or producing propositions that most of them are consummated before we hear of the propositions. When by accident they come to New York, we are slow in acknowledging receipt and almost never investigate the propositions on their merits.

. . . . . .

Primarily, we should decide as far as possible what amount of money we wish to spend annually in acquiring foreign holdings, and where we wish to spend it. We should organize a department which would occupy itself exclusively with foreign possibilities and be held responsible if other people develop a serious production without our being protected.

We should have representatives in all fields where there is a serious production, in order to obtain prompt reports of developments and avoid surprises. For those countries where we wish to make investment it would be necessary to have scouting parties to give us the general information so that we could appreciate offers and opportunities which would come to us through our representatives in the fields where there is already production.

In this same commentary Sadler advocated exploratory efforts in virtually every area in the world where petroleum was believed to exist in commercial quantities.

In 1919 the Foreign Producing Department was established, with Sadler in charge. It is not clear what relationship was contemplated between the new department and those domestic producing operations headed by A. F. Corwin. Sadler's aggressive personality, however, rapidly established the foreign division as a distinct entity. Sadler reported directly to Teagle and the board. Corwin necessarily participated in many matters relating to foreign production, but Sadler's was the voice of authority and he even began to encroach on Corwin's designated responsibilities in the domestic producing branch of the organization. In 1926 the Foreign Producing Department, as such, ceased to exist, and an all-embracing Producing Department was organized, under Sadler's direction, with foreign and domestic divisions.

Organizational lines in the foreign producing business were extended and strengthened as the importance of the foreign business grew. In 1919 a producing office was established in Paris, and Harry G. Seidel, who had presided over Româno-Americana destinies in the war and immediate postwar years, was placed in charge. This office served as a clearing-house and co-ordinating agency for most of the European and Near East producing activities, although no company policy was formulated there.

Geological information was compiled, tabulated, and forwarded to 26 Broadway, as was all information of importance relating to European petroleum affairs. The rapid changes that were taking place in foreign operations at the time were ample justification for the establishment of this branch headquarters and, in 1924, of the European Committee.[46] This committee was composed of Jersey's leading European managers and was most intimately concerned with marketing affairs. The conferences of these high executives, however, provided occasions for discussion of all phases of the foreign business; in certain instances company policy was formulated there. The European Committee was particularly effective in those not infrequent situations where differences between Continental and American operating methods had to be called to the attention of the men at 26 Broadway. In all cases the Jersey board attached great weight to the recommendations of this important group.

As early as the middle of 1920 Sadler was able to report that the company had already come close to fulfilling the promise of Teagle's January, 1920, statement. In a detailed memorandum the head of the new department traced existing activities, or the desire for participation, in actual or potential producing properties in Mexico, Romania, Russia, Venezuela, Poland, Bolivia, Morocco, Algeria, Tunis, Madagascar, Spain, Iraq, Persia, Palestine, Argentina, Brazil, Alaska, Egypt, China, and the Dutch East Indies.[47] Jersey Standard was openly committed to the race for world petroleum supplies, and a sequence of important events now began to unfold in response to that commitment. Functional lines dividing one branch of the business from another were transgressed, and all phases of the company's foreign activities became implicated in the web of international political intrigue.

Chapter 11

The Quest for Crude Oil in the Middle East
1919-1928

BEFORE 1918, efforts of the Jersey Company to expand foreign crude oil reserves had been directed primarily at territories adjacent to foreign markets which the company wished to develop. In certain instances—the Dutch East Indies, for example—competitive strategy and the particularly valuable nature of the crude oil were governing considerations which more than offset unfavorable geographic factors. In other areas—Mexico was one—unfavorable political and competitive conditions were outweighed by advantageous geographic factors. In all cases the search for reserves was influenced by numerous circumstances quite apart from the mere knowledge that oil was present in a given region.

In the immediate postwar years such considerations lost some of their restrictive influence upon company plans. A greatly expanded tanker fleet, together with rapid advances in pipeline construction technology and in drilling techniques, helped to overcome physical obstacles which in prewar years were regarded as forbidding. More important yet was the prospect of a great postwar boom in business and the fear of a world-wide oil shortage. At a time when the growth of large integrated competitors was pronounced, such a shortage posed a serious threat to the Jersey Standard organization, which in 1918—despite considerable progress in the direction of more nearly complete integration—was producing only 16 per cent of the crude oil consumed in its refineries. It was for these reasons that the company was forced to abandon its somewhat selective foreign producing program and to commence seeking crude oil reserves wherever they might be found, almost irrespective of location, competitive circumstances, political difficulties, or the nature of the crude.

Nowhere is the urgency of Jersey Standard's quest for foreign producing territory better illustrated than in Mesopotamia and Persia. Few operational incidents reveal in so concentrated a setting the variety and scope of problems encountered by the company in attempting to pursue its foreign objectives in an altered postwar world. The pages that follow trace the Mesopotamian experience in detail, both because of its far-ranging significance and because a true understanding of Jersey Standard's aims and methods can best be achieved by re-creating something of the flavor of time and place and circumstance. The Persian story is presented in broad outline, not only because it is less important than the Mesopotamian episode in terms of tangible results, but also because of the similarity of background, extenuating circumstances, goals contemplated, and methods employed in the two areas.

The account of Jersey Standard's efforts both in Mesopotamia and in Persia is a composite of many historical episodes, some of which reach back into the nineteenth century. Selected facts from an adventurous background of commercial conflict must be set forth in order to establish the situation which the company faced in 1919, when it turned its attention to the potentialities of oil supplies in the Middle East.

RIVALRIES AND ALLIANCES, 1901-1919

At the turn of the century the Sultan of the Turkish Empire numbered among his rambling and loosely governed dependencies the region of Mesopotamia—today the independent nation of Iraq. Immediately to the east, the desert wastes of Persia—or Iran, as it later came to be known—stretched from the Persian Gulf to the Caspian Sea. The presence of petroleum in those largely inhospitable regions had been noted in the century before Christ by the Greek historian Herodotus. Oil seeps were plentiful, and asphalt played an important part in the enduring architecture of the ancient civilizations that flourished and died there. Euphrates boatmen impregnated their wicker *gufas* with tar, and pagan rites were performed before the mysterious flames of Baba Gurgur.[1] These facts attracted commercial notice as soon as the growing petroleum industry began to offer incentives for a world-wide search for oil supplies.

As early as 1888 Turkish Sultan Abdul Hamid had caused a survey of the oil regions to be made, appropriating immense tracts of land for his own personal benefit. The infiltration of independent explorers and representatives of large and established oil concerns commenced, and it was not long before British and German interests—both commercial and political—were in conflict.[2]

In 1904 a Deutsche Bank consortium obtained a railroad and mining concession, but the consortium was pressed for working capital with which to pursue its objectives. The British-dominated National Bank of Turkey possessed capital, but found its ambitions blocked by the German-held concessions and by strongly entrenched German influence in the murky realms of Turkish politics. It was clear that the circumstances called for an alliance between British and German interests.[3]

The task of channeling the intense ambitions of these bitter rivals and effecting a conciliation of opposing interests owed much to the skillful mediation of Calouste Sarkis Gulbenkian, a young Armenian whose father and uncles were prominent merchants of Russian oil. Gulbenkian had studied the Turkish oil regions and was well versed in Turkish politics. Some called him the Talleyrand of oil diplomacy. In the complicated negotiations which were undertaken between the British and German groups, Gulbenkian's genius was evident.[4]

In 1912 an accord was reached and the Turkish Petroleum Company, organized in 1911, became the vehicle for consolidating the interests of the various groups. To this company the Germans were to turn over their mining concessions, studies, reports, and priorities. The division of shares in the company later became the subject of an important controversy. Gulbenkian relates, in contradiction to the claims of other participants in the venture, that a 40 per cent interest was put at his disposal, to be used for the purpose of obtaining the participation of oil groups capable of carrying out the practical work of exploration and exploitation. Gulbenkian, according to his own account, personally retained a 15 per cent interest, turning the remaining 25 per cent over to Deterding and the Royal Dutch-Shell.[5]

While these plans to develop the petroleum resources of Mesopotamia were maturing, an attempt was being made by officials in nearby Persia to peddle a sixty-year concession to some half-million square miles of territory in the regions east of the Sultan's domains. This concession covered all of Persia, except the five northern provinces which clustered in a crescent around the southern shores of the Caspian Sea. In 1901 an adventurous Australian miner named William Knox D'Arcy took a mighty gamble and purchased the concession.[6]

Notwithstanding the numerous and spectacular oil seepages, D'Arcy's early efforts were not successful, and he soon exhausted his capital. At this stage in the development the British Naval Fuel Committee induced the Burmah Oil Company, Limited, a British organization which was then doing a large business in India, to come to D'Arcy's assistance. In 1905 a concession syndicate was formed. Capital for further exploration in Persia was provided, chiefly by the Burmah Company, and exploratory operations were continued. By 1908, however, the capital of the syndicate was nearly exhausted; orders were dispatched from London directing D'Arcy to abandon drilling. D'Arcy was then working in the Bakhtiari hills, about 145 miles from the Persian Gulf—an area known to the natives as Maidan-i-Naftun. Before these instructions reached their destination, D'Arcy's drill had punched into the Asmari lime formation, and a rush of oil flowed over his derrick.[7]

Developmental efforts following on the heels of the discovery were restricted in scope by the remoteness of this region from important world markets and trade routes, the rugged nature of the terrain, the outbreaks of violence among the native tribes, and the primitive economic state of the country. In 1909 the Anglo-Persian Oil Company was formed to take over and develop the D'Arcy concession. By 1914 thirty wells had been sunk at Maidan, although only twelve of these were actually drilled into the pay formation. All these twelve were flowing wells, but since the company did not have facilities for disposing of the oil, all were wholly or partly shut in. In 1912 a refinery was constructed at Abadan, near the head of the Persian Gulf, and a pipeline was laid across the desert to the field at Maidan.[8]

These developments were examined with interest by Winston Churchill, then First Lord of the Admiralty, and in 1914 the British government invested £2,200,000 in the Anglo-Persian Oil Company. This state undertaking was conceived in order to encourage the development of fuel oil supplies for the Royal Navy, to assure the procurement of those supplies at a reasonable cost, and to free Britain of dependence upon non-British suppliers.[9] With such formidable backing, Anglo-Persian became a factor of importance in the world industry.

Now the hitherto separate paths of the Anglo-Persian Oil Company in Persia and the Turkish Petroleum Company in Mesopotamia began to converge, and the mighty force of British imperialism forged a significant link between oil operations in the two countries.

The British government, established in Persia and cognizant of the potentialities of Mesopotamia, brought strong pressure to bear to obtain an interest in the Turkish Petroleum Company. The measures employed to achieve this end need not be examined here: the pertinent circumstance is that on March 24, 1914, a document was signed at the British Foreign Office which provided that the shares of the Turkish Petroleum Company should be allotted 50 per cent to Anglo-Persian, 25 per cent to the Royal Dutch-Shell, and 25 per cent to the German group. The 15 per cent interest claimed by Gulbenkian, who had been excluded from the negotiations, was swallowed up. Both the Royal Dutch and the Anglo-Persian companies consented, in return, to grant Gulbenkian a beneficiary 2½ per cent interest in the Turkish Petroleum Company for life, without voting rights. Gulbenkian professed his stupefaction at what he characterized as "a preposterous usurpation of power crushing a minority interest without ever consulting or asking the latter's advice."[10]

The aggrieved Gulbenkian at once sought the advice of leading lawyers in England, who told him that his rights could not be thus arbitrarily extinguished, and that the signatories to the 1914 agreement must finally come to satisfactory terms with him. Gulbenkian thereupon resumed his active participation in the management of the Turkish Petroleum Company, pending final settlement of the dispute.

While these events were taking place, the directors of the Turkish Petroleum Company were simultaneously endeavoring to obtain a new concession from the Turkish government which would replace the somewhat indefinite German concessions upon which the company had predicated its existence and operational plans. Early in 1914 certain assurances were extended by the Turkish Ministry of Finance, and the draft of a new concession was prepared. Before this draft could be ratified, the outbreak of war interjected entirely new elements into the tangled situation.[11] Turkey entered the war on the side of the Central Powers. Great Britain confiscated and sequestered the German-held shares of the Turkish Petroleum Company. British expeditionary forces were dispatched to the Middle and Near East to protect Empire interests there, and British agents set to work with Lawrence of Arabia to precipitate a general Arab uprising against the Turkish Sultan.

In 1915 secret negotiations, which Gulbenkian may well have initiated and in which he appears to have served as intermediary, were said to have been commenced between the British and French governments to turn over to the latter the 25 per cent interest of the German group in the Turkish Petroleum Company. Gulbenkian relates that Deterding hoped, by assisting the French to acquire this interest, to gain the favors of France for the Royal Dutch-Shell and thereby pave the way for seizure of at least a part of the French market which Jersey Standard had hitherto largely supplied.[12]

An agreement was at length reached whereby the British government promised that the German shares would be ceded to the French government at the end of the war. The entire subject of Franco-British spheres of influence in the Middle and Near East was defined and set forth in the so-called Sykes-Picot Agreement of 1916.

The Armistice, in turn, introduced new conditions, necessities, and demands. British and French disagreement over the terms of the Sykes-Picot Agreement was ironed out, and a new compact, secretly arrived at, was signed on April 24 and 25, 1920, and made public soon after.[13] This, the San Remo Oil Agreement, shocked American oilmen and legislators alike out of their complacency.

The basic purpose contemplated by the agreement was to consummate a Franco-British petroleum alliance. A separate agreement had already been reached at the San Remo Conference which specified that Great Britain be assigned a protective mandate over Palestine and Mesopotamia, while France was granted a mandate over Syria and Lebanon. The petroleum pact of April 24-25 awarded France a 25 per cent interest in Mesopotamian petroleum—in other words, the German shares in the Turkish Petroleum Company—and the French were to permit construction of two pipelines from Mesopotamia through French-mandated territories to the Mediterranean. France and Britain agreed to co-operate in supporting the interests of their nationals in subsequent endeavors to acquire oil concessions elsewhere.[14] Britain thus recognized the 1916 promise to allow France participation in Mesopotamia, while France realized her long-standing ambition of obtaining a foothold in the Levant and a newer ambition, born of the war experience, of gaining a direct interest in petroleum supplies.

A potential threat to Jersey Standard ambitions had already been posed by the working partnership between the Royal Dutch-Shell and the increasingly formidable Anglo-Persian Oil Company. The Anglo-French oil alliance of 1920 compounded that threat. With the British and French governments making common interest with the Jersey Company's chief international competitor, and with both governments motivated by intense nationalism, Jersey Standard could scarcely expect to obtain their co-operation in re-establishing its foreign business. Company records present no conclusive evidence on the subject, but it is not unreasonable to surmise that the new competitive alignments not only were working against Jersey Standard's re-entry into the French market, but also were exerting an unfavorable influence on the company's efforts to repossess its German tankers and to recover from Britain its Romanian war losses.

The publication of the San Remo Oil Agreement caused a world-wide stir. Statements contained in company records indicate that, though Jersey men suspected that something was brewing in Europe, they were unprepared for the document that was flaunted in their faces. The company's usually comprehensive intelligence system had failed to yield vital information. At 26 Broadway there was ignorance as to the details of the various concession claims in Mesopotamia, the detailed geologic potentialities of the region, the past and present political situation there, and the relative influence of the various groups participating in the Turkish Petroleum Company. Very little detailed information was available about Anglo-Persian operations in Persia.[15] A lively scramble ensued, therefore, to obtain detailed information—political, economic, and geological. Jersey Standard's reactions to the San Remo pact need not be further set forth here, however, for they form the subject of the next section of this chapter.

Other reactions were voiced. Coming at a time when America was already aroused to the peril of diminishing domestic supplies and pervaded by a distrust of British imperialism, the San Remo Agreement provoked fervent outbursts in the American press.[16] The chief protest, based as much on moral as on economic or political grounds, was that the pact was a brazen violation of the mandatory principle of equal rights to all the Allies—a principle that Great Britain and France had openly supported at the very time these two nations were secretly working out their discriminatory petroleum agreement. Was the United States, which had done so much to win the war, now to be excluded from participation in commercial opportunities in the defeated nations? This was the question of the day, and European diplomats were not slow in parrying it with a question of their own. Was the United States entitled to such participation when it had renounced the League of Nations and withdrawn into isolationism?

JERSEY AMBITIONS AND THE OPEN DOOR

On February 24, 1919, while the political fate of the defeated but defiant Turkish Empire was being pondered around European conference tables, Walter Teagle addressed a memorandum to four of his fellow directors. This note establishes the beginning of a serious interest by Jersey Standard in the possibilities of Middle East oil.

Relaying information received from an unnamed informant in London, Teagle wrote:[17]

The future of the present Persian fields is particularly promising. There is every reason to believe that these Persian fields are large in extent and that they extend over into Mesopotamia. . . . In the settlement of the division of Turkey, consideration should be given to the oil possibilities. In this connection it should be recalled that John Worthington always stated that undoubtedly the Euphrates Valley would produce a large quantity of oil. I am wondering if there is any way we can get into the oil producing end of the game in Mesopotamia.

Worthington, the former head geologist of the company, had visited Persia and Mesopotamia in 1910 in connection with the largely unsuccessful endeavor by Jersey Standard to obtain at that time an entry into foreign producing fields.[18] Thus a decade had intervened between receipt of encouraging field reports and effective action by the Jersey directorate. In this interval the Standard Oil Company of New York had acquired a few concessionary rights to acreage in Palestine, Syria, and European Turkey, though no drilling had actually been done.[19] Jersey's tardiness was by no means incomprehensible. In 1910 the potentialities of the Near and Middle East had been nebulous at best, and at the time the area was less promising than many others, such as the Dutch East Indies.

By 1919, however, all factors had combined to produce fertile soil for the seed of Teagle's suggestion to take quick root. In March of 1919 Director F. D. Asche was asking Corwin, head of domestic production operations, if a geological map of Mesopotamia was available. At this same time several government officials were expressing the opinion that American companies should interest themselves in Middle East oil. Already the rumors of American exclusion by British interests were being heard. As early as August, 1918, pressure and subterfuge had been employed by the British to gain access to New York Standard's Near East concession data, and in March of 1919 that company reported to the State Department its conviction that the British would not allow any American company to operate in British-mandated territories.[20] "It occurs to me," Asche confided to Corwin, "that we may want to make some representation to our Government on this question." Corwin sent a map to Asche and suggested that a note be delivered to the State Department indicating the desire of the company to explore Mesopotamia.[21]

Jersey Standard, unaware of the exact nature and extent of the political obstacles which it faced, seemed determined to force the issue into the open. One month after Teagle had called the attention of the directorate to Mesopotamian oil, E. J. Sadler was in Paris talking with American delegates to the Peace Conference about the still vague prospects of a British monopoly in Mesopotamia. Sadler took a gloomy view of such an eventuality, and the opinion was voiced in company circles that British domination would be a greater menace to Jersey's business than a German victory would have been.[22]

In the summer of 1919 plans were made for a geological expedition to Mesopotamia. Jersey men in both Europe and America endeavored to contact former Anglo-Persian employees who might be able to supply information about the country. Sadler informed Hunt that political conditions in the Middle East were such that an Englishman had best be employed to make the journey. There was, however, some difficulty in finding a qualified geologist who was willing to accept the assignment, and before a suitable candidate had been selected all plans for an expedition were placed in abeyance. The British military authorities in Bagdad had refused permission for any American geological parties to prospect in Mesopotamia. A similar prohibition had already been laid on the New York Standard geologists in Palestine and Turkey.[23]

The events that had been and were taking place behind British military censorship in Mesopotamia may be reconstructed from Jersey Company records. In 1917 the British military authorities had acceded to a proposal made by the Anglo-Persian Oil Company that it should drill for oil near Bagdad. A complete refinery, with a capacity of about 1,600 barrels daily, was purchased by Anglo-Persian in New Zealand, dismantled, and shipped to Diyala, seven miles south of Bagdad, where it was placed in operation. The drilling program appears never to have got under way, but a small production was obtained at Kiayarah, 39 miles south of Mosul, from five shallow wells sunk by the German garrison prior to its retreat. In 1918 Anglo-Persian and Royal Dutch-Shell geologists arrived on the scene with instructions to make as rapid a reconnaissance as possible. Under the protection of the British occupational forces they commenced a very intensive survey of Mesopotamia.[24] This survey was actively under way in the fall of 1919, when Sadler was reporting that the frontiers of the region were irrevocably closed to American survey parties.

The Jersey Company, acting on the basis of the best information that could be gathered, launched a protest with the State Department.[25] The Open Door—equal rights of exploitation to all—was again on its way to becoming a *cause célèbre.*

In October of 1919 the State Department, in direct response to the company's protest, communicated to the British government its hope that no discrimination against American nationals would be permitted in the occupied territories. The British Foreign Office replied that, until the political status of Mesopotamia should have been determined, no oil reconnaissance parties would be allowed to work there, nor would any concessions be granted nor any oil operations permitted except those necessary to support the occupational garrison. Appropriate orders were thereupon issued by the Foreign Office. Upon receipt of instructions from London, the resident Anglo-Persian manager forbade further exploration by a Royal Dutch-Shell party which was then at work. On January 10, 1920, the American Consul at Bagdad reported to the Secretary of State that no further permits were being issued for survey parties.[26]

The horse, however, had been stolen before the door was closed. The Royal Dutch-Shell and Anglo-Persian already had much of the geological information which Jersey Standard lacked and which now, technically, all parties were banned from seeking. This exclusive information was certain to be of inestimable value when the matter of Mesopotamian concessions came up for discussion and negotiation. Worse than this, however, was the fact that, despite Foreign Office instructions, reconnaissance by the Royal Dutch-Shell and possibly by Anglo-Persian as well actually continued after the Foreign Office prohibition had been pronounced. Survey parties were still active as late as 1921. The Anglo-Persian field manager himself reported that Royal Dutch-Shell geologists were later able to produce a complete and detailed map of territories that these geologists had been forbidden to enter.[27]

Having failed to get a survey party into Mesopotamia, Teagle and Sadler now adopted a plan of action designed to block, insofar as possible, the exploitation by Anglo-Persian and the Royal Dutch-Shell of their initial advantage. Sadler left Paris, called briefly in Bucharest to look into Româno-Americana affairs, and then proceeded to Constantinople. Here his Annapolis background stood him in good stead. The cruiser *Galveston* was in Constantinople at the time, and its commander was Captain Greenslade, an Academy classmate of Sadler's. Furthermore, Rear Admiral Mark L. Bristol was serving as United States High Commissioner to Turkey. In this friendly naval atmosphere Sadler talked at length with Bristol about the Mesopotamian situation, and on January 8, 1920, sent him a letter which contained a clever and far-reaching suggestion:[28]

It is our intention to persist in the attempt to explore the territory, but until the situation is entirely clear, and all interested parties have had an opportunity to explore the territory, we feel that it would be the greatest injustice to allow any concessions to be taken. We, of course, appreciate that the nationals of all allied and associated countries should be equally at liberty to operate on an entirely impartial basis, but in order to guarantee such a basis we believe that no concession taken since the beginning of the war in 1914, up to the present, should be held valid.

Furthermore, in view of the fact that it is at least probable that some exploration has been done under protection of the British Government in the meantime, we believe that impartial treatment of all nationals could only be ensured by prohibiting the taking out of concessions until one year has elapsed from the time when exploring parties are allowed to travel freely, for purposes of investigation, in the territory in question.

The timing of Sadler's request was propitious, for it came at the precise moment when American alarm over domestic oil supplies and British economic imperialism was approaching a climax. Admiral Bristol, thoroughly aroused to the British threat, communicated Sadler's suggestion to the State Department, where it was viewed with favor. There was some diplomatic difficulty, to be sure. In view of the previous Foreign Office assurances that no reconnaissance was being permitted, the State Department could not translate the Jersey Standard proposal into an official diplomatic representation without plainly implying that the Foreign Office assurances were worthless.[29] By May of 1920, however, the mandate over Mesopotamia had officially been assumed by Britain, and copies of the still secret San Remo oil pact were in the hands of Jersey Standard and the State Department. The State Department was then willing and able to take a stronger stand.

On May 12, 1920, United States Ambassador Davis communicated to Lord Curzon, British Secretary of State for Foreign Affairs, the official State Department views as to the principles which ought to be applied in mandated regions, and invited an expression of British views "in order to reassure public opinion in the United States." This, by diplomatic standards, was a sharp note. It charged that Britain had been preparing quietly for exclusive control of oil resources in Mesopotamia, and it demanded that Americans be awarded rights commensurate with those accorded to the nationals of other countries.[30]

When the San Remo Oil Agreement was made public in July of 1920, still further and more positive diplomatic steps were possible. On July 28 Secretary of State Bainbridge Colby addressed another sharp communication to Lord Curzon. This note charged that Britain's attitude toward Mesopotamia constituted a grave infringement of mandatory principles

You Can Drive an Auto to Gasoline—but

New York Evening Journal, January 29, 1920

SOMETHING THEY ALL RECOGNIZE

New York Tribune, May 22, 1922

previously laid down by the League of Nations and accepted by Britain. This charge, which was also being voiced in European circles, could not effectively be denied. Curzon, in replying to Colby on August 9, categorically denied that the San Remo Agreement excluded other interests from Mesopotamia and pointed out that, though His Majesty's government was willing in principle to discuss the whole matter with the United States government, the subject of mandates was one which could be considered only at the Council of the League of Nations by the signatories of the Covenant.[31]

To a Democratic administration which had unsuccessfully fought for American participation in the League, this was a biting diplomatic retort. On November 23 Colby forwarded to Curzon a powerful representation, which incorporated the exact demand that Sadler and Jersey Standard wished to press. Colby flatly challenged Curzon's statement that the San Remo Agreement permitted freedom of action to Americans and denied that the Turkish Petroleum Company had any existing rights to the oil resources of Mesopotamia. Curzon replied with a detailed defense of the validity of the Turkish Petroleum Company rights.[32]

Now the issues were in the open: Jersey Standard and the State Department were united in an attack upon the British Foreign Office–Turkish Petroleum Company alliance. British and European observers held to the view that this attack was not only bold, but brazen, considering the prior rights of the parties at interest. Americans, on their part, were incensed at the secret division of war spoils among the European Allies and were not reticent about announcing their candidacy for a just share of whatever concessions Turkey might surrender at the peace conferences, even though the United States had never declared war on that country.

Jersey Standard concentrated its hopes upon further and yet stronger assistance from the State Department. Early in 1921 the Republican administration of Warren Harding took office and almost at once made clear its intent to carry forward the oil policy that had been so vigorously initiated and promoted by the retiring Democrats. A strong stand was taken, as we shall see, against expropriation of American interests in Mexico. Strong diplomatic opposition was also voiced to Dutch discrimination against Americans in the East Indies. A settlement of the Panama Canal dispute with Colombia helped to pave the way for the oilmen in that then unfriendly land. These manifestations of a forceful philosophy were not lost upon the British Foreign Office.

In August of 1921 Lord Curzon solicited, in conciliatory tones, the further views of the United States in respect to the Middle East mandates. Secretary of State Charles Evans Hughes replied in two notes, which adhered to the previous view of Sadler and Bainbridge Colby, that the rights of the Turkish Petroleum Company were invalid. In December the British replied that no changes in the terms of the mandates would be undertaken without prior consultation with the American government. The hope was also expressed that Great Britain would be able, at an early date, to give the United States satisfactory assurances in the Mesopotamian controversy.[33]

This retreat of the British from their original stand cannot be explained in simple terms. One important factor clearly was the attitude of the State Department. By adopting a consistently firm tone and persisting in demands which were couched in highest moral tones, the American government had made the position of the Foreign Office ethically untenable before the watchful world. Sadler and Jersey Standard, moreover, had supplied the State Department with a most telling argument. The validity of the Turkish Petroleum Company claim actually was highly questionable. The overwhelming weight of evidence indicates that what this company held was not a concession but the promise of a concession—and this from a defeated and discredited monarch who was soon to be dethroned as well. When, therefore, the State Department persisted, even through a change in the national administration, in attacking the claim, the British position became not only ethically but legally difficult.

Other factors as well were involved in the British retreat—some subtle, some obvious, some secret, and all, in aggregate, important. It would appear that Britain at this time regarded any prolonged and serious dispute with the United States as highly undesirable—American support, both moral and financial, was desperately needed for the rebuilding of Europe and Asia. Small controversies, such as the tanker expropriation episode, might well serve useful diplomatic bargaining purposes, but a major dispute with the United States was to be avoided, even if at some cost.

Britain was in trouble in Mesopotamia, and oil royalties could not be poured on these troubled waters until the American objections were either met or laid and the Turkish Petroleum Company turned into a going concern. An Arab revolt swept the territory in 1920, and in 1921 Feisal, backed by British arms, was crowned an uneasy monarch. Mesopotamia became known as Iraq. Nationalism was rampant in the Middle East, and Iraqi patriots, restive under British rule, were voicing embarrassing demands for competitive bidding on their oil resources. Winston Churchill, now the leading advocate of Empire oil, was accused at home of having loosed the British lion in a desolate morass. Turkey, having lost Iraq by the 1920 Treaty of Sèvres, had formidable forces under arms and was menacing the disputed Turkish-Iraq border territories, some of which included the most promising of the oil regions. The British garrison force in Iraq was reported to have been dangerously weakened.[34] The dissonant clamor of these conflicts all but drowned out the voices in the Admiralty Office.

Yet another explanation has been offered, however, for Britain's yielding before the American objections. In his memoirs C. S. Gulbenkian states that the Anglo-Persian, the Royal Dutch-Shell, and the French groups in the Turkish Petroleum Company were bitterly opposed to any entry by the Americans, and that the initial Foreign Office attitude toward American demands for an Open Door in Iraq was dictated by pressure from these oil interests. Gulbenkian then relates that, after the American government had taken its strong stand, Sir William Tyrell, British Permanent Under Secretary for Foreign Affairs, approached him for advice. Gulbenkian cannily surmised that it was better to give the Americans a share in the Turkish Petroleum Company than to run the risk of letting them loose to compete in Iraq for concessions when the Turkish Petroleum Company in reality had a poor claim to priorities there. Perhaps he also discerned, in the American demands, an opportunity for settling his private quarrel with the dominant interests in the Turkish Petroleum Company. Gulbenkian's advice to Tyrell, therefore, was to summon the leaders of the Royal Dutch-Shell and the Anglo-Persian groups and impress upon them unequivocally that it was in the national interest that the Americans should be admitted as soon as possible. Tyrell agreed, and issued emphatic directions to this effect.

To his memoirs Gulbenkian appended a letter from Tyrell in which Gulbenkian is referred to as being "instrumental in bringing in American participation." Quite apart from this document, however, the weight of evidence substantiates Gulbenkian's account. It may well have been that the words of this great compromiser were decisive, coming as they did at a time when many other forces were pressing in the same direction.

THE AMERICAN GROUP OFFERS TERMS

While diplomatic notes were passing between Washington and London and the partners in the Turkish Petroleum Company were endeavoring to decide what attitude they should take toward the American challenge,

Van H. Manning, former director of the Bureau of Mines and at the time research director of the American Petroleum Institute, was urging the formation of a syndicate of the principal American oil companies for the purpose of operating in the Middle East or elsewhere abroad. Secretary of Commerce Herbert Hoover also supported the idea, but there was opposition from the industry. New York Standard took the position that only those companies which had already established an interest in the areas in question should be included.[35]

At this point Jersey Standard, apparently abandoning its independent efforts to organize an Iraq venture, exerted a decisive influence on the situation. Support by the State Department, which was certain to be needed in the difficult negotiations still ahead, could not be assured if the Jersey Company, hitherto the chief instigator of the Iraq controversy, remained the only party at interest. The State Department could not well support the claims of a single American company to the exclusion of other American companies—particularly since that company happened to be Standard Oil, so lately the object of legal attack and investigation in government circles. Those who were shaping Jersey's Middle East policy grasped the necessity at an early date. On September 27, 1921, Sadler outlined the situation and his own views in a letter to Teagle:[36]

Answering your memorandum dated September the 23rd regarding the investigation of Mesopotamia and Dr. Manning's connection therewith, I agree with your idea that the Standard Oil Company cannot hope to get the serious backing from the State Department if it attempts to enter the Mesopotamian field alone.

I believe it will be necessary to take some other interests with us and a part of whom, at least, should be outside of the subsidiaries. I also think that we should select the associates carefully and keep the list as small as possible. Personally, my suggestion would be the Standard Oil Company of New York, Sinclair, Doheny, Texas, and it seems to me necessarily, the Gulf.

I think the effect of any success in Mesopotamia would result in bringing all these people into competition with us in the Mediterranean and that the association is highly undesirable except to gain the support of the State Department, except for the Standard Oil Company of New York, who have adjacent markets to Mesopotamia and would be naturally buyers and associates if operating in Mesopotamia.

Teagle already was at work along these lines. Early in September he lunched with A. L. Beaty, E. L. Doheny, and H. F. Sinclair—presidents, respectively, of The Texas Company, the Pan-American Petroleum and Transport Company, and the Sinclair Consolidated Oil Company. All three men indicated their willingness to participate. By the end of October Teagle had obtained the assent of J. W. Van Dyke, president of The Atlantic Refining Company; C. F. Meyer, vice-president of Standard of New York; and G. S. Davison, vice-president of the Gulf Oil Corporation. On November 3, 1921, these seven companies drafted a joint letter to Secretary of State Hughes indicating their desire to investigate prospective oil-bearing areas in Iraq.[37]

The general plan which now was contemplated called for the formation of a joint American geological expedition to Iraq. Both Dr. Manning and Herbert Hoover were consulted, and the backing of both was obtained.[38] The broaching of a proposal for an American expedition suggests that at this time (early fall of 1921) the policy of the American companies was directed not at an alliance with the Turkish Petroleum Company but rather in the direction of an independent joint American effort in Iraq. Agreement among the partners of the Turkish Petroleum Company to invite American participation forestalled this alternative.

By June of 1922 the formalities of organizing the American participation had been discussed and agreed upon. A company was to be created as the vehicle for the undertaking.[39] Such a joint corporate type of organization, which not too many months earlier would probably have been censured by the Federal Trade Commission as a violation of antitrust statutes, was now tolerated as a part of the current official interest in promoting foreign trading activities.

A. C. Bedford thereupon called with confidence at the State Department to ascertain the government's attitude in relation to the contemplated private negotiations with the British. The Department stated its desire not to prolong the diplomatic dispute needlessly, nor "so to disregard the practical aspects of the situation as to prevent American enterprise from availing itself of the very opportunities which our diplomatic representations have striven to obtain." Private negotiations would not be objectionable, stated the Department, provided that any reputable American company which wished to participate was not excluded and provided that the legal validity of the Turkish Petroleum Company claim was not recognized unless after impartial arbitration. Sensing that the earlier diplomatic attacks on the Turkish Petroleum Company claim might now prove embarrassing to the American group wishing to do business with that company, the State Department further informed Bedford that it had no objection to any efforts the Turkish Petroleum Company might make to obtain a new or confirmatory concession in Iraq.[40] This conference cleared the way, and in July of 1922 Teagle departed for London to open the negotiations.

Those negotiations followed a tortuous and often discouraging course. On the one side, representing the seven American oil companies then interested in participating in the Iraq development (Texas and Sinclair subsequently withdrew), stood Walter Teagle, ably assisted by Montagu Piesse, Jersey Standard's distinguished British counsel. On the other side, representing the Turkish Petroleum Company, stood Deterding of the Royal Dutch-Shell, Sir Charles Greenway of the Anglo-Persian Oil Company, and Colonel F. Mercier of the French group, together with their legal advisers, geologists, operating men, and sundry other retainers.

Efforts to resolve the serious discrepancies in viewpoint of the various parties commenced in an atmosphere of considerable mistrust, which time deepened rather than alleviated. The Europeans, who appear to have viewed the American intrusion with fundamental antagonism and suspicion, attempted constantly to outwit not only Teagle, but one another as well. Teagle himself soon found ample cause to mistrust his distinguished antagonists. Two weeks after his arrival he communicated to Bedford in New York a warning that there was reason to believe his cables were being intercepted.[41]

On August 5 Teagle, having presented the initial American terms, returned to New York. For some time thereafter the negotiations were continued by correspondence and through the representation of Piesse, who was held in highest esteem by all parties. Basic differences assumed serious dimensions, and new issues came to the surface. By December of 1922 the Americans were ready to withdraw entirely from the complicated negotiations.

In the interval between August and December the only point that had been definitely settled was that of voting procedure—one vote for each group represented. The percentage participation to be allotted to the Americans was still undecided, though Teagle privately had declared his willingness to accept as low as 20 per cent, provided that a working agreement was signed governing the distribution to the participants at cost of such oil as might be discovered. Greenway had signified a willingness to grant the American group the stock it wished out of the Anglo-Persian block, provided Anglo-Persian received a 10 per cent overriding royalty on all oil produced by the Turkish Petroleum Company. Deterding and Mercier, though happy to be thus relieved of the necessity for surrendering any of the stock of the Royal Dutch-Shell and French groups, did not look with pleasure on the price of their deliverance. It seemed reasonably clear that the percentage finally awarded the American group would be determined by the sacrifices that group might be willing to make on other controversial points.[42]

One of these sacrifices—and one which was held by the American State Department to be of greatest importance—was that respecting the right of members of the Turkish Petroleum Company to seek concessions on their own account. The Royal Dutch-Shell, Anglo-Persian, and French groups were already bound by a so-called self-denying ordinance to seek concessions in Iraq and elsewhere in the old Ottoman Empire only through the Turkish Petroleum Company. In view of the State Department's attitude, Teagle necessarily took the position that the Turkish Petroleum Company, whatever its constituent ownership might be, must hold no monopoly in Iraq that would exclude development there by other parties.[43]

Teagle's proposal that the Turkish Petroleum Company become a non-profit organization, delivering its oil at cost to the participating groups in accordance with a prearranged working agreement, was another stumbling block. Teagle was informed that such a plan would be decidedly objectionable to Gulbenkian—who was interested in dividends, not crude oil. Furthermore, the Iraq government, like Gulbenkian, was looking for a share in the profits. Neither Gulbenkian nor the Iraqi could possibly be satisfied unless the participating groups paid the full market price for their respective shares of the company's crude oil.[44]

These were by no means the only complications. Continuously, it must be remembered, the pressure of political events exerted an unsettling influence upon the efforts of the American companies to gain their objectives in Iraq. Devious Turkish diplomacy now became a factor of immediate importance.

SMASHING THE POLITICAL BARRIERS

The Turkish nation had risen from defeat in 1921 to crush an invading Greek army and force upon the Allies the necessity for making a new peace treaty. For this purpose a conference convened at Lausanne in November of 1922. There were many issues of importance, but oil usurped the center of the stage. A border dispute involving the oil regions flared between Turkey and Iraq, and the Turks, possibly with a view to the discomfiture of the Turkish Petroleum Company and its political champions, suddenly began to look with favor on the ancient claims that derived from Sultan Abdul Hamid's appropriation, in the nineteenth century, of lands for his private purse. The first Lausanne Conference failed to resolve any of the problems raised, and the conference broke up with dubious prospects of peace in the Middle East and considerable doubt as to the security of the Turkish Petroleum Company's position there.

In April of 1923 the second Lausanne Conference was convened. For the same transparent bargaining purposes that led them to espouse the cause of the Hamid heirs, the Turks now revived and reaffirmed an old concession claimed by Rear Admiral Colby M. Chester, an American. This spectacle of the Turks freely supporting concessions to lands covered by the claims of the Turkish Petroleum Company was a disquieting one to the groups interested in that company. Stirred at the conference by the revival of the Chester concession, the British attempted, on their part, to obtain from Turkey a reaffirmation of the Turkish Petroleum Company's 1914 promise of a concession. This diplomatic sally constituted an attempt once and for all to put an end to the American contention that the Turkish Petroleum Company held no valid concession. Had it succeeded, the bargaining position of the American group would have been almost untenable. Joseph Grew, chief of the American delegation at the conference, protested vehemently, and the British were forced to abandon their effort. Bitter European attacks were leveled at the United States. "Europe for the Europeans, and Oil for the Americans" was one phrase that was coined. Contemporary comments held that Grew's action constituted a "bland diplomatic way of announcing that America would not permit any sharing of the loot behind her back, and that when it came to oil, the Standard Oil would insist on its share."[45]

The British, meanwhile, were negotiating an agreement with King Feisal of Iraq. The demand was for the issuance, by the Iraq government, of a new concession to the Turkish Petroleum Company. Midway in these negotiations was interjected the insistence of the American State Department that the Open Door principle be incorporated in the concession. This demand was unwelcome to all parties concerned and almost caused a breakdown in the talks. The Iraq government was particularly adamant in its desire to deal with only one contracting party, rather than an indeterminate number. The British government, however, gave the Iraqi to understand that until the Turkish Petroleum Company concession was granted, the British would not allow the new constitution of Iraq to be ratified. In March of 1925 the concession agreement was signed.[46] The agreement provisions which are pertinent to the narrative may be summarized as follows:[47]

Articles 1-3: The Iraq government to grant the Turkish Petroleum Company exclusive rights to produce, refine, and sell petroleum in Iraq, excepting the Transferred Territories and the vilayet of Basra, for a period of 75 years, dating from March 14, 1925.

Article 4: A geologic survey to begin on November 14, 1925.

Article 5: By November 14, 1927, the company to select 24 rectangular plots of 8 square miles each on which to conduct its subsequent operations.

Article 6: Not later than March 14, 1929, and annually thereafter the Iraq government to select not less than 24 rectangular plots of 8 square miles each to be offered for competitive bidding by any parties interested.

The Turkish Petroleum Company or a prospective lessee to indicate plots to be offered. The auction to be conducted by the company and the company eventually to receive the money.

Thirty per cent of the company's pipeline to be available for lessees' oil.

The agreement was admitted by all parties to be imperfect, but it seemed the best that could be drafted with any hope of acceptance. Articles 5 and 6 technically embodied the American Open Door demands, but opinion differed as to the efficacy of these provisions. The State Department apparently was satisfied; this was an essential consideration. In April of 1925 *The Lamp*, in an innocuous article, hailed the granting of the concession and reported that the agreement gave "every nation interested an equal opportunity in Iraq."[48] This viewpoint was a prevalent one. Since, however, the Turkish Petroleum Company retained almost complete control over the competitive bidding and could reject offers or enter higher bids of its own, the Open Door was a shadow and not a reality. Gulbenkian later stated that the impression that the whole world would participate in the exploitation of oil in Iraq was "eyewash."[49]

In 1926 the vexing boundary dispute between Turkey and Iraq was settled by the final award to Iraq of the territory in question.[50] The only obstacle then standing in the path of oil development in Iraq was agreement as to the terms upon which the American group should be allowed to participate. The negotiations had undergone many vicissitudes since December of 1922.

Of the protracted controversies that characterized the years from

1922 to 1928, only the major obstacle to a successful accord requires detailed study. This was the attitude of C. S. Gulbenkian toward Teagle's proposal to limit profits of the company. All other issues were compromised, but Gulbenkian was unswerving. He held, moreover, a position of great power.

THE "GOLD SHILLING GENTLEMAN"

The Gulbenkian dispute flared into the open in the fall of 1923. At that time the internal quarrel over his shares and rights in the Turkish Petroleum Company was still unsettled. Holding steadfast to the opinion of his solicitors that his rights could not be traded away, as the Royal Dutch-Shell and Anglo-Persian strategists had attempted to do in 1914, Gulbenkian offered to submit his case to arbitration. This offer was declined by the other parties—a clue, perhaps, to the merits of Gulbenkian's case. Gulbenkian began, at the same time, to assail the draft of agreement prepared by the American group. In a letter to Heinrich Riedemann, Gulbenkian summed up his objections in terms of mutual interest:[51]

From conversations I have had on this side, I rather gather that my remarks and criticisms are not palatable to many of our friends; but I am sure that in the long run they will readily see that my criticisms were well-founded and in the broader interests of the Turkish Petroleum Company as a whole and of the shareholders individually and separately. In my modest opinion, that Working Arrangement [the proposal to distribute the company's oil at cost] should be done away with, and in its place, the Company should be allowed to sail its own course as an independent concern working to make profits. Prima facie, this suggestion may be open to criticism on fiscal and other grounds, but my experience teaches me that clumsy and one-sided arrangements are far more harmful in themselves than the theoretical economies it is thought to effect in one direction or another.

This letter also contained a none-too-subtle threat that, if profits were done away with, Gulbenkian would bring suit to protect what he characterized as "my private interest . . . which I have retained after personally bearing without remuneration all the expenses incidental to my work in this business, after voluntarily ceding at their par value without profit all the previous holdings I had in order to facilitate the Company's career and progress."

In a letter to A. C. Bedford soon after this, Teagle recorded his private opinion that it was "natural and logical" for Gulbenkian to object to the proposed profit limitation. "If we were in his position," Teagle declared, "we would do so too."[52]

The stalemate continued through 1924—the Americans insistent upon their demands and Gulbenkian firm in his refusal to submit to Teagle on the profit issue or to surrender to the Turkish Petroleum Company groups on the participation dispute. Over this period the members of the American group were progressively less burdened by the urgency of their need for crude oil reserves. The days of shortage and alarm over American supplies were gone. Jersey Standard's domestic production in 1923 was 25 per cent higher than in the preceding year, while total industry production in the United States increased 31 per cent. The great Los Angeles, Smackover, and Tonkawa fields poured their flood into the pipelines and there was talk of a crude oil surplus in the United States.[53] The Royal Dutch-Shell and Anglo-Persian groups, on the contrary, were becoming increasingly anxious to effect a settlement with the Americans in order that development work in Iraq might commence.

For more than two years, however, Gulbenkian stood squarely in the path of a settlement between the Turkish Petroleum Company and the American group. In September of 1924 one of Teagle's lieutenants wrote as follows:[54]

Referring to Gulbenkian's attitude as set forth in cable of 13th September from Messrs. Wellman and Riedemann. The other groups appear to infer that we are under obligation to assist them in cleaning their stable. Such is certainly not the case, and it has always been clear—over the last two years—that they were to take care of him but we retaining the right to approve of any agreement they entered into with him.

For some time Teagle held strictly to this viewpoint, insisting that the Gulbenkian dispute was of no concern to the Americans and that it must be settled before a final agreement on American participation could be reached. This stand, which was a source of much concern to the Anglo-Persian representatives, immensely enhanced Gulbenkian's bargaining position, for Greenway and Deterding must necessarily come to terms with him before settling with the American group. Teagle, it seemed, was playing directly into Gulbenkian's hands.[55]

Neither, it appeared, was Gulbenkian any more likely in the future to agree to the American demands than he had been in the past. He not only held to his earlier refusals to accept a limitation on profits, but he advanced the claim that, since the Americans had agreed to allow the Anglo-Persian group a 10 per cent overriding royalty on all oil produced, he, as a partner who had also surrendered shares in the company, was likewise entitled to a royalty. Gulbenkian stipulated that this should be a gold shilling per ton of production, and he subsequently was referred to by Riedemann as "the Gold Shilling Gentleman." Teagle considered this royalty prohibitive, and for a time it seemed as though negotiations would collapse in their entirety.[56]

Teagle pointed out that royalties proposed for the Iraq government, the Anglo-Persian group, and for Gulbenkian would total 26⅔ per cent of production—all this, said Teagle, on a prospect that was the "wildest kind of a wild cat." Sadler, who had been busy in South America and the Dutch East Indies and had ceased to play an active part in the Iraq controversy, was even more pessimistic. A staunch advocate of independent competitive effort under any conditions, he argued against participation in Iraq under the proposed terms.[57]

Abandoning at last the contention that Gulbenkian was the problem of the Turkish Petroleum Company alone, Teagle made arrangements to see him personally. Riedemann was also present at the meeting. Jersey records include no information on the conversation, but Gulbenkian speaks of it in graphic fashion in his memoirs.

Teagle and Riedemann originally proposed, Gulbenkian states, that he be given a penny a ton royalty, in lieu of any other benefits to which he might be entitled:

I cannot forget the technical arguments put forward by Mr. Teagle to convince me that my rights ought to be amply satisfied with their proposal. Oil technology has always been my weak side and I certainly could not compete with Mr. Teagle's wide knowledge in that direction.

Backed by his solicitors' opinion that the demands of the Americans, as well as the secret and open attacks on him by the Anglo-Persian and Royal Dutch-Shell groups, were "all bluff," Gulbenkian remained firm.

The chorus of recrimination against him mounted steadily in volume. Gulbenkian relates that an effort was made by the Anglo-Persian group to apply British Foreign Office pressure to make him capitulate. He also states that he was misrepresented before the Foreign Office and accused of making difficulties for the Americans. The Foreign Office was helpless, however, in the face of Gulbenkian's willingness to arbitrate and the refusal of Greenway and Deterding to accept such an offer. Neither did it appear that the State Department could effectively intervene in a matter of internecine strife such as this. An attempt to buy out Gulbenkian failed, as did several attempts to get him to agree to a compromise. Teagle was becoming progressively more irritated and privately accused Gulbenkian of wrecking the entire effort at international co-operation. One of Teagle's advisers stated that the only way to "scotch" Gulbenkian was to isolate him before the public as an obstructionist.[58]

Riedemann apparently sensed that Teagle's temper was wearing thin, and took the liberty of cautioning his superior in no uncertain terms. Gulbenkian's position, said Riedemann, was extremely strong, and the compensation offered him was neither right nor proper. This significant opinion was almost simultaneously reinforced by a strong letter from Montagu Piesse. "We must not lose sight of Gulbenkian's point of view," wrote Piesse, "for he would say that the effort at international co-operation is being wrecked by the American Group demanding unreasonable terms from him, and this is the kind of a controversy I think we should avoid." Piesse also hazarded the opinion, in contradiction to that apparently expressed by Teagle, that Gulbenkian was very anxious to come to terms.[59]

THE FINAL PHASE

To the men who were wearily traversing these difficult avenues of negotiation, the prospect of having some fresh and relatively uncontroversial subject to discuss must, indeed, have been a welcome one. It seems almost incredible that in spite of all this time-consuming turmoil, intrigue, and calculation—which might fairly be said to have commenced as far back as 1890—no one yet knew for sure whether or not there was oil in paying quantities in Iraq! Not until April of 1927 did a Turkish Petroleum Company drilling bit grind into the hot Mosul sands.

The operational preliminaries to this long-awaited event necessarily were almost as protracted as the negotiations in London. The field reports gathered by the Anglo-Persian and Royal Dutch-Shell geologists from 1918 to 1921 had not been implemented by detail work since that time. Anglo-Persian operations in neighboring Persia, however, were closely watched for indications that the rich formations there trended toward the Iraq border. This information was closely guarded, and Jersey Company files contain ample evidence of the company's efforts to ascertain what was taking place. In 1923 oil strikes close to the Iraq border gave a hopeful clue. Two years later plans for the geological party specified in the Turkish Petroleum Company's 1925 concession from Iraq were fairly launched. The American group, while not yet admitted to participation in the company, asked for and was granted the right to be represented in the survey party.

When the expedition departed, in September of 1925, it consisted of seven Anglo-Persian men and three representatives each from the Royal Dutch-Shell, the French, and the American groups. Professor Hugo de Bockh, of the Anglo-Persian Oil Company, was placed in charge. The American group was headed by E. W. Shaw, an independent consultant of long experience. From the start, de Bockh dominated the party. The Americans were decidedly restricted in their actions and were not consulted on many matters. Shaw, however, worked under these difficulties with good grace and much tact, as did Professor A. C. Trowbridge and S. L. Mason, the other American representatives. Shaw's letters from the field were guarded in tone but contained significant news, nonetheless.[60]

The main body of geologists, wrote Shaw from Bagdad, spent five weeks working up the Euphrates; then moved northeast to Kirkuk, northwest to Mosul, and south to the border of the vilayet of Basra. De Bockh was pessimistic and condemned structures that Shaw thought were suitable for first operations. There were difficulties with the natives. One guard was shot, and a platoon of soldiers was assigned to the party.[61]

By March of 1926 the expedition had completed its mission, and unofficial reports began to flow into New York. The American geologists reported that de Bockh had disparaged structure after structure, and the Americans found themselves in fundamental disagreement with his geological theories and his recommendations as to drilling sites. All three of the American representatives felt that the official report of the expedition would be far less optimistic than the situation warranted. There was some doubt, too, as to whether the Americans would be given full information —a danger, wrote Shaw, that was considerably lessened by the shining diplomacy of Professor Trowbridge, who by virtue of his personal talents had worked into the key position of collator of data. Shaw, who was known to be conservative, voiced the considered opinion that he knew of no oil region in the world where the promise of drilling was greater than in Iraq.[62] This opinion was substantiated by Trowbridge and Mason, and it intruded into negotiations a note both of optimism and of warning.

As late as January of 1926 Teagle and the American group were still persisting in their original demands. The following exchange of cables indicates the spirit of the negotiations at that time:

Teagle to Deterding   January 14, 1926

Referring your cable December twenty-ninth American Group had meeting Monday last and after carefully considering entire subject felt obliged to cable Nichols [Manager of the Anglo-Persian] that they could not modify their previous position which had been approved by our State Department. I want to express my personal appreciation of the efforts which you have made to bring about a settlement with Gulbenkian. It is incomprehensible to me that British Foreign Office should not view this attempt at international cooperation as being too important to admit of its being wrecked solely as the result of the inflexibility of one selfish individual and am confident you will agree with me in this view.

Deterding to Teagle   January 15, 1926

Many thanks for your telegram. Quite agree with your protest especially as some Government departments here appear to think the big companies are to blame for trying to squeeze G[ulbenkian]. I think it would do good if your State Department would express opinion similar to your opinion and mine to other governments concerned.

Teagle was privately advised, however, that State Department intervention over the Gulbenkian dispute would take the diplomatic pressure off the shoulders of the Anglo-Persian and Royal Dutch-Shell groups and shift it to Gulbenkian—an objective which both companies were anxious to accomplish.[63] The impasse, it seemed, was incapable of resolution unless some new factor was added to the situation. By March of 1926 this very thing had apparently come to pass. A new spirit was in the air, and it may well be that the geological opinions voiced in the interval by E. W. Shaw were responsible. It was becoming increasingly obvious that a settlement with Gulbenkian was imperative.

Meanwhile, operations in Iraq had actually commenced. In a formal report presented in London on September 2, 1926, Dr. de Bockh had recommended ten drilling locations. Drillers were signed on, and rigs were purchased, shipped, and moved onto location. At 11:30 on the morning of April 5, 1927, King Feisal in person threw the switch, and Palkanah Number 1 began drilling.[64]

The Kifri and Jabal Hamrin structures, lying approximately halfway between Kirkuk and Bagdad, were favored above all others by de Bockh, and four test wells were started there. The fifth well projected was Baba Gurgur Number 1, on the Kirkuk structure. This had been deemed by Shaw to be one of the most promising locations of all, and it was at his urging that this well was included in the list of those to be drilled first.

Between April and September much progress was made, but there were difficulties. Storehouses and roads had been poorly located and had to be changed. Even before drilling had commenced, the camp physician committed suicide, three coolies at Palkanah were gassed—two fatally—and the Injareh camp was shot at in the night by natives. Later the drilling superintendent resigned, and there were delays in the delivery of equipment. The London office persisted in sending substitutes for the predominantly American equipment, which were "just as good" but which would not work. The fire hazard was high in the camp tent colonies, and smallpox broke out.[65] Nevertheless, the great question was soon to be answered by the ceaseless grind of the rotaries.

In May of 1927, negotiations in London began to take a turn for the better. Even before this time Teagle, possibly influenced by the favorable geological reports, had definitely decided that the Americans should go into the Turkish Petroleum Company without a working agreement as to profits. This was a major concession, but a major difficulty also arose. The French suddenly advanced the viewpoint that all participants in the company should be bound not to engage individually in producing operations either in Iraq or within the boundaries of the old Turkish Empire anywhere outside Iraq. This demand was regarded as most objectionable by the American group. "I am personally convinced," Teagle commented, "that the attitude of the French Group in this matter is prompted by Mr. Gulbenkian's representations to them."[66]

If this was indeed a last-minute bargaining move by Gulbenkian, who was close to the French, it succeeded. Teagle countered with an offer that, if the French would relinquish their demands and suitable provisions were made for ensuring the Open Door in Iraq, the American group would abandon its insistence on a settlement of the Gulbenkian royalty demands prior to American participation. It was resolved, moreover, that Gulbenkian must receive an unqualified 5 per cent interest in the company, and that each of the other participating groups should hold a 23¾ per cent interest.[67]

While the American group thus persisted in its discouraging quest for Iraq crude, the supply situation in the United States underwent further changes which might well have been considered sound justification for withdrawal from the Turkish Petroleum Company controversy. Amidst scenes of great excitement the Seminole pools in the Mid-Continent began to come in; Jersey Standard was informed that The Carter Oil Company had extensive and promising acreage in the area. New fields, improved production methods, and better refining techniques all contributed to a veritable deluge of oil in the United States. Crude prices dropped sharply, and *The Lamp* began to carry articles dealing with "the oil problem." Teagle's attitude underwent no perceptible change. He continued to hammer away at Gulbenkian.

By July of 1927 a general agreement seemed imminent. Palkanah Number 1 was then drilling below the 1,900-foot level, while Baba Gurgur Number 1 and Kaiyarah Number 1 had been spudded-in. Anglo-Persian employees in Bagdad were becoming outspoken in their charges that the Americans were delaying negotiations until the Iraq oil regions had been proved.[68] This was not true, for a major forward step had been taken to reach real accord. Teagle agreed that the French group should contract with Gulbenkian to purchase from him at market rates his 5 per cent share in the crude oil produced. This proposal at once resolved Gulbenkian's objections to receiving his royalties in oil; at the same time, it satisfied Teagle's desire to have the principal production of the company made available to the participants at cost.[69]

By the middle of October, four bits on the choice Palkanah and Jabal Hamrin locations were unsuccessfully probing the 3,500-foot level where de Bockh believed the Asmari lime would be encountered. On the Baba Gurgur location, more recently spudded-in, there was less of an air of expectancy. Here, it was believed, the Asmari lime was only 2,600 feet below the surface, but the drill had barely passed the 1,500-foot mark. It was at noon on October 15 that a premonitory roar sent an astonished drilling crew scrambling off the rig, and Baba Gurgur Number 1 came in—a majestic gusher.

Telegrams and cables sent the message flashing to London—Paris—New York. Teagle received the news from Montagu Piesse:

Struck oil at Baba Gurgur well no. 1 in main limestone rock at 1,521 feet on Oct. 15. Estimated flowing flush production 50,000 bbls. daily thru 10% inch casing, quality 34 Beaumé. Well under control.

Two days later Piesse informed Teagle that the well was then flowing 90,000 barrels daily and was to be closed in, pending completion of storage and pipeline facilities.[70]

Here was the dramatic culmination which gave meaning to an almost unprecedented commercial experience of thirty years' duration. Baba Gurgur Number 1 marked, in a sense, the end of one chronicle and the beginning of another.

On July 31, 1928, the so-called Red Line Agreement, representing the final compromise of all the bitterly contested issues, was formally signed. The provisions require only a brief summary here, for detailed analysis carries with it the necessity for recounting events that belong to a later historical period.

The American group was admitted to a 23¾ per cent interest in the Turkish Petroleum Company, which in 1929 became known as the Iraq Petroleum Company. The American group vested its interests in the Near East Development Corporation, organized in 1928, shares in which were held as follows:

Atlantic Refining Company, The	16⅔ per cent
Gulf Oil Corporation	16⅔ per cent
Pan American Petroleum and Transport Company	16⅔ per cent
Standard Oil Company (New Jersey)	25 per cent
Standard Oil Company of New York	25 per cent

Gulbenkian received his 5 per cent interest, and the Royal Dutch, the Anglo-Persian, and the French groups each took a 23¾ per cent share. Teagle's working agreement covering delivery of oil to the participants at cost was included, subject only to a private understanding that Gulbenkian's share of oil should be purchased from him at market value. Anglo-Persian received its 10 per cent overriding royalty on all production of the company.[71]

The agreement took its name from the fact that the members of the Turkish Petroleum Company bound themselves not to operate, except through the company, within an area bounded on the map by a red line. This area embraced virtually all of the old Turkish Empire (see map on page 307). Certain complicated exceptions were made to this restriction for the ostensible purpose of incorporating the Open Door principle in the agreement. Articles 5 and 6 of the 1925 convention between the Iraq government and the Turkish Petroleum Company were included. Hence the members of the American group and others were allowed to bid independently for subleases of territory in Iraq which the Turkish Petroleum Company did not select for its own operations, subject, of course, to control by that company over the bidding procedure. In areas outside Iraq but still within the Red Line area, the American signatories might bid for concessions; if, however, they were successful in their bids, they were not to engage in operations on the concessions obtained until they had first offered the other members of the Turkish Petroleum Company

IRAQ AND THE RED-LINE AREA
July 31, 1928
Reproduced from the Original Map

The dotted line (on the original map a red line) drawn on this map is intended to follow the following lines:

A-B   The frontier defined by the Treaty of Berlin of 13th July 1878 and by the Treaty of San Stefano of 3rd March 1878.

B-C   The frontier demarcated by the Turco-Persian Frontier Commission in 1913-14 on the basis of the Protocol signed at Constantinople on the 4(17) November 1913 excepting in sectors a-b and c-d where the red line is intended to follow the line of the previous de facto frontier described on pages 139 and 140 of the Minutes of the Frontier Commission in a note dated the 1/14th October 1914 by the Russian and British Commissioners.

D-E   The limit of the territorial waters of the Arabian peninsula excepting the Sultanate of Koweit and the Farsan Archipelago.

E-F   The Frontier defined by the Anglo-Turkish Convention of 1st October 1906.

F-G   The red line is intended to follow the decision of the Conference of London on the 13th February 1914 in execution of Article 5 of the Treaty of London of 17/30th May 1913 and Article 15 of the Treaty of Athens of the 1/14th November 1913.

G-H   The frontier defined by the Treaty of Constantinople on the 16/29th September 1913.

H-A   The limit of the territorial waters of Turkey in the Black Sea.

Source: SONJ, Recs.

the right of equal participation. Insofar as any oil company not a party to the Red Line Agreement was concerned, the Open Door concept as it applied to Iraq was accorded nebulous recognition at best, though the agreement could not prevent any such company from engaging in activities outside Iraq. In return for their interest in the Turkish Petroleum Company and its promising concession in Iraq, the five participating American companies in effect renounced their claim to independence of action anywhere within the boundaries of the old Turkish Empire.

THE JERSEY SALLY IN PERSIA

The 1901 concession to William Knox D'Arcy, which formed the basis for the subsequent successful operations in Persia by the Anglo-Persian Oil Company, had excluded the five northern provinces of Azerbaijan, Gilan, Mazanderan, Asterabad, and Khorasan. These areas were deemed to be covered by a grant made to Russian interests in 1896. After his visit to the area in 1910, Jersey's scout, John Worthington, had reported that information was vague and—in contrast to Mesopotamia—that the prospects of obtaining oil were visionary.[72] Evidences of petroleum, however, subsequently were discovered, and geologists evolved the theory that some of the Persian formations were associated with the rich Baku oil regions to the north.

Russian and English interests had long competed for economic privilege in Persia. In 1916 this intermittent struggle for precedence was renewed when the Persian cabinet issued to Akakie Khostaria, a Russian, an oil concession covering four of the five northern provinces. The fifth province (Khorasan) was largely desert and was believed to be geologically unpromising for the discovery of petroleum.

Political rather than economic events shaped the history of oil development in northern Persia. The specter of Russian aggression dominated Persian politics. Persian leaders alternated between fear of offending Russia and fear of falling under Russian domination. The Khostaria concession, which had been granted at a time of crisis between the two nations, almost immediately came under attack in political circles in Teheran, the Persian capital, and in 1919 its validity was still the subject of hot dispute. Teheran politics were a quagmire of confusion and intrigue.

In that troubled state of affairs both Jersey Standard and the Anglo-Persian Oil Company discerned opportunity. In the fall of 1919, while Sadler was in Constantinople seeking information about developments in Mesopotamia, John D. Rockefeller, Jr., obtained letters of introduction which enabled Sadler to talk with Persian officials about the possibilities of a Jersey Standard concession in the northern provinces.[73]

Meanwhile, Sir Charles Greenway, leader of the Anglo-Persian Oil Company, had purchased for his company a half interest in the Khostaria concession.[74] Throughout 1920, while Sadler was engaged in an investigation of the Persian project, the Anglo-Persian group was exerting strong pressure in Teheran to have the *Majlis,* or national assembly, ratify an agreement which would allow Anglo-Persian to commence operations in northern Persia.

Anti-British sentiment in Persia, however, was strong. Certain political groups were anxious to rid the nation of British as well as Russian domination, and there was a manifest determination in government circles to block any attempt by the Anglo-Persian group to expand its already formidable Persian interests into a complete monopoly of the country's oil resources. In 1921, moreover, the Persians made an agreement with the Soviet government not to grant concessions in the northern provinces to citizens of a third nation. Russian agents, who were active in Teheran and controlled a portion of the press, played upon resurgent Persian nationalism to advance their own ends. The Russian Minister in Teheran told a Jersey observer that it was only a question of time before Russia would get its "Persian omelette."[75] The oil-concession issue became a political pawn, and considerations for the national economic interest were submerged in the conflicting personal ambitions of Persian leaders. At the same time, however, pro-American sentiment was being nourished, and some Persian leaders were looking to America for disinterested assistance in solving Persia's vexing political and economic difficulties.[76]

In September of 1921 the Persian government agent empowered to carry on concession negotiations in New York offered a definite set of terms: Jersey Standard would receive a 55-year concession to the five northern provinces in return for a loan of $5,000,000 to Persia; royalties of 15 per cent of gross production were to be paid (Jersey men wanted this reduced to 10 per cent); and within two years after commencing operations the Jersey Company was to turn over to the government 50 per cent of the area leased. This offer to the Americans was greeted with alarm by the Anglo-Persian group. In October of 1921 the British government lodged a protest with the State Department against the proposed concession on the grounds that the Khostaria concession of the Anglo-Persian Oil Company was still valid. The Russian government, at the same time, protested strongly in Teheran against the proposed breach of the Soviet-

Persian agreement of 1921, and threatened military action unless the offer to the Americans was withdrawn.[77]

The difficulties which beset Jersey's plans might well have justified abandonment of the Persian venture. A company informant in Teheran had written that were he asked whether one should invest £50 in northern Persia at that time, he would answer "No!" Even if the concession should be obtained, the only outlets for crude oil were north to the Black Sea or south to the Persian Gulf. The northern route was blocked by the Russians, and the southern route, which would have involved pipelines across five hundred miles of the most wild and desolate country, was blocked by Anglo-Persian.[78]

A. C. Bedford, who was in London in November of 1921, talked with Greenway and subsequently took a strong stand that Jersey Standard should not be a party to the repudiation of the Khostaria concession. This attitude virtually precluded an independent attempt by Jersey Standard to enter Persia and is of some interest in view of the almost simultaneous action by the company in urging the State Department to challenge the validity of the Turkish Petroleum Company concession in Iraq. Legal opinion, however, indicated that, while the concession of the Turkish Petroleum Company in Iraq was probably invalid, the Khostaria concession in Persia might very well be sustained if it should be submitted to international arbitration.[79]

The situation in late 1921, then, was a virtual stalemate. The Persian government had professed a desire to grant the concession to Jersey Standard and was definitely determined not to give it to the Anglo-Persian group. A disposition was manifest in Teheran, nevertheless, to use the Anglo-Persian claims as a bargaining tool to force better terms from the Americans. The British were determined not to withdraw, yet could not hope, under existing circumstances, to have their Khostaria concession confirmed by the *Majlis*. They may have discerned in an Anglo-American alliance the opportunity of bolstering the rapidly deteriorating British political and economic position in Persia.[80] The Jersey Company, for its part, was unwilling to proceed with negotiations with the Persians while conflicting claims were in existence. The strong stand of the Russian government was a further deterrent, and there is evidence that Teagle, Bedford, and Sadler were unwilling to cross the Anglo-Persian group in Persia for fear of imperiling the more important negotiations simultaneously going on for American participation in Iraq.

On February 6, 1922, a formal agreement was signed by Jersey Standard and the Anglo-Persian Company which established the conditions for a joint participation in Persia. The Anglo-Persian group purchased the outstanding 50 per cent of the Khostaria concession still held by Russian interests and then sold a half interest in the concession to the Jersey Company for £178,000. This disputed concession was to be held in abeyance by the two companies in favor of the new concession which Jersey Standard had been trying to obtain. Jersey and the Anglo-Persian Company agreed to divide equally the underwriting of the $5,000,000 loan which had been demanded by Persia and to form a company to own and operate the new concession. Voting control of the new company and division of the costs and operating returns were to be shared equally, but Jersey Standard was to provide the management.[81]

With the British-American conflict thus resolved, Sadler actively endeavored to reach a final agreement with the Persian negotiator. Teagle talked with Thomas W. Lamont, of J. P. Morgan & Company, about the $5,000,000 Persian loan. Ten days after the Jersey–Anglo-Persian agreement had been signed, the Morgan firm advanced an interim loan of $1,-000,000 to the government of Persia, to be repaid either out of the $5,000,-000 loan then being negotiated or from royalties paid by Anglo-Persian on its operations in southern Persia. Matters at last seemed to be going smoothly, and Sadler notified the State Department that negotiations for the new concession were "about completed."[82]

Those observers who were familiar with the course of Persian politics were scarcely surprised by what happened next. On February 28, 1922, the agreement which Sadler and the Persian agent had worked out in New York was repudiated by the Prime Minister of Persia, who declared that the Anglo-Persian Oil Company must have no interest in the new concession. This pronouncement was backed by the *Majlis,* which secretly voted to refuse approval of the joint British-American participation.[83]

While all aspects of this turn of events were being probed, a new threat suddenly materialized. News was received at 26 Broadway that Harry F. Sinclair had made a bid in Teheran to obtain the northern concession for his Sinclair Exploration Company. Bedford was informed that Sinclair had offered a $7,000,000 loan to Persia, to be secured by tobacco and opium revenues.[84]

Bedford held to the opinion that Sinclair's activities were a bluff, but by June of 1922 the threat had become so serious that the Jersey Company filed a protest with the State Department and prepared a statement to be released for publication in case the concession was granted to its rival. In this statement the company planned to minimize the value of the concession to Sinclair, in view of the Khostaria rights, and to chide Sinclair for doing that which Jersey Standard had refused to do—namely, become a party to the repudiation of a prior concession. Secretary of State Hughes told Bedford that the policy of the State Department was to act impartially when two American companies were in conflict, even if one seemed to have a better legal case than the other.[85] The British Foreign Office was equally unable to provide assistance, for the Persians had indicated that interference by the detested British Legation would immediately cause the concession to be given to Sinclair.

Faced with adamant opposition to the British in Teheran, the threat that Sinclair might get the concession, and the apparent inability of either the State Department or the Foreign Office to take effective action, Jersey Standard and Anglo-Persian capitulated. On June 30, 1922, assurances were extended that the Jersey Company would deal with Persia in its own name and would wholly own, control, and manage the proposed concession. The Anglo-Persian interests were to be satisfied with a nonsecret contractual side arrangement with Jersey covering British participation in costs and returns.[86] On August 22, 1922, a revised draft of the concession was prepared incorporating these terms.

In the meantime, the Persian cabinet had fallen. The Jersey Company was informed that Sinclair had taken advantage of the political crisis to enlist the support of a large number of deputies in the *Majlis*. Countering this development was the fact that an American advisory commission headed by A. C. Millspaugh, former foreign trade adviser to the State Department, was leaving for Teheran to take charge of Persian finances. Millspaugh had been urging that, from the standpoint of ultimate advantage to the Persian government, the concession be granted to Jersey Standard. Notwithstanding the hope that Millspaugh's presence in Teheran would assist the Jersey cause, however, the opinion was expressed that the company could never expect to win out unless it was willing to pay "baksheesh" for support in political circles in Teheran. It became increasingly evident that the old Serbian proverb, "He who has God for his uncle can easily get to Heaven," was peculiarly applicable to political affairs in Persia. Guy Wellman, Jersey's counsel in the negotiations, stated that if it was necessary to "take care of" government officials, the company had best withdraw. "It would be a mistake, aside from ethical grounds," Wellman wrote to Sir John Cadman, "for us to bid on this basis, among other reasons because it would discredit in the public estimation the new American advisers who are going to Teheran, and would meet with the disapproval of our own State Department."[87]

For more than a year the *Majlis* considered whether to grant the concession to Jersey Standard or to Sinclair. Certain of Sinclair's terms were better, and pressure was applied to force Jersey to match them. Jersey's association with the Anglo-Persian group, even under the modified agreement of August 22, continued to be a major obstacle to the successful conclusion of negotiations. It was believed, on the other hand, that Sinclair would not be able to enlist reliable bankers to underwrite the loan upon which the Persians had conditioned the concession.[88]

For a time Jersey's prospects visibly brightened. The Morgan representatives indicated that they were still willing to consider an additional loan to Persia, provided that terms were favorable and the investment market propitious. In Teheran the American economic advisers, headed by Millspaugh, were hard at work and were achieving satisfactory results in their task of reorganizing Persian finances. Millspaugh had allied himself with the Minister of War, Reza Khan, who was the most powerful figure in Teheran political circles. One advantage to Jersey Standard from the alliance with Anglo-Persian had become obvious: the British were assisting Millspaugh in stabilizing the financial situation. The latter, at the same time, was pointing out to Teheran officials the advantages of allying themselves with the stronger of the competing interests—in his opinion the Jersey-Morgan group.[89]

Concession terms continued to be discussed for several weeks longer, and the Jersey Company indicated a willingness to meet all demands of the Persian government. Only the attitude of Teheran toward the private Jersey–Anglo-Persian working agreement remained to be determined. On September 21, 1923, a meeting was held between Sadler, Wellman, the Persian negotiator, and the Persian Minister to the United States. The Persian representatives unequivocally declared that the Anglo-Persian Oil Company had no valid claims in the northern provinces and that Teheran would tolerate no agreement between Jersey Standard and the British.[90]

This not unexpected stand placed the Jersey Company in an impossible situation. Unable to obtain the concession even with Anglo-Persian as a silent partner, and unwilling as a matter of principle to repudiate its agreement with the British to participate jointly in Persia, the Jersey board met on September 28 and voted to suspend negotiations. The opinion was expressed, however, that if conditions changed the Persian matter might be reconsidered.[91]

Sinclair's representatives continued to be active in Teheran, and late in 1923 a false report appeared in the American press that Sinclair had been given the concession. A new request by Jersey Standard for government support elicited once again the pronouncement from Charles Evans Hughes that the State Department, while upholding the Open Door principle, would not make a choice between competing American interests. The Jersey Company was publicly attacked in the United States for allying itself with a British group for the supposed purpose of defeating another American company. To this charge the company replied, through the columns of *The Lamp,* with a frank and detailed account of the entire affair. This article called attention to the possible validity of the Khostaria concession and showed how the Jersey–Anglo-Persian alliance had been formed some time before the commencement of Sinclair's efforts. The article received wide publicity, and Jersey's observer in Persia expressed consternation over the "brazen" disclosure of relations between the two companies.[92]

Early in 1924 the Teapot Dome scandal over the leasing of naval oil reserves exerted a temporary influence upon the struggle in Persia. The indictment of H. F. Sinclair helped to eliminate him as a candidate for the Persian concession and raised hopes in some quarters that Jersey Standard's bargaining position in Teheran would be enhanced. Intermittently throughout 1924, 1925, and 1926 the possibility of reopening negotiations came up for discussion at 26 Broadway. New factors, however, exerted discouraging influences. The Russians had made progress in setting their own petroleum industry in order, and Russian oil was beginning to compete seriously in Near and Middle East markets. Any hope that might have existed for getting Persian crude out by way of the Black Sea was banished by the unfriendly attitude of the Soviet government. Agreement upon American participation in Iraq was near, too, and this may have caused the Jersey Company's interest in Persia to wane. In 1927 the deadlock over British participation in the northern provinces had not been broken; and, though Jersey Standard still retained a nominal interest in the Khostaria concession, the Jersey board indicated a decisive unwillingness to pursue the project further.[93]

Jersey Standard's endeavors in Iraq and Persia demand summation and invite comparisons.

Viewed together and in broad perspective, the two episodes yield an informative impression of the strategic and administrative sides of the foreign business. In the Iraq negotiations the bold touch of Walter Teagle was abundantly attested, and his reputation as a strategist suffered little from the fact that he was ruffled and defeated by the greatest strategist of all—Calouste Sarkis Gulbenkian. Not the least of Teagle's accomplishments was his success in holding the American group together in a solid front—a sharp contrast to the faction-ridden ranks of the Turkish Petroleum Company.

One segment of the massive Jersey Standard organization was shown at work—suffused in that work with great energy and confidence. A dozen highly competent men and a forceful new department played significant roles. E. J. Sadler was second only to Teagle in the initial planning stages of the Middle Eastern ventures. Sadler took his place on the Jersey directorate in 1920 and unquestionably exerted considerable influence upon his superior. A. C. Bedford proved, in the Persian transactions, to be a skilled, if cautious, negotiator. He appeared often in the background of the Iraq negotiations as well—a contact man of great prestige whose services as such must not be ignored or minimized. The two lawyers, Guy Wellman in New York and Montagu Piesse in London, were wise and conservative, attributes that were particularly valuable at many points in the negotiations. Both helped to maintain the diplomatic entente which was so vital for success. Among these men the greatest informality prevailed, but the informality yielded effective and speedy and well-considered decisions. There were, of course, far larger issues involved than the efficacy in action of the new Teagle administration and the new Foreign Producing Department.

The most obvious and pertinent question of the many raised by the Iraq and Persian episodes is why Jersey Standard's ambitions were so effectively thwarted in Persia—at the very time when success was being recorded in Iraq, where the difficulties were fully as great. It seems clear that the alliance with the Anglo-Persian Oil Company condemned the venture in Persia to failure, but the Jersey Company had little choice. Bedford was convinced that the concession which the Persians wished to grant to Jersey Standard alone could not have been sustained in the face of the prior claims of the British. In any case, the strength of the Anglo-Persian group in the Turkish Petroleum Company might have been enough to force the Jersey Company into the ill-fated agreement to cooperate in Persia.

Failure in the one venture and success in the other seem, in the final analysis, to have derived from the attitude of the State Department and the Foreign Office. The British had taken a strong stand in Iraq to clear the path for the Turkish Petroleum Company. In Persia, however, the Foreign Office apparently lacked sufficient diplomatic leverage to beat down rampant anti-British sentiments. Intervention on behalf of the Khostaria concession in northern Persia would almost certainly have imperiled Anglo-Persian's much more important D'Arcy concession in southern Persia.

In the Iraq controversy Teagle had successfully appealed to the State Department for assistance in overcoming the intransigent attitudes of foreign powers which stood in the path of Jersey Standard's ambitions. After some initial encouragement, however, American diplomatic support for Jersey in Persia was not forthcoming. The attitude of the State Department in supporting the joint American venture in Iraq and in refusing to assist the Jersey Company alone in Persia was consistent and just. There was, indeed, no other possible attitude for the Department to take once the competitive ambitions of Sinclair in Persia had been announced. In this case the men at 26 Broadway had, perhaps, overestimated the strength of the Jersey Company in dealing, unassisted by solid backing from the American petroleum industry, with difficult foreign political situations. The failure in Persia, however, was more than counterbalanced by success in Iraq, and the importance of Jersey Standard's quest for crude oil in the Middle East as a factor in accelerating a major shift in American foreign policy stands clear.

Once again, as so frequently had been the case in Jersey Standard history, the issue of means versus ends was raised. In winning the larger issue of partnership in the Turkish Petroleum Company, Teagle had been forced to surrender on all major points but one (the working agreement). The Jersey Company had freely adopted such measures of aggression and defense as were demanded for success. To be sure, the fact that in order to get into Iraq the American group accepted restrictions upon their freedom of action elsewhere in the Middle East where oil was subsequently discovered in rich abundance does not support an adverse judgment of events to 1928. This decision clearly and logically grew out of the bright contemporary prospects in Iraq and the almost complete lack of prospects elsewhere within the Red Line area. There is justification, however, for a conclusion that insofar as Iraq was concerned the Open Door principle, eagerly espoused by the Americans in their initial efforts to obtain participation in the Turkish Petroleum Company, had been flaunted—in spirit if not in letter—once participation had been assured. To achieve the primary goal, the American group had sacrificed whatever had to be sacrificed. The quest was successful, though the cost was high. With a tenacity unshaken by either the opposition faced or the powerful deterrent of flush production from new fields in the United States, Teagle and the Jersey board pursued the essential objective—expansion of foreign crude oil reserves. The counsel of expediency for the most part prevailed, but the way was thereby prepared for entrenchment of American petroleum interests not only in the Middle East but also in other areas abroad where successful penetration was dependent upon a solid alliance between American government and business.

Chapter 12

Pursuit of the Oil Mirage in Europe
1919-1927

THE EFFORTS of Jersey Standard's leaders to develop a large production in the Middle East should not be allowed to obscure efforts that were simultaneously being made to expand producing operations in Europe. Under the general direction of Everit J. Sadler, a broad geological investigation of every European possibility was under way. Expectations were not always high, but the organization was determined to be thorough in guarding against the discovery by competitors of any major field in areas adjacent to Jersey Standard markets.

The establishment in 1922 of headquarters in Paris by the Foreign Producing Department has already been noted. European capitals were buzzing with oil deals, and Sadler wished to have reliable observers in the thick of the excitement. Harry G. Seidel was a competent and experienced man to head the new office, which soon was moved from its original home with the Bedford Petroleum Company, S.A.F., to rather sumptuous quarters on the Champs Élysées. Early in 1922 Winthrop P. Haynes was transferred from a Mexican assignment to head the geological staff in Paris. Under him at various times worked from one to five other geologists. A draftsman, a translator, a photographer, and a stenographer completed the office staff. Immediately after his appointment Haynes left on a field trip to Czechoslovakia.[1]

In 1922, 1923, and 1924 oil possibilities in France, Italy, Czechoslovakia, Spain, Tunis, Egypt, Arabia, Abyssinia, and on the north, east, and west coasts of Africa were investigated. These efforts yielded little, for Jersey Standard was interested only in major fields. A large amount of geological information was compiled and tabulated, nevertheless, and the Paris office served as a listening post for news from Russia and the Middle East.

Liaison with New York was maintained through William Warfield, Sadler's assistant, but Sadler himself occasionally visited Paris. These visits were for the most part short and hectic. Sadler ignored office routines and called meetings of the staff at all hours of the day and night. The men in Paris found the head of the Foreign Producing Department to be a hard driver. He was impetuous, outspoken, impatient with excuses, insistent upon promptness, and implacably opposed to evasiveness. His keen sense of the relative importance of the various producing projects cleared the air and imparted direction and vitality to office affairs.

In 1926 he caused the activities of the Paris office to be restricted sharply, in order to concentrate on more promising prospects elsewhere. By that time a large number of investigations had been completed; Haynes was spending three-quarters of his time on purely administrative work. The decision was therefore made to limit European efforts chiefly to Poland and Romania. Statistical functions were transferred to New York, and the gathering of published geological information was abandoned. Haynes was released for tasks where his wide geological knowledge could be of greater service to the company. The European search had proved disappointing, but well justified, nonetheless, from a defensive viewpoint.

NEW WELLS AND TROUBLES IN ROMANIA

Difficulties plagued company efforts to revive the Romanian producing venture.[2] Conflicting governmental attitudes were in evidence. On the one hand, Romania's desire to encourage the rebuilding of the petroleum industry was manifest, yet here, as in so many other places in the world, inflation impeded recovery from the war, and intense nationalism was stirring. Jersey men noted an increasing disposition on the part of the Liberal Party in power to discriminate against foreign capital. In 1919 reports of impending nationalization were circulated. In 1920 a plan was proposed by the government to lease promising state lands to the large oil companies in return for a loan of £20,000,000. This project never materialized, and cash concession offers from foreign interests were refused. Instead, the best state lands were turned over gratis to political friends of the government, which then participated only on a royalty basis. At the same time, Jersey Standard's efforts to obtain a satisfactory settlement of its Romanian war-damage claims were beset by delays and rebuffs. Since Romania was destitute of funds and Jersey men knew that any Romanian settlement would necessarily be on a credit basis, the company persisted in its attempts to obtain a settlement of some kind from Britain.

The Romăno-Americana staff did what it could under adverse conditions to increase production. A staff of from three to five geologists working under E. T. Hancock concentrated their attention upon the company's existing acreage in an effort to improve well yields and tap deeper pay sands. Some success was encountered at Baicoi, but the prolific Moreni wells were showing signs of exhaustion and at no time from 1919 to 1924 was total production more than half that of the record year 1914. Hancock reported that delays in starting up the drilling program after the war, together with bad luck on some of the first wells started, had been costly. Competitors beat the company to flush production from new pay horizons.

In July of 1924 a blow was dealt the Romanian venture which Jersey men felt might well prove, in time, to be fatal. The government passed a new mining law which provided for nationalization of the subsoil and prohibited the granting of concessions on state lands to foreign companies. While such companies were not deprived of their old concessions, severe restrictions in favor of Romanian-owned enterprises were laid upon them, and the lure of concessions on the state lands was used to encourage foreign concerns to "nationalize" (that is, to turn over a minimum of 55 per cent of their stock to bona fide Romanian citizens).[3]

The smaller companies took immediate steps to grasp the opportunity thus extended. Steaua-Romăna, the former Deutsche Bank subsidiary, was already owned largely by Romanians. Jersey Standard and the Royal Dutch-Shell, however, declared their intention of resisting nationalization and protested that the new law was confiscatory and illegal.

Teagle declared that as little Romanian crude as possible should be exported—". . . foreign oil companies in their own interest should now do everything possible to bring pressure to bear on Romania to have this law repealed, or at least the discriminatory clauses thereof modified so that foreigners would be given an equal opportunity with Romanian nationals."

"The one way to do this," Teagle concluded, "is to make it difficult for Romania to find a market for all its finished products."[4]

Jersey's operations were encountering other difficulties. Drilling and operating costs were high, and a report prepared in March of 1924 had stated that the Romăno-Americana organization lacked punch and needed overhauling. Alarm was expressed at the rapidly rising cost per barrel of oil produced. Sadler was informed that, though the local management had been given unlimited freedom by 26 Broadway, results had not been forthcoming. The conclusion must be drawn that that management was inefficient.[5]

Some progress, however, was being made. Româno-Americana was able, because of the indefinite wording of the new mining law, to acquire about 1,500 acres of new land, and the geologists defined several new structures. Production increased somewhat in absolute volume, but reports forwarded to 26 Broadway indicated a relative decline in Româno-Americana production from 22 per cent of the country's total in 1921 to 7 per cent in 1926—a direct result of the discriminatory restrictions on foreign-owned companies.

Efforts to pressure the government into repealing the unfavorable legislation were not successful. Early in 1928 Teagle briefly considered opposing the loan that Romania was then seeking from the United States. Seidel, however, pointed out that such action partook more of the nature of an act of revenge than of constructive policy which would bring lasting advantage to the Jersey Company. The prevailing conclusion came to be that, since Romania had proved to be a high-cost crude oil producing area, Jersey policy should be to extract the largest amount of profit from the existing investment—with a minimum of future expansion and the smallest possible additional capital investment.[6] At the end of 1927 Romania, like Persia, had yielded few satisfactions, and was viewed by the Jersey directorate with dimming hopes. The protracted war-damage claims controversy was one of the very few uncertainties that were dissipated in this troubled period.

On July 5, 1928, Austen Chamberlain, speaking for the British government, declared that the facts and circumstances of the destruction of Româno-Americana installations in 1916 were not such as to establish a claim against His Majesty's government.[7] Jersey's legal advisers held that the English doctrines of law were questionable, but they viewed the Chamberlain note as an unusually strong and ably prepared document. In September of 1928 the Jersey Company notified the State Department that it would abandon its claim on Britain and open negotiations with the Romanian government.[8] In May of 1929 a settlement with Romania was concluded.

This settlement called for the payment of principal and accrued interest in bonds maturing at regular intervals from 1929 to 1965. The German settlement, effected in 1919, had awarded the company additional damages, upon which heavy interest charges had accrued. In 1929 Jersey men summarized the situation in these terms:[9]

Actual losses, recorded in the Româno-Americana war-damage account

Loss of physical property.........................	$ 4,693,800
Loss of products.................................	2,473,500
Loss of storehouse material.......................	836,300
Total loss....................................	$ 8,003,600

Awards

From the Romanian government...................	$10,205,500
From the German government....................	6,250,000
Total awards................................	$16,455,500

Excess of awards over losses, taken to represent
lost profits for the five years from December, 1916,

to December, 1921..........................	$ 8,451,900
An annual average profit of.......................	$ 1,690,380

Accrued interest on the Romanian debt to the date of settlement totaled $6,326,600, while by the end of 1929 the interest on the German debt had grown to $4,013,400.[10]

Since Româno-Americana's average annual profit for the 1914-1916 period was equivalent to approximately $2,865,000 and operations had been steadily expanding up to the time when political difficulties had interfered with production, the profit compensation figure was conservative. A serious discrepancy also existed between the amount of the original Jersey Standard claim ($95,700,000 in all) and the sums finally awarded. Jersey men believed that they were entitled to the actual value, as contrasted to the book value, of their property—this value to be measured in terms of prices prevailing at the time of settlement. The settlements, however, appear to have been based on the book value of the property, valued at the prices prevailing in 1916.

The total of $16,455,500 in awards, however, was not all that the Jersey Company could credit against its Romanian war-damage accounts. Some of the wells that had been included in the claims as being totally destroyed were subsequently restored to production. Since the salvage operations were not concluded until many months after the damage claims had been filed, the restored value of these wells was not included in computing the net damage for which the claims were entered. Certain awards of money and material were also made to Româno by the German-owned Vega and Steaua refineries to cover equipment confiscated by them during the war. Both these refineries agreed to process Româno crude oil at a substantial discount while the Teleajen refinery was being rebuilt.[11]

Any judgment as to whether Jersey Standard had fared well or poorly in the settlement of its Romanian war claims and awards is necessarily contingent upon a decision as to whether cost or replacement value of the destroyed property should have formed the basis for settlement. The question of the fairness of the awards, however, has only academic pertinence. The important point was not the amount of the awards but the amount of the payments, and the matter of collections on the large outstanding German and Romanian debts was one which in future years was to yield Jersey Standard few satisfactions.

THE ATTEMPT AT INTEGRATION IN POLAND

Producing operations in Poland, undertaken by Jersey Standard interests in 1922, returned unbroken losses and inconsequential yields of oil.[12] A managerial failure in this venture provided insight into larger forces which were at work at 26 Broadway. Here, too, was to be seen that by no means uncommon situation where losses were borne in one branch of the business in order to sustain profits in another.

Production in the Polish petroleum industry had been declining since 1909. Extremely difficult drilling conditions had discouraged wildcatting, and the division of the heavily populated land into very small holdings made leasing of adequate plots difficult. The oil industry had been intensively developed over a period of many years. Refining capacity exceeded producing capacity by 50 per cent, and competition had been keen. Import and export restrictions and duties hampered the flow of crude oil and refined products into world markets, accentuating the internal difficulties. Marketing within Poland was regulated by a government-controlled cartel.

These problems were not unfamiliar to Jersey men. Before World War I the DAPG had developed an efficient and profitable marketing system in the Posen area. The Nobel petroleum interests had built a more loosely integrated distribution network in eastern Poland and in adjacent Russian territories. Both the DAPG and the Nobels planned to resume operations as soon as the boundaries of the new Polish state were established by the Versailles Treaty and subsequent peace conferences. Both faced the prospect of greater operating difficulties and even more intense competition than had existed in 1914.

In 1919 the Nobels formed an alliance with the Posener Bank and set up the Nobel Brothers Oil Industrial Company in Poland, Limited, ("Polnobel") to handle the marketing business. This potential DAPG competitor also acquired an old refinery at Libusza and two drilling leases at Boryslaw. Despite these preparations, the Nobels, whose industrial empire in Europe and Russia had been greatly disturbed by the war, appeared anxious to enlist the aid of Jersey Standard capital and possibly to forestall Jersey Standard competition. In August of 1919 F. E. Powell, head of Jersey's former British affiliate, the Anglo-American Oil Company, Limited, informed F. D. Asche that the Nobels were willing to dispose of certain segments of their European petroleum marketing system. This intelligence caused a stir at 26 Broadway, and steps were at once taken to arrange a meeting between Jersey and Nobel representatives. On November 21, 1919, a conference was held between Gustav Nobel, Emanuel Nobel, James A. Moffett, Jr., and Sadler, at which plans were drawn for a merging of Polish marketing interests. Riedemann, of the DAPG, was subsequently consulted, and the advice of the three Jersey men was unanimous. On December 31, 1919, the Jersey board approved the purchase of a 25 per cent share in the Nobel company. The Posener Bank retained its previous 50 per cent participation, while the Nobels held the remaining 25 per cent interest.[13]

The actual management of the enterprise had been in the hands of Nobel representatives, but shortly after the purchase a joint management was set up. Leigh Ballenberg, an accountant in whom Teagle had placed great trust while in Canada, was sent to Poland in 1920 to represent the Jersey Company in the direction of Polnobel. Ballenberg was to report to F. D. Asche, director in charge of foreign marketing.[14]

Managerial lines of authority were not clear-cut. Ballenberg found that his associate manager had been extravagant and even dishonest in the conduct of company affairs. In 1921 the Nobel co-manager was discharged, and Ballenberg was placed in charge. At 26 Broadway, moreover, there appeared to be little interest in the Polish venture. Far greater problems were demanding the attention of the Jersey directors.

Ballenberg himself was no producing man, but he concurred heartily with the necessity for obtaining additional producing territories to support the refinery which, in turn, was to supply the products from which the company hoped to make its profits. He was faced with an operating loss of $375,000 which had accumulated under the preceding management. There were no funds with which to support a drilling program.[15]

At this point Jersey directors Sadler and S. B. Hunt visited Poland to look into producing possibilities. Both men believed that with modern equipment the company might be able to produce oil on a commercial basis. This conclusion was verified by the opinion of four company geologists assigned to investigate Poland. A Producing Department memorandum dated June 28, 1922, summarized the situation:[16]

We feel it is justified to enter Galicia with a producing company, and although we do not anticipate a very large production, we believe that our operations will pay out satisfactorily from a producing standpoint. Furthermore we will directly protect our Sales Company, which at the present time, although having the largest sales in Poland, is threatened with the impossibility of securing sufficient crude oil and products to maintain their present position.

Sadler went further and stated that the refining and marketing organization was doomed to operate at a loss indefinitely unless something was done in production.

The Nobels, however, were financially unable or unwilling to put additional capital into Polish operations, with the result that the burden of expansion fell upon Jersey Standard. In 1921 a new company—Towarzyskwo "Olej Skalny," Społka Akcyjna (hereafter referred to as Olej Skalny)—was organized to engage in producing operations. At the same time new capital was invested in Polnobel, the marketing and refining company. This refinancing was undertaken jointly by the Jersey Company and an affiliated French holding company, the Compagnie Standard Franco-Américaine. Jersey Standard interests emerged dominant in both Polnobel and Olej Skalny, the Jersey Company and Franco-Américaine together contributing $4,250,000 out of the $6,000,000 investment in the two Polish concerns.[17]

Olej Skalny was placed under the direction of Seidel, in the Paris office. Exploration and drilling programs were inaugurated, and extensive acreage was acquired in the Bitkow district of southeastern Poland. These operations were not generally successful. Drilling time averaged from three to five years per well. While notable progress was made in improving techniques, in some districts the average drilling cost per well ran as high as $200,000. Royalties to landowners ranged from 10 to 35 per cent of gross production.

Losses were consistently recorded by Olej Skalny. Each year requests were forwarded to 26 Broadway for Jersey to make up the annual deficit.[18] This poor financial showing would have occasioned less alarm had producing goals been met. The Libusza refinery required 1,200 barrels of crude daily, but in no year from 1922 through 1927 did production from the Polnobel and Olej Skalny leases at Boryslaw and Bitkow exceed an average daily net output of more than 800 barrels. Moreover, both fields were old, the future prospects for production there were dim, and the company geologists had not been successful in locating new structures. Supplies of Polish crude available for purchase were almost nonexistent, and prohibitive tariffs kept out foreign crude.[19] Thus the basic objective of the producing venture had not been attained.

Had marketing operations of the Polnobel been successful, the losses incurred by Olej Skalny might have been borne cheerfully. Ballenberg, however, was having his own troubles in refining and marketing. In 1924 the two companies showed a combined operating loss of $457,000. The refinery proved to be faultily constructed, and expensive alterations were required. The old DAPG marketing system was showing fair returns, but the former Nobel installations appeared poorly adapted to modern conditions and were returning losses. Requests by Ballenberg for additional funds to finance the modernization of Polnobel facilities were denied by 26 Broadway in an effort to reduce still further waste and loss. In May of 1924 Polnobel was placed under the unofficial supervision of H. E. Bedford, Jr., head of Jersey's French affiliate and a member of the European Committee. This move was instituted to facilitate communication between Ballenberg and top-level Jersey Company management.[20]

Early in 1925 the Polish situation had reached a point where high-level decisions were required. Teagle immediately demanded—and apparently in no uncertain terms—to be informed what was the matter and who was to blame. A jurisdictional dispute of some intensity at once flared up. Investigations were launched; a score of lengthy reports and memoranda were written. The responsibility for failure was laid by the Foreign Trade Department upon Seidel. H. E. Bedford, Jr., stated that both he and Ballenberg had repeatedly called attention to the fact that no profits could be expected in Poland until production had been increased. These warnings, said Bedford, had not been heeded in New York. Sadler penned a withering letter to Teagle in defense of his assistant. Seidel's responsibility, Sadler asserted, was confined to the Olej Skalny, and the Polnobel management had been under the supervision of F. D. Asche. Bedford and Sadler agreed that Ballenberg's management had been forced to face exceedingly difficult operating conditions, and that lack of financial support and attention by the Foreign Trade Department had deprived the local management of a fair opportunity to prove its ability.[21]

Teagle made no attempt to dodge his share of the blame. He wrote to Riedemann: "I feel that in large measure we are indirectly responsible for the situation existing. In other words, the question of management and method of procedure has not been followed up by us as it should have been, having in mind the large investment we are making."[22]

The agitated comments and charges in 1925 present ample evidence of confused and conflicting lines of authority. There is no question, of course, that difficulties and possibly loss would have been encountered in any case. Oil-finding in Poland had, by the very nature of existing operational circumstances, only a limited chance of success. Lacking adequate protection in the form of controlled production, the marketing effort had an equally small chance of returning a profit. Then, too, the government restrictions upon trade created many difficulties and rigidities. The Nobels had been unable to contribute either money or aggressive management to the joint enterprise which they had been so eager to undertake.

These factors, many of which could have been anticipated and some of which could have been corrected by careful analysis and prompt remedial action, had escaped Teagle's notice. His hierarchy of trusted lieutenants appear, in this instance, to have failed him. It may be that a few men were trying to do too much with a simple organization. Sadler, on this occasion as in the discussion of policy in the Iraq affair, had evidenced an increasing disposition to disagree sharply with the man beside whom he had worked in closest rapport for many years.

The subsequent course of the Polish business may be summarized in a few words. Late in 1925 the Polnobel and Olej Skalny companies were merged, and a single firm, the "Standard-Nobel w Polsce" Spolkałka Akcyjna (the Standard-Nobel Company in Poland, also called "Polnobel"), was formed. Shares in the new concern were held 21.4 per cent by the Jersey Company, 18.4 per cent by Franco-Américaine, 21.4 per cent by the Nobels, and 38.8 per cent by smaller groups. By this consolidation a closer co-ordination of the marketing, refining, and producing functions was obtained, and in both 1926 and 1927 a small operating profit was recorded. The basic problem, however, continued to be that of crude oil supplies. Peak production of 388,000 barrels annually was obtained in 1928, a quantity approximately sufficient to supply the Libusza refinery. Company production thereafter declined rapidly, and geological efforts were unavailing. The old situation of an extensive marketing division with a very limited supply of products to sell was not corrected, and in 1937 the Standard-Nobel Company sold out to Socony-Vacuum.

Limited success was not, to be sure, the universal end for Jersey Standard's producing ventures abroad, but the company's experiences both in Romania and in Poland merit attention along with the more prolific efforts that were simultaneously being made in other parts of the world. The chief interest of the Polish venture lies in the implicit revelations of internal managerial stresses at 26 Broadway and of the difficulties that accompanied efforts toward integration of functions in the oil industry. An even broader thesis is suggested by the fact that Jersey Standard recorded postwar failures in areas where the organization had been able to operate profitably in prewar years. Expectations based upon Jersey Standard's earlier prestige and operating record, it appeared, could not always be realized in a postwar world where traditional economic patterns were being disrupted by social and political movements too powerful for the businessman to control. This conclusion was being forced even more dramatically and decisively upon the consciousness of Jersey executives by concurrent events elsewhere in Europe.

THE NOBEL ALLIANCE OF 1920

On the broad Caucasian isthmus lying between the Black Sea and the Caspian the postwar problems of a troubled world became magnified into seething revolt. For centuries invading and retreating hordes had streamed through the mountain passes separating Persia from Russia. Successive waves of migration from the East to the West left vestiges to populate the area with dissident ethnic groups. Baku, the best port on the Caspian Sea and the commercial capital of the region, had a cruel and bloody past. From time beyond record this door in the wall between Europe and Asia had been coveted and fought over by Russians, Arabs, Persians, Tartars, and Greeks.[23]

The history of man's interest in the petroleum deposits at Baku and adjoining settlements on the Apsheron Peninsula extends back to the pre-Christian era. Burning gas seepages were the object of devotion by pilgrims who came from every part of Asia to the shrines erected by Zoroaster and his followers. A century before Drake drilled his historic well at Titusville, Pennsylvania, a primitive plant for treating raw naphtha had been constructed in the Caucasus. As in Romania, hand-dug wells were numerous. In 1863 a refinery had been built at Baku, and in 1871 the first drilled well in the Baku area came in. Extensive development of the region along modern lines dated from 1875, when the Nobel brothers had begun to invest large amounts of capital in Russian refining and producing properties.[24]

In 1910 the Nobels had materially extended their control over Russian production by concluding a supply agreement with the major Baku firms.

In this same year several tremendous gushers came in at the Grozny fields, 200 miles northwest of Baku, and by 1916 Russian production totaled 70,000,000 barrels, or about 15 per cent of total world production. In that year companies in which the Nobels had an interest produced 33 per cent of the Russian crude, refined 40 per cent of the Russian production, and supplied 60 per cent of the Russian domestic consumption. Most of the growing Russian output was barged up the Volga River to internal markets, and only a small percentage (9 per cent in 1913) was pumped through the 550-mile-long Baku-Batum pipeline or carried by the Transcaucasian railroad to world markets.[25]

In 1917 prevailing processes of economic development began to be twisted by violent and rapid political upheavals. The October Revolution in Russia inspired Bolshevik uprisings in the oil fields, where the workmen had long suffered from harsh treatment and low wages. In April of 1918 the Caucasian provinces of Armenia, Georgia, and Azerbaijan took advantage of the prevalent unrest to declare their independence of Russia, Turkey, and Persia. In August of 1919 the government of Azerbaijan asserted its sovereignty over the Baku fields, assuming control of the petroleum industry there. British garrison forces evacuated Baku, but they continued to hold the strategic port of Batum. Volunteer armies of Caucasian peasants and tribesmen took the field to oppose Bolshevik attempts to conquer the newly formed Caucasian republics. Oil operations came to a virtual halt, typhus broke out, and confusion prevailed.[26]

The Jersey Company's interest in Caucasian oil and oil fields derived quite naturally from the desire to expand the company's oil reserves abroad. Baku oil, which before 1918 had not been directly available to the Jersey organization, could be brought to Mediterranean markets at considerably lower transportation costs than the Western Hemisphere stocks with which the company was supplying these areas. Russian supplies could, moreover, provide a timely substitute for war-impaired Romanian production. A more particular incentive was provided by the knowledge that advantageous trades might be made in the prevailing troubled state of affairs in the Caucasus. Many small operators at Baku, hard pressed for money, were anxious to sell interests in their properties to anyone who could guarantee cash payment. The Azerbaijan government, moreover, was reported to have on hand very large stocks of refined products which it had accepted as collateral for government loans advanced to the local oil operators for the purpose of preventing a complete collapse of the industry. These seemingly advantageous circumstances prompted the Jersey board to move without its customary careful deliberations and investigations. The initial commitment to action, however, was on a relatively small scale and was recognized at 26 Broadway as a speculative endeavor.[27]

On January 7, 1919, the Jersey Company concluded a contract with the Azerbaijan government for the purchase of eleven plots of undeveloped government land in the Baku district. This contract was worked out at meetings in Paris between H. E. Bedford, Jr., head of Jersey's French affiliate, and members of an Azerbaijan European mission. The agreement called for payment by the Jersey Company of 6,000,000 francs (about $320,000 at existing exchange rates). Half of this sum was paid over when the contract was signed; the remainder was to be paid when the plots were actually turned over to the company.[28]

The bargain-basement atmosphere in the Caucasus attracted the interest of others besides Jersey Standard. The Royal Dutch-Shell group was negotiating to expand properties acquired before the war and to purchase refined stocks in storage in the fields and at Batum. Agents of many smaller companies were at hand, and the Turkish, Italian, French, and German governments had all evinced an interest in opportunities created by the fluid political situation. The Anglo-Persian Oil Company appeared to be standing aloof for the moment at least, but Britain's interests were certain to be protected by British military control over the Batum end of the strategic pipeline which constituted the only practicable way by which large amounts of oil could be exported from Baku. The Standard Oil Company of New York endeavored to close a purchase contract with the Azerbaijan government which would virtually have monopolized all transportation facilities out of Baku for a six-month period, but the company was thwarted by strenuous representations made by the Royal Dutch-Shell to the British commanding general of the area.[29]

Throughout 1919 several highly interesting Russian possibilities were brought to the attention of the Jersey directors. Sadler recommended that an investigation be launched of Russian producing prospects—a subject on which the company had no recent information.[30]

Meanwhile, conversations with the Nobels about the marketing alliance in Poland were under way, and it appeared that the Nobel contact might have even wider implications. On November 5, 1919, Sadler and Moffett, who was then serving as understudy to Asche in Jersey's Foreign Trade Department, met in Paris with Emanuel and Gustav Nobel and their assistants. After the Jersey men had mentioned that their company was considering an entry into Russian producing operations, the Nobels expressed their hope that a way could be found to avoid severe competition between Jersey Standard and the Nobel interests in Russia. The Nobels suggested a co-operative venture and said that the time was opportune for the purchase of additional producing properties. Moffett and Sadler were informed that the Nobel group controlled 50 per cent of all Russian production and might be willing to dispose of as much as one-half of its Russian investments.[31]

F. E. Powell, head of Anglo-American, forwarded a strong recommendation to 26 Broadway that the co-operation of the Nobels be obtained at any cost, both to facilitate the possible Russian entry and to prevent the Nobels from making connections that might be unfavorable to Jersey Standard or to Anglo-American, Jersey's important British customer.[32]

For several days the Jersey board considered the Russian matter. On November 13 Asche cabled Moffett that, if an investigation of the Russian fields by Sadler proved to be favorable, the Jersey Company might be willing to associate with the Nobels in a Russian venture. Financial information on the Nobel enterprises was forwarded to 26 Broadway, and Sadler began to map out the itinerary of his trip.[33]

Motivations underlying the Nobel offer are not difficult to discern. The Nobels wished to forestall competition from Jersey Standard in Russia, were anxious to obtain financial assistance from 26 Broadway, and desired to enlist American support for the struggle against Bolshevism which the Nobels and their local managers clearly foresaw. It was also evident that the actions of the State Department in extending diplomatic assistance to American business interests abroad had materially influenced the Nobels' opinion as to the expediency of forming American connections.[34]

In Constantinople, Sadler completed his preliminary studies of the Mesopotamian and Persian situations, as noted earlier, and on December 14, 1919, he departed for Novorossisk. For three weeks he vigorously investigated conditions at Baku and Batum, talking with many important political, military, and commercial people and taking copious notes. Sadler also sounded out several of the Baku producers about the possibilities of purchasing refined products.

Sadler's report on his Russian trip, which was received at 26 Broadway early in March of 1920, was a masterly combination of thoroughness, order, and logic. Generally speaking, Sadler reported, the Russian oil regions were not only a production engineer's dream but a wildcatter's paradise. Sadler found that the Nobels were by all measures the most prominent group in the industry, the Royal Dutch-Shell being their chief competitor. The Nobel properties were in good condition, notwithstanding the chaotic circumstances that had prevailed over the past three years. The Nobel refinery at Blacktown, near Baku, was the largest in all of Russia and had been the first in the world to install a continuous distillation battery (in 1881). In 1919 the Nobels were doing 45 per cent of all Russian refining, while Shell did 25 per cent.[35]

The conclusions Sadler presented were carefully defined and qualified. Production prospects definitely justified an entry into the Caucasus, and Sadler was sure that under normal conditions the Jersey Company could operate profitably there. The political situation was unpredictable, but Sadler felt that if no more than five million dollars was invested the opportunity for gain would be greater than the risks involved. The most desirable way of entering the area would be a partnership with the Nobels, but only with the understanding that the Nobels should modify their asking price to take full account of the many uncertainties and dangers involved.

These recommendations were examined with great interest at 26 Broadway. On March 13, 1920, A. C. Bedford cabled Sadler at Bucharest and instructed him to open negotiations. Two weeks later Sadler met with Gustav Nobel in Paris.[36]

While talks were going on between Sadler and the leader of the Nobel enterprises, company plans matured for the purchase of a large quantity of Baku refined products. Early in March a contract had been concluded with four principal Baku companies (including the Nobel interests) for the sale to the Jersey Company of 64,000 tons of kerosene. These companies had been anxious to prevent Jersey from making purchases from the Azerbaijan government, which had been purchasing oil supplies at the fields at distress prices. Jersey Standard agreed to refrain from dealing with the government for a specified period of time, provided that the producers were able to guarantee the company the supplies it wished. This the producers were able, with some difficulty, to do, and the oil began to be loaded on tankers at Batum.[37]

Political conditions in the Caucasus, however, had taken a turn for the worse. In April of 1920 the feared and the expected happened. The Bolsheviks invaded Azerbaijan, overthrew the government, executed such officials as could be found, and seized the Baku fields. On July 7 the British evacuated Batum. With all the Nobel property in Russian hands and reportedly nationalized, the entire question of Jersey Standard participation was altered in dramatic fashion.

Negotiations with the Nobels, nevertheless, were not broken off. At the very time that the Bolsheviks were seizing the property in which the company was seeking to purchase an interest, the Jersey directors agreed to advance $500,000 to the Nobels to purchase additional interests in producing properties at Baku for the joint account of the two companies. The question at once arises as to why the Jersey men could possibly have considered an investment in the Caucasus after the Soviet seizures.[38]

The Russian Revolution and the acts of the Bolsheviks were viewed with abhorrence by the Western world. In 1920 the feeling was very strong that the reign of terror could not last. A steady stream of "reliable" reports from Russia told not only of internal dissension in the Communist Party, but of administrative chaos which would inevitably result in a complete breakdown of the revolutionary movement and a return to a conservative form of government. It seemed inconceivable that any system of government based upon the complete repudiation of established moral principles and the renunciation of private property rights could for long prevail in the world of the twentieth century. Jersey men, like a great many others, awaited the collapse of the Soviet regime with confidence and took steps to place themselves in an advantageous position for the time when the collapse should come.

There was, of course, an appreciation at 26 Broadway of the risks involved. Teagle outlined to A. C. Bedford the decision which must be made. "If we feel that the internal situation in Russia is such as to make an investment there questionable, then we had better stay out altogether."[39]

The temptation was a great one, nevertheless. Teagle concluded in his note to Bedford:

Personally, while recognizing that twelve to fifteen million dollars is a very large figure, and also recognizing the uncertainties as to the stability of any investment, whether in Russia or in Azerbaijan, still at the same time if we ever expect to be a factor with direct financial interests in this large producing area, it seems to me that there is no other alternative but for us to accept the risk and make the investment at this time. If we do not do it now, I think we will be debarred from ever exercising any considerable influence in the Russian producing situation.

Teagle felt that the matter was of sufficient importance to justify a letter of information to John D. Rockefeller, Jr. Teagle told Rockefeller that Sadler, whom he called "one of our ablest producers," had strongly recommended the investment in question and that eight of the nine board members had approved of the transaction. Rockefeller replied that he knew of no reason why the matter should not be decided on its merits.[40] John Bassett Moore also gave as his opinion that the entry into Russian production was exclusively a business question. These expressions contain the barest suggestion that the ethical aspects of any transaction which the Jersey Company might enter into in Russia had already become a matter of passing concern. So doubtful did it seem at the time, however, that the Soviet experiment would survive its troubled youth that the decision was made on the basis of business considerations alone. These considerations were ably set forth by Riedemann in a letter to Teagle:[41]

The Standard Oil Company has very large investments in Europe to protect, and for the supply of their various organizations there the Standard Oil at present has to rely on shipments from America exclusively. We have no second basis of supply in reserve that would assure us of any quantities to speak of. The Russian field is a proven rich field with a potential production *far* in excess of the crippled Russian home consumption, and very favorably situated for the supply of Europe. It is bound to come back sooner or later, and if it should do so without our having a strong hold on its production, it may mean, in the hands of our competitors, a very severe menace to our European investments, especially if the development of the oil situation in America should reduce the surplus available for export more and more.

This line of reasoning was decisive, particularly since it was reinforced by the knowledge that, if the Jersey Company did not accept the opportunity offered them, the Nobels would probably form an alliance with the British. Action by the State Department, moreover, removed any legal barriers which might have stood in the way. In July of 1920 the Department announced the removal of restrictions upon trade and communication with Soviet Russia. Firms availing themselves of the opportunity for doing business in Russia, however, were to do so at their own risk. This last pronouncement indicated clearly that the company could expect no diplomatic support for its Russian enterprise. Nevertheless, on July 30, 1920, the Jersey-Nobel alliance was consummated.

Teagle's cautious opinion was that the Jersey Company at that time had best not appear as the owner of property in Russia. The agreement with the Nobels, therefore, was made through the Schweizerische Handels-und Beteiligungs-Aktiengesellschaft, the same useful Swiss company which had been the vehicle for the purchase of the Pure Oil interests in Germany in 1911. Through this company Jersey Standard agreed to purchase half of the Nobel family interests in the Nobel Brothers Petroleum Production Company, which, in turn, owned interests in some 28 Russian subsidiaries. For the half share in these interests the Jersey Company agreed to pay the sum of $11,500,000.[42]

There were two complications. In the first place, the Nobels personally owned only 20 per cent of the stock of the Petroleum Production Company. The estimated additional expenditure of $5,000,000 necessary to acquire a majority interest was to be shared equally by Jersey Standard and Nobel, and steps were at once taken to acquire the needed stock.[43]

The second complication arose from the fact that not only were all the Nobel properties in Soviet hands, but 26,000 out of the 36,000 shares of the Petroleum Production Company owned by the Nobels were in Russia—also, presumably, in Soviet hands. The agreement as to payments by the Jersey Company was conditioned upon these circumstances. Upon receipt of certificates representing 13,000 shares of Petroleum Production Company stock Jersey Standard agreed to pay to the Nobels over a two-year period the sum of $6,568,000. By December 31, 1922, all of this money had been paid. The balance of $4,932,000 on the original purchase price was to be paid when the remaining 5,000 shares were delivered and the Nobel properties were restored by the Soviet government.[44]

Viewed by hindsight this agreement, calling for the down payment of more than $6,000,000 without real security or any assurance of fulfillment of the contract, appears to have been one of the most ill considered ever made by a Jersey board. Teagle, the directorate, Sadler and Teagle's astute European lieutenants, the Jersey Legal Department, and consultant John Bassett Moore all approved of the transaction. Such unanimity is the best possible indication of the prevailing conviction that the Russian troubles were of a transitory nature. The risks, though obviously underestimated by the Jersey men, were admitted. The bargain was a colossal one—control of a half or more of the Russian petroleum industry for only $14,000,000! Had Fate turned a genial countenance upon this transaction, it would possibly have been hailed as among the most brilliant ever consummated in the petroleum industry.

SOVIET OIL AND THE FRONT UNI

With the Nobel alliance an accomplished fact, the Jersey directors focused their attention upon the chances of early restitution to the rightful owners of the private property which the Soviet government had seized. Uneasiness increased at 26 Broadway as the months went by and Communism refused to die. Teagle took steps to determine the attitude of the State Department.

Even after the partial lifting, on July 7, 1920, of the American interdict on Russian trade, the official attitude of the State Department toward commercial relations with or in Soviet Russia was far from encouraging. On August 19, 1920, Teagle notified the Secretary of State of the Nobel agreement and the reasons that had led the Jersey Company to make the alliance. The Department, Teagle wrote to Gustav Nobel, could provide no assistance but had expressed its unofficial satisfaction.[45]

There were many disquieting rumors about the activities of competitors—activities that directly involved the oil properties in which Jersey Standard had so hopefully purchased its multimillion-dollar interest. Gustav Nobel reported to Teagle that the Royal Dutch-Shell had made large purchases of producing territories in the Grozny area. Deterding, it was rumored, had determined to control the Russian production, since he looked upon it as the greatest source of supply for the near future, and was dickering not only with the dispossessed private owners but with Krassin, the crafty Soviet commissar of petroleum.[46]

Even rumors such as these were less disquieting than the report that Krassin was negotiating with the Anglo-Persian Oil Company. It was becoming increasingly obvious that Britain, under the leadership of Lloyd George, was not disposed indefinitely to refuse negotiations with Russia and was more and more inclined to take advantage of whatever opportunities for the development of trade and industry the Soviet might offer.[47]

These alarming stories, coming from many quarters and in many versions, indicated beyond doubt that all petroleum properties in Russia, including the Nobel-Jersey interests, were being placed on the auction block by the Soviet government. The Jersey Company contemplated an effort to have the State Department protest to the British government against any Anglo-Persion–Soviet negotiations, but Gustav Nobel objected that this would mean too much publicity. A. C. Bedford suggested that consideration be given to the feasibility of joint action in Russia by the Jersey Standard, Nobel, Anglo-Persian, and possibly French and Italian interests.[48] Behind this suggestion lay the well-defined fear that either the Royal Dutch-Shell or the Anglo-Persian group might conclude a deal with the Soviet government that would exclude all other parties from participation in Russia.

In March of 1921, Montagu Piesse, Jersey's English counsel, was invited by Sir Charles Greenway, leader of Anglo-Persian, to a conference with Krassin. Krassin stated that it was unsafe for him to make any agreement with Anglo-Persian alone, but suggested a joint Anglo-Persian–Jersey participation in Russia. The Soviet commissar stated that his government would commandeer the entire production of the Grozny field, offering one half jointly to Anglo-Persian and Jersey Standard and retaining the remainder for internal consumption. The two companies would be given the right to exploit state lands and build a pipeline to the Black Sea. Krassin avoided the stigma of dealing in stolen goods by stipulating that Jersey and Anglo-Persian should pay a fair price to the original owners for any oil taken from their property. The actual treatment that the former owners would receive under such a proposal was, however, dubious at best, and the Krassin plan could scarcely be viewed as other than a forced liquidation of heavy Royal Dutch-Shell investments in the Grozny area. Greenway, nevertheless, was anxious to enter into this arrangement and indicated that the approval of the British government would be forthcoming.[49]

Piesse forwarded this intelligence to 26 Broadway. John Bassett Moore conferred with Secretary of State Hughes, who stated flatly that he would not approve any Jersey Standard agreement with the Soviet government. Hughes declared that Russia was a "gigantic economic vacuum" and indicated that the United States government would pursue a policy of watchful waiting. Teagle himself was suspicious of Krassin's offer. "I have no confidence whatever," he wrote Piesse, "in any promises or commitments which the Bolshevik government might give."[50]

A sharp cleavage of opinion about company policy appeared in the ranks of management in the spring of 1921 and was not resolved in the months which followed. State Department hostility and Teagle's deep suspicion of the Soviets precluded any deal with Krassin, while great divergence of opinion as to the imminence of the Soviet collapse made the men at 26 Broadway reluctant to accede to the desire of the European representatives to acquire additional Russian producing properties from their former owners. To Riedemann, who was closely following the course of events, Teagle confided that the Jersey Company had already gambled in Russia all the money that could be justified by the existing situation. These were the prevailing circumstances when the Genoa Conference convened in April of 1922.[51]

One purpose for calling the Genoa Conference between the Allied gov-

ernments and Soviet Russia was to review and improve the confused relationships between the Soviets and the Western nations. Lloyd George's
vision of a world united and made harmonious by mutually advantageous
trade pacts was to be translated into reality. The Russians came to the
conference strengthened by the obvious eagerness of the British to trade
and confident that advantageous bargains could be obtained through
promises to make restitution to former owners for the private property
that had been seized. The United States government declined to participate in the proceedings, but declared, nevertheless, its firm conviction
that either confiscated property in Russia must be returned to its former
owners or a fair compensation must be paid those owners.

A suspicious press reported that representatives of the great international oil companies were present in force. No sooner had the conference
convened than a flood of rumors and accusations began to appear in both
European and American newspapers. The Royal Dutch-Shell was reported
to have concluded a secret agreement with the Soviet government involving the confiscated oil properties of many private owners. This story was
given wide credence and nearly disrupted the conference. French and
Belgian groups which had small holdings in Russia protested bitterly
and agreed to merge their interests in a fight against any agreement involving the properties they hoped to regain from the Russians. Teagle
drew up the following memorandum, dated April 14, 1922, for presentation to the State Department, though the records do not indicate whether
this note was actually delivered:

> The Standard is vitally interested in any proposition which may come before the
> Genoa Conference, or which may be discussed informally among the representa-
> tives there, looking to a disposition of either Government oil lands or oil lands
> which have been expropriated by the Soviet Government from private owners,
> and desires to protest against any recognition of any nationalization of privately-
> owned oil properties, or any disposition of oil properties so nationalized.

Charges were publicly aired that in their quest for preferential agreement with Russia the oil companies were undermining the conference.
Jersey Standard was implicated along with the rest, and the directors
caused F. D. Asche to issue a public denial of certain charges that the
company was active behind the scenes at Genoa.[52]

Asche's statement was less than the whole truth and implied a greater
aloofness by the company from events at Genoa than actually was the
case. John A. Mowinckel, then head of Italo-Americana, Jersey's affiliate

in Italy, talked with conference officials and remained in close touch with Washburn Child, American Ambassador to Italy, and Colonel Logan, the American representative to the reparations committee at London, both of whom were present at Genoa. Mowinckel suggested that the Italo-Americana boardroom at Genoa be made available for the private office use of Ambassador Child, and he channeled a steady stream of information to 26 Broadway about conference developments. The widespread belief that Jersey Standard, like the Royal Dutch-Shell, was negotiating with the Soviet government, however, was unfounded. Krassin called on Mowinckel several times, but Mowinckel voiced the company's viewpoint that the moment was not opportune for entering into negotiations. The company's participation in the conference was confined to the gathering of information. This policy of watchful waiting was not abandoned even in the face of alarming rumors of the activities of competitors.[53]

The conference at Genoa was concluded at the end of May. Mowinckel expressed his relief that it was over without having resulted in undue publicity for the Jersey Company or having produced any "disagreeable surprises." The prevalent belief was that the path had been cleared for future action, for, despite the many press reports, it appeared that no concessions had actually been granted by the Russians at Genoa.[54]

To the intense alarm and irritation of the men at 26 Broadway, however, rumors continued to circulate that various oil groups had entered into agreements with the Russians to take over and operate the confiscated properties of others. Teagle advised A. C. Bedford to try to have a "good strong article" prepared for insertion in the *Saturday Evening Post,* as well as shorter articles in the *Wall Street Journal* and other periodicals, pointing out the "absolute insecurity" of any kind of dealings with the Soviet government. Should any statement appear linking Jersey Standard to such transactions, he told Bedford, the company should issue a public denial containing the statement that Jersey Standard believed in the sacredness of private property, whether in Russia or elsewhere.[55]

Meanwhile, Deterding had indicated a willingness to enter into an agreement for joint action with the Jersey-Nobel partnership looking toward an effort to regain the confiscated properties of both parties.

The Jersey men and the Nobels had for some months been willing and anxious to come to a definite understanding with the Royal Dutch-Shell about Russia. As early as February of 1921 Deterding had assented to the principle of co-operation, but he had taken no subsequent action. It may well be that Sir Henri believed he could succeed alone and that only after failure to come to terms with the Russians at Genoa had he come to appreciate the formidable nature of the forces he sought to control. Certainly Deterding's attitude underwent a pronounced change in the closing days of the Genoa Conference. Sir Henri also was obviously disturbed by the Anglo-Persian–Jersey entente in northern Persia. On May 24, 1922, Deterding and Heinrich Riedemann held a long conversation in which the Shell leader denied that he had made any agreement with the Soviet government and stated that their two organizations should make a verbal agreement to co-operate in Russia.[56]

On learning of this meeting Teagle expressed his belief that Sir Henri probably wished to block any possible agreement between Jersey Standard and Anglo-Persian for joint action in Russia. Teagle also confessed that many of the Jersey men felt that if they were to enter the verbal agreement Deterding desired, he would keep it only as long as it suited his own best interests.[57] It was in an atmosphere permeated with suspicion, therefore, that the Jersey–Nobel and the Royal Dutch-Shell groups began to draw together.

On July 21, 1922, Teagle, Riedemann, and Asche met with Gustav Nobel and Deterding in London and reached a general understanding on policies to be followed in Russia. On the following day Nobel and the Jersey men discussed the project further, after which Teagle retired to his hotel to draft the final version of what had been proposed. On July 24 the so-called "London Memo" was ready. This paper was signed by neither the Jersey–Nobel nor the Royal Dutch-Shell group, the memo being, as Teagle told Bedford, merely for the purposes of information and for avoiding any possibility of future misunderstanding. The London Memo, which discreetly omitted any mention of Russia, specified that complete indemnification for the seized properties should be demanded—or, if that did not prove feasible, then restitution of the properties and indemnification for damages should be sought. Both parties agreed not to commence independent negotiations with the Russians. In case an "approach" was made to either group, the other was to be notified. Deviations from the agreement were not to be made without giving thirty days' notice.[58]

This was the first positive step toward the creation of what came to be known as the *Front Uni* by the major oil companies against Communist Russia. The London Memo, however, was at best a vague and negative document. In September of 1922 further conferences were held to implement and broaden the July agreement and to decide what specific steps could be taken to force Russia to restore or make restitution for the confiscated oil properties. At these conferences, which were held in Paris and were presided over by Deterding, representatives were present not only of the Shell, Jersey, and Nobel companies, but also of thirteen other firms (including the Franco-Belgian group) whose properties in Russia had been expropriated. An agreement similar in its terms to the London Memo was drawn up, and committees were appointed to deliberate upon common defense measures. The Jersey Company gave its assent to the agreement, but refused, upon the advice of Teagle and Riedemann, to put its name to any formal document. "We ought to avoid at present," Riedemann explained, in a note to A. C. Bedford, "taking any open initiative from which a blame could be fixed on us to the effect that we are at the bottom of the opposition against Russia."[59]

No sooner had it been created and broadened, however, than the *Front Uni* felt the impact of the disintegrating forces of self-interest. With consummate skill the Russians continued their policy of playing one great oil company against another, while endeavoring, at the same time, to build up a national petroleum industry and to obtain desperately needed foreign capital. World economic trends favored the Soviet strategy. Depressed commercial conditions that had prevailed throughout 1921 yielded to reviving trade demands, and the need for petroleum products began to exceed available world supplies.

Many concerns had entertained concession offers from the Russians, but no oil company had dared, in the last analysis, to brave the moral storm which would certainly have burst upon any company that acquired the confiscated Russian properties of others. The purchase of oil supplies, however, presented fewer practical and ethical objections than did the purchase of seized oil properties. Those who wished to evade castigation could always claim that at least some of the oil stocks that the Russians were offering had been produced on state lands. This new temptation was too great to be resisted.

Reports were received late in 1922 and early in 1923 that Deterding's organization had made substantial purchases of oil from the Soviets. Since the Paris agreement of September, 1922, had clearly stated that none of the participating groups should deal with the Russians in any way detrimental to the common interest, the news of these Shell transactions caused intense consternation among the other parties to the Paris pact. Sir Henri was severely censured both in public and in industry circles. The London *Financial News* attacked the Shell purchases as a breach of the Paris agreement and went on to state: "For the Royal Dutch-Shell to pretend they can purchase products derived from nationalized properties of all the members of the International Consortium without infringing the above agreement is, to put it mildly, astonishing."[60] This threat to the solidarity of the *Front Uni* drove Jersey's leaders to debate and decide upon a definite company policy in respect to the purchase of Soviet oil supplies.

The Jersey Company itself, though tempted, had purchased no oil from the Soviet government. The DAPG, however, had purchased at least two cargoes of Russian oil. These purchases were not initiated by Jersey's German affiliate, but came about through a supply-sharing arrangement which had been concluded between DAPG and certain German competitors. The last of these transactions, involving 7,500 tons of petroleum products for DAPG, had been concluded shortly before the Paris agreement was drawn up in the middle of September, 1922. Immediately thereafter, it became apparent that the purchase of oil from the Russians was to become a major issue. Riedemann wrote to New York for instructions.[61]

The situation confronting the Jersey directors was a most difficult one. The desirability of supplying Jersey's European and Mediterranean markets with purchased Russian products was daily becoming more obvious. Riedemann of the DAPG, Mowinckel of Italo-Americana, and Speth of the American Petroleum Company all wrote to 26 Broadway to complain that their competitors were bringing in cheap Russian oil. Purchases by Shell and by French interests were disturbing to the Jersey representatives in Europe. News was received, moreover, that the independent Vacuum Oil Company, which had been purchasing Romanian stocks from the Jersey Company to supply markets in Egypt, wished to substitute Russian oil in this trade.[62]

Notwithstanding these pressures, F. D. Asche cabled to the European men that, although the directors fully appreciated the growing importance of Russian supplies in the European marketing situation, assistance or relief in any form to the Soviet government might have an adverse effect upon the larger issue of the return of confiscated properties. Riedemann's response to this declaration was tinged with skepticism. "The decision not to purchase Russian products," he wrote, "has been taken from a political point of view. I quite understand this and I am in sympathy with it to some extent. From the marketing viewpoint I regret that the decision had to be taken." Gustav Nobel, however, agreed wholeheartedly with the Jersey Standard policy of total abstinence; he stated that, since the Soviet government could not hope to get out of its difficulties without assistance from the large oil companies, a boycott would materially hasten the return of private property to its rightful owners.[63]

Teagle was beginning to entertain serious doubts, and in 1923 he wrote to Riedemann in a pessimistic vain:[64]

We have a large amount invested in Russia, and while eventually I believe the investment will work itself out and the purchase be justified from the position it gives us there and the earnings derived therefrom, still at the same time I am equally convinced that instead of sitting up with a sick child of this character and nursing it along for years, we could have taken the same amount of money and invested it elsewhere in the oil business in such a way that the investment would have immediately become productive.

Frankly I cannot but feel that in the last two or three years some of the bets we have made—and among others the Russian one—could be criticized from the standpoint of not being as conservative as good business judgment prompts. Please do not think I am a pessimist, for such is not the case, but I am not entirely satisfied in my mind that some of our recent investments, particularly in foreign producing possibilities, can be in every way justified.

Riedemann, in turn, reported certain new developments of interest. A shipment of confiscated lumber to England by the Russians had been protested by the original owners, and a British court had refused to entertain the owners' claims. A similar incident had taken place in Germany, and Riedemann concluded that the fact of confiscation and nationalization would soon be widely accepted. Riedemann took an expedient attitude toward the Russian dilemma:[65]

Certainly the situation in Russia is very abnormal and represents an unprecedented case. The participation of a government in industrial and business enterprise as in Russia is new and unheard of in the history of business, and I wonder whether financially strong concerns capable of so doing will not be found willing to develop the enormous wealth of Russia under given conditions if these should remain for some time longer as they are. None of us like the thought of helping Soviet ideas, but if others should be willing to come in, what would then have been the use if we had kept aloof?

The hope that purchases from the Russians could be entirely prevented by verbal agreement between Jersey Standard and the Shell, Riedemann told Teagle, was not bright. Gulbenkian himself had frankly admitted as much to Riedemann. The practical thing to do, the astute leader of the DAPG concluded, was to combine with the Royal Dutch-Shell in a formal way—perhaps a joint company—and purchase Soviet oil for the common account of both concerns. There was no hope of an effective Russian boycott, but joint purchasing might channel the flow of Russian oil in beneficial rather than harmful directions.[66]

For eighteen months a quiet but intense struggle went on within the Jersey Company over the decision to set up a joint company for trading in and with Russia. Many practical problems stood in the way of making such a company operative; negotiations with the Royal Dutch-Shell were protracted by disagreement over details. Teagle took the position that, pending consummation of the new agreement with the Shell, the Jersey Standard boycott of Russian oil was still in effect. He also believed that Deterding was similarly bound to remain aloof until the new plan matured. Holding to this conviction, Teagle was able to persuade both the Vacuum Oil Company and the Standard Oil Company of New York to refrain from purchasing Russian oil until negotiations with Deterding were concluded and the situation was clarified.[67]

Throughout 1923 and the first six months of 1924, however, the greatest confusion prevailed. In the face of new offers from the Soviet to dispose of their oil at less than prevailing world prices, the *Front Uni* virtually dissolved. In April of 1923 the Royal Dutch-Shell unexpectedly concluded a large purchase of kerosene (estimated by Jersey men at from 150,000 to 200,000 tons) from the Russians. In accordance with the terms of the pending joint agreement, half of this purchase was offered by Deterding to the Jersey Company. Teagle was profoundly disturbed and refused to take the kerosene. Both Teagle and Riedemann believed that the purchase had been badly timed and constituted a disastrous breach in the *Front Uni*. Gulbenkian, too, had vigorously opposed this precipitate action on the part of his impetuous associate. The Vacuum Oil Company and the Standard of New York men, on their part, quite logically held that it was no longer possible for them to continue the "no-purchase" policy, and they were particularly annoyed by the fact that the Royal Dutch shipped the oil it had purchased into markets supplied by their companies.[68]

Dissenting voices were raised within the circle of Jersey men who were concerned with Russian policy. E. J. Sadler expressed the opinion that ". . . the first use that the Royal Dutch will make of this association will be to divide with us the odium of purchasing stolen goods from Russia." F. D. Asche was opposed to purchasing goods of "questionable title." James Moffett, like Teagle, was deeply suspicious of the Soviet government. F. H. Bedford, Sr., head of Jersey's lubricating oil marketing division in Europe, was adamantly opposed to dealing with the Russians.

Director S. B. Hunt stated unequivocally, "I am against buying stolen goods." Riedemann, however, declared that the boycott of Russian products could hurt only the Jersey Company itself, and that an agreement with the Royal Dutch-Shell was imperative in order to avoid "surprises."[69]

New elements were injected into the tangled situation. There were reports that the Anglo-American Oil Company, Limited, and certain German and French firms as well had closed contracts for Soviet oil; both Standard of New York and the Vacuum Oil Company had also begun to negotiate with the Russians. Deterding, in turn, became alarmed and chided Teagle and Riedemann about the activities of Jersey's one-time affiliates. "The difficulty with Henri," Riedemann reported to Teagle, "is that he cannot realize that the dissolution decree is effective and observed and that there is no longer any common control or management among these former subsidiaries." Riedemann bluntly pointed out to Deterding that the Royal Dutch-Shell bore the responsibility for making the first purchase from the Soviet government. In a letter to Teagle, Riedemann expressed concern that not only Deterding but the general public as well believed Standard of New York, Anglo-American, and Vacuum to be Jersey Standard companies and that their purchases made the Jersey Company's pronouncements appear inconsistent. Sir Henri took the position that no joint agreement could be signed until Teagle brought New York Standard and Vacuum Oil back into the *Front Uni*. Teagle responded that he could not be responsible for the action of those companies and could keep them out of the Russian market only by supplying their Mediterranean requirements—a task that was almost impossible until Jersey's Romanian production increased.[70]

Meanwhile, in February of 1924, the British government extended official diplomatic recognition to the struggling Soviet regime. Italy immediately followed this precedent, and it seemed probable that France would soon do so. Rumors of purchases of Soviet oil by many companies continued to pour into 26 Broadway, and Teagle began to waver in his determination not to purchase. To Riedemann he confided: "From the experience of the past two and a half years . . . it would appear that we are more or less clouding the issue and fooling ourselves in adhering to what has been our view on this subject to date." Asche, too, had begun to believe that practical rather than ethical considerations should now govern company policy. Guy Wellman, the farsighted and cautious counsel who was assisting Teagle in the Iraq negotiations, continued to argue in forceful terms that there was absolutely no difference between buying products known to have come from stolen properties and buying the stolen properties themselves.[71]

The logic and strength of such objections were fully admitted by Teagle, but Jersey Standard's position of being the only company resisting the Russian temptations had become intolerable. "I am really afraid," wrote Riedemann to Asche, "that we shall have to swallow the distasteful pill and accept the dictates of the present situation."[72] Reluctantly the decision was made at 26 Broadway. Early in 1924 the Jersey Company was at last ready to do business with Russia.

There was much to be done before an effective purchasing program could be launched. While discussion continued over details of the joint purchasing agreement with the Royal Dutch-Shell, Teagle was able to persuade Standard of New York and Vacuum to abstain from making independent purchases from Russia. Both firms agreed to let either Jersey Standard or the Royal Dutch-Shell do the bargaining, accepting a share in whatever might be obtained. Deterding, too, had given every assurance that he would make no more independent moves, and for the time being, at least, the *Front Uni* seemed once again to be secure. On November 26, 1924, the agreement with the Royal Dutch-Shell was signed, and shortly thereafter a joint trading company (popularly known as the "Construction and Development Company") was incorporated in Liechtenstein.[73] Provisions were included whereby other parties to the existing *Front Uni* might be allowed to subscribe to shares in the company—control, nevertheless, residing with the original participating groups.

Return of or just compensation for confiscated Russian properties continued to be the primary objective of the co-operative undertaking. Teagle had never ceased to insist on this point—nor, to be sure, had Deterding. From the very beginning Teagle and Deterding had hoped that a strong and united front might force the Russians to come to terms. That hope had all but vanished on occasion, but now, with the agreement signed, Teagle, Deterding, and Riedemann began to discuss how the joint purchasing program might be directed to bring pressure upon the Soviet government to accomplish the larger objective.

Both Mowinckel, head of Jersey's Italian affiliate, and Riedemann vehemently condemned the policy of making small purchases of whatever stocks the Russians wished to offer. Both men, and Deterding as well, favored the negotiation of a long-term contract for all of Russia's export petroleum—the contract being conditioned on restitution for confiscated properties. By December of 1924 discussions along these lines with Russian representatives in London had been launched. Apparently because neither Jersey Standard nor the Shell wished to deal directly with the Russians, the negotiations were handled by F. E. Powell, of the Anglo-American Oil Company, Limited.[74]

Personal factors at once complicated the proceedings. Powell and Riedemann did not get on well together, and it was only after an exchange of letters with New York that Powell consented to accept the advice and assistance of the German leader, the best informed of all Jersey men on the subtleties of the Russian situation. Deterding, who at one point had not been reluctant to trade with the Russians, had become markedly antagonistic toward the Soviet government and was insisting on terms which virtually precluded any hope of concluding a contract. Jersey men believed that Deterding's recent marriage to Lydia Koubeyaroff, a White Russian who was bitterly opposed to any dealings with the Soviets, was exerting an important influence upon the negotiations.[75]

Teagle himself, increasingly preoccupied with other aspects of the company's far-flung business, complained of the demands made on his time by the Russian situation. These demands had been visibly increased since June of 1924 by the tragic death in a motor accident of the trusted and hard-working Asche. James A. Moffett assumed Asche's responsibilities, but Moffett required time to master the intricacies of the foreign business. In a significant and frank letter to Riedemann, Teagle wrote:[76]

> As I look back over what we have done during the past six or eight months, I am rather impressed with the fact that a matter so important as this Russian purchase situation should have been handled by us without really giving the subject the consideration which its importance justifies. Mowinckel, probably more than anyone else, deserves the credit for really bringing forcibly to our attention in just what direction our present policy would seem to be leading. It is certainly to be regretted that we have so many things to do and our business day is so fully occupied that somehow or other we seem to make mistakes which could have been avoided if we had really spent the time necessary to think the matter through to a logical conclusion.

The next five months brought little solace or relief to the Jersey Company's hard-pressed president. The Jersey Standard and the Royal Dutch-Shell leaders found themselves in fundamental disagreement on the procedure to be followed in dealing with the Soviet government. Deterding and Gulbenkian contended that a policy of procrastination would force the Russians to their knees. Riedemann vigorously denied this and pointed to the fact that the Russians were successfully setting up a world-wide marketing system of their own and were finding buyers for their export surplus. Riedemann also pointed out to Deterding that neither Vacuum nor Standard of New York could be restrained indefinitely, and that these two firms alone promised Russia an outlet for more than 100,000 tons of kerosene annually. Gulbenkian replied, however, that anti-Soviet feeling in Britain had become so bitter, as a result of Communist agitation in the Balkans, that the time was inauspicious for a big deal. The Soviet government, moreover, had indicated its unwillingness, as a matter of principle, to grant an export monopoly to an international cartel.[77]

Teagle confessed to Deterding that his present thought was to temporize and see what might develop in the next two months. "Frankly," he wrote, "I am still sorry that we ever started trading with these people, but having done so it seems to me that we are now a good deal in the position of the hunter who had ahold of the bear's tail—he couldn't let go." To Riedemann he confided his alarm over the expenditures reportedly made by Communist agents in America for propaganda purposes. Were not the directors of American companies which purchased from Russia overlooking the best interests of their stockholders, Teagle asked, in making these purchases and supplying, in part at least, the funds used by the Reds in their attack upon private property rights? Both Teagle and Sadler were concerned that, if the Russians were allowed to get away with their spoils, an example would be set for all "irresponsible governments."[78]

From May to September of 1925 the question of what to do was pondered in greatest detail. Basic disagreements were not resolved. Deterding and Gulbenkian continued to procrastinate, Riedemann continued to call for a definite policy, and Teagle fluctuated between reluctance to urge a deal with the Russians and the desire to obtain Russian products for the Jersey Company's Mediterranean markets. A suspicion planted in Teagle's mind by his experience in the Iraq negotiations took root. He wrote to Riedemann:[79]

Frankly, I am rather at a loss to understand what is in the back of Gulbenkian's mind. . . . Has it ever occurred to you that what he has in mind is that if he can postpone the actual negotiations between the Shell and ourselves it might be possible for him to so arrange matters with the Russians as to be in a position somewhat similar to the position he is today occupying in the T. P. Co. [Turkish Petroleum Company] matter?

Riedemann discounted this possibility and chided Teagle for his suspicions and for his apparent failure to look at the Royal Dutch alliance from a broad viewpoint:[80]

It seems to me that the really big future interests of the large oil concerns begin to run parallel with each other more and more and sometimes I have wondered whether it is possible that some of us lose sight of this fact by paying *too* much attention and sacrificing *too* much time to the technical and routine side of our business. Surely, we ought to do everything to bring our organizations to the highest standard of technical perfection possible, but this after all is not the only, nor even the main thing in our business. . . . As I have said above, it seems to me that so far as the general policy is concerned our road in all our business outside the United States is converging more and more into a parallel course with Deterding's. . . . While I believe that some of us will not share this opinion and will still feel that the old policy of splendid isolation is the only policy for the S. O. Co. to follow, I am afraid that this opinion is based on a purely inside American point of view and that a good many of those who hold it would change their opinion if they saw the international relations and developments from the outside.

On October 8, 1925, an important meeting was held at 26 Broadway between representatives of the Jersey, Standard of New York, Anglo-American, and Vacuum Oil companies. Vacuum and Standard of New York had an immediate need for 940,000 barrels of kerosene for their Mediterranean markets. The Jersey Company could supply only 540,000 barrels from Romania; the remainder would have to be shipped from the United States. Figures were submitted showing that Vacuum and Standard of New York could supply their need with Russian products at a saving of $501,250 over the cost of the Jersey-supplied oil. Both companies requested, in consequence, that a supply contract be negotiated with the Russians. After exploring all alternatives Teagle agreed to do as they wished and dispatched instructions to Peter Hurll, manager of the Bedford Petroleum Company in France, to obtain the assent of Deterding and to start negotiations.[81]

This decision was extremely distasteful to Teagle, yet, as he told Riedemann, he saw no alternative but to acquiesce in the conclusion reached by their "New York friends." Hurll's negotiations, however, were delayed, and new doubts were voiced by Jersey men. Moffett returned from Europe convinced that no purchases of Soviet oil should be made. Late in October Riedemann came to New York and, in marked contrast to his earlier views, indicated his acquiescence with Moffett's opinion. Apparently Riedemann's sentiments were based less on ethical grounds than on the observed difficulties of getting the Russians to agree to terms which would be satisfactory to Jersey Standard and the Shell. Deterding himself was still convinced that, if the *Front Uni* could be sustained a little longer and all purchases from Russia avoided, the Soviet government would soon

be forced not only to yield better supply terms but to agree to some settlement for the confiscated properties of the Shell and the Jersey-Nobel
group. Under the terms of the joint agreement Deterding's assent to any
negotiations was necessary, and the Jersey Company was by no means
prepared to abrogate that agreement.[82]

Deterding's hope failed to take account either of the pressing needs of
Vacuum and Standard of New York or of the fact that these concerns had
no investments in Russia and consequently had no direct interest in forcing a settlement of the confiscated property question. Early in November
the two companies announced their intention, not only of instituting direct negotiations with the Soviet government for the purchase of 60,000
tons of kerosene, but also of declining to make any joint purchases with
the Jersey-Shell group.[83]

Efforts by Teagle to patch up the rapidly deteriorating situation were
not successful. Deterding expressed his impatience at what he felt to be a
shortsighted attitude on the part of New York Standard and Vacuum
and stated that there were only two roads open: either to bid for the
whole cake or refrain entirely from any purchasing. Deterding also
hinted that if these two companies bought Russian oil without restraint
the result would be a serious fight. Teagle expressed his private opinion
that the whole matter was complicated by the hatred for the Shell entertained by New York Standard's C. F. Meyer.[84]

Hurll, in commenting on this new development, was concerned with
more than the breach in the *Front Uni*:[85]

One has often mentioned the odium which might become attached to the
Standard in the event of it becoming known that we were negotiating with the
Soviets. I think you will agree with me that we, the S. O. Co. (N.J.), will not
escape this even though said negotiations are conducted by the New York Co.
instead of by ourselves. The public do not differentiate between the New Jersey
Co. and the New York Co., and even though we desired to make any explanation as to this, it would be useless to do so, as in the eyes of the public all and
every one of our affiliated and friendly concerns are looked upon as "The
Standard Group."

Teagle's answer to Hurll gave evidence of a profoundly agitated
state of mind:[86]

I appreciate fully the logic of the views advanced by you in your letter under
review, and it is just possible that for the reasons you point out the decision
reached may not be in our own best interest. You Englishmen have a saying
that one gets "fed up;" this is exactly the way I feel on this Russian situation.
I have spent more time and thought during the last two or three years on it

than on any other one matter, and as far as I can see now, without accomplishing anything.

A note, bitter in tone and scarcely consistent with earlier intents of the Jersey Company and its leaders, acquainted Riedemann with the sentiments of Jersey's president:[87]

In view of the fact that the Standard Oil Co. (N.J.) through the Nobels prior to the war controlled about fifty per cent of the Russian exports, it is apparent that the action taken not alone by the Vacuum but also by the Standard Oil Co. of New York, in purchasing stolen oil from the Soviets, is in fact nothing less than purchasing, in part at least, oil stolen by the Russians from the Standard Oil Co. (New Jersey).

You will realize further that affording the Soviet a market for petroleum not only is actually becoming a receiver of stolen goods, but operates to encourage the thief to persist in his evil courses by making theft readily profitable.

"Man is a strange being," Riedemann replied, "and in spite of all disappointments he still starts every year with new hopes. So let us do the same."[88]

The new year did, indeed, bring new hopes. It also brought such a confusion of considerations as to bewilder even those who were directing the course of the company's foreign affairs. For Jersey, however, the new year also introduced the beginning of the end of the Russian nightmare.

In March of 1926 Teagle learned that the Vacuum Oil Company had purchased Russian refined products at prices which, according to best estimates, were well below Russian costs of production. Teagle and the directorate agreed that, if more of such low-priced stocks were offered, they must be purchased in order to prevent them from getting into the hands of competitors and thence finding their way into Jersey Standard's markets. The board voted forthwith to reopen negotiations with the Russians. Deterding gave his assent, and the bargaining was entrusted to Riedemann and Hurll.[89]

There is little need to follow the course of these negotiations in detail. Over the ensuing months the original desire to remove low-priced offerings from the market was expanded into the old plan for a long-term contract which would tie up all the Soviet export supplies. Both Vacuum and Standard of New York were willing to refrain from purchasing for at least a year. Teagle drew up a set of provisions which he felt must be included in the contract. Foremost among these was the clause which stated that a fixed percentage of the purchase price should be paid into a London bank, in trust, for the indemnification of former owners of property in

Russia.[90] This was a highly significant inclusion, reaffirming in strong tones the position Teagle and the Jersey board had consistently taken in every instance where the company had attempted to purchase Russian oil.

Deterding, who by the terms of the joint agreement was to receive a half share in whatever might be purchased, urged Teagle not to be hasty, for he was confident that the Soviet government was desperate and would collapse before the year was out. Riedemann did not share Deterding's optimism and doubted from the beginning that an agreement could be pushed through in the form prescribed by Teagle.[91]

Hurll, too, criticized the contract conditions laid down by Teagle as unrealistic. Teagle, however, refused to shoulder the responsibility for changing them and stated that the matter was one for Riedemann, Hurll, and the other European lieutenants to decide on the basis of their intimacy with the situation.[92]

This, for Teagle, was a new and decidedly uncharacteristic attitude. His apparent unwillingness or inability to take a strong stand left his associates confused and imparted a note of indecisiveness to the situation. Riedemann, who might well have exerted constructive influence at this critical time, was forced by ill health to give up business and go to Biarritz to take a cure. Late in 1926, moreover, C. F. Meyer became impatient with what he characterized as pussyfooting and sidestepping by the Jersey Company and went ahead with independent negotiations with the Russians for 150,000 tons of kerosene for Standard of New York's Indian market.[93]

This was not the only obstacle thrown in the path of the negotiations currently under way in Paris between Hurll and the Russians. Deterding continued to urge delay and showed an increasing disposition to intrude upon the discussions. Teagle cabled a sharp message that his actions were confusing the situation. It also appeared that the talks were being impeded fully as much by disagreements among the Jersey men as by inability to agree with the Russians.[94]

As the new year opened, however, it appeared that despite such difficulties an agreement with the Soviet government had been all but reached. The Russians had even agreed that 5 per cent of the purchase price should be set aside for indemnification of former owners. It was felt, however, that as a measure of protection to the Anglo-American Oil Company, Limited, a large Jersey Standard customer, some guarantee must be included in the contract to hold shipments of Russian products into the British market to a stipulated yearly minimum. Anglo-American, Anglo-

Persian, and Shell—the three principal English marketing firms—were to agree to take a definite quantity of Russian products annually, the Russians agreeing on their part not to ship more than 20,000 tons of oil in excess of these amounts into Britain. Representatives of all three firms tentatively agreed to such an arrangement, but at this point Sir Henri arrived in London and the atmosphere abruptly changed. Deterding declared that a Russian arrangement at that time was politically inexpedient in Britain. Sir John Cadman agreed. Hurll found himself blocked and had no choice but to suspend negotiations entirely.[95]

The collapse of negotiations in January of 1927 seemed to be the signal for the outbreak of pent-up emotions. Deterding's reaction was one of undisguised pleasure. "I am so glad," he wrote to Teagle, "that nothing came of these Soviet deals. I feel that everybody will regret at some time that he had anything to do with these robbers, whose only aim is the destruction of all civilization and the re-establishment of brute force."[96]

Deterding's sentiments on the Standard of New York and Vacuum purchases, however, were of a different tenor. For some time Sir Henri apparently had not realized that the two firms intended to ship their latest purchases of Russian oil into India, where the Shell had large markets. In July of 1927 Deterding suddenly awoke to the fact. At once he cabled his New York representatives, threatening an oil war and a press campaign. For Vacuum and Standard of New York there was, of course, a degree of wry justice in the situation, for Deterding's first purchases of Soviet products had been shipped into their markets. In answer to Sir Henri's threats, both firms declared that they had been dragged into buying Russian oil in the first place by Deterding's own actions.[97]

Sir Henri's press campaign was initiated, and it at once implicated Jersey Standard. In America, as in Great Britain, public antipathy toward Communism was at a high pitch; press notices of the Russian purchases by Vacuum and New York Standard, appearing in July of 1927, disturbed the Jersey directors greatly. Hurll's earlier admonitions that the public would not differentiate between the actions of these companies and those of Jersey Standard proved prophetic. Teagle, for example, was accosted by former Ambassador James Gerard, who said he thought it was a "damned outrage" that Standard Oil should be dealing with the Soviet government and that he would like to see a popular move started to boycott Jersey products—irrespective of the fact that he owned more than 5,000 shares of Jersey stock![98]

On July 19, 1927, the Jersey board issued a public statement denying that the company had any trade relations with the Soviet government or that, in the face of the existing overproduction in the United States, the Jersey Company was buying Russian oil to displace products of American origin in European markets. The statement went on to point out that negotiations with the Soviet government had collapsed through failure of the Russians to recognize private property rights. The concluding paragraph read as follows:[99]

> Such confusion may have resulted from the fact that there are now various separate and independent companies which either bear the Standard Oil name or are popularly characterized in that manner and it therefore seems advisable that the position of the Standard Oil Company (N.J.) in this Russian matter be defined as above.

This release was literally incorrect only in respect to the reasons given for the collapse of the Russian negotiations. By implication, however, the July 19 statement denied that Jersey Standard had ever taken the initiative in seeking to purchase Russian oil, and it patently contradicted the fact that one of the chief goals of Jersey men had been to substitute Russian for American oil in Mediterranean markets.

On July 21 the *New York Times* reported that Vacuum and New York Standard men were incensed at the implications of the Jersey Standard release. The press hailed the statement as a sign that a split had occurred in the "Standard Oil group." The *Times* flatly contradicted the company's implication that it had purchased no Russian oil and resolutely refused to differentiate between activities of Jersey, Standard of New York, and Vacuum.[100]

In view of this rash of unfavorable publicity Teagle caused company records to be scanned with care for proof to support a further and more specific denial that Jersey Standard had ever purchased oil from the Russians. The result of this investigation revealed that total purchases of Russian oil actually consummated by affiliated companies had been less than 40,000 tons. Most of this oil had been acquired as a result of contracts with jobbers rather than through direct dealings with the Soviet government; some of the purchases had been made by local European managers over the protests of 26 Broadway.[101]

These figures and Jersey Standard's protestations, of course, failed to reflect the several unsuccessful attempts which had been made to conclude a purchase agreement with the Russians, and the company was in a distinctly vulnerable position in attempting to avoid its share of the public stigma. The controversy with Standard of New York and Vacuum, however, had its beneficial aspects. As Teagle put it:[102]

The thinking people in Europe, for the first time, now realize that there is a real and genuine difference between one Standard Oil Company and another. This realization could only have been brought about by the publicity which the newspapers have given to the matter.

The conflict between Deterding and the New York Standard and Vacuum men, however, flared violently. In September of 1927 Deterding launched a price war in many parts of the world. Meyer, visibly perturbed by Deterding's particularly drastic price cuts in India, called on Teagle to ask what Sir Henri's intentions might be. Teagle told Meyer frankly that Deterding considered that he had been double-crossed and that he was highly incensed. The Jersey Company, said Teagle, intended to remain neutral.[103]

Hurll reported to Teagle that Sir Henri seemed obsessed in his determination to fight anyone or everyone dealing in what Deterding considered to be stolen oil. Riedemann, back in harness again, informed Teagle that Deterding was so angry at Meyer that he was losing his cool judgment and sense of proportion and no longer was balancing causes and results as he was always accustomed to do. Teagle, on his part, became alarmed at the price war and urged Riedemann to try to restore order. Early in November of 1927 Riedemann saw Deterding and reported that ". . . the pressure was still too high to permit a dispassionate discussion."[104]

These sulphurous outbursts of Deterding's were an intensification of the attitude he had consistently taken since 1924. Despite the fact that, while the Royal Dutch-Shell had set the precedent for purchasing confiscated Soviet oil in 1923, it was the subsequent bitter hatred of Deterding for the Russians which had gone far toward preventing the consummation of a joint contract with them in 1925, 1926, and 1927. Once Deterding had made up his mind to fight the Russians, he fought them with unswerving passion, yielded to no temptations, and absolutely refused to recognize the fact that companies such as Vacuum and Standard of New York were impelled by entirely different motivating circumstances from his own.

Pressure from many directions, within as well as outside of his own organization, finally calmed Sir Henri. Meyer had difficulties with his Russian contract and finally consented to let Jersey Standard supply his company's Indian requirements. Peace was at length restored in the industry. The Baba Gurgur gusher in Iraq promised a welcome substitute for Russian oil, and the Jersey directorate indicated a decided unwillingness to concern itself further with either a Soviet contract or a boycott. "Personally," Heinrich Riedemann confessed, in the fall of 1927, "I have buried Russia."[105]

At the end of 1927 there was little to be counted as gain. The Jersey Company was faced with the unpleasant near-certainty that its investments in Russian producing properties were permanently lost. These investments included $160,000 paid to the Azerbaijan government in 1919 and approximately $8,800,000 expended from 1920 to 1925 to obtain the interest in the Nobel properties. The hope that Russia might be forced into making some kind of restitution had been blasted. Jersey's leaders were universally bitter over their experience.

Had Teagle followed his original inclination to have nothing to do with the Russians, the Jersey Company would have escaped much grief and condemnation. Wherein lay the errors and what was to be the final judgment upon the Russian episode? As so often is the case in history when all evidence is weighed, there can be no clear-cut judgment. Jersey policy ranged from the astute to the naïve.

Of Teagle's unswerving determination not to purchase the confiscated Russian producing properties of others there can be absolutely no question, and the fact is well established that the Jersey Standard organization made no large direct purchases and very few indirect purchases of oil from the confiscated fields. In 1924 and 1925, however, the company was ready and anxious to break the boycott and strike a trade with the Russians. The consummation of negotiations was prevented only by Deterding's obstructive tactics and the seemingly unrealistic insistence of Teagle and the Jersey directors that original property owners be reimbursed for purchases of oil from their properties. On the other hand, no private commercial boycott of Russia such as was attempted by the *Front Uni* could possibly have succeeded at a time when the nations of the world were extending recognition and trade offers to the Soviet government. The foreign policy of Britain and France in particular exerted a decisive influence upon not only the practical but the ethical aspects of the situation.

In these hard months the Jersey leaders proved to be eminently human. The tremendous investment in Nobel properties had been a grievous and costly error, though certainly not without justification in hoped-for returns. The calculated risk had been taken, and the stake had been lost. To regain it the Jersey Company men—driven to desperate measures and encouraged in their course by the counsel of expediency—subjugated personal feelings to what were believed to be the best interests of the company. This was surely an understandable dilemma and one not unfamiliar in the ordinary course of human affairs. The verdict was accepted with a sense of profound relief that what was felt by most of these men to be an ethical mistake was a practical mistake as well.

Management of the Russian affair gave evidence of yet another dilemma. Walter Teagle was caught in the web of his own genius. He had taken such a detailed part in Jersey Standard's business as to make himself virtually indispensable in each operational department. As that business continued to grow and become more complicated, Teagle found that he had assumed responsibilities far in excess of what any man could hope to meet. At one crucial stage in the Russian situation, for example, when Teagle was desperately being urged to come to Europe, he was inextricably involved in a legal tangle in the Refining Department. Teagle himself had realized the serious implications of the demands upon his time and had already begun the organizational changes which would correct the situation. Nevertheless, the Russian operation appears to have suffered from lack of strong leadership in its concluding stages.

Quite aside from errors, however, no small part of the failure recorded in Russia by the Jersey Company, its allies, and its rivals came about as a result of the great skill with which the Soviet leaders avoided being traded out of their strong bargaining position. It seems reasonably clear in retrospect that the Russians had originally hoped to attract foreign capital and management to restore the prostrate petroleum industry, but they had been unwilling to accede to the conditions originally offered both by the Royal Dutch-Shell and by the Anglo-Persian Oil Company. Once a measure of internal recovery had set in after 1922, all hopes for major foreign concessions or for the return of property to its former owners vanished. Cleverly the Russians used their growing oil supplies to break the alliances which sought to throttle them. So diverse were the interests involved and so great were the opportunities for profit from bringing Russian oil into European and Mediterranean markets that any attempt at boycott was foredoomed to failure. Perhaps the basic error of leaders of the world petroleum industry lay in failing to gauge the magnitude of the economic, political, and ideological forces they sought to contain.

One further subject would seem by its far-reaching importance to merit review. Company documents which unfold the story of the Russian experience provide suggestive evidence bearing upon certain of Teagle's broad business philosophies and upon his business and personal relationships with Sir Henri Deterding.

Between Teagle and Deterding there existed great understanding, unbounded mutual admiration, and a rich mutuality of personal likes and professional experience. The relationship stopped short of true friendship, for the essential quality of complete trust was lacking, at least on Teagle's part. Teagle's letters give ample testimony on this point. Never for a moment did Teagle cease to regard the Royal Dutch-Shell as other than a deadly competitor. Riedemann sensed this and argued against it. The Russian episode indicated the length to which Teagle was willing to go, but here temporary alliance as the weapon of expediency twice proved to have a dull edge indeed. Teagle and the directorate must have emerged from the Russian experience strengthened still further in their knowledge that transient co-operation with major competitors was not an infallible solution for commercial and political problems of the day.

Chapter 13

Probing Drills in the Tropics
1918-1927

IN TERMS OF success in achieving basic producing objectives, Jersey Standard's postwar efforts in Latin America and the Dutch East Indies are unparalleled in importance. There, in the years from 1919 to 1928, the organization found that for which it was concurrently fighting with such tenacity and futility in Poland, Persia, Romania, and the Caucasus.

In early postwar years the Transcontinental Petroleum Company was multiplying its acreage and wells in Mexico; operations on the La Brea Estate in Peru were being pursued with vigor; a tremendous concession was acquired in Colombia; plans to explore Argentina, Ecuador, and Bolivia were being translated into action; company geologists were traversing the deadly jungles of Venezuela, where already Jersey Standard had sunk nearly half a million dollars in concessions; and the NKPM, still stubbornly drilling, was fighting for more concessions in Sumatra.

These endeavors provide further illustrations of the broad policies and political circumstances which have been described in some detail in preceding chapters and which therefore can be touched upon henceforward in summary fashion. At the operational level, however, the ventures in Latin America and the Dutch East Indies presented problems of a unique and unusually trying nature which both tested and shaped the new Foreign Producing Department.

NATIONALISM TRIUMPHANT IN MEXICO

In 1919 Tampico, the nerve center of the Mexican petroleum industry, was at the dizzying height of its oil-boom prosperity. The contest for Mexican oil was at its peak, and Jersey Standard interests were in the thick of the fray.[1]

A combination of favorable and ominous portents had attended Jersey Standard's entry into Mexican producing operations in 1917 through pur-

chase of the Transcontinental Petroleum Company (Compañía Transcontinental de Petróleo, S.A.). Transcontinental's first well in the Pánuco
district was gauged at 70,000 barrels of oil daily. An active lease campaign had been inaugurated. E. J. Sadler, who for one year had headed
the Mexican organization, was pressing hard for expansion. On the other
hand, the Doheny and Royal Dutch-Shell companies held a commanding
lead in Mexico. Furthermore, the Carranza constitution of 1917 threatened nationalization of the subsoil. Hatred of foreign corporations was
being nourished in revolutionary circles of the day.

Recognition of Carranza's government by the United States, however,
had been conditioned on the assurance that the lives and Mexican property rights of American nationals would be protected. Carranza had
privately told United States Ambassador Fletcher that American oil interests, whose welfare was increasingly important to the war effort, would
not be molested to any extent under the terms of the 1917 constitution.[2]
These assurances and the belief that the United States would insist that
they be observed gave Jersey executives confidence that their investments
in Mexico would be relatively safe.

For the five years during which this hopeful attitude prevailed, Transcontinental's operations grew rapidly. The first company well in the southern Mexican field came in late in 1918 and was expected to be good for
50,000 barrels daily. Total production (Appendix 2, Table VII) increased
phenomenally between 1918 and 1921. The Jersey Company's investment
in Transcontinental shot up from $4,429,000 at the end of 1918 to $32,247,-
000 in 1922, the highest point reached. In addition, very large sums were
loaned by the parent company to finance operating expansion by the
affiliate. The number of Transcontinental employees increased from 751
in 1918 to 3,313 in 1920.[3]

The early 1920's, however, proved to be the peak of growth. Intrusion
of salt water into the southern producing districts proved disastrous and
led, in 1923, to the complete abandonment of the Tuxpan area by
Transcontinental. Exploratory effort in northern Mexico failed to yield
acreage of comparable productivity to that which had been lost. Jersey
Standard's tardiness in getting into Mexico clearly had cost the company
the cream of the light-gravity Tuxpan crude. Even more serious than
this and other operating difficulties, moreover, was the fact that political
conditions had become progressively less favorable to profitable operations. As early as 1921, both Teagle and Sadler expressed their disillusionment and their concern for the company's investment. Sadler, bold

expansionist though he was, advised that expenditures in Mexico be strictly limited. In March of 1921 Teagle expressed doubt that the investment would ever be recovered. He urged Sadler not to look to the future but to concentrate his attention upon "the best ways and means to return us the largest part of our present investment in Mexico during the next year and a half."[4]

This startling change from an attitude of great hope to one of marked pessimism on the part of men who, as we have seen, were not easily discouraged is readily explained by the sequence of political events from 1919 to 1921. Political and economic factors thereafter combined to prolong the uncertainties and bring about a steady liquidation of Transcontinental's producing ventures.

In 1918 the Carranza government issued a series of decrees which were drawn up with the object of making effective the national ownership of the subsoil. These decrees levied heavy rentals on developed petroleum lands; a 5 per cent tax was imposed on all oil produced. Permits were to be obtained for all drilling activity. All leases which had been or were subsequently obtained from surface property owners were to be "manifested"—or submitted to the state for confirmation.

Jersey Standard refused to conform to the manifestation and drilling-permit requirements, holding that to do so would constitute recognition of the claim that the nation owned the subsoil. The United States government at once protested the decrees, saying that it "could not acquiesce in any procedure . . . resulting in confiscation of private rights and arbitrary deprivation of vested rights." Jersey's legal counsel, C. O. Swain, asserted that the situation was so serious that the oil companies soon would be unable to fill fuel contracts serving American industry, railroads, public utilities, and the mercantile marine. Swain held that there was no hope for any change in Mexican policy unless strong pressure was applied by Washington. He urged the withdrawing of diplomatic representatives and the sending of warships to Mexico, as had been done earlier to protect American interests.[5]

The several protests of the State Department at length caused the Carranza administration to postpone the deadline for manifestations and to agree to issue provisional drilling permits to companies which, like Transcontinental, had refused to recognize the nationalization principle. This arrangement, unfortunately, was to apply only to lands owned or leased before May 1, 1917, the effective date of the Carranza constitution, and upon which positive developmental steps had been taken. Since

Jersey Standard had entered Mexico so belatedly, most of Transcontinental's lands had been acquired after that date. Company objectives were further threatened by loose government interpretations of what, under the 1917 constitution, comprised national reserves. Here political matters stood until the assassination of Carranza in 1920 and Obregon's succession to office.[6]

Some new leases had been acquired, even in the face of such difficulties. The implicit hope was that, even if nationalization became effective, surface owners or lessees would be given some kind of preferential right to the subsoil mineral deposits. Transcontinental, with far smaller holdings than its rivals, was hungry for acreage.

Not only the 1918 decrees but the general revolutionary atmosphere exerted a depressing influence on Transcontinental's business. The 1917 constitution contained labor regulatory provisions which substantially increased the cost of operations. In the fields there was a general decline in worker morale, a great amount of interference by labor inspectors, and an increase in union activity. The demands of the newly organized labor forces became progressively broader. These trends culminated in 1924 in a general labor uprising which affected both Transcontinental and its competitors. The Jersey men, after much discussion and some disagreement among themselves, resolved to take a firm stand. This attitude grew out of a belief that surrender to the unions would be but a further step toward encroachment by the government on the company's business. A compromise settlement was at length agreed upon by the unions and the Association of Petroleum Producers in Mexico, but this proved to be only a temporary truce. In all these negotiations the Jersey-Transcontinental executives indicated a willingness to meet many of the demands of labor, but to resist any measures giving the unions a voice in the conduct of the business. It was clear that the gulf between management and workmen was widening and that a mutual effort at understanding and cooperation was giving place to a struggle for control.[7]

Banditry was rampant in the fields. A regional counterrevolution against Carranza in one instance forced Transcontinental to purchase protection by making forced "loans" of some $60,000 to the current military chief of the state of Vera Cruz. In 1922 and again in 1924 Transcontinental camps were raided and sacked, with attendant paralysis of producing operations.[8]

The political climate, meanwhile, did not improve. On July 1, 1921, the new government headed by Obregon levied a 25 per cent increase in the export tax on oil. Transcontinental, together with other leading American concerns in Mexico, protested strongly. Jersey Standard and certain other companies withdrew their tankers from the Mexican trade for three months, with the result that the industry was nearly paralyzed. The State Department was reluctant to make protests, apparently feeling, in this particular instance, that such protests would not be heeded. Both Sadler and Teagle pointed out the absolute necessity for obtaining as high a profit per barrel from Mexican crude as was obtained, for example, in Mid-Continent operations. Mexico, Jersey men claimed, had ceased to be a low-cost producing area. Prices had fallen, the heavy Pánuco crude was not comparable in value to American crude, and the life expectancy of all Mexican fields appeared to be far less than had once been commonly supposed.[9] The Jersey Company released the following tabulation of costs per barrel:

Average value of Mexican light crude oil in the U. S.		$1.30
Average operating cost of Transcontinental for four months in 1921, exclusive of depletion	$0.31	
Royalties	0.05	
Average cost of transportation to various points in the U. S.	0.43	
Mexican taxes under decrees of 1921	0.36	
Total costs		1.15
Profit per barrel		$0.15

On the basis of this margin, some 166,660,000 barrels of crude would have to be produced to cover the company's investment in Mexico.[10]

In April of 1922 a committee of oil executives consisting of Teagle and Swain, Doheny (Mexican Petroleum Company), Sinclair (Sinclair Oil & Refining Company), Van Dyke (The Atlantic Refining Company), and Lufkin (The Texas Company) arrived in Mexico City to confer with Adolfo de la Huerta, Secretary of Finance, about the troubled petroleum situation. Teagle summarized the demands of the American committee in the following words:[11]

With regard to the further development of Mexican petroleum resources, we endeavored to make it plain that the oil industry will have no future in Mexico unless an intensive effort to find new fields of production be undertaken and successfully prosecuted; that such effort cannot be undertaken until and unless the government shall have completely removed the unusual hazards created by domestic legislation, oppressive taxation and unreasonable and unnecessary departmental regulation and supervision, and shall extend to the oil industry its cordial co-operation and encouragement.

Several meetings were held with de la Huerta, at which various compromise proposals were exchanged, including one for an American loan
to Mexico. Teagle maintained that lands leased after May 1, 1917, should
be exempted from nationalization, a request which could have been
granted only by a complete denial by the Mexican government of the
revolutionary principles it had adopted. The fact became obvious that no
real progress was being made toward a solution, and the conferences were
succeeded by direct negotiations between the State Department and the
Mexican government.

In 1923 at the so-called Bucareli Conferences, Obregon stated that
lands leased before 1917 would not be nationalized, provided that positive
developmental acts had been performed.[12] This so-called "Extra-official
Pact"—actually a gentlemen's agreement—was merely a reiteration of
Carranza's earlier compromise, and Transcontinental, with its later acquisitions, was in no way assisted. Teagle warned that the company's
operations would necessarily be curtailed. Such action was, in fact, already under way. By 1922 the number of Transcontinental employees had
declined to 931 from the high of over 3,300 in 1920. In 1923, however, a
rich strike was made on company acreage in the Cacalilao district, adjoining the old Pánuco field on the northwest. Company production, in
consequence, increased to a peak of 58,700 barrels daily, and the discovery appears to have strengthened the company's determination to continue the political fight.

This resolution was of little avail. In 1925 a new and drastic mining
law was passed in the Mexican Congress, despite vigorous protests
from the State Department. This law, while providing for issuance of
confirmatory fifty-year concessions on preconstitutional holdings, specifically called for nationalization over a period of years of the subsoil of
land which, though privately owned before 1917, had been leased and
developed thereafter. This blow fell much harder on Transcontinental
holdings than on the very much larger concessions of Doheny and the
Royal Dutch-Shell and increased still further Jersey Standard's competitive disadvantage.[13]

The passage of the 1925 law precipitated something of a crisis. Transcontinental's operations were once again restricted. The company was
refused drilling permits because it did not apply for confirmatory concessions; lands within its holdings were granted to others as state property. As a result, in part, of representations and protests by the oil
companies, diplomatic tension between Mexico and the United States

increased almost to the breaking point. Ambassador Dwight R. Morrow was dispatched to Mexico by President Coolidge with instructions to keep the United States out of war.[14]

By 1928 the liquidation of Jersey's Mexican producing venture had been carried far. Loans to Transcontinental, which in 1922 were outstanding in the amount of $12,000,000 and were a source of much concern at 26 Broadway, had all been repaid by 1924. From 1925 through 1927 every possible penny was wrung out of the Mexican affiliate. Dividends paid by Transcontinental to the Jersey Company over these three years totaled $35,131,000, an amount representing all current earnings and a substantial portion of the earnings accumulated in preceding years. Assets were depreciated, receivables and inventories liquidated, and outstanding accounts settled. The investment in Mexico, which stood at $32,247,000 in 1922, had been pared to $8,660,000 by the end of 1927.[15]

Thus the Mexican experience, unlike the contemporary venture in Russia, was by no means a chronicle of financial loss. Notwithstanding the earlier protests of Teagle and Sadler that the Mexican business was unprofitable (as, indeed, it was at the time their statements were issued), Jersey Standard had been able to amortize roughly three-fourths of its investment, after recording on that investment total net earnings for the 1918-1927 period of $45,692,000.[16] Refining, transporting, and marketing profits earned on the millions of barrels of Mexican crude exported by Transcontinental in these years must be acknowledged as well, though such profits cannot be determined. The strategic advantage of having the Mexican stocks available to meet the expanding fuel oil market must also be taken into consideration.

In the light of these rough summary statistics, the bitterness with which the Jersey men (and those of other companies as well) opposed the revolutionary movement is readily comprehensible. In simplest terms, the intermittent conflict from 1918 to 1928 derived from the attempt of the Mexican government to appropriate a major share of the profits that were being taken out of Mexico by foreign businessmen as a result of exploitation of the nation's natural resources. Obviously that share of operating returns devoted to improving the welfare of the workmen and of the country at large was deemed inadequate by the Mexicans. On the other hand, it seems likely that any course pursued by the oil companies would have been condemned in the intense antiforeign atmosphere of revolutionary Mexico.

Jersey Standard executives staunchly defended what they considered to be their legal rights. Their determination to stand on principle in Mexico was bolstered by the company's concurrent success in developing low-cost production elsewhere in Latin America. All precedent indicated the legal validity of such a position. Their lack of faith in the various revolutionary administrations with which they endeavored to deal was not entirely unjustified. Faced with frequent repudiations of promises by the Mexican government, they resisted what to them appeared—in Mexico as in the Caucasus—to be a movement of transient pillage. The strength and prevalence of this attitude help to explain the apparent willingness of the American companies, Jersey Standard foremost among them, to carry diplomatic intervention to the point where relations between the two nations were seriously impaired. Jersey men could have argued that, had force rather than words been employed by the United States government, the world-wide drift toward nationalization of private property might well have been checked and respect for established concepts of international law restored among the wayward members of the family of nations.

Concern for the broader aspects of the Mexican venture molded company policy in an important way. On several occasions Jersey executives indicated that they would have accepted major compromises, provided that those compromises did not involve sacrifice of the principle of private ownership and control of productive facilities. Jersey men knew that if they surrendered on this issue they would destroy the standing of their case under international law, as well as under the law of Mexico as they understood it. Even more important, surrender in Mexico would inevitably react to the company's disadvantage elsewhere in Latin America, where the struggle between private business and resurgent nationalism was also being grimly fought.

In 1927 C. O. Swain held that "with a determined front maintained by our State Department and by the companies themselves and by the pressure of economic considerations, the way will eventually be paved to the working out of a solution that will not involve the surrender of the principle. . . ."[17] In this hope, admittedly none too bright, the Transcontinental venture, though sapped of its vitality, was allowed to stay alive.

STABILITY AND EXPANSION IN PERU

At times it must have seemed to the Jersey directors that the political winds of the day were incapable of blowing good for their company. In Peru, however, the year 1919 ushered in an era of satisfactory operating conditions which contrasted sharply with the situation then prevalent in Mexico.

With the succession of Augusto B. Leguia to the Peruvian presidency in 1919 the tax issue, which for four years had hampered operations by the International Petroleum Company Limited, took a new turn. A businessman and former President of Peru, the new chief executive was sympathetic to business and believed that foreign capital and management were necessary for the effective development of Peruvian resources. Leguia was obviously friendly, as a matter of broad principle, toward International and its objectives.[18]

Leguia, however, could not afford to be unduly solicitous of International's interests. His political position was insecure, and Peru was stricken by financial adversity. The government needed tax revenue from the petroleum industry, and it was politically necessary for Leguia to make as stiff a bargain as that industry could possibly bear.[19] The new President proved to be not only a skillful negotiator but a man of considerable courage as well.

New discussions were inaugurated by R. V. LeSueur, International's able counsel, of the issues which the Peruvian Congress in 1918 had agreed to submit to arbitration. Having learned something from the earlier unpleasant experiences in Peru, the company also employed a Peruvian expert in public relations. LeSueur's personal standing in Peru, which always had been high, was further enhanced by his marriage into a distinguished Peruvian family.

By the close of 1921 LeSueur had come to the conclusion that the company must accede to Leguia's request for a financial grant to Peru of $1,000,000. When Teagle and G. Harrison Smith, president of International, gave their assent, the way was cleared for action. Leguia at once threw his support behind the export tax bill—reasonable in its terms— then pending in the Peruvian Congress and the measure was enacted.[20]

Meanwhile, in August, 1921, a treaty between Great Britain and Peru was signed which was in substance an "agreement for arbitration" of the La Brea y Pariñas controversy. The Peruvian government entered into this pact pursuant to the special legislative authorization of 1918. The pact provided for submission of the dispute to international arbitration and for formation of an arbitration tribunal. It also provided that, if the two governments concerned should agree upon a settlement prior to the rendering of an award by the tribunal, then such settlement should be incorporated in a tribunal award.

Early in 1922 the two governments did, in fact, arrive at a settlement, which was duly presented to the tribunal and was issued as its award in April of that year. The award established the area and boundaries of the property and the subsurface or "mineralized zone" as proposed by the company, fixed a special tax in commutation of surface and production taxes on the property for the next fifty years, guaranteed that the export tax then fixed by law would not be increased for twenty years, provided for the payment by the owners of the property of $1,000,000 to the government of Peru in full settlement of all claims up to the end of 1921, and specified the revocation of the government resolutions of 1915 whose applicability to the property had precipitated the controversy. A letter from Leguia also promised that he would recommend that International be given preferential treatment in the granting of further concessions in Peru.[21]

Thus was finally settled by a process of negotiation and compromise a controversy which had kept Jersey Standard interests in Peru in a turmoil since 1915. The settlement gave promise of stable operations to the company and assured income to Peru.

The hopes nourished by this settlement were borne out by operating returns. International's investment in fixed assets (including refining and marketing installations) increased from $48,144,000 before depreciation at the end of 1921 to $71,854,000 at the end of 1927.[22] The number of employees grew from 2,552 at the beginning of 1922 to 6,143 in 1927. The foreign staff increased from 249 to 340 over this period. Production (Appendix 2, Table VII) increased steadily, being obtained entirely from the La Brea y Pariñas Estate. Efforts at exploration elsewhere yielded few results either to International or to its competitors. The Royal Dutch-Shell, which endeavored to obtain a foothold in Peru, was forced by the absence of promising oil indications on land outside the La Brea concession to withdraw from the country.

On its Peruvian properties Jersey Standard was presented, for the first time on an extensive scale, with the opportunity for carefully regulated development of an oil structure. International's control of the whole Negritos field enabled the company to conduct important experiments with field repressuring and to develop a program to keep production at the most efficient rate from a long-time engineering and economic point of view. Thus was laid in the 1920's the foundation for a system of unit operation which two decades later was to be described as the most efficient in the world.[23]

Operating conditions were exceptionally advantageous. The Estate was on the coast, so that no transportation problem was involved in getting the oil to an ocean loading point. Drilling was relatively easy, the producing wells being shallow and the oil-bearing sands thick. The crude oil produced was of high gravity. Lack of water was one serious drawback that necessitated heavy expenditures for equipment, and, of course, housing and all utilities and schools had to be furnished the workmen and their families.

Though anti-American feeling in Peru continued to be fanned by Mexican propaganda and though internal opposition to Leguia's administration continued strong, Jersey Standard's position in Peru throughout the 1920's was secure to an extent quite unprecedented in any foreign producing venture. The example of a Latin American government and a large foreign corporation working in considerable harmony and to mutual advantage was a valuable one before the Latin American world. This state of affairs in Peru may well have had an important bearing on contemporary developments in neighboring countries to the north.

THE DE MARES CONCESSION IN COLOMBIA

Colombia's great Magdalena River, flanked on both sides by dense jungle, flows northward out of the high Andes to the Caribbean Sea. To the east of the river and about 350 miles from its mouth lay an area of oil seepages. Spanish explorers, visiting the region in 1536, named it Las Infantas in honor of the royal princesses of their homeland.

In 1905 Roberto De Mares, a Frenchman, obtained an oil concession in the region which included Las Infantas. The concession covered an area of 2,061 square miles, stretching 70 miles along the Magdalena and Carare rivers, at an average depth of 30 miles. By 1915, however, De Mares had failed to raise funds for development and was looking for buyers. Several American firms, including Jersey and the famous wildcatters M. L. Benedum and J. C. Trees, were interested. Jersey's geological scout, F. C. Harrington, visited the area in 1915, but no action was taken by the directorate. In 1916 the Benedum and Trees group formed The Tropical Oil Company, boldly took an option on the De Mares concession, and began the search for oil.[24]

This search constitutes one of the epics of the oil industry. The De Mares concession itself was a wilderness—a land of steaming temperatures, unbelievable rainfalls, and none-too-friendly native tribes. Transportation facilities consisted of river boats and canoes, and the caprices of the Magdalena made navigation difficult. Since the war was at its peak, Benedum and Trees were at first unable to obtain the necessary drilling rigs. Three old rigs, monuments to an earlier drilling effort in Colombia, were at length located. From these a single workable drilling unit was pieced together. This was shipped by river steamer to Barranca-bermeja, the nearest landing point on the Magdalena to the drilling sites. Native dugouts carried the dismantled rig 18 perilous miles up a branch stream into the interior. Operations were commenced, and in April of 1918 the discovery well was drilled in.[25]

With the help of some additional equipment, The Tropical Oil Company drilled three wells in 1918. One of these was a big producer, but, since facilities were lacking with which to run tests, no one knew how big. Three wells alone, moreover, could not furnish a conclusive idea of the value of the De Mares concession. Nevertheless, the Infantas structure had been proved. In 1919 the concession was formally transferred, with the consent of the Colombian government, from De Mares to Tropical. The discoveries touched off a fever of speculation and excitement.

No sooner had Tropical drilled its discovery well than a new petroleum law was drafted in the Colombian Congress. The consensus was that this law—which levied heavy taxes and royalties, declared all ventures to be public utilities, and limited the life of concessions to thirty years—was unfavorable for the development of Colombia's oil resources by foreign capital.[26] Nevertheless, the Jersey Standard organization, suffused in 1919 by energies which had been lacking or constrained four years earlier, swung into action.

A party of geologists led by A. V. Hoenig, Carter's producing expert, was dispatched to examine the Tropical properties. At the same time James Flanagan was sent by Teagle to conduct a separate investigation. As was usual, Flanagan's connections were carefully concealed, even from the other company investigators. While Hoenig and the geologists were making their way up the Magdalena, Flanagan reported to Teagle at length not only on petroleum matters, but on Colombian geography, history, politics, religion, social conditions, and public opinion.[27]

Arthur F. Corwin, who was actively following the news from Colombia, took the position that while the new mining law in Colombia was being drafted the oil companies would do well not to try to influence the legislation. Corwin feared that any appearance of interference might produce a more stringent law than would otherwise result. This viewpoint apparently prevailed, for the mining bill was passed substantially in the form in which it had been drafted. Jersey's chief counsel believed that, despite the objectionable features of the bill, profitable operations could still be carried on. Teagle, displaying at this time an impatience with the situation and a disposition to fight first and compromise later, declared that the only practical course was to exert whatever influence the company could to have the legislation withdrawn.[28] Here matters stood while the men at 26 Broadway awaited reports from their investigating parties.

The first estimates to reach 26 Broadway held that the De Mares concession was worth perhaps $1,660,000. Hoenig's final report to Corwin, in September of 1919, raised this valuation to $5,000,000. Hoenig carefully qualified his recommendations with the statement that, though the Tropical properties were undoubtedly valuable, information was too limited and the gamble was too great to merit paying such amounts as Benedum and Trees might be expected to ask. Corwin and S. B. Hunt agreed with this conclusion, but Teagle, refusing the advice of his experts, seemed determined to push ahead.[29] Negotiations were at once opened with Benedum and Trees for the purchase of Tropical by the International Petroleum Company. Once again the tremendous force of Teagle's convictions committed Jersey Standard to a major gamble. But this time Jersey's president was right, and the doubters were wrong.

The owners of Tropical proved to be hard bargainers. As one of the Jersey negotiators told Corwin: "Your friend Mike Benedum sat across the table with a look on his face like a Sunday School superintendent and tried to persuade us that the property was worth $500,000,000. . . ."[30]

Teagle continued to urge the purchase. "There are very few real sure things in the oil game, especially in the producing end," he told International's president, "and the individual or corporation that does not take some chances never gets very far."[31] By no means the least important motive behind the desire to buy Tropical was the fact that the De Mares concession had come to have a special competitive advantage, since it contained more favorable conditions than could be acquired in any new concession under the Colombian mining law of 1919. In August of 1920 the bargain was finally struck; the Jersey men agreed to exchange 1,804,-534 shares of International stock, of a par value of $33,000,000, for all the shares of The Tropical Oil Company.

The concession thus obtained, as amended by the Colombian government for transfer, contained (in essence) the following major provisions:[32]

1. The company to establish a refinery sufficient to meet the national requirements of Colombia within 2 years of the date of the concession transfer.

2. Exploitation of oil resources on the concession not to be abandoned during the life of the concession.

3. The concession to run for 30 years from the beginning of exploitation operations.

4. A royalty of 10 per cent of the gross product to go to the government.

5. The concession to be deemed a public utility, subject to all regulations prescribed for same under Colombian law.

6. Government inspections to be permitted as a guarantee of fulfillment of the company's obligations.

7. The concession to be declared void if any obligations specified in the concession were not fulfilled.

The name of the purchased company was retained, but a new organization was established. Representatives of the Tropical group were admitted to the International board of directors. Five International men, in turn, were appointed to the eight-man Tropical board. J. C. Trees was named president of Tropical, but G. Harrison Smith, the president of International and the vice-president of Tropical, was designated as the managing executive of the company. Smith, in turn, delegated the task of active management to Alex McQueen, International's vice-president. Smith and McQueen conferred often with Teagle, who continued to follow Colombian affairs with intimate attention to details. Sadler, as head of Jersey's foreign producing operations, advised on exploration and producing developments. Other Jersey specialists were called in as needed. Indeed, Tropical's local operating executives had little independence of action in matters pertaining to larger management issues.[33]

The task of developing the De Mares concession was at once faced. Time was a factor of importance in any concession limited to the span of thirty years. The physical problems that stood in the way of exploitation, however, were scarcely amenable to rapid solution.

A party of specialized experts headed by W. S. Smullin, one of the Tropical directors, was at once dispatched to conduct a further examination of the De Mares concession and make specific recommendations upon procedures to be followed. Churning their way up the Magdalena in a chartered launch, the party found as few signs of civilization as had the explorers who had preceded them. Three years of work by the pioneers of The Tropical Oil Company had scarcely scarred the jungle.

The investigators found absolutely no accommodations of any kind, either at Barranca or Infantas, suitable for habitation by white men. There seemed to be little that could be done to overcome the handicaps of a wretched climate and a primitive transportation system. Tropical disease was rampant, and the local natives were mostly diseased, undernourished, and unaccustomed to the discipline of regular labor. Neither man nor nature presented a pleasing prospect, but there definitely was oil in the jungle along the mid-Magdalena.[34]

The period from 1921 to 1924 was chiefly one of preparation. Many operations of varying character were simultaneously undertaken—building of living quarters, utilities, terminal facilities, gathering lines, and a refinery (at Barranca); opening trails and building roads through the jungle; acquiring craft for transportation on the Magdalena; studying the geology of the more accessible parts of the concession; surveying; building wellsites; getting production under way. Farms were even established to provide cattle, hogs, casaba, bananas, and other food for the employees.[35]

The center of interest and the focal point of all these ancillary operations was the drill. A geological reconnaissance of the whole concession was carried out, and detailed studies were made of the northern half. Ten structures were outlined. In the first year of exploration alone, some sixty work camps were established. Geology in the early 1920's, however, was a poor friend to the oilman in regions where surface indications were buried beneath swamp water and jungle vegetation. The decision was made to drill the already proved Infantas anticline. The road from Barranca to Infantas was completed. At the latter place drilling headquarters, living accommodations, a commissary, and a small hospital were established.[36]

Drilling commenced in March of 1921. By the end of June, 6 new well locations had been selected and cleared. By October, 4 strings of rotaries and 9 of cable tools were at work; 7 additional strings of cable tools had been ordered. Nothing could be more dramatic to an oilman than the simple statistics contained in Tropical's operating reports. Of the 74 wells completed in 1926, 72 were producers! By the end of 1926, 141 producing wells and 5 dry holes had been drilled, while 7 additional wells had been abandoned because of drilling difficulties. Production (Appendix 2, Table VII) tripled from 1924 to 1925, increased eightfold in 1926, and more than doubled again in 1927. In 1927 the net production of oil from the Colombian operation actually surpassed that of every other producing venture by Jersey Standard interests anywhere in the world, excepting only The Carter Oil Company's in the Mid-Continent.[37]

The De Mares wells were not deep—the 60 that had been drilled on the Infantas and La Cira structures in 1926, for example, averaged only 1,941 feet. Cable tools were used at first, but subsequently the field managers discovered that rotary and combination rigs produced a much cheaper footage. In 1926, drilling costs per foot averaged $63.77 by cable, $19.12 by rotary, and $11.07 by combination rigs. Such results blasted the pessimism of men like Sadler, who even as late as 1924 had written, "From today's standpoint, it is an open question whether the undertaking will be profitable or not."[38]

No less important than the actual progress of drilling were the efforts by Tropical to create a reasonably efficient working force from untrained and physically below normal candidates and to make the jungle habitable for oil workers. Mistakes, misunderstandings, shortsightedness, and some failures marked the progress from ignorance to hard-won managerial comprehension of the great difficulties involved. The problem of effective liaison between the fields and Toronto and New York was magnified many times not only by geographical distance but, on occasion, by fundamental disagreements between field and office men on ways of solving the problems of labor management and jungle conquest.

The discouraging, magnificent, and, in the end, successful effort by Jersey men to shield the oil-field workers from the paralyzing menace of jungle disease has been reserved for summation in the last section of this chapter. The story of Tropical's efforts to recruit, maintain, and enlarge a labor force may be briefly recounted here as a further illustration of the mutual tribulations which arose out of the impact of modern business necessities upon a primitive civilization.

It has always been the policy of Jersey Standard companies, for economic as well as political and legal reasons, to employ, insofar as possible, the nationals of the countries in which they are operating. Tropical drew upon two reservoirs of labor, hiring largely through contractors. At first the company hired workers living in the immediate area in which it was operating. These were of a river-lowlands racial mixture, poor in health and physique and of few skills. A better class of worker, more robust of body and keen of mind, soon was found in the mountain country. In the early years the turnover of national workers averaged as much as 30 per cent a month.

Tropical management was at first discouraged, but as time passed a better and more stable working force was built up. A visitor to the fields noted, in 1924, that the Colombian drilling assistants had become so skillful that American drillers preferred them to American derrick men. Another observer at the end of 1925 wrote International's president that the Colombians were performing difficult classes of work in a satisfactory manner and that the sales and marine departments, the case and can factory, the power and ice plant, and the woodworking shop were staffed almost exclusively by the nationals. "I can see no reason," this visitor wrote, "why the native, if given the opportunity, could not do most of the work around a rotary drill, as he has proved himself capable of doing any ordinary routine work under competent supervision."[39]

The Colombian worker, however, was showing unmistakable evidence of his unwillingness to be led without protest into a new pattern of life. The labor laws of Colombia were liberal, though they were far from being as radical as were the Mexican laws. Colombia, like other Latin American countries, assiduously protected its workers from foreign employers, though enforcement against national employers lagged. From 1924 onward the pressure of a Colombian labor movement was felt, and from the beginning this movement was nourished and channeled by the efforts of radical agitators.[40]

From the time when it commenced development of the De Mares concession, Tropical had offered terms to labor which appear to have been better than prevailing industrial standards in Colombia. This was done with the conscious objective of attracting superior men and of holding them against the tendency of the Colombians (like other peoples unaccustomed to regular employment) to work for only a short period of time. Tropical was conceded to be among the highest wage payers in Colombia. Shift work was on an 8-hour basis, with extra pay for overtime and two weeks of vacation with pay annually—more liberal conditions than those then prevailing in the oil fields of the United States. The best evidence that working conditions were good by Colombian standards may be inferred from a favorable report made by a government investigating commission in 1924 and, more especially, from the fact that even *El Espectador,* a persistently adverse critic of foreign oil interests, had good things to say about Tropical's treatment of its men.[41]

Managerial relations with the workmen, however, are difficult to assess. Special skills, long experience, and great patience were required to supervise a continually changing corps of men who were below par physically, unused to regular work, and often of difficult temperaments. There was, unfortunately, a rapid turnover in local supervisors as well as among the workmen. Management, from the lower supervisory group to the top, was under terrific pressure to get work done. The American drillers in particular were a hard-driving lot, unaccustomed to jungle conditions, often dissatisfied with their assignments, and none too patient with the Colombians. In addition, there was the gulf between management and worker brought about by differences in language and culture. These circumstances, irrespective of the good pay and hours and benefits, were fertile grounds for the rooting of labor trouble.

Local adjustments were made when difficulties arose, but the problem of labor relations never, in those years, was attacked in any over-all way. The situation was somewhat reminiscent of labor relations in the Jersey Company itself in the years from 1911 to 1918. Tropical depended on wage raises and specific concessions rather than on a general program based on broad concepts of employee relations.

Colombian labor was stirred by outside influences. Agitators pointed their efforts not only against the employers but against the conservative ruling element then in power in Colombia. From 1922 on, therefore, Tropical had to contend on the one hand with frequent disturbances of its labor force by agitators centered at Barranca and, on the other hand, with government inspections and the mediation of the national police in times of strife. There was a nearly constant state of unrest. In 1924 a widespread strike affected Tropical and other companies as well.

Tropical's labor experience over these years seems to confirm the thesis that the Colombian workmen, under the increased demand for their labor and the higher wages paid by foreign employers, were beginning to feel their strength and raise their demands. Quite inadvertently, it seemed, the foreign companies in Colombia, as elsewhere in Latin America, were helping to spark a revolution for which they were not loved by Colombian businessmen or the government nor given credit by labor. Labor, indeed, made opposition to the foreign companies a rallying point for support in its political struggle.

Despite all such difficulties, however, Tropical had succeeded in proving not only that the De Mares concession was valuable, but that Colombia held great promise as an oil-producing region. The results of Tropical's operations encouraged other companies, which had watchfully stood by, to enter upon their own developmental projects. By 1926 the Colombian oil boom was in full play. Rival organizations, however, were handicapped by the early and highly successful start made by Tropical. Jersey Standard interests, for once, had taken the lead in opening an important new producing area.[42]

Tropical's pioneering could have been accomplished only by a company with rich financial resources. There is, of course, no way of assessing the cost of the Colombian project to individuals in terms of hard labor, disease, and personal danger. By the end of 1927 a total of $23,521,000 had been expended on plant and development, total assets of the company amounting at that time to $92,113,000. Eight arduous years of development lay behind, but in 1927, the first full year of producing, transporting, refining, and marketing activities, net income from all branches of operation was $6,943,000.[43] As always seemed to be the case when a company developing production in a relatively undeveloped country had at last begun to make profits, political threats to the continuity of profitable operations were beginning to be heard. Nevertheless, Teagle was able to congratulate his Canadian associates upon what he characterized as "a truly great achievement." There were many Colombian expressions of satisfaction that such a monumental effort had been made to put Colombia on the world oil map.

The success that Tropical had attained would not have been realized, regardless of oil at Infantas and the successful efforts of the producing organization to find and produce it, if there had not been an efficient outlet to ocean shipping points. In 1926 such an outlet was provided by the Andian pipeline. The efforts to provide this outlet for the oil of the jungles of the mid-Magdalena taxed the resources of the company in many ways and gained for it both praise and blame. Praise for the conspicuous success in building the line in the face of tremendous physical obstacles; blame for the way in which permission to lay the line was obtained.

Efforts to obtain the concession for a pipeline from Cartagena to a point on the Magdalena close to Las Infantas began in 1919, even before final arrangements had been completed for taking over The Tropical Oil Company and the De Mares concession. There were several reasons why the pipeline project was not carried forward by Tropical. Jersey men were uncertain as to the nature of the pipeline rights granted by the De Mares concession and feared that those rights would be construed narrowly by the Colombians. As in the United States, a company operating a pipeline was liable to regulation in its entirety as a common carrier. It seemed best, therefore, to separate the producing and transporting functions.[44]

On June 30, 1919, the Andian National Corporation, Limited, was formed as an affiliate of the International Petroleum Company to carry forward the Colombian pipeline venture. James W. Flanagan was made the operating manager, his initial tasks being to get the pipeline concession and acquire terminal facilities. Such an assignment would have offered formidable difficulties under the best of circumstances, but in this instance there was a special obstacle. Any company known to have substantial affiliations with interests in the United States would inevitably encounter serious opposition. There was deeply ingrained resentment in Colombia over the role played in 1903 by the United States in the establishment of the Republic of Panama on what had been Colombian territory. The fact that a treaty for the settlement of the long-standing disputes growing out of the Panama affair was being debated in 1919 and 1920 tended to irritate old wounds and make this a far from propitious time for the Jersey Standard organization to seek new concessions in Colombia.

Cognizant of the prevailing antipathy to United States interests, company executives concluded that it was necessary to minimize the Jersey Standard affiliation and represent the undertaking as Canadian—a contention which had legal if not operational validity. Andian was, in fact, the Canadian subsidiary of a Canadian company. Among the directors were several Canadians of prominence, including Sir Herbert Holt, president of the Royal Bank of Canada, which enjoyed great prestige in Colombia.[45]

The pains which Flanagan took to conceal the American affiliation of the company he headed points up an issue in business which has had tremendous significance but comparatively little dispassionate appraisal. Taking a position in 1919 which perceptive executives of a later day would probably have rejected, the men of the Jersey Standard organization appear to have held that their responsibilities in Colombia did not extend beyond disclosure of immediate legal facts and adherence to policies which were legally correct. While secrecy was essential in achieving objectives, they justified their actions by their conviction, based on experience, that the goals sought were substantially equitable from the point of view of both the company and the nation.

Flanagan's initial efforts to obtain a pipeline concession were handicapped by a number of other situations besides the inherent hostility of Colombians toward the United States. In Colombia, as in Peru, there was an upsurging of national feeling, quite apart from the Panama question, which expressed itself in political opposition to foreign business interests generally. In the extreme factionalism of Colombian politics the rooted prejudice against such interests was used to win support. At the same time, other oil interests, eager to get a foothold in Colombia, constituted a far from insignificant factor in the opposition to Andian's objectives.

There is little need to detail the methods used by Flanagan in winning support for his project. Following the route of legal correctness, he nevertheless laid himself open to the accusation that he misrepresented his true affiliations. Forbidden by his superiors to use more direct means to influence legislation, he employed to the utmost his talent for winning influential friends.[46]

Nevertheless, by the summer of 1920 the pipeline project had reached a stalemate. Flanagan believed that nothing further could be accomplished until the pending treaty between the United States and Colombia had settled the Panama affair, which was then disturbing the local political situation. Flanagan returned, therefore, to the United States and began to work for the ratification of the treaty in the United States Senate. Through his mediation Carlos Urueta, the Colombian Minister to the United States, and Senator Fall, of the Senate Foreign Relations Committee, were brought together and Fall's support was enlisted. Flanagan also took up the Colombian matter with United States Senators Lodge, Hitchcock, and Underwood, as well as with President-elect Harding and others. In April of 1921 the treaty was ratified after a long struggle in the United States Senate.[47]

Soon afterward Flanagan returned to Colombia, and by early 1922, working with infinite patience, had succeeded in obtaining the lands and concessions necessary for the construction of terminal facilities at Mamonal, near Cartagena. Efforts to obtain the pipeline concession itself were for a time frustrated by the increasing instability of the Colombian political situation, but Flanagan's skill and personal influence and the recognition by many influential Colombians of the importance of the project to Colombia again brought a workable compromise. In September of 1922 the pipeline concession was finally granted, though the terms were far less favorable than those originally sought. Flanagan himself considered that the Andian concession had been the "cleanest business of its kind that has ever been accomplished in this country," and that all his expenses had been for a "clearly defined and legitimate purpose."[48]

Actual construction of the pipeline commenced in 1925, under the direction of D. O. Towl, Jersey's pipeline expert. Physical difficulties encountered in laying the line were enormous, and it was not until June 10, 1926, that the first oil from the De Mares concession arrived at the Mamonal terminal. By December 31, 1927, Andian financial statements recorded a net investment of $26,800,000, and in the year 1927 a profit of $5,000,-000 was made.[49]

Even before the line-laying had commenced, however, the Andian concession had become the subject of bitter controversy in Colombia. Flanagan's American connections were revealed. His Colombian supporters were assailed for their pro-United States sympathies. To be sure, President Ospina's support of the concession was applauded by many, and the engineering achievement was admitted even by Andian's enemies to have been outstanding. In many political circles in Colombia, however, American oil diplomacy, whatever its justifications and achievements, was in disrepute. The true cost of the effort to obtain a concession under these prevailing conditions was to be counted in terms of distrust, misunderstanding, and animosity, which were often to obscure the positive value to Colombia of the operations of Tropical and Andian in that country.

THE SEARCH IN ECUADOR, ARGENTINA, AND BOLIVIA

Jersey Standard's search for oil in Ecuador, Argentina, and Bolivia may be summarized briefly—not because of lack of interest, opportunity, effort, or adventure in those countries, but because in each instance company hopes were destined to fall short of fulfillment. Each experience had certain unique aspects, but operations followed the same general pattern that has been examined in some detail in preceding pages and chapters.

Jersey men had hoped that Ecuador, into which extended the same arid coastal shelf upon which the La Brea Estate was situated, might prove as productive as Peru. Geological characteristics were much alike in both countries. The Santa Elena oil seepages in Ecuador were not dissimilar in appearance or in early history to those at Negritos. As early as 1917, therefore, Teagle had initiated inquiries and sent a representative to acquire leases. The project was turned over to the International Petroleum Company.[50]

Jersey's scout, referred to in company correspondence as "Mr. B.," began to acquire leases with the secrecy customary and perhaps essential in such transactions. Flanagan also was dispatched to Ecuador, where he quickly made the acquaintance of a number of influential people and soon was able to forward his customarily thorough report of political and economic conditions and the activities of rival oil companies.[51]

From the beginning, however, Jersey's efforts in Ecuador ran into trouble. The exposure of "Mr. B." as a Standard man caused widespread antipathy. Standard was described in an impassioned plea against foreigners before the Ecuadorian House of Representatives as a boa—"the hissing of which is heard on the shores of the Zambesi and the Lualaba, which swallows little birds like Nicaragua and chokes powerful antelopes like Mexico."[52] In 1919 Ecuador passed a new petroleum law which brought all subsoil mineral deposits, on private as well as on public land, under government control.[53]

By 1921 International had acquired considerable acreage, all subject, of course, to the stringent requirements of the new mining law. The first well was drilled in 1921, and several others were drilled in succeeding years. This was not a big operation, and no oil was discovered. The only tangible benefits consisted of the geological information that was accumulated in prospecting and drilling.[54]

The search in Argentina, on the contrary, was launched on an extensive scale, with large expenditures. Sadler in 1917 had recommended entry into producing operations in Argentina and Bolivia, but both projects had been overshadowed by developments in Mexico which at the time were considered much more promising. By the early 1920's, however, the rapid growth of Jersey's markets in Argentina furnished a motive which was all the more compelling because a heavy duty on imported oil interfered with the profitable supplying of the company's Campana refinery with Peruvian or Mexican crude. Tax laws, on the other hand, encouraged local mining ventures by granting a five-year exemption.[55]

Geologists were sent to explore the oil regions. Some acreage was picked up at Neuquén, 500 miles to the southwest of Buenos Aires; at Salta, near the Bolivian border; and at Commodoro Rivadavia, on the coast south of Neuquén, where the government was engaged in producing operations. Drilling began in 1922 with three strings of tools, the project being incorporated under the name of the Standard Oil Company of Argentina. By the end of 1927 Standard of Argentina was employing 85 Americans and 1,915 nationals, had invested $11,600,000 in producing operations, and could show a daily average production of only 765 barrels of oil.[56]

These indifferent results were the outcome, in large measure, of competition from the Argentinean government, which had entered oil production in the first decade of the century. A government decree in 1923 established the Dirección General de Yacimientos Petrolíferos Fiscales, an official agency to carry on government oil operations. The YPF, as it was called, was strengthened by subsequent legislative acts in 1925 and 1927, receiving large grants of the most promising state lands. In 1925 a government refinery was established near Buenos Aires, and the trend toward an integrated national industry was well confirmed.[57]

The chief proponent of government operations and monopoly was General Enrique Mosconi, whose influence was felt in other Latin American countries as well. As administrator of the YPF, Mosconi was especially critical of foreign oil companies and advocated legislation designed to hamper and eliminate private enterprise. In a much heralded speech in Mexico early in 1928 Mosconi characterized Jersey Standard as a hempen rope and the Royal Dutch-Shell as a silken rope—"both might hang us."[58]

Thus, in Argentina as in Mexico, Jersey Standard interests were caught up in a sweeping national movement which by 1927 had already severely restricted private development of oil resources. The full strength of this movement, moreover, was yet to be felt. It is clear in retrospect that little could have been done to stay or divert the trend.

The Bolivian operation suffered neither from the extreme political adversity which curtailed Jersey's Argentinean and Mexican ambitions nor from the dearth of oil which caused the company to lose interest in Ecuador. Transportation was the severely limiting factor in Bolivia. The Bolivian market itself was restricted. A major pipeline operation would have been required to transport oil to Argentinean outlets or to Chilean ports on the west coast. A. F. Corwin calculated that the only feasible way to transport oil from the fields at Santa Cruz to Buenos Aires would be by a 500-mile pipeline to the Paraguay River and a 700-mile river-barge haul. The pipeline alone would cost $12,000,000. To reach the Chilean coast at Antofagasta would require 1,100 miles of transport through the Andes and a lift of 14,999 feet to cross the mountains.[59]

The Jersey men, nevertheless, decided to acquire concessions in the Bolivian fields. "The whole interest in such fields," Corwin told Teagle, "is in the assurance gained by holding large areas available for production in the distant future when the fields now in sight will either diminish or fail to supply the increased consumption."[60] This undertaking was launched, it should be remembered, at a time when concern over American oil supplies was beginning to become acute.

Negotiations opened in 1920 led to the acquisition of the Braden concession (approximately 1,285,000 acres) and the Richmond Levering concession (2,471,000 acres) in southeastern Bolivia. Both concessions gave to the company broad development rights; both were subject to an 11 per cent royalty and other taxes. In 1921 the Standard Oil Company of Bolivia was organized to carry on development work.

Operating problems were not unlike those which were being faced in northern Argentina. Supplies for both areas were shipped by rail from Buenos Aires to Tartagal, the last station on the rail line. From Tartagal to the northernmost drilling sites in Bolivia, however, was a distance of nearly four hundred miles. The central portion of the Bolivian concessions, where most of the drilling activities were concentrated, was fairly level, semiarid, sparsely settled, and dismally dreary country. There were a few villages and an occasional hacienda in the more fertile valleys, but one could travel for days without seeing a human being, and the trails were not always easy to follow. Until roads were constructed or improved, only the high-wheeled native wagons drawn by mule teams would be able to make the trip to the fields. It was by this primitive means of transportation that the first drilling rigs were sent in. The wellsites in the north, while among the most scenic ever selected by Jersey geologists, often required the construction of scores of miles of roads in rugged terrain. Some 200 carts and 800 mules were employed in this phase of operations alone. Such roads as did exist were soon so churned up by the heavy traffic as to become almost impassable. The rivers, wide and often full of quicksands, were too numerous for bridging and had to be forded. For the three months of the rainy season they were completely impassable, and for three additional months or more they could be crossed only on muleback.[61]

Slowly and at great expense the roads were laid and the supplies moved up. By 1926 the company had surveyed its properties and established eleven work camps. Four strings of tools were operating—two in the south, just across the border from Argentina, and two 350 miles north. Some production was obtained, but not enough to justify the very heavy expense of a pipeline to the outside world. By the end of 1927 output was averaging 71 barrels per day. Jersey Standard's total investment in Bolivia then stood at $11,400,000.[62] This expenditure, like the expenditure of an approximately equal amount in Argentina, was not considered too high an amount to invest in the future of a district where reasonable luck at drilling and a shift in the political winds might conceivably place the company in an exceptionally advantageous position. Chances were taken and many bets were lost—but this was the oil business and Jersey Standard, fortunately, could afford to make many bets.

THE ENTRY INTO VENEZUELA

From August, 1921, to June, 1928, Venezuela appeared to the Jersey directors to be another one of the company's poor gambles. Year after year there had been the same discouraging repetition of dry holes and of moving on to another location. New roads to build; new clearings to make; new camps to construct and new wells to spud-in—a seemingly endless succession. Millions of dollars were expended. The Standard Oil Company of Venezuela had become almost a standing joke among local oilmen. The director in charge of the venture began to be known at 26 Broadway as "the nonproducing production director." But the work went on—and at last the incendiary news: Monat Number 1 had come in at Quiriquire![63]

Much oil history had been enacted in Venezuela before the first Jersey scout slung his pack upon a burro and set out into the jungle. It was the Royal Dutch-Shell which had pioneered. Sir Henri Deterding liked to boast that Maracaibo was his most perspicacious hunch.

As early as 1880 the United States Consul at Maracaibo had reported home about the fountains and wells of petroleum, urging the importance of the Venezuelan petroleum resources and complaining that, while Americans were uninterested, Europeans had definitely taken note of Venezuelan possibilities. Substantial efforts soon followed by Americans and others to exploit the large asphalt deposits in Venezuela, but large-scale oil operations did not begin until after 1912, when the Royal Dutch-Shell took its first concession.[64]

Jersey Standard had kept in touch with Venezuelan developments through its marketing agencies in South America. Venezuelan oil was particularly interesting because of its proximity to the coast and its consequent adaptability to shipment by tanker to the United States and Europe. In 1915 and 1916 company geologists toured the country and reported their observations. No action was taken at 26 Broadway, in part because by that time there were few promising lands still unleased and also because new regulations, promulgated in Venezuela in 1915, discouraged further oil development by foreign capital.[65]

By 1919 many circumstances had changed. Teagle was president of the Jersey Company, and the search for foreign crude oil reserves was being aggressively expanded. New Venezuelan regulations, passed late in 1918, facilitated foreign participation in Venezuela. These regulations, strict in their terms, still were somewhat more liberal than the laws of Mexico and Colombia. The Caribbean Petroleum Company, a Royal Dutch-Shell subsidiary, was in the process of relinquishing some of its less promising concession lands, and these were coming on the market.[66]

Again Jersey Standard sent its scouts into Venezuela. Early in 1919 Carter's A. V. Hoenig, accompanied by a geologist, made a tour of western Venezuela to block out a program in case Jersey Standard should decide to commence operations. The geologist did not pause to inspect the Maracaibo Basin (which subsequently proved to be the richest oil region in Venezuela), explaining that "anyone who stays there a few weeks is almost certain to become infected with malaria, or liver and intestinal disorders which are likely to become chronic."[67]

The geologist was unenthusiastic about the regions he visited and indicated that geological, legal, and operating conditions in Venezuela were not particularly favorable. He conceded that business considerations might dictate an entry, but he warned of the expense, concluding, "Because of the heavy responsibility involved in developing that territory I do not wish to become one of its sponsors."[68]

Hoenig was more optimistic. He reported upon developments by the Caribbean Petroleum Company and surmised, "The fact that they have spent millions there leads us to suspect that there is considerable oil in this country."[69]

Company records fail to indicate what sequence of events followed at 26 Broadway upon the reception of the Venezuelan survey. It seems more than likely that in this instance, as was the case in Colombia, Teagle was determined to push ahead. In the fall of 1919 a new party of Jersey geologists arrived at Caracas and for eight months carried on surveys in the unleased areas south of Lake Maracaibo. At approximately the same time, T. R. Armstrong arrived in Venezuela armed with authority from the Jersey board to seek concessions.[70]

Armstrong was a Texan of means who had been educated at Princeton. As familiar with the Spanish language and the Latin American people as with his own tongue and countrymen, he appears to have been an excellent choice for Jersey's Venezuelan mission. The political situation Armstrong faced was in some respects unprecedented, and his first move was an understandable but very costly mistake.

In Venezuela in 1919 was to be found none of the instability and chaos of Mexico; none of the vacillations of an insecure national administration as in Peru; none of the factional democracy of Colombia. Venezuela was ruled by a dictator who brooked no uncertainties except those of his own making.

Juan Vicente Gómez, an Indian from the Andean region, ruled Venezuela despotically, but with great native intelligence and administrative capacity. Political opponents sooner or later fled the country or ended up in prison. Supported by the army and a clique of friends and relatives, Gómez sat like a feudal baron in his mountain fastness behind the barracks city of Maracay and manipulated the executive, administrative, and judicial affairs of state almost at will.

Like Díaz of Mexico, Gómez was friendly to foreign capital and businessmen. Having seen his country nearly fall under the control of foreign powers early in the century through failure to pay or service its external debts, Gómez was determined to make Venezuela financially independent and strong. Like Díaz, he welcomed the foreigner who gave promise of helping to develop his country. World War I had proved to him that his pro-German sympathies had been inexpedient; by 1919 Gómez had begun to cultivate a new friendship with the United States. No doubt he also saw in the Americans a potential check on the British, who had come to occupy a strong and nearly unchallenged position in Venezuela. Preston McGoodwin, United States Minister to Venezuela, was on friendly terms with Venezuela's dictator. Word had come in a roundabout way to McGoodwin that the Gómez government might give preference to Jersey Standard because of its reputation and standing.[71]

The situation facing Armstrong, therefore, appeared to be propitious— so much so that Armstrong believed he could eliminate those initial procedures, so costly in time and money, which had come to be considered indispensable for success in dealing with any Latin American government. The usual practice, particularly on the part of Americans, was to establish a household on a grand scale, entertain lavishly, and carry on negotiations through intermediaries who were alleged to have great influence. Graft, traditional and universal as it had become, was not condemned, provided that the gratuities were adequate, graciously dispensed, and given to the right people. Armstrong was determined to circumvent this ritual.

"The General," he confided in a memorandum, "has them all bluffed, in my opinion. Since he is the man who has to pass on the question ultimately I believe more is to be accomplished by approaching him direct than thru some sycophant whose standing may not be as good as we are led to believe."[72]

The American Minister arranged an audience, and on December 12 and 13, 1919, Armstrong met with Gómez and made known Jersey's desire to negotiate for a large concession. Gómez scribbled a few words on a card and instructed Armstrong to see Dr. Torres, the Minister of Development, saying, "If he does not give you what you want, come back and see me again." On December 15 came the meeting with Torres. After introductions, the usual exchange of courtesies, and expressions of *amistad*, Armstrong handed Torres the note from Gómez. Armstrong records in his memo: "It seemed to me to startle him considerably and he read the back of it before the front and then said we should have every consideration, etc., etc., and that we needed no intermediary." Detailed discussions followed in which Armstrong not only specified Jersey's concession plans but also signified the company's hope that Venezuela's petroleum legislation would be liberalized.[73] All seemed to be going smoothly.

On January 14, 1920, Armstrong filed applications for five concessions, which had been carefully mapped out by company geologists, in the free territory south of Lake Maracaibo. On the very day these were filed, applications were filed for virtually the identical areas by Julio Mendez, son-in-law of Gómez! After the usual processing, including legislative approval, the concession was granted to Mendez, who, in turn, sold it to Addison M. McKay, the secret agent in Venezuela of the Sun Oil Company.[74] Armstrong had learned his first lesson in Venezuelan oil politics.

Unsuccessful thereafter in several efforts to acquire a blanket concession by dealing directly with Gómez, Armstrong was nevertheless able, in 1920, to obtain close to 3,000,000 acres of exploration concessions scattered throughout Venezuela.[75] These lands, many of which had been given up by the Caribbean Petroleum Company, were purchased from American companies dealing in Venezuelan oil leases. Some additional properties were secured from Julio Mendez. The purchases from Mendez resulted in an improvement in the company's standing in local political circles, though the properties he had offered were not particularly desired by the company and even included 1,700 hectares (4,200 acres) of land under Lake Maracaibo. The manager of the West India Oil Company, who was then in charge of Jersey's concession activities in Venezuela, told the men at 26 Broadway that they had better order a good boat so that in case the concession proved of no value as an oil property they could go into the fishing business.[76] Time was to prove this jibe ill chosen, but in 1920 underwater drilling techniques were in their infancy and old-time oilmen could still scoff with impunity.

Development of these various concessions was believed to be contingent upon a revision of Venezuelan petroleum legislation. Armstrong had urged such revision from the very beginning of his Venezuelan assignment. McKay, of the Sun Oil Company, likewise advocated a change, and representatives of several American companies, including Armstrong and two Sun Oil Company lawyers, drew up a proposed law which apparently was influential in determining the legislation that was finally adopted. McGoodwin, the American Minister, urged that the oil industry and the government should look upon themselves as a partnership in the development of Venezuelan oil resources for their mutual advantage.[77] After much discussion and debate in the Venezuelan Congress, a new law was finally passed in July of 1922.

This law was a milestone in Latin American petroleum legislation. It was looked upon at the time as the most favorable mining law in Latin America, yet its provisions were strict and Venezuelan interests were well protected. Slight modifications were later made, but basically the law remained unchanged and proved a workable one for two decades.

By the terms of the 1922 legislation all oil operations were classed as public utilities. Concessions, which were limited to forty years, could be granted to foreign corporations domiciled in Venezuela, provided that foreign governments owned no interest in such corporations. Provision was made for granting larger concessions. However, only half the lands specified in exploration concessions—in parcels not larger than 500 hectares—could be retained for exploitation; the remainder was to be turned over to the government as national reserves. Rights to import supplies without taxation and to transport, refine, and market oil produced were conferred with the concession grant. Specifications covering government inspection, drilling methods, treatment of workmen, and reports to the government were included in the law. Tax rates and various fees and charges were established. A reduction in royalties was made from 10 to 7½ per cent of production from underwater acreage.

The importance of this law, as it proved, lay not only in its terms, but also in the way in which it was administered. With minor exceptions, relations between the oil companies and the government under the 1922 regulations were satisfactory. The oil industry enjoyed a sense of security unprecedented in degree in any other Latin American country, including Peru. The oilmen soon learned that Gómez respected contracts.

In the summer of 1920 Jersey Standard prepared to investigate such concessions as it then held. By autumn several field parties were at work in the Falcón coastal area, the Maracaibo Basin, the mountainous states southeast and south of the lake, and in eastern Venezuela. The search was perhaps even more difficult, adventurous, and hazardous than that in Colombia. Inland transportation facilities were primitive or nonexistent. The terrain to be explored ranged from desert plains to swampy mangrove jungles. The geologists traveled by boat or native canoe where possible, but often the only means of travel was by muleback. The survey parties usually consisted of two geologists with a few assistants, including a national to take care of the pack animals, a guide, and a cook. Assignments took weeks or even months to complete. In many jungle areas geological observations were nearly impossible.

Jersey's first Venezuelan well was spudded-in on August 31, 1921. Oil was discovered in commercial quantities, but the wells soon played out and the quarter-million-dollar tanks which had been built in anticipation of continued production served only as a reminder of the hazards of the oil business. In December of 1921 the Standard Oil Company of Venezuela was incorporated to take over the existing organization, and work went forward.[78]

In December of 1922 all Venezuelan operations were stimulated by the news that the Los Barossos well of the Royal Dutch-Shell in the La Rosa field in the Maracaibo Basin had blown out at a depth of 1,500 feet, with an uncontrolled production estimated at 100,000 barrels daily.[79] The oil output of Venezuela began to climb, but Jersey Standard as yet had been unsuccessful.

Work camps were established at many points, and the drilling was continued under incredible difficulties. Disease struck at almost all who entered the country. Buildings and derricks erected in the swamps rotted away while still new; equipment was brought in with difficulty and sometimes could not be taken out. Large inventories of equipment parts were required, and local customs regulations sometimes caused delays in obtaining vitally needed materials.

Company concessions in western Venezuela encompassed the heart of the Motolone Indian country. This warlike tribe resented and fought the intruders. At Camp Perija, about 200 miles from Maracaibo near the Colombian border, an American driller was slain by an arrow as he sat on the porch of the mess hall. Several other attacks were made. The drilling superintendent armed his men and cleared away all jungle growth within arrow range of the camp buildings. The Indians were a particular menace to the dugouts bringing passengers and supplies up the small jungle streams. Despite all precautions, one river convoy was ambushed and dispersed and the supplies were looted.[80] These were by no means the only difficulties faced.

Many non-Jersey men were hired as drillers; some of them came from fields in eastern United States and were unfamiliar with the latest drilling methods in use in the Mid-Continent and the Gulf Coast districts. It was four years before the company learned that rotary drills were far superior to cable tools in most parts of Venezuela. There was a high turnover among the American employees; two of the top managers were replaced by Carter men. Among the Venezuelan nationals in the company service such abstractions as loyalty to a company or good work for the sake of doing a good job held little meaning. The incentive of working for pay lasted only until a little money had been earned. Only very slowly did a cohesive and efficient operating organization begin to take form, despite the fact that an extremely close watch upon the Venezuelan venture was maintained by the Foreign Producing Department in New York.[81]

As the months went by and Jersey drills failed to find oil on company lands, other means were employed or contemplated for obtaining a share of the Venezuelan crude which was by then so richly flowing on the concessions of many companies. Contracts were made by Standard of Venezuela to develop parts of the holdings of other organizations. One of the most important connections of this kind was that with the British Consolidated Oilfields, Limited, for development at Buchivacoa, in the state of Falcón, northeast of Lake Maracaibo. The Jersey men found no commercial production and, although the financial outlay was covered by the British, Jersey Standard was blamed in England for losses sustained by speculators in the stock of the British company.[82]

In the spring of 1926 another possibility was mentioned by Teagle in a letter to Sadler. Teagle had learned from a conversation with Gulbenkian and Deterding that the Royal Dutch-Shell might be willing to sell a large share in the Colón Development Company, another of its Venezuelan subsidiaries. Deterding had asserted that his company had more land in Venezuela than his organization could handle. Teagle doubted that Deterding would sell anything that he considered valuable, and yet he was interested in the proposition. "Mr. Moffett and I think," Teagle wrote to

Sadler, "we have invested so much in wildcatting in Venezuela without results, that the acquisition of producing property would not only place us in a position of actual producers but also give us something from which to derive some income to help defray the current operating expenses." Such was to be the policy of the future, but in 1926 Deterding's offer was declined. In his autobiography Sir Henri chided the Jersey men by pointing out that the concession they had declined had later begun to produce regularly at the rate of 20,000 barrels daily.[83]

Poor local management and inordinately bad luck were probably the two chief causes of Jersey's failure to find oil in Venezuela between 1921 and 1928. It is clear that in some instances at least the field-trained oilmen were at fault in failing to follow the advice of their geologists. Tardiness in replacing cable tools with rotary drills was also a factor in the prolonged failure to find oil. Both managerial and operating skills improved with experience, however, and bad luck could not last forever. The lowering of rotary tools into Monat Number 1 at Quiriquire—drilled by cable tools without success in 1924—was symbolic. Old failures were the scene of new efforts, and the Jersey Standard organization could afford the high cost of persistence. That persistence, coupled with a somewhat ponderous adaptiveness, in 1928 was to usher in a dramatic new sequence of events in Venezuela.

A TASTE OF OIL IN THE DUTCH EAST INDIES

The determination of the Jersey board not to surrender to the Royal Dutch-Shell in Sumatra and Java had kept the Naamlooze Vennootschap Nederlandsche Kolionalc Pctroleum Maatschappij (the NKPM) alive for several difficult years. This corporate offspring of Jersey's Dutch affiliate had been able to obtain only discarded, meager, and barren concessions up to 1913, when the Dutch government suspended its mining laws and refused to grant further concessions to anyone.

This impasse was broken by the passage of a new mining law in 1918, but the influence in Holland of Deterding's organization was still formidable. Jersey's ambitions to acquire grants in the great and promising government reserve in Sumatra, the Djambi, were still blocked by Deterding's aspirations to add this tract to the already extensive Royal Dutch-Shell holdings.

Impelling economic factors lay behind the desire to obtain commercial production in the Dutch East Indies. Chief among these was the nature of the crude, a light-gravity product that yielded rich proportions of gasoline. Deterding had proved that Sumatran gasoline could be sold economically in European markets. In postwar months the demand in those markets was growing rapidly, while supplies from alternate sources (Romania, Poland, Russia) had, for one reason or another, been curtailed. Beyond this was the competitive desirability of attacking the Royal Dutch-Shell where it was strongest—in the Orient. This objective could not, because of the distances involved, be accomplished with North American or even Latin American stocks; if, however, the Jersey Company could build a producing and refining organization in Sumatra and work out some means of marketing its products, Deterding could be challenged in the East.

In 1920 this objective was far from attainment. The NKPM had acquired a few more concessions from third parties, but no commercial quantities of oil had been found. In 1921 a new application was made for a half of the Djambi, but the request failed to pass in the Dutch Assembly and a large part of the government reserve lands were awarded, instead, to the Royal Dutch-Shell. This action was protested by Jersey Standard to the American State Department, which, in turn, protested to The Hague that the Dutch government discriminated against American nationals. The Dutch replied that the act of the United States government in excluding the Royal Dutch-Shell from naval preserves in the United States also constituted an act of discrimination. In this somewhat petulant diplomatic exchange no mention was made by the Dutch of the fact that while Jersey Standard at this time was producing only enough oil in the Dutch East Indies to support a skimming plant with a capacity of 100 barrels daily, the Royal Dutch-Shell interests in the United States were producing over 5,000,000 barrels of crude annually.[84]

Despite the rebuff, the Jersey Company continued, with strong diplomatic backing, to solicit concessions. Drilling also went on, but the NKPM field operations were not viewed with satisfaction by the Jersey directorate. The local field superintendents and engineers, though good men in their line, continued to clash with the Dutch colonial government officials and agencies. Life in the islands, it appeared, was very cliquish, and foreigners were not accepted on an equal footing with the resident Dutch. Efforts to find for the NKPM a qualified Dutch chief executive were not successful. Teagle expressed the opinion—significant in view of developing managerial difficulties in other foreign areas—that the local troubles were a result of failure to make any one man in the Jersey organization responsible for the affairs of the NKPM as a whole.[85]

Enthusiasm for the East Indian venture was at a low ebb when, in August of 1922, the Talang Akar wells began to come in. This property, situated 80 miles from Palembang in south Sumatra, was one of the concessions that had been discarded by the Royal Dutch-Shell. The NKPM had been drilling on it unsuccessfully for several years before the pay horizons were finally struck. The discovery well was by no means spectacular, and it was only after a half-dozen wells had come in—one with an initial production of 2,000 barrels daily—that Jersey men began to take notice.[86]

Eighteen months after oil had been found, in fact, both Sadler and Hunt were urging that the NKPM be sold to the Standard Oil Company of New York. Both men felt that an effort should be made instead in the new California fields. Teagle took a strong stand against this:[87]

I feel that we should leave nothing undone to push as energetically as possible the operations of our foreign producing department rather than in the expansion of our domestic producing department business to a district like California. In other words, if we have the capital and talent available for further expansion of our producing operations, then I certainly would favor the employment of the same abroad rather than here in the United States.

Once again Teagle's viewpoint prevailed, though it is interesting that in this instance Jersey's president was using Sadler's old arguments in disputing what seems to have been a decided change of opinion on the part of the head of the company's foreign producing operations.

By December of 1926 the NKPM had drilled 27 wells at Talang Akar, of which 24 were producing. By the end of 1927 the NKPM was producing more than 4,000 barrels of crude oil daily. Teagle had held that a daily output of from 4,000 to 5,000 barrels was sufficient to give the Jersey Company some leverage in the local marketing situation and also provide some gasoline to meet Royal Dutch-Shell competition in Europe. Thus an important end had been attained, despite the fact that Deterding's organization controlled 5,000,000 acres in the Dutch East Indies, while the NKPM had only 68,737 acres under lease.[88]

In 1925 the construction of a refinery at Palembang was commenced, and the quest for additional concessions was energetically pushed. Circumstances had swung in the company's favor since the failure, in 1921, to get into the Djambi. The Minister of Colonies who had vigorously supported the Royal Dutch cause had been succeeded by another, who, so Jersey's European representatives reported, had had quite enough of Deterding's dictation. There was evidence in other quarters, too, that the feeling was growing in Holland that Deterding's organization had too strong a hold on the government.[89]

Sir Henri, who had been disappointed in the results achieved in the Djambi, was sufficiently concerned about Jersey Standard's new concession request to state that he would oppose the Jersey land bill unless equivalent grants were made to his own company. On the other hand, said Deterding, if the petitions of both companies were entertained together, he would do all in his power to see that the bills were passed. Teagle was advised by his Dutch associates to stand fast and not allow The Hague to gain the impression that the Jersey Company was dancing to the tune of Royal Dutch pipes. Teagle himself felt, no doubt as a result of his experience in co-operating with Deterding in Russia, that Sir Henri might delay the concession bills indefinitely. He told Deterding flatly that the Royal Dutch-Shell could do as it pleased, but that Jersey Standard intended to go its own way.[90]

On July 17, 1928, the Jersey concession bill became law. Knowledge that the State Department was watching the progress of the bill was certainly a dominant factor in its passage. After more than fifteen disheartening years and the investment of about $20,000,000, the turning point had come. The new concession granted NKPM 625,692 additional acres of land, some of which was highly promising from a geological viewpoint. At the same time, the 35 wells producing on the Talang Akar property at the end of 1927 caused company geologists to double their earlier estimates of oil reserves there. Plans were initiated to double the capacity of the Palembang refinery.[91] Once again, it appeared, persistence bordering on obstinacy had retrieved a cause which many Jersey executives had considered hopelessly, expensively lost.

THE WAR AGAINST TROPICAL DISEASE

Jersey Standard's struggle against tropical disease formed an integral segment of Latin American producing operations and constituted a dramatic phase of relations between private business and national interests there. In Latin America doctors soon came to be recognized as an integral part of the oil-producing organization. Without them the search for petroleum reserves might well have failed, and in certain areas the political brew, already seething, might have boiled over even sooner.

A word of explanation is necessary in order to establish the background of the company's medical experience in tropical producing operations. The Jersey Standard Medical Department was established in 1918 as one part of an extensive employee benefits program instituted in that year. Under this program the company had established for its employees sickness, accident, retirement, and life insurance policies. Following the example of the insurance companies, a medical director was employed who was to be responsible for reducing the medical risks of the program. Such was the limited purpose first contemplated, but the medical service very soon began to expand beyond its initial restricted objectives.[92]

Dr. Willard J. Denno, the first medical director, was well trained in teaching, public health, internal medicine, and state medical organization. In 1919 the department, still small and still in its experimental stages, began to grow.[93] Dr. Alvin W. Schoenleber, then a colonel in the United States Army, was engaged to serve as medical director of The Carter Oil Company. Schoenleber's experiences with Carter, together with the functionings of Denno's office at 26 Broadway and the growth of the medical staff in the refining and marketing branches of the business, will be touched upon in subsequent chapters.

Denno's new assistant entered his career in industrial medicine with many misgivings. When he first had called upon Dr. Denno, Schoenleber found the medical director quartered in a small and dingy office adjoining an equally small and poorly equipped first-aid room. Work then under way appeared to be confined to physical examinations and the treatment of minor accident cases. Schoenleber already knew that the "company doctor" in general had a poor professional and public reputation, in some cases being forced as a precautionary measure to submit to the supervision of private practitioners. There were few precedents to suggest that a worth-while career might be pursued in the field of industrial medicine. There were, indeed, very few opportunities of any kind for full-time employment as company physician.

Six difficult months with The Carter Oil Company established Schoenleber in the medical organization, and also apparently revealed to Dr. Denno and the Jersey directors the need and the opportunity for more extensive field work. Late in 1919 Schoenleber was dispatched to survey and reorganize, if possible, the medical services of the Transcontinental Petroleum Company in Mexico.

Transcontinental's local manager freely admitted that the company had been too busy getting oil out of the ground to devote much attention to medical matters. For more than 6,000 persons, counting workers' families, living in Transcontinental field camps, the half-time services of one doctor were provided. No sanitary or preventive medicine was practiced.

Even the quarters for American employees, while fairly comfortable, lacked sanitary maintenance. Mexican workmen lived in shacks, without a pretense of public health measures. Hospital facilities in the field were sufficient only to take care of minimum requirements of the American staff and of serious accident cases among the nationals employed. The assumption was made that the Mexicans had always shifted for themselves and would continue to do so. At Tampico, with its thousands of foreign and Mexican residents, there were virtually no hospital facilities.

Schoenleber found that to do anything worth while in preventive medicine he would have to destroy all existing native camps and build entirely new ones. The situation had virtually gone out of control, particularly in view of the failure of the southern fields and the slow liquidation of Jersey's Mexican producing venture. Neither the Jersey Company nor the local management was willing to expend substantial sums of money until the political hazards of the day were removed. The field hospital, however, was enlarged and the medical staff increased. Some cleanup work was attempted, though this program did not progress far enough to exert appreciable influence upon sickness rates. In Tampico Schoenleber cooperated with a local physician in planning and persuading the oil companies to build the modern 200-bed Gorgas Hospital. At the same time, the duplication of payment for medical services among the refining, producing, and tanker operating units was eliminated. Jersey's medical missionary left Mexico dissatisfied with the results he had been able to achieve and aghast that the oil companies should have commenced large-scale operations in the semitropics without adequate medical facilities. Schoenleber was convinced that, with medical foresight and knowledge available in the beginning, any new producing venture could be carried through with spectacular economies in human life and suffering.

This belief was almost immediately put to a test. Schoenleber had no sooner returned from Mexico than he was sent to join the party of specialists who were investigating the recently purchased De Mares concession in Colombia. His reports painted an appalling picture of human misery.

All the people in Colombia, Schoenleber reported to Dr. Denno, were sick. Malaria, hookworm, and amoebic dysentery were widely prevalent, while dengue and blackwater fever and other tropical diseases were plentiful. The smallpox, respiratory, skin, intestinal, and venereal infection rate was high. Lepers walked the streets in some of the smaller villages. Colombia had no national health supervision and appeared to have made no progress in sanitation or public health since the days of Spanish colonization. There were few doctors of any kind and only a handful of competent ones. Colombians of means went to the Canal Zone for medical treatment. Not one up-to-date hospital was to be found in the entire country, nor were there any training schools for nurses. The incidence of disease was high, and geographic conditions were such that the cost of combating disease was heavy. The nation was too poor to help itself; there were no leaders with the administrative capacity or the scientific training to carry out a public health program even if funds had been available.[94]

Armed with assurance of support from 26 Broadway, Schoenleber began to plan his campaign for the scientific medical guidance of a large-scale tropical producing venture. Almost at once the dream was shattered by the tumultuous realities of oil-boom operations. Camp sites were dictated, not by considerations of healthful living conditions, but by the necessities of oil-field technology. Since only the drill could determine exactly where the main field camps would be, permanent health measures on a large scale could not be undertaken in advance. In the process of development it was all too obvious that the camps would be occupied before they could be made sanitary. Worse still, most employees would have to be crowded together in unsatisfactory temporary quarters, a situation which inevitably spelled excessive sickness rates.

First measures, therefore, were of an emergency nature. Schoenleber wired New York, asking that three qualified doctors and several nurses with army field experience be employed as soon as possible. A field hospital was set up at Barranca, and the doctor who had accompanied the original Tropical Oil Company group was persuaded to stay on as a member of the new organization. Another temporary field hospital was set up at Las Infantas, tentative sanitary regulations were announced, medical stores were requisitioned, plans were drawn for a permanent base hospital, and a resident medical director was appointed to carry through the program which had been laid out. Schoenleber then returned to New York to assume the dual posts of assistant medical director of Jersey Standard and medical director in New York of The Tropical Oil Company.

First reports from Colombia were disheartening. In one month in 1921 the annual malaria admission rate was reported as being 1,300 cases per 1,000 employees. The rate in the worst camp in Mexico, by way of comparison, had been 500 cases per 1,000, while the average in Mexico was 250 cases per 1,000. The amoebic dysentery rate in Colombia was unbelievably high, with an annual admission rate in 1921 of 750 cases per 1,000 employees.[95]

Local administrative difficulties began to develop. Clashes occurred between Tropical's local manager and the resident chief physician over medical and sanitary procedures. The former had obstructed vital medical work and the latter had been aggressively undiplomatic. Both men were replaced.

Schoenleber and McQueen, the International Petroleum executive in Toronto who had charge of Colombian operations, got on well together, but, despite McQueen's orders to the field managers, co-operation with the Medical Department was not forthcoming at the local level. The resident managers, it must be noted, were under tremendous pressure to get production started. Medical services of the kind contemplated were costly and time-consuming. No one, least of all the battle-scarred oil veterans, knew for certain that such measures would be effective. Returns in terms of dollars were impossible to assess, and the managers resented the charging of large medical expenditures against the cost of operations for which they were responsible. The support of Teagle and McQueen required positive demonstration if the medical service program was to survive local indifference and hostility. Armed with further assurances of that support, Schoenleber returned to Colombia and laid down the medical law in decisive terms.

From the time of this visit forward, progress was rapid. The long-delayed and much hampered antimosquito and sanitary campaigns were actively pushed. In one year the malaria rate for American employees dropped 50 per cent; in two years 90 per cent. The influx of new workers from the state of Antioquia introduced a malaria strain into the region which reinfected many resident workmen, but soon the malaria rate among all nationals in the company's employ was trending permanently downward. Many other gains were recorded.

Hospital facilities for all employees were steadily extended, both at Barranca and in the field. Water supplies were safeguarded, and the Rockefeller Institute was persuaded to intensify its activities at Barranca to control the sources of hookworm infection. The company itself decided, in addition, to give all employees a standard course of treatment for this and other chronic diseases. Complete medical and hospital service was provided without charge for all employees, both contract and national, and for all members of their families who were authorized to live in company camps. Camp construction and sanitation were steadily improved. To the more persistent critics of sanitary measures in the worker colony, the Medical Department pointed out that contagion bred there was not likely to respect the barriers of nationality or rank.[96]

The lessons learned on the De Mares concession were put to good use in laying the Andian National pipeline. Here, where working conditions were exceptionally difficult, even by Colombian standards, the medical division accomplished remarkable results. Sickness and accident rates were held to what would have been normal for pipeline work in the United States.

In these various efforts to achieve and maintain a level of public health hitherto unknown in such regions, some errors were made. One of the more serious was the company policy toward venereal disease. Following the practice established in the army, and in keeping with the very decided will of Jersey management, the Medical Department adopted a callous attitude toward venereal cases. The prevalent philosophy was accepted that such diseases could be kept under control by punishing the victims. Company doctors were allowed to treat cases on a private fee basis, but the management extended no assistance or benefits, docked the pay of men absent from work for such causes, and charged hospitalized patients $10 per day for their rooms. Experience in time showed that the frequency rate of infection was increasing rather than decreasing and that the poor treatment received in most cases was resulting in a higher than average percentage of complications. The efforts of the Medical Department to reverse their earlier position and adopt a more liberal policy encountered stiff opposition. One unidentified Jersey director is said to have objected that the new plan placed a premium on venereal disease and just encouraged men to go out and contract it. Nevertheless, the doctors in time had their way, and venereal infection victims were eventually treated exactly like other sick employees. A reduction in working time lost was recorded; even the director who had so vehemently denounced the policy change was heard boasting that Tropical's new and radical approach to the venereal disease problem had saved the company money and reduced the incidence rate.

By the time producing operations in Colombia were in full swing there were about fifteen doctors and one dentist on the local staff. Half these men were Colombians, and, as local licensing restrictions became more strict, the proportion of Colombian doctors increased. Difficulties were encountered in persuading medical personnel to stay on. Turnover was rapid; very few American doctors remained for more than one contract term, and most of the Colombians did not stay that long. In spite of this, some outstanding men served and contributed to the Tropical health program. Continuity of policy and management was perpetuated by close attention and control from the medical headquarters at 26 Broadway. The precedent for the application of modern medical science was well established by Jersey Standard in Colombia, and the techniques of application were learned by hard experience. The medical service of The Tropical Oil Company grew to be recognized as an outstanding achievement in tropical medicine, both curative and preventive. "This is the way we did it in the Tropical" came to be a favorite slogan, which helped to sell modern medical practices to many a doubting field manager in the Jersey Standard organization.

In Peru, however, conditions were believed to be different. McQueen is reputed to have laid great stress on the healthful influence of sand and sun in killing germs. Jersey's medical men were suspicious, but they could not invite themselves in for an investigation. This was one of the subtleties of the Jersey Company's relations with its affiliates. In a new venture, such as that in Colombia, the parent company experts dominated the planning and early management. An established operation such as that of the International Petroleum Company Limited in Peru, however, was allowed great freedom from control by 26 Broadway as long as satisfactory results were forthcoming. The headquarters medical staff was up against the practical reality that no service could be rendered an affiliate unless aid was requested by that company—or unless conditions were judged to be sufficiently bad to justify intervention at a high managerial level. McQueen's contention that Peru was one of the most healthful places in the world served to block an investigation by the Medical Department of conditions there.

A careful examination of medical reports from Talara and Negritos by the experts at 26 Broadway at length yielded enough information to show, on the basis of information supplied by International's own Peruvian physician, that conditions were by no means so favorable as the International directors had assumed. The seeds of doubt were planted, and Schoenleber was invited to accompany International executives on their next trip to Talara.

The Peruvian medical establishment was permeated with traditional concepts which had grown up under the British managers from whom Jersey Standard, in 1913, had taken over the La Brea concession. The British staff had been well cared for, but little consideration was given to the workmen employed. It was assumed that they would take care of themselves, as they always had done. The first company doctor had occupied a high social position, but he had no influence nor was he expected to take any interest in matters of general welfare. The local operating manager was the supreme authority, reserving for himself all control over such matters as medical policies, public health, housing, and even hospital construction. Twice a year the doctor submitted a requisition for supplies to the manager, who with great ceremony would go through the already modest list, congratulating himself in direct proportion to the number of deletions he could make. So meager were the purchases as to give rise to interesting stories about the instruments the doctor was forced to make in the smithy shop so that essential surgery could be performed. The economy in medical outlays was viewed as an illustration of operating efficiency.

This penurious medical policy carried over to the new International management, under which the old local staff remained virtually unchanged. Two lone doctors attempted to serve the needs of a colony of workers and their families which numbered some 25,000 persons. The physician in charge, a typical old-school, ultraconservative British gentleman, was perfectly satisfied. He greeted Schoenleber's suggestion that two additional doctors be added to the staff as "an unnecessary extravagance." The company had just completed construction of a new 6-bed hospital to serve a population of over 12,000 people at Talara. The resident physician was well pleased with what he termed "a very generous gesture on the part of management."

Sanitary conditions within the staff compound, Schoenleber found, were fairly good, though this circumstance was largely nullified by the close proximity of the camps provided for the Peruvians. There conditions were unspeakable. The rat population was enormous, and epidemics of bubonic plague had frequently raged. Smallpox outbreaks were perennial affairs. The resident doctor in charge, moreover, told Schoenleber that he had been puzzled by the common occurrence of a sickness which had all the textbook symptoms of beriberi, a disease then believed to be confined to the rice-eating populations of the Orient. Schoenleber found that beriberi was indeed prevalent—the direct result of the meager supply of fresh vegetables in the area. McQueen had been right. But for the sun and the absence of rain, few indeed would have survived such unbelievable conditions as existed.

By a remarkable coincidence, even while the Jersey Medical Department had the La Brea operation under surveillance, an astonishing climatic change occurred. The parched nature of this section of coastal Peru derives from the cold Humboldt Current, which hugs the shore along the west coast of South America to a point about a hundred miles north of Talara, where it is diverted westward into the Pacific. North of that point of diversion the warm El Niña Current produces an abrupt change to a climate marked by heavy tropical rainfall and a country blanketed by jungle vegetation. Occasionally—every forty years according to legend— the Humboldt Current mysteriously changes direction and wanders out to sea, being replaced by the warm waters from the north. One of these temporary transformations commenced in 1924. Rainfall in this and the following two years was increasingly heavy. Property damage was extensive, for the International camps had been constructed to meet prevailing desert conditions. Roads, rail lines, shops, and wells were washed away or made useless. The pumping station on the Chira River, which provided fresh water for Negritos, was put out of commission. The barren desert sands brought forth a veritable jungle of luxuriant growth. Birds, insects, and animals which most natives had never before seen in these regions began to appear. With them came the anopheles mosquito—and malaria. By 1925 the infection rate was higher in the Talara-Negritos region than in the Panama Canal zone; beriberi flourished as floods cut off the Talara population from its normally inadequate fresh food supplies from the Chira Valley. Under these exceptionally adverse conditions the work of reorganizing the Peruvian medical service was carried forward.

A new 75-bed hospital was approved for Negritos and a 50-bed field hospital was constructed at Lagunitos, one of the producing centers near Negritos. Additions to the Talara hospital increased its capacity to 100 beds. As soon as such facilities became available, a more liberal policy was adopted for the hospitalization of sick employees and their families. The medical staff was increased to eight doctors, a dentist, several technicians, nurses, and some sanitary inspectors. This staff would still have been inadequate had it not been for the company's great success in training Peruvian first-aid men to assist the doctors. Many of these men became exceptionally competent and reliable. Their skill bore witness to the high native intelligence of the Indian peons who formed the bulk of the working force. This staff provided free medical service not only for the company camps, which grew to contain about 35,000 persons, but for an additional 15,000 nationals living in villages as much as 50 miles distant, who came to the International hospitals for surgical treatment.

The entire population of the International settlements was vaccinated against smallpox and typhoid fever, and a modern water plant was constructed. In one sweeping stroke the existing native camps were condemned; in three years completely new quarters were constructed for the entire camp population. These new camps provided larger houses, wider streets, improved plumbing, a laundry, and garbage-disposal facilities. Pigs, chickens, and goats were no longer allowed to roam at will through houses and streets, but were confined in pens. New school buildings and playgrounds were constructed for the children—clubhouses and recreational facilities for the adults. The festering slaughter houses and markets were replaced with new buildings with screens and cement floors.

The effects of these measures could not be assessed in a short period of time. The most spectacular result was a sharp drop in infant sickness and mortality rates, which had hitherto been appalling. Schoenleber told the local manager of plans which would save even more lives. "We don't know what to do," the manager replied, "with those already saved by the medical department." This was an apt tribute to the medical progress that had been made in Peru, and a profound reflection upon the sociological forces that had been unleashed by the transforming touch of modern industry and science.

In Venezuela the failure to get large commercial production up to the end of 1927 had restricted the scope of the medical problem. The Jersey Medical Department participated in the planning and early developmental stages of this producing venture, but early efforts in Venezuela suggested that the Jersey directors had yet to learn that adequate medical care could not be conditioned upon success in finding oil.

The medical service in Venezuela followed the wildcatters. At the end of 1925 the local medical division consisted of 3 doctors, 4 first-aid men, and about 34 peons (employed chiefly in sanitation work). Four Venezuelan doctors cared for employees in areas where medical service was not otherwise available, and a company operating in Guanoco in northeastern Venezuela furnished limited hospital services. These medical facilities were generally inadequate to cope with the staggering local health problem. In 1924 the sickness rate in Venezuela was 1,332 per thousand employees, as compared with 1,159 in Colombia, 477 in Mexico, and 228 in Peru. The Medical Department at 26 Broadway continually pressed for greater expenditures, but until 1927 the small scale and the lack of success of operations apparently discouraged management from approving adequate medical appropriations. When the doctor in charge left Venezuela, Schoenleber wrote: ". . . if it is decided not to return Dr. Greenwood we will find it almost impossible to employ a good man if we are honest with him and let him know the conditions under which he will have to work."[97] After 1927, however, the medical service in Venezuela was rapidly brought up to a standard comparable with that attained earlier in other tropical producing ventures.

In Argentina the work of the local medical department attracted much favorable notice in circles outside the company. There, as in Bolivia, Venezuela, and Colombia, the doctors and their assistants initially worked under primitive conditions and performed miracles of professional skill and human endurance. At Tartagal a 50-bed hospital was constructed. The local manager was a strong supporter of the medical service, and a diplomat as well. The Tartagal facilities were opened for use by such adjacent Argentinean communities as could not be served elsewhere, and an extensive health campaign was carried out in the employee camps which attracted the attention of the national government. Standard Oil of Argentina's chief surgeon took a leading part in helping to control a plague epidemic that broke out in the north and somewhat later established the first training school for nurses in Argentina.

This pattern of effort was duplicated, though on a much smaller scale, in Bolivia. In the Dutch East Indies, where the need for medical reform was great, the Jersey staff did not take a hand until 1927. There was still, at the close of 1927, much to be done in many parts of the world, but already the precedent for reorganization had been well established and the central department at 26 Broadway had achieved a reputation which was not confined to the Jersey Standard organization.

Until The Tropical Oil Company commenced operations in Colombia, few companies had taken full advantage of the hard lessons learned during the construction of the Panama Canal. In Jersey's producing venture on the De Mares concession those lessons were applied for the first time on a large scale. In most respects this was a radical departure from industrial precedent because it gave the prevention of disease an equal status with curative medicine. It was especially drastic from the viewpoint of local managements, which thereafter were required to expend enormous sums of money to sanitate the field camps. A new item had been added to the operating budget; to some the addition initially seemed unnecessary.

Certainly the conservative attitude of the field managers (and some high executives in home offices) was a major obstacle to medical progress. The prevailing viewpoint was that, though the highly paid staff employees should receive the best of care, the native workmen should be left to practice such remedies as were traditional. Since no sickness benefits originally were paid, there was no particular incentive to keep the men well. Arguments that operating costs were increased by workmen suffering from chronic diseases and that high labor turnover resulting from sickness was expensive were usually passed off as theoretical. Once a broad general health program had been placed in operation, however, the results were too obvious to ignore. The breaking down of initial barriers of suspicion was one of the great achievements of Jersey's new medical division. The idea was firmly established, both at 26 Broadway and in the central offices of at least a few affiliated companies, that if a new venture did not have sufficient prospects for success to justify ample expenditures to protect the health of the employees, then that venture was too risky for the Jersey Standard organization to undertake.

Some gains from the medical program in Latin America were slow to appear, but they may well have been far-reaching nevertheless. Local managements were not long in finding out that government officials and others of influence who visited the camps were more interested in the hospitals, baby clinics, and sanitary projects as they applied to the national workmen than they were in the industrial activities. Such exhibits, though obviously not intended to serve only in this capacity, were good antidotes for the propaganda that foreign corporations were draining away the lifeblood of the Latin American nations. There is no way of assessing the public relations aspects of the medical work done in Colombia, Peru, Argentina, and elsewhere. An enlightened medical policy was not enough to stem the larger forces at work, but certainly by such means the sharp edge of nationalism was somewhat blunted.

The fact was that, although the investment in medical and sanitary work in the tropics paid handsome and immediate dividends to the companies, it was the community at large that reaped the greatest rewards. The influence of such work as was done spread far beyond the confines of the company camps and touched people who had never been treated in a Jersey Standard clinic. The labor turnover in all the Latin American operations was high, and eventually most employees and their families returned to their home villages. Each year the Jersey Standard affiliates turned out, in effect, hundreds of graduates who had lived under sanitary conditions far superior to any they had known and enjoyed the advantages of modern medical care. As these former employees scattered throughout the country they not only served as walking advertisements of what modern medicine could achieve, but they also carried information of great value to the communities in which they took up residence. Thousands of nationals, moreover, were trained as technicians, nurses, and *practicantes* in company hospitals. Of such skills the Latin American nations were in direst need. In a way, too, the company clinics prepared the way for the downfall of the alien doctor. The facilities of company hospitals provided hitherto unknown opportunities for the intern training of young Argentinean, Colombian, and Peruvian doctors—men who were later to take leading roles in stimulating and organizing the public health services in South America. Thus it was that the influence of the Jersey Standard medical service, successfully directed at the primary goal of increasing profits, permeated in both subtle and direct ways the very fabric of a civilization.

Possibly as early as the end of 1927—certainly by the middle of 1928—Jersey Standard's operations in Latin America and the Dutch East Indies could be regarded as a success. Receipts had not as yet caught up with expenditures in these areas as a whole, but crude oil was beginning to flow in satisfactory volume—this had been the primary goal. Such an operating record, obviously, is not explicable in terms of persistence alone.

Teagle had consistently refused to permit local distractions to obscure long-range objectives. When Sadler and Hunt had wavered, Teagle had stood firm. Repeatedly Jersey's president enunciated for the benefit of his directors the basic necessities of the foreign producing program. There is no evidence that Teagle was beset by misgivings about the Latin American or East Indian operations as grave as those which preyed upon him in his direction of the company efforts in Europe.

Looking upon the 1920's from the vantage point of after years, the fact is plain that the expenditure of capital and effort in Latin American countries enjoyed, from the very beginning, a greater chance of satisfactory return than similar expenditures in the Eastern Hemisphere. These countries to the south were swinging into a new economic orbit. American capital was beginning to compete seriously with and even replace European capital. German commercial penetration had been stalled, and Britain's interests were widely dispersed. As soon as the first vessel had threaded its way through the Panama Canal, the United States government conceived an impelling interest in preventing European economic aggression in the Western Hemisphere. All these factors favored company ambitions—though, as in Mexico, local trends of an opposing nature sometimes produced both temporary and enduring difficulties. Jersey records are not sufficiently complete to support a conclusion that the company and its executives found it easier to deal with the small, undeveloped, and faction-ridden Latin American countries than with the strong adversaries faced in Europe and the Middle East, but a surmise of this nature is difficult to resist. Influential groups in each of the Latin American countries wished to develop the native resources and realized that foreign capital was necessary for such development. In much of the Eastern Hemisphere, on the contrary, the political unit was often a colony or a mandated territory rather than a small independent nation. Economic development in many areas there had long since achieved a state of comparative maturity; almost everywhere were to be found extremely strong and well-entrenched groups who stood ready to fight any American entry.

The expenditures in Mexico, Peru, Argentina, Ecuador, Bolivia, Colombia, Venezuela, and the Dutch East Indies, therefore, had been well directed—at worst they could be regarded as a reasonable gamble. Mistakes of policy and management, understandably enough, were made. The existing organization was clearly inadequate to meet the tremendous demands placed upon it by simultaneous expansion into many areas. This deficiency was remedied as rapidly as possible. Necessary managerial adaptations had been made rather rapidly, largely because of the administrative capacity of Sadler and his assistants. Each individual producing venture was closely regulated by 26 Broadway. Inexperience, to be sure, provoked temporary maladjustments, but increasingly close liaison was built up between the fields and the home office. This co-ordination of efforts did not, unfortunately, appear to be so effective in the highest levels of management, where some disagreement over the direction and extent of the total producing effort began to appear.

On a broader plane, the men at 26 Broadway proved to be no more flexible than most of their contemporaries in other lines of business enterprise in adapting to the new spirit which was smoldering in some places and flaming in others. There was an obvious disinclination to regard Latin American nationalism as a permanent force, and there was a correlative determination to seek and expect a return to the economic philosophies and methods which had prevailed in 1914. Thus local pride was often trampled upon, and the forces of nationalism were strengthened still further.

Jersey men chafed at the restrictions that were placed upon them, often after heavy financial commitments had been made and much effort expended to obtain production. At the same time, few Latin American politicians dared to do otherwise than attack the foreign corporations. The contest between private and national interest, nevertheless, eliminated neither profits for the oil companies nor gain for the nations. In seeking and getting the crude oil it needed, Jersey Standard (and other oil companies as well) contributed in an important way to economic development and the advancement of general well-being in Latin America. One of the great misfortunes of that decade was the common failure by both businessmen and the political leaders of undeveloped countries to recognize the basic mutuality of private and public interest and to substitute co-operation for strife. The rewards for the victor in the struggle, however, seemed too rich to admit of compromise, and there still were few precedents in history for co-operation.

Chapter 14

Crude Oil for the North American Refineries
1919-1927

IN 1927, as in 1919, Jersey Standard refineries in the United States and Canada were running nine-tenths of all crude oil processed by the Jersey organization throughout the world. The efforts to supply crude oil for the immediate needs of Jersey's American and Canadian refineries therefore continued to be of dominant importance. Some foreign crude supplies, notably Latin American, were utilized, but the oil search was principally confined by economic circumstance to Canada and the United States. As in earlier years, the crude oil procurement program had dual facets. What the Jersey Company and its affiliates could not produce themselves, the organization was forced to purchase from others.

While the struggle for foreign crude reserves was replete with episodes of a dramatic and nonrecurrent nature, much of the domestic procurement program moved forward in routine and familiar patterns. Even Teagle, Sadler, Bedford, and the others—the master strategists of the Jersey organization—spent by far the largest part of their time determining where petroleum supplies should be obtained, what supplies should be sent where, in what amounts, and with what expected results. This, as surely as the weighty negotiations for the petroleum resources of foreign nations, was the oil business.

The routine, of course, was far from being the tedious. In the early and middle 1920's an undercurrent of excitement surged through the domestic procurement program. Established patterns were shattered, reformed, and shattered again with bewildering rapidity by the wildcatter's drill, while new philosophies and new techniques boisterously intruded upon complacency.

PETROLEUM SUPPLIES—THE POSTWAR ENIGMA

The Jersey directors in 1919 pursued a seemingly clear, if somewhat difficult, line of procurement policy. Total Western Hemisphere production by the Jersey affiliates was averaging 59,000 barrels daily, of which 18,000 barrels were required for the various refineries in Mexico, Cuba, Peru, and Argentina. This left a balance of 41,000 barrels, plus stocks in storage, available to meet crude runs in the Canadian, Louisiana, and eastern seaboard refineries totaling about 178,000 barrels daily.[1] Most of the remainder was acquired by purchase—by continued heavy reliance upon independent suppliers not subject to control by 26 Broadway.

Possible future trends were anxiously surveyed. The Caddo Parish wells, from which the Standard Oil Company of Louisiana was obtaining two-thirds of its production, were showing declining yields. Production by The Carter Oil Company was off sharply as a result of declining output in the El Dorado, Healdton, and Cushing fields in the Mid-Continent. Both Louisiana Standard and Carter had been purchasing heavily, to be sure, but in postwar months the Jersey directors pondered the problem of finding supplies to meet a booming market for petroleum products. Crude prices rocketed upward: Oklahoma crude from $2.12 in 1918 to $3.35 or more per barrel in 1919; Gulf Coast crude from $1.50 to $2.50. Finished-product prices followed on the golden path.

In the face of the impending supply crisis company policy could follow only one line: push production, purchase whatever supplies were available at less than prohibitive cost, and alter refinery runs to obtain maximum yields of the products in shortest supply (gasoline and fuel oil).

Jersey Standard, like many other American companies in a similar plight, turned hopefully to Mexican supplies for relief. George McKnight, secretary of the Manufacturing Committee, summarized certain limitations to this remedy. The Bayway refinery, he told Teagle, might run light Mexican crude in place of Mid-Continent. On paper the shift promised greater earnings per barrel. The practical difficulties, however, were that gasoline and kerosene yields would be less, the sulphur impurities greater, the repairs to apparatus excessive, and the depreciation in refinery equipment greater. Moreover, McKnight prophetically asked, would the supply of Mexican crude be certain enough to justify making the necessary conversion of refining facilities?[2] Despite these technical difficulties, Mexican crude oil did, as indicated in preceding chapters, materially help to meet the postwar supply crisis in North American markets.

In 1917 and throughout a part of 1918 Jersey considered sending Carter into Texas. Political considerations, however, appear to have dictated the alternative of purchasing an interest in a company already established in the state, allowing it to operate with a high degree of local autonomy. Two outstanding possibilities existed.

With the approbation of the Jersey board and the reassurance of Jersey's legal counsel in Texas, Teagle opened negotiations early in 1918 with Edgar Marston for the purchase of the Texas Pacific Coal and Oil Company, which only a short time before had brought in the important Ranger field in north Texas. A price was quoted by Marston, and the two leaders arranged a subsequent meeting to close the deal. When he met Jersey's president some six weeks later, however, Marston carried in his pocket a telegram informing him of new strikes on the company's extensive acreage. Marston doubled his price, and Teagle refused to buy.[3]

Late in 1918 consideration began to be given at 26 Broadway to the purchase of stock in the Humble Oil & Refining Company. This Texas concern had grown out of the intense dissatisfaction of small independent producers in the Gulf Coastal area with their relations with the major oil companies which controlled the pipelines and constituted the principal purchasers of crude oil in the region. In 1916 the Gulf Coast Oil Producers' Association was formed with the hope that in collective voluntary action lay an antidote for the individual weakness of the independents. A year later W. S. Farish, head of the Association and partner in one of the Texas producing concerns, took a further step and joined with two other groups of producers to form the Humble Oil & Refining Company.[4] Humble thereupon became the fifth largest producer in Texas. The company also operated a small refinery and topping plant; in 1918 it had commenced to build up a marketing division of bulk plants and stations.

Producing prospects were promising, but the newly organized group was badly in need of working capital. The Jersey Company, with ample funds, inadequate producing capacity, and a proved interest in securing a foothold in Texas, was the obvious prospect for a deal. A personal friendship between Farish and Teagle, who had worked side by side on the Petroleum War Service Committee and had hunted together, facilitated the contact. Soon after Farish had indicated his group's willingness to dispose of a part of their interest in the business, a party of Jersey experts journeyed to Texas, surveyed the properties, and returned a favorable report to 26 Broadway.[5] Not the least of the considerations involved for Jersey Standard was the opportunity for bolstering the organization through the addition of a group of able and experienced producing men.

Teagle wished to purchase a 60 per cent interest in the company.

Director George H. Jones held that a 51 per cent interest would be sufficient to comply with the Jersey policy of acquiring at least a majority
stock interest in affiliates. The Jersey Legal Department was reluctant to
recommend the purchase on any terms. Humble leaders wished the
venture to be a 50-50 partnership, for they were unwilling to return to
Texas and tell their stockholders that they had sold a majority interest in
the company to the Standard. This last viewpoint prevailed. On January
29, 1919, the Humble representatives signed an agreement calling for the
sale of a 50 per cent interest in the company to Jersey Standard at a price
of $17,000,000.[6] After the agreement had been signed, C. O. Swain, head
of the Jersey Legal Department, instructed Jersey's Houston attorney to
purchase five shares of the Humble stock on the open market in order
to assure the Jersey Company of majority ownership. This cautious
gesture was of little meaning. The Humble men retained actual control,
and in Texas—where echoes of earlier legal actions aimed at curbing
Standard Oil interests had not died out—it could not be otherwise.[7] Local
autonomy, moreover, was traditional with Jersey, and in this case was
doubly assured by the need for experienced producing executives.

Both Jersey Standard and Humble obtained what they wanted; it was a
near-perfect bargain. Humble received the financial backing it needed
without sacrificing autonomy. Jersey Standard not only was assured of a
greater actual and potential domestic crude production, but obtained the
services of an able purchasing organization to remedy that dangerous
dependence upon non-Jersey crude suppliers to which Sadler had pointed
with alarm a year earlier. The Humble purchase immediately added an
average daily production of 16,500 barrels to Jersey supplies, plus an additional 7,500 barrels daily which Humble was purchasing at the wells.

Operational returns at the end of 1920 clearly reflected the efforts
which were being expended to bring crude oil supply into balance with
demand. Purchases by affiliated companies had increased substantially.
Humble alone, in 1920, had bought an average of 34,000 barrels daily.
The crude production of all three companies had increased. Louisiana
Standard's production had actually tripled as the Homer field came in
with yields unprecedented in Louisiana since the early years of the
Caddo field. Notwithstanding these efforts, considerable quantities of
crude were being withdrawn from storage. Carter's crude stocks, for
example, were depleted by some 2,000,000 barrels in 1920—a decline of
about 16 per cent in the Carter Company's total stored supply.[8]

Before the end of 1920, however, total crude production in the United States had caught up with and passed crude consumption. Tanks which had been emptied across the nation began to fill again. The postwar boom in business hesitated in its spiraling course, and then began to recede.

The year 1921 opened on a note of hesitancy which abruptly changed to one of great alarm. General business conditions deteriorated rapidly. Prices of crude oil and finished stocks wavered briefly at their peaks and then plunged. In the space of a little more than five weeks prices at the well for various grades of crude fell 50 per cent. "The unfortunate part of the whole situation," wrote the head of Jersey's refining organization, "is that we are so blocked with products at our New York plants that we are having to curtail running instead of increasing to take advantage of the present low crude prices."[9] Notwithstanding some withdrawals during 1920, Jersey Standard, like most of the oil companies, was caught with large stocks of expensive crude. In three weeks Mid-Continent crude oil prices fell 50 per cent. By April of 1921 quotations declined from 1920 highs of $3.50 per barrel to $1.75. Shortly thereafter prices went to $1.00. Tank-wagon prices for gasoline and kerosene were down 5 cents per gallon; lubricating oil was off 20 cents a gallon; fuel oil down $1.05 per barrel. "Economy in operation is now the chief factor and the one which demands our constant and conscientious consideration," was Teagle's message to the company. Jersey operations were progressively curtailed, and the working force was reduced. By June of 1921 crude supplies and reserves, held eight months earlier to be dangerously inadequate for the needs of the nation, were seemingly far in excess of those needs. Mexican crude supplies, hailed in 1920 as indispensable to the American economy, were attacked in 1921 as a source of dangerous competition for American producers. Overproduction and ruinous prices almost overnight became the industry's problem.[10]

Company policy makers in mid-1921 faced a perplexing enigma. Seldom had the true supply situation been more difficult to assess. Was the 1920 peak an effective gauge with which to measure future demand? Or was crude oil overproduction, even after recovery from the 1921 slump, to be a chronic condition? Faced with the necessity for deciding whether petroleum reserves were too great or too small, the Jersey Standard directors chose to place their faith in continued over-all expansion of the American economy and in the long-term growth in world consumption of petroleum products.

BEGINNING OF THE DELUGE

The astronomical crude prices prevailing in 1919 and 1920 stimulated drilling activity all over the United States. Never before, even under the impact of war demands, had so many wells been sunk or such vast areas been tested for petroleum deposits. The fields that came into production as a consequence of this extraordinary effort—Homer, Hewitt, Burbank, Mexia, and many others—continued to pour forth their flood in 1921, oblivious of the crashing price structure and the market glut. Wildcat drillers continued, though less enthusiastically, to search for new fields, for this was their livelihood. Most operators in established fields continued to exploit their acreage, for if they did not get the oil their neighbors would. No force of law or ethics was as yet strong enough to exert a decisive restraining influence, though even oilmen had begun to protest against the oversupply which they themselves had precipitated.

Then, the quick price purge of 1921 having run its course, a new cycle commenced. Dollar sales volume turned upward, and it became obvious that the market's appetite for petroleum products was not to be easily satiated. The depressive influence of industry stocks in storage soon lessened, for such stocks, at the most, were equivalent to only a few months' consumption. Refiners tried to forget about their large stocks of high-priced crude and hastened to take advantage of prevailing low crude prices. Producers sought in increased output to compensate for the low profits they were receiving per barrel. Recklessly—lavishly—the search for oil went on. Carter, Humble, and Louisiana Standard all were encouraged to persist in their efforts to expand their control over crude oil reserves.

Humble's production in Texas leaped from 21,000 barrels daily in 1920 to 47,000 barrels in 1923, the year of flush production in the great Powell field. From a position of fifth largest producer among Texas oil companies in 1917, the Humble organization had risen, by 1921, to first.[11]

For Louisiana Standard the Homer field, discovered in January of 1919, was a bonanza—one of those dazzling episodes where the policy of buying protective leases in unproved but promising areas paid fabulous dividends. While, in 1920, Louisiana Standard was producing only about 12 per cent of the total output at Caddo, 2 per cent of the De Soto district production, and 1 per cent of the Red River field total, at Homer the company wells were accounting for 20 per cent of all oil produced. Producing Department profits leaped from $523,000 in 1919 to $8,454,000 in

1920, and then held at $1,626,000 in 1921, despite plunging prices and a rapid decline in the Homer output.[12]

In the absence of effective control over production, rapid depletion was the inevitable fate of the new fields. No well-ordered producing department could rest for a moment on laurels won in any single district. The measure of success, rather, was a sequence of profitable participations. While the Homer production curve was flattening, Louisiana Standard scouts were picking up scattered leases here and there where wildcat operations had indicated the possibility of new fields or extensions of old. The company itself did almost no wildcat drilling.

Just north of the Louisiana border in Arkansas lay El Dorado, the quiet rural center of Union County. No oil in commercial quantities had been found in this area, but good oil showings had been encountered nearby at Stephens and a large gasser had been drilled at El Dorado. Louisiana Standard picked up about 50 leases in the Stephens-Smackover-El Dorado triangle as a precautionary measure. On January 10, 1921, the Busey-Mitchell interests completed their Armstrong well Number 1, and the El Dorado boom was on. Louisiana Standard's leases at Stephens proved of limited value, but the company immediately bought into the El Dorado development, and in 1922 obtained a peak production there of 772,000 barrels. Within a few weeks of the El Dorado discovery in Arkansas, the Haynesville field in north central Louisiana was proved. A wild leasing and drilling campaign followed, but Louisiana Standard had acquired four leases there prior to discovery and was able to operate profitably on a modest expenditure. In the spring of 1922 Smackover, lying a few miles north of El Dorado, became the scene of yet another oil bonanza. Here Louisiana Standard had leased several thousand acres. This became the company's most productive field, surpassing, in 1925, even the flush production of 1920 in the Homer district. In none of these fields, however, were profits comparable to the price-inflated returns of 1920. At El Dorado and Smackover waste was prodigious. Gas was burned in giant torches or vented into the air. Millions of barrels of oil stood in open storage at the mercy of the elements while frantic efforts were pursued to complete pipeline and rail extensions. At Smackover a price of 50 cents per barrel was posted by the major purchasing companies, but producers lacking transportation facilities offered their crude for as little as 20 cents per barrel. As at Homer, production at both El Dorado and Smackover reached an early peak and began a precipitous decline.[13]

The Smackover field represented the culmination of five years of remarkable luck. After 1925 Louisiana Standard production fell far behind that of Carter and Humble. The company was not aggressive in adopting the new exploration techniques which were coming into vogue, and an ultraconservative leasing and drilling program proved inadequate to offset declining yields in established fields. The failure to emphasize production, however, reflected conscious policy rather than managerial neglect. The strategic location of its pipeline and refinery facilities and the low crude prices which persisted after 1921 dampened local enthu-

Table 11: **NET CRUDE OIL PRODUCTION AND ESTIMATED RESERVES**
Standard Oil Company of Louisiana, 1912-1927

Crude Oil Production, 1912-1919

In thousands of barrels per year

Principal Fields	1912	1913	1914	1915	1916	1917	1918	1919
Caddo, La.	1,745	2,935	1,865	1,721	1,337	1,021	1,001	923
De Soto, La.	....	25	437	180	80	46	31	21
Homer, La.	....	....	....	....	....	....	....	470
Red River, La.	....	....	....	514	498	219	130	86
Total	1,745	2,960	2,302	2,415	1,915	1,286	1,162	1,500

Crude Oil Production, 1920-1927

In thousands of barrels per year

Principal Fields	1920	1921	1922	1923	1924	1925	1926	1927
Caddo, La.	742	644	582	612	563	584	565	541
De Soto, La.	18	14	9	6	5	7	9	9
Homer, La.	4,263	3,277	1,446	1,029	781	612	548	490
Red River, La.	77	65	49	41	30	25	23	30
El Dorado, Ark.	....	643[a]	772	288	300	313	328	297
Haynesville, La.	....	14	640	288	167	132	73	64
Smackover, Ark.	....	....	331	1,619	1,726	4,347	4,075	3,010
Bellevue, La.	....	....	256	392	248	134	108	76
Other	....	....	....	53	71	56	84	168
Total	5,100	4,657	4,085	4,328	3,891	6,210	5,813	4,685

Estimated Recoverable Reserves as of January 1, 1912-1927

In thousands of barrels

1912	no data	1916	10,340	1920	9,502	1924	12,990
1913	14,459	1917	8,557	1921	9,702	1925	10,168
1914	12,445	1918	7,267	1922	9,417	1926	23,318
1915	10,361	1919	6,244	1923	12,991	1927	19,980

[a] Includes small production from Stephens, Ark., leases.
Source: SONJ, Valuation Reports, Field Summaries.

E. M. CLARK

E. J. SADLER

H. RIEDEMANN

C. J. HICKS

F. A. HOWARD

W. C. Teagle and E. J. Sadler escort Queen Marie of Romania
on trip to New Jersey refineries in 1926

F. H. Bedford, F. D. Asche, T. J. Williams, and J. A. Moffett, Jr.

Boardroom at 26 Broadway in 1924

Entrance to 26 Broadway in 1919

26 Broadway after enlargement in the 1920's

Service station in New Jersey in early 1920's

Service station in New Jersey in 1927

German curb pump in 1924

German river barge in 1927

Distributing station in Sweden

Fueling airplane with Eco-Essence in France

Well in western Venezuela in 1922

Bulk plant in Brazil in 1920

Mule team carrying equipment to the fields in Argentina

Carrying equipment to the fields in Venezuela

River boat in Venezuela

Inspection party at the Palembang office in 1924.
Standing, F. Horstmann, W. Haynes, local doctor, L. J. Farley, M. Balfoort, and
G. S. Walden; seated, H. G. Seidel, S. W. Emery, K. Armstrong, and A. F. Corwin

Pile driver on dock construction at Songei-Gerong

Carrying pipe in the Dutch East Indies in 1924

Laying a line in a Sumatran field

Drilling a well in the Dutch East Indies in 1924

Songei-Gerong in the Dutch East Indies in 1926

Landing at site of Barranca refinery in Colombia

Clearing the Colombian jungle

The road to Seminole in 1927

siasm for an extensive producing program. The Louisiana organization continued, instead, to purchase Louisiana, Arkansas, and Mid-Continent crude in large amounts.[14]

The Carter Oil Company, meanwhile, emerged from a sequence of operating experiences ranging the tumultuous decade from 1915 to 1925 as a solid, substantial, and reliable concern, not given to ostentation and not, it appears, so vitally concerned with operating efficiency as with the number of barrels of oil it could produce from its wells. In 1919 J. Edgar Pew's post of operating head of the organization was given to R. M. Young, a highly intelligent and forceful man who had risen in the company from the position of auditor. Young's first innovation was to remove Carter bookkeeping from the cuffs of the field managers and instill in the organization a sense of cost-consciousness. The company, however, tended increasingly toward conservatism, and Young's later administration was reported to be tinged with favoritism and lacking in drive. Practical men dominated the operating organization from top to bottom. Young lacked the technical background to back his geologists and engineers in the frequent disputes which flared between the old producing school and the new. Carter in this era, it is said, never adopted any new technique until it had been declared obsolete by its rivals. Like Louisiana Standard, however, Carter enjoyed a run of success that did not derive from gamblers' luck alone.[15]

Since 1915 the company's fortunes in the Mid-Continent had been characteristically fickle. Millions of dollars had been spent for producing properties at Cushing and Healdton, Oklahoma, and at El Dorado, Kansas, but these rich fields were declining at the very time (1918-1920) when crude stocks were most desperately needed. Because of the aggressive leasing program of J. Edgar Pew, however, Carter held extensive protective acreage in many parts of the Mid-Continent.

Early in 1919 the Hewitt pool, near Healdton in south central Oklahoma, was discovered. Carter at once developed some good production from two leases held there and, in 1920, augmented its original holdings by the purchase of 14 additional leases. In 1921, when the field reached peak production, Carter's net output exceeded 2,000,000 barrels, or 16 per cent of total field production.

Even as this field was becoming the company's largest producer, there were exciting developments in the Osage country in the northern part of the state. For many years after 1872, when the federal government had moved them to their new reservation on deserted lands along the Arkansas

River, the Osage Indians had been desperately poor. Then had come the discovery of a number of small oil and gas fields. Under Section 3 of the Osage Allotment Act of 1906 all oil, gas, and other minerals on this reservation were to be reserved for the Osage tribe as a unit. Leases for operating properties there were to be made with the Osage tribal council, subject to the approval of the Secretary of the Interior. From 1912, when the first Osage oil and gas lease auction was held at Pawhuska, Oklahoma, to 1918, when the western half of the Osage country was first opened for public leasing, a total of nine auctions had been held. Some 179,000 acres of land were disposed of for $13,196,000, and several small pools were discovered.[16] Carter had developed a small production on the eastern reservation lands.

The opening of the western reservation sections at the Pawhuska auction on December 9, 1918, aroused great speculative interest. This was unexplored territory, and Carter, the Gypsy Oil Company, the Marland Oil Company, and others all picked up leases in a few scattered tracts and began to drill test wells. Carter chose from among the vast expanse of rolling prairie a site 22 miles west of Pawhuska at Burbank, an inconsequential little trading settlement.

By September of 1920 Carter, which was first to drill in the field, had completed one well—a gasser. A second well was started, but before this could be completed the Marland Oil Company, on May 8, 1920, brought in a 150-barrel well nearby. Carter's second well came in as a small producer soon afterward, and subsequent drilling rapidly spread over the Burbank field in all directions from the two discovery wells. The boom was on, and the Pawhuska auctions became the scene of a frantic scramble for acreage—an Osage Monte Carlo, as historian Carl Rister describes it, at which millions of dollars were made and lost by highly competitive and sometimes capricious bidding.[17] That the industry was even then plagued by a superabundance of oil meant nothing. The Carter Oil Company, with 10,000,000 barrels of crude in storage, upon which large inventory losses had already been taken, was an enthusiastic participant.

Under J. Edgar Pew, Carter had paid many a handsome bonus for proved or promising acreage in an effort to establish the company in the Mid-Continent fields. For the 160-acre Manuel lease and the 165-acre Yahola lease at Cushing (the latter with 13 producing wells on it) bonuses of $460,000 and $400,000 respectively had been paid in 1915. In that same year the company had expended $591,714 to acquire the 100-acre Ward lease at Healdton, which had 8 producing wells at the time of purchase.

At El Dorado, Kansas, in 1916, Carter paid $1,148,524 as a bonus for the 240-acre Wilson lease with its 8 producing wells. Other bonus payments in these fields had been far lower. At the prolific Hewitt field Carter's largest bonus had been $150,000—and this for 600 acres of land. The Pawhuska auctions broke all records.

For the 35 Osage district leases taken prior to the discovery of the Burbank pool, all but one of which were undrilled, Carter had paid an average bonus of $35,609 for each 160-acre section. The first lease acquired subsequent to the Burbank discovery was the 160-acre Bait lease, on unproved land, for which Carter in June of 1921 paid a bonus of $351,000 to the Osage tribe. A second 160-acre section was leased in this same month for a bonus of $300,000. In 1922 three more unproved 160-acre sections were bid in by Carter at Pawhuska for bonuses of $160,000, $117,500, and $500,000. The highest bid ever made at the Pawhuska auctions appears to have been one of $1,990,000 by the Midland Oil Company, but Carter was not far behind. In 1923 six 160-acre plots, all unproved, were acquired by the company at a total bonus cost of $2,776,815—the individual payments ranging from $127,000 to $1,025,000. In 1924 three more sections were leased at bonuses of $230,000, $310,000, and $405,000.[18]

The development of the Burbank field was orderly, though veteran oilmen have since regretfully speculated as to how much more oil the magnificent Cherokee sand formation might have yielded under a scientifically controlled rather than a highly competitive drilling program. Possibly because of the high initial cost of the leases, most of the drilling was done by the large companies, and the wells were limited, by mutual agreement, to one for each 10 acres. By September of 1921 Carter was the biggest producer in the field, a position which the company appears to have held through July of 1923, when the pool reached its peak and began to decline.[19]

This episode in Carter's history highlights several phases of the company's operating policies and problems. By no means the least interesting question is that raised by the enormous bonus payments. Had company management, in point of fact, been seduced from reason by the intoxicating tempo of the Pawhuska auctions?

A compilation of 13 of the high-bonus leases acquired by Carter in the Osage district in the 1921-1924 period shows a total amount paid in bonuses of $4,850,315. The leases encompassed 2,000 acres, and on this land, by the end of 1924, the company had drilled 154 producing wells and 5 dry holes. The value of the oil produced, after deducting the one-fifth royalty specified by the government on all wells making more than 100 barrels daily, had totaled $14,570,000 by the end of 1927, at which time many of the wells were still young. This figure was more than sufficient to cover not only the bonus payments but drilling and development costs (in other words, the capital outlay), annual operating expenses, and yearly allowances for depreciation and depletion.[20] If Carter management had gambled on the Osage tribal lands, the fates had been good and the company was able to escape the stigma of extravagance. To the charge that the Osage spree scarcely contributed to that reduction in crude stocks which many oilmen held to be essential for the health of the industry, the old answer could still be given that what Carter did not take its rivals surely would.

Consumption of petroleum products in the United States continued to expand at a rapid rate, although in each year from 1921 through 1926 substantially larger quantities of products were manufactured than were sold or exported. The deluge of oil grew heavier, and the total crude stocks in storage increased enormously.[21]

Jersey's stable natural gas companies did not feel the impact of expansionist philosophies, but crude oil production from properties originally operated by these companies increased modestly. The gas of all the companies was carefully treated for its precious gasoline content. In 1920 the 35 absorption plants of the natural gas affiliates produced 32,000,000 gallons of gasoline, or about 4 per cent of total gasoline output by the Jersey organization in the United States. Little effort was made to expand markets for natural gas in West Virginia, Pennsylvania, and Ohio. Gas supplies in the old Appalachian fields being restricted, a policy was followed of limiting the amount of natural gas sold and spreading the available supply out, at higher rates, over a maximum span of years. In 1921, for example, the hope was expressed that natural gas consumption in those areas could be cut in half.[22]

In the newer producing districts of the Mid-Continent and the Gulf Coast the problem was one not of gas shortage but of surplus. Plants for extracting casinghead gasoline from gas were rapidly constructed by Louisiana Standard, by Humble, and by Carter.[23] With vastly increased production of crude oil by Carter and Humble and with increasing gasoline yields at the Jersey refineries, however, the output of casinghead gasoline and the activities of the natural gas companies became progressively less significant parts of the over-all producing program.

In 1925 the Hope Construction & Refining Company, which in 1918 had

Table 12: NET CRUDE OIL PRODUCTION AND ESTIMATED RESERVES
The Carter Oil Company, 1912-1927

Eastern Division, Crude Oil Production, 1912-1925

In thousands of barrels per year

Year		Year		Year		Year		Year	
1912	918	1915	703	1918	778	1921	721	1924	604
1913	925	1916	695	1919	814	1922	652	1925	640
1914	807	1917	760	1920	997	1923	618	a	

Western Division, Crude Oil Production, 1915-1921

In thousands of barrels per year

Principal fields	1915	1916	1917	1918	1919	1920	1921
Blackwell, Okla.	....	1	7	310	347	250	276
Burbank-Osage, Okla.[b]	....	....	25	79	317	385	1,445
Cushing, Okla.	2,810	758	534	374	214	149	206
El Dorado, Kan.	....	79	2,775	2,529	1,287	744	595
Healdton, Okla.	69	830	1,174	947	644	458	402
Hewitt, Okla.[c]	....	....	....	....	42	1,105	2,155
Nowata, Okla.	....	90	232	98	77	55	41
Okmulgee, Okla.	....	8	20	7	129	204	462
Salt Creek, Wyo.	....	....	....	....	....	....	21
Other	....	229	210	198	278	460	757
Total	2,879	1,995	4,977	4,542	3,335	3,810	6,360

Western Division, Crude Oil Production, 1922-1927

In thousands of barrels per year

Principal fields	1922	1923	1924	1925	1926	1927
Blackwell, Okla.	278	451	211	334	244	177
Burbank-Osage, Okla.[b]	2,588	3,253	3,304	2,933	2,014	1,294
Cromwell, Okla.	....	....	....	....	787	602
Cushing, Okla.	1,074	681	498	405	389	293
El Dorado, Kan.	509	441	373	541	456	382
Healdton, Okla.	354	323	302	281	262	242
Hewitt, Okla.[c]	1,515	1,318	1,040	880	945	770
Nowata, Okla.	35	29	27	20	29	44
Okmulgee, Okla.	821	304	691	1,465	109	110
Salt Creek, Wyo.	185	495	358	267	181	123
Seminole, Okla.	....	....	....	....	783	17,080
Other	410	349	315	261	353	2,272
Total	7,769	7,644	7,119	7,387	6,552	23,389

Western Division, Estimated Recoverable Reserves, 1915-1927

In thousands of barrels per year

Year		Year		Year		Year	
1915	7,154	1919	13,013	1922	28,489	1925	19,706
1916	10,373	1920	18,487	1923	28,487	1926	22,927
1917	15,526	1921	26,750	1924	28,825	1927	48,094
1918	14,929						

[a] These properties turned over to Hope Construction & Refining Company in 1925.
[b] Includes Burbank pool after 1919.
[c] Includes Boynton pool after 1921.

Source: SONJ, Valuation Reports, Field Summaries.

taken over the oil-producing properties of the natural gas companies, received a further increment to its scattered holdings. In that year the Carter Eastern Division, which was recording a meager production and steady operating losses in the old fields in West Virginia, Ohio, and Kentucky, was liquidated. Unsatisfactory prices for Appalachian stocks, together with competition from top-grade Mid-Continent and Texas crudes, were the causes held responsible for the poor showing. Such leases as were not taken over by the Hope Company were sold outright, and efforts were made to absorb the 660 Eastern Division employees elsewhere in the Jersey organization. From a sentimental viewpoint, wrote Corwin to A. V. Hoenig, then the leader of the Eastern Division, the move was a cause for regret. Here lay a historic segment of the Jersey business —an operation which in its heyday had been prosperous and colorful, a fertile training ground for men who later rose to prominence in the oil industry.[24] Dynamic transition, however, was the essence of the producing business. There was little room for sentiment or—as Jersey men learned in Canada—for operations that consistently failed to justify the hopes with which they had been undertaken.

Imperial Oil, Limited, had not succeeded in lessening the dependence of its Canadian refineries on imported crude.[25] The embryonic producing organization established at Teagle's insistence, however, was still alive, and one more effort was made. In 1919 the field staff was expanded, and a strenuous leasing and exploration campaign was launched in Alberta and the Northwest Territories.

In 1920 a much-publicized gusher was brought in at Fort Norman, on the Mackenzie River 2,000 miles north of the international boundary, but this well was soon closed in for lack of profitable outlets for the oil. Other efforts to locate new fields were unsuccessful, and in 1921 Imperial purchased proved properties in the Turner Valley, Alberta, field. From these a small production was obtained. By the end of 1921 some $4,500,000 had been expended on exploration, wildcatting, and leasing. The objective of heading off efforts by the Royal Dutch-Shell to obtain a blanket exploration concession in Canada appeared to have been realized, and perhaps this in itself was sufficient justification for the efforts and money expended. Sadler, however, was anxious to abandon all drilling in Canada, which, he felt, had been dictated more by political than by economic factors. Imperial executives continued to look hopefully to The Carter Oil Company for crude supplies, and to urge upon the Tulsa management the great strategic importance to Imperial of developments in Wyoming and Montana.

The Carter men were not easily swayed by such importunings, and there was some passing friction over efforts by Sadler, Hunt, Corwin, and others at 26 Broadway to have the company devote serious attention to fields which, if they proved up well, would greatly benefit the Imperial refining organization across the border. Imperial executives envisaged a flow of Carter crude from Wyoming and Montana to the new Regina and Calgary refineries comparable to that of Carter's Mid-Continent crude to the Sarnia plant in Ontario. As early as 1916, in fact, supplies of purchased Wyoming crude had begun to travel the tank-car route to Plentywood, Montana, and thence by Imperial pipeline to Regina.

This well-conceived ambition was at least temporarily thwarted by production difficulties and by the one-pool-at-a-time psychology of Carter management. The executives in Tulsa consistently concentrated upon areas, wherever located, which promised large immediate producing returns. Carter was a producing specialist, and Carter men had as little feeling for refining necessities as most Imperial men had for production problems. Cushing in 1915; Healdton in 1916; El Dorado in 1917; Hewitt in 1919; Burbank from 1921 to 1923—thus went the Carter record. Opportunities elsewhere were sacrificed, although (as Burbank in particular demonstrated) the policy of concentration had its rewards as well as its costs. Not until 1923, when the Burbank lease-play was well advanced and Carter production was established there, did the company begin in a serious way to consider those producing possibilities in the Northwest which were agitating Imperial executives. In this instance the Jersey policy of cajoling rather than commanding its affiliates was a cause of belated co-ordination of organization-wide effort.

Carter geologists had pointed out the opportunities in the Northwest much earlier than 1923, but their reports had not stirred the Tulsa management to decisive action. Even Jersey experts seemed reluctant to believe that Montana held any real promise as a petroleum-producing area. There were, to be sure, great difficulties attendant upon operations both in Wyoming and in Montana.

The Salt Creek field, in Natrona County, Wyoming, had been opened in 1908, but the inaccessibility of the region discouraged rapid development of what eventually became one of the largest light-oil fields in the world. In 1921 and 1922 Carter purchased a number of marginal properties at Salt Creek and elsewhere in the Wyoming oil districts. Much turbulent history was being enacted there. Claimants of mineral rights clashed with placer-mining claimants. Instances of claim-jumping were not unknown, and the use of armed "lease-riders" was widespread. There were also conflicts between homesteaders and drillers, and the courts tended to favor the homesteaders over the oil companies. On two occasions Carter drillers were run off their leases at gunpoint. The story is also told that one small but particularly aggressive oil company (which made its "stake" at Salt Creek and subsequently became well known and respectable) posted gunmen on the buttes to drive off rival exploration parties. Even if valid claims could be obtained, the royalty rates were high. On its eleven Salt Creek properties, all of which were on land leased from the government and most of which Carter shared with other oil companies, sliding scale royalties ranged up to one-third of all crude oil produced. Transportation difficulties there were of the near-insuperable variety.[26]

In Montana, as in Wyoming, natural obstacles were imposing. The discovery of the Sunburst pool in the so-called Sweet Grass Arch area, some seven miles south of the Canadian border, sent Carter geologists hastening to the region in 1920. Two years later two properties were acquired. Field conditions were primitive, roads were poorly suited to the movement of heavy drilling equipment, the climate permitted operations only during a part of the year, and the flow of oil was not encouraging. Had Carter been successful in Montana, the Imperial refineries might have benefited immensely, but such was not to be the case. Imperial was forced to rely primarily upon purchased supplies for such Sweet Grass crude as was needed.

Neither did Carter succeed in acquiring enough Wyoming crude to satisfy Imperial's needs. In both Wyoming and Montana the difficulties involved in obtaining adequate production were too great, and perhaps the effort expended was too small. The peak of Wyoming returns came in 1923, when net production from Carter properties at Salt Creek totaled 495,000 barrels of crude, an amount roughly equivalent to one-third of the Regina refinery runs in that year.[27] At the end of 1925 The Carter Oil Company was looking anxiously for some new bonanza, but there seemed to be a singular lack of enthusiasm in Tulsa for searching out a Cushing or a Burbank in the Northwest.

The producing returns scanned by the Jersey directors in January of 1926 yielded unmistakable evidence that the deluge of oil might soon diminish, in important specific localities if not in total. Louisiana Standard, it was true, had smashed all its own previous records as a result of its ventures in Arkansas, but Humble leases at Powell were diminishing in productivity and efforts elsewhere in Texas had proved disappointing. Every one of Carter's fields was declining—some rapidly. It was obvious that Oklahoma would soon be "finished" as an important oil-producing region and that Oklahoma firms would have to move elsewhere—thus ran the reasoning of veteran oil-seekers of the day.[28] The cautious Carter management, discouraged in the Northwest, disheartened by an uneventful year in the Mid-Continent, and prevented by organizational reasons from making a bid in Texas, unenthusiastically scanned the well-worn geological maps of its home territories. Management was concerned, too, with contingent issues which at one time had been considered inconsequential and superfluous to the producing business but which, by 1920, had become too conspicuous to be ignored any longer.

NEW MEDICINE FOR OLD FIELD MALADIES

Experienced oilmen grumbled that producing problems were growing more numerous with the passing of years. What very probably was happening, of course, was that difficulties once shrugged off as inevitable and incurable were now, in the early 1920's, being emphasized and subjected to the searching attention of specialists in the fields of law, of medicine, and of natural science. Only a few of these difficulties need be mentioned to establish the fact that the deluge of oil had precipitated a double torrent of uncertainty and of change. The vicissitudes that beset The Carter Oil Company may be taken as illustrative of those encountered in greater or less degree elsewhere in the Jersey Standard producing organization.

While anxiety over the large capital outlays in the Osage district of Oklahoma was rapidly being alleviated by the flow of Carter wells, legal problems of a formidable nature were faced by the Carter management. In 1916 the Supreme Court of Oklahoma had held that the traditional oil lease form was invalid, since it could be surrendered at will by the lessee but not by the lessor and hence lacked true mutuality. This decision, which would have invalidated at least 90 per cent of Carter's leases, fortunately was reversed in 1918 by the Oklahoma court. There were other leasing difficulties which were more permanent.

Long before the Burbank boom, Indian leases had proved a prolific source of trouble. Even the elementary question of who was an Indian— upon which the validity of many an Osage lease rested—could not always clearly be answered. The informal marital habits of the tribes made it next to impossible, in some instances, to trace and obtain clear titles. Forgery and perjury were commonplace, and a thriving business was done in Tulsa and elsewhere by professional claim disputants. Not until 1928 was the Statute of Limitations extended to cover Indians, with the result that until that time the oil companies continually found themselves fighting suits which supposedly had been settled earlier. In substance, no Oklahoma Indian title carried with it any real security, and exploration efforts were seriously restricted. Carter made it a practice to buy up both sides of important disputes, then referring the particular question to the Department of the Interior for settlement. Many properties were drilled without any assurance of ultimate ownership. This was a policy which only the largest companies could afford to pursue. Many of the small operators, unable to assume such risks, confined their activities to Kansas or to those sections of Oklahoma not subject to federal control.[29]

The reputation of the Carter Company for fair dealing, established under J. Edgar Pew, was strengthened still further in the chaotic legal tangles of the early 1920's. The influence and prestige of James A. Veasey, Carter's chief counsel, began to spread. The company fought its cases squarely, complained of no conspicuous discrimination against the major oil companies in local courts, lived up to its agreements, and settled legitimate claims promptly. Louisiana Standard and Humble were similarly openhanded. The Carter small-claims men, whose task it was to keep minor disputes out of court, followed close behind the drillers, making friends with the local residents and carrying with them checkbooks and the authority to make settlements without reference to the Tulsa office. Few other companies permitted their field agents such liberties, and few other Carter operating policies were so productive of good will as this one. Slowly the immensely complicated matter of leasehold law began to crystallize under the cumulative weight of adjudication. State legislatures and courts, like the federal government and for many of the same reasons, began to exhibit a comprehension of the problems and the necessities of the large oil companies, as well as of the small.

Despite local managerial rigidities, too, oil-field methodology was improved in several important particulars. In 1919 Dr. A. V. Schoenleber (the physician who later directed the fight against tropical disease in Latin American producing operations) was dispatched from New York to assume the position of medical director of the Carter Company. Here was a seemingly routine, necessary, simple, and painless effort by the parent company to elevate an important subsidiary operation to a new plane of efficiency. Nevertheless, Schoenleber's reception by the Tulsa manager was frosty, and he was told that no office space was available. This medical mission was saved only by the timely intervention of James J. Conry, then Carter's production manager and later to succeed R. M. Young as president of the company. Conry, a veteran who had served under Sadler in Romania, was quick to confess the crying need for a medical reorganization, and he promised to help Schoenleber bring it about.[30]

Carter's new medical director found that both the old field camps and those springing up in new producing districts had been planned with only elementary consideration for proper sanitation. The fact that the oil companies knew very little about sanitation was less surprising to Schoenleber than the obvious failure of those companies, Carter included, to make any real effort to learn. Worse yet, the public health departments in Oklahoma and other Mid-Continent oil states had virtually ignored the existence of health hazards in the boom towns and field camps.

Surveying the medical and hygienic deficiencies in the field was easier than correcting them, for there was no spontaneous demand among the older oilmen for a medical service. They had been raised in a rough school; their toughness and devil-may-care approach to the hazards of the oil business, disease included, were their badge of honor. No man was considered a real oil veteran until he had been through a bout of typhoid fever.

Schoenleber outlined a program of sanitary measures to be taken in all new camp construction—measures which would obviously benefit the employees and cost the company enough to jolt management out of its prevailing indifference. Strict and far-reaching regulations were drawn up so that standards in the older camps would be brought up to the level of the new camps as quickly as possible. Responsibility for the new program was placed upon the shoulders of the field managers, and for several harried weeks Schoenleber traveled from one camp to another to note progress and make his presence felt in the organization. A grading system was evolved to stimulate rivalry between camps, and local pride was stirred.

Real progress, however, depended directly upon the enforcement powers of the new Medical Department. These were soon tested. One field manager seemed determined to ignore the regulations and to make an issue of Schoenleber's authority to interfere in matters which always had been the sole concern of the production superintendents. After repeated failures to achieve the co-operation he wished at this camp, the medical director took the case to Conry. The recalcitrant manager was called to Tulsa and summarily discharged. Thereafter the medical program moved forward rapidly, and Carter took its place among the leaders of the industry in the practice of industrial hygiene.

The progressive spirit varied greatly in intensity among the various Jersey Standard affiliates—a circumstance which clearly reflected the high degree of local autonomy tolerated by 26 Broadway. The Carter medical reorganization preceded measures of comparable scope in the Louisiana Standard and Humble organizations, but both Carter and the Louisiana Company lagged behind Humble in adopting the new techniques of exploration which were revolutionizing the search for oil in some sections of the United States.

The geologist rapidly assumed a position of major importance in oil-producing organizations. In 1919 petroleum geology was a relatively new specialty, and emphasis up to that time had been laid upon surface observations. The possibilities of surface geology, however, were rapidly being exhausted by the relentless exploratory efforts of the oil companies. Moreover, surface structures frequently failed to conform to underlying structures; on the Gulf Coast even normal outcroppings were hidden under the coastal-plain deposits.

Emphasis began to shift to subsurface geology, although surface exploration and mapping continued to be an important phase of oil-finding. The Humble geologic staff, under the leadership of Wallace E. Pratt, was a leader in the new methodology. Early in 1919 the number of Humble geologists was increased from three to ten. A systematic collection of subsurface cores and drill-cuttings was commenced, and a research laboratory for the study of these samples was established in Houston. In 1920 Humble began to employ micropaleontology—the study of microscopic fossils contained in well samples—as an aid in finding oil. Subsurface exploration was further facilitated by the rapid evolution of techniques for obtaining cores and other rock samples from the depths of the earth.[31]

Careful analysis of bits of evidence gathered by many means and in many places yielded a growing knowledge of the contour and composition of subsurface structures. This knowledge not only was helpful in the location of promising structures and the outlining of new oil fields; it also contributed in an important way to the formulation of new theoretical concepts. The discovery, for example, by Pratt and the Humble geologic staff that faulting was responsible for oil accumulation at Mexia and Powell was an important one for the industry, since faults had hitherto generally been considered only as the means for allowing oil to escape from a formation.

While work along such lines was being actively pursued, various geophysical instruments for mapping underground structures were being introduced on an experimental basis. It was not, however, Jersey Standard's producing affiliates that took the lead in the initial introduction of these geophysical devices. In 1922 the Rycade Oil Corporation brought from Hungary the torsion balance, a delicate instrument which helped to locate the various rock strata by measuring their respective gravitational pulls. In 1923 the Marland Oil Company began to use the refraction seismograph, imported from Germany. This instrument measured the depth and character of buried formations by means of dynamite-generated shock waves. The magnetometer, which probed the subsurface by recording magnetic variations in rock strata, also came into experimental use. By 1924 Marland, Rycade, Gulf, Roxana, and other companies were all using one or more instruments for exploring structures in the Gulf Coast area. German instrument makers and consulting experts began to advertise in America. Several of the major oil companies either set up their own geophysical departments or hired geophysical crews from the contract companies, which were being organized in increasing number.[32]

In 1924 Humble took steps to organize a geophysical department, and by April of 1925 a Humble seismographic crew was in the field. In December of 1925, Humble was using nine seismographs, four torsion balances, and two magnetometers. Gulf then had ten seismographs and three torsion balances at work; Roxana, fifteen or more torsion balances; Atlantic, one seismograph; Marland, two seismographs and one torsion balance. The Rycade Oil Corporation, which earlier had been using ten torsion balances in the field, had completed its exploration work for the time being. By the end of 1925, Humble had surveyed about 1,100,000 acres with its new instruments and had located two prospective drilling sites.[33]

The precedents in exploration of Jersey's producing affiliate in Texas were followed only belatedly elsewhere in the organization. Carter's geological department under L. Murray Neuman had begun to experiment with the possibilities of micropaleontology and core studies soon after 1920, but the company lagged well behind others in augmenting subsurface geology with the complex new geophysical instruments. In 1926, when the initial experimental stage was drawing to a close, Carter began to use both the torsion balance and the magnetometer, but without any conspicuous success. Louisiana Standard, which was doing very little exploration work of any kind, appears not to have adopted any geophysical apparatus. Both these companies, to be sure, were conducting their exploration outside the Gulf Coast salt-dome area, the only place where geophysical instruments were being used successfully. Late in 1925 Româno-Americana geologists were actively engaged in subsurface studies in the Romanian fields. The Schlumberger system of electrical measurement of structures was in use at Baicoi, and the company management enthusiastically reported to 26 Broadway that no other Romanian company had been so aggressive in testing new exploration techniques. Standard Oil of Venezuela did not begin to use the torsion balance and coring techniques until 1927, although inquiries had been initiated by the local management as early as 1924.[34]

In geophysics, as in certain other phases of the oil business, the component segments of the Jersey organization demonstrated a conservative viewpoint. By the end of 1927 only the Humble Company had made any real progress in reorganizing exploration techniques. The transition, nevertheless, had commenced. When the detection of a salt-dome structure by Humble geophysicists in 1927 resulted, in the following year, in the discovery of the important Sugarland field, even the more cautious members of the producing organization were won over to the use of geophysical instruments.

The new field technology of the 1920's was by no means confined to exploration techniques. Electric power began to be more widely utilized for drilling as well as for pumping. Rotary drilling techniques were improved, and, in the early 1920's, this system of drilling spread from the Gulf Coast into the Mid-Continent. By 1927 the rotaries, which offered the advantages of speed in drilling and economy of casing, were rapidly displacing cable tools in most of the oil-producing regions of the nation. Better drill pipe, such improved alloys as stellite for drill bits, and a large number of minor improvements (many of them emanating from the makeshift machine shops set up in the fields) reduced drilling costs and enabled progressively deeper holes to be drilled. Rigs, tools, tanks, pipe, couplings, and all kinds of production accessories began to come under technical scrutiny in a sustained effort to improve designs and lower costs. On January 11, 1927, John R. Suman, a specialist of outstanding reputation, joined the Humble organization as director in charge of petroleum engineering. Following precedents set by the University of Pittsburgh in 1912 and the University of California in 1915, the Missouri School of Mines instituted a course in what was then known as "oil engineering," and in 1923 graduated four men, two of whom later went to work for Carter. The University of Oklahoma, the Colorado School of Mines, the University of Southern California, and the University of Pennsylvania all established courses in petroleum engineering between 1923 and 1928.[35]

Improvements in oil-finding and recovery methodology were accompanied by increasingly strenuous efforts to supply remedies for the profligate waste and the periodic oversupply situations that had long troubled the industry. The conservation movement, which achieved its real momentum after 1927, received encouragement and leadership from both the Carter and Humble companies, as well as from executives at 26 Broadway. But first, the basic issues and problems and remedies required clarification.

From the beginning of the oil industry the only effective and widespread remedy for overproduction had been storage. In performing this vital function the large operators, much calumniated though they were in so doing, measurably helped at times to preserve some semblance of industry stability by keeping part of the excess off the market and enabling small producers to obtain an outlet for their oil. The Jersey organization, which at the beginning of 1922 owned a fourth of all crude oil in storage in the United States, was an integral and important part of this stabilizing force. Nevertheless, the remedy diminished in effectiveness as the malady became more malignant. The nation's crude oil stocks mounted fast after 1922, but, even so, tankage construction failed to keep pace with crude oil production. The rule of capture, a healthful accelerator in earlier days when demand seemed likely to outrun supply, became an unstabilizing force as the supply of oil continued to outrun demand.[36] Certain individuals in the industry became aroused to the necessity for holding oil in its natural reservoirs in the earth until it was called for in the markets of the world.

Paradoxically, this concern about oversupply was accompanied by a fear of oil shortage which led to the development of a movement to conserve the national oil resources. In the early 1920's conservation efforts were directed largely at control of surface waste. The legality of intervention through states' police power to prevent waste had been established as early as 1900 by a decision of the United States Supreme Court. Many state regulations had, accordingly, been promulgated governing the drilling of offset wells, the plugging and casing of wells, and gas waste. The oil companies themselves had already made some voluntary moves to prevent physical or economic waste, or both. Carter and Humble both advocated wider spacing patterns in developing new fields, and both adopted ten-acre spacing of their wells. In 1919 Humble joined with Gulf to recommend voluntary prorationing of pipeline facilities among the wells in the Burkburnett field. Nevertheless, the problem of waste had not been attacked in a fundamental way.

In the 1920's attitudes in the oil industry toward the emerging conservation movement varied greatly. Many of the small operators held, with much justification, that measures restricting output penalized those firms which lacked the financial resources to indulge in such forbearance—however much larger the eventual yield of oil might be. Men like Jersey's Teagle, Carter's Young, and Humble's Farish showed a strong preference for industry self-regulation. They, like most oil executives of the day, accepted the older forms of regulation to prevent flagrant aboveground waste. These regulations were obviously beneficial and did not seriously interfere with established producing methods. Both the Jersey Standard producing men and their contemporaries, however, were initially reluctant to co-operate in efforts to restrain production in the interests of greater ultimate oil-field recovery. This attitude undoubtedly owed something to the prevailing heavy demands and high prices for crude oil. There was also well-founded doubt that effective control of production could be achieved by voluntary co-operative efforts, and in any case co-operative measures to restrict production clearly fell within the twilight zone of restraint of trade. The alternative to voluntary self-regulation—more government control—was decidedly unwelcome. But the major explanation for prevailing attitudes in the early 1920's was ignorance. There was little understanding of reservoirs and their behavior, and, consequently, little appreciation of the extent and nature of oil and gas wastage, the relationship of excessive drilling and unrestrained production to ultimate field recovery, or the nature and sources of the energy that performed the vital function of moving petroleum in its reservoirs and lifting it to the surface of a well.

A process of education was under way, but the process was a slow one. In 1923 the American Petroleum Institute, in response to the prodding of E. W. Marland and Henry L. Doherty, named a committee of four men to investigate and report on the production and conservation of oil. The report of the committee, of which Doherty and Teagle were members, pointed to the need for action to forestall harmful legislation aimed at regulation and control of the industry. It stated that, because of existing laws, oil-producing operations by the industry were accompanied by "great waste and the violation of all the important principles of conservation." Doherty worked out and presented a proposal which called for compulsory field regulation under federal control.[37]

Though industry leaders, including Teagle and Farish, in general agreed with Doherty's diagnosis of industry problems, they held his solution to be impractical and unconstitutional.[38] In January, 1925, the board of the American Petroleum Institute, of which Farish and A. C. Bedford were then members, indicated its flat disapproval of the Doherty plan. Anticipating this opposition, Doherty had already carried the issue directly to the President of the United States.

In December of 1924 President Coolidge had set up the Federal Oil Conservation Board to investigate the problems of the waste and long-term supply of the nation's oil resources. Both Teagle and Farish were apprehensive over the implicit threat of interference by the federal government. In January of 1925 the two men, then vacationing on the Norias Plantation in Georgia, addressed a long letter to A. C. Bedford, stating as their opinion that it was imperative for the American Petroleum Institute board to take a strong stand one way or another—either in direct opposition to the idea that effective conservation was possible or in favor of wholehearted co-operation with the Conservation Board. The co-operative course which both men favored envisaged the development of a code regulating production by the industry and the modification of existing state and federal antitrust laws so as to make such voluntary remedial action legally feasible. On January 12, 1925, Bedford proposed a resolution to the American Petroleum Institute offering full co-operation with the Federal Oil Conservation Board. The resolution was adopted, and a committee of eleven members was appointed to study the problems of the industry.[39]

This so-called Committee of Eleven, of which Farish was a member, returned a report which was firm in its denial of waste and made no suggestions for action. It ignored Doherty's plan for field regulation by the federal government and went as far in denying any danger of a shortage of oil supplies as the conservationists had gone in exaggerating the danger of imminent exhaustion of reserves.[40] The truth of the matter, made evident only with the benefit of hindsight, appears to be that contemporary lack of knowledge about reservoir behavior robbed both sides to the controversy of any sound basis for argument. Time proved the Committee of Eleven right on the question of imminent shortage.

Farish, the leading producing man in domestic operations of Jersey affiliates, set forth his personal views in response to a questionnaire sent by the chairman of the Federal Oil Conservation Board to leading executives in the industry.[41] Denying the right of federal or state governments to control overproduction, Farish instead advocated legislation to permit voluntary joint agreements among pool operators to accomplish that end. He denied that there was any danger—imminent or remote—that oil supplies in the United States would be exhausted, or that there was currently any substantial overproduction or waste in the industry.

These statements must be evaluated in the light of existing circumstances. Like most oilmen, Farish was apparently thinking in terms of aboveground waste, in the reduction of which some progress had been made. Moreover, in 1925 the most crucial problem facing Humble was not waste resulting from general overproduction, but rather the difficulty of obtaining adequate supplies of particular types of crude oil. It seems fair to conclude, however, on the basis of later testimony by informed oilmen themselves, that the position taken by Farish and the Committee of Eleven was influenced to a substantial degree by fear that an admission of the charges of waste leveled at the industry would result in the imposition of some form of government control.[42] This fear reflected, in part at least, a lack of confidence in the scientific premises upon which proposals for regulation were then based.

After 1925, the knowledge of reservoirs was developed by scientists and communicated to industry leaders at an accelerating pace. Discussions and papers at meetings of the American Petroleum Institute, the American Institute of Mining and Metallurgical Engineers, and the American Institute of Mechanical Engineers were helpful in disseminating information about the behavior of oil in its underground reservoirs. Meetings of the Association of Petroleum Geologists and the American Bar Association also contributed to a larger understanding of pertinent issues. Public hearings instituted by the Federal Oil Conservation Board in February of 1926, together with the temperate report of the Board the following September, did much both to spread knowledge of conservation principles and to lessen oilmen's fear of federal attention to their problems. And finally, a flood of oil from new fields late in 1926 dramatized the necessity for action to restore and perpetuate some measure of equilibrium between crude oil supply and demand.[43] In 1926, executives of the Jersey Company and its affiliates began to give positive support to the conservation movement.

As the year progressed, Farish—by this time president of the American Petroleum Institute and a figure of national importance—was an increasingly outspoken proponent of field regulation in the interest of more efficient and orderly production. Statements made in his addresses bore little resemblance to those of the previous year and showed the influence on his thinking of growing knowledge of reservoir behavior. No longer undertaking to defend the industry against all charges, he acknowledged that waste, both surface and underground, was widespread and serious and stated that the industry lacked cohesion and intelligent direction. While advocating a program of reform by the industry on a voluntary basis, Farish also urged specific extensions of state regulation—for example, he recommended in June, 1926, that the state of Texas establish adequate regulations to conserve gas energy in field reservoirs.[44]

Teagle, who had been among the first to protest against waste and overproduction, continued to urge constructive action by the industry in order to forestall possible harmful federal government action. Carter's James A. Veasey, meanwhile, was urging remedial conservation measures upon the Oklahoma legislature and oil-producing concerns. His address before the American Bar Association in September, 1927, stands as a landmark in the history of the development of American oil conservation law.[45] Both Veasey and Farish became members of committees established under government and professional auspices in contemporary efforts to arrive at some satisfactory solution to the problem of too much oil. On all sides there were much talk, some action, considerable hope, many fears, and a large amount of disagreement. By the end of 1926 conservation, like geophysics, had yet to be widely accepted in principle, much less tested universally in practice.

NEW SUPPLIES, NEW SUPPLIERS, AND NEW ROUTINES

The Jersey directors at 26 Broadway publicly expressed their satisfaction that by 1926 the producing affiliates were supplying a far larger share of the crude oil requirements of the organization than at any time since 1911. In private, however, much concern was being manifested over the formidable problems encountered in obtaining the remainder of the supplies that were needed. The duality of the procurement program was still a fact; purchasing policy was still commanding the continuous attention of the managers of the business.

The crash of crude oil prices in 1921 called for a quick policy decision.

Should the organization risk similar huge inventory losses in the future by continuing to pile up stocks regardless of price? A Manufacturing Committee memorandum dated June 30, 1921, supplied the answer and set the procurement pattern for Jersey and its affiliates. "We do feel," the statement read, "that every bit of crude tankage which we now have should be full of cheap oil before the crude market goes up." Stocks of crude held by the Jersey Company and its affiliates increased from 37,774,140 barrels in January of 1921 to 52,189,856 barrels a year later.[46]

The domestic supply situation was changing rapidly and forcing Jersey Standard to probe new procurement channels. Production from the Signal Hill, Huntington Beach, and Santa Fé Springs fields in California began a sharp rise. From January, 1922, to September, 1923, crude production in California almost tripled. Hitherto, California crude supplies had exerted comparatively little influence on the industry east of the Rocky Mountains. As early as September of 1922, however, West Coast crude oil surpluses began to come into competition with Gulf Coast and Mid-Continent crude.[47] The economical movement of California stocks was facilitated by the postwar surplus of tanker tonnage.

By 1923, when West Coast production totals began to rival those of the Mid-Continent, California gasoline prices commenced to affect market quotations in New York, which previously had been based primarily on the Mid-Continent and Gulf supply situations. On June 20, 1923, Teagle reported to A. C. Bedford that California production during the preceding week had resulted in a surplus over local requirements and storage facilities of 200,000 barrels, which were destined for shipment to eastern United States. Any efforts to restrain production in the Mid-Continent, Teagle stated, would therefore be futile, and a reduction in crude prices was the only way to bring supply and demand back into balance.[48]

In September of 1922 Teagle opened negotiations with K. R. Kingsbury, president of the Standard Oil Company (California), for the purchase of California crude. Teagle wished to obtain the West Coast stocks in order to cover a Jersey contract to supply the United States Shipping Board with 745,000 barrels of fuel oil monthly. The dickering that ensued was reminiscent of Teagle's earlier efforts to come to terms with Cowan of Indiana Standard over the Burton-Humphreys process rights. Kingsbury, no doubt, was fully aware that Teagle wanted the heavy California crude as a hedge against the possible decline of Mexican imports; Teagle, in turn, pointed to the low value of the California crude in view of flush production at Smackover, Goose Creek, Hull, and other Mid-

Continent and Gulf fields, which were yielding crudes suitable for fuel oil and little else. Terms were at length struck, and during 1923 the Jersey Company purchased 19,572,443 barrels of crude and fuel oil from the California Company. An additional purchase of 5,018,903 barrels of crude and fuel oil was made in 1923 from other California firms.[49]

These purchases represented a substantial departure from earlier established procurement routines. Between April 17 and June 5, 1923, Jersey purchases from The Prairie Oil & Gas Company, which had totaled 3,000,000 barrels of crude over the preceding half-year, were entirely suspended for a period of five months, after which they were resumed at a much reduced rate.[50] This severance of an old alliance was not, however, exclusively a result of the competition from California—as Prairie men seem to have believed. Carter and Humble were purchasing and producing more heavily than ever, and acquisitions of Mid-Continent crude stocks actually increased in 1923, despite cessation of purchases from Prairie. Jersey policy clearly was directed at the goal of concentrating, wherever possible, a larger percentage of the purchasing business within the confines of the organization and keeping the commissions and handling profits at home.

The record of crude runs in Jersey Company and Louisiana Standard refineries during 1923 shows the supply situation as it then existed:[51]

	Barrels	
Lubricating and light crudes		
Appalachian	3,456,550	
Mid-Continent	24,316,665	
Ranger (Texas)	2,606,630	
Mexia and Powell (Texas)	5,142,120	
North Louisiana & Arkansas	7,026,980	
Gulf Coast	1,767,413	
Peruvian	481,800	44,798,158
Fuel crudes		
California	20,991,880	
Smackover (Arkansas)	1,339,550	
Light Mexican	7,304,745	
Heavy Mexican	4,983,245	34,619,420
Total crude runs		79,417,578

The appearance of California crude in markets accessible to Jersey Standard was by no means the only unsettling influence of the day. Each new Mid-Continent or Gulf Coast field discovery set Jersey pencils scribbling. Purchasing contracts were under constant scrutiny, and the procurement program was altered almost daily as market conditions fluctuated. Despite the existence of a more or less continuous crude oil buyers' market after 1921, the major purchasing companies began to display an increasing disposition to improve the effectiveness of their buying techniques. This well-defined movement was a reflection of the fact that, even though business was brisk and crude prices were generally low, competition in refining and marketing was growing tremendously. On a broader plane, the new awareness of costs demonstrated the prevailing militant concern of American businessmen with efficiency at all levels of operation.

Jersey and its purchasing affiliates continued to acquire crude oil at prices specified in long-term contracts or at posted market prices, as they had done before 1918. Contract prices were determined to a very large extent by the relative bargaining power of the contracting parties, the existing posted prices being taken as a starting point for negotiations. As we shall see, an important modification in this contractual procedure was introduced in 1923.

Posted prices, which governed the noncontractual purchases, were established by large individual purchasing firms in accordance with each firm's estimate of prevailing and potential conditions of supply and demand. Repeated federal investigations failed to disclose any evidence of substantial collusion between these buyers, and Jersey Standard records contain no hint of collective action. Prices posted by the major purchasers, however, changed almost simultaneously—a condition that has been noted by economists and historians in other industries where the number of buyers (or sellers) is small. Certain companies acted as price leaders, though not consistently. Of the 48 price changes made in the Kansas-Oklahoma-North Texas district from January 1, 1922, to June 30, 1927, Prairie initiated 25, Magnolia 6, Humble 7, Sinclair 4, Marland 4, and Texas 2. These figures omit the North Louisiana-Arkansas-Oklahoma area where Louisiana Standard was actively purchasing in this period. Nevertheless, it seems safe to conclude that Jersey's three producing and purchasing affiliates were not exerting strong price leadership in either rising or falling markets, despite the fact that aggregate purchases by Humble, Louisiana Standard, and Carter exceeded those of any other single company or group of affiliated companies in the Mid-Continent.[52] This reluctance by the Jersey organization to act as crude oil price-maker possibly derived in part from tradition and in part from unwillingness to assume a position so vulnerable to public criticism.

Before 1910 prices paid by purchasers at the well in many instances had taken into account minute variations in the gravity of the crude oil. For several years after 1910, however, available supply and transportation costs had been the chief determinants of Mid-Continent, Gulf, and Wyoming crude prices. One explanation for this change unquestionably was the increasingly strong sellers' market for crude then prevailing. Efforts to recognize quality variations necessarily were restricted in a period when oil of any kind was sought at almost any price.[53]

With new and more intricate refining processes and lower refining profit margins came a need for increased attention to the gravity of the crude oils run. Greater discrimination in refining called forth greater discrimination in procurement pricing. Even minor differences in crude oil gravity were beginning to spell the difference between profit and loss. The Jersey Company, for example, found that with its new cracking equipment it could profitably utilize large quantities of the lower grades of crude in the manufacture of gasoline; hence there existed a real incentive to adopt some pricing system that differentiated between low- and high-gravity offerings. The abundance of crude in 1921 and thereafter, moreover, probably facilitated the introduction of a selective pricing system which producers might well have rejected had they correctly fathomed the trend toward low-grade crude utilization and had their bargaining position been as strong as it was formerly.

The classification of crude prices in accordance with a gravity scale began again in the Mid-Continent in October of 1921, when the Gypsy Oil Company posted a 25-cent differential on crude of 38° gravity or better. In July of 1922 The Texas Company also began to quote on a gravity basis. Humble and the Cosden, Sinclair, Prairie, and Empire companies had followed by November of 1922. In January of 1923 Jersey Standard set up its own gravity price scale. Further recognition of the importance of quality variations (as well as available supply and transportation costs) in crude pricing was afforded in Jersey's 1923 contracts for California crude. These contracts specified that the contract price should be established only after distillation analysis had demonstrated the exact nature of the crude. This method was also inaugurated in the company's Mid-Continent purchase contracts.[54]

Crude pricing, at the same time, began to be tied directly not only to the proportions of finished products that might be recovered from a given crude, but also to the market prices of those products. This was a step far beyond earlier practice, when posted prices at the well were determined only very roughly, indirectly, and belatedly by prevailing prices of gasoline, kerosene, fuel oil, lubricating oils, and the other end products. In 1923 the Jersey Company evolved a pricing formula for California crude which was tied to gasoline and fuel oil prices on the East Coast. These were the illustrative figures which Jersey men worked out:[55]

Terms: Price paid for crude to be 60 per cent of prevailing prices
        of products obtained from the crude
Computation of contract price per gallon:

60 per cent of Newark tank-wagon price for motor gasoline			$0.1290
60 per cent of bunker fuel oil f.o.b. Bayonne			0.0243
Approximate yield per barrel of crude:			
10.5 gallons gasoline at	$0.1290		$1.3545
31.5 gallons fuel oil at	$0.0243		0.7650
Total			$2.1195
Less freight San Pedro to Atlantic seaboard			0.8500
Contract price of oil per barrel			$1.2695

The contract which embodied these pricing provisions was drawn in May of 1923 with the California Petroleum Corporation and called for the delivery of 36,500,000 barrels of crude over a three-year period—an amount which would have been roughly equivalent to 20 per cent of total Humble, Carter, and Louisiana Standard purchases projected over the three-year period at their 1923 rate. Difficulties with the price formula commenced almost at once. While the first deliveries under the California Petroleum Corporation contract (some 900,000 barrels) were made at a price of about 2.5 cents per barrel over posted field prices, product prices soon declined so that California Petroleum was receiving under the contract formula only 57.69 cents per barrel for its crude as compared with the posted price of 70 cents. T. A. O'Donnell, head of the California Petroleum Corporation, protested vigorously, with the result that in January of 1924 Teagle caused the contract to be modified so that prices paid actually exceeded posted field prices. This action, in effect, destroyed the pricing formula and caused Teagle's refining managers to grumble over his unwillingness to hold O'Donnell to the original terms.[56] The episode well illustrates the broad attitude of Jersey's top management toward contractual relationships—and the occasional disposition of second-line management to take issue with that attitude when it cost the company money.

For a few weeks late in 1923 and early in 1924 Teagle considered the possibility of joining with O'Donnell to form a company and build a topping plant in California to process the crude which Jersey Standard was purchasing. Jersey's lawyers approved the plan but the directorate hesitated, despite the saving in transportation costs that would have accrued.[57] The old fear of antitrust proceedings may well have been voiced, but there were strong economic objections. A number of Gulf Coast rail lines filed revised rates in 1924 which made the heavy Smackover crude from Arkansas available to refiners at much lower cost; at the same time the volume of Mexican crude imports temporarily spurted. Sadler voiced the opinion of many when he charged that the movement of California crude to eastern markets was "unnatural" and could persist only under exceptional conditions. The decisive factor in causing the scheme to be laid aside, however, was probably a decline in production from the new California fields. So rapid was this decline, in fact, that by the middle of 1924 O'Donnell was unable to deliver the amounts specified in his contract, which was thereupon revised from 36,500,000 barrels to 3,680,000.[58]

In view of the uncertainties of Mexican supplies, the Jersey Company still wished to buy large amounts of the heavy California crude to cover its fuel oil commitments, but could do so economically only if California prices remained low enough to justify transportation costs to the Jersey refineries. As production increases slowed on the West Coast, however, prices began to climb. As a result, Jersey's purchases of California stocks continued through 1924, 1925, 1926, and 1927 in far smaller amounts than in 1923. After 1924 all contract prices for such crude were related to prevailing posted prices in the field, and no effort was made to incorporate in subsequent contracts any formula tying crude prices to the prices of finished products. In most cases, indeed, Jersey was forced to pay a premium over posted field prices in order to obtain such supplies as the company felt it needed.

Purchases of Mid-Continent stocks, upon which the Jersey Company relied to meet the constantly growing demand for gasoline, continued heavy. Every effort was made to acquire such Mid-Continent and Gulf crudes as were particularly adapted to the manufacture of fuel and lubricating oils. On March 21, 1923, the Jersey Company entered into a contract with the Marland Oil Company which called for the delivery in 12 months of 6,000,000 barrels of crude to Carter and 2,000,000 barrels of gasoline to Jersey Standard. Prices named were those being quoted in the field by the principal purchasing companies; the Jersey Company advanced a loan of $2,000,000 to Marland which was to be considered as an advance payment under the contract. Over the next few months additional contracts were made with Marland for large amounts of crude. By April of 1927, when the takings from Marland were terminated, Carter and Jersey Standard had purchased 27,300,000 barrels of crude, for which $60,021,587.29 was paid. Jersey men figured that Marland must have netted a profit of $3,000,000.[59] Purchases by Humble, Carter, and Louisiana Standard also continued to expand, while Colombian crude from the De Mares concession began to become available in quantity for export to the United States. The Colombian crude proved suitable for the manufacture of low-cold-test lubricating oils and placed the Jersey Company in a particularly good competitive position relative to other refiners, to whom only the heavy coastal crudes were available as a suitable source of supply for such stocks.

The fact that the Colombian crude was produced from Jersey-financed wells by an affiliated organization by no means guaranteed, however, that Jersey Standard could acquire this crude on its own terms. Price haggling between parent company and affiliates on this and other occasions indicates very clearly how large a measure of independence existed in the corporate family. Jersey's refining men and Alex McQueen, of International Petroleum, disagreed over pricing the Colombian crude. Teagle and Imperial's president, G. Harrison Smith, joined in the controversy. At length a price was set which was somewhat less than the Canadians wished to receive and a little more than Jersey refiners thought they should pay. The men at 26 Broadway also appeared to feel that their Texan as well as their Canadian associates were charging the Jersey Company a higher price than should attach to a very large volume of oil moving to a regular customer—and higher, perhaps, than would have been the case had that customer been an independent company. Bargaining over crude prices in this period was particularly sharp between Jersey and Humble. "Some day," Teagle wrote, "I hope to be successful in locating the exception which will prove the absolute correctness of the rule that no matter what you pay for crude, the producer is never satisfied."[60]

On matters of broad importance, however, the affiliates looked to the Jersey directorate for guidance. Both pricing and inventory policy continued through 1924, 1925, and 1926 to be subjected to analysis and change, the affiliates patterning their action more or less in accordance with the wishes of the Jersey board. Efforts to remedy the recognized deficiencies in existing crude pricing systems were not successful, and by 1926 no substantial and permanent crude pricing innovations had been adopted. It had become apparent by then that the Jersey Company and its affiliates could purchase crude oil only by paying the competitive price ruling in the various producing districts, regardless of what the company's own product market prices might indicate as the correct value of the crude. Even the choice of withdrawing from crude markets where posted prices seemed too high could not always be exercised at will, for the organization was forced to maintain its connections with producers and keep its pipelines and other fixed facilities employed.[61] In its efforts to inaugurate more effective pricing techniques Jersey Standard, mighty though it was, found itself circumscribed by competitive pressures and traditions, even as its most puny competitors.

Storage policy, on the contrary, presented greater opportunities for independent decision and action. Late in 1924 an important modification in procedure was being inaugurated by Jersey Standard in the face of an opposing industry-wide trend.

Total crude stocks stored by the industry had increased 179 per cent between December 31, 1920, and December 31, 1924. The Jersey organization had followed this trend, though total Jersey stocks had grown only 78 per cent over the period. Anxiously leaders of the industry probed the causes and implications of the tremendous and increasing stores of oil. Teagle reported, in a masterly and detailed analysis, that the situation had grown out of repeated overestimates by the industry of the amounts of crude that would be needed each year to meet market requirements. The reason for the overestimation appeared to lie in failure by the major companies (Jersey Standard included) to realize that vast improvements in cracking techniques had doubled the yield of gasoline—the major product—from crude, and that better methods of processing natural gas had helped to supply the clamorous gasoline market without touching crude stocks at all. One barrel of crude was going as far in 1924 as two barrels had gone in the years before cracking equipment was in widespread use. The result of failure to assess correctly the true worth of stored supplies had been a panic-tinged bidding up of crude prices each year in anticipation that the summer seasonal peak of gasoline demand would exceed current production and cause heavy drafts on stored crude supplies, large portions of which had been tanked at higher than prevailing prices. Teagle might well have added that oilmen had not yet forgotten the numbing fear of shortage which had taken possession of them in 1919 and 1920. Thus crude oil supplies in storage had not served their economic purpose of stabilizing the price structure by flowing forth with each advance in prices. The stored stocks had been too sticky in periods when crude prices were advancing—and the price rises had served only to stimulate production, which further increased those stocks.[62] The cost of carrying the crude stocks, moreover, had been enormous.

This was the situation, but what could be done about it? Teagle made no attempt to deny that Jersey, too, had maintained excessive stocks, and he pointed to the obvious fact that the company could not by itself bring about a more healthy situation in the industry.

Nevertheless, Teagle began to practice his preaching. Jersey Standard could afford to do what most smaller companies could not: that is, write down the value of its crude oil reserves in storage and bring them forth at a competitive price. This course of action commenced on a small scale in 1924, when Teagle urged Humble to cut its stocks. The Texas affiliate responded with a reduction of 2,000,000 barrels in 1925. Carter reduced its stocks by 1,780,000 barrels. At the end of 1925 total stocks held by Jersey, Humble, Carter, and Louisiana Standard were down 4,558,000 barrels from the level of the preceding year-end. Percentage-wise this drop was small (7 per cent of the Jersey organization total and 1 per cent of the industry total), but the decline worked in two ways. Jersey's excessive stocks were reduced, with attendant savings in storage costs and decreases in carrying risks, and the company was able to restrict its expanding purchases by just the amount of crude that it took from its tanks. It is possible that this action helped to ease in some small measure the competitive pressure on crude prices that was stimulating production. The precedent established by the new policy would have been even more valuable than the practical effect of the policy upon the industry—but it was not followed. Total industry stocks of crude leaped 14,000,000 barrels, or 3 per cent, between 1924 and 1925.[63]

On November 1, 1925, Jersey Standard crude stocks, standing at 61,698,789 barrels, were equivalent to 194 days' supply for the domestic refineries at their 1925 level of activity. This figure was better than the industry average of 213 days' supply, but still it was large. The company, however, was able to report empty storage capacity equivalent to 15,597,000 barrels of crude—evidence that the reduction program had achieved some results.[64]

By June of 1926 stocks held by Jersey, Humble, Carter, and Louisiana Standard had decreased an additional 8 per cent. The hope was expressed that Carter, for example, might reduce its stored stocks by as much as 50 per cent during 1926. The laborious process of reduction continued in the face of opposing industry trends. The question of how much crude to draw from storage was an infinitely complicated and delicate one, and the Jersey directorate did not push withdrawals to such a point as to produce a drastic decline in production or a major deceleration in purchases by the organization. The persistence in working stocks down, nevertheless, was remarkable in view of industry conditions. It almost seemed as though Teagle and his associates had already sensed, by some intuitive process, what lay undiscovered deep beneath the prairie at a crossroads settlement forty-five miles southwest of Oklahoma City.

Table 13: **CRUDE OIL PURCHASES COMPARED WITH PRODUCTION**
Standard Oil Company (New Jersey)
Affiliates in the United States, Mexico, and Canada
1912-1927

	Barrels per day							
	P U R C H A S E S							**Total Production by These Companies**
Year	Carter	Humble	Louisiana Standard	Domestic Gas Cos.	Trans-continental Pet. (Mexico)	Imperial (Canada)	Total Purchases	
1912	381	....	6,573	25	....	690	7,669	7,469
1913	429	....	8,645	69	....	744	9,887	11,596
1914	318	....	14,885	120	....	596	15,919	9,021
1915	45,763	....	21,157	143	....	1,358	68,421	17,083
1916	11,488	....	14,407	162	....	4,490	30,547	13,400
1917	6,557	....	17,988	156	....	9,817	34,518	20,087
1918	8,659	....	27,512	178	284	11,213	47,846	21,335
1919	3,865	7,449	19,352	186	2,360	9,889	43,101	54,250
1920	4,498	33,908	24,533	316	36,034	9,256	108,545	87,491
1921	7,585	44,660	29,805	248	22,573	12,859	117,731	103,653
1922	8,241	48,913	42,216	214	26,439	13,452	139,475	79,248
1923	30,897	51,936	35,626	239	9,586	10,858	139,142	141,460
1924	46,727	68,214	52,010	207	37,473	11,701	216,332	127,166
1925	59,792	86,254	45,745	211	42,353	10,941	245,296	136,184
1926	53,752	100,245	36,805	448	30,762	28,021	250,033	94,343
1927	46,178	165,960	13,765	427	15,846	26,117	268,293	122,760

Source: SONJ, Stat.

DEBACLE AT SEMINOLE

In March of 1926 Teagle was in west Texas. Jersey's ebullient leader related in a letter to E. M. Clark that he planned to spend ten days there and in New Mexico. "Ostensibly," Teagle archly reported, "the reason for this trip is to catch some trout, but the real reason is to get a general idea of this particular section of the country."[65] This was the vigilance which made Teagle a great oilman—the vigilance that ignored low prices and excessive supplies, those twin opiates which deadened the perceptiveness of many a producer.

It was by no means contradictory that Jersey men should urge restriction of crude output in the industry at the very time they were themselves bending every effort to acquire new producing property. Old fields would fade out in time, and their decline must be matched by new discoveries. One encounter with the specter of shortage had been enough for oilmen of that decade. And no one company, lacking any assurance that effective conservation measures would be worked out, could afford to stand aside while competitors brought in and dominated a major field. Prices were not so low that an important discovery could not make crude oil available to favored refiners at still lower prices. The search went on for the oil which most oilmen agreed was already too plentiful.

Among the many places where Jersey interests searched was Oklahoma's Seminole County. The first major oil strike here had come in March of 1923, when the Wewoka pool near the eastern border of the county was brought in. An excited boom ensued, and the wildcatters roamed the district seeking other pools. In October the Cromwell pool to the north was discovered, further excitement was generated, and more intensive exploration was stimulated. For twenty-eight months thereafter, however, no major finds were made.[66]

The Carter Oil Company geologists had noted the potentialities of Seminole County's echelon fault-lines at an early date, but they thought that the most promising land lay west of the area where the first discoveries had been made. Carter men in later years liked to recall that the geologists of a major competitor believed the central and western part of the county to be barren of promising formations, with the result that their company acquired no protective acreage there. Carter itself, of course, had also made embarrassing mistakes in various places, but Seminole was not one of them. The company's first leases were taken in 1922. These were four in number and comprised a total of 220 acres—all centered in Seminole City. The highest bonus paid was only $5,993.[67]

Even after the Wewoka and Cromwell discoveries, Carter continued to concentrate upon the still unproductive central and western county sections. From December 31, 1922, to December 31, 1926, the company carried on what subsequently proved to be one of the most spectacular domestic leasing operations ever conducted by the Jersey Standard organization. Convinced that oil was present and with careful surface geology as its only guide, Carter leased hundreds of acres of land stretching in a crescent from Earlsboro through Seminole City and south through Bowlegs, a hamlet that could boast of a picturesque name and not much else.

It is axiomatic of the producing business that the glory of discovery seldom goes to those who lay the groundwork. Carter's leasing program did not escape notice. Before a Carter rig ever had been set up in Seminole County several small operators were drilling madly on leases adjacent to those picked out by head geologist Neuman and his staff. On March 1, 1926, Morgan and Flynn's Ingram well Number 1 drilled in at Earlsboro. A week later the discovery well in the Hunton lime formation of the Seminole City pool was brought in by the Indian Territory Illuminating Oil Company. On April 21, F. J. Searight discovered yet another pool, which subsequently bore his name, four miles north of Seminole City. On July 26 the Fixico Number 1 well at Seminole City, on which a local resident and his wife had staked most of their possessions, began to produce from the Wilcox sand at a rate which soon went to more than 6,000 barrels daily.[68]

The Greater Seminole area, as the district embracing these separate pools came to be called, went wild. Carter found that its leases literally plastered the Earlsboro, Seminole City, and Searight pools, and then—to make the record perfect—Carter's leases south of Seminole City were found to straddle the Bowlegs and Little River pools, discovered, respectively, in January and July of 1927.

Now the economic fat was in the fire, but no one of the thousands of drillers, lease-hounds, roustabouts, shopkeepers, supply agents, builders, pipeliners, lawyers, contractors, livery keepers, card sharps, or ladies of easy virtue who descended upon the Greater Seminole district stopped to ponder economic implications.

Carter, caught with its rigs down, frantically rushed in tools, cables, engines, casing, pipe, lumber, and the thousands of accouterments which went into the drilling of oil wells. The first company well in Greater Seminole was spudded-in at Seminole City six weeks and one day after discovery of the pool and came in as a producer two months later, making a total of 77,980 barrels before year-end. Major companies and fly-by-night outfits scrambled for leases. Oil and water pipeline connections were pushed to completion, and earthen storage tanks were hastily shoveled up. Transportation facilities all but collapsed under the impact of the boom; trucks sank half out of sight in the red mud of what once had been quiet country lanes. Production in the district went to 120,000

DRILLED WELLS AND CARTER LEASES IN GREATER SEMINOLE DISTRICT
as of July 1, 1929

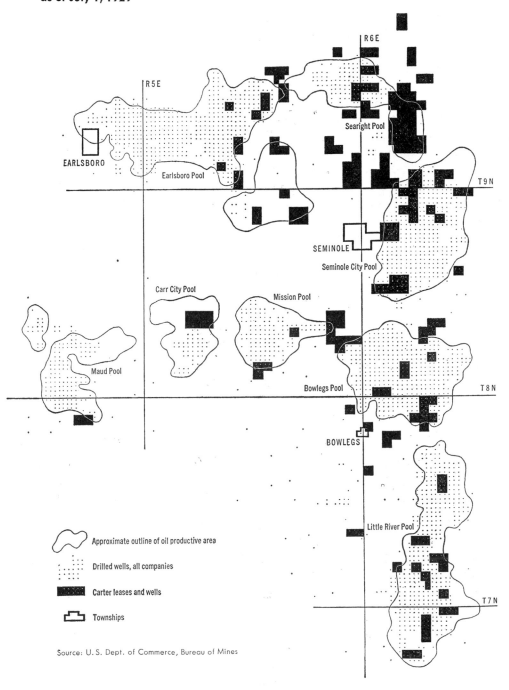

R6E

R5E

Searight Pool

EARLSBORO

Earlsboro Pool

T9N

SEMINOLE

Seminole City Pool

Carr City Pool

Mission Pool

Maud Pool

Bowlegs Pool

T8N

BOWLEGS

Little River Pool

T7N

Approximate outline of oil productive area

Drilled wells, all companies

Carter leases and wells

Townships

Source: U. S. Dept. of Commerce, Bureau of Mines

barrels daily before the year was out; some experts even hazarded a guess that an output of 150,000 barrels daily might be reached. On November 3, 1926, the worried operators agreed among themselves to restrict their drilling activities until storage and transportation facilities equal to the load could be built. On November 29 the bans were lifted. On April 24, 1927, production was at the rate of 342,000 barrels daily.[69]

There were few legal formalities and little order. Carter pushed its line connections through without stopping to inquire who owned the land or what the damages might be. Behind the line crews came the claims men, checkbooks literally in hand.

Drilling in the Greater Seminole district was wantonly competitive. Fine talk about conservation was drowned out for a time by the rush and roar of oil. Rotaries were used more widely than in any other previous Mid-Continent field. The technique was to drill with maximum rapidity to the overlying Viola sand, pull the string, and punch through to the oil-soaked Wilcox sand with cable tools. Carter geologists sat in Tulsa scanning the well logs that came in, trying to map the structural trends. Amazement grew as the cumulative reports began to indicate one of the most chaotic subsurface structures any of the experts had ever encountered. One well might record the Viola sand at 5,000 feet, while the offset well showed it at 4,500 feet. Then came revelation. The mad drilling pace was resulting in crooked holes. In one astonishing instance a Magnolia Company well was actually drilled into a Carter offset, with interesting producing results. Soon a device was evolved to determine whether or not the holes were going straight. This consisted of a bottle half filled with acid. Suspended in the well for a time, the acid etched a line on the bottle which gave a rough measure of the degree of vertical deviation. The Carter drilling superintendents, in a clear-cut case of old school versus new, refused for a time to allow any "newfangled stuff" to be dropped into their wells. The geologists won out only after demonstrating that vertical deviation was costing as much as $8,000 of unnecessary drilling expense on some wells.[70]

In one respect Carter was progressive—too progressive. S. F. Shaw, an engineer employed by the Guggenheims in Mexico, had worked out a method of forcing the water out of flooded silver mines by injecting compressed air. Shaw was employed by the Amerada Company to see if he could increase the flow of oil wells by injecting compressed air or gas into the well by a small pipe run down through the casing, to force or lift the oil to the surface. Shaw's first experiments failed, but in 1926 Carter employed him, and the experiment was tried again at Seminole—this time with a more powerful compressor. Shaw succeeded—brilliantly. A Carter well which had dropped in production from 1,000 to 200 barrels daily responded to the gas lift with an output of 1,200 barrels. Another well, which had declined from a peak of 3,000 barrels daily to the point where it was regarded as worthless, responded with a daily production of 4,000 barrels and then went to 6,700 barrels.[71]

Carter, noting that the gas lift not only boosted production but brought up oil exceptionally rich in light fractions, at once applied the method to its other wells. Competitors followed as rapidly as possible, and by July of 1927 Greater Seminole output was 514,000 barrels daily. The Seminole City pool reached its peak within a year of discovery—a record for a major American field.[72] Reservoir energy in the Seminole pools was prematurely exhausted, millions of barrels of oil which might have served for many years as a rich reserve were lost in the earth, the oil market was glutted by the oil that was raised, prices broke, and the operators came together again to institute remedies which already were too late. This, in substance, was the story of one of the nation's greatest light-oil fields.

Carter's producing record at Greater Seminole, understandably enough, was impressive. On April 21, 1927, the company recorded a peak production of 90,957 barrels daily, or about 27 per cent of total output in the district at that time. This was said to be the greatest amount of oil any company had ever taken in a day from a single field in Oklahoma or Kansas to that date.[73]

All but 160 of the 1,640 acres under lease in the Seminole City pool at the end of 1927 had been acquired by Carter before discovery of the Hunton lime, and the 160 acres leased after that time had been acquired before discovery of the Wilcox sand, from which the richest returns were recorded. In the Bowlegs pool Carter held 1,000 acres, of which 880 had been acquired before discovery. A similar proportion prevailed at Earlsboro, Searight, and Little River. By the end of 1928 the Carter drilling record on 3,700 acres in the Greater Seminole district comprised 153 producing wells and 53 dry holes and abandonments. The highest bonus paid per acre was $75,466 for the 40-acre Stepney lease at Earlsboro, acquired a year after discovery of the pool. Since Carter had purchased so much acreage before the boom started, the average bonus cost of the company leases was exceptionally low—most of the bonuses ranged from $1,000 to $3,000 for 40-acre plots. The largest initial flow from any Carter well was 7,005 barrels daily, from a well on the 40-acre Walker lease at Bowlegs, but many other wells made from 3,000 to 5,000 barrels. The most prolific lease was the Killing 120 acres at Seminole City, acquired on June 19, 1924, for a total bonus of $1,800. Twelve wells were drilled there—all producers—and yearly output rose from 34,737 barrels in 1926 to 3,301,560 in 1927, declining in 1928 to 1,868,628.

In 1927, the peak year at Seminole, Carter produced over 17,000,000 barrels of oil from its wells at Seminole City, Searight, Earlsboro, Bowlegs, and Little River. The company also acquired productive acreage in the older field at Cromwell. Carter's Greater Seminole production for 1927 was about triple the combined output of all the company's other fields (Table 12), approximately equal to the total combined output of Humble and Louisiana Standard in that year, and equivalent to 25 per cent of all crude produced throughout the world by Jersey Standard affiliates. Two and one-half per cent of all crude oil produced in the United States in 1927 came from Carter wells. Carter's stocks in storage leaped 4,000,000 barrels, and Teagle's program of inventory reduction—brilliantly justified by the events of 1927—was threatened.[74]

The complexion of the American oil economy was altered, not only by Seminole but also by major discoveries in Texas. The Prairie Oil & Gas Company, with large stocks of relatively costly crude in storage, endeavored for a time to hold the price line at Seminole by offering to take 35,000 barrels daily at prevailing prices if other large buyers would do the same. Within the Jersey organization there was some support for an effort at price maintenance. "Technically," wrote the head of the Jersey refining organization to Teagle, "the situation for the industry as a whole, from a supply standpoint, is not good, but I fail to see how a cut in prices will have any beneficial influence. It will not prevent the drilling of a single well in any of the proven pools, and unless a radical slash were made would not influence any wildcat operations. The cutting of prices, therefore, simply means less total revenue to the industry and increasing financial difficulty in carrying the burden of overproduction. Lower prices will not increase consumption."[75]

Teagle and the Jersey board, however, appear to have had enough of what Teagle, at least, had long believed to be a preposterous relationship between prevailing crude stocks, crude production, and crude prices. On February 22, 1927, Carter cracked the already sagging Mid-Continent price level by posting a graduated scale of price reductions for various grades of crude. For 33° crude the decline was 20 cents per barrel; for Seminole crude (41° and 42° gravity) the cut amounted to 28 cents.

Prairie, Sinclair, Gypsy, The Texas Company, and other large operators immediately followed Carter's unexpectedly asserted leadership. At the same time Humble also led the market in posting lower prices in Texas. Mid-Continent prices, already down from 1926 highs of over $2.05 per barrel, were dragged down from $1.75 in February to $1.22 in March, carrying with them prices in every field in the United States and in many fields abroad.[76]

The cause of conservation in all its varying and controversial phases was publicized as never before. Even the more conservative industry leaders hastened to lend support to efforts that might forestall severely restrictive federal legislation. W. S. Farish exerted strong leadership in the conservation movement. Throughout 1927 practical efforts were launched by Humble directed at conservation of gas energy in the fields, at control of production through voluntary prorationing of field output, and at achieving unitized field operations by voluntary agreement among the operators or through outright control of an entire producing structure by the company.[77]

By February of 1927 Farish had become convinced that the petroleum industry, united though it was in believing that something should be done, was opposed to remedial legislative action. Teagle, while favoring modifications of antitrust laws to permit voluntary action by the industry, was reluctant to entrust industry problems to politicians. Forcefully Jersey's president reiterated his earlier attacks upon prevailing price and storage policies.[78]

In May of 1927 Teagle and Carter's Veasey discussed the need for curtailment of production at Seminole with the Secretary of the Interior and the chairman of the Federal Oil Conservation Board. As a result of this conference Teagle called a meeting of leading oilmen at New York, at which the decision was reached to restrict the drilling of wells. Subsequent agreements were made restricting field output—which, to be sure, had already passed its peak. At the same time Farish and Teagle, at the suggestion of Secretary of Commerce Hoover, presented a plan to the Secretary of the Interior for voluntary unitization of field operations. Jersey's magazine, *The Lamp*, which closely reflected prevailing sentiments at 26 Broadway, carried a long article stressing the probability that the industry could solve its own problems and the desirability that it do so. In the same issue Veasey warned that, if industry leaders failed to put their house in order, the demand for legislative control of production would become irresistible.[79] Humble led the way by instituting a voluntary program of prorationing in the Yates field, the first major effort of this kind in the United States.

By June of 1927 Farish had so far departed from the thinking of his mentor, friend, and hunting companion as to state that the industry was powerless to help itself and that "the only solution to the trouble the oil industry is in is government control and help. . . ." Farish worked actively through the American Petroleum Institute to build up sentiment in favor of state gas conservation laws. In December of 1927 a Committee of Seven set up by the Institute reported in favor of such legislation.[80]

It was clear that disagreement in the industry over practical conservation measures had not been resolved, nor had concern about the effect of antitrust laws on co-operative remedial action been alleviated. By the end of 1927 only stopgap conservation efforts had been inaugurated. Nevertheless, the reckless extravagance of that year had caused all oilmen to recognize the magnitude of their problem and to ponder long-range remedies. This was progress of an important, if intangible, kind. Behind the gaudy luster of events at Seminole could be discerned the still amorphous form of a maturing industry.

PROGRESS TOWARD AN INDEFINITE GOAL

The need had been sensed somewhat earlier, but in 1917 E. J. Sadler had defined the most important single objective toward which the Jersey Standard organization must work. The goal was a nebulous one and defied exact limitation. Company-controlled production must be increased to bear a higher ratio to company crude oil consumption. No one knew exactly how high this ratio might be or should be, and for many years, indeed, there was little thought that any question would ever arise as to how much crude should be produced and how much purchased. From 1918 to the mid-1920's the goal had been to produce as much as possible, given the limitation that management must also devote time and funds to maintaining other branches of the business in a healthy condition. Great progress was made, as we have seen, in this direction.

In 1923 Sadler sounded a new note:[81]

As a policy question I think it is our interest that legitimate producers in the Mid-Continent are not put out of business. I also think it is our interest for the long look ahead that The Carter Oil Company be a purchaser of crude from a few of the large producers in the Mid-Continent field to supplement their own production in order to fill the Oklahoma pipeline and supply our steamers and refineries in the future. I do not anticipate that we will ever produce all the

crude that we need for our business, and even doubt if it would be desirable to
do so.

Company policy had veered slightly as the hazards of production and
the tremendous costs and risks of storage increased and became more
fully appreciated. There probably would always be substantial reliance
on purchased crude, and, indeed, there were compelling economic and
political reasons for continuing to offer an outlet for the oil of small
producers. The old objective of reducing dangerously heavy reliance on
independent suppliers, however, was unchanged, and toward this goal,
too, real progress had been made.

The total results of Jersey's crude oil procurement policies at home and
abroad for the years from 1911 through 1927 may be recorded with both
conclusiveness and simplicity, and some phases of Jersey's performance
may be compared with general trends in the industry. The vital question
of the cost of company progress is not easily answered, though some suggestive figures may be cited. The equally vital matter of comparing and
relating the procurement program to the development of other branches
of the business is best left for the final chapter of the volume.

Table 13 in the present chapter and additional statistical material in
Appendix 2 yield many conclusions as to procurement trends. The salient
points can be noted briefly here.

Net crude production by Jersey Standard affiliates in the United States
increased fourteen times from 1912 to 1927, but crude throughput in Jersey's refineries in the United States increased only two and three-quarters
times over the period. The initial difference between crude production
and consumption was so great, however, that, even after its relatively
faster increase, crude production in 1927 was still far below refinery runs.
In 1912 total company production was equivalent to 11 per cent of total
refinery throughput; in 1918 to 16 per cent; and in 1927 to 44 per cent.
The trend toward more nearly complete integration was broad and unmistakable. A comparison of total production and refinery runs by the Jersey
Standard organization in 1912 and 1927 yields further information of
interest.[82]

In contrast to the fourteenfold production rate increase by Jersey affiliates in the United States, total production by the industry between 1912
and 1927 approximately tripled. Jersey Standard had done far better than
the average producer. In 1925, the latest year in the period for which
detailed comparative figures are available, total net production by the
organization in the United States of 33,000,000 barrels was equivalent to

5 per cent of industry production. In that year Prairie produced about 13,600,000 barrels, California Standard 55,000,000, Atlantic 3,300,000, Indiana Standard 20,200,000, Shell-Union 48,300,000, Standard of New York 27,900,000, The Texas Company 21,200,000, Tide Water 25,900,000, and Gulf 36,500,000.[83] From a woeful deficiency in controlled crude oil

	Net Production			Refinery Runs		
		Barrels of Crude Oil per Day				
	U. S.	*Western Hemisphere*	*World*	*U. S.*	*Western Hemisphere*	*World*
1912	7,469	7,469	11,091	93,209	96,995	101,437
1927	112,380	181,606	189,911	349,295	420,773	434,321
Increase	104,911	174,137	178,820	256,086	323,778	332,884
Percentage increase	1404	2331	1612	275	334	328

Source: SONJ, Stat.

production in 1912, the Jersey organization had fought its way to the position of the fourth largest producer in the domestic industry.

Abroad, the producing program had already begun to yield decisive results, and the groundwork had been laid in many areas for even greater gains. Jersey Standard's total foreign production rate recorded a twenty-two-fold increase between 1912 and 1927; in 1927 Jersey affiliates accounted for 8 per cent of total production outside the United States.

The over-all picture of changing crude supply sources is presented on a yearly basis in Appendix 2, Table VII, but the following summary tabulation of total net crude oil production by Jersey Standard and its affiliates is useful:

	1912		1927	
	Barrels per Day	*Per Cent of Total*	*Barrels per Day*	*Per Cent of Total*
U. S. and Canada	7,469	67	112,976	59
Europe	3,622	33	4,908	3
Latin America	none		68,630	36
Dutch East Indies	none		3,397	2
Total	11,091	100	189,911	100

Reliance upon non-Jersey suppliers had lessened as crude oil production by the parent company and its affiliates had grown. From 1912 to

1927 the gap between crude runs, on the one hand, and production, on the other, appears to have narrowed greatly. The increasingly heavy utilization of Humble, Carter, and Louisiana Standard as purchasing agents also had the effect of moving the Jersey organization a step nearer to its sources of supplies and helped still further to complete the pattern of integration which had been distorted in 1911. In 1912 the largest purchases for the organization had been made by The Ohio Oil Company (19,000,000 barrels), in 1919 by Prairie (19,400,000 barrels), and in 1927 by Humble (60,600,000 barrels).

Producing efforts over the decade ending in 1927 had shown tremendous fluctuations in costs and returns (Table 14), but the primary task of building up substantial production for the organization had been performed by Humble, by Carter, and by Louisiana Standard at an over-all profit. Returns varied considerably for these three principal producing branches of the Jersey organization, and it was Louisiana Standard, the smallest producer of the three, that showed the largest profit and the most stable earning record. Total net earnings of the Louisiana producing department for the period amounted to $23,912,000. Humble was next with earnings of $18,846,000, while Carter showed earnings of only $3,272,000.[84] Carter's poor showing was in part the result of tremendous deficits in 1921 and 1922—presumably the result of heavy inventory losses. Humble was able by a change in inventory costing methods to avoid posting an inventory loss of several million dollars in 1921, and the company gradually averaged out over a period of years the high cost of crude oil stored in 1920. When the profits made by each company are weighted by the quantity of oil each produced, Humble—which in 1921 was appropriately called "Teagle's sick baby"—would seem to have emerged in 1927 as the most effective producer of the three. Such a conclusion, however, fails to take adequate account of the tremendously speculative nature of the producing business. Only the returns for a much longer span of time than nine years would balance out the element of luck and constitute a significant clue to relative effectiveness.

Not even a broad treatment of producing profits can be undertaken, moreover, without noting the substantial and changing influence upon such profits of the charge that oil producers in the United States made for depletion. Recognition of depletion as a cost of doing business was first officially extended by the federal government in 1913, though oilmen had long realized that an allowance of some kind must be made to cover not only the wearing out of their equipment but the using up of their raw material—the oil in the ground. The Revenue Act of 1918 greatly enlarged statutory relief to the oil industry by broadening the base for property valuation, thereby enabling substantially higher depletion charges to be made than had been the case previously. The fact should be noted that producing profits in the 1920's, when liberal depletion allowances were permitted, are not strictly comparable with producing profits of later years when amendments of regulations, interpretative opinions of the Bureau of Internal Revenue, judicial decisions, and changes in federal administrative policy resulted in substantial reductions in allowable charges. Had producing profits of the 1920's been calculated on cost bases allowed a decade later, such profits would have been higher than those recorded. Inconsistencies arising out of procedural changes, of course, color many, if not most, of the statistical series upon which the historian is forced to rely so heavily. The issue of depletion is singled out only because of the degree of its importance to the oil industry.

In Jersey Standard producing history the year 1927 marks a division point comparable in vividness to the year of the dissolution. As in 1911, external events were pressing hard on the policy makers of the organization. For ten years following the dissolution decree the Jersey directors had seen only short intervals when scarce and costly crude oil had not been the rule and the problem. In 1921 the reversal commenced. In 1926 there had been momentary hope in some quarters that supplies would not swamp demand, but the events of 1927 dramatically confirmed the trend inaugurated six years before. Policy in 1927 had to be reformulated to meet the acknowledged and apparently chronic condition of too much oil—this was the primary problem of the immediate future. In 1927 the production expansionists were in disrepute, and the immediately ensuing years were to bring them little glory. Still hidden from the view of the industry's prophets was that further day when the territorial crude oil reserves which Jersey Standard so tenaciously sought and finally acquired were to have a new meaning and purpose and value.

Table 14: NET EARNINGS FROM CRUDE OIL PRODUCING AND PURCHASING
Standard Oil Company (New Jersey) and Affiliates, 1912-1927

Earnings — Dollar figures in thousands (Parentheses indicate net loss)

Earnings	1912	1913	1914	1915	1916	1917	1918	1919
DOMESTIC								
Jersey Standard[a]	$ 689	$ 991	$ 596	$ 1,035	$ 1,145	$ 395	$ 3,135	$ 2,267
Carter	738	1,121	62	452	3,323	5,739	2,734	(965)
Louisiana Standard	140	2,423	(306)	(396)	298	649	606	523
Humble	—	—	—	—	—	—	—	(631)
Other	31	21	7	9	11	19	8	(1)
Total domestic	$ 1,598	$ 4,556	$ 359	$ 1,100	$ 4,777	$ 6,802	$ 6,483	$ 1,193
FOREIGN								
Canadian								
Imperial	—	—	$ 220	—	—	—	—	—
Latin American[b]								
Transcontinental	—	—	—	—	—	—	$ (606)	$ 1,096
International Pet.	—	—	—	—	—	—	—	1,124
Other	—	—	—	—	—	—	977	762
Total Latin American	—	—	—	—	—	—	$ 371	$ 2,982
European								
Româno-Americana	$ (92)	$ 993	$ 1,036	$ 453	$ 658	d	d	$ 265
Other	—	—	—	—	—	—	—	—
Total European	$ (92)	$ 993	$ 1,036	$ 453	$ 658	d	d	$ 265
Total domestic and foreign	$ 1,506	$ 5,549	$ 1,615	$ 1,553	$ 5,435	$ 6,802	$ 6,854	$ 4,440

Earnings as percentage of Jersey total producing and purchasing earnings[c]

	1912	1913	1914	1915	1916	1917	1918	1919
Domestic	106.1	82.1	22.2	70.8	87.9	100.0	94.6	26.9
Canadian	—	—	13.7	—	—	—	—	—
Latin American	—	—	—	—	—	—	5.4	67.2
European	(6.1)	17.9	64.1	29.2	12.1	d	d	5.9
Total	100.0	100.0	100.0	100.0	100.0	100.0	100.0	100.0
Jersey producing and purchasing earnings as percentage of Jersey total earnings[c]	4.3	12.1	5.2	2.5	7.6	6.5	8.8	9.2

[a] Net earnings on purchases of Mexican and other crude oil.

[b] The figures reported on Jersey statements and contained in this table fail to give a completely accurate picture of the profits which were being made in certain segments of the producing organization, notably in Latin America. From 1920 through 1927, for example, International Petroleum reported total net profits of $95,151,556. As its share of those earnings, however, the Jersey Company recorded only $23,880,000 actually received in dividends and special payments, and it is this amount which finds its way onto the Jersey books and is recorded in this table. Conversely, the Jersey accounts also fail to reflect the large expenditures made by the organization in Venezuela, since the returns of the Standard Oil Company of Venezuela were not consolidated with the parent company. All such balancing factors considered, the given figures

Table 14 (cont.): NET EARNINGS FROM CRUDE OIL PRODUCING AND PURCHASING
Standard Oil Company (New Jersey) and Affiliates, 1912-1927

Dollar figures in thousands (Parentheses indicate net loss) — Earnings

1920	1921	1922	1923	1924	1925	1926	1927	
								DOMESTIC
$ 4,841	$ (1,676)	$ 1,516	$ 716	$ (3,452)	$ (311)	$ 215	$ (108)	Jersey Standard[a]
3,951	(7,093)	(8,636)	851	(1,474)	5,869	7,571	3,197	Carter
8,454	1,626	2,499	1,409	56	3,224	4,263	1,858	Louisiana Standard
3,462	(628)	412	2,297	5,169	8,601	5,531	(5,367)	Humble
26	(9)	3	(1)	26	(6)	(1)	(2)	Other
$ 20,734	$ (7,780)	$(4,206)	$ 5,272	$ 325	$ 17,377	$ 17,579	$ (422)	Total domestic
								FOREIGN **Canadian**
—	$ (90)	$ (16)	$ (3)	$ (11)	$ (1)	$ (11)	—	Imperial
								Latin American[b]
$ 13,158	$ 6,453	$(2,225)	$ (40)	$ 8,445	$ 14,121	$ 1,862	$ 839	Transcontinental
397	11,734	1,564	768	2,272	1,525	2,253	2,240	International Pet.
—	—	—	—	—	—	—	(23)	Other
$ 13,555	$ 18,187	$ (661)	$ 728	$ 10,717	$ 15,646	$ 4,115	$ 3,056	Total Latin American
								European
$ 7	$ 166	$ 86	$ 1	$ 73	$ 185	$ (1,097)	$ (402)	Româno-Americana
—	1	1	—	—	—	—	—	Other
$ 7	$ 167	$ 87	$ 1	$ 73	$ 185	$ (1,097)	$ (402)	Total European
$ 34,296	$ 10,484	$(4,796)	$ 5,998	$ 11,104	$ 33,207	$ 20,586	$ 2,232	**Total domestic and foreign**

Earnings as percentage of Jersey total producing and purchasing earnings[c]

1920	1921	1922	1923	1924	1925	1926	1927	
60.5	(74.2)	(87.7)	87.9	2.9	52.3	85.4	(18.9)	Domestic
—	(1.0)	(0.3)	e	(0.1)	e	(0.1)	—	Canadian
39.5	173.6	(13.8)	12.1	96.5	47.1	20.0	136.9	Latin American
e	1.6	1.8	e	0.7	0.6	(5.3)	(18.0)	European
100.0	100.0	(100.0)	100.0	100.0	100.0	100.0	100.0	Total
23.1	31.0	(10.4)	10.7	13.7	29.9	17.5	5.5	Jersey producing and purchasing earnings as percentage of Jersey total earnings[c]

for producing earnings would appear to be highly conservative.

[c] Since the percentage figure for any one earnings classification is determined not only by the actual amount recorded in that classification but also by earnings and losses in each of the others, no attempt should be made to trace year-to-year variations in one classification without careful reference both to other percentage classifications and to the pertinent dollar figures. All

functional earnings figures given in SONJ, Fin. Recs., for the years 1912 through 1924 have been adjusted by the authors to match, insofar as possible, the account classifications employed in those records in the years 1925 through 1927.

[d] Comparable data not available.

[e] Less than 0.1 per cent.

Source: SONJ, Stat.

Chapter 15

The Changing Transportation Pattern
1919-1927

INTEGRATING THE PIPELINES

B Y 1920 the Jersey Company had made great progress in building up
those branches of the business which had previously required heavy
dependence upon nonaffiliated companies. No serious effort, however,
had been made to alter the existing pattern of pipeline transportation.
Jersey Standard continued to rely heavily upon the pipelines of the Prairie
Pipe Line Company and connecting carriers for the movement of crude
oil east to the seaboard refineries. In 1919 Jersey called upon these lines
to move 75,000 barrels daily for the Bayonne and Bayway refineries alone.
Prairie lines also served some of the Carter fields, initiated the flow of
considerable quantities of Mid-Continent oil south to Baton Rouge and
north to the Imperial refineries, and formed the Arkansas connecting link
between the lines of Louisiana Standard and the Oklahoma Pipe Line
Company. The Prairie organization also produced or purchased large
quantities of crude for the Jersey Company and its affiliates.

For many years this system had operated with great efficiency. Relations between the Jersey Company and its one-time affiliate were harmonious. As Prairie's largest customer, Jersey Standard expected and
usually received excellent service. The working partnership derived particular effectiveness from the fact that the grip of large companies on
the nation's petroleum transportation system had remained a tight one.

Up to 1918 neither the dissolution decree of 1911 nor the common
carrier decision of 1914 had succeeded in forcing the pipelines to serve
the needs of the small independent producer—or, indeed, the needs of
anyone they did not wish to serve. This situation continued to prevail
through the 1920's. Producers lacking a pipeline affiliation of their own
still were forced to sell their output at the well to the pipeline companies
—a necessity which continued to give rise to highly agitated controversies

over prices and takings. Even where producing areas came to be served by several rival networks, independent producers found themselves unable in many instances to obtain the prices they wished or to stir up strong competitive bidding for their supplies among the pipeline companies.[1] This condition, primarily the result of overproduction and large surplus stocks of crude, was blamed on the selfishness of the pipeline operators. Many small producers continued to believe that the remedy for their plight lay in forcing the pipeline companies to perform the common carrier function and transport the producers' oil to markets away from the fields. This alternative was blocked by the continued refusal or inability of the lines—all of which were busily employed in supplying the needs of established customers or affiliates—to act as common carriers and by the Interstate Commerce Commission's continued laxity in promulgating new regulations or enforcing old ones which would force the lines to do so.[2] From 1918 through 1927 Jersey Standard's domestic pipeline affiliates continued, with few exceptions and despite their common carrier designation, to carry only the crude oil of the Jersey organization. This was true of other lines as well, but many of those changes regarded as desirable by federal regulatory bodies were nonetheless coming about.

Pipeline rates, described as exorbitant by the Federal Trade Commission in 1916, had increased still further by 1920. These rates were set at the highest level possible, competing railroad rates rather than pipeline costs being the chief determinant of the maxima.[3] When buying oil from Prairie in the years before 1918, the Jersey Company could afford the high transportation costs involved, for other Prairie customers were paying the same fees and most of those customers were not competing with Jersey Standard anyway. There were as yet relatively few pipelines serving Jersey competitors. Many competing companies were being forced to obtain their oil through even more costly transportation channels than the pipelines. This advantageous situation was profoundly altered between 1920 and 1927.

The failure of existing pipeline systems to act as common carriers, coupled with the lure of high profits in pipeline transportation, the general expansion of the oil business, and the rapid growth and integration of a number of independent oil companies, all contributed to a rapid growth of competing lines. Between 1919 and 1927, total pipeline mileage in the United States increased very rapidly. Some of the growth was in lines operated by companies never affiliated with the old Standard Oil group.[4] The result inevitably was to create a depressive influence on rates.

More and more companies came to enjoy advantages in overland transportation equivalent to those long enjoyed by Jersey Standard. As competition in refining and marketing, in consequence, became more intense, the Jersey Company began to exert pressure upon Prairie to cut its transportation charges and reduce its crude oil quotations. In 1921 Prairie declined to adopt Teagle's plan of tying crude prices to the prices of finished products. Increasingly thereafter Teagle and a cost-conscious Jersey directorate manifested a desire to eliminate, wherever possible, the Prairie gathering charges and handling commissions of 30 cents per barrel. Jersey men felt not only that these charges were too high, but that Prairie had not been aggressive in tapping new sources of supply. The more nearly complete integration of pipeline transportation came to be a necessity almost as pressing as that which somewhat earlier had directed the drive for greater control over crude production. Here was yet another manifestation of the true, if belated, efficacy of the dissolution decree.

Even while the organization was relying heavily upon Prairie, Jersey affiliates were gradually extending their own pipeline network. The strategic location of the Oklahoma Pipe Line Company–Louisiana Standard trunk line facilitated the servicing of new fields in northern Louisiana, southern Arkansas, and Oklahoma with Jersey-controlled lines. By 1920 the Humble Oil & Refining Company had completed a 275-mile trunk line in Texas from the Ranger pool to the Gulf Coast terminus at Texas City. From the terminals of these lines in Texas and Louisiana crude oil could be carried by tanker to the eastern refining centers, thus lessening Jersey's dependence upon Prairie and the overland pipeline system from the Mid-Continent to the Atlantic seaboard.

Late in 1923 the Oklahoma Pipe Line Company started construction on a 165-mile line extension from the pumping station at DeQueen, Arkansas, to the Hewitt field in southern Oklahoma. Representatives of Jersey, Carter, Humble, and the Oklahoma Company conferred and agreed that Carter and Humble production and stored stocks in southern Oklahoma could keep this line running at capacity, delivering over a two-year period approximately 14,000,000 barrels of crude. This amount of crude could be handled by the new line 31 cents per barrel cheaper than by Prairie lines. The total two-year saving of $4,400,000 would pay for the line.[5]

Pipeline operations of Louisiana Standard furnish further examples of the field-by-field process by which dependence upon Prairie was reduced. In 1918 the Louisiana system had consisted of a 267-mile trunk line from Ida, in the northwest corner of the state, to Baton Rouge. Short feeder lines reached west to the Caddo field and northeast to the De Soto-Crichton district. The system at that time was capable of delivering 50,000 barrels of crude daily at the Baton Rouge terminus. Steel tankage with a capacity of 3,222,300 barrels had been constructed along the line.

Ten years later, and after the expenditure of approximately $15,000,000, the capacity of the main trunk line had been increased to 90,000 barrels daily, and new tankage with a capacity of 4,840,000 barrels had been built. The increase in line capacity was roughly equivalent to the growth in average throughput at the refinery—from 43,790 barrels daily in 1918 to 98,682 barrels daily in 1927. By 1927, feeder lines and extensive gathering systems served the Homer, Haynesville, El Dorado, and Smackover districts, in addition to the older producing areas at Caddo, De Soto, Cotton Valley, and elsewhere. Louisiana Standard had also purchased the gathering system of The Prairie Oil & Gas Company in the southwestern part of Arkansas.

The growth process was not simply a matter of building new lines whenever a new field was discovered. In some instances there was a choice between allowing Prairie to serve the field or having the Louisiana Company build its own lines. Whenever such a choice was offered, Jersey policy, for reasons already noted, was to dispense with the services of Prairie and confine the gathering and carrying profits within the organization. This decision was made the easier for the relatively short distances and consequently small capital expenditures involved. In other cases the company apparently was forced to lay its own lines because Prairie failed to build the necessary connections.

In all instances where new pipelines seemed to be needed, field production potentials were carefully studied, but even then mistakes were sometimes made. In 1921 and 1922, for example, the Homer pool declined so rapidly as to threaten the company's investment in lines and tanks in that section of northern Louisiana. Before the pipeline managers had fairly begun to worry, however, the development of large production at Haynesville, El Dorado, and Smackover transformed the Homer line into a tremendously valuable asset. Impressed by the flow of oil in these areas, the Pipe Line Department then commenced to discount the future importance of Oklahoma crude oil supplies to the Baton Rouge refinery. A section of the main trunk line from Ida Station northwest into the Mid-Continent was forthwith reduced from a daily capacity of 40,000 to 25,000 barrels in order to obtain urgently needed pipe for the El Dorado district system. No sooner had the pipe been moved than the north Louisiana–

south Arkansas boom began to subside and Oklahoma fields to pour forth new floods. These capricious pranks of nature made planning a gamble, but with infrequent exceptions the Louisiana Standard Pipe Line Department, like the Producing Department, enjoyed extraordinary good fortune in the early 1920's.

There were, nevertheless, chronic political difficulties. These derived in part from the universal agitation to make pipelines act as common carriers and in part from a purely local situation that was endowed with particularly unpleasant connotations.

In 1917 the Pine Island extension of the Caddo field was discovered, and the hopes of many small property holders there were raised. Huey P. Long, already well started on his spectacular political career in Louisiana, had invested $1,050 in a Pine Island well. Long offered to sell his interest to Louisiana Standard for $12,000, but Dan Weller, vice-president of the company, refused to bid higher than $8,500 for the property. Shortly thereafter the Louisiana Company was faced with a temporary over-supply of crude and curtailed its purchases in the Pine Island district. Property values plunged, and Long was unable to dispose of his holdings at any price. Louisiana Standard had made a bitter enemy.[6]

Louisiana's aggressive and vocal political dictator-to-be was not a man to regard his loss with resignation and to accept it merely as one of the vagaries of a highly speculative business. Long claimed that the Louisiana Company had curtailed purchases with the express intent of freezing out the independents. Company men retorted that available evidence wholly disproved this charge, pointing out that Louisiana Standard had, in fact, gone out of its way to offer its pipeline facilities to producers in the Pine Island field who could find purchasers for their oil.[7]

Here, clearly, was a further case where Jersey interests stood firmly by their business convictions and legal rights, conceding nothing to political expediency. This may, indeed, have been the wise course, for Huey Long, like many ambitious office-seekers before him, possibly discerned political advantage in assailing Standard Oil interests and might have done so under any circumstances. In his powerful position as chairman of the Louisiana Public Service Commission Long launched an attack upon Louisiana Standard.

On December 8, 1922, the Commission ordered the company to show cause why, by virtue of its pipeline operations within the state, it should not be classified in Louisiana (as it had been since 1914 in interstate trade) as a common carrier. Long went even further and claimed that the refinery itself was a public utility and should be regulated as such.[8]

The Louisiana Company accepted the challenge at once, and a spirited political and legal fight ensued. Long's efforts to bring the company under strict regulation were frustrated, but the threat, coupled as it was with increasingly burdensome federal regulation, was sufficiently serious to impel the company to divorce its pipeline operations from its other activities. On January 13, 1923, the Pipe Line Department was separately organized as the Standard Pipe Line Company, Incorporated. This move was similar in nature and purpose to those corporate divorcements which had followed the 1914 pipeline decision of the United States Supreme Court. No company wished to submit to regulation and public audit in its entirety because of the activities of one branch of the business alone.

Dramatic and disturbing though it was to those who participated, the Huey Long affair of 1922 cannot be viewed as more than a parenthetical incident in the main story. Despite such difficulties and some errors, the overland transportation function in each year after 1919 was more fully integrated into the master operating plan of the Jersey organization. In the period from 1919 through 1927 trunk pipeline mileage owned and operated by Jersey Standard affiliates increased about 112 per cent, as compared with a total increase in trunk-line mileage in the United States of 73 per cent. At the same time, the Jersey Company was moving in other directions to minimize the delivered cost of crude at its refineries. The cumulative result of these various efforts was to undermine the dominating position the pipeline companies had held since early in the century in the movement of Mid-Continent crude oil to the refining centers on the Atlantic seaboard.

Chief among those forces which dealt certain of the pipeline companies a heavy blow in the early 1920's was increased competition from water carriers. In earlier years the bulk of the Jersey tanker fleet had been profitably employed in carrying Mexican crude to the United States and Canada and in transporting refined products from the United States to Europe. Both traffic patterns had been disrupted in postwar years. The Mexican export situation was highly uncertain, and after 1919 the European trade was dull. The tanker fleet, meanwhile, had expanded considerably in the war years. Tankers themselves were larger and more economical to operate than those of the prewar years. Thus, at the very time when unprecedented quantities of crude oil were being produced in the field and demanded at the refineries, the service of a large tanker fleet was available and ocean shipping rates were low. Between January 1.

1920, and June 30, 1922, Jersey moved 85,981,000 barrels of crude to the Atlantic Coast by tanker, as against 42,738,000 barrels by pipeline. The pipeline companies, having raised their rates by 25 per cent in 1920, stubbornly held them at the new level for several critical months while formidable competitive forces were generating. Prairie had already incurred the displeasure of Jersey men by imposing new regulations governing types of crude which it would transport.[9]

Because of the somewhat unusual postwar tanker situation, eastern refiners were able, as we have seen, to take advantage of booming California production and low crude prices on the West Coast. California crude began to move by tanker from San Pedro and other loading points around through the Panama Canal and into Atlantic markets to compete with and displace Mid-Continent stocks shipped overland by pipeline. The reader will recall from the preceding chapter that this movement reached an early peak in 1923, in which year the Jersey Company alone purchased and shipped close to 21,000,000 barrels of California crude— an amount equivalent to one-quarter of all crude run in Jersey's domestic refineries in that year. In view of that same availability of tankers which was bringing West Coast crude into eastern markets, Teagle, McKnight, Jones, and others in high managerial circles were manifesting the keenest interest in relative shipping costs of Mid-Continent stocks. In 1922 the company began to swing still more of its bountiful and traditional carrying patronage from the transcontinental pipelines to its own pipelines and tanker fleet.

Comparative cost figures were convincing, if not startling. In March of 1922 Teagle was given the following information on relative costs of Mid-Continent crude delivered to Bayonne and Bayway by pipeline and by tanker:[10]

	Delivered Cost per Barrel	
	Pipeline	*Tanker*
Well price of crude	$2.0875	$2.00
Commission	0.10	0.10
Gathering charge	0.20	0.20
Pipeline charge	1.0063	0.40
Loading expense	none	0.03
Boat charge	none	0.35
Total cost	$3.3938	$3.08

This was not the complete cost picture, however, for against the tanker rate could be laid the profits accruing to the Jersey organization if it per-

formed the handling and shipping functions itself—as it did when shipment was by tanker from Baton Rouge. The tanker shipment figures per
barrel were as follows:

| | Per Barrel | | |
	Rate	Cost	Profit to Jersey Standard Affiliates
Commission	$0.10	none	$0.10
Gathering charge	0.20	$0.08	0.12
Pipeline charge to Baton Rouge	0.40	0.20	0.20
Loading expense	0.03	0.01	0.02
Boat charge	0.35	0.26	0.09
Total	$1.08	$0.55	$0.53

With these profits figured in, the delivered net cost to the Jersey Company was $0.8438 per barrel less by tanker than by pipeline. The yearly
saving in shipping by tanker the 38,500 barrels daily of Mid-Continent–
North Texas pipeline mixture being run at that time by Prairie for Jersey's
account was calculated at $11,887,500.[11]

"To continue to use the common carrier facilities," Teagle wrote,
"means eventually putting us out of business, as at the present existing
pipeline rates the Eastern refineries cannot successfully compete with the
refineries located at the Gulf, due entirely to the difference in the pipeline
transportation charges."[12] The cost differential between Mid-Continent
crude delivered at Gulf and at Atlantic seaboard refining centers, of
course, had always existed, but in 1922 competition was pressing upon
the refiners as seldom before in the history of the oil business, and the
cost situation was coming to have a new urgency.

In July of 1922 Prairie cut its rates by 12½ per cent. Further cuts in
rates on Texas crude ranging up to 50 per cent were made in October of
1923 as the California crude movement began to affect the entire competitive situation and cut seriously into the pipeline business.[13] These rate
slashes were not enough to close the gap between pipeline and tanker
costs and halt the loss of overland traffic. For several months in 1923,
indeed, Jersey Standard suspended altogether the movement of crude oil
by pipeline to the eastern refineries.[14]

The transportation cost to the Jersey Company of Mid-Continent crude
shipped over the Prairie–Illinois Pipeline–Tuscarora route to Bayonne at
the new rates was down to $0.7675 per barrel. This same crude, however,
could be sent by Oklahoma Pipe Line and Louisiana Standard Pipe Line

to Baton Rouge and thence by tanker to Bayonne at a cost of $0.56. In November of 1923, only a month after the most recent Prairie rate cut, the Jersey refining men were asking Teagle if Prairie could not be persuaded to lower its rates still more. The eastern connecting lines were also eager to bring this about in order to give themselves some business.[15]

Correspondence and the compilations of data in connection with the rate-reduction issue showed clearly to what point Jersey's own pipeline operations had been built up. In April of 1922 domestic refinery requirements had called for 137,500 barrels of crude delivered daily at Gulf and Atlantic seaboard plants. Jersey's affiliated pipelines and the tanker fleet were then capable of providing 86,500 barrels, and the balance of 51,000 barrels was being taken from the transcontinental pipelines. Figures on affiliated pipeline capacity furnished to Teagle in November of 1923, however, indicated that the goal of integrating the pipeline transportation function had been achieved. Normal refining requirements of the organization at that time were for 150,000 barrels of Mid-Continent crude daily. The combined lines of Louisiana Standard and the Oklahoma Pipe Line Company were capable of capacity deliveries to Baton Rouge of 90,000 barrels daily, while the Humble lines in Texas, if run at maximum peaks, could provide 60,000 barrels daily at the ocean loading terminal at Texas City. It was expected, furthermore, that the California traffic would soon diminish, releasing more tankers and reducing ocean shipping rates. Theoretically, at least, the Jersey organization was completely independent of the pipelines which had so long provided the vital link between fields and the eastern refineries.[16]

With a keen instinct for the competitive aspects of the situation, Teagle declared that the company should not seek a further rate reduction for the overland traffic. Since Jersey Standard owned a far larger tanker fleet than its domestic competitors and had built up its own pipelines to deliver the required crude at ocean loading points, the existing cost differential in favor of water transportation benefited the company. The relatively high pipeline rates penalized those competitors who were forced through lack of tanker facilities to ship their crude overland. Even if the high pipeline rates drove such competitors to charter tanker tonnage, the Jersey Company could still deliver crude to the refining centers in its own tankers at a lower cost than could be obtained on a charter voyage.[17]

In taking issue with Teagle, E. M. Clark, representing Jersey's Atlantic seaboard refining interests, was quick to point out that capacity operation of company-controlled lines was a physical impossibility. Operating breakdowns would occur, Clark declared, and the Carter, Louisiana Standard, and Humble wells could not be depended upon to produce the requisite quantities of crude. It was true that by the end of 1923 most of the crude run by the Jersey refineries was being shipped through company pipelines and in company tankers, but Clark believed that the old ties with Prairie and the other carriers and suppliers should not be entirely severed. There might well come a time when the company would need crude from Prairie, which had accumulated large stocks in storage. Prairie, moreover, was connected with a large number of old, small wells in Kansas—a source of supply which was not unimportant and to which no other company could economically gain access. Clark concluded, therefore, that Prairie and connecting carriers should be asked to bring their charges into line with tanker rates, and that the Jersey Company should continue to utilize the overland shipping routes and purchase some crude from the nonaffiliated companies.[18]

There was yet another factor to be considered—the position of Jersey's affiliate, the Tuscarora Oil Company, Limited. Before 1918, when the seaboard refineries were receiving virtually all of their Mid-Continent oil by overland routes, the shipments had traveled by Prairie and Illinois Pipe Line Company lines to the western boundary of Pennsylvania. There the shipments were split up—some to travel the northern route over lines of the independent New York Transit Company; some to go across Pennsylvania through the Tuscarora lines. As overland traffic decreased in the early 1920's, the New York Transit route was abandoned by Jersey in order to give its affiliate in Pennsylvania whatever business was left.[19] By 1923, however, this business had shrunk to less than one-fourth its earlier volume, and Tuscarora was in a precarious condition. A further decrease in overland traffic might put the company out of business.

In 1924 the issue of rate reduction was actually taken up with Prairie but, while some reduction in gathering charges and commissions appears to have been made, the pipage rates were not altered. In 1926 the cost differential still favored the tanker route for Mid-Continent crude. Despite a general increase in crude consumption in Jersey's eastern refineries over the years from 1921 to 1927, the shipment of crude oil overland had decreased. In August of 1926 Teagle reported that Tuscarora was virtually out of business, and he doubted that the Tuscarora lines would ever again be used for the movement of Mid-Continent crude to the Jersey Company's seaboard plants.[20]

In 1927 many signs pointed toward the end of the era of lavish pipeline profits—to the doom of the old tradition that the real money in the oil business was made in transportation. Pipeline earnings of most of the eastern and Mid-Continent carriers for the years from 1921 to 1927, nevertheless, averaged out at a high though declining level. Prairie's earnings, which averaged 42.3 per cent on invested capital in 1921, were far from insignificant by 1926, when a return of 22.1 per cent was realized.[21] While the earnings of Prairie, the Illinois Pipe Line Company, the New York Transit Company, and other carriers that had participated heavily in the eastward movement of Mid-Continent crude showed sharp decreases after 1921, the earnings of Jersey's pipeline affiliates (Tuscarora excepted) moved spectacularly upward as the flow of crude was diverted from the old traffic pattern to the new. These earnings are presented in Table 15. The fact that pipeline profits of integrated competitors also were increasing rapidly suggests that the experience of the Jersey Company was by no means unique.

Pipeline rates had been criticized by the Federal Trade Commission intermittently since 1916. From 1921 to 1924 Jersey Standard, while calling upon Prairie and connecting carriers to reduce their rates, had posted high rates on its own affiliated lines. By 1926, however, Jersey executives were coming to entertain a modified viewpoint. Before this time it had mattered little whether Humble, Louisiana Standard, and Oklahoma Pipe Line Company rates were high, since these lines were carrying oil only for the Jersey organization. The flood of crude in 1926 and 1927 precipitated a situation where Jersey Standard, hitherto predominantly a crude oil purchaser, wished to sell some crude to nonaffiliated companies. This crude could not be priced at a competitive level unless the high pipeline tariffs in effect on the Jersey-controlled lines were modified. The Jersey marketing and refining men, moreover, were hard pressed by competition and were asking for a more equitable (from their viewpoint) interorganizational allocation of profits. On November 20, 1926, after several months of controversy, the decision was made at 26 Broadway that the affiliated pipeline companies should reduce their commissions from 10 cents to 5 cents per barrel and the gathering charges from 20 cents to 12½ cents.[22]

The Jersey rate changes were not viewed with equanimity by Prairie representatives, who at that time were contemplating an effort to restore their own gathering charges and commissions to the old level. Harsh words were spoken in private, and the threat was voiced that if Jersey Standard persisted in its course steps would be taken to spur the Inter-

Table 15: PIPELINE NET EARNINGS
Jersey Organization and Other Carriers

Net Earnings Expressed as Percentage of Invested Capital[a]

(Parentheses indicate net loss)

	1921	1922	1923	1924	1925	1926
Jersey Standard group						
Humble Pipe Line Co.	b	31.8	37.3	53.9	48.7	30.7
Oklahoma Pipe Line Co.	7.3	12.5	31.5	33.3	33.6	34.7
Louisiana Standard	b	b	21.0	37.7	39.6	59.1
Tuscarora Oil Co.	18.7	22.5	6.5	(2.9)	0.7	(8.8)
Imperial Pipe Line Co.	9.1	15.0	10.1	9.4	7.2	12.0
Selected other carriers, nonintegrated						
Prairie Pipe Line Co.	42.3	33.8	26.5	19.3	24.4	22.1
Illinois Pipe Line Co.	22.8	16.8	11.9	11.4	15.0	14.8
New York Transit Co.	6.9	5.6	5.1	3.9	3.9	(0.1)
Selected other carriers, integrated						
Magnolia Pipe Line Co.	6.1	7.6	11.5	15.5	17.5	32.3
Gulf Pipe Line Co. (Texas)	4.2	12.4	5.6	14.7	17.3	20.0
Texas Pipe Line Co. (Texas)	19.2	28.5	17.3	22.2	26.7	28.3
Gulf Pipe Line Co. (Oklahoma)	(1.3)	47.8	41.1	37.9	38.5	52.1
Texas Pipe Line Co. (Oklahoma)	22.6	15.2	8.4	8.3	15.3	17.4

Jersey and Affiliates' Net Pipeline Earnings[c]

Dollar figures in thousands (Parentheses indicate net loss)

	1919	1920	1921	1922	1923	1924	1925	1926	1927
Domestic									
Humble Pipe Line Co.	$ 260	$ 569	$3,291	$2,819	$ 3,037	$ 4,191	$ 5,949	$ 5,661	$ 8,843
Oklahoma Pipe Line Co.	124	(192)	553	806	2,831	4,501	4,838	4,869	7,534
Louisiana Standard	342	107	28	205	5,632	11,516	11,167	12,602	7,262
Tuscarora Oil Co.	841	854	974	1,021	310	(61)	130	(183)	555
Total domestic	$1,567	$1,339	$4,846	$4,851	$11,810	$20,147	$22,084	$22,949	$24,194
Foreign									
Imperial Oil (Canada)	b	b	b	b	$ 101	$ 100	$ 60	b	b
Româno-Americana (Romania)	$ (9)	d	$ 1	$ (1)	1	5	3	$ 6	$ 53
Total foreign	$ (9)	b	$ 1	$ (1)	$ 102	$ 105	$ 63	$ 6	$ 53
Total	$1,558	$1,339	$4,847	$4,850	$11,912	$20,252	$22,147	$22,955	$24,247
Total pipeline earnings as percentage of total Jersey earnings[e]	3.2	0.9	14.3	10.5	21.2	25.0	19.9	19.5	60.0

[a] Taken from Federal Trade Commission, *Prices, Profits and Competition in the Petroleum Industry*, 352-353.
[b] Comparable data not available.
[c] Taken from SONJ, Fin. Recs.
[d] Too small to measure.
[e] Since the percentage figure for any one earnings classification is determined not only by the actual amount recorded in that classification but also by earnings and losses in each of the others, no attempt should be made to trace year-to-year variations in one classification without careful reference both to other percentage classifications and to the pertinent dollar figures. All functional earnings figures given in SONJ, Fin. Recs., for the years 1912 through 1924 have been adjusted by the authors to match, insofar as possible, the account classifications employed in those records in the years 1925 through 1927.

state Commerce Commission to effect a dissolution of pipeline subsidiary ties. Teagle ignored the threat. The only consideration to which Jersey's politically intrepid leader attached importance was whether economic considerations justified a return to higher rates. Opinion within the organization supported the cut, and the lower rates were left unchanged.[23]

As the early 1920's had marked the peak of the high profit era for Prairie, the Illinois Pipe Line Company, New York Transit, and others among the nonintegrated carriers, so did the rate change in 1926 herald the eventual end for the Jersey pipeline affiliates of the time when rates were determined by arbitrary considerations quite apart from actual line construction and operating costs. In 1927, however, that end was still far from sight. The pipeline affiliates had risen in the years since 1919 to a position of importance in the Jersey organization unprecedented since 1911. Pipeline earnings for the 1919-1927 period averaged about one-sixth of all earnings of Jersey Standard and its foreign and domestic affiliates. It was chiefly a matter of bookkeeping, to be sure; but while competition was squeezing the producing, refining, and marketing branches of the business, pipeline earnings were building a rich surplus against which could be charged the downward adjustment of costs in any sorely pressed area of operations. The advantages of integration proved to be no less in 1927 than in the years when John D. Rockefeller was beginning to build up his oil business.

GROOMING THE MARINE ORGANIZATION

No other branch of Jersey's business had been stimulated so greatly by the effort of war as the Foreign Shipping Department. The physical condition of the tanker fleet had never been better than it was at the close of 1919. Half the 44 vessels sailing under the Jersey flag were less than three years old; 27 other tankers were owned by affiliates. This combined fleet of 71 ships was the second largest privately owned tanker fleet afloat, being surpassed only by the Royal Dutch-Shell armada of 100 vessels. Other oil companies owned far fewer tankers: Standard of New York and affiliates 33, Anglo-American 29, Anglo-Persian 24, Gulf 22, Pan-American 20, Texas Company 15, Burmah Oil 10, and Standard of California 10.[24]

Despite the size of the Jersey Standard fleet, however, a shortage of ocean-going tonnage hampered operations in immediate postwar months. This shortage, together with the far-reaching legal precedents involved, imparted urgency and importance to efforts by the company to obtain possession of and title to the eight DAPG tankers which had been seized in German ports in 1919 by the Allied Supreme Economic Council and placed in British custody.

Despite the unforeseen obstacles and hostility which had attended Jersey Standard's initial efforts to take over these vessels, American diplomatic protests were at length successful in obtaining a temporary and compromise solution to the tanker controversy. On June 7, 1920, the Reparations Commission concluded an agreement with the United States government which provided that the eight vessels be turned over to the United States Shipping Board for operation, the question of ultimate disposition being submitted to an arbitration court composed of one American and two British members. The Shipping Board thereupon turned the tankers over to the Jersey Company, which was to receive a managing fee of $1,000 per month for each vessel. By this time, however, the shipping shortage had so far lessened that the company was actually considering the sale of certain of its ships.[25]

For six more years the controversy continued. Three of the eight tankers, which were found to be unfit for transoceanic trade, were sold at auction and the proceeds (slightly less than £18,000) turned over to the Reparations Commission in accordance with the 1920 agreement. The Jersey Company operated the five remaining vessels in its own trade. Jersey's legal advisers appeared to feel that it was merely a matter of time and protracted diplomatic quibbling until the Reparations Commission would be forced to surrender before the virtually unassailable evidence of Jersey Standard's interest in the assets of its German affiliate.[26]

At last the arbitration court appointed under the 1920 agreement returned its decision. On April 5, 1926, the court declared that the company had not established any foundation for its claims to the ownership of any of the tankers under litigation, nor was it entitled to any indemnity whatsoever. The tankers, together with all proceeds from operation, were ruled to be the property of the Reparations Commission and were awarded to the British government. To this decision the American member of the three-man tribunal dissented, but the verdict was final.[27]

The five vessels were then sold at auction, and the Jersey Company turned over to the Reparations Commission for credit to the British Board of Trade the sum of $623,937.13, representing the net profit realized from the operation of the tankers for six years. Jersey acquired two of the five tankers at a total cost of £160,000. The three remaining ships were sold to British and Italian interests for £105,000.[28]

If the $383,443 in management fees received by the company over the period and the benefits accruing from the possession and use of the vessels in its own trade are taken into consideration, the Jersey Company's actual loss was probably not large. To Jersey men, however, the tanker episode appeared an outrageous act of expropriation on the part of the Reparations Commission and its British-dominated arbitration court. Such a judgment may well have been valid on strictly legal grounds, but it ignored strong countering arguments. Whatever claims Jersey Standard could make on the grounds of ownership and invested capital, the DAPG was a German company in respect to its charter, management, and operations. In prewar years Jersey executives had deliberately fostered the idea that the company was German in every essential respect. During the war the DAPG organization, willingly or otherwise, had provided material assistance to the Kaiser's armies. The Reparations Commission, it appeared, had looked to the operational reality and the Jersey Company had taken refuge in legal precedents. Both sides to the dispute were clearly motivated by considerations of expediency.

Other difficulties, more routine in nature but perhaps of even greater total significance, were faced by the Foreign Shipping Department in postwar years. With the rapid growth of the fleet and the turmoil of war had come increasing departmental rigidities and inefficiency. The tanker operation traditionally was a difficult one to administer, and the central organization was forced to rely to a certain extent upon the capabilities of the ship captains. Control of the vessels appeared to have been less carefully maintained than it might have been. Graft in the taking on of fuel, supplies, and cargoes at outports still flourished. Turnover among the tanker crews was unbelievably high. The seamen were unruly, discontented, obligated by few loyalties, and continually stirred by union agitators. An estimated 80 per cent of the unlicensed personnel on Jersey vessels were members of the Industrial Workers of the World.[29] Of these conditions the Teagle administration was well aware, and while the Foreign Shipping Department was adjusting its operations to a peacetime basis, remedial plans were being drawn up.

Over the years from 1919 to 1927 the company's marine business was a barometer of trends and events in many other branches of operation. Amidst the interminable detail of extant voyage schedule records, certain broad movements stand clear. These are evident in the figures in Table 16.

While the Mexican trade was rising and falling with shifts in the revolutionary tides, a broad and strong increase was taking place in Jersey's Atlantic coastwise business. This reflected not only the movement

Table 16: TANKER SHIPMENTS AND EARNINGS
1919-1927

Net Marine Earnings, Standard Oil Company (New Jersey) and affiliates, 1919-1927

Dollar figures in thousands *(Parentheses indicate net loss)*

	1919	1920	1921	1922	1923	1924	1925	1926	1927
Jersey Standard	$14,141	$26,783	$11,600	$7,361	$7,867	$ 8,787	$3,400	$5,620	$10,421
Humble	a	a	59	(19)	51	(325)	21	a	a
Imperial Oil, Canada	(66)	711	(1,532)	(536)	1,125	1,351	264	(361)	2,812
Transcont. Co., Mex.	(296)	(5)	(6)	(6)	(1)	(7)	a	a	a
DAPG, Germany	a	a	a	a	a	a	559	288	a
La Columbia, Italy	a	a	845	76	215	200	134	161	322
Total[b]	$13,779	$27,489	$10,966	$6,876	$9,257	$10,006	$4,378	$5,708	$13,555

	1919	1920	1921	1922	1923	1924	1925	1926	1927
Marine earnings as percentage of Jersey's total earnings[c]	28.6	18.5	32.4	14.9	16.4	12.4	3.9	4.9	33.5
Marine earnings as percentage of Jersey's net investment in tankers[c]	40	67	19	14	16	22	10	15	19

Petroleum and Petroleum Products Carried in Jersey-Owned and Jersey-Chartered Tankers[d]

Thousands of barrels

Trade	1919	1920	1921	1922	1923	1924	1925	1926	1927
BULK:									
Atlantic coastwise	10,955	14,508	19,851	21,923	26,366	40,229	54,048	58,486	50,945
Mexican	20,112	37,710	38,303	35,349	18,561	26,392	29,653	29,791	25,983
Transatlantic	5,560	5,557	4,846	7,322	5,456	5,233	5,317	4,579	5,627
CASE:									
South American	e	e	e	e	1,564	2,529	3,559	3,233	3,679
Californian	....	....	....	994	24,863	20,723	5,034	3,677	6,146
South American	1,631	1,236	1,208	998	1,068	1,450	1,725	1,668	1,287
European	99	133	17	f	f	f	f	f	f
African	25	121	13	f	f	f	f	f	f
Total	38,382	59,265	64,238	66,586	77,873	96,556	99,336	101,434	93,667

a Comparable data not available.
b Earnings of Dutch tankers not available.
c Since the percentage figure for any one earnings classification is determined not only by the actual amount of earnings recorded in that classification but also by earnings and losses in each of the others, no attempt should be made to trace year-to-year variations in one classification without careful reference both to other percentage classifications and to the pertinent dollar figures. All functional earnings figures given in SONJ, Fin. Recs., for the years 1912 through 1924 have been adjusted by the authors to match, insofar as possible, the account classifications employed in those records in the years 1925 through 1927.
d Does not include figures for operations of affiliates.
e Included in Atlantic coastwise total.
f Handled by Foreign Sales Department and not included in Marine Department summaries.
Source: SONJ, Fin. Recs.; annual reports of the Marine Dept., 1921-1927.

of Mid-Continent and Gulf crudes that was starving the transcontinental pipelines, but the further fact that Jersey vessels could be used to best advantage in areas where competition from low-cost foreign tankers was prevented by law. Relatively few Jersey ships plied the transatlantic route—this business was turned over to the vessels of foreign affiliates. The California traffic, in turn, came at a providential time when Mexican shipments were down and surplus tanker tonnage was promising to become a problem of major dimensions. When the California business declined, an increase in Atlantic coastwise and Mexican traffic and in the movement of bulk cargoes to South American markets helped to take up the slack. These well-meshed vacillations of trade produced a stabilizing influence upon the profit level. Shipping rates, like pipeline rates, bore little reference to operating costs. Profits were usually possible if cargoes could be obtained, but high losses accrued from idle vessels. Jersey Standard and its affiliates appear to have been extraordinarily adroit in keeping their vessels employed, a circumstance which derived both from the broad opportunities offered by the company's international business and from a careful grooming of the marine administrative organization.

The reorganization commenced in April of 1920 with the formation of a so-called Shipping Committee. David T. Warden, the head of the Foreign Shipping Department, was appointed chairman; assistants were named to attend regularly scheduled meetings at which departmental affairs were discussed. Jersey director James A. Moffett, Jr., was designated an ex officio member in order to facilitate a harmonious correlation of marketing and transportation requirements. Three months after this preliminary step had been taken, the Foreign Shipping Department itself became the scene of extensive changes.

Warden, whose achievements in setting up the Foreign Shipping Department and directing the tremendously difficult marine war effort far outshine such shortcomings as appeared in his administration, left the company. He was replaced by Robert L. Hague, who had given up his position as marine superintendent of the Standard Oil Company (California) in 1918 to serve as chief of the construction and repair division of the United States Shipping Board. The name of the Foreign Shipping Department was changed to the Marine Department, and Hague attacked the problem of bolstering fleet morale and efficiency.

The basic feature of the reorganization was the institution of an incentive plan whereby bonus payments ranging up to 35 per cent of officers' salaries and to 10 per cent of crew wages were made for the attainment of predetermined standards of performance. These standards sought to encourage reasonable care and economy in the use of stores and supplies, the elimination of accidents, the avoidance of unnecessary repair bills, and the maintenance of a high level of operating efficiency. In an effort to win over the loyalty and co-operation of the crews, great emphasis was placed upon clean and comfortable living quarters and good food aboard the tankers. An additional bonus, 10 per cent of wages plus one vacation week with pay, was provided for crew members who stayed in the company employ for a year. All possible measures were adopted to achieve a quicker turnaround of the vessels at both ends of their voyages.[30]

The years 1920 and 1921 produced many gains, but there were difficult operational problems to be solved. In the postwar surge of optimism many new vessels had been ordered. This expansion program seemed eminently justified in 1920, when high shipping rates were coupled with heavy traffic in Mexican crude to produce tremendous profits. Ships for which contracts had been placed at the height of the postwar boom, however, were still being delivered to the Jersey Company when the business collapse of 1921 began to shake the petroleum industry. In January of 1921 freight rates from North Atlantic ports to Europe were $25.00 per ton; by July the rate had fallen to $5.50. Despite the sharp decline in business early in the year, ten new tankers were delivered to the Marine Department. By fall business had revived, but the company still found it necessary to keep twelve tankers tied up. The cost for the year of these idle ships totaled $1,090,000. Shipping interests complained of the inability of American vessels to compete with foreign, and the demand grew in shipping circles for a government subsidy. On such of its vessels as the Jersey Company was forced to utilize in the transatlantic trade, depreciation charges and lay-up expenses were frequently absorbed in departmental overhead in order to permit the cargoes to be delivered at competitive rates.

As rates fell and business declined, the American Steamship Association, of which Jersey Standard was a member, recommended a wage reduction of 25 per cent, the virtual elimination of all overtime pay, and the cancellation of closed-shop agreements made between the Association and the maritime unions in the closing months of the war. Union representatives refused these demands, and the issues were taken before Admiral Benson of the Shipping Board. Benson sided with the Association, but he recommended that the wage reduction be limited to 15 per cent. On May 1, 1921, the Association members, Jersey Standard included, adopted the Shipping Board recommendations and placed them in effect. A nationwide shipping strike was promptly launched by the marine engineers.[31]

These events, whatever the justifications involved, were scarcely calculated to assist Hague's efforts to build up the loyalty of the marine organization. The strike lasted six weeks and was abortive from the beginning. Engineers leaving Jersey ships were promptly replaced. Tankers were routed to trouble-free ports so that there was little or no interference with Jersey operating schedules. The measures adopted on May 1 resulted in an estimated saving to the company for the year of $450,000.

Paradoxically enough, while wages were being cut and overtime eliminated, the efficiency bonus plan was paying premiums. During 1921 about 20 per cent of the Marine Department seagoing personnel became eligible for payments totaling $130,000. Turnabout time was reduced by a full 25 per cent and loading time by 33⅓ per cent, in part because skilled company representatives were stationed at important outports to supervise the cargo handling. So vigorously did the Marine Department enforce its port schedules, in fact, that the foreign affiliates complained of inability to meet what they characterized as unreasonable dispatch and demurrage conditions, which were, in consequence, modified.

Economies were also reported in repair costs and provisioning, and Jersey saved $1,475,000 by setting up its own insurance reserve instead of insuring with commercial underwriters. Two physicians were assigned to the department to inspect vessels, pass on sanitary conditions, and examine new crew members, while the *Ships' Bulletin* was started with a view to promoting closer contacts between the afloat and the ashore staffs. Altogether, the year had not been devoid of tangible benefits. Shipowners generally numbered as the most important among these the abrupt shaking down of war-inflated labor costs to what they considered a more realistic peacetime level.

Throughout 1922 the supply of tankers continued to exceed demand, and competition for business was keen. The company kept an average of twelve ships tied up, but held the out-of-pocket loss to a minimum of $126,600 by utilizing the vessels for floating storage of oil. Shipping rates declined an additional 38 per cent in the transatlantic service, 40 per cent in the coastwise trade, and 40 per cent in the Mexican trade. Hague devoted much attention to the condition of the fleet, but no new vessels were added during the year. Rigid economies were practiced afloat and in the offices; statistical procedures were thoroughly overhauled. Operating costs per hundred-ton-mile were reduced from 7 cents in 1921 to 5 cents in 1922, and a further wage reduction became effective. Bonus payments to officers in 1922 totaled $122,000, while the turnover of licensed personnel decreased 30 per cent from the level of the preceding year. Little progress, however, appears to have been made in winning the cooperation of the crews, and Hague was concerned over the possibility of another strike. Hague also expressed disappointment that the ship subsidy bill, which the Jersey Company had supported in Congress, had become entangled in the common carrier controversy and was finally drawn in such a way as to exclude from benefits all companies that carried their own cargoes.

On April 25, 1923, Jersey tanker crews again went on strike for higher wages. This walkout, however, was short-lived. By June the departmental reorganization appeared to have gone through its most grueling stages. Shipping rates were still low, but business was improving. The easing of both external and internal pressures provided the leaven of employee benefits with a more propitious atmosphere in which to work. Wages and salaries were increased approximately 10 per cent, labor turnover decreased markedly, and efficiency bonuses totaling $247,500 were dispensed to officers and crews. Operating performance of the tankers improved demonstrably. Shipping costs per hundred-ton-mile declined to 4.8 cents. Jersey Standard established a school for ships' cooks, placed in operation a new marine warehouse at Bayonne, and compiled a marine stores and equipment catalogue to facilitate effective requisitioning of ship supplies. The twelve immobilized tankers were emptied of their stored cargoes and dispatched to California to participate in the oil rush there. The turning point in departmental affairs had been reached, and there was optimism in the offices.

All marine engineers of the day were looking at their old ships and wishing they were Diesel-powered. Rapid progress had been made abroad in the few years since the war in developing the marine Diesel engine. By 1923 this type of installation was showing a saving of from 10 to 20 per cent in transportation costs over the oil-burning steam engine. The cost of converting old vessels was very high and relatively few conversions were made, but all new construction contracts placed by Jersey from this time through 1927 called for Diesel units. In 1923 two 14,000-ton, 11-knot Diesel ships were commissioned at the Howaldswerke at Kiel and delivered to the DAPG. Orders for three additional tankers were placed in German yards for the account of European affiliates. The Jersey

fleet was pruned and prodded to new performance levels, with the result
that the close of the year 1924 brought an abundance of satisfying reports—lower labor turnover, reduced operating costs, higher earnings.
The insurance reserve showed a cumulative credit of $4,185,000, and it
began to appear that considerable new tonnage might be necessary. Ten
old ships were sold, but orders for twelve new ones, all Diesels, were
placed abroad. There, Hague reported, they could be built for half what
they would cost in the United States. If foreign-registered and manned
by European crews, the vessels could operate 9 per cent cheaper than
equivalent American tonnage.

By 1925 the Marine Department reorganization had established a plane
of efficiency from which departures in the ensuing two years were relatively minor. Operating costs had stabilized at slightly under 5 cents per
hundred-ton-mile, and the outport representatives were effectively supervising cargo handling, repairs, and foreign requisitioning of stores and
supplies. The Jersey fleet did not grow in numbers, but the fleets of the
Canadian, German, Dutch, and Italian affiliates expanded considerably.
In 1926 vessels owned and chartered by the foreign affiliates carried
14,624,000 barrels of petroleum products in the transatlantic trade—more
than three times the volume handled by the Jersey Company itself in
this trade.

When temporary shipping shortages occurred, Hague chartered tankers.
In 1927, for example, 36 per cent of the total Jersey cargo movement was
in chartered vessels. In the offices of the Marine Department was manifest a strong disinclination to indulge in that flamboyant optimism which
had laid so many keels in 1919 and 1920. There was, indeed, no outstanding reason to hope for a return to the rates of 1920. A vastly expanded
world tanker fleet proved adequate, in general, to handle the steady and
large increase which had taken place in the carrying trade. Shipping
rates, in consequence, showed a tendency toward weakness.

Jersey's marine profits slumped sharply in 1925, but by 1927 they had
again attained a more than modest level. The psychology of rigid economy
appears to have survived the months of departmental retrenchment and
to have persisted in years when earnings were high. No wage increases
were made for American personnel between 1923 and 1927, the burden
of building employee morale being placed upon good food, clean quarters, the benefits program, and the *Ships' Bulletin*. The efficacy of such
measures remained to be fully tested, and the most that could be said in
1927 was that Hague had made an effort to follow an enlightened labor

policy with a group of employees who seemed to most steamship owners at that time to be anything but enlightened themselves.

By the end of 1927 the Jersey fleet numbered 38 ships, nearly four-fifths of which were less than ten years of age. One of these was the 21,000-ton *John D. Archbold,* the second of that name and the largest tanker in the world at the time of its christening. The ships of the 1919 fleet had been of younger average age, but they numbered no Diesels among them. A third of the Jersey organization's 1927 fleet was Diesel-propelled, and that fleet, if older, was better managed, better organized, and better cared for. The policy of utilizing foreign-registered ships to the fullest extent possible had resulted in an expansion in tankers owned by affiliates from 27 in 1919 to 54 in 1927. The trend was clearly toward a re-establishment of the situation which had prevailed before the mass transfers of German tankers in 1914, but with the added stipulation that the Jersey Company must itself own sufficient tonnage to meet the requirements of the American coastal trade, from which foreign-registered vessels were excluded. As in the days before 1914, the foreign affiliates enjoyed considerable freedom, within the broad policy limits established at 26 Broadway, to manage their own marine affairs.

The Jersey Company and its affiliates had failed to match the fleet increases of the Royal Dutch-Shell or of Anglo-Persian, which added 48 and 59 tankers, respectively, to their rosters between 1920 and 1927. Nevertheless, other tangible and conventional measures indicated that these had been outstanding years for the Jersey Marine Department. Profits had never reached the levels prevailing when Hague assumed his post with Jersey Standard, but this had been an exceptional period and Hague had no control over the subsequent course of shipping rates or the volume of business. Such cost factors as his department could control were carefully controlled, and the way was thereby well paved for the time when operating expenses and managerial efficiency would come to have a critical importance indeed.

Chapter 16

The Rising Tide of Competition
1919-1927

THE AUTOMOBILE was the marvel of the decade and the pride of the society which it was altering. In 1920 no oilman believed, as some had in 1914, that the future prosperity of the industry was to be based on fuel oil. The automobile had come to be the most important external influence on the domestic business of Jersey Standard and of most American oil companies.

After 1918 the consumption of petroleum products continued, with only minor interruptions, to increase. Gasoline sales were a solid floor supporting the oil trade through two fleeting periods of economic adversity. Kerosene, though relatively neglected by the mass market in America, was still a major product line in Europe and South America. Fuel oil, lubricating oils, and specialty products continued to find many growing markets at home and abroad. The combination of rising demand, growing supplies of cheap crude, a vastly improved transportation network, and great advances in refining techniques held forth a promise of tremendous profits to the oil industry.

Unfortunately for the maximum fulfillment of this promise, there were other factors to be reckoned with. Those competitive forces unshackled in 1911 and successively constrained thereafter by a business recession and by a war burst forth at last. In the decade commencing in 1920 the dissolution decree and the revolution in motive power came together with a staggering impact. The American petroleum industry was buffeted, shaped, and energized. In simplest terms, Jersey executives found that they were selling more and more for less and less. Only in 1921 were profits small, but in all the years from 1919 through 1927 the making of profits required exceptional managerial diligence. This prosperity was not without its challenges, and it left a deep imprint upon the business philosophies of the oil executive.

COMPETING CAUTIOUSLY IN DOMESTIC MARKETS

At a time when competitors were bold and their number was increasing, Jersey Standard's caution in serving an expanding domestic market bordered on timidity. The conservative attitude that prevailed at 26 Broadway may have been unfortunate, but it was defensible. Standard Oil still had many public enemies, and the perplexing economic crosscurrents of the 1920's were difficult to explain to those who could not or would not understand the oil business.

Many Congressmen had noted the bitterness and frequency of complaints that crude oil prices were at or very near the break-even point and that many small producers were professedly losing money. How, then, was it that gasoline prices were so high as to cause complaints from the motoring public? A Congressional committee headed by Senator LaFollette sought to find out, and in 1923 it returned a damning report on conditions allegedly prevailing in the petroleum industry since 1920.

The Standard Oil Trust, LaFollette appeared to believe, was conspiring simultaneously to squeeze the small producer and rob the consuming public. The report of his committee charged that there was collusion among the Standard Oil companies disaffiliated in 1911, that gasoline prices were arbitrarily determined, that exorbitant profits were being made, and that operations by the Standard companies were characterized by waste and extravagance.[1]

This report exploded in the petroleum industry like a bomb. The Jersey Company lashed back at LaFollette in the May, 1923, issue of *The Lamp*. The guarded tones with which that publication usually discussed controversial issues were abandoned. The company accused the LaFollette Committee of suppressing evidence and of "rigid adherence to a set purpose, which was obviously the substantiation of a charge of domination and corrupt practices on the part of the so-called Standard companies." Teagle, the company asserted, had been refused the opportunity to submit statistical evidence to the investigators, and the investigation had been lacking in competent direction and thoroughness. Point by point the LaFollette Committee charges were discussed in various articles in *The Lamp*, the evidence of fact and of reason being brought to bear upon them with great force. A study by R. L. Welsh, secretary of the American Petroleum Institute, called attention to errors in the statistical methods employed by the committee and even in the basic figures employed. Warren C. Platt, editor of an important petroleum trade paper, went even further and suggested that the figures might have been willfully falsified.[2]

Certain of the committee findings—such as that "the dominating fact in the oil industry today is its complete control by the Standard companies"—were patently untrue. Such utterances, flaunting or misconstruing available evidence, were typical of the old sensation-seeking attacks of the trust-busting days gone by. An objective estimate of all points raised by the 1923 report indicates that the evidence submitted in rebuttal of the charges was more convincing than that presented by the investigating committee. There is little doubt that the LaFollette report was, as A. C. Bedford described it, "frankly a political document."[3] The charges, however, received far wider publicity than the denials, and the political atmosphere was reminiscent of the earlier years of Jersey Standard's penance. The most favorable interpretation of the 1923 investigation is that it, like the American buyers' strike of 1921, was a reflection of popular protest against economic conditions which were widespread and the fault of no one company or group of companies or industry. Jersey's leaders, while outraged, were deeply impressed.

Not until almost five years later was the miasmal cloud, which had hung over the petroleum industry since the LaFollette Committee returned its findings, partially dispersed. In December of 1927 the Federal Trade Commission published the voluminous results of a survey of prices, profits, and competition in the industry.[4] This report was critical of certain phases of operations in the industry, but at the same time it contradicted many of the charges and implications of the LaFollette survey. Though the 1927 report persisted in the virtually meaningless statistical groupings of "Standard Oil Interests," it did make clear, at last, the reasons for that peculiar behavior of gasoline prices which was nourishing suspicions of restraint of trade in the petroleum industry. The broad and well-illustrated conclusion reached by the Federal Trade Commission was one familiar to every oilman but imperfectly understood by the public—that in most instances it was futile to attempt an explanation of prevailing price levels of refined products in terms of prevailing prices and supplies of crude petroleum at the well. Only the long-term trend of prices was affected by conventional supply-demand relationships; at any given moment that relationship might be gravely disturbed by conditions, practices, and unpredictable events peculiar to this complex industry.[5]

Against a reviving market for gasoline in 1922 the petroleum industry charged the costs of still subnormal demand and consequent low prices for other refined products. This situation was unfortunate for the motoring public but entirely normal in an industry which depended for its existence upon the total return from all its product lines. Much more than by-product economics, however, was involved. As Teagle himself had already noted, pessimism over crude supplies had become a chronic malady in the oil business. Though every oil company was frankly anxious to maximize its profits, it was the lingering fear of shortage rather than a deliberate conspiracy which was subverting the workings of the law of supply and demand in the period under investigation. Each spring for three years (1924, 1925, and 1926), for example, gasoline prices advanced in the face of prevailing low crude oil prices, tremendous stored reserves, and adequate crude oil production. One explanation given for these increases was that they merely represented restoration of prices to "normal" levels following cuts which had been made in the preceding winters for the purpose of stimulating off-season buying. A strong psychological factor, moreover, was at work. The price leaders in the industry, awed perhaps by the immensity of the demand which they were responsible for meeting, had become fearful whenever even small drafts were made on their reserves in storage—which, to be sure, were equivalent to a few months' supply at best. Ignoring current supply-demand relationships, these companies in the three successive years set price levels in anticipation of shortages which never developed. This was a communal error of judgment in a business that had always been intimately affected by the laws of chance. For its bad guesses the industry itself paid the penalty in the form of sharp price reactions in the closing months of each year— and in finally provoking, in 1927, a condition of crude oil oversupply that shook the oil trade to its foundations. This, in barest outline, was the political and economic framework within which Jersey Standard marketing policies and practices of the 1920's were molded.

The essence of Jersey Standard's marketing effort between 1919 and 1927 is not to be found in a description of which products were delivered to the trade and in what quantities, but this information is essential nonetheless. The chart on page 189 and Appendix 2, Tables X-XIII, present the best statistical compilations of such data that could be gleaned from existing company records. The trends revealed there are ones already familiar—the intensified extensions of movements already under way before 1918. Deliveries of refined products in the United States by the Jersey organization increased some 133 per cent over the years 1919 through 1927. Since the domestic business done by Jersey's new affiliate in Texas accounted for only about 9 per cent of this increase, the growth in deliveries must be attributed predominantly to the growth of demand in established market territories rather than to any substantial geographic expansion of selling effort. With Humble's share of the business subtracted, the resulting 124 per cent increase in Jersey's volume of trade matches rather closely the rise in total consumption of oil products in the United States over the period (144 per cent).[6]

The rate of growth varied widely among the major product classifications. The chart on page 189 indicates to what extent kerosene was being displaced by other lines. Table XII in Appendix 2 compares company trends with those in the industry and shows that between 1919 and 1927 Jersey lost ground to competitors in gasoline and kerosene deliveries, while improving its position in fuel and lubricating oils. The net exchange slightly favored the company. In 1919 the Jersey organization accounted for approximately 10.1 per cent of the domestic refined product deliveries in the United States; in 1927, for 11.0 per cent.[7]

The great absolute increases in gasoline deliveries which took place over the period, of course, are readily explained by the tremendous expansion in the number of automobiles in operation. Lubricating and gas oil deliveries reflected the influence of a level of general industrial activity which was rapidly approaching an all-time peak. Great growth in the demand for fuel oil derived from this same economic tempo and from an accelerating rate of conversion to Diesel power units by the fleets of the world. These were the years of the business millennium, and the uses for petroleum products were legion.

Jersey's basic marketing policy was to ride the boom, maintain its prevailing share of the business, and increase the operating efficiency of its distributing organization. No reorganization comparable in scope to that which had been brought about in the Foreign Shipping Department was deemed necessary, but there were some changes. Concern over organizational formalities and over the need for co-ordinating groups characterized the early years of the Teagle administration to a marked degree. On May 15, 1919, the Marketing Committee was established—or, more accurately, re-established, since this committee had been an active one in the years before the dissolution. T. J. Williams, who had headed the Domestic Trade Department of Jersey Standard since 1908, was named chairman. Other members, at various times, included representatives of each of the major geographic and product divisions of the business. Top-level direction of domestic marketing activities changed rapidly, for the leaders in this branch of operations were mostly older men. Williams relinquished his committee chairmanship in August of 1919, when he was elevated to a Jersey directorship, and was succeeded briefly by C. E. Young, the head of the Newark Division since 1890. Young retired in 1921 and was replaced by J. H. Senior, of the West India Oil Company. Williams supervised marketing affairs at the directorship level for only a short time. In 1922 Teagle brought the hard-hitting G. W. Mayer from Toronto to fill the vacancy caused by Williams' retirement. Mayer, in turn, retired from the directorate in 1925, and his marketing responsibilities were passed to fellow director J. A. Moffett, Jr. A new domestic trade committee was formed, with some of the administrative functions hitherto performed in branch offices being centralized at 26 Broadway.[8]

At the operational level the spirit of change which pervaded the Marketing Department derived more from external pressures than from the accelerated rate of managerial succession. Even before 1919 many of the economic, contractual, and personal ties which initially inhibited the effective working out of the dissolution decree had ceased to exist. After 1919 the petroleum industry rapidly began to assume a form which perhaps it might have taken much earlier had the Standard Oil Trust never existed. The Atlantic Refining Company burst out of its traditional territories in Pennsylvania and Delaware and began to market in New England in competition with Standard of New York and in the southern coastal states in competition with the Jersey Company. Standard of New York followed this precedent by acquiring outright control of Magnolia, which competed with Louisiana Standard in Arkansas and with Humble in Texas. The Tide Water Oil Company, in which Jersey Standard owned a large though not controlling interest (23 per cent in 1927), began in postwar months to market actively in the New York area. These manifestations of the prevailing expansionist psychology among former members of the Jersey family were dwarfed by the efforts put forth by The Texas Company, the Gulf Oil Corporation, and other firms in the so-called "independent" group.[9]

The gasoline market was a rich prize, competition centering in efforts by the rival oil companies to obtain retail outlets. In their respective territories both Jersey Standard and Standard of New York were left far behind in the initial postwar rush for service-station affiliations. The origins of the so-called lease-and-license program are not easily traced, but in the early 1920's several companies, seeking what they conceived to be their proper share of the eastern seaboard market, vigorously began to utilize such means for obtaining exclusive outlets for their gasoline in Jersey territories. These agreements stipulated that the hitherto independent station owner should, in return for a generous consideration, lease his station to the oil company, operating the station thereafter under a license from the company and handling only that company's products. In effect, the lease-and-license plan amounted to a concession to dealers from prevailing tank-wagon prices.[10]

With only eleven service stations owned outright in 1919, the Jersey Company's contacts with the retail gasoline market were extremely vulnerable to attack. The marketing men at 26 Broadway, however, were slow in perceiving the danger. Despite warnings and protests from the Newark and Baltimore division-office representatives, no authorizations were forthcoming to allow Jersey marketers in the field to employ lease-and-license agreements as a means of obtaining and holding retail distributors. In 1918 the company did 75 per cent of the motor fuel business in the Baltimore area, but by 1920 the figure had shrunk to 20 per cent. By 1924 the number of Jersey-owned service stations had grown to 87, but competitors appear to have been expanding their owned retail stations even more rapidly. This same comparative situation prevailed in respect to bulk gasoline distributing stations in Jersey's Newark and Baltimore sales divisions. Between 1919 and 1924 the company increased the number of such stations by 60 per cent (from 410 to 654), while competing bulk stations grew almost 80 per cent in number (from 250 to 447). Jersey's share of the gasoline business declined, in consequence, from 58 per cent of the total in 1919 to 47 per cent in 1924.[11]

One popular explanation for Jersey's widescale entry into service-station ownership and operation in 1925 is that this move was made in order to provide more up-to-date and adequate facilities for the motorist. These, however, were derived advantages. The real motivating force lay in the discovery that by 1924 the company had come to have an unsatisfactory large-dealer representation in the heavily populated centers of its territories. At the same time, company delivery equipment was being employed to haul gasoline many miles into the country to supply small dealers. Competitors—The Texas Company in particular—were making serious inroads on Jersey's business. Through extensive recourse to lease-and-license agreements with station owners The Texas Company was able, for example, not only to wean retail outlets away from the Jersey Company, but also to attract the business of jobbers with the promise of assured service-station outlets.[12]

The real explanations for Jersey Standard's lack of drive in the critical years between 1919 and 1924 may only be surmised. The Legal Department was intensely (and from the viewpoint of the marketers, excessively) concerned with the legality of special inducements to dealers. An attitude of "wait and see what happens to competitors" prevailed. In the Marketing Department itself top management was old and had been trained in an era when company markets had been relatively secure. Even Mayer, who with great determination had fought off challenges to Imperial's markets in Canada in the years preceding his assignment with Jersey, was beginning to tire at last and was persuaded to postpone his retirement only by the personal urgings of Teagle. Certainly the concept that the entire marketing situation had been dramatically altered was one which the older men could not be expected to grasp readily. It may be more than coincidental that company policy was brought under critical review at about the same time that direction of the department passed from Mayer to the young and aggressive Jimmy Moffett.

In 1924 the Marketing Committee held a joint conference with the Jersey Board of Directors and with field executives. The legal viewpoint prevailed; Jersey's marketers were denied permission to utilize exclusive-agency contracts. A program of owned service-station expansion, however, was recommended at this important meeting as an antidote for the lease-and-license activities of competitors. This program was immediately put into effect.[13] Louisiana Standard, which up to 1924 had owned few retail stations, also began to push the expansion program. Humble did little at this time. Over the course of the next two years the Jersey organization made considerable progress in building and buying stations, but it still lagged behind many of its competitors and other oil companies, who were simultaneously acquiring stations at an extraordinary rate.

Standing in the way of more rapid Jersey expansion was a cautious ruling that all station acquisitions be approved in advance by the Legal Department, which took the position that the acquisition program should always leave a reasonable amount of business available to competitors. The delays attendant upon obtaining such approval were so costly, however, that in 1925 the policy was established of requiring Legal Department authorization only when the number of Jersey's own service stations exceeded 30 per cent of the total number of vending stations, including garages, in any community, or when the volume of company sales through its own stations and other retail outlets exceeded 30 per cent of total retail gasoline sales.[14] In practice, authorizations were often given in areas where the company owned as many as 75 per cent of the stations in the community.

Nevertheless, the competitive situation continued to deteriorate. Sinclair undertook an extensive eastern expansion program and cut seriously into Jersey's tank-car sales to jobbers. The lease-and-license program of competitors was intensified. A Supreme Court ruling sustained the legality of the practice of lending pumps and tanks to dealers and of confining the use of such equipment to the dispensing of the lending company's oil. This ruling was interpreted by many marketing companies as permitting the extension to station operators of many additional inducements— a practice conceived in and nourished by increasing competitive pressures. Abnormal rentals were paid by some companies for exclusive sign-display privileges at stations. Driveways, canopies, and even complete stations were constructed, and equipment of all kinds was installed without cost to the station owners in return for exclusive patronage. Informal agreements were frequently made to extend price concessions to dealers consenting to an exclusive relationship. Many service stations were granting special prices to commercial vehicles and selling coupon books to non-commercial buyers at prices that approximated wholesale levels.[15]

The intensity of these competitive pressures is perhaps explicable in terms of the dynamic nature of the market. The era of crude oil scarcity had been supplanted, because of prolific field discoveries, by one of rapidly mounting supplies. In all market areas new competitors were trying to effect entry. Drastic measures were necessary in order to attract business from established firms. Jersey Standard, enjoying a large percentage of the available business in its marketing territories, found it expensive to attempt to compete with newcomers who initially attacked in localized segments of the markets in which the Jersey Company did business. The cumulative effect of the loss of one small outlet after another, however, was becoming serious. Much of the company's bulk distribution system, moreover, had been established at a time when deliveries from bulk plants were made by animal-drawn wagons. As a result, bulk stations were seldom more than 25 miles apart. New competitors, by taking advantage of the long hauls made possible by motor-vehicle transportation, were able to build effective distribution systems around a relatively small number of bulk plants. Not only was entry into the business facilitated by motor-truck deliveries, but Jersey Standard was forced to the trouble and expense of shifting an established distribution pattern.

Jersey field representatives complained bitterly and with increasing frequency that, though the company had finally authorized the loaning of pumps and tanks, they were still at an extreme disadvantage in trying to hold their trade. In July of 1925 another joint conference was called between representatives of the Marketing Department and the Jersey board, at which the admittedly serious competitive situation was discussed. The marketers were discouraged. Everyone agreed that the company was rapidly losing much of its prestige in the field of domestic marketing, and that this loss could be stopped only by drastic measures. Discussion centered in the possibility of alterations in the company's price structure.

Jersey pricing policy, a particularly delicate matter, had been influenced more by legal and traditional considerations than by prevailing competitive conditions. As had been the case before 1919, the company's tank-wagon price for gasoline was taken by the industry as the official market price in Jersey Standard sales territories. In the years when the company enjoyed an almost unchallenged position in its markets, that price level had been set to permit a very comfortable margin of profit. By 1924 the fact had been demonstrated that Jersey's price was well above the level called for by the prevailing competitive situation. The company continued, nevertheless, to adhere so rigidly to its prices that competitors enjoyed a practical guarantee of immunity against retaliation when they offered local price concessions to obtain business.[16]

Jersey's reluctance to match these concessions may have derived in part from failure of the directors to appreciate the seriousness of the existing market situation, but the principal reason lay in the conviction of the Legal Department that local price reductions were not defensible against the federal Clayton Act and state anti-price-discrimination statutes.[17] Jersey must lower its prices over wide segments of its territories or not at all. The July, 1925, conference was therefore confronted with a difficult and contradictory situation.

At last a recommendation was made and adopted that Jersey's tank-wagon prices be revised in an effort to cut the wide margin between wholesale and retail prices which hitherto had allowed competitors to make generous concessions to dealers and still earn a profit. Henceforward state-wide price levels were made to fluctuate with changes in average competitive prices prevailing in each state where the company marketed.[18] In view of the frequent charges of the day that gasoline prices were too high, this decision has particular interest. Had competitive pressures been less acute, Jersey policy, unless modified by public opinion alone, might well have produced that very situation which critics of the industry believed to exist. Too many competitors, however, had squeezed under the ample price umbrella, and the Jersey Company was forced to do that which had been unnecessary earlier—reduce the size of the umbrella.

The action of July, 1925, had a beneficial effect upon business volume, and in the following year the Legal Department devised ways by which the company hoped to meet local competitive situations effectively, legally, and without necessitating further general state- or territory-wide price reductions. Jersey retail dealers were authorized to quote special prices to operators of commercial vehicles when it could be proved that competitors had initiated such practices. Company jobbers were also authorized to meet competitive price concessions to station owners, provided that proof of such concessions could be produced. This policy of defensive pricing, however, the Jersey marketers characterized, for many reasons, as "most unsatisfactory." In 1926 the so-called factorage agreement was inaugurated as a counter to competitive concessions to retail station operators.

Under the factorage arrangement the Jersey Company concluded regular consignment agreements with dealers, allowing them a commission based upon station rentals and the prevailing competitive differential between tank-wagon and service-station prices. Since the courts had ruled that in such transactions the title to the goods passed directly from the consignor to the final purchaser and never vested in the middleman, the Jersey Company was able to argue that the varying commissions allowed its factors did not constitute a discriminatory price transaction under the one-price laws because no sale of merchandise was involved. In practice, the circumstances under which such agreements were permitted by the Legal Department were carefully delineated, the chief concern being that no local monopoly situation be created. Relatively few of the proposed factorage agreements, however, failed to win the approval of Jersey's lawyers.[19]

By the end of 1927 Jersey's efforts to sharpen its competitive weapons had not proved outstandingly successful; marketing policy was essentially conservative and far from what many men in the Marketing Department wished. On only very special occasions did the company extend inducements to dealers other than the loan of pump and tank equipment; hence the company continued to be handicapped in its efforts to obtain and hold exclusive outlets. As a result, Jersey distributors grew restive and sometimes took matters into their own hands, on one occasion precipitating a lawsuit in which The Texas Company charged that Jersey marketers were stealing customers.[20] Efforts to institute effective and prompt counteraction against new marketing schemes introduced by other companies were impeded by the delays involved in clearing proposed measures through the Legal Department. The company suffered most severely, too, from its attempts to compete legally with small local dealers who were not subject to federal and state anti-price-discrimination laws and with certain large operators who appeared willing to place a liberal construction on the practices permitted by those laws. In this particular situation the highly conservative viewpoint entertained by the Legal Department was probably wise—if costly. With public protests being heard again, it is not surprising that these able lawyers should have attempted, in the face of tremendous temptations, to perpetuate the cautious attitude which had evolved in the troubled times and urgent necessities of the company's earlier history.

The Jersey board was itself to blame in some particulars for the difficulties experienced by the marketers in holding their position in the retail gasoline trade. The equipment loan program was impeded by failure of the company to provide an adequate supply of pumps and tanks.[21] An Advertising Committee had been formed in December of 1921, but advertising expenditures were not greatly increased in the face of the first surge of competition after 1919, and they did not exceed a million dollars annually until 1927. Brand policy reached a climax of indecision at the very time when the competitive situation was at its worst.

Up to 1918, as we have seen, the Jersey Company marketed a wide variety of products under a wide variety of trade names. The "Standard Motor Gasoline" mark was not registerable and could not, in any case, be used outside the company's old marketing territories without infringing the rights of other Standard Oil companies. After 1911 the once-mighty Standard Oil name was, in effect, a tremendous liability, yet all the forces of sentiment and many considerations of logic militated against its abandonment. In 1920, when the United States copyright laws were altered to permit the registration of descriptive brand names, Jersey at once registered the "Standard" mark with the Patent Office. Plans were formulated to register this name in several states and to apply it to all company products as rapidly as possible. The Legal Department at once objected that, in view of the probable inability to prove the company's right to the exclusive use of the mark, such a course was inadvisable.[22]

This clash of opposing considerations led, as might be expected, to a compromise solution rather than to a bold renunciation and a fresh start. Jersey men began to experiment with names to which the cobwebs of history still clung, but which could still be used in other Standard Oil territories without fear of infringement. *Stangas—Sonjol—Jerzene;* so went the suggestions. On February 3, 1923, C. A. Straw, the director of the patent and trade-mark division of the company, hit upon *Esso.* This name, embodying as it did the phonetic rendition of the old Standard Oil monogram, met with considerable favor. A design coupling "Esso" with the "SO" monogram was worked out and submitted for registration. In a faint foreshadowing of things to come, Standard of New York promptly objected to the use by the Jersey Company of the monogram. This part of the mark was therefore dropped, and the word "Esso" alone was registered.[23] The new trade-mark was held in abeyance pending further consideration of the brand question.

The next step in the history of Jersey Standard's present family trade-mark involved what finally proved to be one of the happier episodes in the marketing story from 1919 to 1927—the bringing out of an exceptionally high grade of motor fuel. This move was made imperative by the action of competing companies in bringing out benzol-treated blends of gasoline of relatively high antiknock rating.

As early as 1919 the Jersey Company had considered the possibility of bringing out a premium-quality, benzol-treated gasoline. It was decided, however, that there was no substantial demand for a better fuel than straight gasoline and that well-directed sales effort would soon drive out the competitive premium fuels. The company was reluctant, moreover, to encourage the manufacture and sale of a competitive fuel produced by an industry in no way related to petroleum, particularly since facilities for benzol production had been greatly expanded during the war years.

This policy soon proved to be a mistake. In the face of rising popularity of premium-grade gasolines the Jersey Company began to purchase benzol, substantial quantities of which were added to the company's gasoline in 1921 and 1922. Jersey marketers, however, continued to complain that the quality of the product being supplied to them by the Jersey refineries was not adapted to prevailing market requirements. In 1924, therefore, the company placed a premium-quality antiknock gasoline on the market under the name of "Standard Ethyl Gasoline"—the first fuel marketed by the company which contained tetraethyl lead. A serious manufacturing accident at Bayway, however, caused such widespread public fear of ethyl gasoline that the new product was withdrawn and a benzol mixture substituted pending further experiments. Teagle asked for a distinctive new trade-mark for the benzol-treated product; Straw again suggested "Esso." This name was considered and approved at the marketing conference of February, 1926, thenceforward becoming the generic name not only of the new premium gasoline but, in time, of the entire company line at home and abroad.[24]

Esso gasoline was first placed on the market in April of 1926 at a premium of five cents per gallon above the service-station price for "Standard Motor Gasoline." Even before the difficulties with ethyl had been resolved (Chapter 17) and the benzol blend replaced, Jersey men were convinced that their product was better than any other. An advertising campaign was launched which called for the expenditure of $375,000 in the first year.[25] Public response was gratifying, and Esso gasoline started its career auspiciously by helping Jersey's hard-pressed marketers to regain some of the ground that had been lost to competitors.

At the end of 1926, the only year for which such statistics are available, the Jersey Company, with approximately 43.2 per cent of the total business, was still by far the largest marketer of gasoline in its own territories. Gulf was second with 13.6 per cent of the total, and Texas was third with 12.7 per cent.[26] In Louisiana Standard territory the same relative situation prevailed: the Louisiana Company commanded 35.5 per cent of the gasoline market, Gulf 12.3 per cent, and Texas 7.9 per cent. The Jersey organization was doing a smaller total gasoline business through retail outlets than either Gulf or The Texas Company, which marketed in 26 and 44 states, respectively. Jersey Standard, however, enjoyed the advantages of concentrated effort in 11 states. In 1927 the company was still, despite its troubles, in a favored position to exert market leadership, provided that the requisite skill and verve could be mustered within the organization to defend against the continuing market assault.

Jersey Standard's position in the bulk trade to large customers was also a strong one—stronger in 1927, in fact, than in 1919, for it was in this trade that the company had recouped the relative losses suffered in the retail gasoline market.

Statistical evidence bearing upon the trade outlets through which company products moved to market after 1919 is fragmentary, but it appears that deliveries to other large oil companies and large industrial consumers continued to exceed by a substantial margin the quantity of products sold to small jobbers, retailers, and the public. In January of 1927 Teagle testified before the Federal Trade Commission that over 60 per cent of the company's total domestic sales of all products were made in tank-car and barge lots, and that the principal extension of the company's business since the dissolution decree had been in the bulk rather than in the tank-wagon trade.[27]

This was true even of gasoline, despite a conclusion to the contrary in the Federal Trade Commission report of 1927. In 1919 some 47.5 per cent of Jersey's domestic gasoline sales were made through its own marketing divisions, while 50.9 per cent went to Standard of New York, an amount constituting 61.5 per cent of the total gallonage which that company, in turn, sold. Despite Jersey's drive to build up its own retail outlets after 1919, bulk gasoline sales continued heavy. In 1924 about 47.8 per cent of the company's total domestic gasoline sales were made to Standard of New York; in 1927 the New York Company was still depending on Jersey Standard for over 50 per cent of its gasoline sales requirements.[28]

There were, in addition, other very large sales contracts of fuel oil to the Shipping Board, the United American Lines, the International Mercantile Marine, the Hamburg-American Line, North German Lloyd, the Italian and French navies, and other shipping interests. It was the close attention of Jersey management to obtaining business of this kind, rather than the well-publicized and more dramatic effort in the retail trade, which enabled the company to show a slight relative gain over competitors in the total volume of business done in the 1919-1927 period and to record substantial earnings in each year except 1921.

At the close of 1927 Jersey Standard could count many gains in domestic marketing. Of these the greatest, perhaps, was the change in public attitudes. Gasoline prices, in falling in the mid-1920's to the lowest point since 1915, had negated the dire prognostications of dollar-a-gallon motor fuel which had been voiced in the years from 1920 to 1923. The oil industry—temporarily at least—had ceased to be the target of public censure. Even more important, the Federal Trade Commission in its 1927 report made some unprecedented statements and published some remarkable evidence. The Standard Oil companies, it appeared, were generally conceded to be fair competitors and a stabilizing force in an industry which had changed, during the past twenty years, from one in which there was a high degree of monopolistic control to one in which freedom of competition generally prevailed.[29] Jersey's gasoline marketers, smarting under competitive attack and writhing under restraint, could find solace in the knowledge that the fact of their forbearance had been noted and at least obliquely commended.

STRENGTH AND COMPROMISE
IN THE FOREIGN TRADE

Jersey Standard's profits from foreign marketing continued to exceed those made in the domestic trade—often by a very wide margin. This circumstance derived both from long-established priorities abroad and from great flexibility in the face of a rapidly changing market environment. In no other area of operations did the traditional policy of allowing its affiliates freedom in governing their own affairs have such important and favorable results. Yet, at the same time, those affiliates of necessity looked often to the parent company for tangible assistance and for policy guidance. The demands of the foreign trade were for alert adaptability in the field and for sympathetic cognizance at 26 Broadway.

These requirements were competently fulfilled by the existing organization. In 1919 the foreign affiliates were still guided by the strong men of prewar years—Riedemann in Germany, Speth and Maquinay in Belgium, Klaare and Horstmann in Holland, Holm and Hauan in Scandinavia, Mowinckel in Italy, and Senior in South America. All were men of great ability and long experience. To their number had been added some younger men, new to the ranks of top management, such as Henry Bedford, Jr., and Peter Hurll in France and F. H. Bedford, Jr., who was in charge of both the domestic and the Continental lubricating oil business. The Jersey directorate, itself thoroughly conversant with the intricacies of the foreign business and sensitive to its potentialities, was strongly commanded by an ingenious, persevering, and fearless leader—Walter Teagle. The Export Trade Department continued, under the general supervision of director F. D. Asche, to be the staunch managerial unit that it had been without interruption since early in the century. D. L. Harper headed the department at the operating level and continued after 1924 to serve efficiently under Asche's successor, James A. Moffett, Jr. The lines of communication between 26 Broadway and all marketing offices abroad were open and well defined; administrative techniques were clearly understood; mechanical procedures were familiar.

Most important of all, the new Teagle administration was encouraging close policy and operational liaison between foreign marketing, domestic marketing, producing, refining, and transportation units of the organization. Commencing in 1924 the permanent members of the European Committee met two or three times weekly in Paris to pool information about marketing, refining, and producing, to co-ordinate these activities, and to regulate petroleum stocks and the movement of tankers. Periodically through the year conferences, which provided opportunities for extensive surveys of Continental developments, were held with the heads of the various European affiliates.

Jersey Standard wealth and experience were pitted against unfavorable trends of formidable dimensions. Inflation and general economic chaos disturbed the postwar European market to an important extent. Intense nationalism was as hostile to Jersey foreign marketing interests as to the company's efforts to expand foreign production. The threat of state petroleum monopolies appeared in many places, and in many places was more than a mere threat. Competitors, new and old, sought to strengthen their position before Jersey Standard could form new competitive alignments to replace those disturbed and broken by the war. The most important of those competitors were foreign corporations, whose freedom from American antitrust statutes permitted them to combine and operate boldly. As late as 1926 the Jersey Company was still sensitive to the possibility of antitrust prosecution on the basis of its foreign holdings. Company lawyers recommended a policy of caution abroad as well as at home, even though such a policy might place the company at a competitive disadvantage. Indeed, one reason for the operational freedom granted the foreign affiliates admittedly lay in the fear that any obvious control from 26 Broadway would precipitate a legal attack on the company by the Department of Justice.[30] As subsequent paragraphs reveal, however, the advice of the Legal Department was not so inhibitory in the foreign as in the domestic trade.

The foreign-trade policy of the organization was intimately linked with foreign producing objectives. Teagle and Sadler had irrevocably committed the company to the expansion of crude oil reserves abroad and had enlisted the support of the American State Department. The maintenance of strong foreign markets was equally essential in order that Jersey might establish a well-integrated foreign business and stay strong abroad.

At the same time, however, the demands of the foreign trade had to be measured against domestic price and supply trends, for as late as 1927 most of the products sold abroad still were being refined in America from American crude stocks. Decisions called forth by the competitive situation abroad could, and often did, conflict with the dictates imposed by domestic conditions.

Pricing required a particularly delicate managerial touch, for Jersey's foreign prices were determined primarily by American crude oil prices (and, of course, by ocean shipping rates), while the European market price level reflected the influences of foreign crudes—particularly Russian. Jersey Standard was able not only to market successfully abroad in these years of increasing competition, but in general to charge slightly higher prices in the export trade than at home.[31] This pricing differential, prevailing despite the necessity for transporting refined products thousands of miles, was made possible by declining crude price levels in America, by the great efficiency of the Jersey tanker fleet, by failure of Galician and Romanian crude oil production to match the increases in European demand, and by the political squabbles that delayed the development of Middle East oil reserves. To a considerable extent, foreign price levels also showed the influence both of agreements between competitors to divide markets and of Jersey Standard's very strong marketing position in certain areas.

Profiting generally from its ability to get better prices abroad than at home, the Jersey Company also directed its price policy at meeting specific competitive and supply situations. Two export price schedules were maintained—published prices and so-called inside prices. Published prices formed the basis for most of the business with nonaffiliated companies, while the lower "inside" prices were quoted principally to affiliates. D. L. Harper felt that a differential of at least ¼ cent per gallon should be maintained between the two schedules. Actually, the gap was sometimes very much wider than that.[32]

To retain the large foreign business done with the Anglo-American Oil Company, Limited, and the Vacuum Oil Company—neither of which was an affiliate—the Jersey Company at least occasionally extended to them the privilege of its "inside" prices. Most of the foreign affiliates were not informed of the prices quoted by Jersey to the others, and the parent company sometimes differentiated in these family quotations in order to allow a particularly hard-pressed affiliate to meet a local competitive situation.[33] The necessity for such secrecy within the foreign-trade organization may well have derived from prevalent jealousy among the gifted but often temperamental leaders of the European affiliates.

Prices were also changed in order to swing the American supply point for the foreign trade to whatever loading port was most advantageous in view of the domestic supply and refining situation. This practice was provocative of protests from the foreign managers. In March of 1924, for example, freight rate differentials and prevailing East Coast price schedules favored the loading of European-bound tankers at New York rather than at Gulf ports. The foreign affiliates saw no reason why they should not take advantage of this situation to draw their requirements from Bayonne and Bayway, yet the Jersey Company wished them to take their supplies from Baton Rouge, where stocks were so excessive that the refinery there faced a curtailment of operations. In consequence, New York inside prices on export kerosene and gasoline were advanced ¼ cent per gallon in order to drive the trade to Baton Rouge. The affiliates would no doubt have preferred that Baton Rouge prices be cut ¼ cent to accomplish the same end.[34]

Three years later the supply situation reversed itself completely. The Manufacturing Committee advised the Export Trade and Marketing committees that excess stocks existed in New York and that at least 40 per cent of the foreign-trade requirements should be drawn from Bayonne and Bayway, particularly since the Baton Rouge refinery at that time was having difficulty in producing the quality and quantity of products required abroad. Price schedules, however, then favored loading at the Gulf, and the foreign affiliates objected to taking supplies from New York. The Manufacturing Committee was unwilling to cut New York prices because the refineries there were already operating at a loss, while a rise in Gulf prices was out of the question under prevailing competitive conditions.[35]

Riedemann complained that the DAPG was paying a cent per gallon more for gasoline purchased f.o.b. New York than the prevailing Gulf prices. Moffett replied that Jersey's export prices were generally in line with competitive quotations, but that sometimes sellers of distress gasoline or concerns anxious to win trade from Jersey might offer special concessions. Moffett then went on to point out to Riedemann the long-term advantage of trading with a stable concern which could guarantee supplies at all times. Teagle wrote Riedemann a rather sharp note, stating that he would "dislike very much to be obliged to admit that in order to sell its current output, the Jersey Company had to discount the quality of its products by naming a price for the same that was invariably lower than that of any of its competitors." Mowinckel, siding with Riedemann, tartly suggested that if the New York refineries could not meet Gulf prices they should withdraw from the export trade and Jersey should enlarge its refinery facilities at the Gulf.[36]

These exchanges, which may be traced interminably in the Jersey records, illustrate the difficulties encountered by the men at 26 Broadway in guiding, for the general interest, the diverse operations of the foreign affiliates, and in curbing the natural inclination of the foreign managers to advance their particular corporate interest. The specific problems met in the various marketing areas form the subject matter for the remainder of this section of the chapter, but the general trends and cumulative results of all foreign marketing operations should first be set forth briefly as a background for the individual case studies.

Although Jersey Standard and its affiliates were supplying only about 10 per cent of the total domestic market, Jersey exports in the 1919-1927 period ranged from 25 to 41 per cent of total exports of refined products from the United States (Appendix 2, Table X). These figures have validity only in measuring Jersey's foreign business against that of other American companies. In terms of world trade, foreign deliveries of the Jersey organization were approximately 12 per cent of total foreign consumption of crude oil and refined products in 1912, 18 per cent in 1919, and 19 per cent in 1927. In 1927 Jersey's foreign gasoline sales were equivalent to 30 per cent of all gasoline consumed outside the United States in that year.[37] No satisfactory base has been found with which to compare the volume of Jersey Standard's foreign trade with that of specific foreign competitors over a period of time. A set of figures for 1927, however, indicates that of the total consumption of refined products outside the United States, the Jersey organization supplied 23 per cent; the Royal Dutch-Shell 16 per cent; the Anglo-Persian Oil Company 11.5 per cent; Russian suppliers 6.5 per cent; and all others (for the most part American companies) 43 per cent.[38]

Growth and high profits characterized the foreign trade from 1919 to 1927, but both volume growth and earnings varied widely among marketing areas. In 1919 deliveries to Europe were at a low level, but solid earnings in Canada were responsible for higher total profits in Jersey's business outside the United States than at home. The European trade revived somewhat in the following two years and in 1921 helped to offset heavy losses at home, but the derangement of European currencies interfered with exports to the area. After 1921 Canadian operations returned a steady and substantial profit. Earnings of European affiliates fluctuated in response to the highly competitive situation prevailing there, never regaining the predominant importance they had held before the war. The industrialization of Latin America, however, continued to accelerate, and it was the tremendous growth in this business which accounted for the great increase in Jersey Standard's total foreign marketing earnings between 1919 and 1927.

In 1927, as had been the case in 1912, by far the greater volume of export deliveries went to affiliated companies. In 1912, 63 per cent of export deliveries went to affiliates and 37 per cent to other customers. Of that 37 per cent, Jersey's one-time affiliate and still good customer, the Anglo-American Oil Company, Limited, took 54 per cent. In 1927, 64 per cent of export deliveries went to affiliates and 36 per cent to other customers, with Anglo-American taking 70 per cent of the deliveries to nonaffiliates. In the interval between these two dates Jersey's British friends consistently took about one-fifth of all Jersey's export deliveries.[39] Space does not permit a detailed analysis of markets in each year from 1919 to 1927, but Table XIII in Appendix 2 illustrates the extent and proportion of Jersey's foreign trade in the three major product lines (gasoline, kerosene, and fuel oil) in the representative year 1924.

The voluminous figures by which Jersey clerks recorded the course of Jersey's foreign trade were reflected in widely disparate circumstances in many parts of the globe. The most outstanding episodes in particular countries will serve to exemplify the nature and direction of the foreign marketing effort after 1919, though sight must not be lost of the importance of the routine, day-by-day, invoice-by-invoice transactions by which company products were made to move into the markets of the world.

In both Canada and Latin America Jersey Standard affiliates enjoyed a dominating position in the oil trade. Neither Imperial Oil, Limited, nor the Latin American affiliates, however, followed a passive course. Great efforts were expended in both areas to fend off growing competition and preserve or improve upon the favorable situation prevailing in 1919. Those efforts led to divergent results in the two areas.

In Canada the drive for market outlets was comparable in timing to that launched by Jersey Standard in the United States. Widespread Canadian prosperity and a program of large extensions of the paved roads in the provinces provided expanding markets for gasoline, fuel oil, lubricants, and asphaltic compounds. With market expansion, however, came a flood of competition. Imperial fought to hold its dominant position in the Canadian market by all means at its command. Prices were cut to meet specific competitive challenges, and improvements were continually sought in quality and service. Bulk station outlets were multiplied; great promotional effort was exerted in all markets. Abandoning in 1920 the device of operating service stations through a hidden affiliate, Imperial entered into the retail gasoline business directly and began to expand the

number of its owned station outlets. An increasing amount of trade, however, was channeled through independent jobbers.[40]

In some respects, at least, it seems clear that the Canadian business
was conducted in ways no longer expedient or possible in the United
States. Certain competitors who became too strong were bought out. In
western Canada an agreement with competitors sought to control cut-
throat business tactics. Imperial favored a high tariff on refined products
and in one instance offered concessions to independent operators who
were agitating for tariff reduction. Pressure was also brought to bear
upon railroads in Alberta to keep competitors in that area from obtaining freight-rate reductions on refined products. When competition with
Shell interests became acute on the west coast of Canada, a plan was
considered to stir up sentiment against Shell because of its foreign ownership—an issue, however, which Imperial could not push because of its
own vulnerability on this ground.

Notwithstanding these efforts, Imperial lost business to competitors.
Although aggressive marketing tactics were employed at certain times
and in some places, company response to the challenge of growing competition in many instances was conservative. Between 1921 and 1927 the
company's gasoline sales more than doubled, but Imperial's share of the
gasoline market slipped from 79 to 66 per cent of total. This same trend
characterized the other product lines as well. Marketing earnings remained relatively steady (Table 17), but this stability was a danger signal in an era when business was booming and profits might have been
increasing. The policy of "salesmanship, quality, and service" was not
enough. Imperial's attempt to hold its very large percentage of the far-
flung Canadian market was perhaps somewhat less successful than the
Jersey Company's attempt to preserve a more modest share of the business in concentrated segments of the market in the United States.

In Latin America a different situation prevailed. Jersey's position there
was strong in 1919 and did not, in general, become less so with the passing of years—except in Argentina, where, as noted earlier, steps were
being taken to build a national petroleum industry, and Venezuela, where
tariffs discouraged importation of refined products. Standard Oil of Brazil
and the West India Oil Company continued to push the substitution of
directly managed offices and substations for the old commission-agency
type of distributor. On the west coast and in Peru, however, Jersey
Standard continued for a time to rely heavily upon the British mercantile

Table 17: NET EARNINGS FROM MARKETING
Standard Oil Company (New Jersey) and Affiliates
1919-1927

Earnings	Dollar figures in thousands (Parentheses indicate net loss)								
Domestic	1919	1920	1921	1922	1923	1924	1925	1926	1927
Jersey Standard	$ 3,491	$ 4,315	$(1,182)	$ 5,749	$12,000	$ 9,358	$ 4,508	$ 7,735	$12,321
Louisiana Standard	532	702	(733)	766	783	1,015	(225)	1,863	2,341
Humble	60	110	79	(6)	(36)[a]	34	133	36	165
Other	3	22	8	25	27	9	(10)	119	166
Total domestic	$ 4,086	$ 5,149	$(1,828)	$ 6,534	$12,774	$10,416	$ 4,406	$ 9,753	$14,993
Foreign									
Canadian									
Imperial Oil	$ 3,554	$ 4,922	$ 2,014	$ 3,260	$ 4,160	$ 3,985	$ 3,762	$ 4,404	$ 4,847
Latin American									
West India Oil Co.	$ (435)	$ 1,588	$ 1,338	$ 2,875	$ 1,041	$ 4,969	$ 7,694	$ 8,876	$ 8,008
Standard Oil Co. of Brazil	1,089	(955)	(2,099)	(680)	(732)	909	3,156	3,387	1,933
Other	—	—	—	—	—	—	20	196	18
Total Latin American	$ 654	$ 633	$ (761)	$ 2,195	$ 309	$ 5,878	$10,870	$12,459	$ 9,959
European[c]									
American Pet., Belgium	[a]	$ 322	$ 55	$ 154	$ 52	$ 395	$ 185	$ 263	$ 140
American Pet., Holland	$ 1,461	1,409	863	641	561	548	1,283	624	657
Bedford Pet. Co., France	45	84	(34)	(109)	(63)	156	96	151	(50)
Det Danske, Denmark	1,167	375	60	1,677	752	(122)	939	1,079	1,168
DAPG, Germany	[a]	[a]	271	3,087	90	(978)	549	571	969
Pet. Import Cie., Switzerland	[a]	[a]	161	(656)	(98)	109	100	(13)	(167)
Italo-Americana, Italy	641	762	580	1,150	591	329	639	931	(336)
L'Economique, France	—	—	—	65	58	(33)	280	146	47
Other	(3,136)[b]	1,788	23	6	(21)	180	81	424	412
Total European	$ 178	$ 4,740	$ 1,979	$ 6,015	$ 1,922	$ 584	$ 4,152	$ 4,176	$ 2,840
Total	$ 8,472	$15,444	$ 1,404	$18,004	$19,165	$20,863	$23,190	$30,792	$32,639

Earnings as percentage of Jersey total marketing earnings[d]

	1919	1920	1921	1922	1923	1924	1925	1926	1927
Domestic	48.2	33.3	(130.2)	36.3	66.7	49.9	19.0	31.7	45.9
Canadian	42.0	31.9	143.4	18.1	21.7	19.1	16.2	14.3	14.9
Latin American	7.7	4.1	(54.2)	12.2	1.6	28.2	46.9	40.4	30.5
European	2.1	30.7	141.0	33.4	10.0	2.8	17.9	13.6	8.7
Total	100.0	100.0	100.0	100.0	100.0	100.0	100.0	100.0	100.0
Total marketing earnings as percentage of Jersey total earnings[d]	17.6	10.4	4.1	38.9	34.0	25.8	20.8	26.2	80.7

[a] Comparable data not available.
[b] Includes loss on lubricating consignments of $3,136,000.
[c] In certain cases includes dividends paid by European companies to Jersey Standard rather than Jersey's proportionate share of earnings.
[d] Since the percentage figure for any one earnings classification is determined not only by the actual amount recorded in that classification but also by earnings and losses in each of the others, no attempt should be made to trace year-to-year variations in one classification without careful reference both to other percentage classifications and to the pertinent dollar figures. All functional earnings figures given in SONJ, Fin. Recs., for the years 1912 through 1924 have been adjusted by the authors to match, insofar as possible, the account classifications employed in those records in the years 1925 through 1927.

Source: SONJ, Fin. Recs.

houses to reach the important nitrate, railroad, mining, agricultural, and municipal customers. These mercantile firms were well established, had strong political and industrial connections, and were generally well regarded in the area which they served.

One significant postwar trend was the steady increase in bulk shipments to South American markets. This movement reflected the large increase in trade and the extension to many of these countries of the same efficient methods of bulk distribution which had long prevailed elsewhere in the Jersey marketing system. Coincidental with this trend toward bulk rather than case and can shipments was the gradual increase in marketing activities of Jersey's Canadian-owned affiliates, whose success in obtaining production in Peru and Colombia has already been traced. The terms of the De Mares concession in Colombia had stated that The Tropical Oil Company (affiliate of Imperial's affiliate, the International Petroleum Company Limited) must supply the nation's needs for petroleum products. This proviso was not difficult to meet, since the existing market was limited and tariffs protected the kerosene trade against imported oil. Competition in gasoline from Shell interests, however, was keen.

The sale of products from Tropical's Barranca refinery commenced in May of 1922, and by 1924 the West India Oil Company had withdrawn from the Colombian market.[41] Production of the De Mares wells on the upper Magdalena was restricted until the local market could be built up and the Andian pipeline completed. Tropical's managers set a policy of rigidly maintaining low prices and undertook an extensive campaign to educate the Colombian natives to the advantages of kerosene lamps and stoves. Efforts were made at the same time to persuade industrialists to convert their river boats, railroads, and furnaces from wood fuel to oil. Available records fail to indicate the profits earned in supplying the Colombian market, but sales increased from 73,543 barrels of refined products in 1922 to 987,852 barrels in 1927. In 1926, with the completion of the Andian pipeline outlet from the fields to the sea, the sale of Tropical oil for export commenced. This trade was handled for Tropical by the International Petroleum Company Limited, which forwarded information on the specifications of the Colombian crude to Atlantic, Vacuum, Anglo-Persian, and other potential customers.[42]

Jersey's marketing position in Peru, as in Colombia, was strengthened by the closely integrated nature of producing, refining, and marketing operations. International Petroleum, which had direct jurisdiction over Peruvian producing and refining activities, did a large local business in products refined from La Brea crude oil at the Talara plant. In Peru, as in Colombia, political considerations dictated that prices be held to absolute minimum levels, International's gasoline quotations at Lima being reported on occasion as the lowest in South America. Much of this local business was actually handled for International on a commission basis by the distributing firm of Balfour, Williamson & Company, Limited. International also served large export markets with Peruvian crude and refined oil. Crude exports rose from an average of about 2,000 barrels daily in 1918 to more than 14,000 barrels daily in 1927, and went to Imperial's refineries at Vancouver and Halifax, to Jersey's refineries in the United States, and to affiliated plants at Havana and Campana, Argentina, and elsewhere. Refined products went chiefly to the west coast of South America, where they were distributed by the West India Oil Company and by Balfour, Williamson.

In this export trade there was spirited competition with Grace & Company, the Union Oil Company (a Royal Dutch-Shell affiliate), and the Anglo-Mexican Petroleum Company, Limited. International was forced, in consequence, to modify its old relationship with the British merchants, who proved to be less aggressive and efficient than the situation demanded. By 1927 some of the business in Peru and on the west coast handled by Balfour, Williamson and other commission houses had been entrusted to the West India Oil Company. Inspectors were also employed to supplement the efforts of the agent concerns. Otherwise, the agency system of distribution by which Jersey Standard had entered the Latin American market remained unchanged.[43]

This same trend toward direct participation in marketing was evident elsewhere throughout the world where the Jersey Company and its affiliates distributed refined petroleum products. In a great many areas, to be sure, the marketing function had been closely integrated since late in the nineteenth century, and in one district an opposite course was dictated by peculiar local circumstances. This last-named situation came about in the East Indies when the Talang Akar field at last rewarded the persistent efforts of Jersey's Dutch managers with production in marketable quantities and caused the building, in 1925, of a refinery at Palembang. Local markets in the area were small, and in any case Jersey's affiliate, the NKPM, had not developed an adequate marketing organization. Sale of the Palembang output, therefore, was turned over to Standard of New York, to which the Far Eastern market had fallen at the time of the dissolution decree.[44]

Jersey marketers on the opposite side of the world also confronted the problem of marketing channels and found it to be hedged with formidable difficulties. The prewar alignment by which Jersey Standard had supplied approximately two-thirds of the refined products consumed in France had been shattered. The tight grip of the French Refiners had been broken by their failure to meet the war emergency and by the subsequent formation of a government oil consortium that took control of imports and accepted the offers of any firms which could guarantee deliveries of petroleum products. Adroit maneuvering by C. S. Gulbenkian during the war years had strengthened the position of the Royal Dutch-Shell in the French market. The political atmosphere was extremely hostile to Jersey Standard, the French national oil interest had become allied by the San Remo Oil Agreement with Jersey's English and Dutch rivals, and proposals for a government petroleum monopoly were being advanced. Jersey, on the other hand, could count as surviving assets the friendship of some of the most important French oil-distributing firms, the sympathetic influence of the important Banque de Paris et des Pays-Bas, and the profound experience of the members of its own European Committee with the ephemeral vicissitudes of the Continental oil trade.

The government consortium which imported and directed the subsequent distribution of all oil products in France in the closing months of the war was perpetuated through 1919 and 1920—to the considerable annoyance of Jersey marketers. Restrictions thereafter were relaxed somewhat, but a licensing system was instituted whereby import privileges were restricted to a cartel group consisting of the old French firms and such new participants as the government wished to favor. It was clearly evident that the French government was determined to keep a close watch on the trade.[45] In the face of these obstacles, the Jersey Company promptly entered into complicated transactions to regain as much of its old market as was feasible.

Two principal and interrelated objectives were sought. The first was to commence marketing directly in France, introducing those efficiencies which had been so notoriously lacking under the French Refiners' monopoly of earlier years. Such a course spelled competition with former allies; therefore, the second objective was formulated of enlisting the financial participation of those allies.

In March of 1920 Jersey formed L'Economique, Société Anonyme de Distribution de Pétrole et Essence. L'Economique—or Eco, as it came to be called—was to undertake the actual bulk distribution of gasoline and kerosene in the French market. In October of the same year the Compagnie Standard Franco-Américaine was incorporated. A majority of Franco-American shares (51 per cent) was taken by the Banque de Paris, five influential French leaders being induced to sit on the nine-man board by a promise that 10 per cent of the net profits of this holding company would be paid to the directors. The founding purpose of Franco-American was to carry on a search for crude oil in France and the French colonies. When that search proved costly and unproductive it became necessary, in order to retain the essential good will of the French interests, to seek profits for the company in some other direction. Accordingly, the Jersey Company agreed to permit Franco-American to purchase up to 20 per cent of the capital stock of Eco.[46]

At the same time it was thus enlisting the support of French banking interests, Jersey moved to make agreements with such of the old Refiners group as had not already allied themselves with the Royal Dutch-Shell and other competitors. By these agreements the company hoped to assure both the co-operation of potential market rivals and the all-essential link with national distributors who were licensed under the prevailing cartel system to participate in the importation of petroleum products into France. In April of 1920 Jersey signed a contract with La Pétroléenne Société Anonyme—formerly the prominent firm of Fenaille & Despeaux—which specified that La Pétroléenne should have the right to subscribe to 11.175 per cent of the Eco stock; that it should not compete with Eco in the bulk trade; and that Jersey Standard should supply it with a minimum of 800,000 barrels annually for two years of refined products or crude and a maximum of up to 75 per cent of La Pétroléenne's total requirements. La Pétroléenne agreed, in turn, to sell at cost to Eco up to 11.175 per cent of that company's bulk requirements.[47]

Contracts of this same type were also drawn up between Jersey and Desmarais frères (11.175 per cent participation in Eco); with Paix & Cie (4.36 per cent participation); with Lesieur & Fils (2.5 per cent participation); and with the Raffinerie de Pétrole du Nord (1.915 per cent participation)—all former members of the French Refiners group. These negotiations, however, were never consummated.[48]

The immediate results of these complicated maneuvers were, first, to assure Jersey Standard initially of about 50 per cent of a market which was becoming increasingly competitive and, secondly, to permit Jersey to introduce in France, through Eco, the system of tank-wagon bulk deliveries, service stations, and the improved Gilbert & Barker dispensing equipment which had proved so effective elsewhere. The distribution of gasoline by tank wagons commenced in November of 1920, and soon "Eco" stations were dotting the countryside. Jersey's long-established affiliate, the Bedford Petroleum Company, S.A.F., continued to push the sale of lubricating oils in France, though this business proved to be far from remunerative.[49]

Meanwhile, competitors had not been idle. Anglo-Persian interests acquired control of Paix & Cie, Lesieur & Fils, the Raffinerie du Nord, and other distributors, while the Royal Dutch-Shell, in addition to buying into established firms, set up a distributing company of its own. Jersey men began to fear that their remaining French associates would not be satisfied with the prevailing agreements, should Eco develop the French business in a wholehearted way.[50] Jersey endeavored, accordingly, to guarantee control over certain important distribution outlets by outright purchase. By 1921 Jersey Standard had acquired a 48 per cent interest and Franco-American a 9 per cent interest in the Compagnie Générale des Pétroles pour L'Eclairage et l'Industrie, marketers in the Marseilles area and another one of the old Refiners cartel. Protracted negotiations also commenced which led, in 1923, to the acquisition by Jersey and Franco-American of a 48 per cent interest in La Pétroléenne. The addition of these companies to Jersey's interests significantly altered the division of business in France. In 1915 all Jersey's shipments to France of gasoline and kerosene were delivered to nonaffiliated companies (the French Refiners). In 1922 the deliveries of these two major product lines were divided approximately 63 per cent to affiliates and 37 per cent to nonaffiliates. By 1927 affiliated companies were receiving 85 per cent of Jersey's total deliveries to France of these products.[51]

Competitive alertness in protecting outlets, the drive to extend the company's direct participation in French marketing, and an aggressive promotional campaign for "Eco" gasoline and kerosene enabled the Jersey Company to maintain a strong position in the French market.

The company's introduction of gasoline pumps and bulk storage at French service stations preceded similar efforts elsewhere on the Continent by others. At the close of 1927 Jersey Standard interests were still predominant over those of any other competitor in the French gasoline, kerosene, and lubricating oil business. Earnings of Jersey's affiliates in this trade, however, reflect the keen competition which prevailed and seem to have been less than imposing. Table 18 gives an approximation of the returns to the Jersey Company from the operations of its French affiliates between 1919 and 1927 and indicates the division of the French market among major competing groups in 1928.

Not only sharp rivalry but great uncertainty as well prevailed throughout the middle 1920's in the French petroleum industry, and the political environment became even more hostile than it had been in 1919. In 1925

Table 18: **FINANCIAL RETURNS**
   and Division of Business in the French Market

Earnings or Dividends of French Affiliates[a]

Dollar figures in thousands (Parentheses indicate net loss)

	1919	1920	1921	1922	1923	1924	1925	1926	1927
Bedford Petroleum Co.	$ 45	$ 84	$(34)	$(109)	$(63)	$ 156	$ 96	$ 151	$ (50)
Cie Standard Franco-Américaine	—	—	—	8	63	(115)	(23)	69	9
Cie Générale des Pétroles[b]	—	—	—	25	3	14	—	47	34
L'Economique	—	—	—	65	58	(33)	280	146	47
La Pétroléenne[b]	—	—	—	—	—	151	—	247	172
Other	—	—	—	—	—	—	—	14	2
Total	$ 45	$ 84	$(34)	$ (11)	$ 61	$ 173	$ 353	$ 674	$ 214
As percentage of Jersey's total marketing earnings	0.5	0.5	(2.4)	(0.1)	0.3	0.8	1.5	2.2	0.7

Division of Business among Competitors, 1928

Thousands of tons per year

	Vacuum Oil Co.	Jersey Standard	Royal Dutch-Shell	Anglo-Persian	Jersey Standard Percentage of Total
Gasoline	109	324	265	167	37
Kerosene	25	51	46	20	36
Lubricants	42	125	7	11	68
Fuel Oil	5	....	228	112	....
Gas Oil	4	4	50	26	5
Asphalt	....	19	54	2	25
Total	185	523	650	338	31

[a] Does not include Jersey's earnings on shipments of gasoline, kerosene, and fuel oil to nonaffiliated companies and to the French government. These shipments totaled approximately 11,800,000 barrels in the years 1919 through 1921. For the years 1922 through 1927, shipments of these three products to nonaffiliated companies totaled 5,900,000 barrels, as compared with shipments to affiliates of 11,600,000 barrels.
[b] Dividends paid to Jersey Standard. Earnings figures not given.
Source: SONJ, Fin. Recs.; memo, H. E. Bedford, Jr., to Teagle, Apr. 12, 1929.

licensing restrictions were placed upon the industry. The French government, moreover, favored maintaining supply relations with Russia and Romania in order to avoid dependence upon the large international oil groups. Romanian and Russian oil imports, in consequence, increased markedly after 1925. Russian manipulation for an even larger supply contract was discerned behind the passage, in April of 1926, of Socialist-supported French legislation which specified that a state petroleum monopoly might be established under certain conditions. This alarming bill, which Jersey Standard interests opposed bitterly but with futility, was followed by an effort on the part of the government to bring about a voluntary agreement between the national petroleum company already in existence (the Compagnie Française des Pétroles, S.A.—created in 1924 to take up the French participation in the Turkish Petroleum Company) and the major oil companies to co-operate in dividing the French market. This effort to establish a national marketing cartel failed, through the admitted reluctance of the private companies to consent to the certain sacrifices involved in a regrouping of interests along government-conceived lines.[52]

At the close of 1927, therefore, Jersey Standard and its major competitors alike were faced with the possibility and even the probability that the French government would effectuate the state monopoly already authorized, or take some other drastic action to obtain that control over the French market and marketing profits which many politicians held to be desirable and expedient. Once again it appeared that Jersey interests were stubbornly defending commercial rights which had long been recognized as inviolable but which now were being discredited and renounced in many capitals of the world. It was not long after 1927 that at least one company observer concluded that failure to co-operate with a national commercial endeavor—whatever the sacrifice in dollars or in principles— invariably provoked retaliatory legislation which was more costly to private interests than the original government proposals.[53]

Few Jersey marketers throughout all of Europe, in fact, were destined in that turbulent decade to know the meaning of tranquillity. The business of the American Petroleum Company in Holland and in Belgium (where in 1919 a separate corporation of the same name was set up) was one of the few instances in Europe where Jersey efforts were characterized by stability and prosperity. In neither country were serious government restrictions encountered, and in each the position of Jersey's affiliates was well established. In Holland the American Petroleum Company held close to 80 per cent of the market—a situation which appears to have annoyed Sir Henri Deterding greatly. Up to 1923 voluntary price agreements existed among the major competing groups not to underbid one another for the business of established customers, though competition for new business was sharp. In 1924, however, the Royal Dutch-Shell launched a price war in order to enlarge its share of the market. Jersey's affiliate responded with an active drive to improve the mechanics of gasoline and kerosene distribution.[54]

Italy, too, was a relatively stable market, though less prosperous than that in the Lowlands. Government price regulations and restrictive taxation were introduced, but commerce was not immediately menaced by serious threats of state monopoly. The Italo-Americana organization, through which the bulk of Italy's war needs for petroleum had been channeled, continued to be the principal oil importing and distributing agency. Available evidence does not indicate whether prewar agreements to divide the market with competitors continued in effect after 1919, but the presence of competition in Italy is suggested by the introduction of improved distribution facilities—service stations, Gilbert & Barker pumps, and tank-wagon deliveries. Contrary to the experience of the American Petroleum Company (Holland), which continued through 1927 to sell far more kerosene than gasoline, sales of motor fuel by Italo-Americana began as early as 1920 to surpass those of kerosene. A considerable business also was done in supplying fuel oil to the Italian Navy and to industrial consumers. Italo-Americana also shipped petroleum products into Tripoli, Albania, Tunis, Algeria, Malta, and Switzerland.[55] Operations in this last-named country provide a particularly illuminating example of Jersey's postwar foreign-trading methods.

The Petroleum Import Compagnie was the Jersey Standard distributing unit in the Swiss market. This company, which obtained its principal supplies by tank car from Italy and by barge up the Rhine, was under the independent direction of resident Swiss managers. In Switzerland, as in France, the war years had brought state control of the petroleum industry. Imports were handled by the government and channeled to private distributing firms, which received a fixed but generous commission on sales to consumers at state prices. At the close of the war some thirty firms had built up a prosperous gasoline trade in various local areas. These small companies feared that when state control was abolished they would lose their business to Standard Oil and the Royal Dutch-Shell. The Swiss government itself was disposed to perpetuate its profitable import monopoly and was considering legislation to accomplish this objective. Jersey men felt, on their part, that the local firms had become very firmly entrenched and that the Swiss people, with their militant fondness for local canton institutions, might not readily be won over by a large, nationwide sales organization, however efficient it might be.

Emil Harneit, the leader of the Petroleum Import Compagnie, and Heinrich Riedemann, who served on the directorate of the company, worked out a solution not unlike that adopted in France. Harneit made contracts designating twenty-five of the *most* important Swiss firms as agents of the organization for the sale and delivery of gasoline. These firms preferred such an arrangement to the uncertainty of government contracts under a state monopoly, and the first result of Harneit's stratagem was to rob the pending monopoly bill of its principal support. The bill failed to pass.

The second result was to obtain for Jersey's Swiss affiliate a large share of a market in which Jersey Standard had hitherto participated only to a minor extent. In 1924 the retail distribution system was improved along lines already followed in France, and by 1927 the Petroleum Import Compagnie was supplying 70 per cent of the refined oil and 45 per cent of the gasoline trade in Switzerland. Royal Dutch-Shell interests, which had held virtually all of the gasoline market in 1914, were doing 37½ per cent of the total gasoline business in 1927. The Swiss trade was not, however, a remunerative one—probably because Jersey Standard had to grant low prices on its supply contracts in order to hold the loyalty of its agents. Jersey men were also dissatisfied with their inability to take a hand directly in marketing activities.[56]

In the postwar Scandinavian trade some of Jersey's difficulties derived from internal friction among the leaders of its affiliated companies. In August of 1919 director F. D. Asche was in Copenhagen trying to repair an open break between Christian Holm, the head of Det Danske, and the leaders of the Norwegian refining and marketing companies which up to that time had been affiliates of Det Danske and under Holm's direction. The strong antipathy which had sprung up during the war between the Danish and Norwegian nations was accentuated by the marked personal antipathy between Holm and the Norwegian leaders, with only one of whom Holm was on speaking terms. Teagle commiserated with Asche and told him the mission of conciliation was such as should be given only to one's worst enemy![57]

Asche, however, attacked the problem in his calm and painstaking way and soon worked out a solution. The interest of Det Danske in the Norwegian companies was taken over by the Jersey Company, and the Norwegian leaders, who had gained stature and experience during the war years, were given freedom to run their own business. This remedy, though scarcely palatable to Holm, had the practical effect of strengthening the incentive of the Norwegians to develop the local trade and to fight a pending state monopoly bill.[58]

At about this same time Hans Olsen, general manager of the Nobel petroleum marketing organization in Europe, asked Holm to "be reasonable" and stop competing with the Nobels in Finland. Otherwise, Olsen stated, the Nobels would be forced to compete with Det Danske in other Scandinavian markets. Teagle was opposed to having Det Danske enter into any joint enterprise in Finland and was sure that Holm and Olsen could never work together harmoniously. Holm, however, was convinced that protection against Nobel competition was essential, and he pushed the matter hard. In April of 1920 an agreement finally was made between the Nobels and Jersey Standard. A joint marketing company—Finska Aktiebolaget Nobel-Standard—was formed, in which Jersey owned 40 per cent of the stock, the Nobels 30 per cent, and Finnish interests 30 per cent. Both Det Danske and the Nobels thenceforth marketed in Finland only through the new company, which drew its supplies of refined products from Jersey Standard.[59]

Operations of the Nobel-Standard Company in Finland were conducted in a reasonably satisfactory manner, the market being stabilized to some extent by price agreements with the Royal Dutch-Shell, the principal non-Jersey competitor in the region. At the close of 1927 Nobel-Standard and Jersey's other Scandinavian affiliates were returning fair profits, but there were many troublesome problems. Competition was felt in Finland from importers of Polish refined products. Moffett also complained that, as had happened in other joint ventures with the Nobels, the burden of providing working capital had fallen entirely on the Jersey Company. The men at 26 Broadway became concerned over the amount of money borrowed by their Scandinavian affiliates, insisting in certain cases that dividends be reduced or eliminated until the debts to Jersey had been scaled down. Holm took personal offense at this recommendation and had to be reassured that no lack of confidence in his management was implied. Jersey fiscal policies also encountered opposition from the large minority interests (about 48 per cent) in the Norwegian companies. Nor had all the ill will between Holm and the Norwegians died out. In Denmark, moreover, anti-American agitation had been stirred up by British trading firms, which contended that Denmark should draw its supplies from Britain, its principal customer for farm products. This movement was strengthened by the action of the United States government in raising tariffs on Danish products.[60]

There seemed to be no end to the number, variety, and size of the troubles in Europe. Even tiny Iceland succumbed to the lure of statism and in 1922 abruptly declared operative a state monopoly over petroleum importation and distribution which had been authorized a decade earlier. This action had been rumored some weeks in advance, but Holm and the local Icelandic manager were confident that no monopoly would be declared. Det Danske had supplied the needs of the nation for thirty years, and the Icelandic ministers were said to have admitted that prices under a government-controlled system of distribution would necessarily be higher than those hitherto prevailing. Behind the monopoly proposal, however, were the secret promptings of the British Petroleum Company—an affiliate of the Anglo-Persian group with which Jersey men at that very time were conducting negotiations for joint action in the Middle East. No sooner had the monopoly been proclaimed than the Icelandic government entered into a three-year exclusive supply agreement with this company.[61]

Jersey men, both at 26 Broadway and in Europe, were indignant over this turn of events and the way it had been effected. A protest was launched with the American State Department. F. D. Asche took preliminary steps to oppose a loan which Iceland was seeking in the United States and to persuade the United States Tariff Commission to institute retaliatory measures. Plans for an active counterattack, however, were held in abeyance, since opposition to the state monopoly was developing among consumers in Iceland. Finally, in 1924, pressure exerted by the United States Minister in Copenhagen was successful in getting the Icelandic Parliament to promise that the exclusive contract with the British Petroleum Company would be canceled at the earliest available opportunity, and that other firms would be given a chance to bid for supply contracts.[62]

Neither in Poland nor in Romania did Jersey marketing endeavors encounter great success. The joint enterprise with the Nobels in Poland (Chapter 12) was hampered by government restrictions, by internal managerial difficulties, and by a failure to develop adequate production to serve the needs of the distributing organization. In Romania the major competing oil companies continued to market through Distributia, the joint distributing agency. Political uncertainties were paralyzing, and for much of the period sales were made at price levels fixed by the government. Earnings from Româno-Americana's marketing division were inconsequential; even though export taxes were high, the bulk of the company's oil continued to be shipped elsewhere. Meanwhile the Romanian public was unable to obtain the supplies it needed, and small competitors waxed fat by selling oil illegally at prices above the government-imposed ceilings.[63]

Conditions were much better in Spain than in most of the European marketing areas in the early 1920's, but by 1927 had become much worse. In 1922 Jersey's supply contracts with local marketing firms enabled the company to supply 62 per cent of the total Spanish market demand. Competition from the Royal Dutch-Shell—holding 38 per cent of the trade and strenuously endeavoring to obtain more—was keen, and Jersey Standard was none too certain of the continued patronage of the firms with which it had agreements. The company, therefore, pursued a policy in Spain similar to that followed in France.

In 1922 a controlling interest was purchased in the Industrias Babel y Nervión, Compañía anónima, the largest of the Spanish marketing firms. Negotiations were also commenced to effect a fusion of some kind with all the Spanish firms, which had already merged their purchasing and transportation interests in a joint company. This organization, the Société Espagnole d'Achats et d'Effrètements (also known as the Sociedad Espagnolea de Compras y Flitamentos), had been formed in 1893 and strengthened in 1923. On May 1, 1923, agreements were concluded by which Jersey Standard and its recently acquired Spanish affiliate purchased a half interest in the Société d'Achats. One of the considerations involved was a loan to the Spanish group of $1,000,000. The Société d'Achats agreed, in turn, to take from Jersey at least 80 per cent of the supplies required by its members. This agreement was hailed as one of the most favorable ever concluded by the Jersey organization in Europe, and the company seemed assured of at least two-thirds of the Spanish trade. This satisfaction was short-lived. Competition from the Royal Dutch-Shell, which marketed through its own distributing company, continued strong. At the end of 1924 the Société d'Achats had increased its share of the market to 72 per cent and was able to report good profits, but thereafter the Shell Company gained steadily, and by June of 1926 the Société was doing only 57 per cent of the business.[64]

With all the attention of competing firms focused on efforts to enlarge their share of the Spanish market, the sudden threat of a state monopoly came as a shock to the industry. Motives behind the monopoly proposal were similar to those prompting identical action in other countries. By taking over the industry and eliminating the profits of private distributors the government hoped to obtain a source of badly needed revenue. On June 30, 1927, a monopoly decree was issued. Sir Henri Deterding made common interest with the Jersey Company and rushed to Madrid to see what could be done, but at the end of 1927 Jersey's Spanish venture was embroiled in turmoil. D. L. Harper voiced the only possible note of hope implicit in the situation. "If," he wrote, "the Spanish government is to get the revenue it anticipates through the monopoly, there is no way this can be done except by a radical increase in prices of products to the consumer. This should give an excellent argument for combating the contemplated monopoly in France, and if the monopoly issue must be met sooner or later, Spain is the best country to try it in."[65]

In Germany, too, the monopoly issue was raised in postwar years, but this was by no means the greatest difficulty faced by Heinrich Riedemann in attempting to restore what once had been Jersey Standard's most lucrative foreign market.

In 1919 F. D. Asche visited Riedemann in Zurich and reported to Teagle that the German leader was in a very disturbed state of mind and clearly showed the strain he had been under. Sadler verified this news and reported that "the delicate situation confronting him in his own country through his action to protect our interest is making life most uncomfortable for him." Riedemann was greatly perturbed over the outcome of the 1917 exchange by which Jersey had sold its shares in the DAPG to the Riedemanns, accepting as collateral the securities held by the Riedemann family in the United States—which securities, in turn, had been appropriated by the Alien Property Custodian. Riedemann believed that the Jersey Company should protect the family against any loss arising from a transaction which, he claimed, had been consummated solely for the purpose of protecting Jersey's interests. Teagle promptly cabled instructions that Asche should assure Riedemann he would suffer no loss on the confiscated securities. The Jersey Company pledged a sum equivalent to the value of the securities, and in due course the DAPG shares which the Riedemann family had acquired in 1917 were returned to Jersey.[66]

Riedemann then set about to buy back the half interest (4,500 shares) in the DAPG which, for political reasons, he had been forced during the war to sell to the Stinnes combine and to the Hamburg-American Line. In September of 1921 Riedemann was able to report to Teagle that he had repurchased the 2,250 shares held by Stinnes for $850,000 in gold, after "trading Stinnes down to the last dollar." Stinnes made a profit of $470,000 on the transaction, but, Riedemann stated, "If I could have safeguarded the position of the DAPG during the war by the sacrifice of a couple of millions, I would not have hesitated to do so." For political and business reasons Riedemann allowed the Hamburg-American Line to retain 562 of the 2,250 shares they had held.[67]

Jersey's able German manager, relieved of his personal anxieties, began with vigor to rebuild the German business. Asche and Riedemann approached the German government and offered long-term supply contracts on favorable terms in return for a guarantee that competitive conditions in the German petroleum industry would be restored to and maintained on the basis prevailing before August 1, 1914. The specific outcome of this request, which would have given the DAPG a large majority of the German market, is not revealed in the company records. Riedemann was successful, however, in concluding a supply agreement between the DAPG and the government. Some time later Riedemann remarked that this contract had forestalled the threat of a state monopoly in Germany.[68]

Inflation of the currency impeded recovery from the paralysis which gripped German business in 1919. The DAPG struggled along, keeping its stocks very low and doing business on a cash basis until the inflationary spiral had run its course and the German mark had been stabilized. In 1924 Riedemann was able, at last, to report to Teagle that this had come about. The DAPG, he claimed, was the only petroleum company in Germany that had been able to make any money. In that year Riedemann felt sufficiently sure of his position in the German market to turn down a proposal by the Deutsche Bank for a merging of interests, though the possibilities of such an alliance admittedly were tempting.[69] In 1925, 1926, and 1927 small but increasing profits were reported in the German trade. Over the 1919-1927 period, however, the business and earnings of the DAPG amounted to only a fraction of those reported in earlier years. Complete recovery in Germany waited upon submergence of the economic consequences of Versailles by still more compelling national trends.

Viewed in perspective, Jersey's foreign marketing experience between 1919 and 1927 illustrates the proverbial dilemma of irresistible forces encountering immovable obstacles. In many areas the company would have fared worse than it did had world markets not been thirsty for petroleum. Competition, however, was growing abroad as at home. The basic rivalry still was between Jersey Standard and the Royal Dutch-Shell. In certain countries the two mighty adversaries made restraining agreements, but these were not important in broad consequence or in precedent. Neither company had shown, by 1927, any serious intention of endeavoring to come to a sweeping agreement to support international prices and divide international markets. The Jersey Company, always powerful, evidenced extraordinary skill in its competitive efforts and decisively outmaneuvered the Royal Dutch in several markets. The drive for customers introduced great conveniences and great efficiency in regions where distribution facilities had hitherto been archaic. Neither the Jersey Standard nor the Royal Dutch-Shell organization, however, was sufficiently strong or skillful to arrest the forces of nationalism.

The mania that possessed nations in the 1920's grew out of circumstances too complex and numerous to consider here. Everywhere the need for augmented tax revenues was acute. National factions were vigorously employing antiforeign appeals in their efforts to strengthen themselves politically. In most countries the parties in power were decidedly reluctant to relinquish controls imposed on private industry in the war years. This disinclination, it should be noted, was strengthened by almost universal suspicion that the great international oil combines were secretly striving to achieve a monopoly which would wring small consumers and nations alike with its iron fingers. So deep was this distrust that responsible governments hastened to forestall the eventuality, and in so doing often created by state fiat the very conditions they were guarding against. For its unsavory reputation the world petroleum industry could only blame its leaders, fighting with all the means at their command—the worse as well as the better—to channel the forces of militant nationalism and to restore an economic system which was not to be restored. If aggressive response to dynamic challenge was a crime, the international petroleum industry of the 1920's was not unique in sinning.

Chapter 17

The Drive to New Performance Levels
in the Refineries, 1919-1927

BETWEEN 1911 and 1918 Jersey Standard had not been outstandingly successful in effecting major refining-process improvements. Competitive pressures were not sufficiently acute nor had changes in market demand been sufficiently drastic to force the company to scrap any substantial part of its huge investment in plant facilities. The Burton-Humphreys gasoline cracking process of Indiana Standard sufficed to meet such transformations as did occur. Jersey's Manufacturing Committee was predominantly concerned with the immediate problem of co-ordinating refinery schedules with other phases of the business and getting the most out of the existing plant. In 1918 neither the men nor the organizational devices were at hand to effect the drastic technological revitalization which was necessary. In greater or less degree this same stagnancy pervaded many other oil companies. Pure research on petroleum refining processes was confined largely to university laboratories and to the workshops of independent chemists.

The months following the Armistice brought upheaval. The tremendous surge in demand for gasoline not only was difficult in itself to meet with existing facilities, but it raised flamboyant hopes of still greater expansion in the future. The unleashing of pent-up competitive forces imposed on all refiners the necessity for modernization—and for elimination of the costly licensing of new processes from competitors or potential competitors. At the same time, several long-pursued lines of experimentation gave positive indication of culminating in practical devices for cracking gasoline. Industry leaders began to look at their stills with a critical eye, and one of the first to do so was Walter Teagle.

ORGANIZING FOR TECHNICAL PROGRESS

In 1918 Teagle was anxious that the Jersey Company should develop its own gasoline cracking process. Both financial and technological considerations were involved. By 1919 the deficiencies of the Burton-Humphreys process were beginning to loom as large as its merits, great though these were. Despite improvements which reduced excessive coke formation and local overheating, the operating cycle of the cracking stills was relatively short. This was a batch process, and as such it was not well suited to the requirements of high-capacity, low-cost operation. The process also required a clean distillate for charging stock and could not operate on crude or fuel oils of any sort, or on high-sulphur-content distillates produced from California, Gulf Coast, Mexican, and other crudes. The very stocks that were most abundant in the postwar months were those which the Burton-Humphreys cracking process could handle least advantageously.[1]

What Teagle contemplated amounted to a potential revolution of refining technology as then practiced in the Jersey Standard organization. The

Table 19: **BURTON PROCESS ROYALTIES**
paid to Standard Oil Company (Indiana)
by Standard Oil Company (New Jersey)
and Affiliated Companies, 1915-1924

Jersey Standard Refineries					Louisiana Standard, Imperial, and Humble Royalties [a]	
Year	Gross Profits	Royalty Paid	Maintenance and Depreciation	Net Profits		
1915	$ 233,163	$ 58,291	$ 105,210	$ 69,662	1915	$ 30,000
1916	4,234,768	1,058,692	341,955	2,834,121	1916	74,000
1917	3,754,608	938,052	420,843	2,395,113	1917	262,000
1918	3,486,353	871,588	420,843	2,193,922	1918	787,000
1919	2,730,956	682,739	578,659	1,469,558	1919	894,000
1920	3,792,274	948,068	971,651	1,872,555	1920	375,000
1921	(681,746)[b]	none	987,432	(1,669,179)[b]	1921	369,000
1922	7,937,554	437,840	1,133,498	6,366,216	1922	643,000
1923	3,286,133	373,360	1,064,848	1,847,925	1923	516,000
1924	3,384,956	472,784	1,053,577	1,858,595	1924	232,000

[a] Profit and cost figures not available.
[b] Net loss.

Source: *U. S.* v. *SOC (Indiana)* et al., II, Book of Petitioners' Exhibits, 1185, 1225.

backing by the directorate was strong, too, for the cost of technological backwardness was being carefully and clearly counted out for all to see by the steady flow of Burton-Humphreys process royalties from the Jersey till to the coffers of Indiana Standard. By the end of 1919 these royalties had accumulated to the considerable sum of $3,609,000 (Table 19). The prospect of a booming gasoline market indicated that future payments would be even greater. Teagle was spurred to action, however, not only by the practical and immediate desirability of eliminating the large royalty payments, but by his own interest in petroleum chemistry and by a far-ranging hope of fostering great technical progress in the industry, which he felt had been backward. Many other Jersey men shared these aspirations. A will to be efficient and progressive was well defined in the organization, but strong leadership was needed.[2]

The Jersey directors looked to the one outstanding place where a new leader might be recruited. E. M. Clark, superintendent of Indiana's Wood River refinery, was a promising candidate. With a background of common-school education, Clark, who in 1918 was forty-eight years of age, had worked his way from the post of railway telephone operator to mastery of a highly complex technology. Clark's work and training under Burton had been outstanding, his inventive abilities were marked, and he was uninhibited in his scientific attitudes.

A. C. Bedford spoke to Dr. Burton about obtaining Clark's services, and Burton stated categorically that Clark could not be spared. Bedford, with that rare feeling for the quotable answer which he often exhibited, quickly replied, "We do not want anyone who *can* be spared!"[3] Late in 1918 Clark came to the Jersey Company as general manager of the Bayway refinery at an annual salary of $18,000. With him he brought two of his staff: Dr. N. E. Loomis, a former physics and chemistry professor at Purdue, who had been with Clark at Wood River for only three months and already was considered by Clark to be a highly valuable assistant in research; and J. R. Carringer, trained in practical refining and cracking-still development work, who came to the Jersey Company as assistant superintendent of Bayway. The Clark team thus combined experimental and operational skills of a high order. These men were given virtually a free hand in working out a new cracking process. In effect, their task was to raise Jersey Standard from the position of one of the more conservative large refiners in America to one of the most progressive.

Clark at once set to work at Bayway. His was a technical assignment, and almost immediately it became apparent that Jersey's deficiencies could not be remedied without substantial administrative changes. Clark's initial efforts took place in a far from sympathetic environment. Research effort throughout the organization was not co-ordinated so as to proceed without conflict along lines of predetermined usefulness. Since all research effort had hitherto been directed only at solving specific and limited problems, wide gaps existed in knowledge of the fundamental facts of petroleum. In the Jersey Company, as in other units of the petroleum industry, progress had been hampered for years by the conviction of practical refiners that common sense, prior practice, and conventional engineering were sufficient to ensure larger and better refineries. Up to 1919 applied chemistry had played a relatively small part in the improvement of refining processes in the industry, and theoretical chemistry almost no part at all. Even the justly famed Burton-Humphreys process had owed its origin as much to the art of the refiner and the boilermaker as to the knowledge of the scientist.[4] Jersey Standard desperately needed the services of E. M. Clark to solve the immediate problem of perfecting a new cracking process. But to inaugurate a sweeping new research program, as Teagle wished, and to enlist the aid of science and scientists in the business required much more than the employment of a gifted inventor.

Had Clark not been a perceptive administrator as well as an inventor, the development of Jersey research might well have been delayed many years. Burdened from the moment of his arrival at Bayway with a tremendous load of responsibility, Clark was quick not only to discern the organizational deficiency but also to encourage the institution of those measures directly responsible for elevating Jersey Standard to a new position in the refining branch of the industry. Criticized bitterly for many things by some of his contemporaries, the role he played in the formation of Jersey's Development Department, nevertheless, was a vital one.

While serving under Dr. Burton in the Indiana Company, Clark had had ample opportunity to observe the administrative problems growing out of the cracking patents. As soon as the basic patent had been issued in 1913, Indiana Standard found itself engaged in two active and interlocking ventures—the technical improvement of the new process and the simultaneous handling of the patent situation in such a way as to derive the largest possible earnings from licensing. These circumstances brought about a loose and temporary form of organization for technical progress involving Indiana's manufacturing experts, the Chicago patent law firm of Dyrenforth, Lee, Chritton & Wiles, and two consultants—Ira Remsen of Johns Hopkins and Robert A. Millikan of the University of Chicago. Frank A. Howard, an engineer and junior partner of the law firm, was assigned the task of co-ordinating the work of the three groups.[5]

Installed in makeshift quarters at Bayway, Clark demonstrated a keen interest in technical progress outside the Jersey Company. Realizing that the patent consultants then employed by the company were not conversant with the most recent developments in the oil industry, Clark caused more and more of Jersey's patent work to be shifted to Dyrenforth, Lee, Chritton & Wiles, which firm, he knew, was thoroughly cognizant of contemporary trends. In the spring of 1918 a voluminous correspondence developed between Clark and Howard, his former legal consultant, about various research projects of mutual interest. Howard stated his opinion that an experimental engineering department should be established in the Jersey Company.[6]

Clark showed Teagle the Howard letters and recommended Howard highly. Soon thereafter Teagle began to correspond directly with Howard and to utilize the services of the Chicago attorney. Clark continued to press upon Teagle the wisdom of forming a research division, and at Teagle's request he asked Howard to outline a plan for such an organization. The suggestion was one which was well calculated to appeal to Jersey's president—himself an enthusiastic advocate of bold administrative moves looking toward closer control over the rambling Jersey organization. By June of 1919 Teagle had agreed in principle, and he summarized his conclusions in a letter to A. C. Bedford:[7]

Since you have been away I have felt more than ever before the need for a thoroughly organized and competent research department under an able executive, such a department not to be confined merely to chemical research, but to general research in connection not only with the production and refining of our products, but with the sales end of our business as well. There are, I am convinced, a number of products that could be manufactured in addition to the lines which we are at present manufacturing, and the manufacture of those products undoubtedly would result in enhanced profits to the company. The General Electric and other concerns of a like character lay a great stress upon their research department. They consider this department on a parity in importance with the manufacture and sales end of their business. Our research department up to date is a joke pure and simple; we have no such thing, and on your return here I am anxious to discuss with you this entire question.

"Dear Walter," Bedford replied, "This is intensely interesting and practical. We should give the whole subject most careful consideration and plan out a definite Department along some such lines as suggested."

Howard then set forth in a letter to Clark his general notions as to how the agreed-upon goal might most effectively be sought. "Co-ordination," he wrote, "can only be accomplished from the top." Existing personnel and equipment, Howard went on to say, should be utilized to the fullest possible extent, but someone should be given authority to mold the organization into a new form. This person presumably should be hired from outside the company, since all qualified company executives were already overburdened. The hypothetical new executive should promote the effective gathering of technical information from sources outside the company and correlate that information with the needs and ambitions of the company. He should also foster the spirit of scientific analysis in the Jersey refineries and have the power to co-ordinate manufacturing, process and chemical research, marketing, and patent policies.[8]

To these principles both Clark and Teagle agreed. The search for a man to head the new branch of the business led, after several candidates had been considered and rejected, to Howard himself, who agreed to take a six months' leave of absence from his partnership and try to get the new department organized. On September 27, 1919, a formal notice was issued to all department heads informing them of the establishment of the Development Department, of which Howard was to be the manager.[9]

On October 8, 1919, Howard submitted to Teagle a tentative form of organization. The basic theory he advanced, acquiesced in by Clark and accepted by Teagle and the directorate, was that new ideas and inventions on which the technical progress of the company might be based would arise in the main from external sources, and that the primary job of the Development Department would be to uncover these ideas, test them out, and carry them forward to some practical end. If original ideas of merit emerged from Jersey laboratories so much the better, but the new plan was not aimed at fostering creative research. The new branch of the business was to be, literally, a development rather than a research department. Four main divisions were envisaged. The information division was to report on technical progress inside and outside the petroleum industry. The experimental or development division was to perfect new processes and the equipment for carrying them out on a practical basis, whatever their origin. The research laboratory was to serve the developmental division and engage in scientific pioneering on its own account whenever able to do so. The patent division was intended primarily to keep the company out of legal trouble and, secondarily, to get the maximum possible revenue out of patent licensing.[10]

A vigorous search was at once launched for men to fill the blank places on the organization chart which Howard had drawn up. Jersey's chief chemist, Dr. Clarence I. Robinson, headed the research division. Upon Robinson's retirement in 1921 the position was given to C. O. Johns, an experimental chemist in the United States Department of Agriculture. Howard sought and obtained permission to utilize the services of Ira Remsen, president emeritus of Johns Hopkins and one of the leading organic chemists of the day, as a consultant. Remsen was to receive $100 per day to advise on chemical research problems. Howard also received permission to engage the consulting services of Warren K. Lewis, head of the chemical engineering department of the Massachusetts Institute of Technology, at an annual retainer of $2,500 for a maximum of 50 days of work per year. Lewis, whose experience and reputation alike were wide, was to advise on problems relating to distillation processes. Robert Millikan, like Remsen an expert with whom Howard had become intimate through his work for Indiana Standard, was not retained as a consultant but offered advice on the hiring of scientists to round out the Development Department roster. N. E. Loomis was placed in charge of the developmental division.[11] By February of 1920 the department organization had crystallized in the form shown in the chart on page 527.

Clark's position in the company was not clearly spelled out in correspondence of the day, but in effect he dominated the entire manufacturing establishment at the subdirectorate level and shared with the Manufacturing Committee the difficult responsibility of translating general policies enunciated by the Jersey directors into effective action at the operating level. Conversely, Clark was also responsible for analyzing operational problems, reducing them to essential details, transmitting them to the Jersey board, and obtaining from the board a clear policy pronouncement that would permit appropriate action to be taken. The formation of the Development Department in itself was an excellent example of the upward dissemination of a recommendation and downward diffusion of a major policy decision. In practice, refining policy normally originated in the recommendations of second-line management.[12]

Clark's position initially was circumscribed with great practical difficulties. While supervision of the routine problems of what and how much to make was vested in the Manufacturing Committee (of which Clark was a member), Clark assumed the major responsibility of directing the frequent process alterations called forth each time an important new source of crude oil supply was tapped by the producing and purchasing branches of the business. Clark's part in the research and development program necessarily continued to be an active one, for this was his special field and particular talent. The organization of the Development Department, however, relieved him of much detail work, and the task of perfecting a new cracking process fell heavily upon Loomis and his assistants. Clark himself continued to work upon various improvements in the Burton-Humphreys process.

The year 1920 was characterized by much groping. However clearly

ORGANIZATION CHART OF THE DEVELOPMENT DEPARTMENT
of Standard Oil Company (New Jersey) in 1920

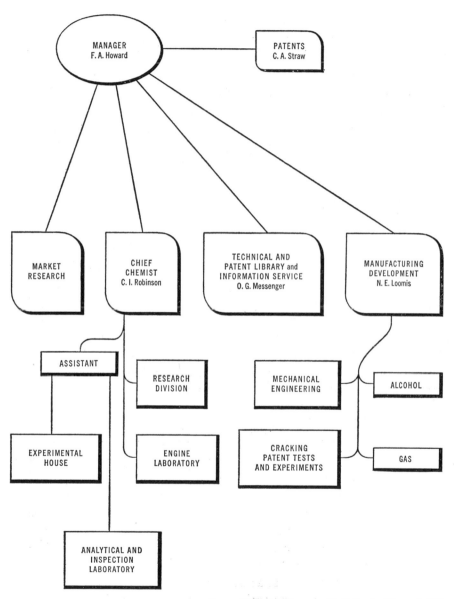

MANAGER
F. A. Howard

PATENTS
C. A. Straw

MARKET
RESEARCH

CHIEF
CHEMIST
C. I. Robinson

TECHNICAL AND
PATENT LIBRARY and
INFORMATION SERVICE
O. G. Messenger

MANUFACTURING
DEVELOPMENT
N. E. Loomis

ASSISTANT

RESEARCH
DIVISION

MECHANICAL
ENGINEERING

ALCOHOL

EXPERIMENTAL
HOUSE

ENGINE
LABORATORY

CRACKING
PATENT TESTS
AND EXPERIMENTS

GAS

ANALYTICAL AND
INSPECTION
LABORATORY

Source: SONJ, F. A. Howard to W. C. Teagle, February 5, 1920

Howard had delineated the functions of the Development Department, the success or failure of this administrative experiment and of the entire development program depended upon the success of Howard and of Clark in obtaining the co-operation of the existing organization. Clark encountered not only strong opposition to his technical ideas but personal antagonism as well on the part of the old-school refiners in the organization. Despite Teagle's strong support Clark was often frustrated in his efforts to influence the Jersey board, and apparently he did not initially enjoy the complete confidence of the directors. Not until Clark himself became a director, in December of 1920, does it appear that he was able to exert the authority necessary for fulfillment of his responsibilities.

In the first year of his service with the Jersey organization Howard gave ample evidence of great administrative capacities as well as of a firm grasp of legal and technical problems. Howard felt very keenly, however, his lack of experience in the field of refining. Despite the fact that the new department head was made a member of the Manufacturing Committee, conflicts developed with the operating branches of the manufacturing organization. Howard was not adequately supplied with current information, statistics, and forecasts. Misunderstanding prevailed in the company as to the exact functions of the Development Department; some persons regarded it as a division of the Manufacturing Department and others as an appendage of the Bayway refinery, where the research and development program came to be centered. George McKnight, chairman of the Manufacturing Committee, was not backward in telling Howard that the Development Department was inclined to work too independently of the committee. These evidences of transitional difficulties were matched by reports of remarkable progress.

At the close of 1920 Howard was able to report that the Development Department numbered 55 employees and had cost the company $327,000 in operating expenses over the preceding year—a sum well calculated to make the directorate sit up and take note of the fledgling group at Bayway. All divisions were functioning well, the Department was in close touch with all developments in the field of producing and manufacturing which could possibly concern future technical operations of the company, and the several developmental projects which had been undertaken were well advanced. The Department had also followed experimental work being performed in the automotive industry. Teagle's keen interest, close attention, and strong support at the top administrative level unquestionably constituted a dominant explanation for the successful establishment of the Development Department. Howard also noted his great indebtedness to Clark in getting the development program organized.[13] The tremendous potentialities of the Teagle-Clark-Howard team were clearly evidenced even before the exact direction and scope of the reorganizing effort could be discerned.

The Development Department had not been in existence for long before Howard discovered that much time was being expended on routine technical chores. He warned Teagle that such endeavors, helpful though they unquestionably might be to the company and its affiliates, were incapable of showing any direct returns. This handicap was inescapable, but Howard moved in other directions to build up the prestige and efficiency of the research and development program. Teagle was urged to become a member of the American Chemical Society and the Chemists' Club of New York, in order that "the administration of the company be known to have a scientific outlook in the technical world." Howard also recommended that the Jersey Company become a member of the Manufacturing Chemists' Association.

Early in 1922 the old Inspection Laboratory was incorporated in the Development Department in order to centralize the performance of routine testing operations and minimize duplication of work. On September 25, 1922, the patent section of the Development Department was incorporated as the Standard Development Company. This last-named step, suggested by Howard, had its origins in the legal necessities of the research program. Jersey was threatened, as we shall see, by complex and dangerous patent litigation. If the company continued to hold in its own name the patents under which it was operating, there was a risk that minor or preliminary legal actions would prejudice the company in defending future damage claims. There was also the danger that loss of the legal battle would result in sharing with rival claimants some of the past profits earned under those patents. Vesting the patents in a separate corporation lessened this danger and also facilitated transactions with inventors, promoters, and firms who were seeking licenses from Jersey to use the processes and products developed in the Jersey laboratories. Jersey Standard, accordingly, transferred all its patents to the Standard Development Company.[14]

Further efforts were also made to obtain improved co-ordination between the research division and the various operating branches of the business. In 1922 regular periodic conferences were instituted between the Manufacturing Committee, the refinery managers, the refinery general superintendents, the General Engineering Department, and the Development Department. Two years later a committee was formed to facilitate direct co-operation between the Manufacturing Department and the Development Department, with particular emphasis upon the prompt exchange of information. Howard still believed there was room for improvement and continued to press for better liaison. Early in 1924 he told McKnight that the business had grown faster than the organization and that all executives, in his opinion, were so heavily overburdened that there was inadequate time provided for necessary co-ordination meetings. The Manufacturing Department, Howard pointed out, functioned not as an integrated unit but as a loose federation of divergent interests. Time and energy were being wasted in reconciling conflicting views on technical matters. Neither had it been possible to secure the necessary degree of co-operation among the various refineries. After a careful examination of the administrative make-up of the manufacturing departments of Indiana Standard, Standard Oil of California, and the Union Oil Company of California, Howard proposed several changes, among which were a strengthening of centralized control over refinery affairs and a more careful delineation of the duties of the various members of the Manufacturing Committee.[15]

E. J. Sadler, too, had persistently criticized the manufacturing establishment and pointed to the need for a control group of some kind which would harmonize the work of the manufacturing, marketing, and staff divisions. The joint urgings of Sadler and Howard and a carefully detailed memorandum from Sadler to the directors resulted in the creation, in September of 1925, of the Co-ordination Committee, composed of four directors and a staff organization called the Co-ordination Department, which was headed by McKnight's assistant, Orville Harden. The functions of this committee and department were to allocate crude oil runs among the various refineries in the most effective possible way, having reference to available crude supplies and prices, transportation facilities and costs, refinery capacities, and market demand for refined products. The new co-ordinating group, being staffed at the top by high-level executives, was more successful than those committees previously formed at lower administrative levels in the company to carry out certain of these duties. At the close of 1926, however, Howard still was profoundly disturbed by new administrative problems that had been raised by the great expansion of the business since 1920.[16]

Where, Howard asked, was the effective dividing line between Jersey

Standard's operating and holding-company responsibilities? The broad repercussions raised by this question are considered in the final chapter of this volume. Howard, in speaking of his own department, had a clear and logical answer. The Development Department was attempting to engage in too many kinds of work for the available facilities and personnel. Better results would unquestionably have accrued by limiting activities, but the pressure from all sources to tackle new problems had been impossible to resist. The future of the company, moreover, was vitally dependent upon expansion rather than restriction of research effort.

"My own view of the proper policy for an expansion of research and development work in the Jersey interest," Howard wrote, "is to build up the technical staffs of subsidiary and affiliated operating companies."[17] The Inspection Laboratory, the Patent Division, and certain phases of research-laboratory work requiring expensive physical testing apparatus were proper holding-company functions, he went on to state. On the other hand, those developmental assignments closely allied to operating problems should be considered as the proper functions of the operating affiliates. A greater volume of research and developmental work should, in substance, be undertaken by the affiliated companies. The Humble Oil & Refining Company had progressed the furthest in this direction, but a definite policy pronouncement from 26 Broadway was needed. The whole program would require careful co-ordination to prevent duplication of effort and facilities, and the separation of holding-company and operating-company functions would unquestionably necessitate a major organizational change.

Howard's feeling in 1926 that major problems still lay unsolved should in no way be allowed to obscure the outstanding achievements which had been recorded since 1919. The research and development program had yielded returns of inestimable value to the company. Many knotty administrative problems were faced and resolved. The number of employees in the Development Department had tripled, and all tangible measures indicated that the development program as conceived by Howard and made a reality in 1919 by the joint exertions of Howard, Clark, and Teagle was one of the most solidly based and forward-looking changes ever instituted in the manufacturing branch of the business. An appreciation of this fact is necessary for a proper understanding of the specific episodes related in subsequent sections of this chapter, while those episodes, in turn, throw additional light on the effectiveness with which Jersey Standard had organized for technical progress.

THE CONTINUING SEARCH FOR
BETTER REFINING PROCESSES

In 1919 and 1920 high profits and the threat of a petroleum famine imparted a zest to the search for refining-process improvements which fully matched the enthusiasm of the seekers for new crude oil reserves. The search took many directions. Effort was made to increase the quality and lower the manufacturing cost of all petroleum products, while at the same time the magic of chemical engineering was bringing new products out of the crude-oil barrel like rabbits out of the conjurer's hat. The focus of attention, however, was on gasoline.

One goal was higher yields. If 50 instead of 25 per cent of a barrel of crude could be converted into gasoline at a reasonable cost, the result would be a substantial reduction in the exhaustion rate of known crude reserves. Prevailing high crude prices, too, could be spread over more gallons of gasoline, thereby strengthening profit margins against the growing pressure of competitive price reductions.

Another goal was manufacturing flexibility. Refiners had long complained that their costly equipment—tailor-made for the type of crude which was most plentiful at the time the equipment was installed—quickly became obsolete when new supply sources were tapped. Depreciation rates were high, for most of the known refining methods took a frightful toll of pipe and stills. The petroleum refiners, through no fault of their own to be sure, had yet to achieve that mastery over automatic techniques which had been commonly found in the textile industry of a century or more before and in many other mechanical industries at the halfway mark of the nineteenth century. The demand of the day was for a refining process that could handle a wide range of crude oils and distillates, separate the by-products precisely, operate for long periods of time without shutdowns, and depend to a minimum degree on fallible human judgment.[18] All over the world men were hopefully working on countless divergent schemes to accomplish one or all of these desiderata.

A man in Indianapolis had concocted a white powder which, he averred, dissolved in water to form an efficient motor fuel. An engineer in Germany had developed a marvelous device for exploding air under pressure which would eliminate petroleum fuels altogether. Dozens, literally, of back-shed scientists discovered "revolutionary" distillation processes. Some of these people actually held patents, and they therefore looked suspiciously at the experimental work that was going forward in the big oil companies. An old company pensioner indignantly wrote to John D. Rockefeller, Jr., to say that his plan to double the yield of gasoline from charging stock had not been given a fair hearing by the Jersey men. An inventor in New Jersey, working on synthetic alcohol, claimed that he held a patent on pressure distillation which antedated the Burton-Humphreys process.

These claims could not be dismissed summarily, for among the chaff might well be found some grain. Howard's Development Department performed an invaluable service in relieving hard-pressed Jersey executives of the onus of investigation. Company policy in dealing with inventors who wished to make Jersey Standard their partner was clear-cut. As Howard wrote:[19]

The invariable rule which we have had to adopt for our own protection is that we cannot receive communications or any information concerning any secret process or invention. All information given to us must be without reservation or any obligation of secrecy or special trust or confidence on our part. Any other course would keep us perpetually in hot water with inventors who imagined that we had violated some fancied special obligation we owed them.

While Howard was scrutinizing the steady stream of technical reports, patents, and rumors channeled to his office from all branches of the organization at home and abroad and occasionally making inventions of his own in oil processing, Clark, Loomis, and the development staff were laboring on the chief Jersey project—the perfection of the tube-and-tank cracking process.

Certain features of this process had already been worked out by Clark before he left the Indiana Company to come to Jersey Standard. The principle was simple, but practical difficulties were great. Of these the most imposing was the danger—the inevitability, almost—that the work at Bayway would infringe one or more of the scores of patents that had already been issued. Russell Wiles, Howard's former law partner in Chicago, served a friendly warning, in fact, that the Jersey experiments were likely to result in infringements upon the Burton patents. Howard disagreed, and the work went forward.[20]

Clark had demonstrated that if the charging stock destined for cracking in the Burton stills was brought to cracking temperature during forced circulation through a coil of tubes and then discharged into the main still chamber, cracking would continue in the still chamber, even though the still was not itself being heavily fired. Coke would form in the still, to be sure, but with a reduction in direct heating the danger of a hot bottom was minimized. Because of the rapid circulation of the oil, coke did not form readily in the tubes, such coke as was formed there being swept along into the still. Thus, by applying heat at that stage of the process where coke formation and deposition were negligible and by minimizing or eliminating altogether the heating of that part of the apparatus where a substantial part of the cracking and consequent coke deposition took place, it was possible not only to operate the entire process without danger for considerably longer periods of time than had hitherto been possible, but also to utilize stocks which formerly could not be handled because of their high coke-deposition rate. The use of the tube coils also increased the still output over a given time, effected economies in fuel consumption, and permitted utilization of higher pressures in the cracking process.[21]

The Jersey men first conceived these advantages to be particularly pertinent to the problem of reducing to fuel oil the highly viscous Mexican crude which was then so plentiful. To this restricted objective the initial experiments of Clark and Loomis in 1919 were directed. Almost at once, however, they envisaged the broader purpose of making the continuous tube process a practical substitute for the Burton-Humphreys batch process in manufacturing the entire range of petroleum distillates. The first experimental tube stills were erected at Bayonne in 1919, and a number of these units were constructed at Tampico to work on Pánuco crude. The chief result of the first efforts was a serious fire at Bayonne, after which the experiments were transferred to Bayway and carried forward in four units there under the auspices of the newly created Development Department.[22] The collective ideas of Clark, Loomis, and Howard were combined to form the basic design for what later became known as the tube-and-tank process.

It was at this point, early in 1920, that the value of Howard's new department was dramatically demonstrated. Among the scores of technical reports and queries which crossed Howard's desk was one which recalled to him a faintly familiar name. While he had been working on patent matters in Chicago before coming to the Jersey Company, Howard had purchased for one of the meat-packing houses the rights to a patent relating to the hydrogenation of fatty oils. Carleton Ellis, the inventor from whom this purchase had been made, now wished Howard to look over some other patents he held.[23]

These patents had grown out of experiments in distillation conducted by Ellis over a period of several years. In 1916 Ellis discovered a practical way of making alcohol from light petroleum distillates. The Melco

Chemical Company was thereupon formed to manufacture isopropyl alcohol by the Ellis process, a pilot plant being constructed in Bayonne. Both Clark and C. I. Robinson were aware of the Ellis experiments and were interested in the possibilities of synthetic production of alcohol. In 1918 the Jersey Company had purchased the rights to the Ellis alcohol process. What Ellis called to see Howard about, however, was not this process but his conviction that his earliest patents covered and antedated the tube-and-tank process being evolved at Bayway. Ellis believed that he held product claims covering the Burton cracked gasoline as well.[24]

Howard, to whom such claims were commonplace, was not at first unduly alarmed. In January of 1920 he reported to Teagle that Ellis must abandon the idea that his patents would make him a fortune—actually, Howard stated, they had a nuisance value to Jersey Standard of not in excess of $5,000. A more careful investigation subsequently caused Howard to change his mind. In December of 1920 he told Teagle that the Ellis patents definitely covered all cracked gasoline produced by Jersey Standard and that they were an outstanding menace. Ellis was well aware of this fact and was proving to be a hard trader. His price to the Jersey Company for the exclusive right to all his inventions was $225,000, and Howard urged that the offer be accepted at once. Ellis, it appeared, had taken into account only the nuisance value of his early patents and his product claims on cracked gasoline. His later patents, Howard reported, were of tremendous value to the Jersey Company for the tube-and-tank cracking principles they disclosed and covered. If this fact became known to Ellis, he would certainly recall his offer. Teagle approved the transaction on the same day he received Howard's report. On January 18, 1921, the Ellis patents were acquired by Jersey Standard, Ellis himself being retained to consult with the company.[25]

With this legal obstacle removed and with the additional benefit of Ellis' experiments made available, the Jersey tube-and-tank process was ready for commercial exploitation in the spring of 1921. The fact that this process was subsequently referred to by many as the "Ellis process" should not be allowed to obscure the full facts of its parentage. Had there been no Ellis patent, the independent work of Clark, Howard, and Loomis might well have been honored in name as well as in fact. History knows few more difficult tasks than that of tracing the true ancestry of invention. Even the validity of the Ellis paternity claim was soon to be challenged.

Experimental licensing arrangements were concluded by Jersey in 1921 to permit the Beacon Oil Company in Massachusetts and the Owl Oil Company in Oklahoma to install the tube-and-tank process. A royalty of 10 cents per barrel of charging stock was fixed. These licenses, however, did not indicate that a liberal sublicensing policy had been established. Both Teagle and Howard felt that a passive licensing course should be followed until legal and technical difficulties had been resolved. Nor did installation of the tube-and-tank units proceed rapidly in the refineries of the Jersey organization. Howard reported, that although the year 1922 found Jersey Standard with a new cracking process, the $20,000,000 worth of Burton stills then in place were more than sufficient for immediate needs at that time of diminished business activity. "We are in the unhappy situation," he told Teagle, "of a man with a rented suit of clothes on, a new suit of his own in his hands, and no place to make a change."[26]

In 1923 there were only 6 tube-and-tank batteries in operation in the New Jersey refineries—as compared with the 150 Burton stills operating there. Humble's new Baytown refinery, opened officially in April of 1921, was equipped with old-style stills which actually were obsolete before they had even commenced to operate. For this circumstance the Jersey technicians who helped to plan the refinery were heartily condemned by the Texans. Widespread adoption of the tube-and-tank process, however, waited upon a clarification of the legal issues involved, and it was not until the fall of 1923 that the new units could safely be installed. By the end of 1926 the Jersey Company and its affiliates were operating 118 of the new cracking units and had 45 more under construction.[27]

Jersey's Bayway refinery became the center of cracking operations and the laboratory where Clark, with the men whom he had trained or brought from Indiana, tested a rapid succession of new ideas. Conflict between the Bayway group and the older Jersey refining men was inevitable. When the boom of 1920 dictated an expansion of Bayway facilities, C. H. Haupt, head of the General Engineering Department, reached up to an office shelf and pulled down a set of blueprints prepared years before for just such a contingency. Clark's indignation was that of the scientist; he curtly told Haupt that if he had no new ideas he should retire. Many others who had grown up in the conservative Jersey family felt the impatience of the new manager with established procedures. W. C. Koehler, the Bayonne manager, was not sympathetic with Clark's new technical ideas, and no cracking units were installed in Jersey's largest plant. In Louisiana the dogged and gifted Louis Link continued his own line of experimentation on batch-type crude distillation stills in almost complete defiance of Clark's conviction that effort should be centered in perfecting continuous-process units. This controversy split the ranks of Jersey technicians and caused the Manufacturing Committee to send a seven-man team to Baton Rouge early in 1922 to investigate the merits of the alternate systems. The committee report proved most of all the difficulty of teaching old refiners new tricks. Three of the investigators came to the test confirmed batch-process men—and left in the same state of mind. Three others came as continuous-process advocates; they, too, came away with unmodified convictions. The seventh (from the Sarnia refinery) concluded that continuous stills were best for light distillates and batch stills for heavy.[28]

Stubbornness unquestionably was rooted in the ranks of the organization. Clark, on the other hand, apparently went too far and too fast for some of his associates, such as Charles G. Black, chairman of the Manufacturing Committee, who was elevated to the directorate the same time as was Clark. A man of genius and great strength, Clark—like many such men—was not sympathetic with those entertaining opposing views. His influence was a tremendously virile one, however, and Clark stimulated all with whom he came in touch. In a remarkably short space of time after his arrival, all the refinery managers and superintendents were wondering if their plants were as good as they had hitherto believed.

Many processes felt the impact of the stirring spirit. Two new products were added to the Jersey line—Flit, an insecticide, and Sealite, a foam composed of glycerine, glucose, and glue which was poured on the surface of stored oil to reduce evaporation losses. The company commenced the manufacture of synthetic alcohol under the Ellis patents. Efforts were also expended to improve the yield and quality of lubricating oils, both properties having suffered from the emphasis on obtaining maximum gasoline yields in the cracking process. Much attention was focused, too, on regulating the viscosity of motor oils at low winter starting and high summer operating temperatures.[29]

Earlier experiments were continued on fractionating towers in order to increase the precision with which various distillates were separated in the refining process. Link's success in utilizing five different towers on his stills was reflected in the fact that the Baton Rouge refinery was able to ship natural white distillates without the usual acid treating or redistillation. In 1921 Jersey's chemical engineering consultant, W. K. Lewis, set up the first of his so-called bubble towers at Bayway. So well did these units perform that soon this improved fractionating system was being installed elsewhere in the refinery organization.

With this line of endeavor well in hand by 1924, Lewis turned his attention from the overhead equipment of the cracking stills to the stills themselves and began to work on vacuum distillation. This process had long been known, but practical difficulties had discouraged development even in the face of the realization that the vacuum process yielded gasoline with a high antiknock rating. Lewis, working with the Development Department, constructed at Bayonne the first continuous-flash vacuum still. This was experimentally successful, but the need for the process at the Bayonne refinery had passed even before the completion of the still. It was the Humble manufacturing organization that finally translated Lewis' vacuum-distillation work into a commercially successful process.[30]

The Clark-Howard-Loomis team, meanwhile, continued to improve the tube-and-tank units, principally in the direction of increasing the pressures utilized in the cracking apparatus. In 1922, experiments indicated that an increase in pressure from 250 to 350 pounds brought improved results. It was not many years before apparatus was being designed to withstand pressures in excess of 1,000 pounds. In 1923 Loomis reported that refiners were no longer trying to achieve maximum gasoline yields at the expense of all else, and that efforts were under way to control the cracking process and avoid excessive destructive distillation in early stages of treatment. The prevailing tendency was to return to the earlier goal of obtaining cleaner separation in the initial distillation process of products naturally present in the crude, and subsequently operating upon them as market conditions dictated. The greatest advantages of the tube-and-tank process over the Burton stills had already proved to be high output and the capacity for handling a wide range of stocks.[31]

Between 1914 and 1927 the average yield of gasoline obtained by American refiners had been doubled (from 18 to 36 per cent). As nearly as can be ascertained, these percentages were approximated by the Jersey organization. The gradual increase in production of cracked gasoline, both by Jersey Standard and by the industry, is indicated by the figures in Appendix 2, Table IX. These tangible achievements were recorded in the face of some pronounced failures, both technical and administrative. By 1927 no satisfactory steel had been developed for the tubes in the cracking apparatus, with the result that depreciation of equipment was rapid. Lack of proper instruments impeded the progress of experiments in all lines of cracking, and the flood of cheap crude in 1927 discouraged efforts to maximize the yield of lubricants. Louis Link steadfastly refused to abandon his batch stills—his opposition to Clark seemingly inspired by a powerful sense of destiny. In 1927 the Jersey manager was still dispatching investigating committees to Baton Rouge, and it was not until 1931 that Clark was able to obtain the adoption of his own refining methods in the Louisiana Company.[32]

Notwithstanding this conspicuous exception, much of the conflict between the scientists and the "practical men" in the organization had been resolved by the end of 1927. Increased understanding derived from prolonged association, extreme viewpoints on both sides being modified somewhat. If some of the older men seemed to be unduly conservative, it was because their broad experience in the business had taught them of the pitfalls which existed at every turn of the path. The young scientists were dynamic, but inexperienced. Real progress came from a synthesis of experience and of new ideas—not instantaneously, but by imperceptible degrees over the months and years.

Two episodes in particular did much to win respect and acceptance for the Jersey scientists. Neither the experiments with tetraethyl lead nor the efforts to produce petroleum fuels from shale and coal could have been carried far without the aid of the most advanced scientific knowledge of the times. Both lines of endeavor contemplated and bade fair to achieve such eminently practical goals as to impress even the most reactionary. Both experiments, however, depended for final success not only upon new ideas but upon the accumulated skills of a generation of practical refiners.

The need for improved motor fuels was emphasized by the great progress of the automotive industry. By 1916 it was apparent that research in the petroleum industry had been inadequate to meet the needs of the industry's largest customer. Each new engine design had raised compression pressures slightly, with resultant increases in power and better mileage per gallon. Continued development of the automobile engine along such lines was circumscribed by the disposition of higher compression engines to knock excessively. In layman's terms, the problem was that gasoline vapor in the cylinder head tended to explode, rather than burn. Initiative to discover a remedy was taken not by the petroleum refiners but by Charles F. Kettering, director of the General Motors Corporation's research division.[33]

In 1916 Kettering turned over the results of his own earlier experiments to Thomas Midgley, Jr., a recent Cornell graduate. Midgley's initial work at Dayton established the basic facts about engine knock. Subsequent efforts were directed toward the discovery of some substance which could be added to gasoline to prevent or reduce knocking. In 1919 Howard interested Teagle in the problem. There was some talk of a cooperative research program by the petroleum and automotive industries to keep gasoline quality in step with engine improvements. Laboratory experiments were planned by Howard and Clark and launched at Bayway in 1919 to check Midgley's work and to try to find better compounds to reduce knocking.[34]

Throughout 1920 experiments directed toward the common goal were independently conducted under Midgley at Dayton and under Howard at Bayway. Formal co-operation between General Motors and Jersey Standard was confined to the exchange of information on seasonal and territorial variations in the quality of gasoline and motor lubricants. Jersey assured General Motors, however, that it was willing to assist in the distribution of an antiknock additive if a suitable one could be found. In its early research efforts, Howard stated, the Jersey Company actually was "one jump ahead of Kettering." When Kettering announced, early in 1920, that aniline would serve to stop engine knock, experiments at Bayway had already established the fact that aniline stopped the knock at low speeds but aggravated it at high speeds.[35]

Howard's assurance, however, was premature. On December 9, 1921, the search finally culminated in Midgley's discovery of the remarkable antiknock properties of tetraethyl lead. E. I. Du Pont de Nemours, Inc., co-operating with General Motors, worked out a method of manufacturing this compound, and on February 2, 1923, "Ethyl" gasoline was first placed on public sale by a service station in Dayton operated by The Refiners Oil Company. General Motors incorporated the General Motors Chemical Company to distribute tetraethyl lead, which Du Pont manufactured at a specially constructed plant in Deepwater, New Jersey. During 1923 ethyl gasoline was sold in many stations throughout the Middle West. In August of that year General Motors announced that sufficient ethyl fluid would be allotted in Jersey marketing territory to process 13,000 gallons of gasoline per day. Midgley visited the Jersey Company and other large eastern refiners to see if they would undertake the distribution. General Motors' terms included a charge for the ethyl fluid at the rate of 3 cents per gallon of gasoline treated—the ethyl gasoline to be sold at a 5-cent margin above regular grades. General Motors also agreed to finance local advertising in its own name in the territories where the gasoline was to be sold. These terms were not satisfactory to Jersey—particularly the provision that no extra margin of profit on ethyl gasoline was to be allowed the distributor.[36]

Midgley's 1921 discovery had not put an end to Jersey experiments, but it had changed their direction. The Du Pont process of manufacturing tetraethyl lead was unsatisfactory in many particulars and expensive. Jersey chemists, assisted by the advice of Remsen and Robert Millikan, worked to find either a better method of manufacturing tetraethyl lead or a better antiknock additive. In 1922 the problem of manufacturing tetraethyl lead was turned over to Professor Charles A. Kraus of Clark University, a leading authority on metallo-organic compounds. His efforts culminated early in 1924 in a manufacturing process which made possible a reduction in the selling price of tetraethyl lead from one cent per cubic centimeter to less than one-fifth cent, thus rendering obsolete the Du Pont process.[37] This sparkling piece of applied research—clear evidence alike of Jersey's aggressive new spirit in technological matters and of the effectiveness of the development organization—virtually dictated a Jersey Standard–General Motors alliance.

On August 18, 1924, the Ethyl Gasoline Corporation was incorporated to develop, manufacture, and distribute tetraethyl lead. Jersey Standard and General Motors held equal interests. Kettering was named president; Howard and Midgley, vice-presidents. Teagle, Howard, Clark, and Moffett served on the original board of directors along with six General Motors men. Exclusive rights under all appropriate Jersey and General Motors patents were transferred to the new corporation, and distribution of ethyl fluid to the petroleum industry was begun.[38] The manufacture of the fluid by the new process was commenced on an experimental scale at Bayway, in Dayton, and in Deepwater. The Jersey Company began to advertise *Standard Ethyl Gasoline*—the providential answer to competition from premium-grade gasolines of competitors.

The danger of the manufacturing process had been well demonstrated by a number of cases of lead poisoning which had been reported in the Dayton laboratories and in the Du Pont plant in Deepwater. On October 26, 1924—only three weeks after all department heads had been called to witness a triumphant demonstration of the remarkable new fuel in one of the offices at 26 Broadway—a minor manufacturing accident precipitated a catastrophe at Bayway. Dozens of workmen were found to have been affected by the tetraethyl lead, and five men died. Jersey management was appalled at the tragedy. Manufacturing operations were suspended. Medical and chemical investigators rushed to the scene. A review of manufacturing experience elsewhere revealed fatalities at Dayton and at Deepwater, with a very large number of less acute cases of lead poisoning being reported at both places. While there was no attempt or desire on the part of the manufacturers to hide or gloss over the grim facts, misinformation and exaggeration were rampant in the press. Ethyl gasoline, the sensation-seeking publications reported, was deadly. The public shrank in dismay from what had promised to be one of the most outstanding contributions yet made to automotive development. The state of New Jersey and several communities in other states as well placed a ban on sale of the new product.[39]

On November 3, 1924, the Jersey Company announced the withdrawal of ethyl gasoline from its markets. The State Board of Health was called in and apprised of company plans. The attitude of the state authorities was reasonable, and there was no hysteria at the professional level. A carefully written and accurate article appeared in the December, 1924, issue of *The Lamp,* which pointed out that the danger lay in manufacturing the concentrated ethyl fluid and that there was no hazard involved in using ethyl-treated gasoline. On May 5, 1925, the Ethyl Gasoline Corporation suspended the sale of ethyl fluid and invited the office of the Surgeon General of the United States to conduct an investigation. The work of this investigating committee was supplemented by experiments conducted by the United States Public Health Service, the Bureau of Mines, and Columbia University. All reported that ethyl gasoline was not harmful to the motorist, automotive mechanic, or the service-station operator. Safety precautions and regulations governing the manufacture and handling of the concentrated fluid were established, and on June 1, 1926, the Ethyl Gasoline Corporation again placed ethyl fluid on the market.[40]

The Jersey Company, having placed great hope upon the new premium product as a means of combating serious competition in its domestic gasoline markets, was faced with a difficult decision. Should the company start in again to market *Standard Ethyl Gasoline* in the face of still current and widespread public fear? Dr. W. Gilman Thompson, the company's medical adviser, strongly counseled Teagle to abandon ethyl. Teagle confided to Clark his own fear that the moment the company put ethyl back on the market "all the black-leg lawyers over the country will start gunning for us." Howard held that Jersey Standard could ill afford to become involved in further incidents which would lose for the company the confidence of the public health authorities. The market situation, on the other hand, was serious. Some competitors had developed benzol-treated motor fuels superior to Jersey's standard grade, and some companies had commenced to market ethyl gasoline aggressively as soon as the Ethyl Gasoline Corporation lifted the ban on the sale of ethyl fluid.[41]

It was this situation which brought about the decision, already noted in the preceding chapter, to abandon *Standard Ethyl Gasoline* and bring out a new product under the trade name of *Esso*. This new blend, placed on the market in April of 1926, was made from crudes carefully chosen for their antiknock properties. For a short time in 1926 the product which was sold in North and South Carolina as *Esso* contained tetraethyl lead, but the Jersey Company studiously avoided advertising the fact and confined its notice to the pump-plate statement required by law: "Ethyl gasoline containing ethyl lead. To be used for motor fuel only." Elsewhere in its marketing territories the Jersey Company (and Louisiana Standard) used benzol as an antiknock agent, a policy which soon was adopted in the Carolinas as well. Because of the great care exercised in choice of crudes and in the refining process, *Esso* was fully equal in quality to any competitive products and superior to many of them. *Esso*'s knock rating of from 0 to 1½ was actually superior to that of the *Standard Ethyl Gasoline* marketed by Jersey before the suspension. The manufacturing disadvantage, however, was formidable, since benzol was costly and there was difficulty in obtaining adequate crude of the desired quality.[42]

Jersey's cautious policy of refusing to use tetraethyl lead in some of its gasoline—and of refusing to advertise the fact when it did use it—precipitated further complications. At the end of 1926 the Ethyl Gasoline Corporation had yet to show a profit. Manufacturing operations had been centered in the Deepwater plant of Du Pont and no further serious trouble was experienced from lead poisoning, but market acceptance of ethyl gasoline was slow. E. W. Webb, president of the Ethyl Gasoline Corporation, charged that two factors were hampering profitable development. The first was the attitude of the Buick organization, which had advised its dealers that ethyl gasoline would ruin engine valves. The second was Jersey's promotional emphasis on *Esso*.[43]

"It has been difficult for us," Webb told his fellow directors, ". . . to explain the fact that although the Standard Oil Company of New Jersey owned half of our company nevertheless it was not selling Ethyl gasoline, but another antiknock claimed to be better by their salesmen than Ethyl."[44]

This acutely awkward situation—essentially a result of Jersey caution in the face of potential public censure—was relieved somewhat in 1927 when the Ethyl Corporation at last began to do an active business and show good profits. At the end of that year, however, the Jersey Company was still refusing to incorporate "Ethyl" in its brand name and was not a large customer for the product which it was indirectly engaged in selling to others and into the development of which company money, energy, and skill had been poured.

No such marketing enigmas were promised by Jersey Standard's contemporary interest in the production of oil from shale and coal—a matter to which company executives devoted even more attention than they did to tetraethyl lead. The beginning of the story may be traced here briefly, for while this line of endeavor eventually developed into a major episode in Jersey Standard history, the events from 1920 to 1927 were of a preliminary nature.

One result of the fear of petroleum shortage which gripped the country, the industry, and the Jersey organization in 1920 was the awakening of an interest in substitute sources of crude oil. Refiners had long known that oil could be produced from shale, but the process was not believed to hold promise of commercial success under prevailing economic conditions. The Jersey Company, however, began in the early 1920's to cast a speculative eye at the oil-shale deposits in the West and at the Athabasca tar sands in Canada. The Canadian deposits were ruled out, but in 1921 the company actually purchased 22,000 acres of shale lands in Colorado against the possibility that a commercially practicable oil-extraction process might be developed.[45]

Interest in shale soon diminished to a vanishing point as reports were received of technical developments in Germany. There during the war years the problem of oil shortage had been acute. Starving for natural raw materials, the German petroleum and rubber industries alike had tried to stay alive with the aid of chemistry. The incentive of national emergency produced experimental work of promise. Further research was fostered in postwar years by German tariff policies and by inflation. The hard-pressed German government was doing all in its power to reduce costly dependence on foreign manufactured articles. German capitalists, at the same time, mistrusted their paper profits and poured money into research projects and new industries in an effort to avoid taxes and the demand by stockholders for dividends. Friedrich Bergius, continuing experiments which he had commenced in 1910, was close to success in perfecting a commercial process for the synthetic production of mineral oils. His hydrogenation, or coal-liquefaction process as it was called, consisted of combining hydrogen with powdered brown coal under conditions of high temperature and pressure to form a derivative very much like crude oil. The Bergius patents were taken over by the Badische Aniline und Soda Fabrik, one of the several large chemical firms which were merged in this period into the combination known as I.G. Farbenindustrie.[46]

Jersey's interest in hydrogenation may be effectively dated from a letter written by Teagle to Riedemann on October 14, 1920. The Development Department would like to be fully informed, Teagle told his German friend and associate, of the progress made during the war in extracting oil from brown coal. Riedemann answered that he thought the Jersey Company should engage a scientific specialist to study the problem. "The fact is," he wrote, "that we shall have to expect a large increase in the German oil production from coal and that . . . we must be prepared that for every ton produced in Germany, a ton of the same product will be imported less." Ira Remsen, who was in close contact with German developments, also felt that Jersey should investigate, an opinion that E. M. Clark likewise shared. Howard suggested that Ross H. Dickson, one of his assistants, be sent over, and in 1922 this was done.[47]

Dickson reported, after extensive investigations in Germany, that the hydrogenation process was far from a commercial reality. In 1924, however, after Dickson had departed, Bergius made further improvements in his apparatus. Riedemann admitted that he was skeptical in some ways, but deeply worried by the knowledge that certain astute European financiers were backing the hydrogenation experiments. It was at this point that a tangential development in the ethyl gasoline business influenced the course of Jersey Standard's nascent relations with the German chemical industry.

Officials of the Ethyl Gasoline Corporation were interested in the progress of the Badische firm in developing iron carbonyl as an antiknock agent. Discussions with Badische were carried on by Jasper Crane, European manager of Du Pont, and a contract was concluded by the Ethyl Corporation, settling a dispute over patent rights on noncarbonyl additives. In 1925 officials of the Badische organization arrived in the United States to carry on patent negotiations with Du Pont. Howard, urging the importance of the hydrogenation work being carried on by the German firm, arranged that the visitors tour the Jersey plants. This visit resulted in an invitation to Howard to visit the great research center at Ludwigshaven.[48] Thus the tenuous ties, momentarily weakened by Dickson's report in 1922, were kept from breaking.

In 1926 Howard visited Ludwigshaven. So impressed was he by the progress there in synthetic production of oil that he urged Teagle to enter into an agreement with I.G. Farben to launch a joint program of research. Teagle and the Jersey board approved in principle. Further conferences were arranged in Germany at which Teagle, Howard, Moffett, Riedemann, and other top-level Jersey executives were present. On September 27, 1927, a contract was signed between Jersey Standard and I.G. Farben which outlined a course of co-operation in the development of the hydrogenation process in the United States. The Jersey Company made no cash payments, but bound itself to a program which involved the expenditure of millions of dollars. Jersey was to have the right to use the hydrogenation process in the United States upon payment of a fair royalty to I.G. Farben. The German firm was to retain its United States patents and control the licensing of the process to other parties, but, as compensation for development costs incurred, was to pay Jersey one-half of all American royalties collected.[49]

In effect, the Farben contract gave Jersey Standard (which, like other American companies, had done virtually no effective work in the field) access to the tremendously valuable knowledge and experience of the Germans—in return for the guarantee that Jersey would engage in research efforts which probably would have been undertaken in any case and under far less propitious circumstances. This was possibly among the most advantageous transactions ever concluded by the Jersey Company, one which soon was to benefit the American petroleum industry generally and was to make possible the strengthening of the nation for the conflict that lay ahead. That it later formed the basis for a bitter attack upon the company by the federal government and resulted in widespread public disapprobation was another of those ironic pranks of history so familiar to Jersey executives whose memory went back to the chill days of the dissolution decree.

Quickly the hydrogenation project took form. Contemplating the vast research program that lay ahead, Howard called again on the advice of W. K. Lewis. Lewis suggested Robert T. Haslam, one of his associates at the Massachusetts Institute of Technology, to head the project. Haslam was given leave of absence, but he never returned to his academic post. Baton Rouge was chosen as the site of the new laboratory. Haslam picked Robert P. Russell, assistant professor of chemical engineering at the Institute, to head the research center, which was staffed largely by junior faculty members of MIT and of its affiliated School of Chemical Engineering Practice.[50] Though the fact was not at first obvious, the Jersey Company in this one step covered much of the imposing gap which so long had yawned between applied and creative research in petroleum technology. Synthetic rubber was only the most spectacular of the many developments which traced all or parts of their origin to the new science center in Louisiana. Here lay the start of an action-packed chapter in Jersey's technological history.

At the close of 1927 no observer familiar with the efforts of Teagle, Clark, and Howard to push the Jersey Company forward to a position of technical leadership in the industry, or with the perfection of the tube-and-tank and other processes, or with Jersey's flirtatious excursions into the field of manufacturing chemistry—could say that the nine preceding years had been uneventful or devoid of tangible gain, though many developments were still in a formative stage and many capital expenditures had yet to show a return.

THE BATTLE OF THE PATENTS

Jersey's efforts to be progressive in technology were conditioned at one point by a legal situation of incredible complexity. The tube-and-tank process was the direct issue, but the sequence of events—the attacks, the counterattacks, the remedies for open warfare in the industry—affected all the work that the Development Department was contemplating or carrying forward.

In 1919 four cracking processes which promised rivalry for the Burton process of Indiana Standard were in various experimental stages. These were the tube-and-tank process of Jersey, the Holmes-Manley-Adams process of The Texas Company, the Cross process of the Gasoline Products Company, and the Dubbs process of the Universal Oil Products Company. Each of these groups held patents or patent applications based, not on the art or theory of cracking itself, but on means by which the common goal of pyrolytic cracking could be achieved. Since those means necessarily involved the exposure of oil to heat and pressure in a reaction chamber, it was not surprising that infringement claims were soon heard.

In 1916 the Universal Oil Products Company sued Indiana Standard for infringing the original Dubbs patent. This patent, applied for in 1909, had not been issued until 1915. Indiana men claimed that it had been unlawfully altered during its course through the Patent Office to cover the principles disclosed in Burton's 1913 patent. The Universal Oil Products Company, backed by J. Ogden Armour, was aggressively inclined; and it appeared that the Dubbs patent—whatever its merits or legality or originality—was to be employed not so much for manufacturing purposes as for a weapon with which to attack all other holders of cracking patents.[51]

The Dubbs suit, which wore on for some years, was the beginning of the battle of the patents. By 1920, however, this suit was not the most important issue, and it may be disregarded for present narrative purposes. The greater danger perceived by Indiana Standard in that year was the issuance to The Texas Company of the Adams patents.

The Adams patents had been applied for in 1909 by a Brooklyn inventor, were acquired in pending form by The Texas Company in 1915, and formed the legal basis for all subsequent experiments carried on by that company. When the basic Adams patents finally were issued by the Patent Office in 1920, Indiana Standard and its Burton-process licensees at once began to look up defense material to meet the expected attack upon them by The Texas Company, for it was apparent that the Adams applications had been molded in the Patent Office in a broad form well suited for such an attack. On July 23, 1920, The Texas Company actually wrote a warning letter to Indiana Standard. Jersey, Louisiana Standard, Standard of New York, Humble, Standard of California, and other licensees under the Burton process all were concerned, for all were liable for damage and back-royalty payments if The Texas Company made good its infringement claims.[52]

What promised to be a tremendous patent suit, however, never materialized. To be sure, the Adams patents held by The Texas Company clearly antedated the Burton patents of Indiana, but in endeavoring to perfect its Holmes-Manley-Adams process The Texas Company found that it must incorporate certain additional features that were covered by the Burton patents. When this fact became evident, Indiana in turn threatened The Texas Company with an infringement suit. The stalemate was resolved by the Indiana-Texas Company agreement of August 26, 1921.[53]

By the terms of this agreement each party consented to withdraw its infringement claims and allow the other the use of all its cracking patents, granted or pending. Each company guaranteed, in effect, to protect the other from any damages that might be assessed in court action against any of the patents exchanged, and Indiana was granted the right to sublicense Texas patents to existing licensees of the Burton process.[54]

Indiana Standard had other reasons for concluding this agreement than the immediate one of avoiding a direct clash with The Texas Company. Indiana men were well aware that Jersey Standard had obtained the Ellis patents and was on the verge of making the tube-and-tank process practicable. This development threatened to put an end to the royalties which the Jersey organization was paying to Indiana for use of the Burton-Humphreys process. At that very time, in fact, Indiana was being forced by Jersey to reduce the royalty rate, the stated reason being excessive deterioration of the stills caused by the running of Mexican stocks.[55] Actually, this reduction was an evidence of Jersey's improved bargaining position as a result of work on the competing process.

Indiana, then, was motivated by a desire to protect its royalty revenues from further shrinkage. Not only Jersey's cracking process, but that of Dubbs and also the system developed by Walter Cross, all spelled trouble for Indiana—either in the form of infringement suits (such as the one already started by the Dubbs group) or, in case there was no infringement, in the form of increased competition and diminished royalty revenues from the Burton-Humphreys process. The Indiana Company, in short, seemed about to lose the near-monopoly in the cracking-patent field which it had enjoyed since 1913.

The Dubbs, Jersey, Cross, and Holmes-Manley processes, however, had many features in common. It seemed inevitable that infringement actions would arise among these four groups as a result of the close similarity of the processes which they were sponsoring. Indiana Standard lawyers felt reasonably certain that Texas would win out and dominate the field. If this happened, Indiana would have assured itself, by the provisions of its agreement with The Texas Company, that the stream of revenue from Indiana's existing licensees would not be cut off, even if those licensees abandoned the Burton in favor of the newer processes. Indiana Standard would, by the terms of the agreement, also share in Texas royalties from new licensees—an important proviso if the competing methods should make the Burton-Humphreys process obsolete. Indiana, moreover, would be able to employ the Texas patents for defense purposes in the still unsettled suit which had been brought by Dubbs in 1916.[56] These were the best-laid plans of some of the most astute businessmen in America; they were shattered by Fate's predilection for scorning the logical and the clever.

Even as Indiana Standard men were drawing the terms of the 1921 agreement, events were seemingly falling into the anticipated pattern.

The Texas Company laid its plans to sue Jersey. Jersey, having been notified by the Patent Office that its newly acquired Ellis patents had been granted, promptly began an attack upon Cross. This last-named action commenced three days after the granting of the Ellis patents and was nominally directed at The Pure Oil Company, Limited, a Cross-process licensee. Howard stated that the suit was not inspired by a desire to monopolize the tube-and-tank field, but was intended merely to defend that segment in which the Jersey Company had pioneered. Howard's remarks notwithstanding, Jersey's action appeared to be a highly aggressive form of defense. The Cross patent specifically featured the high pressures toward which Jersey research was pointed, and Jersey's further progress apparently was threatened unless interference could be proved against Cross on other grounds. The Jersey Company not only brought suit, but it caused a notice of the fact to be published in *The Lamp*.[57]

The attitude prevailing among petroleum refiners of the day was a grim one. "He who lives by the sword must die by the sword," said Howard.[58] This remark was made in 1924 and directed at Dubbs rather than Cross, but it appropriately characterized the general feeling prevalent in 1921 and 1922. Tremendous sums were at stake. Since it clearly was a question of attack or be attacked, the Jersey suit against Cross seemed defensible on both economic and ethical grounds. The action, nevertheless, appears in retrospect to have been a managerial blunder of formidable dimensions. Public attitudes toward the large oil companies were again being recast. The benign approbation with which war achievements of the petroleum industry had been greeted was giving way to distress over allegedly exorbitant gasoline prices. The LaFollette Committee had launched its investigation and was seizing upon every incident which could be used to support its hostility toward the large oil companies in general and Standard Oil companies in particular. The Cross suit was cited at length in testimony before the committee. Questions leveled at E. M. Clark were designed to suggest that Jersey had given notice to the trade of its suit against Cross in order to discourage other refiners from installing the Cross process. This undoubtedly was the case, and public revelation of the fact was extremely awkward for the Jersey Company. The examination of Walter Cross himself took a highly damaging turn for Jersey when he testified that the resources of his Gasoline Products Company would be severely taxed in meeting Jersey's damage claims. Notwithstanding the fact that Cross and his company were backed by powerful New York banking interests, the general picture which was painted by the questioning was that of a great and heartless Standard Oil Company crushing a small and hapless competitor.[59] Thus Jersey courted public condemnation to gain ends which might well have been achieved without stigma by allowing Cross to take the initiative in litigation.

The immediate effect of the Jersey suit was to cause Cross to form a defensive alliance with The Texas Company against Jersey Standard. Preliminary talks commenced in June of 1922 and, on January 26, 1923, matured into an agreement. This agreement provided for a pooling of patents in much the same fashion as had the Texas-Indiana agreement of 1921.[60] The patent battle lines were thereby consolidated. By the pooling agreements of 1921 and 1923 Indiana Standard, The Texas Company, and the Gasoline Products Company manned a common and tremendously strong defense line. In direct opposition stood the Jersey Standard forces, apparently armed only with the Ellis patents. The Dubbs–Universal Oil Products Company group was a common enemy of both the major contesting parties and continued to snipe at the flanks.

Some time before this new alignment had taken form, a man by the name of George T. Rogers came to Teagle's office. One of Teagle's business friends in Plainfield, New Jersey, where Rogers lived, had suggested that he go there with his story. Rogers informed Teagle that he had been an early partner of Joseph H. Adams, the patent holder upon whose claims the Holmes-Manley-Adams process of The Texas Company was legally based. In 1907 he had loaned Adams $5,000, Rogers went on to say, and had received from Adams in return a 40 per cent interest in the process. Thereafter the two men had come to a parting of the ways.[61]

Teagle may well have thought that here, figuratively speaking, was another man with a marvelous white powder to sell. He sent Rogers to Howard, and Howard conscientiously studied Rogers' claim. Surprisingly enough, it looked like a valid one—but to what, exactly, was Rogers entitled? Undoubtedly to repayment of his $5,000, and to 40 per cent of whatever Adams had received or would receive in royalties and salary over the years from The Texas Company. None of Jersey's lawyers believed at the outset, however, that The Texas Company could be implicated. It seemed obvious that Texas had acquired Adams' process in good faith and without an inkling that Adams' title was questionable—otherwise millions of dollars would not subsequently have been poured into the Holmes-Manley-Adams process without some effort to buy up Rogers' interest. The facts, however, could be established conclusively only by an examination of the Texas-Adams contract and correspondence. Since The

Texas Company was not likely to permit Jersey lawyers to examine its files, suit would have to be brought by Rogers to force an accounting and disclose on the witness stand the true history and nature of the Adams-Texas Company relationship.[62]

Howard thought the gamble was worth taking—no one could foresee what course the testimony might take. If nothing more, the suit might prove to have a nuisance value in the impending Texas-Jersey patent clash. He agreed, therefore, to have the Jersey Company back Rogers in an action against Adams and The Texas Company, in return for the option to purchase all Rogers' claims for $50,000. At first Jersey's backing was carefully concealed, apparently in the hope that The Texas Company might treat the case as a minor one and handle it carelessly. Rogers' claim was turned over to the outside law firm of Fish, Richardson and Neave, and suit was instituted in the New York courts. The Texas Company promptly offered Rogers $10,000 in settlement, which offer, of course, was refused.[63]

When the course of testimony at length forced the disclosure of the Jersey Standard interest in the Rogers claims, the importance of the suit became evident to all. The case became involved in the legal subtleties of trusteeship and notice; it was doubtful to the very end that Rogers could establish a claim against anyone except his one-time partner. The verdict, finally sustained on June 5, 1923, in a decision by the Appellate Division Court, was a stunning one. The court ruling held, in effect, that The Texas Company was indeed bound by the Rogers-Adams agreement of 1907. Rogers (Jersey) was entitled to 40 per cent of all revenues ever received by The Texas Company under its cracking patents. More startling yet, the fact had been established that the Rogers-Adams agreement contained a somewhat unusual clause that Adams could not put his inventions to use without Rogers' consent. Since that consent had not been obtained, Texas' use of Adams' inventions in its Holmes-Manley process was a violation of the contract, and all licenses issued under the Adams patents were also violations of Rogers' rights. This was only the beginning. Not only was The Texas Company in a bad position, but Indiana Standard, because of its 1921 pooling arrangement with Texas and because it had taken licenses under the Adams patent, was liable to Jersey Standard for possibly all and certainly 40 per cent of its operating profits from all cracking processes, including the Burton-Humphreys, over the entire period that those processes had been in use.[64]

Indiana, however, was protected against the Jersey claim by the warranty of The Texas Company, contained in the 1921 agreement, that the Texas patents were valid. The position of The Texas Company, therefore, was a most serious one. Texas not only owed Jersey Standard 40 per cent of the Texas royalties under the Adams patent, but was liable to Indiana for Jersey's potentially huge claim against Indiana. Were the Jersey Company to press its claims against both companies, Indiana would have to fall back on its warranty and total damages to The Texas Company could have amounted to many millions of dollars.[65]

This was a highly dramatic situation. Absolute control for Jersey Standard of more than half of the cracking capacity in the United States and possible dominance of the entire field waited only upon an affirmative nod from Walter Teagle. Most of America's business leaders of an earlier generation would have relished such an opportunity—there would have been no hesitancy. But this was 1923, and the day had long passed when a dangerous competitor could summarily be destroyed. There was a real danger, too, that if Jersey Standard pressed its claims and Indiana was forced in consequence to do likewise, the action would look suspiciously like conspiracy between two Standard Oil companies to put a rival independent out of business. Jersey declared "live and let live" as its patent policy, sheathed its sword, and handed its erstwhile opponents a pen.

Negotiations between the parties involved proceeded throughout the summer of 1923 and culminated on September 28, 1923, in the "T. I. J." (Texas-Indiana-Jersey) agreement. The fundamental purpose of this pact was to provide "a limited exchange [of licenses] giving to each party the opportunity to proceed with the logical development of his own method without interference from others."[66] The agreement specifically provided a mutual release of all parties from interference proceedings, defined and distinguished the processes of the parties involved, granted to each the right to use and license its own processes at will, and established terms under which each might be licensed to use the processes of the others. Jersey released Cross and the Gasoline Products Company from all claims. Indiana agreed to reduce by 25 per cent the royalties paid by Jersey and Louisiana Standard for use of the Burton process. This reduction was to remain in effect until 1931, after which Jersey and Louisiana Standard were to have the right to use the Burton process without charge.

Since Jersey Standard had no wish to use the Holmes-Manley-Adams process and since it was apparent, even in 1924, that by 1931 Jersey would probably have ceased to use the Burton-Humphreys process at all, the face value of the concessions received by Jersey under the 1923 pooling agreement was surprisingly modest. Nevertheless, an incautious judgment that Jersey Standard was being highly magnanimous should be avoided. The company, it must be remembered, did not dare for political reasons to exploit its legal triumph in too obvious a fashion. Then, too, the possibility was very real that Jersey's tube-and-tank process developments might infringe the Holmes-Manley-Adams patents. No doubt these facts were well appreciated by all parties involved. The prize which was coveted, however, had actually been won. Jersey men were convinced that their tube-and-tank process was far superior to all others, and that the company's emphasis on research—possibly greater at the time than in any other major oil company in the world—would keep Jersey Standard ahead. What was absolutely vital to the company was freedom to go its own way unhampered. For this privilege the Jersey Company, in all confidence, was willing to pay the necessary price of allowing the other signatories that same freedom.[67] Certainly Jersey's handling of the situation bears evidence of a degree of business statesmanship not always displayed by the company in those years.

The 1923 patent-pooling agreement resolved a dangerous and untenable situation in the American petroleum refining industry in a reasonable and workable fashion. From 1919 to 1923—a period which should have witnessed the wholesale modernization of the entire refining industry—the application of the many new cracking processes had been virtually at a standstill. This circumstance is clearly reflected in the statistics presented in Appendix 2, Table IX. Each of the groups sponsoring new cracking systems wished to be free to grant licenses, though Jersey Standard, for one, was not anxious to do so. Had there been no legal impediments, those who wished to license could have done so and those who did not would unquestionably have been forced to do so by the pressure of competition and of public opinion. In any case, the small refiners would have benefited from the research work being performed by the large companies. Yet neither the holders of patents nor the prospective licensees had dared to move. The plight of the engineers planning Humble's new Baytown refinery was by no means unique. Granting or accepting licenses to any cracking process in those years was an open invitation to legal action. The cracking facilities in use in the United States had remained concentrated in the hands of the companies which had developed those facilities, and of the relatively small number of licensees who were strong enough to bear the legal risks involved. In 1924 Indiana Standard had produced 34.82 per cent of all cracked gasoline manufactured in the country, while Jersey, Louisiana Standard, and Humble together produced 24.29 per cent, and The Texas Company 21.94 per cent—a total of 81.05 per cent of the industry's output.[68]

There are grounds, too, for surmising that research had been somewhat stifled through fear that money would be expended only for a competitor's gain. Jersey's considerable devotion to improving the old Burton stills may well have derived from fear of confining its efforts to a tube-and-tank process which might prove to be dominated by someone else. If this was, indeed, the case, all was now changed. A competitive technological race developed, the industry generally became more actively interested in new processes, and each of the patent-pool members continued to license its processes. For years cracking patents had served almost exclusively to restrict progress. After 1923 those same patents conformed more nearly to the basic concept underlying United States patent laws— the encouragement of widespread technological development.

Such, however, were not the views of the Department of Justice, and a new legal conflict began to take form in the shadowland between patent and antitrust laws. The concept and purpose behind patent laws were somewhat anomalous in a nation which had come to abhor monopoly. While the Patent Office was issuing handsomely engraved certificates granting the recipient a seventeen-year monopoly, the Justice Department was enthusiastically engaged in destroying monopolies on sight. It is not surprising that conflicts were frequent between those who held patents and those who enforced the antitrust laws.[69]

In the petroleum industry there was another and more particular source of friction. Refining had grown to be an immensely complex art requiring a high investment in plant. The day of the small refiner was not past, as some claimed, but in the early 1920's the members of this group were individually in a weakened position. Many of them lacked the capital necessary to pay the high first cost of the new cracking equipment (a single tube-and-tank unit cost about $500,000, as compared with $50,000 for a Burton still), and maximum efficiency by modern refining methods could be attained only in a large-scale installation. These smaller refiners quite naturally put the blame on their large rivals rather than on the trend of the times; their protests filled pages of the LaFollette Committee records. A federal suit against the members of the 1923 patent pool was the almost inevitable aftermath of the LaFollette Committee's report.

On June 25, 1924, the United States Attorney General filed suit in the Federal Court for the Northern District of Illinois against Standard of

Indiana, The Texas Company, Jersey Standard, and the Gasoline Products
Company—the primary defendants—as well as against 46 other corporations engaged in refining and selling cracked gasoline. The bill brought
against the defendants charged violation of Sections 1 and 2 of the Sherman Antitrust Act: attempts to monopolize interstate trade in cracked
gasoline and conspiracy in restraint of such trade.[70] A Master in Chancery was appointed by the court to hear and report evidence and return
findings of fact and conclusions of law.

A burst of publicity followed the announcement of the suit. "The greatest attack ever made by the Government on trusts and monopolies," the
New York *Sun* reported. Many newspapers were noncommittal, while the
trade journals sprang to the defense of the accused. The *Oil & Gas Journal,* pointing to one of the most glaring weaknesses of the petroleum industry, made what was possibly the most pertinent comment of all:[71]

> The only way to meet publicity is with publicity. Everybody is using it nowa-
> days, everybody but the oil industry. Even the Government departments have
> their publicity representatives, their "confidential—to be held for release" an-
> nouncements. Occupants of the White House itself have been known to rely
> upon timely and favorable publicity through chosen channels.
> This is the spirit of the age—to get your case before the public. It need not
> be propaganda which is merely an imitation of genuine publicity. The plain
> truth, if you have a good case, is the best publicity always.

Both sides prepared their cases with painstaking care, for the subject
was surrounded by legal and technical complexities of a formidable nature. The government employed as its technical adviser Ralph H. McKee,
professor of chemical engineering at Columbia University. William J.
Donovan, assistant to the Attorney General of the United States, headed
the prosecution. An imposing array of legal talent led by Russell Wiles,
of Dyrenforth, Lee, Chritton & Wiles, represented the oil companies. The
Jersey Company employed John W. Davis and the patent law firm of
Fish, Richardson and Neave, which had handled the Rogers suit so brilliantly. Howard devoted much of his time to the case and appears to
have been as instrumental as any other single individual in planning the
defense strategy. As technical expert for the defense the oil companies
called on Robert E. Wilson, assistant director of research of the Indiana
Company and former director of the Research Laboratory of Applied
Chemistry at the Massachusetts Institute of Technology.[72]

The government opened the attack by contending that the cracking
patents in question were invalid, since they covered principles that had

been disclosed long before the issuance of those patents. The pooling agreements had gone, so the charge ran, far beyond the limits necessary to settle litigation and had resulted in diminished competition between what at one time were rival processes. The patent pool had resulted in restriction of output of cracked gasoline and had enabled unjustified royalties to be levied. The territorial restrictions that Indiana Standard had written into its early Burton-Humphreys process licenses were clearly in restraint of trade.[73]

Upon these charges the oil companies launched a determined legal counterattack. Counsel for the defense objected that the validity of patents could not be attacked in a Sherman antitrust case. This objection was overruled. Wilson, the technical expert for the oil companies, then contributed very convincing testimony in support of the validity of the defendants' patents. Admitting that the theory of cracking was covered by earlier patents, he went on to state why this fact should be discounted. "In my opinion the reason the industry did not adopt any of these prior art cracking processes was because it was not possible by the use of any of them to make commercially useful gasoline, a marketable gasoline, at a profit."[74]

Denying charges of high royalty rates, upholding the legality of licensing agreements, and pointing to the fact that the defendants had been and were still willing to license others to use their cracking processes, the counsel for the defense called attention to the fact that patents were intended, by definition, to be monopolistic and that some restraint of commerce necessarily attached to patents. Indiana Standard, however, was particularly vulnerable to charges of restraint of trade because of the territorial restrictions in certain of its licenses. Defense against this charge centered in the facts that such restrictions were no longer included in licenses or were not actually enforced.[75]

McKee, technical witness for the prosecution, was subjected to a merciless cross-examination. Howard outlined to Wiles the strategy of getting the witness completely committed on so many practical points that upon "testimony of Wilson and myself it will appear that McKee is totally incompetent and unqualified."[76] This plan was followed, and the government's case appears to have suffered because McKee was more familiar with laboratory experimentation than with the actual operation of refineries, whereas Wilson was eminently qualified to testify on prevailing operating conditions and practices in the industry.[77]

The final opinion of the Master in Chancery, returned on December 7,

1927, held that the defendants had procured their patents honestly, with good motives, for the purpose of increasing the supply of motor fuel; that their patents were of great utility and had been the means of increasing the supply of gasoline; that the licensing agreements were made for the purpose of avoiding litigation that would have been detrimental to the defendants and to the public; that the royalties exacted and the restrictions imposed by the licenses were reasonable and within the limits of fair reward contemplated by the grant of patents; that the result of the inventions and their use by the defendants had been to increase the supply of gasoline and lower its cost, all to the benefit of the public; that the defendants had not monopolized nor attempted to monopolize trade; and that in such a case as this one it was unnecessary and improper to search claims and files in order to ascertain the scope and validity of patents.[78]

This sweeping vindication of the oil companies was taken under consideration by the United States District Court. On January 20, 1930, this court, in a two-to-one decision, reversed the findings of the Master in Chancery and ruled that the patent pool was in violation of the Sherman Act and must be dissolved. On April 13, 1931, the United States Supreme Court, by unanimous decision on the part of the eight justices then sitting, in turn reversed the District Court finding, upheld the oil companies, and ruled that the Sherman Act had not been violated.[79]

No final estimate of the charges against the oil companies and of their defensive counterclaims should be attempted from the records of one defendant alone, yet some tentative conclusions may be advanced on the basis of the evidence available. This important legal action grew out of and was influenced by considerations broader than the field of law alone. The Sherman Antitrust Act was (and is) less a law than an expression of national policy, the interpretation of which depends upon the mood of the times. Under this versatile law, or policy, individuals and companies might enjoy certain monopolistic patent privileges or they could be indicted for exercising those privileges, depending somewhat upon who they were and what was their public standing. Public opinion, which the patent-pool members had not only ignored but even flouted, demanded the 1924 indictment, quite irrespective of the legal justifications therefor. The fact that the oil companies were exonerated by a traditionally hostile federal court perhaps constitutes a more valid estimate of the real merits of the charges and defenses than could ever be derived from an examination of all pertinent records. Even if the action brought by the Attorney General's office was unjustified and in some respects unfair, however, it

was by no means devoid of benefit to the oil companies. The case helped
to locate anew for the industry the faintly marked, illogically drawn, and
constantly shifting line of demarcation between the permissible and the
forbidden. Once again and very forcibly the large oil companies had been
put on notice that their own concept of the location of that line was not
the governing one, no matter how formidable were their claims or how
compelling their necessities.

The practical effect of the Supreme Court decision, of course, was to
encourage the maintenance and strengthening of the patent pool. Teagle
and Howard welcomed the end of the "patents-for-revenue" philosophy
which had been fastened on the industry. Both men hailed what they
hoped was the opportunity to forget about patents and get back to manufacturing for revenue. Before this objective could finally be attained, however, the still outstanding Dubbs litigation had to be ended. In 1931 a
group of companies, including Jersey Standard, Indiana, Texas, and several others, finally bought the Dubbs patent rights, at a reputed price of
$26,000,000, and eventually presented them to the American Chemical
Society to assist in raising funds to promote research in petroleum chemistry.[80] To the Dubbs-Universal Oil Products Company group, which in
1916 had formally opened the battle of the patents, therefore fell the distinction of writing the final treaty of peace. Research and development
rather than litigation, it was hoped, would henceforth be the primary
concern of American refiners.

MEASURING THE REFINING ACHIEVEMENT

Much that was taking place in the refineries of Jersey Standard and of
its affiliated companies has necessarily been revealed in tracing the important events that were taking place elsewhere in the business. The
drive for greater efficiency, the reorganization of managerial techniques,
the tremendous qualitative and quantitative fluctuations in crude oil supplies, the growth of markets for refined products, the decided changes in
the transportation system, the highly significant modifications of the product line—all these forces, variously dealt with in preceding pages, produced a substantial cumulative alteration in the refining organization. A
description of that alteration and a translation of those forces into terms
of barrels of oil, investment in plant, and dollars of revenue serve to tie
many narrative threads together.

All the multiple activities at the individual refineries between 1919 and
1927 were conditioned by one dominating factor—growth. Average crude

oil throughput of all the refineries in the Jersey organization increased
61 per cent from 1912 to 1918, a highly creditable performance under
prevailing conditions. From 1918 to 1927, however, throughput leaped
163 per cent. The record of crude oil runs at the various refineries is
presented in Appendix 2, Table VIII, a statistical compilation which reveals many trends.[81]

These figures would undoubtedly have caused the founders of the business to be impressed by the size of the enterprise they had established.
They would have been equally interested, perhaps, in the evidence that
the historic geographic pattern of refining activity was changing. On
many occasions in the years following World War I, questions about the
comparative effectiveness of eastern seaboard and Gulf Coast locations
had been raised.

The only certainty in the oil business was that new oil pools would play
out. Jersey men did not, therefore, like to emphasize too greatly the
proximity of Gulf Coast refinery locations to Mid-Continent, Louisiana,
and Texas fields.[82] Time and again this factor was discounted as a dominant and permanent advantage. Time and again, too, this line of reasoning was shaken by new field discoveries. The Mid-Continent area refused
to go into a permanent decline, and the Gulf Coast fields continued to
confound the prognosticators. As competition increased and refining margins were cut, cost factors weighing in favor of Gulf locations received
increasing consideration.[83]

No clear-cut and final policy decision on location appears to have been
made in the 1919-1927 period, since the geographic factor was only one of
many points that were considered when plans for expansion were made.
The efficiency of Bayway was high, the very heavy investment in eastern
seaboard refinery facilities precluded rapid displacement of those facilities, and the eastern refineries continued to enjoy definite freight advantages in some branches of the trade. In 1924, for example, the necessity
for an increase in over-all refining capacity was met by the decision to
expand both Baton Rouge and Bayway, careful consideration having
been given to crude oil supply points, freight charges, and the comparative efficiency of the two plants.[84]

Nevertheless, over the 1919-1927 period the Gulf Coast refineries came
to surpass their veteran counterparts in the East. In 1924 Baton Rouge
displaced Bayonne as Jersey Standard's largest refinery—measured in
terms of crude throughput. In 1927 average daily crude runs of Jersey's
affiliated Gulf Coast plants totaled 186,000 barrels, as compared with

163,000 barrels run in all Jersey's eastern refineries. This dynamic change from the situation existing in 1919 (when the Gulf area refineries ran 46,000 barrels daily and the eastern refineries 111,000) was in part attributable to the progress of the Humble Oil & Refining Company. Humble's Baytown plant, surmounting great initial difficulties, expanded its output so that in 1927 it was second only to Baton Rouge.[85]

Bayonne output, meanwhile, faltered at its 1924 peak and then fell off sharply. This trend presumably had its origin in the fact that gasoline production was centered in other refineries, while the hoary Bayonne establishment was consigned to lesser glories. Bayway, on the other hand, was the leader in initiating the new gasoline cracking processes and continued to expand at nearly the same rate as the Baton Rouge and Baytown units. A relatively small new refinery at Charleston, South Carolina, was brought into operation in 1920 to assist in meeting the great demand for fuel oil and an expected increase in the use of road asphalt in the Carolinas and Georgia. Throughput of the Eagle and Parkersburg refineries expanded modestly rather than spectacularly with the times, while the Baltimore refinery, helping to supply the active Caribbean market, more than doubled its crude runs between 1919 and 1927.

Jersey's program of expanding foreign refining capacity to service specific foreign markets is also mirrored in the statistics in Appendix 2. Foreign refinery runs bore approximately the same ratio to domestic in 1927 as in 1919. This comparative stability was deceiving, for many changes were taking place abroad.

At Teleajen, Romania, the rebuilding of Româno-Americana facilities destroyed during the war years progressed very slowly. Some crude was run for Jersey's Romanian affiliate by other refineries, but this was a costly makeshift. Threatened nationalization of the entire petroleum industry and actual nationalization of the subsoil discouraged any great program of expansion. In 1927 crude runs were substantially less than they had been in 1914 and 1915.[86]

In no other European country did refining operations achieve a position comparable even to that of Teleajen. Efforts in Poland, Italy, Germany, and Norway provide further illustrations of those political troubles which were vexing Jersey's foreign marketers. The refineries at Trieste, at Allicante, at Bilbao, and at Marseilles (all acquired by Jersey affiliates since the war), the old Korff kerosene plant and the benzol and specialty processing plants in Germany, the Nobel-Standard refinery at Libusza, Poland, and the Vallö refinery in Norway all were very small, though each helped to meet local needs and to overcome local tariff barriers against imported refined products.[87]

The inconsequential performance in Europe was counterbalanced by successful efforts to expand facilities in Canada, Latin America, and the Dutch East Indies. Imperial's cross-Canada refinery chain had been completed in time to meet the 1919-1920 boom. In 1923 a combination of economic considerations led to the building of the Calgary refinery, which had an initial capacity of 4,000 barrels daily. The Imperial refineries continued to lean heavily on advice from Jersey technicians and to follow Jersey's precedent in refining matters. In 1924 the tube-and-tank process was installed in Canada, and Imperial founded its own development department. As was the case with the Humble Oil & Refining Company, Imperial's interest in research preceded by some months Howard's dictum that the burden of development carried by Jersey must be shared by the affiliates. The Canadian market grew and so, too, did competition in refining, but in 1930 the refining capacity of the Imperial organization was equivalent to over 80 per cent of total Canadian capacity.[88]

On the other side of the world construction of the Palembang refinery in Sumatra got under way late in 1925. Teagle and Clark differed as to the capacity required to handle the production expected from the Talang Akar field. Clark was pessimistic, but Teagle insisted on a capacity of at least 4,000 barrels daily (in 1931 crude throughput came close to the 25,000-barrel-daily mark). Construction went forward under the difficulties created by an unfriendly climate and an inadequate laboring force. Permanent housing was built, appropriate health measures were taken (after some serious mistakes), and on December 17, 1926—two weeks ahead of schedule—the new refinery was officially opened.[89] This installation, coupled with the success of Jersey's Dutch affiliate in developing adequate crude oil production, promised in the years to come to make Jersey Standard a factor in the Far Eastern trade and to improve the company's competitive standing in the world-wide contest with the Royal Dutch-Shell.

Jersey's affiliated refineries in Latin America expanded with the market that those refineries were designed to serve. Since this area of operations has already been probed in the chapters devoted to producing and marketing, little more need be said. The Talara plant, benefiting from the momentary stability of political conditions in Peru and stimulated by the direct marketing activities of the International Petroleum Company Limited, nearly tripled its output between 1919 and 1927. The Barranca refinery in Colombia began to turn out refined products in 1922. The Campana refinery in Argentina fell under the dark shadow of nationalization when the Argentine government, in 1923, concluded a contract with Bethlehem Steel for construction of a state refinery at La Plata. This was no small-scale experimental project: capacity of the new refinery was equivalent to two-thirds of the national consumption of kerosene. Despite the growing local market, therefore, Jersey executives were unwilling to expand Campana facilities until political events should have taken a more favorable turn. Efforts of the local managers were directed, instead, at obtaining an agreement to participate in marketing some of the output of the government refinery.[90]

The situation was more acutely unfavorable in Argentina than elsewhere, but in all foreign countries where refining activities were under way or contemplated, Jersey policy was conditioned by very broad considerations involving all aspects—public as well as internal—of the business. Nowhere was this fact better demonstrated than in England. The British market had been dominated for many years by the Anglo-American Oil Company, Limited, Jersey's one-time affiliate. Even after 1911 the Jersey–Anglo-American tie was a close one. Jersey's sales to the British marketing firm had continued large. F. E. Powell, Anglo's leader, was so often consulted on matters of mutual interest that for all practical purposes he was considered a member of Jersey's European Committee. After 1919 the Jersey–Anglo-American position was seriously threatened by increased competition from the Royal Dutch-Shell, the Anglo-Persian Oil Company, a growing number of smaller independents, and a Russian marketing syndicate.

By 1926 it had become evident that preservation of the British market depended on a much closer relationship between Jersey and Anglo-American. Jersey's Legal Department was fearful that an outright merger would be construed by the Justice Department as violating the injunctions contained in the 1911 dissolution decree, but considered that the necessity was worth the risk. In anticipation of the possibility of such a liaison at some time in the near future and to achieve in the meantime the advantages of local refining facilities to match those of competitors, the Jersey Company, in 1926, acquired control of the Agwi Petroleum Corporation, Limited, a small independent concern which owned a refinery at Fawley, Southampton Water.[91] This acquisition promised much for the future and constituted an important forward step in perfecting the pattern of integrated foreign operations.

The postwar Jersey Standard policy of encouraging expansion of the foreign refining network led, in turn, to a reappraisal of the existing method of administering foreign manufacturing activities. Before 1919 the foreign plants had been closely tied to local marketing operations and had come under the general jurisdiction of Jersey's Export Trade Committee. As the number of foreign refineries increased after 1919 and certain of those refineries achieved or promised to achieve a substantial volume of output, administrative changes became imperative. E. J. Sadler, conscious as always of organizational deficiencies, began to urge that these refineries be placed under the supervision of the Manufacturing Department. "One of the criticisms that I have always made about our foreign business," he wrote to Teagle, "is that the foreign refineries are almost never visited by people from the Manufacturing Committee. It is undoubtedly due in part to the fact that the Manufacturing people here are not directly responsible for the foreign refineries." E. M. Clark concurred in this view, and in 1925 a closer working liaison was established between the Manufacturing Committee at 26 Broadway and the foreign plants. Local autonomy was not greatly curtailed in matters of general administration, but refining operations abroad from this time forward received the benefit of technical inspection, advice, and assistance from the parent company.[92]

An examination of the Jersey refining organization as a whole suggests at once that in no two refineries were manufacturing necessities identical—a circumstance that provided the Manufacturing Committee of the parent company with heavy co-ordinating responsibilities. In no two refineries was the product line exactly the same. Humble's new Baytown refinery, for example, initially concentrated upon the production of low-cold-test lubricating oils for the export trade, while many of the foreign refineries devoted their chief attention to kerosene. These wide individual variations were not haphazard; they grew out of carefully calculated adaptations to specific crude oil availabilities and to particular market needs. The operating entity which these dissimilar, and in some cases insignificant, parts collectively comprised was imposing in size and scope. Every commercially useful petroleum product then known to industry and science was being produced by the Jersey Standard organization in approximately those proportions dictated by market demand. That refining organization itself comprised by far the largest in the United States and possibly the largest in the world.

Jersey book figures for investment in plant facilities do not, for statistical reasons that need not be examined here, constitute a reliable measure of long-term growth. Crude throughput statistics, while subject to some limitations, serve the purposes of historical measurement far better and permit comparisons between Jersey Standard and its competitors. In 1925, the latest year in the 1919-1927 period for which such information is available, the combined crude throughput of the Jersey Company, Louisiana Standard, and Humble refineries was almost double that of the next largest refining organization in the nation (Standard Oil of California) and more than 9 per cent (10,000,000 barrels) greater than the combined crude throughput of The Texas Company, the Gulf Oil Corporation, and the Shell-Union Oil Corporation refineries. In 1927 Jersey's domestic refineries ran 15.4 per cent of all crude processed by the United States petroleum industry, while the throughput of all Jersey affiliated refineries at home and abroad comprised 14.3 per cent of total world-industry refinery runs.[93]

These figures take on unusual interest because from 1912 to 1918 Jersey Standard had failed to expand as fast as its competitors. Notwithstanding the phenomenal increase in industry refining activity between 1919 and 1927, the Jersey organization not only held but even increased slightly its share of the total output, both domestic and world-wide. This circumstance derived from the aggressive expansionist policies of the Teagle administration; the quantitative achievement was impressive for the fact that it was accompanied by tremendous advances in technological skill and administrative proficiency.

Size, organizational form, and technical alertness were not, however, ends in themselves. The ultimate goal was profit, and it was to this decisive measure of refinery performance that Jersey executives inevitably devoted great attention. Judged on the basis of realized profit, the 1919-1927 period afforded few occasions for complacency. Manufacturing operations, for many years the principal source of revenue for the organization, in 1921 and intermittently thereafter constituted the least profitable branch of the business. The full extent of this sharp reversal is revealed by the figures in Table 20, covering the entire 1912-1927 period. The chart on page 568 illustrates the alteration which took place in 1921 in relationships between refinery activity and refining earnings.

The factors responsible for the unsatisfactory earnings record from 1921 to 1927 were not confined to Jersey Standard. Other refiners complained about poor business and the pressure on profit margins. The lack of adequate manufacturing-cost summaries precludes any detailed analysis of comparative performance, but such earnings figures as are available for the industry suggest that Jersey's experience was the common one. The situation was generally blamed upon what Jersey's 1927 annual report to the stockholders epitomized as "intemperate and uneconomic" competition. It seems clear that the profound change in supply and de-

Table 20: **NET EARNINGS FROM REFINING AND MANUFACTURING**
Standard Oil Company (New Jersey) and Affiliates, 1912-1927

Earnings	Dollar figures in thousands *(Parentheses indicate net loss)*					
	1912	1913	1914	1915	1916	1917
Refining earnings						
DOMESTIC						
Jersey Standard	$ 4,504	$ 2,858	$ 2,063	$15,939	$17,888	$36,392
Louisiana Standard	1,398	4,904	3,383	5,358	6,125	6,543
Humble Oil & Refining Co.	—	—	—	—	—	—
Other affiliates	817	817	817	817	960	4,153
Total domestic	$ 6,719	$ 8,579	$ 6,263	$22,114	$24,973	$47,088
FOREIGN						
Canadian	$ 711	$ 856	$ 522	$ 1,665	$ 1,671	$ 951
Latin American	111	142	145	186	254	161
European	605	1,288	1,988	2,481	1,931	b
Total foreign	$ 1,427	$ 2,286	$ 2,655	$ 4,332	$ 3,856	$ 1,112
Total domestic and foreign	$ 8,146	$10,865	$ 8,918	$26,446	$28,829	$48,200
Miscellaneous manufacturing earnings						
Gilbert & Barker	$ 25	$ 8	$ 84	$ 473	$ 354	$ 1,113
Interstate Cooperage Co.	99	191	(4)	146	178	79
Other	44	55	26	108	111	151
Total	$ 168	$ 254	$ 106	$ 727	$ 643	$ 1,343
Total refining and manufacturing	$ 8,314	$11,119	$ 9,024	$27,173	$29,472	$49,543

Earnings as percentage of total Jersey refining and miscellaneous manufacturing earnings[d]						
	1912	1913	1914	1915	1916	1917
REFINING						
Domestic	80.9	77.2	69.4	81.4	84.7	95.1
Canadian	8.5	7.7	5.8	6.1	5.7	1.9
Latin American	1.3	1.2	1.6	0.7	0.9	0.3
European	7.3	11.6	22.0	9.1	6.5	b
Miscellaneous manufacturing	2.0	2.3	1.2	2.7	2.2	2.7
Total	100.0	100.0	100.0	100.0	100.0	100.0
Refining and miscellaneous manufacturing earnings as percentage of total Jersey earnings[d]	23.5	24.2	28.8	44.5	41.0	47.6

[a] Includes Standard Oil Co. of New Jersey.

[b] Comparable data not available.

[c] Includes manufacturing earnings previously classified under "Refining, Jersey Standard."

[d] Since the percentage figure for any one earnings classification is determined not only by the actual amount recorded in that classification but also by earnings and losses in each of the others, no attempt should be made to trace year-to-year variations in one classification

mand relationships, resulting from discovery of and unrestrained production from prolific new fields, was exerting an unsettling influence even in those branches of the petroleum industry which normally stood to benefit from weakness in crude oil prices.

In more particular terms, the capacity of American refineries, expanded

Table 20 (cont.): **NET EARNINGS FROM REFINING AND MANUFACTURING Standard Oil Company (New Jersey) and Affiliates, 1912-1927**

		Dollar figures in thousands (Parentheses indicate net loss)							Earnings
1918	1919	1920	1921	1922	1923	1924	1925	1926	1927
$36,265	$27,326	$41,510	$ (9,143)	$ 17	$(2,915)	$ 7,731	$ 3,699	$ 1,080	$(24,594)[a]
8,753	5,685	17,490	(3,715)	7,725	(2,748)	(3,643)	1,820	3,645	(20,907)
—	(1)	(61)	29	(314)	310	412	3,956	4,546	3,629
2,561	2,156	2,372	1,699	—	202	809	809	966	857
$47,579	$35,166	$61,311	$(11,130)	$ 7,428	$(5,151)	$ 5,309	$10,284	$10,237	$(41,015)
$ 1,894	$ 2,004	$ 3,627	$ (987)	$ 2,562	$(2,265)	$ 441	$ 1,031	$ 4,824	$ (1,070)
123	476	988	1,859	(598)	1,713	4,583	2,670	1,563	(776)
[b]	228	36	2,053	1,037	(134)	(141)	652	1,915	1,564
$ 2,017	$ 2,708	$ 4,651	$ 2,925	$ 3,001	$ (686)	$ 4,883	$ 4,353	$ 8,302	$ (282)
$49,596	$37,874	$65,962	$ (8,205)	$10,429	$(5,837)	$10,192	$14,637	$18,539	$(41,297)
$ (377)	$ 944	$ 982	$ 642	$ 1,015	$ 2,208	$ 1,853	$ 1,734	$ 1,732	$ 591
437	(29)	(94)	(955)	(90)	50	37	(108)	(175)	(219)
51	226	45	61	235	209	159	3,379	3,294	3,786[c]
$ 111	$ 1,141	$ 933	$ (252)	$ 1,160	$ 2,467	$ 2,049	$ 5,005	$ 4,851	$ 4,158
$49,707	$39,015	$66,895	$ (8,457)	$11,589	$(3,370)	$12,241	$19,642	$23,390	$(37,139)

Earnings as percentage of total Jersey refining and miscellaneous manufacturing earnings[d]

1918	1919	1920	1921	1922	1923	1924	1925	1926	1927
95.7	90.2	91.6	(131.6)	64.1	(152.8)	43.4	52.4	43.8	(110.4)
3.8	5.1	5.4	(11.7)	22.1	(67.2)	3.6	5.2	20.6	(2.9)
0.3	1.2	1.5	22.0	(5.1)	50.8	37.4	13.6	6.7	(2.1)
[b]	0.6	0.1	24.3	8.9	(4.0)	(1.1)	3.3	8.2	4.2
0.2	2.9	1.4	(3.0)	10.0	73.2	16.7	25.5	20.7	11.2
100.0	100.0	100.0	(100.0)	100.0	(100.0)	100.0	100.0	100.0	(100.0)
64.1	81.0	45.1	(25.0)	25.1	(6.0)	15.1	17.7	19.9	(91.9)

without careful reference both to other percentage classifications and to the pertinent dollar figures. All functional earnings figures given in SONJ, Fin. Recs., for the years 1912 through 1924 have been adjusted by the authors to match, insofar as possible, the account classifications employed in those records in the years 1925 through 1927.

Source: SONJ. Fin. Recs.; Stat.

COMPARISON OF CRUDE RUNS AND TOTAL NET INCOME
Standard Oil Company (New Jersey) and Affiliates, 1912-1927

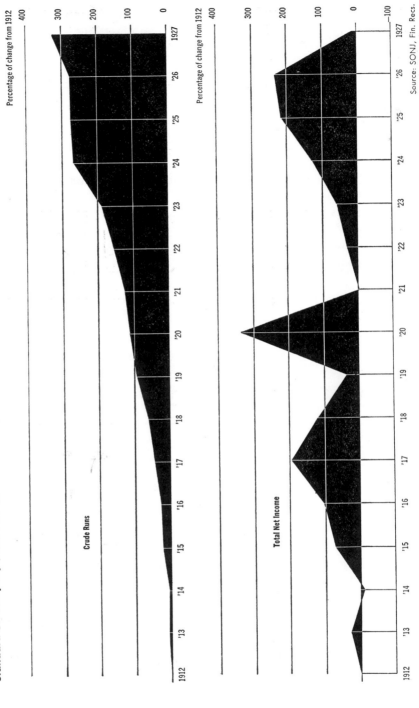

Percentage of change from 1912

Crude Runs

Percentage of change from 1912

Total Net Income

Source: SONJ, Fin. Recs.

sharply in response to high profits in the 1917-1920 period and augmented still further by new manufacturing techniques, had far outstripped the existing market demand for refined products. In 1918 refinery capacity of the American industry was only about 3 per cent greater than prevailing market demand, but in 1927 total capacity was close to 35 per cent in excess of need. Gasoline production was about 632,000,000 gallons in excess of consumption in 1920 and approximately 1,029,000,000 gallons in excess in 1927. Stocks of most refined products (and of crude oil) accumulated at a substantial rate after 1921, and imports, though small in proportion to total consumption, grew very rapidly. Finally, the very comfortable spread between crude-oil and finished-product prices that had persisted over most of the 1912-1919 period appears to have been narrowed considerably thereafter. Whether crude prices after 1920 were still too high in relation to existing supplies (as Teagle believed) or refined product prices were too low (as the Manufacturing Committee contended and the marketers denied), the fact remained that the difference in elasticity between these two crucial commodity price groups was operating to restrict the refinery profit margin.[94]

In April of 1927 came the public announcement that 340 pressure stills at various Jersey refineries had been shut down. The pessimism of company executives at the close of the 1919-1927 era was an echo of general sentiment in the industry. This was not a period of bountiful and obvious fulfillment, nor were the administrative and legal accomplishments of the Jersey Company susceptible of measurement. A victim of uncontrollable and unfavorable economic circumstances, the Jersey refining organization, moreover, had yet to realize the full advantages of the technical modifications that had been undertaken. By 1927 the change from Burton stills to tube-and-tank units had progressed only to the halfway mark, while many highly promising lines of experimentation were still sources of expense rather than of revenue. Many pages of history had yet to turn before a final judgment could be rendered, though in 1927 it could at least be said that realized profits, the source of contemporary dismay, were not really a fair measure of the contemporary achievement.

Chapter 18

The Ideal and the Reality in Labor Relations

ONE OF the distinguishing marks of the Teagle administration was the breadth of the effort made to push the Jersey Standard organization to new performance levels. Critical problems received primary attention, but Teagle and the capable staff of assistants he had gathered around him probed a wide range of possibilities for effecting constructive changes. More and more of the executives had become convinced that the problem of labor relations was as critical as any other, and that progressive endeavor in this field would not only avoid expensive complications, but might even effect a reduction in normal operating costs. The reorganization of the refining branch of the business, therefore, came to involve not only administrative, technical, and legal adjustments, but extensive experiments with the human factor as well.

CRYSTALLIZATION OF A LABOR POLICY

The prime weakness in Jersey's labor relations, which might have been noticed by the directorate at the time of the first Bayonne strike in 1915, certainly had been made obvious by the 1916 disturbance. The Bayonne workmen believed that wage levels and working conditions were at the root of the strikes. The Jersey directors held that professional agitators were responsible. Both viewpoints in large measure were incorrect. The basic cause of the uprisings was the yawning administrative chasm that separated Bayonne management and the men. Jersey Standard's honorable tradition of fair play to the contrary notwithstanding, no workman at the Bayonne refinery had any effective way by which he might air his grievances. In official public statements Jersey directors claimed that any man had the right to bring his complaints to the attention of management. This was the tradition. That it was a living, powerful, and rectifying force in many segments of the organization no impartial observer could deny. It was an effective guide for labor relations wherever just foremen and good local managers were to be found. But the men at Bayonne knew, if the directors did not, that long before they reached the front office with their complaints they would have ceased to hold their jobs. In this place Jersey tradition was not strong enough to overcome the forces of disharmony and indifference. Here the only recourse was to the strike; the men submitted to the leadership of rabble-rousers, radicals, and incompetents because there was no effective alternative. Above all else, the Bayonne strikes showed that Jersey Standard had become too large to be safely governed by traditions any longer. At Bayonne the time had come for mechanisms, not pronouncements. Soon other branches of the operating organization, where until now old methods had sufficed, might expect trouble from that growing cleavage between men and management which was the concomitant of increasing size.

The story is told in many places that at this point A. C. Bedford recognized the need for an appraisal of company labor relations and took steps to obtain the services of a qualified adviser.[1] This is a plausible story, and one which does maximum credit to the Jersey principals involved. There is evidence, however, to indicate that, even after the bludgeoning lessons of 1915 and 1916, the drastic changes required were not initially conceived by Bedford and that Jersey's new labor policy did not originate within the company at all. Certainly the directors continued to hold to their belief that the Bayonne troubles were the fault of agitators and not of basic company policy. What the directorate did finally realize, of course, was that a change must be made in the Bayonne management. Hennessey was soon replaced, and after a time Gifford left the company. Pay levels were advanced to match the continuing rise in living costs. It may well be that these changes would have represented management's final answer to the Bayonne troubles, had it not been for the influence of John D. Rockefeller, Jr.

The retirement of the Rockefellers from active participation in the enterprises in which they held such large blocks of stock had been absolute. John D. Rockefeller, Sr., was busy with his estates and his investments, while an able staff headed by his son John and Frederick T. Gates were supervising the adventures in philanthropic spending with that same meticulous devotion to form and detail which had characterized the building of the fortune. This retirement, nevertheless, did not and could not dissipate the influence which the Rockefellers, father and son, possessed. When a situation in which they were interested, either financially or in principle, seemed to demand action, the Rockefellers had proved willing to act.[2]

After the 1913 Ludlow Massacre, the younger Rockefeller had exerted pressure to bring about a change of management in the Colorado Fuel & Iron Company. He then asked William Lyon Mackenzie King, former Deputy Minister of Labor in Canada, to come to New York. King had traveled all over the Dominion settling strikes. Seeing in Colorado an opportunity to employ his favorite principles of arbitration, conciliation, and organization in industry, he accepted the Rockefeller request to work out a plan that would assure company employees of an easy and clear means for presenting their case. King joined the Rockefeller Foundation and began a study of the Colorado situation.[3] One of his first moves was to enlist the services of Clarence J. Hicks.

Hicks had followed a somewhat unusual path. Drifting here and there in his search for a satisfying career, and driven always by his remarkable affinity for people, Hicks finally accepted the position of senior secretary of the Railroad Department of the International YMCA. Here he became involved in an active endeavor to better working and living conditions among railroad employees by extending the facilities and services of the "Y." His efforts brought him into constant contact both with working-men and with some of the most prominent business and political figures in the country. For this work Hicks showed exceptional aptitude. By 1911 he had achieved invaluable experience and an international reputation. At many points his efforts had crossed the borderline into the then ill-defined field of labor relations.[4]

In 1911 Cyrus H. McCormick brought Hicks to the International Harvester Company to work out plans for improving working conditions and employee morale. This was the formal launching of Hicks' career in labor relations. Four years later, when King sent him to Colorado to put into effect the plan of industrial representation that had been worked out on paper, there probably were few men in America better qualified by training and personality than C. J. Hicks to undertake this experiment.

Confident that Mackenzie King and Hicks were pointing a path to enduring labor peace, John D. Rockefeller, Jr., now brought his influence to bear on the Jersey Company as well and suggested that Hicks be called in for consultation.

To the historian looking back many years later upon the chain of events, it seems as though in this situation, as in the reorganization of Jersey research, the directors were anxious to be progressive.[5] Certainly they were anxious to be fair. But their concepts of fairness had been attacked, and they did not know how to be progressive in labor matters. Rockefeller suggested a way, and Bedford at once grasped the possibilities.

Bedford invited Hicks to leave Colorado and spend a month or two studying labor conditions at Bayonne, Bayway, and the Eagle Works, after which he was to submit his recommendations to the Jersey board. Hicks' report was placed before the directors late in 1917. As might be expected, it recommended the adoption of the plan of employee representation which Mackenzie King had outlined and which Hicks had placed in operation at the Colorado Fuel & Iron Company. The Jersey directors now certainly were confronted with the necessity for an act of faith. The company had long since become accustomed to employing the services of outside experts, but the recourse to a labor consultant was quite unprecedented. The King-Hicks experiment in Colorado had still to stand the test of usage. The Colorado plan followed the pattern both of the proved Whitley Councils in England and of the effective concepts of organization worked out by King while employed in the Canadian Labor Ministry, but the plan had not been widely tested in American industry, where conditions and attitudes were quite different.

The directorate of 1917, however, was ready to follow Rockefeller and Bedford. The Hicks plan was accepted in full, on the one condition that Hicks himself should accept the position of executive assistant to the Jersey president and take charge of the task of remolding employee relations. To this Hicks agreed, though he was reluctant to abandon the developing program in Colorado. The opportunity for working out his ideas on a vast scale in one of the most influential companies in the world was one that he could not spurn.[6]

Hicks wound up his business in Colorado and moved to New York to set up his program, the basic feature of which was the industrial representation plan. This plan provided for periodic conferences between representatives of labor and management in the various departments of the Jersey organization. Employees were to elect their own representatives annually, one for each 150 workers. The joint conferences were to discuss and act upon such matters of mutual interest as wages, hours, working conditions, and particular grievances. An annual meeting of all representatives was to be held, at which matters of interest common to all company employees would be discussed. The Jersey board was to have the right to review all settlements made by the various joint conferences.

Approval of the plan by the Jersey directorate was only the first step.

To make the installation a success Hicks needed the co-operation of local managers and the support of the men. These, with experienced salesmanship, Hicks began to solicit. There were both opposition and suspicion. A great many foremen were hostile, for they saw in Hicks a threat to their authority over the men. Some plant managers also were unfriendly or indifferent, particularly in the first weeks.

In developing his program Hicks was careful to recognize fully the authority of the executives with whom he had to deal. Employee relations men in the refineries and affiliates were made responsible to the managers of their respective divisions, representatives of the central employee relations office at 26 Broadway dealing with the local executives in an advisory rather than an authoritative capacity. This meant, of course, that without strong moral support Hicks could not possibly succeed.

With a rare understanding of the delicacy of his position, Hicks won important backers for his work. Bedford was behind him from the start. Director Seth B. Hunt, one of those who had taken the lead in abolishing the 12-hour day and the 7-day week in the Jersey organization, was an outstanding friend of the industrial representation plan. Hunt never failed in his interest in the employees, and it was to him that the directorate looked for counsel in labor matters. With Hunt, Hicks worked out the details of such proposals as required the approval of the board. Director George H. Jones was another staunch friend of Hicks.

After Teagle had taken over the Jersey presidency he, too, became an increasingly wholehearted supporter. The new president was not, however, a man to walk by faith alone. In Canada the requirements of operating efficiency had been allowed to dictate a different course. Placing what he believed to be the welfare of the company above all else, Teagle had sternly held wages and benefits at the absolute minimum consistent with labor peace and had declared that under no circumstances would the company tolerate unionism. Such an attitude was neither expedient nor intelligent in the new situation that Teagle faced when he came to New York, and Teagle changed his attitude to fit the different conditions. The immediate concern of the new president was to make certain that the new program was solidly conceived and ably administered. Having reassured himself that Hicks was a capable man and that his program offered tangible values to the company, Teagle rallied to the new proposals and imparted to the program in its infancy his appreciation of the broad operational necessities of the business. Teagle's realism, as well as

Hicks' enthusiasm, was necessary if the industrial representation plan was to succeed.

On March 27, 1918, the employees at Bayonne, Bayway, and the Eagle Works elected their representatives. Hicks had not succeeded in allaying all doubts, but with the support of many Jersey officials he had at least put his plan into operation. The installation of the joint-conference procedure was extended to the Charleston, Baltimore, and Baton Rouge refineries, then to marketing, producing, and pipeline units of Jersey and affiliated organizations in the United States and Canada. Charles G. Black in refining, Christy Payne in natural gas, and T. J. Williams in marketing all were given credit by Hicks for getting the plan into successful operation in their respective branches of the business.

The joint-conference system was actually but a quarter part of the entire program. Certain other features were made public at the first joint conference, which took the form of a dinner given by the company on April 1, 1918, at 26 Broadway for the newly elected employee delegates. This was a gala occasion. At the left hand of A. C. Bedford sat C. J. Hicks. To Bedford's right sat Miss Mary Tully, employee representative of Division 13 at Bayonne. The seventy-three employee delegates from Bayonne, Bayway, and the Eagle Works sat and talked with high-ranking company officials, many of whom they had never even seen before. Good feeling and optimism were evident, and glowing words of hope were spoken.[7]

Bedford was greeted with a burst of applause as he rose to speak. "I am sure," he said, "that your kindly greeting to me is indicative of the fellowship with which we are all gathered here tonight." Bedford pointed to the lamentable decline of personal contacts that went with increasing size in a company and urged the employee representatives to take their new responsibilities seriously. He then introduced Walter Teagle, who delivered a brisk, straightforward talk filled with impressive factual references. Company policy, he said, consisted of fair wages and fair working conditions. Welfare work would in no sense be regarded as a substitute for fair wages. Teagle then pointed to the fact that daily-wage increases that had been made since September 15, 1915, totaled 63 per cent for all classes of labor and 80 per cent for common labor. He announced a quite unexpected new general wage increase of 10 per cent, effective that day, and stated that henceforth the company would pay time and one-half for all hours worked in excess of 48 weekly.

C. J. Hicks then arose, and after some general explanatory remarks he announced the inauguration of an extensive program of employee annuities and benefits. Hicks' address was followed by speeches by the refinery superintendents and delegates. It was quite characteristic of the Jersey Company that so many of the officials prefaced their remarks by references to the days when they, too, had been workingmen in the company—fifteen, twenty, and twenty-five years before. James Mulvoy, employee representative from the Eagle Works, was not a polished speaker, but he voiced the thoughts of many when he managed to blurt out, "This is the dawn of a new day for the working man." The industrial representation plan was hailed by both labor and management as a pioneer step in labor relations in America.

The annuities and benefits plan announced by Hicks was a far-reaching one. The company established annuities for all employees who had reached the age of sixty-five years and had been with the company for twenty years or longer. Payments were made at a rate equivalent to 2 per cent of the employee's average salary for the final five years of his service, multiplied by the number of years served. Substantial death, accident, and sickness benefits were also established. These plans, and the annuities as well, were financed entirely by the company.

The third part of the general program of revolutionizing the company's labor relations consisted of staff changes and innovations which seemed necessary to effectuate the first part (the industrial representation plan) and the second (the annuity and benefits plans). A personnel and training department was established. Supervision of the hiring and discharging of the men was centralized in the personnel offices which were set up throughout the organization. This meant, in effect, that those functions that once had been the foundation of the foreman's authority were no longer his to exercise without restraint. It was a most significant change and one that promised profound consequences. The Jersey Company was setting no precedents here. Large segments of American business at this very time were taking similar steps. This was one manifestation of a widespread realization that industrial enterprise had outgrown the administrative techniques evolved in the formative years of the nineteenth century. The foreman, for many years the key figure in the operating structure of manufacturing business, was now being relegated to an increasingly minor role. To Jersey Standard, as to all companies who were making the transition, the dangers involved were great. Degradation of its strongest administrative ally was a high price for any management to pay for the new efficiency. The personnel managers were faced with the formidable and continuing challenge of providing more effective contacts with the men than had the foremen before them. Efforts were made, of course, to persuade the foremen to co-operate in their own downfall.

The general responsibilities of the personnel and training department, as promulgated by Hicks, were to assure the employees of uniform treatment throughout the organization, to arrange the intraorganizational transfer of employees in a satisfactory manner, to ensure the employment and training of suitable candidates for employment, to make certain that employees were not laid off without cause, and to guarantee the men fair treatment generally from the company. Plans for a company-wide safety program were set forth within the framework of the new department, and a medical division was set up at 26 Broadway, with branch offices at the various plants.

Acceptance of the new Personnel Department was greatly facilitated by the sweeping benefits which were announced at the time and which were administered by the various branches of that department. Employees who had entered the armed services after July 1, 1917, were granted bonuses of from 25 to 50 per cent of their annual earnings, the amount depending upon the number of their dependents. In September of 1918 a "Coin Your Ideas" plan was announced, with prizes ranging up to $300 for employee suggestions on improvements in processes, shop practice, or any other operation conducted in conjunction with the company's business. In this same month the company announced another general 10 per cent wage increase. This announcement, made at a joint conference with representatives of the labor forces of the Bayonne, Bayway, Eagle, Baltimore, and Parkersburg plants, explicitly set forth the desirability of tying company wage levels not just to those prevailing elsewhere in the community (the old practice), but to government cost-of-living indices as well.

The fourth feature of Hicks' broad innovations consisted of a formal "joint agreement" drawn up by Jersey management and accepted by the labor force. This agreement, effective April 1, 1918, formalized the plans for the new Employment Department and the joint conferences and established procedures governing discipline, wage adjustments, and right of appeal of the men. Plans were made at the same time to undertake the publication of an employee magazine.

The Lamp was first brought out in May of 1918, clearly following precedents established in 1914 by the Standard Oil Company (California) and in 1915 by The Imperial Oil Company, Limited. Teagle was a strong supporter of the idea, and a man whom Teagle had noticed while in Canada was given the task of organizing the venture. Victor Ross had been the financial writer for the Toronto *Globe*. His book, *The Evolution of the Oil Industry,* had impressed Teagle, and he brought Ross to New York for the specific task of starting *The Lamp*. Ross enlisted the assistance of Jersey's advertising agency, the H. K. McCann Company, in preparing the early releases.

The first issue of *The Lamp* summed up the purpose contemplated for the publication. Ross wrote as follows:[8]

> The mission of "The Lamp" is that much abused word "service." The circumstance that the operations of the company are spread over a considerable territory and the range of its activities is quite comprehensive, has been one of the chief obstacles in the interchange of ideas between the thousands of employees. Its purpose is to introduce the employees of the Standard Oil Company (New Jersey) to each other and to cultivate acquaintanceship into a spirit of fellowship and cordial cooperation.

The entire first issue was devoted to an explanation of the various features of the Hicks program. An editorial entitled "The New Outlook" presented the essence of the company's new policy in terms which today may seem hackneyed but which for the readers of that time were vibrant with hope. For the first time in Jersey's history employees were told, in a detailed, accurate, official, and interesting manner, about the policies that affected their daily lives. They were told much more as well.

The four issues that appeared in 1918 contained a large amount of information about the operating branches of the company and about the men who were making company history. The tone of the publication was factual, and there was no "writing down" to a supposed employee level. Names became personalities. The Bayonne still-cleaners learned what their fellow workers on a Carter well in the Mid-Continent were doing. Managerial attitudes and company policy were frankly set forth. The magazine, while not the first of its kind, compared favorably with other such publications of the day. In 1918 the impact of *The Lamp* already began to be felt throughout the sprawling Jersey empire.

Even when the events of 1918 are viewed in their contemporary context, the conclusion is scarcely debatable that in one mighty surge of effort the Jersey directors, prodded by Rockefeller, Jr., and led by Hicks, had pushed the company almost overnight to a position where it could be regarded not just as a good employer but as among the most progressive in the field of labor relations in America. No one of the many measures adopted in this year of great transitions was unprecedented, but the comprehensive scope and the total effect of all the efforts imparted to company policy an almost revolutionary character. As was so often the case in Jersey history, internal change both reflected and influenced contemporary trends in the world of which the company was a part. Having fought for political democracy in Europe, Americans were evincing a strong concern for industrial democracy at home. The cause of labor had been strengthened by the sympathies of the Wilson administration; wartime federal employment practices had reinforced a progressive tradition. By the time it was laid before the Jersey directors, the plan of industrial representation had already begun to arouse more than an intellectual interest in America. Jersey's revolution was not unique, though it was early and it did, because of the company's prominence, give impetus to the broad social movement of which it was a part.

After 1918 it could no longer be said that Jersey Standard labor policies were ill defined. C. J. Hicks combined much that was old and some that was new in his formulation:[9]

The labor policy of the Standard Oil Company (NJ) is founded first of all on paying at least the prevailing scale of wages in the community; on the eight hour day, with time and one half for overtime; one day's rest in seven; sanitary and up-to-date working conditions; just treatment assured each employee; payment of accident benefits beyond the amount prescribed by the State compensation law; health supervision by a competent medical staff; payment of sickness benefits after one year's service; cooperation with employees in promoting thrift and better social and housing conditions; and assurance of a generous annuity at the age of 65, guaranteed for life after 20 years of service.

A major hope which lay beneath the acceptance by the Jersey directors of Hicks' recommendations was that, by providing generous benefits and effective mechanisms for the settlement of differences between employer and employee, the growing forces of unionization would be checkmated.[10] The ideal that Hicks had outlined for Jersey management was a company-wide one, and the hope existed that in time this ideal could be sought not just in the parent company and a few chosen affiliates but in all segments of the organization. Hicks, John D. Rockefeller, Jr., and some of the Jersey executives even dared to believe that what was being attempted might point a way to permanent labor peace which all American business could follow.

The scope of company efforts, the goals contemplated by those efforts, the individual effectiveness of the various benefits extended, and the sincerity of the good feeling that existed at the time were not open to serious criticism. The great unsolved problem in 1918, rather, was whether the progressive attitude had indeed become a permanent fixture in company labor policy. It remained to be proved that the tremendous momentum built up in the early stages by the Hicks program could be maintained. Nor was it entirely certain that the enunciated doctrine of employee representation would turn out to be practicable. Despite all the fine words and high sincerity of purpose, the program might easily degenerate, under unsympathetic handling, into merely a more sumptuous form of nineteenth-century paternalism.

WORKING OUT THE LABOR PROGRAM

Efficiency was the keynote of the Teagle administration, but insofar as labor policy was concerned this was not the same new concept of efficiency that was straining the ties between labor and management in many American concerns in the experimental and uneasy years of the 1920's. Scientific Management was a drug concocted to cure grievous ailments in the American business system, but like all powerful drugs it was dangerous when misused. In various ways and in many places the workman was carefully being incorporated in the industrial blueprint as a factor of production—not as an individual.

Efforts after 1918 to increase the efficiency of the Jersey organization contemplated, at the very beginning, the rights, the worth, and the limitations of the individual. The reorganization of labor regulations and practices thus was predicated upon a sound basis and commenced in a favorable environment.

Jersey executives, however, were uncertain as to the proper methods and techniques for perpetuating, under rapidly changing industrial conditions, the harmonious relationships which had long prevailed in most segments of the organization, and they were doubtful of their ability to re-establish such relationships in the few places where there had been strife. Members of the laboring force themselves were unprepared for the privileges that were extended to them in 1918. Definitions of the proper role of the employee varied widely, and company management numbered among its members many conservative or downright reactionary individuals. The experiment in labor relations, therefore, was launched in an atmosphere not alone of hope and high expectation, but of uncertainty, inexperience, disagreement, suspicion, and even fear.

The program of employee benefits and joint labor-management conferences, so enthusiastically proposed by Jersey management and accepted by the working force in April of 1918, was accompanied by many other labor and wage developments which were indigenous to the industry and to the times. The study of these essentially routine trends can be confined to a few paragraphs without losing the main thread of Jersey's labor history.

The statistics in Appendix 2, Table XVI, give a fragmentary picture at best of employment trends over the period. The increase in number of employees was far less remarkable than the increase in productivity of those employees. In 1921 combined deliveries of refined products to the home and export trade by Jersey Standard and the Louisiana Company had been equivalent to 2,557 barrels annually per employee; by 1927 such deliveries had risen to 4,908 barrels. These figures were a general reflection of the higher refinery output, the increased efficiency of the transportation system, and the development of extensive marketing facilities which have been discussed in earlier chapters. A further, though still very generalized, illustration of the trend in labor productivity is afforded by the statistics of refinery employment. Refinery throughput per employee (including workers in the Case and Can Department, barrel factory, and chemical and acid works) increased at Bayonne from 8.4 average barrels daily in 1918 to 15.3 barrels in 1927, notwithstanding the fact that this refinery was not so thoroughly modernized as some others. At Bayway, where extensive changes in cracking equipment were under way, daily throughput per employee leaped from 10.6 to 20.8 barrels over the same period. These examples serve to illustrate in a general way what was taking place in varying degrees throughout the organization. The fact is not without interest that, whereas productivity, measured in terms of output per employee, rose by 82 per cent at Bayonne and by 96 per cent at Bayway over the years from 1919 to 1927, productivity in all manufacturing industries in the United States increased about 58 per cent.[11]

Summary wage statistics are even more fragmentary than the figures for total employment. In 1919, again taking the eastern seaboard refineries as an example, Jersey Standard appeared to be making good its often-repeated promise to pay wages equal to those paid elsewhere for similar classes of work. In that year average annual earnings per employee in the New Jersey refineries equaled $1,783, a figure that compared favorably with average annual earnings in all manufacturing industries of $1,158.[12] At Bayonne the annual average was $1,908 and at Bayway $1,866. Further information on comparative wage levels and rates is given in Appendix 2, Tables XIV and XV, but the general account of Jersey wage trends after 1919 is best presented in conjunction with a description of the practices introduced by Teagle's new assistant in labor relations.

The annuities and benefits program and the industrial representation plan of 1918 were rapidly adopted in all branches of the Jersey Company. The major domestic affiliates soon followed the precedent of the parent, as did Imperial Oil, Limited, in Canada. In no case does there appear to have been substantial difficulty in convincing these companies of the basic potentialities of the new program, though enthusiasm varied and there was disagreement over details. The Rockefeller influence was felt elsewhere as well; in 1919 Indiana Standard also adopted a representation plan aimed at bridging the gap between management and labor. In Jersey's foreign affiliates no attempt was made for some time to introduce the Hicks program. Labor practices in those companies were regulated by the local managers according to the dictates of local conditions, the Jersey board confining its regulation to the insistence that trouble be avoided and that the going wage be paid. Abroad, as at home, labor peace was the rule. Certain affiliates like the DAPG in Germany took pride in pension systems and pay scales which were said to be more generous than those generally prevailing in local industry.

Retirement pensions, disability allowances, and death benefits were only a part of the new labor program. The Medical Department, established in 1918 in dingy and restricted quarters at 26 Broadway, rapidly expanded its influence under the leadership of Doctor W. J. Denno. Full-time physicians and nurses took up residence in major branch locations of the organization, and the company constructed a 20-bed hospital for its employees at the Loomis Tubercular Sanitarium in Liberty, New York. The contribution of Jersey's doctors and nurses to Latin American operations (Chapter 13) was perhaps the most spectacular part of the medical program, but this was only one illustration among many of the constructive results forthcoming at the operating level when a progressive, or even a tolerant, attitude was entertained in the top levels of management. This attitude was not entirely a reflection of philanthropic instinct. Support for the new measures from the more conservative members both of Jersey and of affiliated company managements was enlisted by the strictly utilitarian argument that such steps were essential in order to minimize the heavy burden of sickness and disability benefits that had been assumed under the annuities and benefits program. On a wide scale, however, the enlarged medical services were warmly sponsored for reasons in

no way related to financial considerations. Once the expensive initial decision had been made, enthusiasm spread rapidly and even touched those
who had at first been dubious.

Hand in hand with the realization that employees should be protected
in health and assisted in illness went the concept that effort could profitably be expended to place each workman in the spot where his abilities
could best be utilized. No deviation from the generation-old policy of
promotion from within was contemplated. Instead, this policy was carefully spelled out and repeatedly emphasized. Jersey executives took great
pride in stating that when a vacancy appeared in the board chairmanship,
a new office boy was hired. This was a hoary legend, but there was much
truth behind it. Means were devised to enable employees to take better
advantage of the opportunities for advancement. In June of 1919 a Personnel and Training Division was established to set up and supervise hiring techniques and to assist in solving placement and training problems.
Extraordinary effort had always been expended to shift employees to
places where they would be most useful. A central office devoted to this
task simplified the administrative problems involved. Various new training courses, too, were established for the employees, and in some instances
the company paid part of the tuition of those who wished to enroll in
accredited night classes in outside institutions.

These policies all had the merit of building loyalty and reducing labor
turnover. The "Coin Your Ideas" plan, inaugurated in 1918 to reward
employees who contributed valuable suggestions, also had as its primary
goal the enhancement of the individual in the organization and the consequent enlistment of his sympathies and loyalty. Unlike many such
schemes undertaken in other companies and soon abandoned for lack of
interest and results, the "Coin Your Ideas" project was kept alive over the
years and is still in effect today.

The stock-purchase plan of 1921 also sought a strengthening of the
company-employee tie. This proposal was not new even in the Jersey
Standard organization. Imperial had tried it in 1915, and Humble in 1917.
Since both companies had found that the success of the plan was limited
by the inability of many employees to purchase stock even in installment
payments, the 1921 plan was drawn with very liberal provisions. Teagle,
like many other businessmen of the day, was convinced of the merits of
some kind of a limited profit-sharing arrangement.

The par value of Jersey's capital stock was reduced from $100 to $25,
and plans were announced for the issuance of $10,000,000 of additional

stock. Employees could purchase this stock at stipulated prices, which proved in practice and on most occasions to be less than prevailing market values. The company contributed 50 cents for each dollar the employee paid in. All contributions were placed in trust. At the end of five years the employee received a number of shares of stock determined by the amount of his contributions (which were limited to 20 per cent of his earnings), plus those of the company and the cumulative total of interest and dividends, plus an amount representing the distribution of company contributions credited to the account of those who withdrew from the plan prior to its termination.[13]

By 1923 some 11,000 Jersey employees—nearly two-thirds—had heeded Teagle's exhortation to "become capitalists." By 1925, when the first plan terminated, the number of participants had grown to 16,000 (about three-quarters of the working force), and 884,004 shares of stock with a market value of $30,359,485 had been distributed. Of this total, employees contributed $18,490,427 and the company $9,245,214, the balance of the fund having originated in dividend and interest accruals. New stock was promptly made available, and a second plan, limited to three years and ceiling contributions of 10 per cent of employees' earnings, was inaugurated. Company testimonials to the efficacy of the 1921-1925 plan were glowing, though these can scarcely be taken as objective estimates. The wide participation, however, suggests that the stock-acquisition plan was indeed successful in encouraging employee thrift. Allegiance to the company, too, was doubtless strengthened, though only the most sanguine observer would state that the ownership of a share or two of Jersey stock was sufficient to cause a still-cleaner at Bayonne to consider himself a capitalist and a real partner in enterprise with the members of the Jersey board. This was a groping step toward the unification of interests which never had been identical and possibly never could be, yet it was a constructive step, well meant, and executed in a way that avoided many of the serious deficiencies of earlier profit-sharing programs. It was also an expensive measure and, as such, one that was practicable only during good times in a rich company. With the relatively high prevailing level of wages considered, company dollars probably were employed far more efficaciously in the stock-sharing plan than those same dollars would have been in wage increases—a conclusion with which those employees who were unable by circumstance or by disposition to save a part of their earnings would certainly have disagreed.

Most company executives, it is said, looked upon the disbursements credited to the account of labor with real pleasure, and took pride in the reputation for progressive dealing which rapidly was acquired by the Jersey Company and many of its affiliates. Jersey's program, however, was defensive as well as constructive, and there was a ready, if unspoken, appreciation of the fact that the new plans and practices were suffocating by sheer weight of generosity the forces of unionism within the company. Jersey policy was never patently antiunion, but it was strongly and openly committed, nevertheless, to the open-shop principle. The boilermakers' union in the Louisiana Company was not opposed, but rather smothered. In a few isolated instances throughout the organization where work stoppages occurred, the men who had provoked the dispute and scorned the established grievance procedures were not rehired. All this, of course, smacked of paternalism and suggested that the employees received only those things which provident management felt they should have. Only through a careful examination of the actual operation of the industrial representation plan does the true state of the management-labor relationship become evident.

Such an examination is not easy, for the practices of the affiliates were not always in keeping with the procedures and principles established at 26 Broadway. Imperial Oil, for example, lagged fourteen years behind Jersey Standard in granting paid vacations to its employees, while Humble anticipated Jersey's practice by approximately two years. Humble, on the other hand, did not abolish the 84-hour week and adopt the 8-hour day until a decade after the Jersey Company had taken such action, and lagged behind in the safety program which Jersey began to stress in 1920. Even the details of the annuities and benefits program varied somewhat from company to company. No universal judgment, therefore, can be attempted, and the industrial representation plan must be examined at work in as many places as possible.

The essential features of this plan consisted of formal division conferences between elected representatives of labor and an equal number of delegates appointed by management. These conferences were called, either by labor or by management, whenever occasion required. Grievances were aired, petitions submitted, and votes taken on minor issues concerned with working conditions. The superintendent of the division acted as conference chairman and could, if necessary, cast the deciding vote in case of an equal division in the balloting. Major questions such as requests for wage increases could be raised and discussed but not settled. Recommendations on such issues were submitted by the joint conferences to the consideration of top management, as were unresolved minor disputes. No provision was made for the arbitration of decisions handed down by management in response to recommendations forwarded by the joint conferences.

The division conferences were augmented by regular (usually quarterly) works conferences, which were attended by elected labor representatives from every plant division and by an equal number of management representatives. In the larger plants executive councils consisting of a small number of labor and management representatives handled much of the routine business, leaving the general meetings free to deal with special issues. Once a year the Jersey Company sponsored a large gathering of all company delegates, at which the accomplishments of the past year were eulogized over a companionable banquet table.

In the various branches of Imperial Oil, Limited, the industrial representation plan was adopted, but inadequate provisions were made for administering the complexities of the system. Initial confusion, distrust, and inexperience were gradually tempered, but results varied widely among the 90 councils that were in existence by 1930. In some instances unsympathetic or dominating managers made the meetings a mere formality; elsewhere the labor delegates showed a careless indifference to the necessities of the business. In general, however, Imperial was able to report an absence of ill feeling; and as the record of harmonious labor-management relations lengthened, the belief grew that the joint-conference system had proved a success in Canada.[14]

A study of the representation plan in the Louisiana Company yields less favorable conclusions, at least for the years from 1919 to 1927. At Baton Rouge most of the foremen and some of the company executives were opposed to the idea because they believed it would destroy the authority of the foremen over their men. There, as in Canada, the employees greeted the plan with suspicion. A strong paternalistic atmosphere had taken root, and the first joint-conference groups at once earned the cognomen of "Kiss Me Clubs." Early meetings all too often consisted of a brief announcement by management of some new benefit for the employees, followed by a speech of thanks by the chairman of the labor delegates. Discussion of plant affairs often evolved into the stereotyped report, "Everything is going along all right in my department. We are getting along fine." The Negro employees, who had their own delegates and who met with management in separate conferences, were more demonstrative. Managerial announcements were sometimes acknowledged by the delegates with the cry, "Thank God for Standard Oil! Everybody pray for Standard Oil!"[15]

Acceptance of the representation plan at Baton Rouge was marred somewhat, too, by the militant opposition of the AFL boilermakers' union. Samuel Gompers, president of the American Federation of Labor, had taken a strong stand against works councils. In an apparent effort to meet the threat of the new plan, the boilermakers in 1920 called a strike which severely restricted plant activity. Violence was avoided, but the strike lasted nearly a month and was broken only by the superb salesmanship of Hicks himself, who finally convinced the strikers of the merits of his conference system and won the allegiance of the general foreman of the recalcitrant group. The ending of the strike and the acceptance by the union of the industrial representation plan greatly strengthened the working of the plan throughout the Baton Rouge refinery. Three years after the establishment of the first joint council in 1919 the Hicks plan was at least operating smoothly, though not on so thoroughly mutual a basis as had been contemplated by its originator.[16]

In the Humble Oil & Refining Company the Hicks program also fell short of contemplated goals. There, as in the Louisiana Company, the strongly democratic and paternalistic proclivity of the company managers was an obstacle to effective industrial representation. The early management was characterized by an intimate personal touch. Need of a formalized procedure for handling labor matters, not widely appreciated nor admitted by management, unquestionably was less acute than in the eastern refineries. The joint conferences held at Baytown did not often consider important issues such as wages and hours but were devoted, instead, to discussions of such community subjects as thrift, housing, and sanitation. Lack of a municipal government in the new refining community rendered these conferences very useful in such a connection, but this was not the end that Hicks had sought. After two years of experimentation, complaints were voiced that interest in the industrial representation plan was lacking and that hardly more than half the employees were voting at the delegate elections.[17]

The Jersey Company's own experience in attempting to bring management and labor together in the mutual interest was spread over several refineries and two marketing divisions. The minutes of hundreds of joint conferences record a highly interesting story, one which differs somewhat from that told about the early functionings of the industrial representation plan in Louisiana and in Texas. The Bayonne and Eagle Works records will suffice for illustrative purposes, and events in these two refineries may be regarded as more or less typical of what was happening elsewhere.

Observers recall that the first Jersey joint conferences were brief. Just as much time was spent as was necessary for the delegates to report that conditions in their departments were "foine," and for them to smoke the free cigar they received at the start of the meeting.[18] The labor delegates' initial attitude of incredulity and suspicion was prolonged by the fact that management held the stage in the first meetings, a situation which probably was inevitable.

The passive attitude of the labor delegates was short-lived, however, and the announcement phase of the representation program soon passed. By December of 1918 delegates in all the councils had begun to find their voices. At that time dissatisfaction was rife among the boilermakers at Bayonne, Bayway, and the Eagle Works because they were receiving less money than shipyard workers. They requested a pay increase, and the labor delegates submitted statistics which indicated that the Jersey pay scales in general had lagged behind increases in the cost of living. After a study of comparative wage rates, the Jersey board authorized a general 10 per cent increase for all mechanical and process men in the company, effective December 17, 1918.

This satisfactory settlement of a major and apparently justified complaint, plus the admonitions of the refinery superintendents that the men must speak up in meetings, had an immediate and salutary effect. Management was deluged with reports, complaints, and requests. Never, after December of 1918, was there difficulty in ascertaining labor's grievances, minor or major, real or imagined.

There were, of course, misunderstandings and frictions. In some instances uncertainty prevailed over the responsibilities and allegiances of the labor delegates. One labor representative at the Eagle Works reported that he had endeavored to correct a deficiency in his department, but had been told by the men that it was none of his business. General Manager C. E. Graff remarked that in such cases the delegates should employ "a good swift kick or a club"—counsel which Graff, an exceptionally mild-mannered and even-tempered man, certainly did not extend in a literal sense but which indicated nonetheless a profound lack of understanding of the principles involved in the industrial representation plan. Another labor delegate observed that, if the representatives interfered in operations, the foremen would be alienated. This problem of delegate-foreman conflict was a serious one and was mentioned often in the joint meetings.

Initial difficulties probably were accentuated by the tendency of some superintendents to look upon the labor delegates as representatives of and as observers for management. The delegates themselves soon realized the importance of establishing satisfactory relations with the department foremen and of avoiding the reputation of being "company men."

Much attention in the early meetings was devoted to procedures by which grievances were handled. The established routine was for unsettled complaints to pass in successive stages of appeal from the foreman to the division conference, thence to the works conference and, finally, to top management. Bayonne delegates asked that when cases were referred to management for ultimate disposition a decision should be made compulsory within 10 days. This recommendation was adopted. Hicks, who was a regular participant at the joint meetings, suggested that the grievance hearings should avoid the appearance of a trial. The term "plaintiff" was thenceforth abandoned as a part of the grievance terminology.

Soon the labor delegates began to complain of the excessive demands upon their time made by the men. "Noon times they want this and they want that," one representative reported. "I haven't time to eat my lunch any more." Wage increases were constantly being requested, usually by groups of workmen who felt that their particular skills were not adequately recognized. W. C. Koehler, general manager of Bayonne, settled a particularly sharp dispute among the pipe fitters by agreeing to a reclassification of first- and second-class ratings. Simultaneous wage demands by the men in the Bayonne barrel factory, however, were flatly refused. Koehler pointed to the many benefits which the company had granted its employees and said he thought that the employees should be more grateful. Hicks then rose and took sharp exception to Koehler's remarks. The benefits the company had extended, Hicks stated, were not intended to be at the expense of wages.

Month by month the painful educational process went on, with Hicks serving as the mentor of management as well as of labor. Interminable requests for wage increases were processed with increasing effectiveness. Specific inequities were corrected, and Hicks kept a vigilant and detailed watch upon general cost-of-living trends and wage levels in other industries. By August of 1919 the pressure for a general increase was acutely reflected in all joint conferences. Hicks reported that Bureau of Labor Statistics indices justified some action. On August 18, 1919, a general 10 per cent increase was announced. This increase was to be effective only so long as the Bureau indices remained above the level of December,

1918. Two months later the company agreed to distribute tea, coffee, flour, shoes, ham, and bacon at cost to its employees. In the Case and Can Department 1,100 employees agreed on their own initiative to increase their output 10 per cent, a spontaneous gesture of appreciation for the action of the company in taking care of the families of employees serving in the armed forces and of re-employing more than 1,800 men who had been released from military service. The company reported that in the first year of the industrial representation plan 80 joint conferences had been held and 119 controversies discussed and settled. Of the topics raised, 38 per cent involved wages; 10 per cent, working conditions; 9 per cent, promotions and discharges; 8½ per cent, hours; 8 per cent, methods of wage payments; 8½ per cent, workings of the representation plan; 3 per cent, social, housing, and sanitation; and 15 per cent, miscellaneous. Wage decisions had increased the annual payroll about $5,000,000; 9,251 employees were insured for $9,188,000; more than 2,000 employees received sickness disability benefits amounting to $95,000.[19]

In no perceptible degree, however, did requests for further wage increases and adjustments diminish. Managerial attitudes stiffened for a time. A request for extra pay in hazardous occupations elicited the policy statement that the company would pay more for longer hours or for harder work, but not for more dangerous work. The public announcement of some new Rockefeller beneficence called forth the comment in one Bayonne meeting that "if Rockefeller is giving away $100,000 every day, why doesn't he give it to the workmen?" Delegates also mentioned the widespread public charges of profiteering and high prices in the petroleum industry, and criticized the Jersey Company's expenditures on advertising. In January of 1920 Teagle stated that the company did not feel it could grant any new wage increases.

Driven by spiraling living costs in 1920, however, employee demands continued heavy. Management countered with a housing project in Bayonne, while the labor delegates set about compiling figures to prove their contention that an increase was justified under the cost-of-living formula evolved in the preceding year. These figures were considered by the Jersey board in July, and another general 10 per cent bonus was granted.

Two years of vociferous effort under the industrial representation plan, therefore, had given the employees blanket wage increases of 30 per cent and numerous additional pay adjustments in specific occupations. Much of this gain unquestionably would have accrued without representation, for Jersey had never been niggardly. Nevertheless, the necessities of the company employees were more swiftly and effectively met by the joint-conference system than would otherwise have been possible, and labor-management pressures were materially eased in a period that witnessed much unrest in other segments of the nation's industrial economy. A large number of minor adjustments were effected for grievances which otherwise might have gone unremedied.

This auspicious beginning owed much to external circumstances quite apart from the favorable economic trends of the postwar months. In 1918 enthusiasm for "industrial democracy" began to sweep through American business in much the same way that the Scientific Management movement had done five years earlier. Employee representation plans were publicized by studies of the newly formed National Industrial Conference Board and promoted by rulings of the National War Labor Board. Between 1919 and 1922 the number of companies having employee works councils more than doubled. In 1918 Jersey Standard and its affiliates had been the only petroleum companies possessing an industrial representation program; in 1922 there were eighteen oil companies with such plans. Thus was imparted to Hicks' efforts in Jersey's seaboard refineries the momentum of a small-scale industrial crusade.[20]

While the industrial representation plan was proving its worth, Jersey executives did not forego the opportunity of lecturing their employees. This was an oratorical age, and on the American business scene many sound sentiments had not yet degenerated into platitudes. The announcement of the 1921 stock plan before the January works conference at Bayonne was taken by Teagle as the occasion to plead for co-operation and to urge that the men "think of the company as a large family, with each worker a member, not a servant." Hicks, not usually given to moralizing, could not resist noting that the day the meeting was being held was Benjamin Franklin's birthday, a coincidence which lent itself admirably to a brisk lecture on thrift. The well-intended words of inspiration had scarcely ceased to ring in the hall when one of the delegates rose to ask if the Case and Can boys could have a place to smoke—an unfortunately timed request which earned for its sponsor the rather icy comment from General Manager Koehler that this matter would be taken up later.

The year 1921 put the industrial representation plan to severe test. As the depression unfolded, both the 10 per cent bonuses of preceding years were withdrawn. The company laid off 5,200 employees—32 per cent of the total average working force. Hicks worked devotedly to keep alive the enthusiasm of the delegates. In 1922 he introduced a new assistant,

T. H. A. Tiedemann, who had come to the company in 1920 as a safety engineer. Tiedemann traveled from one refinery to another, making acquaintances and studying the conference system. Extraordinary efforts were made by management to keep the employees informed of the pressures that were besetting the business. Comparisons of wages were presented which showed that Jersey laborers were receiving 19 per cent higher wages than those employed in similar work throughout the area. The accuracy and applicability of these figures were questioned by the delegates, as were most of the federal statistics subsequently quoted by the company. One delegate stated that the Teapot Dome scandal proved to his satisfaction that Washington bureaus were not above perverting facts to favor the big oil companies.

In 1922 the joint conferences worked successfully at establishing a uniform code of rate and job classifications among the refineries. There was comparatively little discussion of general wage levels, but much time was devoted to a host of minor matters. A stock answer to employee requests at this time was that the matter "would be looked into." In 1923 wage demands revived, and management, reiterating its policy of paying the prevailing wage, pointed out that on no statistical basis were increases justified. The delegates challenged the company's definition of prevailing wage levels, but the objections carried little weight at a time when the refineries were recording heavy losses. There was, indeed, considerable justification for a further reduction in refinery wages, though such a step appears not to have been considered seriously. A fairly acrimonious dispute flared up over seniority, which finally elicited a policy statement that, all other factors being equal, seniority in the company service was to be the deciding consideration. There was a sharp division of sentiment among the employees over this question. Many felt that ability should be rewarded ahead of seniority, and that service in a department should take precedence over service in the company.

Throughout 1924 and for the ensuing three years the joint conferences continued to be lively. Again and again the wage issue was raised by the employee delegates, but without any great success. On one occasion Teagle answered that he was "surprised and disappointed" to note the request for an increase, since the refining situation was acute and company wage scales already were considerably higher than those of competing companies. This response, as we have seen earlier in this chapter, was well justified by operational circumstances, but repeated rebuffs over the issue of primary importance inevitably were disappointing. Nevertheless, the conference system, still carefully supervised by Hicks, Teagle, and Tiedemann, continued to be an effective medium for the settlement of disputes, and it yielded many benefits. Requests for liberalization of the company's vacation policy resulted in 1924 in the granting of one week of vacation with pay for all employees who had been with the company five years or more. In 1925 two weeks with pay were given to ten-year men. In 1926 all who had worked for the company one year were given one vacation week with pay, while the service requirement for the two-week paid vacation was lowered from ten to five years. This last concession was regarded at the time by Jersey management as unprecedented.

Other tangible gains which accrued as a direct result of requests from the employee delegates included better sanitation facilities, arrangements with a New York bank that allowed employees to use their purchase-plan stock as collateral for cash loans, the adjustment of wage inequities and the institution of an incentive pay plan in the Case and Can Department at Bayonne, and the adjustment of literally hundreds of minor disputes and complaints. Various modifications were also effected in the annuities and benefits program, with the result that pensions under the liberalized 1918 plan were said to be more than double the average pension paid under voluntary private plans in the United States.[21]

The representation program continued to show some weaknesses. Hostility was still prevalent among the foremen; the labor delegates were handicapped in not having access to company files on wages, hours, and job classifications; and in periods of depression the conference system was strained by firm and repeated company denials of wage requests. Despite such shortcomings, many direct and indirect testimonials were voiced to the efficacy of the conference system. In March of 1926 one employee delegate reported that in the seven years of his service in office he had never heard of a single case where a representative had been discriminated against or in any way persecuted for his efforts in behalf of the men. "We as representatives," he concluded, "owe a great deal to management for the courteous manner in which they have received us and the methods by which they treat our grievances."

This comment can stand as a fair summation of the industrial representation plan as applied in the Jersey Company. The stiffness and lack of sophistication on the part of management and the aloofness on the part of the labor delegates which were noticeable in the early meetings had been overcome. In time management and employees became accustomed to working together—by no means an easy task for either group. Examples of management-dominated meetings are not difficult to find, but the evidence is overwhelming that the labor delegates spoke freely and voted without fear on all subjects. Some requests were granted and some were not, but insofar as can be determined from the Jersey records all requests were fully discussed and carefully studied. It could well be argued that in theory the representation program lacked true mutuality, but in practice management clearly exercised its ultimate judicial powers with a restraint that was all the more remarkable because collective bargaining was still a privilege and not a right. Management, in turn, owed a considerable debt to the delegates. The mutual give and take of the joint conferences was an invaluable experience. Perhaps the greatest benefit of the industrial representation plan as it was applied in the Jersey Company was that it enlarged management's understanding of the problems, the necessities, and the collective idiosyncrasies of the employees.

Jersey's own experience indicated that close and sympathetic supervision was essential in order to prevent the representation program from losing its mutuality and hence its appeal to the men. Time and again the presence of C. J. Hicks at the joint conferences served to curb the tendency of management representatives to dominate proceedings. Had Hicks been able to devote that same ceaseless attention to the application of the representation plan in the affiliated companies, the early history of the program in those organizations might have been far different. Teagle's active interest in the workings of the plan also imparted an element of strength and permanence. Although for a time after 1922 Jersey's president steadfastly refused requests for wage increases, and on one or two occasions sharply rebuked or ponderously lectured the delegates, the men showed great confidence in him and often expressed a desire to refer even minor issues to Teagle's adjudication. The precedent of Hicks and of Teagle could scarcely be ignored by second-line management, with the result that the joint conference meetings became important high lights in the operational routine.

Industrial peace prevailed in the Jersey Company. Minor disputes and even occasional walkout threats by small groups at the various refineries constitute no important qualification of the general conclusion. The measures that Jersey Standard adopted in 1918 and thereafter, however, contemplated more than the mere perpetuation of a labor record which had been generally tranquil for a great many years—not only in the Jersey organization but throughout most of the petroleum industry. In labor relations as in technology the company deliberately set as its goal the attainment of an entirely new performance level. The reality was still far short of the ideal, but Jersey men believed that they had demonstrated the means by which enduring reciprocity between management and labor could be assured in a large organization.

Chapter 19

At 26 Broadway

THE CO-ORDINATING responsibilities of the men at 26 Broadway became increasingly complex as the branches of Jersey Standard's business grew in size. Preceding chapters have traced the pageant of operating events; a part of the final chapter may appropriately be dedicated to the correlative development of those staff functions so essential to coherent administration of a prodigiously expanding enterprise.

The course of narrative inevitably leads to the massive granite building overlooking Bowling Green and lower Manhattan. Here reports from the far-flung branches of the business were absorbed in busy departmental offices, classified, condensed, and eventually blended by the directors into workable summarizations of the operating entity. Just so must an evaluation of Jersey history gather and sift many facts and, finally, utilizing some of the summary devices employed by the directors themselves, distill from those facts the essence of what Jersey Standard had been, was, and promised to be.

FISCAL POLICY AND THE GAUGES OF AN ERA

At one level in the organization at 26 Broadway company clerks were meticulously labeling every penny of the billions of dollars that flowed across their ledger sheets. At this level statistical precision was a fetish. Jersey accountants, however, knew that the figures purporting to represent net income were informed guesses at best, and that most asset values inscribed on the books were approximations only. At the accountants' level the goal was not literal accuracy, which was impossible, but plausible approximation and, above all else, consistency. Statistical measurements that held little real meaning when first established became progressively more useful when applied with consistency over a span of years. In the top echelons of management, however, a keen awareness of the flexibility of figures led to occasional decisions to effect broad changes in those figures for purposes which at times were contrary to the dictates of consistency and even of plausibility. Thus the Jersey records came, in time, to represent a curious combination of revelation and obscurity—of minute subdivision and gigantic inaccuracies. Like the records of other corporate enterprises in America, the Jersey accounting system of the period was designed to reveal from within and conceal from without.

The cumulative results of operations in all branches of the business were discernible when the directors gathered in the boardroom at 26 Broadway to report on their specific responsibilities. This high-level personal intercourse served to make effective for control purposes the terse general summaries which were prepared. Few persons outside the narrow circle of the directorate were competent to assess these statements—much less to act upon them. Earnings figures from vastly important areas of operation were hidden in meaningless general classifications. Significant operating units, such as the Andian National Corporation, Limited, and the International Petroleum Company Limited, were buried in the corporate organization, the extent of the Jersey connection being effectively hidden from bookkeepers and public alike. The command of the Jersey Company over the facilities and earnings of partially owned affiliates was imperfectly reflected in published statements and on the Jersey books.

Progress toward greater statistical reality was not lacking, as we shall see, but in 1927 neither the balance sheets nor the income statements adequately met even the very general requirements of investors and investment analysts. In this respect the Jersey Company was not unique in the industry or in the nation. The science of public reporting was in its infancy, and the Jersey directors had only begun to grasp the implications of the fact that ownership of the company was passing into the hands of the general public.

Subject to the limitations discussed in preceding paragraphs and elsewhere in this volume, the total net-income figure measured the immediate success of the enterprise. If profits were not the only gauge of performance, at least they were the most useful and by far the most widely used. Such summary figures were not absolute, however, and became completely meaningful only when related to general profit trends in the industry and in the national economy. Profits were measures of accomplishment, but they also bore a strong causative relationship to administrative decisions. Thus may we discern in Jersey records not only the results of operations but also the basic reasons for changes in method and organization.

The panoramic view of the company's operating record requires answers to two fundamental questions. What were the sources of revenue and

Table 21: TOTAL NET EARNINGS
Standard Oil Company (New Jersey) and Affiliates[a], 1912-1927

Earnings	Dollar figures in thousands (Parentheses indicate net loss)							
	1912	1913	1914	1915	1916	1917	1918	1919
Producing[b]								
Domestic	$ 1,598	$ 4,556	$ 359	$ 1,100	$ 4,777	$ 6,802	$ 6,483	$ 1,193
Foreign	(92)	993	1,256	453	658	—	371	3,247
Total	$ 1,506	$ 5,549	$ 1,615	$ 1,553	$ 5,435	$ 6,802	$ 6,854	$ 4,440
Transporting								
Domestic	$ 1,528	$ 1,811	$ 2,144	$ 4,581	$ 5,855	$ 11,658	$ 13,483	$ 15,709
Foreign	3,304	374	488	762	75	(183)	397	(372)
Total	$ 4,832	$ 2,185	$ 2,632	$ 5,343	$ 5,930	$ 11,475	$ 13,880	$ 15,337
Refining and Mfg.								
Domestic	$ 6,911	$ 8,833	$ 6,369	$ 22,841	$ 25,616	$ 48,431	$ 47,690	$ 36,307
Foreign	1,403	2,286	2,655	4,332	3,856	1,112	2,017	2,708
Total	$ 8,314	$ 11,119	$ 9,024	$ 27,173	$ 29,472	$ 49,543	$ 49,707	$ 39,015
Marketing								
Domestic	$ 1,445	$ 1,442	$ 680	$ 2,243	$ 2,797	$ 3,427	$ 3,791	$ 4,086
Foreign	7,394	10,926	7,692	11,246	13,459	16,920	14,629	4,386
Total	$ 8,839	$ 12,368	$ 8,372	$ 13,489	$ 16,256	$ 20,347	$ 18,420	$ 8,472
Natural Gas								
Domestic(no foreign)	$ 6,606	$ 6,816	$ 6,472	$ 8,255	$ 11,206	$ 12,235	$ 7,179	$ 7,701
Misc. domestic								
Interest	$ 7,049	$ 8,665	$ 4,630	$ 4,491	$ 4,957	$ 4,616	$ 3,445	$ 5,290
Other earnings[c]	(2,721)	(2,731)	(2,139)	(213)	(1,765)	(879)	(21,916)	(32,310)[d]
Total	$ 4,328	$ 5,934	$ 2,491	$ 4,278	$ 3,192	$ 3,737	$(18,471)	$(27,020)
Misc. foreign	895	1,908	716	965	316	12	2	209
Total misc.	$ 5,223	$ 7,842	$ 3,207	$ 5,243	$ 3,508	$ 3,749	$(18,469)	$(26,811)
Total domestic	$ 22,416	$ 29,392	$ 18,515	$ 43,298	$ 53,443	$ 86,290	$ 60,155	$ 37,976
Total foreign	12,904	16,487	12,807	17,758	18,364	17,861	17,416	10,178
Total world	$ 35,320	$ 45,879	$ 31,322	$ 61,056	$ 71,807	$104,151	$ 77,571	$ 48,154
Total net earnings as published	$ 35,108	$ 45,692	$ 31,458	$ 60,777	$ 70,792	$ 80,766	$ 57,284	$ 77,986

Earnings figures as percentages of Jersey's total net earnings[e]

	1912	1913	1914	1915	1916	1917	1918	1919
Producing	4.3	12.1	5.2	2.5	7.6	6.5	8.8	9.2
Transporting	13.7	4.8	8.4	8.8	8.3	11.0	17.9	31.8
Refining and Mfg.	23.5	24.2	28.8	44.5	41.0	47.6	64.1	81.0
Marketing	25.0	27.0	26.7	22.1	22.6	19.5	23.7	17.6
Natural Gas	18.7	14.9	20.7	13.5	15.6	11.7	9.3	16.0
Miscellaneous	14.8	17.0	10.2	8.6	4.9	3.7	(23.8)	(55.6)
Total	100.0	100.0	100.0	100.0	100.0	100.0	100.0	100.0
Total domestic	63.5	64.1	59.1	70.9	74.4	82.9	77.5	78.9
Total foreign	36.5	35.9	40.9	29.1	25.6	17.1	22.5	21.1
Total world	100.0	100.0	100.0	100.0	100.0	100.0	100.0	100.0

[a] The figures in this table, as in all earlier functional earnings tables, represent the Jersey Company's own earnings and its proportionate share of the earnings of affiliated companies. In a few instances, however, only the dividends paid to Jersey by affiliates, rather than Jersey's share of the earnings of those affiliates, were reported. These dividends necessarily have been employed in lieu of earnings figures in arriving at total earnings. It will be noted, too, that in particular years the total net earnings figures in this table vary considerably from those given in the Annual Reports, although there is only a very slight divergence in the totals for the period. For the years 1917 through 1920, this discrepancy arises from retroactive federal income tax adjustments. These adjustments were not allocated in the Jersey operating summaries among the functional earnings classifications presented above. Hence, in order to show those various classifications in this table, the unadjusted book figures necessarily were employed. Distortion from using the unadjusted book figures above is not believed to be significant in scope.

[b] Includes profits from crude oil purchasing by the Jersey Company, as given in Table 14. See also note c of that table.

Table 21 (cont.): **TOTAL NET EARNINGS**
Standard Oil Company (New Jersey) and Affiliates[a], 1912-1927

	Dollar figures in thousands (Parentheses indicate net loss)								Earnings
1920	**1921**	**1922**	**1923**	**1924**	**1925**	**1926**	**1927**	**Total 1912-1927**
$ 20,734	$ (7,780)	$ (4,206)	$ 5,272	$ 325	$ 17,377	$ 17,579	$ (422)	
13,562	18,264	(590)	726	10,779	15,830	3,007	2,654	
$ 34,296	$ 10,484	$ (4,796)	$ 5,998	$ 11,104	$ 33,207	$ 20,586	$ 2,232	$ 146,865
$ 28,122	$ 16,505	$ 12,193	$ 19,728	$ 28,609	$ 25,505	$ 28,569	$ 34,615	
706	(692)	(467)	1,441	1,649	1,020	94	3,187	
$ 28,828	$ 15,813	$ 11,726	$ 21,169	$ 30,258	$ 26,525	$ 28,663	$ 37,802	$ 262,398
$ 62,244	$(11,382)	$ 8,588	$ (2,684)	$ 7,358	$ 15,289	$ 15,088	$(36,857)	
4,651	2,925	3,001	(686)	4,883	4,353	8,302	(282)	
$ 66,895	$ (8,457)	$ 11,589	$ (3,370)	$ 12,241	$ 19,642	$ 23,390	$(37,139)	$ 308,158
$ 5,149	$ (1,828)	$ 6,534	$ 12,774	$ 10,416	$ 4,406	$ 9,754	$ 14,993	
10,295	3,232	11,470	6,391	10,447	18,784	21,038	17,646	
$ 15,444	$ 1,404	$ 18,004	$ 19,165	$ 20,863	$ 23,190	$ 30,792	$ 32,639	$ 268,064
$ 10,880	$ 3,502	$ 14,360	$ 14,962	$ 10,882	$ 11,315	$ 14,613	$ 10,192	$ 157,176
$ 8,331	$ 8,204	$ 4,702	$ 5,404	$ 6,597	$ 7,194	$ 6,357	$ 4,574	
(24,476)[d]	(5,536)	(9,673)	(6,366)	(12,733)	(13,577)	(9,738)	(12,530)	
$ (16,145)	$ 2,668	$ (4,971)	$ (962)	$ (6,136)	$ (6,383)	$ (3,381)	$ (7,956)	
8,276	8,432	330	(667)	1,805	3,735	2,989	2,653	
$ (7,869)	$ 11,100	$ (4,641)	$ (1,629)	$ (4,331)	$ (2,648)	$ (392)	$ (5,303)	$ (32,221)
$ 110,984	$ 1,685	$ 32,498	$ 49,090	$ 51,454	$ 67,509	$ 82,222	$ 14,565	$ 761,492
37,490	32,161	13,744	7,205	29,563	43,722	35,430	25,858	348,948
$ 148,474	$ 33,846	$ 46,242	$ 56,295	$ 81,017	$ 111,231	$ 117,652	$ 40,423	$ 1,110,440
$ 164,461	$ 33,846	$ 46,242	$ 56,295	$ 81,017	$ 111,231	$ 117,652	$ 40,423	$ 1,111,030

				Earnings figures as percentages of Jersey's total net earnings[e]				
1920	**1921**	**1922**	**1923**	**1924**	**1925**	**1926**	**1927**	**Average**
23.1	31.0	(10.4)	10.7	13.7	29.9	17.5	5.5	13.2
19.4	46.7	25.3	37.6	37.3	23.8	24.3	93.6	23.6
45.1	(25.0)	25.1	(6.0)	15.1	17.7	19.9	(91.9)	27.8
10.4	4.1	38.9	34.0	25.8	20.8	26.2	80.7	24.1
7.3	10.3	31.1	26.6	13.4	10.2	12.4	25.2	14.2
(5.3)	32.9	(10.0)	(2.9)	(5.3)	(2.4)	(0.3)	(13.1)	(2.9)
100.0	100.0	100.0	100.0	100.0	100.0	100.0	100.0	100.0
74.7	5.0	70.3	87.2	63.5	60.7	69.9	36.0	68.6
25.3	95.0	29.7	12.8	36.5	39.3	30.1	64.0	31.4
100.0	100.0	100.0	100.0	100.0	100.0	100.0	100.0	100.0

[c] Principal component is yearly charge for general overhead expense, which normally would be allocated among the various preceding operating classifications. It was not possible to construct any basis for allocation, and the figure necessarily was left in the Miscellaneous Earnings classification.

[d] The abnormally heavy charges in these years appear to consist of federal income and excess profits tax adjustments.

[e] Since the percentage figure for any one earnings classification is determined not only by the actual amount of earnings recorded in that classification, but also by earnings and losses in each of the others, no attempt should be made to trace year-to-year variations in one classification without careful reference both to other percentage classifications and to the pertinent dollar figures. All functional earnings figures given in SONJ, Fin., Recs., for the years 1912 through 1924 have been adjusted by the authors to match, insofar as possible, the account classifications employed in those records in the years 1925 through 1927.

Source: SONJ, Fin. Recs.

how was this revenue employed? Table 21 provides a rough answer to the first of these queries.

The figures in this table verify what preceding chapters have emphasized as a conspicuous aspect of the Jersey Standard history from 1912 to 1927—the large relative growth of the producing function and the violent market fluctuations brought about by momentous and often rapid changes in the crude oil supply situation. Revealed in perspective, too, is the dramatic increase in transportation earnings which accrued from expanding fleet operations and from the spread of the pipeline network. The trend of marketing earnings was not so spectacular in terms of overall growth as was the general increase in output of refined products, but for much of the period earnings were characterized by stability which reflected product and geographic diversification. Refining earnings reached a peak of relative importance in 1918 and a peak in absolute size two years later. The losses imposed by inventory declines and low market prices in 1921 were repeated in 1927 on an even more imposing scale. Figures for the more nearly normal years between 1921 and 1927 suggest that the dangerously dominant position once occupied by this function had been modified in a beneficial way—not by curtailment of refinery output or facilities, but by relative expansion of other branches of the business. In contrast to profits in producing, refining, marketing, and transportation, the earnings of the natural gas business were remarkably stable. Relatively small though these earnings appeared, they never ceased to be important as a stabilizing influence.

All this is but a part of a broader picture. From 1912 to 1927 the drive toward a more completely integrated enterprise was a fundamental force in every branch of the business. Viewed in total, the functional earnings figures help to measure the success of the integrating effort; they also show why that effort was so essential. There is no way, of course, by which the very great strategic advantage of a well-rounded enterprise may be measured, but in a financially demonstrable way Jersey Standard benefited from the functional diversity of its business. While profit trends in producing, refining, transportation, and marketing were somewhat similar in broad pattern, important variations in the degree and timing of profit changes in each major operating department had a compensatory effect. In 1922 fair marketing and refining returns and the reliable stream of revenue from the natural gas business helped to offset one of the most unprofitable years the producing division had known for some time. The year 1927, on the other hand, would have been a disastrous one had Jersey Standard been a refining organization alone. The reader may multiply such examples many times with the information provided in Table 21.

Integration was not only functional but geographic. It is the dispersion of Jersey Standard's business throughout the world which provides the most spectacular illustrations of compensatory profits and losses. In 1912 roughly two-thirds of the company's profits were made in the United States; the remainder abroad. This relationship changed each year, as Table 21 indicates, but not until 1921 was there a drastic reversal. In that year profits from foreign producing activities were instrumental in helping the organization to avoid a serious total deficit, almost all the profits that were made in those trying months being made outside the United States. For most years thereafter the foreign producing program, even though still in its infancy and beset by many difficulties, augmented other sources of income in an important way. This was the more remarkable for the fact that the basic purpose contemplated by that program had been not immediate and direct profit but the gaining of assured sources of crude oil supply. Foreign marketing earnings also exhibited an almost uncanny propensity for burgeoning at times when the domestic business was beset with calamities. This nice dovetailing of functional and geographic earnings was only partially fortuitous. Here, in an increasingly well-developed state of integrated enterprise, lay the strength of the Jersey Standard organization and the proof of skillful and farsighted management. Here, too, might be discerned the practical necessity for great corporate wealth and the operational effectiveness of such wealth when skillfully utilized.

In the sixteen years from 1912 through 1927 Jersey's net profits totaled slightly more than one billion dollars.[1] Less than one-third of this sum was paid out in common-stock dividends. The conservative dividend policy established for the parent company at 26 Broadway was followed by the affiliates, although certain of these in which minority interests were large pursued a somewhat more liberal pattern. The Jersey directors appear to have maintained a closer control over this phase of affiliated operations than almost any other. The "Big Board," in turn, apparently enjoyed complete freedom, insofar as the large stockholders of the company were concerned, to set and modify the dividend policy of the organization in accordance with the dictates of the business situation.

Conservatism prevailed in the years from 1912 to 1918, when regular dividend disbursements by the Jersey Company averaged 32.2 per cent of net earnings. After that time an even more cautious financial course was followed. Teagle and the directors were concerned by growing competition, by the large outlays required to finance expansion and improvement in all branches of the business, and by the threatening crude oil supply situation. The dividend rate (20 per cent of undivided par) was not changed until 1926, but after 1918 the ratio of dividends to earnings fell off, averaging 28.9 per cent for the 1919-1927 period. These figures, together with those which are summarized elsewhere in this section, may be traced in some detail in the tables in Appendix 2.

With maturity had come a growing sense of permanence. The Teagle administration clearly conceived its primary responsibility to the stockholders to be the perpetuation of the company as an institution as solid as the government itself. Jersey stock took on an institutional character, actually yielding less to investors at times than did either government or high-grade municipal bonds. Not once in the years from 1916 to 1927 did the annual average ratio of dividends to market price exceed 3.6 per cent. The reasoning of investors which in 1920 drove Jersey Company stock from a low of 570 to a high of 880 was as specious as that which drove it down, in 1921, to the equivalent of 500. The cash dividend rate remained as steady as the grind of a rotary drill in a soft formation. For its stockholders the Jersey management had, it seemed, virtually eliminated the speculation from a fantastically speculative business.

Management found, however, that great wealth could be a great care. The proper utilization of liquid assets was a major and constant concern of the directorate—more particularly, of Jersey's succession of treasurers: A. C. Bedford, Seth Hunt, and George H. Jones. In most of the years after 1918 large sums were tied up in inventory, for reasons and with results that have been discussed earlier. The Jersey Company also continued to act as the banker for the entire organization, and a large portion of the company revenue which did not go into inventory was converted at once into working-capital loans to affiliates. After 1920 the Humble Oil & Refining Company outstripped Carter, Louisiana Standard, and Imperial as the heaviest borrower. Rapid expansion of producing and refining facilities in Texas was made possible largely by the bounteous flow of capital from New York. In December of 1923 the Humble loan account reached a high of $35,000,000.

Jersey funds which were surplus after meeting inventory and loan requirements were invested in government and other high-grade marketable securities. Intermittently from 1922 to 1926 some twenty to thirty millions were placed out in the lucrative call loan market. Most of these short-term loans went in relatively large individual sums to reputable New York financial houses. In December of 1926, for example, the brokerage firm of Jessup & Lamont was indebted to the company in the amount of $23,670,000 for call money which had been advanced. In total the banking functions performed at 26 Broadway were not unimportant as a source of revenue to the parent organization. In several years the Jersey Company's interest income actually was greater than profits in domestic producing or refining or marketing.

Great though the company's earnings appeared in total, the demands of the expanding business were even greater. In 1919 and 1920 nearly $200,000,000 of preferred stock was sold to finance the actual and antici-pated growth of company operations. A. C. Bedford informed the stock-holders that this need would normally have been met by earnings, but that the heavy federal tax burden of the war years made recourse to the capital market desirable. In anticipation of the preferred stock issue the Jersey Company abandoned the New York Curb, where company stock had long been traded, and applied for a listing on the New York Stock Exchange. This change in policy paved the way for a general widening of the market for the company's securities, a necessity which seemed particularly acute in the booming postwar months.

In 1920 Jersey common stock was reduced from $100 par to $25, in order to increase the marketability of the stock and place it in a price range that would permit the newly adopted employee stock-acquisition plan to function effectively. Thereafter, the amount of common stock out-standing increased rapidly. In 1922 a 400 per cent stock dividend was declared, which increased the amount of outstanding common stock by $399,700,000. This dividend helped to reduce a huge surplus which was even then being made still larger by a change in the method of valuing investments in affiliated companies.

The psychological danger of showing too great a balance in the surplus account was one that was well recognized by the Jersey directors, as by most American businessmen. The practice of converting a part of surplus into stock became popular when the United States Supreme Court ruled, in 1920, that stock dividends did not represent taxable income to the recipients. "Too much capital," wrote Teagle to Riedemann, "is a great deal more of a handicap than too little, as it tends to extravagance and inefficiency."[2] To this sentiment some of the smaller companies in the oil industry might well have taken exception.

Further changes in the capital structure were planned in 1926 and put into effect in the following year. Money rates were lower than in 1919, when the Jersey Company had issued its 7 per cent preferred stock. This stock was therefore refunded with a $120,000,000 issue of 5 per cent bonds. The refinancing effected a reduction in annual fixed charges from $14,000,000 to $6,000,000. Some $86,000,000 of common stock was sold at this time to help finance the retirement of the preferred issue.

Company balance sheets (Appendix 2, Tables III and IV) measure the growth of the business and provide a partial answer to the question of how the revenues from operations and from the sale of stock were employed. These financial statements, however, have many limitations for historical purposes. Federal taxation policies, stock-listing requirements, and intermittent efforts by the directors to place more realistic figures at the disposal of the organization produced several important alterations in recording procedures. The most far-reaching of these was a change in the method of showing the parent company's investment in affiliates. Since 1907 these investments had been carried on the books at cost. In order to comply with the listing requirements of the New York Stock Exchange in 1919, however, the company was forced to show its investments in affiliates at a figure representing not what had been paid for those investments, but their actual worth at the time of reporting. All published company statements in 1919 and thereafter followed the procedure of valuing investments at current worth, and in 1922 a start was made at bringing the Jersey books into harmony with the published statements. This adjustment from cost to a current-value basis was made over a five-year period and produced a cumulative write-up in investments and corresponding credits to surplus of approximately $348,500,000. In 1927 the Jersey books and published statements were further changed, in compliance with accounting recommendations formulated for the oil industry by the American Petroleum Institute, so as to present a clearer picture of consolidated account totals for the Jersey organization as a whole. This alteration in reporting techniques seriously impairs the validity of the 1927 balance sheet as a basis for comparison with earlier statements.

Some, though not all, of the various financial adjustments in the Jersey records can be traced back and eliminated so as to yield a rough statement of the actual flow of funds in the company. Table 22 provides this information for the span of years 1913 to 1926, inclusive, as a rule-of-thumb answer to the question of how the Jersey Company revenues were derived and utilized.

Table 22: **SOURCE AND APPLICATION OF FUNDS**
Standard Oil Company (New Jersey)
January 1, 1913, to December 31, 1926

Sources of Funds	Amount	Per cent of total
Jersey Company's own earnings	$ 324,000,000	29
Dividends paid to Jersey Company	361,000,000	32
Depreciation adjustment[a]	89,000,000	8
Sale of common stock	21,000,000	2
Sale of preferred stock[b]	200,000,000	18
Sale of bonds[b]	120,000,000	11
Total	$1,115,000,000	100
Application of Funds[b]		
Refining establishment	$ 127,000,000	11
Marketing establishment	28,000,000	3
Fleet	60,000,000	5
Other assets	19,000,000	2
Investment in affiliates	252,000,000	23
Dividend payments (common and preferred)	415,000,000	37
Working capital	214,000,000	19
Total	$1,115,000,000	100

[a] Estimated for seven of the fourteen years on the basis of earlier and later practice. Other years given in Annual Reports and Listing Statements.
[b] As of December 31, 1926, the preferred stock issue and the bonds sold to retire that issue both were outstanding, the exchange not taking place until 1927. Source: SONJ financial statements, ledgers, journals, and published reports.

Any real measure of Jersey's growth and profits necessarily involves comparison with other companies which are somewhat similar in point of size or in nature of business. So difficult are the statistical problems involved in such a comparison, however, that the effort can be viewed only as an approximation. In Appendix 2, Tables V and VI, the Jersey record is broadly compared and contrasted with that of United States Steel, E. I. du Pont de Nemours, the General Motors Corporation, the General Electric Company, The Texas Company, the Gulf Oil Corporation, Standard Oil of Indiana, and Standard Oil of California. These tables suggest that Jersey Standard's growth pattern was by no means unique, but that the company's dividend policy was more conservative than that of any of these companies except the closely held Gulf Oil Corporation. Jersey's percentage of return on net capital invested in the business ranged from a high of 18.5 per cent in 1920 to a low of 4.0 per cent in 1927, and averaged 8.8 per cent for the 1918-1927 period. This return on capital was not so impressive as the rate for some of the other companies shown in the comparative figures, though it exceeded returns for the petroleum industry in general. For the years from 1912 to 1917, Jersey net earnings averaged 15.8 per cent of invested capital, the range being from 10.3 per cent in 1914 to 21.8 per cent in 1917. For the entire 1912-1927 period earnings averaged 12.4 per cent.

Over the years from 1912 to 1927 growth in size of the organization, as measured by the balance sheets, was tremendous. This growth, as Appendix 1 indicates, took place largely within the framework of the existing corporate structure. Output, measured in terms of barrels of crude oil run in the refineries, increased even faster than did assets, indicating a significant improvement in the efficiency of operations. The increase in output outran by a substantial margin the general rate of increase in world consumption of petroleum products (Appendix 2, Table I). These more or less impressive suggestions of satisfactory performance, however, were overshadowed by the fact that in the years from 1919 to 1927 the Jersey organization was earning substantially less per dollar invested in the business than had hitherto been the case. In the face of high taxes, increasing competition, and, occasionally, low market prices, the great achievement of the 1920's was in keeping profits at or even slightly above the prevailing industry level and in strengthening the entire organization for the operational and financial trials that lay ahead.

EVOLUTION OF THE ADMINISTRATIVE FUNCTION

Preceding chapters exhibit the reflections from many facets of the administrative function performed at 26 Broadway. That function itself must now be isolated and its principal components examined directly.

The top administration of the Jersey Company involved a small number of men and the mechanisms they employed for making decisions and translating those decisions into effective action. Before the men or the mechanisms can profitably be discussed, however, the ultimate sources of administrative authority must be probed. Where, it may well be asked, did company policy actually originate?

After 1918, as in earlier years, voting control of the company resided in the hands of a small group of stockholders. On one occasion, following the Bayonne strikes, the Rockefellers had influenced company policy in an important way, though with the acquiescence of the directorate. Teagle also solicited the views of John D. Rockefeller, Jr., upon the Russian business. These, however, were exceptional circumstances.

After 1918 the authority of the "Big Board" was strengthened by the accelerating diffusion of stock interests. A few figures computed from the detailed information presented in Appendix 2, Table IV, serve to illustrate the movement which was taking place. Between 1912 and 1927 the holdings of Rockefeller interests decreased only slightly—from 25 per cent of total shares outstanding in 1911 to 22 per cent in 1927—but the number of stockholders increased 35 per cent between 1912 and 1918 and 541 per cent from 1918 through 1927. In 1927, to be sure, the dispersion process had only begun to make itself felt, much of the increase in number of shareholders had resulted from the employee stock plans, and the company was still closely owned. The trend, however, was clear. Teagle was far less intimate with the Rockefellers, father and son, than Archbold had been. The Jersey management, which had become strongly professional in character by 1913 at the latest, became increasingly so thereafter, and the administration of company affairs was firmly in the hands of this small and self-perpetuating group of trustees. So normal was this stockholder-management relationship that it would not merit particular notice but for the widespread belief that the Rockefellers were actively directing the company—an impression that exists in some quarters even today.

The point which should be stressed in describing Jersey's top administration is not that it was oligarchic in character but that it was not autocratic. Many of Walter Teagle's natural propensities were certainly autocratic in implication: his prodigious grasp of operational detail, his aggressiveness, his boundless enthusiasm and energy, his instinct to be everywhere and to do everything. For a time following Teagle's succession to the presidency, company management seems to have been more autocratic in tone than had before been the case. Such a situation, however, could not prevail for long. The oligarchic Jersey directorate continued to be permeated by a tremendously strong democratic tradition. Teagle himself not only had, in addition to his other attributes, a personal side which recoiled against the idea of dictatorship, but he was too capable and well disciplined an administrator to indulge his passion for minute and universal supervision to a dangerous degree.

Thus, if the administrative pattern at the directorate level did become slightly warped for a time following Archbold's death, it was resolutely recast along familiar lines. Like Rockefeller and Archbold before him, Teagle developed a corps of extremely capable associates by the simple, if dangerous, process of giving promising candidates a great load of responsibility and the administrative power to go with it. To be sure, the executive selection process was informal and subject to shortcomings. Sadler and Riedemann appear to have been the principal recruiters of top executive personnel: men who caught their eye were most likely to be pushed ahead. Some men, too, owed their promotions to kinship or influence. In later years the fact became clear that there was room for improvement in the executive recruitment and training areas. Nevertheless, the top managerial group which developed under Teagle possessed both ability and balance. The affairs of the company were administered by a process of intimate and constant discussion. Each executive in a position of responsibility was backed by an assistant qualified for permanent succession, or at least able to carry out the duties of the office on a temporary basis. This tradition of management-in-depth was as practical as it was venerable, for most Jersey officials were away from their desks as often as they were behind them. A reservoir of trained executives also existed in the affiliated organizations.

The oligarchy centered in the directorate, but it included certain men who were not directors at the time and at times apparently excluded some who were directors. Significant changes, of course, took place in the make-up of the top administrative group and in the power of the individuals within that group.

The summer of 1925 found A. C. Bedford representing his company before the industry and the public as energetically as ever, but in September he was dead. Those persons who privately had held that this man was only a figurehead soon realized how intimately the employees, the stockholders, and the industry had come to identify the company with the symbol. Jersey Standard had lost a man who was widely respected, who entertained broad and human concepts, and who brought to the directorate a conservative attitude that was not without value in a dynamic business. Not for two decades was Jersey Standard to be so well represented outside the confines of the business as it had been in the closing years of A. C. Bedford's unusual career.

George H. Jones was the new board chairman. This appointment had much to recommend it, though Jones was not and never could be the public figure that his predecessor had been. Jones had no enemies, was reputed to be one of the clearest thinkers on the board, and possessed a phenomenal grasp of detail. Like Bedford, he was a presiding officer who could be depended upon to render valuable services without trespassing in areas where he was not qualified to tread. This was not a common capacity or a mean achievement. It may well be, moreover, that the elevation to board chairmanship of one of the most cautious directors was a move designed to provide a check on the more aggressive element in top management. A tendency had long been manifest in company affairs to thus bracket bold and conservative leaders.

Certain other shifts in the administrative alignment came about as a result of changes in policy emphasis. As might be expected, the prestige enjoyed by the various directors fluctuated considerably over a period of time. The performance of the administrative function, however, was apparently not adversely affected by the ebb and flow of personal influence—or even by the fact that rancor was not unknown in the boardroom. A few episodes must suffice to illustrate this phase of the administrative pattern.

Outspoken and forceful—the self-styled "stormy petrel of the organization"—E. J. Sadler became a persistent critic of the Teagle administration. Once a bold expansionist himself, Sadler vehemently objected to expansion of company interests in areas where violent political conflict could be expected. He detested secrecy and deplored the necessities which made secrecy imperative. He was, at the same time, exceedingly sensitive to inefficiency. His critical analyses of administrative weaknesses were astute, but sometimes caustic. His heavy criticism was taken in good spirit by Teagle, and Sadler's needle-pointed comments were put to constructive use. Opposition, it seems clear, was tolerated in the boardroom, and mistakes were forgiven—at least once. Sadler took full blame, for instance, for the scare buying of crude in 1920 which subsequently caused heavy inventory losses to the company. For his strong and erroneous stand on this issue, Sadler related, he was never chastised—the board assumed full responsibility.[3] In 1927 Sadler was a potent force on the directorate, and his influence in matters of general administration was still strong.

E. M. Clark had gained stature and influence by virtue of his dogged fight against the more conservative directors for improvements in the refining organization. G. W. Mayer, until his retirement in 1925, was close to Jersey's president because of the earlier association in Canada and because Mayer was the hard-driving kind of executive that Teagle admired. Frank Howard's position was enhanced by his brilliant conduct of the affairs of the Development Department—a phase of operations recognized by all the directors as being of great importance. James A. Moffet, Jr., enjoyed a period of considerable influence following the death of Asche in 1924 and the retirement of Mayer in 1925, though this interlude was brief and was beset by increasing antagonisms. Heinrich Riedemann continued to be a close confidant of Teagle and one of his most farsighted advisers.

While the subtle month-to-month shifting of personal influences can scarcely be traced or appraised, it seems clear that a conscious effort was made to avoid the common circumstance of a management within a management. Teagle, though unquestionably very much closer to some of his associates than to others, successfully solicited the assistance of a very large number of executives, held individual jealousies under rein, bolstered individual weaknesses with the collective strength of the administrative group, and insisted upon making the committee system of management a reality. That system, to be sure, more than once in the 1912-1927 period proved too ponderous to cope with specific situations. On several occasions the necessity for rapid response to acute challenges had made it necessary for Teagle and others to assume heavy personal responsibilities, acting only under the restraint of very broad policy formulations.

As the size of the business increased, the administrative function itself was broken down into increasingly specialized divisions. Without exception, the Jersey board was composed of specialists. An increasing number of specialized staff departments served as the eyes and ears and hands of management. Each year the information-gathering process became more complex as new committees were formed to ease the crushing burdens which were being shouldered by existing administrative bodies.

Several of the most important administrative changes that took place over the years have been detailed in preceding chapters—the formation of the Development Department (1919); the creation of the Foreign Producing Department (1919); the subsequent consolidation of foreign and domestic producing into a new Producing Department (1926); the establishment of the Medical Department and of the several divisions required to administer phases of the employee relations program inaugurated in 1918; the formation of the Marketing Committee (1919); and the creation of the European Committee (1924)—to recall the most conspicuous additions and realignments. In the staff departments of the business the increasing managerial burden also produced quantitative and qualitative change.[4]

The primary responsibility of the Accounting Department was to gather and correlate operating cost figures of the Jersey Company, with particular emphasis upon refining statistics. In 1912 this division was staffed by 51 employees; by the middle 1920's it had more than doubled in size. The narrowing spread between refining costs and returns focused attention upon the cost-recording process, but despite the new necessities neither the accounting system as a whole nor the structure of the department was basically altered. By 1927 a complete reorganization was both necessary and imminent.

In 1912 the Auditor's Department, with 21 resident employees, was responsible for supervising the accounts of the affiliates, employing a corps of experts who traveled from one company to another to introduce and maintain reasonable uniformity in accounting procedures throughout the organization. No public auditors were employed by the company from 1912 to 1927. The Comptroller's Department, with 14 employees, combined the figures of the parent company with those of the affiliates to obtain summary statistical analyses. In 1918 the standardized forms for reporting to the parent company were altered so as to provide more detail. In that same year the Auditor's and Comptroller's departments were merged. These changes probably reflected the Jersey Company's action in applying for a listing on the Stock Exchange and the consequent necessity for maintaining records of current fluctuations in the value of investments in affiliates. In 1919 the Charting Division of the Comptroller's Department was established to serve as a clearinghouse and standardizing agency for all printed forms used in the organization—a task of no small dimensions and importance. Despite many added responsibilities the unification of the two departments enabled the auditing, consolidation accounting, and ancillary duties to be performed with fewer employees than had formerly been engaged in the separate divisions.

The Treasurer's Department was a distinct entity, charged with the regulation of investments, loans to affiliates, foreign exchange, and some tax work. In 1912 these duties, of which financing was the least important, were performed by 18 employees. By the middle 1920's the paper work connected with stock issues and employee stock plans had become a major concern of the Department, which had quadrupled in size. A separate division of 11 additional assistants was established to handle employee stock acquisition alone.

The joint efforts of these three departments—Accounting, Comptroller's, and Treasurer's—were aimed at the common goal of providing statistical and financial controls for the management of the business and, after 1918, at furnishing financial statements for public investment purposes. In 1925 the usefulness of statistics as an instrument of control was greatly strengthened. Before this time budgetary planning within the Jersey Company, though long practiced, had been somewhat haphazard. Various operational units had submitted financial requests on a when-needed basis; annual requirements were not always carefully defined. George H.

Jones, then Jersey's treasurer and a devoted advocate of statistical precision, insisted that a budget section be set up at 26 Broadway to study major departmental needs and initiate both special and regular annual requests. No effort was made at this time to budget other than capital expenditures, but Jones did institute the additional practice of preparing an annual budget of cash requirements. He also insisted that the affiliates do likewise and submit their budgets to 26 Broadway for approval.

New functions also were assumed by the Purchasing Department, which numbered 18 employees in 1912 and 76 a decade later. This group had nothing to do with crude oil purchasing, which was handled either by the Manufacturing Committee or, in such cases as involved large contracts, by one or more of the directors. The Purchasing Department was responsible for procurement of the thousands of supply items required in the normal conduct of the business. For many years, however, each refinery did its own purchasing and jealously maintained that local needs could not be serviced adequately by a group of "white-collar men" at 26 Broadway. In 1921 this needless duplication was eliminated by centralizing the purchasing program. Trained buyers were sent to the various plants to study local needs, and requisitions were routed through the central office and combined to facilitate more effective ordering. The parent company appears to have done little before 1927 to make its procurement facilities widely available to affiliated companies, nor was this feasible in many instances. Some assistance was provided affiliates, however, in the procurement of such major contract items as pumps, drilling gear, casing, and fabricated tank and boiler plate.

The Secretary's Department, occupying a strategic position among the various line-and-staff departments at company headquarters, was charged with maintaining a smooth two-way flow of communications between department heads and the boardroom. This was not a large component of the administrative organization (13 employees in 1923), and the functions performed were purely mechanical in nature. Here, nevertheless, was the allegorical horseshoe nail for loss of which a kingdom fell. The hiring, in 1925, of a staff of messengers to deliver routine interoffice mail every twenty minutes, for example, was a perfunctory sort of improvement, but the success of mighty ventures depends upon effective administration, and effective administration is a composite of perfunctory chores well done.

There was nothing perfunctory about the office in which the bimonthly issues of *The Lamp* were born. This was one place among several at 26 Broadway where lines of communication between the company and the public originated. Victor Ross, brought from Canada by Teagle in 1918 to establish *The Lamp,* had remained only long enough to get the publication started and implant in the mind of Jersey's president an enduring appreciation of the necessity for good press relations. Ross returned to Canada in 1919, leaving Northrop Clarey in charge of the newborn magazine. Clarey had worked as financial editor for the *New York Times* and as an advertising executive. His press relations were wide, he was a good copyman, and he knew how to get out a paper with wide audience appeal. The original intent of the publication had been to explain and popularize the new employee relations program. This purpose was broadened under Clarey's management and with Teagle's enthusiastic and detailed support. *The Lamp* became a chatty, useful, and immensely informative house organ. Circulation climbed, but the annual expense of publication from 1918 to 1927 never exceeded $35,000. This, figuratively speaking, was a low-cost wildcat lease which had produced a gusher of pure naphtha.

Public relations in the broad sense of the term was not an integral part of the administrative function, yet many of the staff departments and some of the line executives were concerned with such relations in the performance of their routine tasks of gathering and disseminating information essential to the conduct of company business. The concept of public relations as a field requiring special effort and skill had not been clearly defined, either in the Jersey Company or in American industry generally. As in Rockefeller's day, the basic philosophy appeared to be that good public relations would derive, in the last analysis, from the decent and effective performance of that work for which the organization had been created. To be sure, Teagle appreciated keenly the need for "good publicity." With the exceptions already noted in earlier chapters he also encouraged accurate reporting. There was no thought, however, of combining and co-ordinating the several existing and mutually independent connections which existed between the company and the industry, the public, and the government—much less of seeking important new connections. Teagle believed that every executive and every employee should serve as an emissary of good will. The Treasurer's Department was giving to the financial press the most complete financial summaries ever issued, voluntarily or otherwise, by a Standard Oil company. The press was welcome in company offices. *The Lamp* was telling the employees (and hence the public) everything that could be told, and had even been accused of telling too much. Jersey men had usually answered with a fair degree of frankness the questions of prosecutors, senators, and Federal Trade Commission investigators. All this, Teagle and the directors appeared to believe, was quite enough, and more than many other companies had done.

No department entrusted directly with public affairs, therefore, was added to those divisions at 26 Broadway through which the business, both public and private, of the Jersey organization was regulated. The Publicity Bureau over which J. I. C. Clarke had once benevolently presided had expired by 1918. Ivy Lee, the professional public relations expert, had continued to write speeches for A. C. Bedford, but after Bedford's death in 1925 there is no evidence of activities by Lee in behalf of the company and its officials. In 1927 it appeared that low gasoline prices were building greater public good will for Jersey Standard and the petroleum industry than could have been expected from all the efforts of the nation's best publicists, speech-writers, and editors. The great necessity, in 1927 as in 1912, was deemed to be that the Legal Department keep the company from breaking the law and successfully defend the company against those who charged that it had done so.

The Legal Department, smallest in size of any of the staff divisions at 26 Broadway, was the mightiest. The heads of the operating departments bowed to the edicts emanating from the suites on the sixteenth floor, and the veto power exercised by Jersey's lawyers over press releases was absolute. Teagle, as we have seen, changed his bold strategic plans when his legal advisers looked stern. The more impetuous and ambitious of the young executive group often had occasion to chafe under legal restraints.

Legal affairs of the organization were directed from the central offices, but there was a high degree of specialization within those offices and considerable decentralized legal activity throughout the network of affiliated companies. Mortimer F. Elliott, who served as chief counsel until 1915, also remained for a time in close touch with the legal representatives of those companies disaffiliated in 1911. His correspondence suggests that, while he was intimately consulted on large issues affecting Jersey Standard, he also handled much of the detail work for the company. His successor, C. O. Swain, built up a larger staff as the business increased, concerning himself chiefly with major cases and with matters of broad policy. As had been the case before 1911, most of the affiliated companies maintained a legal staff or retained consultants to handle local problems, though Jersey's Legal Department advised closely on issues involving federal jurisdiction and intercompany relationships.[5]

Over the course of years the company employed many distinguished consultants. John G. Milburn, of Carter, Ledyard & Milburn, conducted the dissolution suit defense and served through 1927 as consulting expert on antitrust matters. Richard V. Lindabury, senior partner of Lindabury, Depue, & Faulks, also was consulted in antitrust matters until his death in 1925. After 1921 the services of John W. Davis were also engaged in this capacity. Charles Evans Hughes was placed on a retainer basis from July of 1925 to December of 1927 and was consulted on international affairs, particularly on Middle East and Russian negotiations. John Bassett Moore's participation from 1914 to 1922 in the tanker and war-claims disputes has already been recorded in some detail. There were many others —patent specialists, Washington representatives, experts in New Jersey corporate and civil law. Particular interest attaches to the employment, in 1920, of J. L. Darnell and Emerson F. Rossmore, for in these appointments lay the birth of a significant new segment of the Jersey Standard administrative organization.

Before 1913 tax work had made as inconsequential drains upon the time of company executives as had tax payments upon the treasury of the company. Nor was any great change envisaged when the federal corporation-income tax was levied in 1913 and war taxes were imminent. Louisiana Standard's first income-tax return was sent by the treasurer to the president of the company for signature accompanied by a memorandum stating that the tax would be paid under protest, since the law was "obviously unconstitutional."[6]

By 1920 it had become apparent not only that the "obviously unconstitutional" law was to be a permanent and consequential financial burden, but that tax accounting had become an intensely specialized and intricate art. The tax regulations, moreover, were subject to constant modification. The Revenue Act of 1918 and subsequent changes in regulations rendered company accounting methods obsolete for tax purposes. The Treasurer's Department, even with help from Accounting and Comptroller's, could not be expected to compute the well-discovery valuations and the depreciation and depletion schedules on producing property that would determine for years to come the allowable charges which Jersey Standard and its affiliates might claim on tax returns. Neither did the producing affiliates possess the necessary knowledge and personnel to attempt the job. Jersey, therefore, enlisted the services of outside consultants.

Rossmore, an independent tax consultant, was retained to give advice on legal aspects of tax returns in general, but he declined an offer to give up his practice and join the company on a full-time basis. Darnell, of the firm of Darnell & Eaton, undertook the forbidding task of computing new valuations of all producing properties for all years back to 1909, and of setting up allowable depreciation and depletion schedules. This assignment consumed twenty-six months, filling many volumes with material of immense historical value. By the time Darnell had set up the new schedules a few Jersey accountants had become well trained in tax procedures; the nucleus of a tax department was in existence. This highly specialized group was formally organized as the Tax Department in 1924. Morris Frey, formerly tax expert for the Guaranty Trust Company, was made head of the new department.[7]

Efforts to bring the accounting system into harmony with procedures prescribed by the Bureau of Internal Revenue were carried still further in 1925 and 1926.[8] The Revenue Act of 1918 had specified, for the first time, that deductions for obsolescence as well as depreciation might be claimed. The Tax Department began to adjust asset valuations on the books to reflect charges for obsolescence, which had been high in the petroleum industry because of the tremendous improvements in cracking equipment, and to give effect to allowable depreciation rates, which varied considerably from those the company had employed. Charge-backs in asset accounts were made to the year 1882. When figures for early years were not available, arbitrary assumptions were agreed to by the company and the Bureau of Internal Revenue. This wholesale effort was not completely successful in reconciling company book valuations with valuations allowed by the Bureau. The stream of new regulations and decisions from the United States Treasury Department made the adjustment process never-ending and at times exceedingly frustrating. The necessities of federal-tax reporting certainly introduced greater accounting consistency and possibly introduced greater realism into the records of the petroleum industry, but the cost to the companies in terms of clerical expense and supervisory effort was enormous.

In 1926 the departmental organization at 26 Broadway was far more specialized than that which had existed fifteen years earlier. Effective subdivision of the administrative function had eased specific burdens, but at the same time it had increased the difficulty of over-all control. Tremendous growth of the business had raised serious doubts about the ability of the parent organization to serve simultaneously as a holding and an operating company. The administrative reorganization of 1927 was the culmination of nearly ten years of sporadic attempts to solve these problems in a realistic manner.

CO-ORDINATION FROM THE TOP

Frank Howard's opinion that co-ordination could be accomplished only from the top was well substantiated by the success of the Development Department in fitting into the rigid, if ill-defined, manufacturing organization that existed in 1919. Efforts originating in the lower echelons of management to harmonize the activities of various departments and committees had not been outstandingly successful. Certainly one of the most conspicuous characteristics of the Teagle administration was the energetic endeavor made to test the universal applicability of the principle enunciated by Howard.

The necessity for a more satisfactory working liaison between various branches of the business became acute when the organization experienced its tremendous postwar expansion in size and complexity. E. J. Sadler was probably the first to perceive that co-ordination, like labor relations, was fast becoming a problem for which top management must assume direct responsibility. As early as 1917 he had pointed to the necessity for correlating producing activities all over the world. In 1919 he had called for close relationships between the headquarters offices and the foreign refineries.[9] At the same time, the sudden demands imposed upon the company by the war effort, together with the industry-wide work of the Petroleum War Service Committee, focused attention upon the mechanisms of liaison in general and on the statistical prerequisites for such liaison in particular. Such efforts and realizations represented a start toward better co-ordination, though these beginnings were either ill defined or concentrated in highly specialized areas. Other steps followed rapidly.

Each of the departmental changes that were instituted in the years from 1919 to 1926 represented an effort to co-ordinate more effectively the activities within the departments, but at the same time much thought was being given to the broader problem. In February of 1922 a statistical committee was formed. The function of this committee was to correlate the various reports prepared by each operating division and to furnish the directorate with summary information about the business as a whole.

This new group was not assigned control responsibilities, but supplied the information upon which more effective control could be predicated. In February of 1923 Jersey Standard went a step further.

Business had slumped after the recovery of 1922. The LaFollette Committee was vehemently charging waste and extravagance in the petroleum industry Teagle himself admitted that many of the inefficiencies which had crept into the business during the war years had not been rooted out, and he forcefully declared that if the oil companies did not clean their own houses the government might attempt to do so. Jersey's president announced that an efficiency committee had been formed to study all departmental operations and make recommendations to the directorate of improvements which should be effected.[10] This new group might conceivably have attacked the problem of co-ordination in a broad and constructive way. Unfortunately, however, no Jersey directors were named to the committee, and a revival of business focused attention upon operational rather than administrative problems. The smaller task was attempted, and the larger waited upon the formation of the Co-ordination Committee in September of 1925.

The Co-ordination Committee, as noted previously, owed its creation to the realization by Sadler, Clark, Howard, and others that such a planning group was necessary. This represented the broadest attempt which had thus far been made to improve managerial liaison at a high level in the organization. As originally constituted, however, the Co-ordination Committee was an integral part of the manufacturing organization and it worked with the Marketing Committee on a coequal basis—an important deviation from the principle that co-ordination should be accomplished from the top. E. M. Clark indicated that co-operation between the Manufacturing and Marketing departments still was not effective when, in December of 1925, he urged Teagle to put Howard on the Marketing Committee.[11]

By February of 1927 a wholesale reorganization had become inevitable. Sadler, Clark, Howard, and Orville Harden were still pointing to many unremedied weaknesses in the administrative structure. Teagle himself appears to have become profoundly disturbed by two circumstances. The first was the tremendous demands that the business was making upon the time and energy of the directors. No man could do the long-range thinking necessary for the guidance of the business when his time was consumed by a succession of immediate managerial problems. The strain of the Russian and Middle Eastern negotiations had left their imprint on

Jersey's leader. He had been deeply dismayed by his occasional inability to fulfill the responsibilities that indubitably attached themselves to the presidency of the Jersey Company as then constituted. Secondly, Teagle had become dissatisfied with the performance of his board of directors. Here was a group of specialists—operating men—whose responsibilities were divided between policy-making for the entire organization and the management of the affairs of their own divisions. The policy-making function had begun to suffer, for the most immediate and obvious duty of the directors—the duty upon which their reputation directly depended— was departmental management. Each of these specialists had shown, at times, a disturbing lack of appreciation of the problems of other departments and of the requirements of the business as a whole. The basic necessity became clear: the policy-making function must be divorced from that of management.[12]

Teagle grasped this concept clearly and exercised strong leadership, but in point of fact initiative for the reorganization of 1927 can be credited to no one person in the Jersey Company; the necessity became clear as a result of the experience, the thinking, and the criticisms of many men. The actual form of the remedy was perhaps influenced most directly by Howard's analysis of the needs of the Development Department. The Jersey Company, Howard held, had failed to distinguish between those functions which properly belonged to a holding company and those which were best exercised by an operating company.[13] This failure was a natural outgrowth of the accident of history that in 1899 made Jersey Standard, until then only one of many Standard Oil operating units, the parent company of the group. The inability or unwillingness thereafter to draw a sharp line between these functions had been provocative of confusion which increased in direct proportion to the growth of both parent company and affiliated operations. By 1927 effective policy-making for the organization as a whole could be assured only by splitting Jersey Standard asunder—and this is what was done.

On August 29, 1927, a new affiliate was incorporated in Delaware: the Standard Oil Company of New Jersey. The Delaware Company, as this company came to be known, took over the manufacturing and marketing functions and assets of its parent, the Standard Oil Company (New Jersey), together with the stock of several affiliates. The new company was headed by Jersey director Charles G. Black. Men active in the management of the seaboard refineries and the Newark and Baltimore marketing divisions were named to key executive positions. At approximately the same time, the Marine Department of the Jersey Company became the Standard Shipping Company, a corporation formed in Delaware on August 3, 1927, headed by E. M. Clark, and staffed with personnel from the old Marine Department.

The final step in divesting the Jersey Company of its operating responsibilities was taken on October 28, 1927, when the Standard Development Company, which had been formed in 1922 to handle patent matters for the Development Department, was reorganized as the Standard Oil Development Company and placed under the direction of Clark as president and Howard as vice-president. To this new company were transferred the Engineering Department, the Research Laboratory, the Standard Inspection Laboratory, and the Development Department—hitherto operating segments of the Jersey Company. Representatives of the chief affiliates engaged in manufacturing—Humble, Imperial, Louisiana Standard— as well as members of the old Development Department organization served on the board of the new company.

When these corporate changes had been completed, the Jersey Company—the Standard Oil Company (New Jersey)—stood as a holding company alone. Its operating departments had become autonomous and more or less specialized affiliates much like The Carter Oil Company and Gilbert & Barker. The Jersey directorate, nominally relieved of operating responsibilities, was to be a policy-making board alone.

This separation of policy-making and management represented a delicate administrative balance. To formulate policy effectively the Jersey directors had to be freed of managerial burdens, but without being divorced from the realities of the business. This fact was recognized, and the make-up of the Jersey directorate was altered to facilitate close contacts between the parent board and the affiliated managements. The number of directors was increased from nine to sixteen. The new members of the board represented specific operating divisions—W. S. Farish, the Humble Oil & Refining Company; Riedemann and Mowinckel, the European interests; Christy Payne, the natural gas companies; J. H. Senior, Latin American marketing; G. H. Smith, Imperial Oil, Limited; C. O. Swain, the Legal Department. The primary responsibility of these men continued to be operational; they were expected to attend the meetings of the "Big Board" only at stated intervals. A five-man executive committee, of which George H. Jones was the chairman, was the nucleus of the reconstructed board; no one of these five directors was to be connected with any of the operating affiliates. Through this combination of five non-managing directors, meeting daily, and eleven divisional managers, meeting with the executive committee at stated intervals, the organization sought to achieve the full advantages and to minimize the dangers of centralized policy-making and decentralized management.

By the end of 1927 the administrative reorganization was still far from a reality. The blueprint had been drawn and many of the formalities had been concluded, but ahead lay months and years of painful experimentation and modification. Co-ordination from the top was still an ideal—remote, intangible, elusive.

The Jersey executives, nevertheless, had vigorously demonstrated a breadth of cognizance. At the operating level these men had succeeded in bringing the major divisions of the business into reasonable balance. The significance of the year 1927 was measured by this fact, and by another. At 26 Broadway administrative theory, if not practice, had completed a great historical cycle. The administrative organization, profoundly disturbed in 1911, had been recast in a form designed to recognize current necessities and to eliminate the structural ambiguities that had grown out of a troubled past. Jersey history was many things, and not the least of these were the efforts of company leaders to control the forces which they and their predecessors had called into existence.

THE CONDUCT OF THE BUSINESS

The great questions which grow out of these years of Jersey's history are issues not of fact but of judgment. Too often the judgment of the historian is regarded as conclusive, instead of merely interesting or, at most, significant. The preceding narration of events can serve as the basis for differing and contradictory assessments, though this circumstance in itself need not be a cause for concern. Business, like human behavior of which it is a manifestation, is full of contradictions. These final paragraphs constitute one assessment only—not conclusive and not oblivious to the fact that judgment must be an intensely personal matter.

This volume tells of the remarkable resurgence of the Jersey Company in an environment that was far from friendly. The progressive success of the company as a profit-making enterprise stands clear. The fact has been noted that profits of the era recorded only a part of the tangible managerial achievement. These assessments of internal performance can serve as the conclusion for a history of only the narrowest kind. The usefulness of the historical effort is vastly enhanced by an evaluation of the means by which company ends were attained, and by an attempt to relate both the means and the ends to the world of which Jersey Standard was so conspicuous a part.

Few forces to which the Jersey Company and the petroleum industry responded were as powerful in degree and as universal in scope as those that derived from the dissolution decree of 1911 and the concurrent hostility of many groups toward the Standard Oil organization. In the opinion of the Supreme Court of the United States that organization constituted a monopoly, with the power to destroy the potentiality of competition. The object of the decree was to dissolve the illegal combination, but not to deprive the defendant corporations of their rights to exist under the laws of the land nor to execute lawful contracts and agreements required in the normal course of business.

Behind the reputable and intelligent justices of the court a motley army had gathered. In the ranks of this army were some who believed, as objectively as any person could believe at that time, that restraint of the Standard Oil combination was wholesome and necessary. There were others—and these were many and vociferous—who wished to make the edict of 1911 a death warrant and who believed that this was what it constituted. The avowed intention of the federal and state governments to strike down monopoly was subtly perverted by the influence of some small businessmen, segments of the rural population, and dedicated reformists into an attack on bigness. These were powerful groups indeed, and they did not lack for political champions, both selfish and sincere. So vast was their following that it is by no means illogical to refer to these groups, their champions, and their sympathizers as "the public"—a concept which they themselves warmly cherished.

The Federal Trade Commission, many Congressmen, and some state agencies abandoned the Supreme Court's incisive interpretation of the Sherman Antitrust Act and accentuated the attack on large corporations. No other course, indeed, was politically expedient or possible at the time. New legal and legislative actions were commenced on all sides. The privileges guaranteed to the Standard Oil companies by the terms of the 1911 decree were bitterly assailed because by such privileges, however legal and however commonly enjoyed throughout the business world, the economic entity of the Standard Oil group could be preserved.

Those who wished to reduce Jersey Standard and its former affiliates to impotence were clever in attacking the normal rights of contract and agreement, and in insisting that the dissolution be absolute and immediate. Had the popular mandate been enforced, most of the Standard Oil companies would have been desperately smitten. It also seems probable that the American petroleum industry would have been completely demoralized and that many consumers would have been either poorly served or not served at all.

These political and legal efforts to destroy a system that had been laboriously molded over the course of a generation to fit an exceedingly complicated pattern of economic circumstances—a system for which there was no practical substitute at the time—fortunately were frustrated. Strictly observing the terms of the dissolution decree, insisting upon the rights guaranteed to it under that decree, and making only such concessions to the public will as were absolutely essential, the Jersey Company survived the shock of the dissolution and then began to grow strong again. This constituted forthright defiance of the public intent—or at least of the intent of powerful segments of the public, who feared that growth would lead to restraint of trade. The defiance was successful because it was unimpeachably ethical and legal, but it was blatant because the company made few effective efforts to disprove the charges made against it or to dispel the fog of misinformation which still shrouded many aspects of the business. Vital contractual relationships, many of which were secret, were established and maintained between the parent company and its former affiliates. The subtle power of influence, exerted throughout the petroleum industry by the Standard Oil companies and their officials, defied all regulatory efforts. Together, the power of contract and the weight of influence gained precious months and years for the company and the industry in which to effect a rational, profitable, efficient, and permanent adjustment to the mandate of the Supreme Court and to the requirements of a dynamic economic trend.

History moved in a momentously ironical cycle to thwart the enemies of bigness. By basic circumstance large units in the petroleum industry were more efficient than small ones. The effect of the dissolution decree, combined with the growth of markets, the discovery of new petroleum reserves, and the manifest inability of Standard Oil companies to compete to the maximum extent of their available capacities, was to permit a handful of the most efficient, best-situated, and most aggressive small operators to grow large. Many of the larger disaffiliated Standard companies, at the same time, had successfully remedied their structural weaknesses and had begun to compete with one another. Thus, in the course of a decade the intent of the Supreme Court to accentuate competition in the petroleum industry was achieved in an orderly way, though the industry continued to be dominated by large corporate groups. The small operator who in 1911 had clamored for the slaying of the Standard Oil Goliath at length found himself trying to survive on a battleground trampled by many giants. The economic position of the small independent remained as precarious as ever, and sometimes he could not afford to be efficient or farsighted. Nevertheless, he performed many services of great value. His continued protests were a constant reminder to the giants to be careful where they put their feet.

The effect of unremitting public attacks, many of which had been launched for eminently selfish purposes, was to make Jersey Standard watchful, sensitive, cautious—and strong. The LaFollette Committee report of 1923 was a reverberating salvo fired by the retreating but not defeated enemies of the large corporation. Certain government agencies had long since openly admitted the necessity for size and integration in the petroleum industry. In 1926 the defeat of the Department of Justice on the issue of patent monopolies was imminent. The Federal Trade Commission, though still suspicious, was formulating unprecedented pronouncements about the healthy state of competition in the industry. In many phases of their thinking petroleum executives had proved to be years ahead of their critics, and in certain areas of operation—notably labor relations and oil conservation—the large oil companies, extremely sensitive to criticism and the threat of regulation, had endeavored to anticipate regulation by voluntary action. A generation of prosecution bordering on persecution had helped to give America an efficient, resourceful, and well-balanced industry.

Quite aside, however, from the obvious effectiveness with which the petroleum industry was serving the American consumer and mending its own fences, broad economic and sociological movements had blunted the attacks on big business. In America the decade of the 1920's was a bustling, competitive, and materialistic age—scarcely less so than the cocky 1840's or the sumptuous 1880's. The system of free private enterprise—slightly regulated—was showering the world with material blessings. Business, particularly big business, was currently regarded by many as the force that would rebuild a disillusioned world. The American public would travel on wheels from cradle to grave, growing rich on common-stock holdings in the interval between. The disturbing and inexplicable radical movement in the ranks of labor would be undermined by taking labor into partnership on a limited basis and by providing new benefits and privileges out of the bounteous profits. The hard-driving American businessman, who in 1911 had been a villain, by 1927 had become a hero. The ivy halls where American business administration was taught were veritable shrines. The world stood in awe of the dramatic potentialities of American business efficiency, though there were some cynical prophets and certain recalcitrant foreign governments.

The Jersey Standard organization, it seems clear, was strangely blessed by its political adversity and visibly assisted by the hyperthyroid environment of the postwar years. Jersey's operating achievements clearly were substantial, and the question may quite logically be raised as to whether those achievements did not stem primarily from the remarkable long-term upswing of the petroleum industry.

The unflattering observation was once made that Sir Henri Deterding had succeeded because he was a plunger operating in a period when even outrageously rash gambles really had an excellent chance for success. This judgment has a trace of truth in it without being substantially true. Teagle, like Deterding, rode the mighty boom of the new oil era. Jersey Standard was favored by many other circumstances as well, the most important of which was the inauguration of that propitious interlude when American foreign policy was militantly directed at obtaining equal rights for the American businessman abroad.

While many of Jersey's handicaps were unique, however, most of the factors favoring company growth were universal in compass. The Open Door abroad was not opened for Jersey Standard alone, nor was increase in the uses of petroleum derivatives confined to those products which bore a Jersey Standard label. Market demand was growing, but competition for markets was growing even faster. Resounding failures were always a possibility in this restless environment. The Jersey Company was able to preserve its competitive position only by exceptional diligence and skill.

Managerial skill, of course, is almost by definition a product of co-operative endeavor, and no large company is a monument to one man's talents alone. Nevertheless, the influence of Walter Teagle upon the course of Jersey Standard history had become remarkably strong at least four years before he assumed the presidency of the company late in 1917, and it did not diminish substantially for more than two decades thereafter. In evaluating the contributions of this man, great care must be taken to avoid the common tendency of regarding public figures as unchanged in character and ability throughout the course of their careers. The essence of Teagle's business life was growth. An empire builder by disposition and capacity, he found his disposition and capacities circumscribed by an age that was unsympathetic toward empire builders. He was an effective leader, however, because he grew with time and changing circumstance. In labor relations Teagle changed from a stubborn opponent to an enthusiastic advocate of the moderately liberal viewpoint. Not without protest, he surrendered on issues in refining, marketing, and production when he realized or was shown that his prevailing beliefs were no longer expedient or pertinent. The Teagle of 1911 was not the Teagle of 1927.

Holding his personal emotions under strong check at most times and attacking daily problems with good humor and calculating logic, Jersey's president, nevertheless, displayed quite normal human frailties. On many occasions he was impetuous and impatient, sometimes he was too sanguine, and more than once he was less than frank. Too often his diplomacy consisted of translating the immense power of the Jersey Standard organization into cold, irrefutable statistics and relying upon the bludgeoning impact of facts upon his adversaries of the moment.

One who has carefully studied these resurgent years of Jersey's history will find it hard to resist the conclusion that Walter Teagle was a great business executive and leader. Surrounding himself with men of high capacity, he utilized those capacities when his own knowledge was inadequate or his vision was dim. Teagle contributed the rare quality of plain common sense to the collective wisdom of the directorate. To that wisdom he applied his particular genius for detail and for organization and for getting things done. Only in the acquisition of foreign crude oil reserves and in the building of a fleet organization did Teagle and his fine managerial team succeed in winning absolute leadership, but in all areas of operation the Jersey Company, after 1918, continually gave challenge both to its domestic and to its foreign competitors.

Like its leader, the organization as a whole exhibited a capacity for adaptation in many operating areas. This flexibility ensured that the company would move successfully forward through a series of difficult business situations in pursuit of strength, balance, and security. On exceptional occasions, however, inconsistency in policy and in practice arose from the necessity for subordinating means to ends, and the ultimate judgment upon company objectives and methods involves recourse to contradictory evidence. Some inconsistencies in company policy and practice, to be sure, were more apparent than real.

Motives of expediency might seem to rob the company's attitude toward labor relations of some of its luster. An examination of that attitude at once reveals the fact that fear of unionism was a strong motivating force in the adoption of the Hicks program in 1918, and there is little question that thereafter labor practices throughout the organization remained heavily tinged with paternalism. For all this, however, labor relations in the organization were indisputably healthy. Executive enthusiasm for the annuities and benefits program unquestionably was predicated upon the human as well as upon the practical advantages. Such labor sentiments as those that were professed throughout the organization are customarily discredited by impartial observers, since so often in the annals of business they have proved to be superficial and meaningless. The high idealism entertained in the years from 1918 to 1921, however, should not be mocked because management subsequently was forced on frequent occasions to exercise its power of veto at the conference table. Students of Jersey's history are in fundamental agreement in reporting a long-continued warmth and mutuality in the relationship between management and labor. This feeling survived isolated disturbances through the course of a great many years to become a living force—deeply submerged at times and quite undefinable, but potent.

So, too, was the case with the Jersey Standard policy of corporate democracy. It is true that the directors feared, for political reasons, to exert obvious control over the affairs of many affiliated companies, and it is no less true that affiliated operations were guided, invisibly but decisively, by policies set at 26 Broadway. These facts might well induce a cynical attitude toward the historical conclusion that local managerial freedom not only existed but also constituted a very positive factor in the flexibility and strength of the organization. In 1923 a traditionally hostile Texas court declared that Jersey Standard, at that time the owner of a 60 per cent stock interest in the Humble Oil & Refining Company, did not control the operations of that company. This decision was surprising only to those who did not appreciate the practical necessity for encouraging local initiative in an organization which was international in scope and whose component segments were operating under a truly astonishing variety of circumstances.

In all its domestic operations the Jersey Company displayed a concern for legality which was often so acute as to be paralyzing. This circumstance does not support a conclusion that company executives were fundamentally more law-abiding than those of other companies. The Jersey Company simply dared not indulge in liberal interpretations of its statutory rights, although most of its competitors could and some of them undoubtedly did so on occasion. Quite apart from the question of expedi-

ency, however, Jersey men and companies were regulated by a strict code
of honor, the core of which was sanctity of the contract. In many cases
it was obviously as impolitic for Jersey to break a contract as to break a
statute, but actually this code was so deeply imbedded in the fiber of
company tradition as to be beyond cynical interpretation. The company's
reputation for integrity spanned two hemispheres. Russia's Krassin and
Venezuela's Gómez trusted a Jersey contract when they trusted few other
oil companies in the world.

Jersey Standard's failings, like its virtues, were functions of time and
place and circumstance. A common excuse offered for the deviations of
the businessman is that he did what others of his day were doing, but
this line of reasoning is valid only if it is not pushed to uncritical ex-
tremities. In its operations abroad the company demonstrated an inflexible
determination to resist rather than to co-operate with the forces of nationalism and to insist upon the privileges set forth in classic formulations
of international law. This determination was based on the belief that
concession on any important issue in any country would prove to be a
fatal precedent. There was much justification for such a stand, but in a
majority of instances the company fared poorly because of tenacious
insistence upon its rights. In those cases where the contest was not with
private competitors but with a nation inflamed with self-interest and
aroused by the spectacle of economic exploitation, rigid adherence to the
traditional pattern often proved, in the end, to be unwise. The underdeveloped countries, to be sure, may have done themselves a disservice
in minimizing the importance of co-operation with foreign capital, but
the Jersey Company too often overestimated its power to deal with governments and grossly failed to gauge the forces of national pride. By
1927 neither side in disputes of this nature was ready to make the necessary compromises.

Implicit in Jersey Standard's foreign policy was an aggressiveness
which not only far surpassed that displayed at home but even appears to
have dwarfed the foreign exertions of the years before 1911. Teagle and
Sadler saw the ominous implication of events abroad and drove the
Jersey Company into the fray a full decade before most other American
oilmen became sufficiently concerned to act. The primary goal of increased crude oil reserves became almost an obsession. The company's
foreign policy was intensely nationalistic in an intensely nationalistic age,
and the way for American participation in the oil reserves of the world
was cleared by the Jersey assault. It seems evident, given the competitive

and political situation abroad, that, without recourse to such measures as were employed, the promising coincidence of Jersey Standard's foreign ambitions and the public interest would have been devoid of profit for both the company and the nation.

Here the issue of inconsistency stands clear. Certain actions of the company and its representatives seemed to be at variance with the very real tradition of business integrity that prevailed in the organization. Side by side with plain evidence of a determined intent to live up to that tradition is to be found equally plain evidence of sporadic recourse to practices long since renounced. In most of the cases in point this apparent contradiction is resolved by evidence that the responsible individuals were sincere in believing that their behavior did not violate contemporary ethical precepts. This evidence must be respected. In other instances, notably few in number, the action of Jersey men is difficult to defend by any set of standards. If, in these years of transition, Jersey leaders often exhibited a degree of business statesmanship worthy of a day not quite come, it is not illogical that they should also have tolerated some of the expedient practices of a day not quite past.

These men had worked with great skill and outstanding devotion to prevailing ideals, as they understood them, to make their company strong. To a marked and increasing extent they conceived this objective to have a broader value than that which was measured by profit alone. Over the course of almost half a century company policy had rarely been careless or extravagant, and never irresponsible. In these circumstances lay the explanation for a remarkable record of public service up to 1927 and an effective promise of enduring corporate and social gain in the years that lay ahead.

Appendix 1

Investments in Other Companies
Standard Oil Company (New Jersey)
1912-1927

This appendix is the result of a lengthy effort to obtain a list of the companies through which the Standard Oil Company (New Jersey) operated in the United States and abroad in the years from 1912 to 1927. These companies, following Jersey's practice, have been divided into three groups according to degree of integration and extent of stock ownership.

The first group includes those companies most closely affiliated with Jersey Standard and whose earnings were consolidated with those of the parent company. Generally, but not always, Jersey owned a majority of the common stock in these companies. Some were referred to as affiliates and others as subsidiaries, the two terms being very loosely employed. For convenience, we have called them "consolidated" companies or Group A companies.

The second group includes those companies whose earnings were not consolidated with Jersey's, although their dividends were included in Jersey's income. In some, the Jersey Company owned a minority of the stock; in others, a majority. In this latter instance the companies were usually passing through a developmental period, as was the case with various producing companies in South America. All these non-consolidated companies are given in List B.

The third group of companies includes those in which Jersey's "consolidated" companies (Group A) held stock. Information about these companies has generally been obtained from the parent company's reports, and in many cases it is not complete. After World War I there is a noticeable shift in the ownership of many Group C foreign companies from Jersey's "consolidated" affiliates to the Jersey Company itself.

For these three groups of companies pertinent data have been obtained on date and place of organization, type of business, capitalization, and Jersey Standard's stock holdings. This information has come from the Jersey Company records, without recourse to secondary sources of data. The names of the companies, which are listed alphabetically, are generally the legal ones, although in certain cases they are the commonly used Anglicized titles, with other forms given in parentheses. The date given for organization is generally the date of incorporation. The given capital stock refers to the amount of stock

631

outstanding and not to the authorized capital stock unless so stated. The holdings are generally given in the currency of the country in which the company operated or was organized.

This list of Jersey's direct and indirect corporate affiliations is not complete, since it is based only on that information available in the Jersey files. The compilation, for example, does not include the affiliates of companies in Groups B and C, except for a few cases of unusual interest when such holdings are mentioned in Jersey Standard records. Difficulty was encountered, moreover, in completing the compilation for the year 1927 because the Jersey files for that year did not provide full information on companies in Groups B and C. Individual reports were used in an attempt to fill in the information, but some few companies may have been missed.

The same company may appear in each of the three lists because of changes in its status during the period. Generally a full description is given in the first list in which such a company appears, with only an indication of ownership in the subsequent listings. Sometimes, because of unusual conditions, the listing of common stock has been supplemented by references to preferred stock and to bonds. This is the case with several European companies. The statements as to amount of stock and to ownership pertain to the end of the year, the time when the affiliates reported to Jersey Standard. Whenever (as happened in a few instances) a company reported conditions earlier in the year, an effort was made to ascertain conditions prevailing at the end of the year.

Group A. "Consolidated" Companies

1. Aktien Gesellschaft Atlantic
   Organized 1891 in Bremen, Germany, to own and operate ocean-going tankers. In 1912 Jersey held 60 per cent of its capital of 1,150,-000 marks. During 1912 and 1913 the company was in the process of liquidation. Its one remaining tanker, *Bayonne,* was transferred to Società Italo-Americana pel Petrolio.

2. American Petroleum Company, "Société Anonyme Belge"
   Organized 1919 in Belgium to take over transporting and marketing in Belgium where American Petroleum Company (Holland) had formerly operated. Capital stock: 10,000,000 Belgian francs in 1919, 15,000,000 from 1920 through 1923, 30,000,000 from 1924 through 1926, and 60,000,000 in 1927. American Petroleum Company (Holland) held all shares in 1919 and then transferred them to its stockholders (see List C). Jersey held 58.8 per cent from 1920 through 1924, and 77.5 from 1925 through 1927. This company also held stock in other companies as given in List C.

3. American Petroleum Company (Holland)
   Organized 1891 in Holland to transport and market in Holland, Belgium, and on the west bank of the Rhine. Capital stock: 12,000,000 florins from 1912 through 1923, and 15,000,000 from 1924 through 1927. Jersey held 51.25 per cent from 1912 through 1924, and 57.92

from 1925 through 1927. Company held stock in various other companies as given in List C.

4. Attapulgus Clay Company
   Organized in 1921 in Delaware for producing and marketing clay for decolorizing petroleum products. Capital stock: $1,500,000 from 1922 through 1925, $500,000 in 1926, and $250,000 in 1927. Jersey and The Atlantic Refining Company each held 50 per cent.

5. Bedford Petroleum Company, Société Anonyme Française
   Organized 1902 in France for marketing lubricants. Capital stock: 1,750,000 francs in 1912, 2,250,000 from 1913 through 1919, 10,000,-000 in 1920 and 1921, 20,000,000 from 1922 through 1924, 30,000,-000 in 1925, and 40,000,000 in 1926 and 1927. Jersey held all shares except for a few qualifying shares, ranging in number from 5 to 40, of 500 francs par. Company held stock in various companies. (See List C.)

6. California Natural Gas Company
   Organized 1910 in California as a natural gas company. A decree for its dissolution was filed in 1916. Jersey held all stock, $350,000, from 1912 through 1915.

7. Carter Oil Company, The
   Organized 1893 in West Virginia as a producing company. Capital stock: $2,000,000 from 1912 through 1916 and $25,000,000 from 1917 through 1927. Jersey held all stock except for qualifying shares, ranging from 4 to 50, of $100 par from 1912 through 1926. In 1927 Jersey transferred its holdings to the Standard Oil Company of New Jersey, and company's financial statements were consolidated with those of its new parent.

8. Carter Oil Company of Delaware
   Organized 1922 in Delaware to hold undeveloped leases in Mississippi and Alabama. Jersey held all stock, valued at $5,000 from 1922 through 1924, and $25,000 from 1925 through 1927.

9. Clarksburg Light and Heat Company
   Organized 1904 in West Virginia as natural gas company. Capital stock: $1,000,000. Jersey held 51 per cent 1912 through 1922, 52.43 from 1923 through 1926, and 52.78 in 1927.

10. Compagnie Commerciale des Produits Pétrolifères
    Organized 1920 in France with capital stock of 6,250,000 francs. In 1922 Jersey held 56 per cent. In September, 1923, a meeting was held to commence liquidation of the company. (See also List B.)

11. Compagnie Standard Franco-Américaine
    Organized 1920 in France as holding company. Capital stock: 10,000,000 francs in 1920, 20,000,000 in 1921 and 1922, 30,000,000

in 1923 and 1924, and 60,000,000 from 1925 through 1927. Jersey held
49 per cent and Banque de Paris 51 per cent from 1922 through 1926.
(See also List B and List C for affiliates.)

12. Compañía Petrolera "Rayón," S.A.

Organized 1925 in Mexico with capital of 100,000 pesos. Jersey held
all stock in 1925 and 1926 and transferred it to the Standard Oil Company of New Jersey in 1927.

13. Compañía Transcontinental de Petróleo, S.A.

Organized 1912 in Mexico to produce, transport, and refine petroleum. Reorganized 1918 with capital stock of 400,000 pesos. Jersey held
all stock from 1918 through 1926 and transferred it to Standard Oil
Company of New Jersey in 1927.

14. Connecting Gas Company, The

Organized 1902 in Ohio to transport natural gas. Capital comprised
8,250 shares in 1912 and 1913 and 13,000 from 1914 through 1927.
Par was $100 from 1912 through 1921, $75 from 1922 through 1926,
and $35 in 1927. Jersey held 4,119 shares from 1912 through 1920, and
4,120 from 1921 through 1927. (See also List C.)

15. Det Danske Petroleums-Aktieselskab

Organized 1888 in Denmark to market in Scandinavia. Capital stock:
6,800,000 kroner from 1912 through 1921, 13,600,000 in 1922 and
1923, and 27,200,000 from 1924 through 1927. Jersey held 79 per cent
from 1912 through 1927. The company held stock in many companies.
(See List C.)

16. Deutsch-Amerikanische Petroleum-Gesellschaft (commonly referred to
as DAPG)

Organized 1890 in Germany to transport and market petroleum products; also operated several gas oil and benzine plants. Capital from 1912
through 1921 consisted of 9,000,000 marks in shares, 21,000,000 in
share warrants, and 30,000,000 in debenture bonds. These issues were
changed to 18,000,000, 42,000,000, and 60,000,000 marks, respectively,
in 1922 and 1923. In 1924 they were reduced to 3,600,000, 8,400,000,
and 12,000,000 new reichsmarks, respectively. In 1926 the share warrants were redeemed in shares, and additional stock was issued so that
shares stood at 18,000,000 reichsmarks. In 1925 debenture bonds in the
amount of 3,000,000 reichsmarks were paid off. In 1926 participating
loan certificates for 9,000,000 reichsmarks were issued. Jersey held 99.91
per cent of shares and share warrants combined and 99.91 per cent of
the debentures from 1912 to 1917. Early in 1917 Jersey sold its shares
to Wilhelm A. Riedemann, who at the end of 1917 transferred them to
Deutsche Verwaltungs-und-Beteiligungs GmbH (a family trust) which
on June 2, 1918, transferred 2,250 shares to Hamburg-Amerikanische
Packetfahrt-Aktien Gesellschaft (Hamburg-American Line) and 2,250

to Aktien Gesellschaft Hugo Stinnes für Seeschiffahrt und Ubersee-handel (Hugo Stinnes Navigation and Overseas Trade Company). After the war Jersey's sale of shares to the Riedemanns was declared illegal by the United States Alien Property Custodian. Jersey Standard arranged with the Riedemanns to take back the shares which they then held and to straighten out payments when international law permitted. Jersey purchased 2,250 shares from the Stinnes' interests on October 31, 1921, and 1,688 from Hamburg-American on June 1, 1922. Jersey's holdings of share warrants and debenture bonds again were adjusted so that the percentages (98.12 per cent) were the same for shares and share warrants combined as for debentures for 1922 through 1927. DAPG held stock in many companies. (See List C.)

17. Domestic Coke Corporation
    Organized 1918 in Delaware to produce coke and the by-products of coal. Jersey held entire stock, which was $3,500,000 in 1921 and 1922, $4,000,000 from 1923 through 1925, and $3,500,000 in 1926 and 1927.

18. East Ohio Gas Company, The
    Organized 1898 and reorganized in 1910 in Ohio to transport and market natural gas in Ohio. Common stock: $10,000,000 from 1912 through 1917, $28,039,000 from 1918 through 1920, and $28,500,000 from 1921 through 1927. Preferred stock remained at $10,000,000 from 1912 through 1927. Jersey held about 75 per cent of the common and preferred from 1912 through 1914 and about 99.8 per cent from 1915 through 1927.

19. East Ohio Producing & Refining Company, The
    Organized 1922 in Ohio to produce oil and absorption gasoline. Capital stock: $600,000 in 1923 and 1924 and $1,000,000 from 1925 through 1927. Jersey held all but 5 shares of $100 par from 1923 through 1927.

20. Gilbert & Barker Manufacturing Company
    Organized 1870 in Massachusetts to manufacture equipment for the oil industry. Jersey held all stock, which was $250,000 from 1912 through 1916, $1,000,000 in 1917, $2,000,000 from 1918 through 1921, and $5,000,000 from 1922 through 1927.

21. Hope Construction & Refining Company
    Organized 1918 in Delaware for production of oil and absorption gasoline. Jersey held the entire stock of $500,000 in 1919, $4,500,000 in 1920 and 1921, $5,400,000 from 1922 through 1925, and $9,500,000 in 1926 and 1927. (See also List B.)

22. Hope Natural Gas Company
    Organized 1898 in West Virginia to produce and transport natural gas. Jersey held all stock, which was $17,000,000 in 1912, $19,000,000

in 1913, $20,000,000 from 1914 through 1921, $25,000,000 from 1922 through 1925, and $26,600,000 in 1926 and 1927. Company held stock in other companies. (See List C.)

23. Humble Oil & Refining Company
Organized 1917 in Texas as a successor to the Humble Oil Company (formed in 1911) for producing, refining, and marketing. Capital stock issued: $25,000,000, 1919 through 1921, $43,750,000, 1922 through 1925, $73,117,575 in 1926, and $73,685,700 in 1927. Jersey's interest was 56 per cent at the end of 1919, 56.37 in 1920 and 1921, 60.77 from 1922 through 1924, 63.06 in 1925, 62.89 in 1926, and 62.63 in 1927. Consolidated with Humble's reports were those of two wholly owned affiliates: Humble Pipe Line Company from 1919 through 1927 and Compañía Petrolera Tamaulipas, S.A., from 1923 through 1927. (See List C.)

24. Imperial Oil, Limited
Organized 1880 in Canada as The Imperial Oil Company, Limited; name changed to above in 1919. Capital stock issued: $6,000,000 (Canadian) in 1912, $10,000,000 in 1913 and 1914, $22,962,500 in 1915, $25,000,000 in 1916, $30,000,000 from 1917 through 1919, $35,256,025 in 1920, $39,222,750 in 1921, $39,605,225 in 1922, $40,026,825 in 1923, $40,485,250 in 1924, $40,697,044 in 1925, $40,871,238 in 1926, and $41,097,388 in 1927. Jersey holdings were 83.875 per cent in 1912, 79.5 in 1913 and 1914, 80.35 in 1915, 77.466 from 1916 through 1919, 77.0 in 1920, 76.2 in 1921 and 1922, 74.8 in 1923, 73.8 in 1924, 74.5 in 1925, 73.2 in 1926, and 72.76 in 1927. Imperial Oil carried on diversified functions both in its own name and through its many affiliates. (See List C.) Consolidated with its reports from 1919 through 1927 were those of a company which changed names twice, ending with Imperial Oil Refineries, Limited, in 1923. (See List C.)

25. International Co., Vaduz
Organized 1922 in Liechtenstein as holding company, with capital of 400,000 Swiss francs from 1922 through 1927. Stock held by Petroleum Import Compagnie from 1922 through 1924 (see List C), and by Jersey from 1925 through 1927. (See List C for affiliates.)

26. Interstate Cooperage Company, The
Organized 1904 in New York to own cooperage works and timber lands in various states. Jersey held entire stock of $200,000 from 1912 through 1927.

27. "La Columbia," Società Marittima (per trasporto di petrolio e derivati)
Organized 1917 in Italy to transport petroleum products. Capital stock: 5,000,000 lire from 1917 through 1920, and 20,000,000 from 1921 through 1927. Jersey held 39.25 per cent from 1921 through 1927. (See List C for other stockholders.)

28. L'Economique, Société Anonyme de Distribution de Pétrole et Essence

Organized 1920 in France by Jersey and French interests to handle the distribution of light products and to hold stock in other companies. Capital stock: 10,000,000 francs in 1920 and 1921, 20,000,000 in 1922, 30,000,000 in 1923, 55,000,000 in 1924, and 70,000,000 from 1925 through 1927. Jersey held 69 per cent in 1922, 59 in 1923 and 1924, 43.9 in 1925, and 53.9 in 1926 and 1927. (See List B for 1920 and 1921 and List C for other stockholders as well as company's holdings of stock.)

29. Marion Oil Company

Organized 1891 in West Virginia as a producing company. Jersey held 50 per cent of capital stock, which was $70,000 from 1912 through 1922 and $50,000 from 1923 through 1927.

30. Oklahoma Pipe Line Company

Organized 1909 in Oklahoma as part of a pipeline system from Oklahoma fields to Baton Rouge refinery. Capital stock: $1,500,000 in 1912, $1,650,000 in 1913 and 1914, $2,500,000 from 1915 through 1917, $4,000,000 in 1918, $5,000,000 from 1919 through 1922, $10,000,000 in 1923 and 1924, and $15,000,000 from 1925 through 1927. Jersey held all but 5 shares of $100 par, 1912 through 1926, and transferred its holdings to Standard Oil Company of New Jersey in 1927.

31. Pennsylvania Lubricating Company, Incorporated

Organized 1895 in Pennsylvania for making mill greases. Jersey owned 60 per cent of its capital stock, which was $50,000 from 1912 through 1914, $500,000 from 1915 through 1921, and $1,000,000 from 1922 through 1927.

32. Peoples Natural Gas Company, The

Organized 1885 in Pennsylvania to produce, transport, and distribute natural gas. Common stock: $9,300,000 in 1912, $10,200,000 from 1913 through 1915, $11,000,000 from 1916 through 1921, and $13,-200,000 from 1922 through 1927. In 1926 and 1927 there was also preferred stock outstanding of $11,280,000. Jersey owned all common stock 1912 through 1927. (See List C for affiliates.)

33. Petroleum Import Compagnie (commonly called Pico)

Organized 1894 in Switzerland as a marketing company. Capital stock: 400,000 Swiss francs from 1912 through 1927. DAPG's former shares (60 per cent) were transferred to Jersey which held them, 1921 through 1927. Pico held stock in a few companies. (See List C.)

34. Raffinerie Française

Organized 1891 in France as a refining company. Jersey held all its stock of 400,000 francs in 1912, but transferred its holdings to the Bedford Petroleum Company, S.A.F., in 1913 and liquidated the company.

35. Reserve Gas Company

Organized 1902 in West Virginia to produce natural gas. Jersey held 11,126 of the 22,250 shares ($100 par) in 1912 and transferred them to Hope Natural Gas Company in 1913.

36. River Gas Company, The

Organized 1894 in West Virginia as a producer and distributor of natural gas in West Virginia and Ohio. Jersey held all 3,000 shares ($100 par) in 1912 and 3,440 of the 3,600 shares outstanding from 1913 through 1927. (Hope Natural Gas held the remainder. See List C.)

37. "Româno-Americana" (Societate Anonimă pentru Industria, Comerciul și Exportul Petrolului)

Organized 1905 in Romania for producing, refining, transporting, and marketing. Jersey held all capital stock, which was 12,500,000 lei in 1912 and 1913, 25,000,000 from 1914 through 1916, 37,500,000 from 1917 through 1919, 150,000,000 in 1920, 200,000,000 in 1921, and 500,000,000 from 1922 through 1927. The company held stock in a few companies. (See List C.)

38. Rotterdamsch Petroleum Entrepot

Organized 1920 in Holland as a bulk forwarding plant for trade on the Rhine. Capital stock: 125,000 guilders, 1920 through 1927. Jersey held all stock in 1922. (See Lists B and C.)

39. S.H.S. Amerikansko Petroleumsko, D.D. (or S.H.S. American Petroleum Company or Standard Oil Company of Yugoslavia)

Organized 1921 in Yugoslavia as a marketing company. Capital stock: 4,000 shares in 1921, 5,000 from 1922 through 1924, and 100,000 shares from 1925 through 1927 (1,000 dinars par). In 1922 Jersey held 92.5 per cent. (See Lists B and C.)

40. Società Italo-Americana pel Petrolio (commonly called SIAPP)

Organized 1891 in Italy for transporting and marketing. Capital stock: 15,000,000 lire in 1912 and 1913, 20,000,000 from 1914 through 1920, 100,000,000 from 1921 through 1924, and 250,000,000 from 1925 through 1927. Jersey owned 73⅓ per cent of stock from 1912 through 1919, 81⅚ per cent in 1920 and 1921, 83⅚ per cent in 1922 and 1923, and 89⅓ per cent from 1924 through 1927. SIAPP held stock in many companies. (See List C.)

41. Société Anonyme Pétrolea

Organized 1900 in Switzerland as a marketing company. Capital stock: 400 Swiss francs, 1912 through 1922. Jersey acquired a 40 per cent interest in 1921 and 33 per cent additional in 1922. During 1923 the business was turned over to Pico and the company liquidated. (See List C for other stockholders.)

42. Stanco Distributors, Incorporated
    Organized 1925 in Delaware to sell Nujol, Flit, and other special products in states where Jersey was not authorized to engage in business. Jersey held all shares of $100,000 capital stock from 1925 through 1927.

43. Stanco Incorporated
    Organized December 30, 1927, in Delaware to prepare specialties. Jersey held all shares of $10,000,000 capital stock.

44. Standard Oil & Refining Company, Limited
    Organized 1920 in England as a patent holding company. Jersey owned entire capital stock of £120,000, from 1922 through 1925. Company then became dormant. (See also List B.)

45. Standard Oil Company of Brazil
    Organized 1896 in West Virginia as Empreza Industrial de Petroleo for refining and marketing in Brazil. Reorganized with new name (above) in 1911. Capital stock: 5,000 shares of $100 par, 1912-1917. Jersey held all but 7 shares from 1912 through 1924 and all shares from 1925 through 1927. (See List C for affiliates.)

46. Standard Oil Company of Louisiana
    Organized 1909 in Louisiana for producing, transporting, refining, and marketing. Jersey held all except a few qualifying shares, which varied in number from 9 to 212½. Capital stock: $5,000,000 from 1912 through 1916, $10,000,000 from 1917 through 1919, $30,000,000 in 1920 and 1921, and $75,000,000 from 1922 through 1927. Consolidated with its reports from 1923 through 1927 were those of its subsidiary, Standard Pipe Line Company, Incorporated. (See List C.)

47. Standard Oil Company of New Jersey (commonly called the Delaware Company)
    Organized August 29, 1927, in Delaware with capital stock of $200,-000,000 which was all owned by Standard Oil Company (N. J.), to assume operating functions of Jersey's business. To it, in 1927 Jersey transferred its own refining and marketing properties and its holdings of stock in The Carter Oil Company, Oklahoma Pipe Line Company, Tuscarora Oil Company, Limited, and six Mexican companies.

48. Standard Oil Development Company
    Organized in 1922 in Delaware as Standard Development Company; name was changed to above on October 28, 1927. Jersey held entire capital of $250,000 from 1922 through 1927. Its business was broadened in 1927 from that of holding patents to include work in development and research which formerly had been carried on by Jersey's Development Department.

49. **Standard Petroleum Co. (Glarus)**
    Organized 1911 in Switzerland as Schweizerische Handels-und Beteili-gungs-Aktiengesellschaft; name changed to above in 1921. Capital stock: 1,500,000 Swiss francs from 1911 through 1927. Jersey held all shares from 1921 through 1927. Company held the stock of various companies. (See Lists B and C.)

50. **Standard Shipping Company**
    Organized August 3, 1927, in Delaware to take over Jersey's Marine Department. Capital stock: 250,000 shares ($100 par), all of which were held by Jersey.

51. **Tagus Oil Company**
    Organized 1919 in Portugal to provide a bunkering station in the Azores. Capital stock: 100 shares of 100 escudos par from 1920 through 1922, and 5,000 shares from 1923 through 1927. Jersey held all shares from 1922 through 1927. (See also List B.)

52. **Taylorstown Natural Gas Company**
    Organized 1889 in Pennsylvania as a producer and supplier of natural gas. Capital stock: $10,000 from 1912 through 1921 and $40,000 from 1922 through 1924. Jersey held 30 per cent from 1912 through 1924, while the remainder was held by Washington Oil Company, a former affiliate to which Jersey's holdings were transferred in 1925.

53. **Tuscarora Oil Company, Limited**
    Organized 1910 as limited partnership in Pennsylvania, taking over the A. C. Bedford pipelines. Except for 36 to 56 shares, Jersey owned all 50,000 shares ($100 par) from 1912 through 1926. In 1927 these holdings were transferred to the Standard Oil Company of New Jersey.

54. **Underhay Oil Co.**
    Organized 1890 in Massachusetts for handling lubricating oil and greases. Jersey owned 98.8 per cent of the capital stock of $25,000 from 1912 through 1927.

55. **United Fuel Gas Company**
    Organized 1903 in West Virginia as a natural gas company. Jersey owned 51 per cent of its capital stock of $6,000,000 from 1912 through 1914. Company was sold before the end of 1915.

56. **United States Petroleum Company, S.A.**
    Organized 1919 in Belgium to deal in lubricants, waxes, etc., in France and Belgium. Jersey held 96 per cent of its stock of 250,000 Belgian francs, 1922 through 1927. Company held stock of The Pure Oil Company, Limited, in 1921 and 1922. (See List C.)

57. **West Coast Oil Fuel Company, Limited**
    Organized 1911 in England to transport fuel oil on the West Coast of the Americas. Capital stock: £100,000. Jersey held 69.94 per cent

of stock in 1912 and 1913 and transferred its holdings to The Imperial Oil Company, Limited, in 1914. (See List C.)

58. West India Oil Company

Organized 1902 in New Jersey to market in the West Indies, Central and South America. Capital stock: $100,000 from 1912 through 1914, $3,000,000 from 1915 through 1924, and $10,000,000 from 1925 through 1927. Jersey held all except 7 shares of $100 par, 1912 through 1927. Company held stock in other companies. (See List C.)

59. West India Oil Refining Company, The

Organized 1882 in Kentucky to refine in Cuba and Puerto Rico when tariff laws favored it. Capital stock: $300,000 from 1912 through 1922. Jersey held 49.8 per cent from 1912 through 1920, 49.7 in 1921, and 79.7 in 1922. In 1919 the company sold its property, including the Belot refinery at Havana, to the newly organized West India Oil Refining Company of Cuba, and became a holding company. Company dissolved in 1923, and its business and property were transferred to company of the same name incorporated in Delaware. (See List C.)

60. West India Oil Refining Company, The

Organized 1923 in Delaware as successor to company of the same name incorporated in Kentucky. Capital stock: $300,000, of which Jersey held all from 1923 through 1927. Consolidated with it were the business and reports of its affiliate, West India Oil Refining Company of Cuba and the latter's affiliate, Standard Oil Company of Cuba. (See List C.)

Group B. Non-Consolidated Companies, 1912-1927

1. Agwi Petroleum Corporation, Limited

Organized 1920 in Great Britain to refine petroleum at Fawley. Capital stock: £300,000 first debenture stock and £1,000,000 share capital, which was increased to £1,500,000 in 1924. Jersey held 68 per cent of the share capital in 1926 and 1927.

2. American British Oil Company

Organized 1924 in Venezuela as a producing company. Jersey held all 5,200 shares of stock (1,000 bolivianos par) from 1924 through 1927.

3. Americká petrolejářská společnost v Ceskoslovensku (American Petroleum Company of Czechoslovakia)

Organized 1921 in Czechoslovakia to trade in petroleum and products. Capital stock: 2,000,000 Czechoslovakian kroner in 1921, which was increased to 9,000,000 in 1923. From 1921 through 1927 Jersey held 60 and Compagnie Standard Franco-Américaine held 40 per cent of the stock. (See List C.)

4. Carwardine (John) and Son Limited

   Organized 1906 in England to process and market candles and soap. From 1925 through 1927 capital stock was 1,500 ordinary and 500 preference shares of £ 10 par. Jersey held 600 ordinary and 250 preference shares from 1925 through 1927.

5. Compagnie Commerciale des Produits Pétrolifères

   Jersey held 56 per cent of the stock in 1920 and 1921. (See List A for further data.)

6. Compagnie Générale des Pétroles pour l'Eclairage et l'Industrie

   Organized 1881 in France as a refiner and marketer of petroleum products in southern France. By 1921 its capital comprised 4,500 founders' shares and 11,500 ordinary shares (500 francs par). In 1924 ordinary shares increased to 27,500 and in 1925 to 43,500. In 1921 Jersey purchased 48 per cent of both types of shares. In 1925 the Jersey holdings were increased to 49.5 per cent of founders' and 53 per cent of ordinary shares. The company held stock in other companies. (See List C for other stockholders.)

7. Compagnie Standard Franco-Américaine

   Jersey held 49 per cent of the stock in 1920 and 1921. (See List A for further data.)

8. Compañía Nacional de Petróleos, Limitada

   Formed in 1905 for producing, manufacturing, and marketing in Argentina as Compañía Nacional de Acietes; in 1909 succeeded by Compañía Nacional de Petróleos, Sociedad in Comandita; in 1911, by company of name given above. Capital stock: 7,500 shares of 1,000 pesos each from 1911 through 1927. Jersey held 65 per cent in 1918 and 1919. (See also List C.)

9. Compañía Transcontinental de Petróleo, S.A.

   Jersey held all stock in 1917. (See List A for further data.)

10. Construction and Development Company

    Organized 1925 in Liechtenstein to hold two Russian contracts with capital of 100,000 francs, which was increased to 900,000 in 1926. Jersey held 25 per cent interest from 1925 through 1927.

11. Empreza Nacional de Petróleos

    Organized 1925 in Brazil for marketing. Jersey held all 4,000 shares of 800,000 Brazilian milreis from 1925 through 1927.

12. Ethyl Gasoline Corporation

    Organized 1924 in Delaware for the manufacture and sale of ethyl fluid for mixing with gasoline, with capital stock of $1,500,000. Jersey and General Motors each held 50 per cent from 1924 through 1927.

13. Field (J. C. & J.), Limited
    Organized 1887 in England as manufacturer and marketer of soap.
    By 1922 capital comprised £ 125,000 of preference and £ 125,000 of
    ordinary shares. Jersey held 30 per cent of both from 1922 through
    1927.

14. Finska Aktiebolaget Nobel-Standard (Nobel-Standard in Finland, Aktie-
    bolaget)
    Organized 1920 for marketing in Finland. Capital stock: 30,000,000
    Finnish marks, which was increased to 40,000,000 in 1926 and 1927.
    Jersey held 40 per cent, the Nobels 30, and Finnish merchants 30. The
    company owned stock in a few other small companies.

15. Grisdale (James) & Sons, Limited
    Organized 1911 in England for making candles. By 1925 its capital
    stock was £ 15,000, of which Jersey held 30 per cent from 1925 through
    1927.

16. Hazelwood Oil Company
    Organized 1873 in Pennsylvania as a producing company. Jersey held
    2,511 shares (36 per cent) valued at $69,053 from 1912 through 1914,
    and sold them in 1915.

17. Hope Construction & Refining Company
    Jersey held all stock in 1918. (See List A for further data.)

18. Industrias Babel y Nervión, Compañía anónima
    Organized 1918 as a marketing company in Spain. Capital stock:
    10,000,000 pesos in 1920 and 1921, 10,300,000 in 1922 and 1923, 13,-
    000,000 in 1924, 15,000,000 in 1925, and 18,000,000 in 1926 and 1927.
    Jersey held 48 per cent in 1921, 46.6 in 1922 and 1923, 51 in 1924,
    57 in 1925, 62 in 1926, and 80 in 1927. (See also Sociedad Espagnolea
    de Compras y Flitamentos, List B.)

19. Interstate Natural Gas Company, Incorporated
    Organized 1926 in Delaware to produce and transport natural gas
    from Monroe, Louisiana, field to Baton Rouge. Capital of 1,000,000
    shares, no par value. Jersey held 375,000 shares, which it valued at
    $1,875,000 in 1926 and 1927.

20. Königsberger Handels-Compagnie
    Organized 1872 to market in East Prussia. Capital stock: 2,300 shares
    (1,000 marks par) from 1912 through 1923; same number of shares
    at 200 new reichsmarks par from 1924 through 1927. Jersey increased its
    holdings from 1,145 in 1921 to 1,424 shares in 1927. (See also List C.)

21. La Pétroléenne, S.A.
    Organized 1920 in France to take over business of Fenaille & Des-
    peaux. Capital stock: 22,000,000 francs in 1920, 40,000,000 from 1921
    through 1923, and 50,000,000 from 1924 through 1927. Jersey held 40

per cent of the capital in 1923, 42 in 1924, 77 in 1925, and 65 in 1926 and 1927. (See List C for other stockholders.)

22. L'Economique, Société Anonyme de Distribution de Pétrole et Essence

   Jersey held 75 per cent of the stock in 1920 and 1921. (See Lists A and C for further data.)

23. Lone Star Gas Company

   Organized 1909 in Texas as natural gas company. By 1912 its capital stock was $3,500,000, of which Jersey held 25 per cent. Jersey holding written off by the end of 1913.

24. Magyar-Amerikai Petroleum résvénytársaság (Ungarisch-Amerikanische Petroleum Aktiengesellschaft or Hungarian-American Oil Company Limited)

   Organized 1921 in Hungary as marketing company with capital stock of 5,000,000 Hungarian crowns. Capital increased to 30,000,000 crowns in 1922, to 300,000,000 in 1923 and 1924, and 1,600,000 pengos 1925 through 1927. Jersey owned all stock from 1921 through 1927.

25. Mineraloel-Raffinerie vorm. August Korff (Bremen)

   Organized 1887 in Germany as Petroleum-Raffinerie vorm. August Korff. Name changed to above in 1922. Capital stock: 1,500,000 marks from 1912 through 1920, 3,000,000 in 1921 and 1922, 6,000,000 from 1923 to 1924, 1,800,000 new reichsmarks 1925 through 1927. Jersey held 47.3 per cent from 1921 through 1923, 48.5 in 1924 and 1925, and 61.5 in 1926 and 1927. (See also List C.)

26. Naamlooze Vennootschap Nederlandsche Koloniale Petroleum Maatschappij (called NKPM)

   Organized 1912 in the Netherlands to secure oil concessions in Dutch East Indies. Capital in 1912 consisted of 5,000,000 florins common stock, which by 1918 was increased to 10,000,000. There were also 100,000 florins of preference shares which were retired at the end of 1925. All common shares were held by Jersey interests in Holland from 1912 through 1925. In 1926 Jersey took over the investment in its own name.

27. Norsk-Amerikansk Petroleums Company A/S

   Organized 1906 for marketing of lubricants and specialties in Norway. Capital stock: 500,000 kroner 1921 through 1927. Jersey held 39.6 per cent from 1921 through 1924 and 39.4 from 1925 through 1927. (See List C for other stockholders.)

28. North Texas Gas Company

   Organized by 1911 in Texas with capital of 5,000 shares ($100 par). Jersey held 3,242 shares in 1912, 3,567 in 1913, and had disposed of the stock by December, 1914.

29. Oesterreichisch-Amerikanische Petroleum-Gesellschaft (Austrian-American Oil Company)

Organized 1921 in Austria to market petroleum products. Capital stock: 5,000,000 Austrian kroner in 1921, 300,000,000 in 1922, 600,-000,000 in 1923, 6,000,000,000 in 1924, and 400,000 schillings from 1925 through 1927. Jersey held all stock from 1921 through 1927.

30. Ohio Fuel Supply Company, The
Organized 1907 in Ohio. Capital stock: 489,210 shares ($25 par) in 1912. Jersey held 65,978 shares (13 per cent) from 1912 through 1916 and sold them in 1917.

31. Oil Trading Company
Organized 1927 in Prague, Czechoslovakia, to take over the business in lubricants and miscellaneous products of the Americká petrolejářská společnost v Ceskoslovensku. Jersey held all the stock of 2,000,000 kroner in 1927.

32. Oil Trading Company (Mineraloel-Handels-Gesellschaft)
Organized 1927 in Vienna, Austria, to trade in lubricants and miscellaneous products in Austria and Hungary. Jersey held all the stock of 500,000 schillings in 1927.

33. Partridge (A. H.), Ltd.
Organized 1924 in England with 25,000 shares (£1 par) for manufacture and sale of candles. Jersey held 7,500 shares from 1924 through 1927.

34. Petroleum Industrie Maatschappij
Organized 1920 in Holland to market fuel oil. Capital stock: 5,000,-000 florins. Jersey held 75 per cent from 1920 through 1923 and 87.5 per cent from 1924 through 1927.

35. Refiners Oil Company, The
Organized in 1915 in Ohio for refining and marketing. By 1926 its capital was 7,878 shares of common, 1,117 of preferred, and 505 shares of participating preferred, all at $100 par. The latter two were increased in number to 1,398 and 608 shares, respectively, in 1927. Jersey held 3,939 shares of common stock in 1926 and 1927.

36. Rotterdamsch Petroleum Entrepot
Jersey held all the capital in 1920, 1921, and 1923. (See Lists A and C for further data.)

37. Shandon Candle Company, Limited
Organized 1924 in the Irish Free State to make and sell candles. Capital of £20,000. Jersey held 30 per cent from 1924 through 1927.

38. S.H.S. Amerikansko Petroleumsko, D.D. (or S.H.S. American Petroleum Company or Standard Oil Company of Yugoslavia)
Jersey held 92.5 per cent of the shares in 1921. (See Lists A and C for further data.)

39. Sociedad Espagnolea de Compras y Flitamentos (Société Espagnole d'Achats et d'Effrètements)

    Organized 1893 and reorganized in 1923 for refining and marketing in Spain. Capital stock: 10,000,000 pesetas in 1923 and 1924, and 15,000,000 from 1925 through 1927. Jersey held 10 per cent 1923 through 1927, while Ind. Babel y Nervión held 40 per cent and other Spanish interests the remaining 50 per cent.

40. Società Italiana Lubrificanti Bedford

    Organized 1925 in Italy to sell lubricants and miscellaneous petroleum products. Capital stock: 10,000,000 lire. Jersey held 20 per cent from 1925 through 1927. (See List C for other holdings.)

41. Société Auxiliaire de Transports

    Organized 1920 in France to transport petroleum products. Capital stock: 1,200 shares (500 francs par) from 1920 through 1922, 4,000 shares in 1923, 10,000 in 1924, and 20,000 from 1925 through 1927. Jersey held 2,000 shares in 1924 and 4,000 from 1925 through 1927. (See also List C.)

42. "Standard-Nobel w Polsce" Spolkałka Akcyjna; Standard-Nobel Company in Poland (also known as "Polnobel")

    Organized 1920 in Poland as Nobel Brothers Oil Industrial Company in Poland, Limited. Capital stock: 100,000,000 Polish marks, which was increased to 200,000,000 within the year, to 520,000,000 in 1921, to 1,170,000,000 in 1922, and to 2,340,000,000 in 1923. In 1925 merged with Olej Skalny and capital doubled and name changed to above. In 1920 the original stock was divided equally between the Nobels and the Posner Bank. Jersey then acquired a 25 per cent interest, the Nobels retaining 25 per cent and the Posner Bank 50 per cent. By 1925 the holdings of the Posner Bank and other local interests were 38.8 per cent, Nobels 21.4 per cent, Jersey 21.4 per cent, and Compagnie Standard Franco-Américaine 18.4 per cent. (See also List C.)

43. Standard Oil & Refining Company, Limited

    Jersey held 30,000 shares in 1920 and 120,000 at £1 in 1921. (See List A for further data.)

44. Standard Oil Company, S.A., Argentina (Standard Oil Company of Argentina)

    Organized 1922 for producing in Argentina. Capital stock: 3,000,000 pesos from 1922 through 1924 and 9,000,000 from 1925 through 1927. Jersey held all from 1922 through 1927.

45. Standard Oil Company of Bolivia

    Organized 1921 for producing in Bolivia. Capital stock: 7,500,000 bolivianos from 1922 through 1927, of which Jersey held all.

46. Standard Oil Company of Peru
    Organized 1926 for producing in Peru. Capital stock: 200,000 Peruvian pounds. Jersey held all in 1926 and 1927.

47. Standard Oil Company of Venezuela
    Organized 1921 for producing in Venezuela. Capital stock: 10,000,-000 bolívares, of which Jersey held all 1922 through 1927.

48. Standard Petroleum Co. (Glarus)
    Jersey held all the shares as non-consolidated in 1920. (See List A for further data.)

49. Standard Trust Aktiengesellschaft
    Organized 1920 in the Free State of Danzig as a holding company for Bapico stock. Jersey held capital stock of 50,000 marks from 1920 through 1922. Company liquidated in 1923.

50. Stewart Storage Corporation
    Organized 1927 in Delaware with capital of $500,000, all of which was held by Jersey.

51. Tagus Oil Company
    Jersey held 100 shares (100 escudos par) in 1920 and 1921. (See List A for further data.)

52. Tide Water Associated Oil Company
    Organized 1926 as a holding company in Delaware. Capital stock: 4,786,479 shares of common of no par value and 727,244 shares of preferred ($100 par) at the end of 1926; changed in 1927 to 4,776,323 and 727,509 shares, respectively. It held 78 per cent of the common stock of Tide Water Oil Company and 94.5 per cent of the stock of Associated Oil Co. in California by the end of 1926. Jersey held 1,078,-123 shares in 1926 and 1927.

53. Tide Water Oil Company
    Organized 1888 in New Jersey. Jersey increased its holdings from 102,094 shares (valued at $4,858,539) in 1912 to 808,592 (valued at $26,683,356) in 1925. The Jersey interest amounted to 43 per cent in 1912 and 40 per cent in 1925.

54. Tide-Water Pipe Company, Limited, The
    Organized 1878 in Pennsylvania. Capital stock: 6,250 voting shares and 13,750 nonvoting at $100 par in 1912 and 1913; changed to 62,500 voting shares in 1914. Jersey held 4 voting shares in 1912 and 1913 and 40 from 1914 through 1920.

55. Towarzyskwo "Olej Skalny," Społka Akcyjna ("Olej Skalny" Oil Company, Limited, The)
    Organized 1921 for exploration and producing in Poland. Capital stock: 25,000,000 Polish marks, 1921 through 1923; 50,000 zlotys in

1924. In 1925 company merged with Nobel Bros. Oil Industrial Co. in Poland, Ltd., taking over the latter's charter. Jersey held 70 per cent and Compagnie Standard Franco-Américaine 30 from 1921 through 1924.

56. United Oil Company
    Organized 1887 in Colorado. Capital stock: $2,700,000. Jersey held 17 per cent from 1912 through 1915, and disposed of it in 1916.

57. Vallö Oljeraffineri, Aktieselskabet
    Organized 1905 in Norway for refining at Vallö. By 1912 its capital stock was 2,500,000 kroner; increased to 4,000,000 in 1926. Jersey owned 40 per cent from 1919 through 1927 while Vestlandske held 21 per cent and Ostlandske 20 per cent.

58. Vestlandske Petroleumscompagni, Aktieselskabet
    Organized 1891 for marketing in northern and western Norway. Capital stock: 1,700,000 kroner 1912 through 1914, 3,400,000 from 1915 through 1919, and 5,100,000 from 1920 through 1927. Jersey held 0.5 per cent of the stock, 1922 through 1927. (See List C for other stockholders.)

In addition, the Jersey Company had small investments in three other oil companies during this period: two in liquidation from 1923 through 1926, Rheinisch-Westfalische Petroleum Gesellschaft mbH and Suddeutsche Petroleums Handels Gesellschaft; and Standard Oil Company of Cuba in which it held two shares in 1927.

Jersey also had investments in several diversified fields: Atlantic Mutual Insurance Company; Baltimore Chamber of Commerce; Baltimore Office Building; Bayonne Housing Corporation; Cascade Paper Company; Charleston, S. C., Dwelling Property; Chemists Building; Community House, Bayway; Exchange Membership; Housing Property, City of Elizabeth, N. J.; Klip Chemical Company; Meeker Foundry Company; Merritt-Chapman & Scott Corporation; Petroleum Casualty Company; Richmond-New York Steamship Company; Schuler Mercantile; and U. S. Daily Publishing Corp. By far the largest investment in any of these was that of $2,000,000 in the Baltimore Office Building in 1927.

Group C. Affiliates of Consolidated Companies

1. American Petroleum Company, "Société Anonyme Belge"
   American Petroleum Company (Holland) held all the stock, valued at 2,500,000 florins in 1919. (See List A for further data.)

2. American Petroleum Company (Holland)
   Standard Petroleum Co. (Glarus) held 11 shares in 1925 and 1926 and International Co., Vaduz, 11 in 1927. (See List A for further data.)

3. Americká petrolejářská společnost v Ceskoslovensku (American Petroleum Company of Czechoslovakia)

Compagnie Standard Franco-Américaine held 40 per cent of the stock, 1921 through 1927. (See List B for further data.)

4. Amerikanische Petroleum Anlagen, GmbH

    Organized 1894 in Germany with principal office at Neuss for shipping and storing petroleum products. By 1912 its capital was 750,000 marks, which American Petroleum Company (Holland) held from 1912 through 1927.

5. Amerikanische Petroleum Anlagen-Saarland, GmbH

    Organized 1924 in Saarbrucken for marketing. Capital stock: 500,000 French francs. American Petroleum Company, "S. A. Belge," held all the capital from 1924 through 1927.

6. Andian National Corporation, Limited

    Organized 1919 in Canada for operating pipeline in Colombia. Original capital 10,000 shares ($100 par—Canadian currency); changed to 1,000,000 shares of no par value in 1925 and to 3,000,000 shares in 1926 (of which 2,125,000 were issued in 1926 and 1927 and were valued on Andian's reports at $21,250,000). Imperial Oil, Limited, listed its investment in Andian at $686,000 in 1921, $1,150,000 in 1922, $965,500 in 1923, and $996,100 in 1924. In June, 1925, Imperial held 996,592 shares which it transferred to Colombia Investment Trust, incorporated in 1925 and wholly owned by International Petroleum Company Limited.

7. Apekol, Amerikanu Petrolejas Kompanija Latvija (Apekol Amerikanische Petroleum Kompanie in Lettland)

    Organized 1924 in Latvia for marketing. Capital stock: 100,000 lats. DAPG held 95 per cent from 1924 through 1927.

8. "Astra" Compañía Argentina de Petróleo, S.A. ("Astra" Argentina Sindicato Petrolifero)

    Organized 1915 in Argentina. Capital stock issued by 1927 was 5,499,375 bolivares (109,987½ shares). Standard Oil Company of Brazil held 723 shares in 1918, 867⅗ from 1919 through 1924, and 927⅗ from 1925 through 1927.

9. Baltisch-Amerikanische Petroleum-Import-Gesellschaft mbH (called Bapico)

    Organized 1919 to bring certain German tankers and local marketing properties under Danzig jurisdiction. Original capital of 250,000 marks was changed to 260,000 guilders in 1923. In 1919 was owned by Wilhelm Riedemann and others; from 1920 through 1922 by Standard Trust Aktiengesellschaft; from 1923 through 1926 by Standard Petroleum Co. (Glarus); and in 1927 by International Co., Vaduz.

10. Brown (J. A.), Sociedad en Comandita (silent partnership)

    Organized 1919 in Mexico to secure leases. Capital stock: 10,000 pesos. Compañía Transcontinental de Petróleo, S.A., held all stock from 1919 through 1927.

11. Câmpurile Petrolifere Baicoi (The Baicoi Oilfields)

Organized 1920 in Romania to explore for oil. Capital stock: 22,000,-000 lei from 1923 through 1927. Româno-Americana held 50.97 per cent from 1923 through 1927.

12. Charleston Natural Gas Company

Organized West Virginia in 1894 with capital of $200,000. Dissolved in 1913. Its statements were consolidated with those of the United Fuel Gas Company in 1912.

13. Columbia Natural Gas Company, The

Organized in 1891 in Pennsylvania as Patterson Natural Gas Company. Name changed to Harmony Natural Gas Company in 1909 and to above in 1926. Capital of $4,500,000 held by The Peoples Natural Gas Company in 1926 and 1927.

14. Compagnie Auxiliaire des Transports Internationaux

Organized 1913 in Belgium. By 1920, capital consisted of 2,800 shares (500 Belgian francs par); in 1922, 2,400 shares (250 francs par) were added. In 1925, both types of shares were valued at 250 francs par. American Petroleum Company, "S. A. Belge," held 100 shares in 1920 and 1921 and 200 from 1922 through 1927.

15. Compagnie Commerciale des Produits Pétrolifères

Bedford Petroleum Company, S.A.F., held 4 per cent of the stock from 1920 through 1922 and Compagnie Standard Franco-Américaine held 20 per cent in 1921 and 1922. (See Lists A and B for further data.)

16. Compagnie du Belge Gaz Catalytique

Organized 1922 in Belgium with a capital of 7,000,000 Belgian francs. Bedford Petroleum Company's holdings stood at 54,039 French francs in 1925 and 1926 and at 105,959 in 1927.

17. Compagnie Française des Pétroles, S.A.

Organized 1924 in France as a successor to Syndicat d'Etudes des Pétroles of 1923, under French government direction, to hold stock in various companies, including the Turkish Petroleum Company. Original capital consisted of 12,500 Class A shares and 37,500 Class B shares (both 500 francs par) to which were added 50,000 new Class B shares in 1926 and 2,500 Class A and 47,500 Class B shares in 1927. Many companies marketing in France took stock, including several in which Jersey Standard had an interest: L'Economique subscribed to 10,000 shares in 1924 but had reduced its holdings to a total subscription of 270 Class A and 2,430 Class B shares by the end of 1927. By 1927 the Compagnie Standard Franco-Américaine had subscribed to a total of 1,270 Class A and 2,430 Class B shares. Two non-consolidated companies also took stock. By 1927 the Compagnie Générale des Pétroles had subscribed to a total of 210 Class A and 840 Class B shares, while La Pétroléenne had subscribed to 667 Class A and 5,333 Class B shares.

18. Compagnie Générale des Pétroles pour l'Éclairage et l'Industrie
   Compagnie Standard Franco-Américaine held 9 per cent of the total stock in 1921, 18 in 1922 and 1923, 25 in 1924, and 22 from 1925 through 1927. (See List B.)

19. Compagnie Industrielle "Atlas," S.A.
   Organized 1905 in Belgium to manufacture lubricants as successor to Leduc Frères. Capital in 1924 was 600 shares at 1,000 Belgian francs each. American Petroleum Company (Holland) held all the shares from 1914 through 1918 and 1 share from 1922 through 1927. American Petroleum Company, "S. A. Belge," held all shares in 1919, 563 shares in 1920 and 1921, and 594 shares from 1922 through 1927. Company held stock in other companies.

20. Compagnie Pétrolifère, S.A., à Gand
   Organized 1891 in Belgium. By 1912 its capital comprised 200 shares at 500 Belgian francs. American Petroleum Company (Holland) held 149 shares from 1912 through 1918 and 1 share from 1920 through 1927. American Petroleum Company, "S. A. Belge," held 149 shares in 1919 and 194 shares from 1920 through 1927.

21. Companhia Maritima Brazileira, S.A.
   Organized 1921 in Brazil as a marine transporter of petroleum products. Capital stock: 5,000 shares at 100 milreis each. Standard Oil Co. of Brazil held all shares from 1922 through 1924 and West India Oil Company all from 1925 through 1927.

22. Compañía de Petróleo Mercedes, S.A.
   Organized 1927 in Mexico to explore and hold leases. Capital stock: 500,000 pesos, all held by Standard Oil Company of New Jersey.

23. Compañía Nacional de Petróleos, Limitada
   Standard Oil Company of Brazil held 65 per cent of the 7,500 shares from 1914 through 1917; Compañía Transcontinental held 65 per cent from 1920 through 1922. International Co., Vaduz, held all from 1925 through 1927. (See List B.)

24. Compañía Petrolera Minerva, S.A.
   Organized 1927 in Mexico to explore and hold leases. Capital stock: 400,000 pesos, of which the Standard Oil Company of New Jersey held 65 per cent.

25. Compañía Petrolera Neuvas Exploraciónes, S.A.
   Organized 1920 in Mexico to explore and secure leases. Capital stock: 50,000 pesos. Compañía Transcontinental held all from 1920 through

1926. The company became dormant after 1925, when it failed to comply with legal requirements.

26. Compañía Petrolera Olympia, S.A.

    Organized 1927 in Mexico to explore and secure leases. Capital stock: 300,000 pesos, of which Standard Oil Company of New Jersey held 99.97 per cent in 1927.

27. Compañía Petrolera Tamaulipas, S.A.

    Organized 1922 in Mexico to explore and produce oil. Capital stock: 1,000,000 pesos. Humble Oil & Refining Company held all the stock in 1922 and consolidated reports with its own for 1923 through 1927.

28. Compañía Petrolera Titania, S.A.

    Organized 1927 in Mexico to explore and hold leases. Capital stock: 300,000 pesos, of which 99.7 per cent was held by Standard Oil Company of New Jersey.

29. Compañía Transportadora de Petróleos

    Organized 1916 in Argentina for marine transport of petroleum products. Capital stock: 300 shares (100 pesos par), which was increased to 1,050 shares (1,000 pesos par) in 1921. West India Oil Company held 296 shares from 1916 through 1920 and 1,046 shares from 1921 through 1927.

30. Connecting Gas Company, The

    Hope Natural Gas Company held 2,375 shares from 1914 through 1927. (See also List A.)

31. Consumer Gasoline Supply Company

    Imperial Oil's investment was $10,000 (Canadian currency) in 1915, $20,000 in 1916, $30,000 in 1917, $50,000 in 1918, $49,500 in 1919, and $500 in 1920 and 1921.

32. Det Dansk-Tyske Petroleums-Kompagni

    Organized 1904 in Denmark. By 1923 its stock was 500,000 kroner, all held by Det Danske from 1923 through 1927.

33. Deutsche Petroleum-Licht-und Kraft-Gesellschaft mbH, Hamburg

    Organized in 1903 in Germany to sell Galician petroleum products but changed to American products in 1906 when DAPG invested in the company. Original name was Wachs & Flössner, Petroleumgesellschaft mbH, Dresden, which was changed in 1917 to Deutsche Petroleum und Beteiligungs Gesellschaft and by 1922 to above. DAPG held all the stock, consisting of 100,000 marks, from 1912 through 1917 and 1921 through 1922. Thereafter, company was in process of liquidation.

34. "Distributia" (Societate Anonimă pentru Distribuirea Produselor Petrolului)

    Organized 1908 to market petroleum products in Romania. Capital stock: 1,000,000 lei (200 shares at 5,000 each) from 1912 through 1927. Româno-Americana held 41 shares in 1912 and 28 from 1918 through 1927.

35. Eesti-Petrol, Aktiengesellschaft, Reval

Organized 1925 to market petroleum products in Esthonia. Capital stock: 4,000 shares of 100 Esthonian kroons each. DAPG held 55 per cent in 1925 and 85 per cent in 1926 and 1927.

36. "Favorit," Petroleum-Kannengeschaft mbH

Organized 1906 as a kerosene peddling company in Prussia. Capital stock: 20,000 marks. DAPG held all from 1913 through 1927. Company existed in name only from 1921 on.

37. Galena-Signal Oil Company of Canada Limited

Organized 1920 in Canada to sell lubricating oils and greases. Capital stock: $1,000,000 (Canadian currency). Imperial Oil, Limited, acquired all the stock in 1927.

38. Ghent Petroleum Company, S.A.

Organized in 1899 to take over business of E. Sudan & Co. Capital stock: 2,000 preferred shares of 500 francs and 2,000 common shares of no par from 1912 through 1927. American Petroleum Company (Holland) held 1,146 preferred and 1,349 common from 1912 through 1918. American Petroleum Company, "S. A. Belge," held 1,146 preferred in 1919, 1,469 in 1920 and 1921, 824 from 1922 through 1924, and 889 from 1925 through 1927; 1,349 common shares in 1919 and 40 from 1920 through 1927. Company in process of liquidation from 1921 through 1931.

39. Groupement Charbonnier Rouen

Bedford Petroleum Company's investment was stated at 877,250 francs in 1920 and at only 80 from 1921 through 1926.

40. Hanseatische Handels-und Beteiligungs-Gesellschaft mbH

Set up in 1917 in Hamburg, Germany, as holding company. Capital: 1,000,000 marks in 1917, which was reduced to 25,000 by 1921 and 500 reichsmarks in 1924. DAPG held all in 1918 and 1919; Standard Petroleum Co. (Glarus) held all from 1921 through 1926 and transferred it to the International Co., Vaduz, in 1927.

41. Hanseatische Petroleum-Handels-Gesellschaft mbH, Hamburg

Organized 1908 in Germany as kerosene peddling company. Capital stock: 20,000 marks, all held by DAPG 1913 through 1927 (valued at only 500 reichsmarks from 1924 through 1927).

42. Hesperus Petroleum-Handels-Gesellschaft mbH

Organized 1908 in Germany as kerosene peddling company. Capital stock: 50,000 marks, all held by DAPG 1913 through 1921. Company liquidated by 1922.

43. Hid Islenzka steinoliuhluafjelag

     Business started in Iceland in 1889 by brokers in Copenhagen. Changed to an office in Iceland in 1907 and organized in Iceland in 1914 under name of Det Islanske Petroleum Company. Its name was changed to Hid Islandske Petroleum Company by 1918 and to above by 1924. Capital stock: 300,000 kroner from 1914 through 1917, 600,000 from 1918 through 1922, 300,000 in 1923, 150,000 in 1924, 75,000 in 1925, and 48,000 in 1927. Det Danske held 94.2 per cent from 1914 through 1916, 93 in 1917, 89.4 in 1918 and 1919, 90 from 1920 through 1922, and 91.7 from 1923 through 1927.

44. Hollandsche Petroleum Vereniging

     Organized 1896 in Holland. Capital stock: 30,000 florins by 1912. Company liquidated in 1913. American Petroleum Company (Holland) held all in 1912.

45. Humble Pipe Line Company

     Organized 1913 as the Southern Pipe Line Company and name changed to above in 1919. Capital stock issued: $15,000 in 1919, $12,-000,000 from 1920 through 1923, $24,000,000 in 1925 and 1926, and $44,000,000 in 1927, all held by Humble Oil & Refining Company, which consolidated the pipeline earnings with its own from 1919 through 1927.

46. Imperial Oil Refineries, Limited

     Organized 1917 in Canada as Imperial Oil, Limited; name was changed to Imperial Petroleum Company, Limited, in 1919 and to above in 1923. This refining company had a capital of $50,000,000 (Canadian currency) from 1918 through 1922 and $500,000 from 1923 through 1927. Imperial Oil held all but 5 shares of $100 par from 1918 through 1927.

47. Imperial Pipe Line Company, Limited, The

     Organized 1914 in Canada to operate a pipeline from Cygnet, Ohio, to Port Huron, Michigan. Capital stock: $280,000 (Canadian currency) from 1914 through 1916 and $680,000 from 1917 through 1927. Imperial Oil held all but 5 shares of $100 par from 1914 through 1927.

48. International Co., Vaduz

     All stock held by Petroleum Import Compagnie from 1922 through 1924. (See List A for further data.)

49. International Petroleum Company Limited

     Organized 1914 in Canada to take over the business of London and Pacific Petroleum Company (organized in 1889), which had a concession in Peru. In 1916 West Coast Oil Fuel Co., Limited, was acquired (see Lists A and C). In 1920 company was reorganized to acquire the assets of The Tropical Oil Co. Capital stock: 100,000 shares preference stock (par value £1 sterling), 1914 through 1927; 1,253,401 shares common stock ($5.00 par value) from 1914 through 1919, 2,601,488 in 1920, and 7,123,544 shares of no par value from 1921 through 1927. Imperial Oil held 99.995 per cent of the preference from 1914 through 1927; 33.8 per cent of the common from 1914 through 1919, 72.3 per cent in 1920, and 56 per cent from 1921 through 1927.

50. Königsberger Handels-Compagnie
    DAPG held 1,145 shares, 1912 through 1916. (See List B for further data.)

51. Kohlenheber Gesellschaft
    DAPG held stock valued at 35,000 marks from 1912 through 1923 and 3,500 reichsmarks in 1924 and 1925.

52. Krooks Petroleum & Oljeaktiebolag
    Organized 1896 in Sweden to market petroleum products. Capital stock: 1,500,000 kroner, 1912 through 1914; 2,000,000 in 1915 and 1916; 4,000,000 from 1917 through 1923; and 6,000,000 from 1924 through 1927. Det Danske held 50.33 per cent in 1912 through 1914, 63 from 1915 through 1923, 72 in 1924, and 73 from 1925 through 1927.

53. "La Columbia," Società Marittima (per trasporto di petrolio e derivati)
    SIAPP held all the stock from 1917 through 1920 and 52 per cent from 1921 through 1927. (See List A.)

54. "La Mediterranea," Società Anonima
    Organized 1906 under the laws of Tunis and Italy and reorganized in 1909 in Tunisia for business in refined oils. Capital stock: 1,500,000 lire frm 1912 through 1927. SIAPP (Società Italo-Americana pel Petrolio) held 65 per cent of the stock from 1912 through 1919 and all for 1924 through 1927.

55. La Pétroléenne, S.A.
    Compagnie Standard Franco-Américaine held 8 per cent of the stock in 1923, 10.56 in 1924 and 1925, and 28 in 1926 and 1927. (See List B for further data.)

56. L'Economique, Société Anonyme de Distribution de Pétrole et Essence
    Bedford Petroleum Company, S.A.F., held 5 per cent of the stock from 1920 through 1923, 6 in 1924, and 6.3 from 1925 through 1927. Compagnie Standard Franco-Américaine held 20 per cent from 1921 through 1927. (See also Lists A and B.)

57. Lianosoff Fils, G.M., Société de Production de Naphte
    Organized 1907 for producing and refining in Russia. Capital stock: 300,000 shares of 100 roubles each. The Nobel Bros. Petroleum Production Co. was among the principal owners with 100,000 shares owned directly and 12,000 indirectly. From 1920 through 1927 the Standard

Petroleum Co. (Glarus) secured 33,200 shares, so that the combined Nobel-Jersey holdings were enough to control the company.

58. Lobitos Oilfields, Ltd.
    Imperial Oil had an investment in this company of $29,595 in 1914.

59. Maatschappij "Pétrolifère," S.A., à Gand
    Organized 1910 in Holland to peddle kerosene. American Petroleum Company (Holland) held all 50 shares at 1,000 florins each from 1912 through 1927. Company liquidated in 1927.

60. Maatschappij tot Detailverkoop van Petroleum "De Automaat" (Petroleum Retail Company "The Automaton")
    Organized 1898 in Holland to peddle kerosene; charter renewed in 1921. American Petroleum Company (Holland) held all 400 shares of stock (1,000 florins par) from 1912 through 1927.

61. Manufacturers Gas Company of Greensburg
    The Peoples Natural Gas Co. held 200 shares at $50 each from 1912 through 1915 and 2,744 shares (for a total investment of $236,450) from 1916 through 1919.

62. Mannheim-Bremer Petroleum-Aktiengesellschaft
    Organized 1896 in Germany for transportation and storage tanks on the Rhine. Capital stock: 3,000,000 marks. DAPG held 75 per cent from 1912 through 1921; American Petroleum Company (Holland) held the remaining 25 per cent from 1912 through 1920. Company in liquidation from 1921 through 1925.

63. Mineral A. G. Wangen near Olten
    Organized 1925 in Switzerland as a local marketing company. Capital stock: 100,000 Swiss francs, all held in 1927 by Petroleum Import Compagnie.

64. Mineraloel-Raffinerie vorm. August Korff (Bremen)
    DAPG held 47.3 per cent of the stock from 1912 through 1916 and American Petroleum Company (Holland) held 7.3 per cent from 1912 through 1927. (See List B for further data.)

65. Naamlooze Vennootschap Hollandsche Maatschappij tot verkoop von zuivere Petroleum (Pure Oil Company of Holland)
    Organized 1898 and reorganized in 1911 in Holland for marketing petroleum products. Capital stock: 500,000 florins held by the Standard Petroleum Co. (Glarus) from 1912 through 1924 and by American Petroleum Company (Holland) from 1925 through 1927. The company for a time held stock in three other Pure Oil companies (London, Berne, and Brussels).

66. Naamlooze Vennootschap Nederlandsche Koloniale Petroleum Maatschappij

American Petroleum Company (Holland) held all the shares from 1912 through 1925. (See List B for further data.)

67. Naamlooze Vennootschap Petroleum Maatschappij "Holland"
    Organized 1922 in Holland to retail petroleum products. Capital stock: 50,000 florins. American Petroleum Company (Holland) held all, 1922 through 1927.

68. Nobel Bros. Petroleum Production Company
    Organized 1879 in Russia for producing, refining, and other functions. Purchased stock in many other companies, often exchanging stock with them. Before World War I capital comprised 2,000 organizers' shares at 5,000 roubles par and 140,000 common shares at 250. The Nobel family and affiliated interests held 25 per cent of the latter. In 1920 it was arranged that Standard Petroleum Co. (Glarus) should take 18,000 of the Nobels' common shares, but by 1927 only 13,000 had been delivered.

69. Norddeutsche Petroleum Gesellschaft mbH
    Organized 1912 in Germany as a peddling company. Capital stock: 30,000 marks. Name changed to above from Norddeutsche Petroleum-Werke GmbH in 1912. Inactive from 1921 on. DAPG held all the stock from 1913 through 1927, but from 1924 through 1927 valued it at only 500 reichsmarks.

70. Nordisk Benzin Compagni, Aktieselskabet
    Organized 1904 in Denmark to market benzine in northern Denmark. Capital stock: 300,000 kroner. Det Danske held all from 1912 through 1927.

71. Northwest Company, Limited
    Organized 1917 in Canada to search for petroleum. Capital stock: $500,000 (Canadian currency), of which Imperial Oil held 28 per cent in 1917, 40 in 1918, 99.9 from 1919 through 1927.

72. Ostlandske Petroleumscompagni, Aktieselskabet
    Organized in 1893 in Norway for marketing of petroleum products. Capital stock: 480 shares at 2,500 kroner from 1912 through 1916, at 5,000 kroner par in 1917 and 1918, and 10,000 kroner par from 1919 through 1927. Det Danske held 254 shares in 1912, 253 shares from 1913 through 1918, and 254 from 1919 through 1927.

73. Petroleum-Handels-Gesellschaft
    Organized 1893 in Switzerland as Schweizerische Petroleum-Handels-Gesellschaft; name changed to above in 1921. By 1912 it was a peddling company with shares of 200,000 Swiss francs and share warrants for 100,000 francs (the latter were eliminated in 1921). DAPG held 60 per cent from 1912 through 1922, and SIAPP held 40 per cent from 1912 through 1923. By 1924 all the shares had been transferred to Pico, which

held them at reduced value, 1924 through 1926, and transferred them in 1927 to International Co., Vaduz.

74. Petroleum Import Compagnie (called Pico)
    DAPG held 60 per cent of the stock of 400,000 Swiss francs, 1912 through 1916, and SIAPP held 40 per cent, 1912 through 1919. SIAPP's holdings were transferred to Standard Petroleum Co. (Glarus) in 1920 and in 1925 to International Co., Vaduz. (See List A for further data.)

75. Pétrolifère Nationale, S.A., à Gand
    Organized 1898 in Belgium. Capital was 100 shares (500 Belgian francs par) 1912 through 1927. American Petroleum Company (Holland) held 100 shares 1912 through 1918 and 1 share 1921 through 1927. American Petroleum Company, "S. A. Belge," held 100 shares in 1919 and 94 shares from 1920 through 1927.

76. Pétrolifère Luxembourgeoise, S.A.
    Organized 1920 in Luxembourg as a marketing company. Capital stock: 200 shares (500 Luxembourg francs par). American Petroleum Company (Holland) held 1 share from 1921 through 1927. American Petroleum Company, "S. A. Belge," held 194 shares from 1920 through 1927.

77. Petrolul Carpatilor Société Anonyme Roumaine
    Organized 1926 as a producing company in Romania. Capital stock: 12,000,000 lei by 1929. Româno-Americana held 100,000 lei in the company in 1926 and 1927.

78. Pure Oil Company GmbH
    Organized 1910 in Hamburg, Germany, to take over two Pure Oil tankers, which were sold during the war. After the war company sold refined oils and in 1927 changed to lubricants. Capital stock: 10,000,000 marks in 1912; changed to 1,800,000 reichsmarks in 1924 and to 20,000 reichsmarks in 1927. Standard Petroleum Co. (Glarus) held all from 1911 through 1926 and transferred holdings to International Co., Vaduz, in 1927. Company held stock in "POCOL" Petroleum Gesellschaft mbH organized in 1909 in Germany.

79. Pure Oil Company, Limited, The
    Organized 1896 in London, England, for marketing petroleum products. By 1922 its capital was £5,000 and by 1923 £10,000. United States Petroleum Company, S.A., held the stock in 1921 and 1922; N. V. Hollandsche Maatschappij in 1923 and 1924; Standard Petroleum Co. (Glarus) in 1926; and International Co., Vaduz, in 1927.

80. Pure Oil Company Gesellschaft für Petroleumvertrieb Berne
    Formed 1921 in Switzerland for marketing kerosene. Capital stock: 300 shares of 500 Swiss francs each, 1921 through 1927. N. V. Hollandsche Maatschappij transferred 298 shares in 1923 to Standard Petro-

leum Co. (Glarus) and latter transferred them to International Co., Vaduz, in 1927. Company was then being liquidated.

81. Queen City Oil Company, Limited, The

    Organized 1896 and reorganized in 1915 in Canada for crude oil storage. Capital stock: $50,000 (Canadian currency); reduced to $25,-000 in 1923. Imperial Oil held 99 per cent from 1918 through 1922 and 98 per cent from 1923 through 1926.

82. Raffineria Triestina di Olii Minerali

    Organized 1891 to produce in Galicia and to refine in Trieste. In 1920 its capital was 5,000 shares at 2,000 lire, held by SIAPP from 1920 through 1927.

83. Reserve Gas Company

    Hope Natural Gas Company held 11,126 shares from 1913 through 1916, 17,626 of the 35,250 shares from 1917 through 1919, and 20,001 of the 40,000 shares from 1920 through 1927. (See List A.)

84. Rheinische Petroleum Aktiengesellschaft

    Organized 1903 in Germany. Capital stock: 100,000 marks by 1912. Liquidated by end of 1922. American Petroleum Company (Holland) held all from 1912 through 1919.

85. River Gas Company, The

    Hope Natural Gas Company held $16,000 from 1913 through 1927. (See List A.)

86. Rotterdamsch Petroleum Entrepot

    DAPG held all stock 1924 through 1927. (See Lists A and B.)

87. Royalite Oil Company, Limited

    Organized 1921 in Canada as a producing and refining company. Capital stock: 40,000 shares of $25 par (Canadian currency), of which only 24,600 were issued in 1921 (no report for 1922). Fully issued 1923 through 1925 and changed in 1926 to 400,000 shares without par. Imperial Oil's investment $207,500 in 1921 and 1922, $399,963 in 1923, and $433,003 from 1924 through 1927.

88. Russian General Oil Corporation, Limited

    Organized 1912 in England as a holding company. Capital stock: 2,500,000 shares at £1 each which were increased to 4,500,000 shares in 1922. The Nobel Bros. Petroleum Production Company held 952,500 shares directly and 105,000 indirectly. It was arranged that shares should be purchased from outsiders so that Standard Petroleum Co. (Glarus) would hold 195,000 shares, but only 191,710 shares were actually secured between 1920 and 1927.

89. St. Paul Petroleum Tanks, Limited

    Organized 1900 in England to take over oil storage installations in

Malta and Gazo islands. Capital stock: £50,000, of which SIAPP held 65 per cent from 1912 through 1927.

90. Schlesische Petroleum-Gesellschaft mbH

Organized 1908 in Prussia as a peddling company. Capital stock: 20,000 marks. DAPG held all from 1913 through 1919. Liquidated by 1925.

91. S.H.S. Amerikansko Petroleumsko, D.D. (S.H.S. American Petroleum Company or Standard Oil Company of Yugoslavia)

Standard Petroleum Co. (Glarus) held 4,250 shares in 1923, 5,000 in 1924, and 100,000 shares in 1925 and 1926. These shares were transferred to International Co., Vaduz, in 1927 which in the same year sold them to Standard Oil Company of New York. (See Lists A and B.)

92. Skandinavisk-Amerikansk Petroleums-Aktieselskabet

Organized 1904 in Denmark for marketing. Capital stock: 6,000 shares (500 kroner par), reduced to 150 kroner par in 1923. Det Danske held 609 shares in 1913, 2,688 from 1914 through 1916, 3,098 in 1918 and 1919, 3,118 in 1920, 5,968 in 1921, 5,982 in 1922, and 5,995 from 1923 through 1927.

93. Skanska Petroleum Aktiebolaget

Organized 1896 in Sweden for marketing. Capital stock: 500,000 kroner in 1912 and 1913, 1,000,000 from 1914 through 1919, and 1,500,000 from 1920 through 1927. Det Danske increased its holdings from 60 per cent in 1912 to 62.5 per cent from 1924 through 1927.

94. Sociedad Anonima Surtidores Wico

Organized 1924 in Argentina to operate street pump concessions in Buenos Aires. Capital stock: 1,000,000 pesos. West India Oil Company held all from 1924 through 1927.

95. Sociedad Naviera Chilena de Transportes

Organized 1923 in Chile for transportation. Capital stock: 400,000 pesos, which West India Oil Company held from 1923 through 1927.

96. Società Anonima Petrolio Estrazione e Raffinazione

Organized 1923 in Italy with capital of 5,000 shares of 1,000 lire. SIAPP held all from 1925 through 1927.

97. Società Anonima "Porto Vado" pel Impianto Escercizio Depositi Olii Combustibili

Organized 1920 in Italy with capital of 2,000 shares at 1,000 lire, of which SIAPP held 40 per cent from 1922 through 1927.

98. Società Importazione Vendita Olii Pesanti

Organized Italy in 1926 for importation and sale of heavy mineral oils in ports of Savona and Vado Ligure. Capital stock: 5,000,000 lire. SIAPP held 80 per cent in 1926 and 1927.

99. Società Italiana Lubrificanti Bedford
    SIAPP held 55 per cent from 1925 through 1927 and Bedford Petroleum Company, S.A.F., held 20 per cent from 1925 through 1927. (See List B.)

100. Società Italiana Rivendita Automatica Benzina
    Organized in 1924 in Italy to market curb-pumps. Capital stock: 2,000,000 lire. SIAPP held all in 1926 and 1927.

101. Società Meridionale pel Commercio del Petrolio
    Organized 1898 in Italy and merged with SIAPP in 1927. Capital by 1912 was 1,000,000 lire, of which SIAPP held 60.7 per cent from 1912 through 1924 and all in 1925 and 1926.

102. Società Nord Africana des Petroles
    Bedford Petroleum Company's investment was 2,250,000 francs in 1927.

103. Società per Gli Olii Minerali
    Organized 1896 in Italy with bulk plants for handling both American and Russian oil and merged with SIAPP in 1927. Capital: 2,400 shares at 42.5 lire in 1912, which was increased to 50 in 1915 and 500 in 1926. SIAPP held 52 per cent from 1912 through 1926.

104. Société Anonyme Pétrolea
    DAPG held 40 per cent 1912 through 1916, and SIAPP 26.5 per cent 1912 through 1922. (See List A for further data.)

105. Société Anonyme pour la Vente des Pétroles, ci-devant H. Rieth & Compagnie
    Organized 1896 in France to trade and transport petroleum products on the Rhine. Capital stock: 495 shares at 5,000 francs by 1912. American Petroleum Company (Holland) held 300 shares from 1912 through 1922 and 100 from 1923 through 1925. American Petroleum Company, "S. A. Belge," held 495 shares in 1926 and 1927. Company in process of liquidation after 1921 and its business absorbed by its parent.

106. Société Auxiliaire de Transports
    Bedford Petroleum Company, S.A.F., held 1,000 shares from 1920 through 1922, 3,900 in 1923, 2,900 in 1924, and 5,800 from 1925 through 1927. Compagnie Standard Franco-Américaine held 3,000 shares in 1924 and 6,000 from 1925 through 1927. L'Economique held 3,000 shares in 1924 and 6,000 from 1925 through 1927. (See also List B.)

107. Société Bedford Ibérique
    Organized 1924 in France to market lubricants and asphalt in Spain and Portugal. Capital stock: 1,200 shares of 500 francs, increased to 4,000 shares in 1925. Bedford Petroleum Company held 31 per cent from 1924 through 1927.

108. Société Tunisienne des Pétroles

Organized 1904 in France and Tunisia, with principal office in Tunis, for marketing. By 1912 its capital was 800,000 francs; increased to 1,600,000 in 1919 and to 3,200,000 in 1926. SIAPP held 65 per cent from 1912 through 1925 and 80.4 in 1926 and 1927.

109. "Sperantza," Societate Anonimă pentru exploatarea și explorarea produselor solului și subsolului

Organized 1899 in Romania for producng. Original capital authorized of 3,000 shares of 500 lei each, of which 2,912 shares were issued by 1921. Capital increased to 36,000,000 lei by 1927. Româno-Americana's holdings increased from 31 per cent in 1912 to 58.7 per cent from 1923 through 1927.

110. "Standard-Nobel w Polsce" Spolkałka Akcyjna (Standard-Nobel Company in Poland) (also called "Polnobel")

Compagnie Standard Franco-Américaine held 15 per cent of stock in 1922, 18.34 in 1924, and 18.4 from 1925 through 1927. (See List B.)

111. Standard Pipe Line Company, Incorporated

Organized 1923 in Louisiana to take over pipelines which had formerly been owned by Standard Oil Company of Louisiana and connecting trunk line in Arkansas owned by Prairie Pipe Line Company. Capital stock: $25,000,000; all but a few shares held by Louisiana Standard from 1923 through 1927. Its statements were consolidated with those of parent.

112. Strassen-Tankwagen Gesellschaft (Street Tank Wagon Business, Düren)

Organized 1903 and liquidated by 1925. Capital was 10,000 marks by 1912. American Petroleum Company (Holland) held 55 per cent from 1912 through 1918, and American Petroleum Company, "S. A. Belge," held 55 per cent in 1919 and 1920.

113. Sudan Frères & Compagnie, Ghent

American Petroleum Company (Holland) held half the shares, valued at 131,579 florins, from 1912 through 1914.

114. Sydsvenska Petroleums Aktiebolaget

Organized 1898 in Sweden for marketing. Capital stock by 1912 of 720 shares (1,000 kroner par); increased by 1917 to 1,600 shares. Det Danske held 361 shares from 1912 through 1916, 922 from 1917 through 1923, and 990 from 1924 to 1927.

115. Technik & Finanz, A.-G.

Organized in 1926 in Switzerland as a holding company for shares of Deutsche Gasoline A. G. Berlin. Capital stock: 1,000 shares (500 Swiss francs par), increased to 5,000 shares in 1927. International Co., Vaduz, held 25 per cent in 1926 and 1927.

116. Towarzyskwo "Olej Skalny," Społka Akcyjna ("Olej Skalny" Oil Company, Limited, The)

    Compagnie Standard Franco-Américaine held a 40 per cent interest from 1921 through 1924. (See also List B.)

117. Transit and Storage Company

    Organized 1917 in Delaware to operate tankers under charter and storage tanks. Capital stock: $100,000, of which 3,009 shares of no par value issued. Imperial Oil's holdings valued at $215,000 in 1917 and 1918 and $300,000 (3,000 shares) from 1919 through 1927.

118. Transit Company, Limited

    Organized 1916 in Canada to rent tank-car equipment. Capital stock: $250,000 (Canadian currency), which was increased to $500,000 in 1919. Imperial Oil held 59.8 per cent from 1916 through 1918 and 49.9 from 1919 through 1927.

119. Vestkustens Petroleum Aktiebolag

    Organized 1895 to market in Sweden. By 1912 its capital stock was 393 shares at 2,500 kroner and, by 1924, 400 shares at 5,000 kroner. Det Danske held 197 shares from 1912 through 1923 and 393 shares from 1924 through 1927.

120. Vestlandske Petroleumscompagni, Aktieselskabet

    Det Danske held 50.58 per cent of the stock from 1912 through 1927. (See also List B.)

121. West Coast Oil Fuel Company, Limited

    The Imperial Oil Company, Limited, holdings valued at $346,846 (Canadian currency) in 1914 and 1915. (See List A.)

122. Westfalische Petroleum Gesellschaft mbH

    Organized 1903 in Germany to trade in petroleum and empty barrels. Capital of 100,000 marks by 1912. DAPG held 75 per cent from 1912 through 1920 and all in 1921 and 1922.

123. West India Oil Refining Company of Cuba

    Organized 1919. Capital stock: $1,595,900, which was increased in 1920 to $4,500,000. West India Oil Refining Company (Kentucky) held all but 5 shares of $100 par from 1919 through 1922; West India Oil Refining Company (Delaware) held all the stock, 1923 through 1927. In 1926 Standard Oil Company of Cuba was formed with $5,000,000 common and $5,000,000 preferred stock to take over refining and marketing property in Cuba. All its stock, except for 2 shares, was held by West India Oil Refining Company of Cuba. The statements for these two companies were consolidated with that of West India Oil Refining Company (Delaware) from 1923 through 1927.

124. Winnipeg Oil Company, Limited
   Imperial's holdings were valued at $915,290 (Canadian currency) in 1919.

In addition, several companies in List A had small investments in a number of other companies. Information on most of these is scanty, and the nature of the business of many cannot be determined exactly. These holdings were as follows:

Petroleum Companies:

Eschweiler Petroleum Import GmbH; Mineraloel Handels und Beteils Gesellschaft; Pechelbronn, S.A. d'Exploitation Minières; Ranney Oil Mining Company; Société Alsace Lorraine des Rech Minières; Société Nationale des Rech et Trait; Société Anonyme Georges Michoud, Lausanne.

Miscellaneous Companies:

Banca del Piccalo com Venice; Brave Water Company; Bulletin des Halles; Central Colos Inc.; Consolidated Sales Book & Wax Paper, Ltd.; Courier des Pétroles; Deutsche Seevericherungs; Goodwill Newfoundland Purchase; Hamburger Luftschiffhallen Ges.; Ioco Townsite Limited; Macoris Light & Power Co.; Monongahela Development Company; Outdoor Advertising, Ltd.; Pennsylvania Linseed Products Company; Perfection Stove Co. Ltd.; Santa Clara Sugar Co.; Schwiemer Hoftenbalm; Società Coop. Turino; Società Generale di esercizi con Automobili; Società Incremento Automobilismo e Sport; Società La Marconi International; Società Telephoni Automatici; Società Termino Electrica Umbra; Société Potasse d'Alsace; Syndicat d'Aviation de Cabourg; Sylvan Manufacturing Co.

Appendix 2

Selected Operating Statistics

Table I: **COMPARATIVE TRENDS IN BUSINESS**
of Standard Oil Company (New Jersey) and Affiliates
1912-1927

	Jersey Company and Affiliates						
			Net Value[a]		Jersey Com- pany Common	World Con- sumption of	Wholesale Price Index
Year	Crude Oil Run to Stills	Net Earnings (Published)	Affil- iates	Jersey Company	Stock High for Year	Petroleum Products	(All com- modities)
1913	+6.9	+30.2	+19.7	−4.5	+4.4	+6.2	+0.1
1914	−3.0	−31.2	+8.2	+4.0	−2.9	−0.6	−2.5
1915	+18.1	+93.2	+14.8	+14.1	+31.3	+10.5	+2.1
1916	+3.1	+16.5	+14.3	+14.5	+25.4	+8.8	+23.0
1917	+14.2	+14.1	+26.2	+19.7	+11.9	+5.5	+37.4
1918	+11.8	−28.1	+23.7	+17.7	−18.3	+6.0	+11.7
1919	+19.9	+34.2	+14.3	+23.6	+22.0	+8.9	+5.6
1920	+18.6	+110.9	+23.6	+27.7	+14.0	+20.0	+11.4
1921	+3.1	−79.4	+3.5	0	−15.6	+3.1	−36.8
1922	+7.6	+36.6	+5.5	+1.9	¦30.2	+10.5	−0.9
1923	+13.9	+21.8	+3.7	+2.8	−12.0	+21.4	+4.0
1924	+27.5	+43.9	+8.8	+5.6	−4.5	+7.9	−2.5
1925	+1.5	+37.3	+10.7	+8.4	+11.8	+5.1	+5.6
1926	+0.2	+5.8	+11.1	+7.5	−2.4	+9.8	+3.4
1927	+13.5	−65.6	[b]	−11.9	−10.8	+4.9	−4.6

[a] Total assets minus current liabilities.
[b] Not available.
Source: World consumption figure from National Industrial Conference Board, The Petroleum Almanac. 341.

Wholesale Price Index from U. S. Bureau of the Census, Historical Statistics of the U. S., 1789-1945, 233. All other figures from SONJ, Fin. Recs.; Stat.; Annual Reports.

Table II: **DIVIDENDS AND INCOME STATEMENTS**
Standard Oil Company (New Jersey) and Affiliates

All dollar figures in thousands except dividends per common share

Cash dividends, Jersey Standard, 1912-1927

	1912	1913	1914	1915	1916	1917	1918	1919
Common stock, total	$19,668	$59,003[a]	$19,668	$19,668	$19,668	$19,668	$19,668	$19,668
Common stock, per share[b]	20.00	60.00[a]	20.00	20.00	20.00	20.00	20.00	20.00
Preferred stock, total[c]	—	—	—	—	—	—	—	1,551

Income statements, Jersey Standard and affiliates,[d] 1919-1927

	1919	1920	1921	1922	1923
Gross earnings[e]	$454,759	$659,573	$478,393	$328,287	$367,334
Other income					
Jersey's portion					
of consolidated affiliates' earnings	43,511	91,839	26,342	33,355	40,788
Dividends from nonconsolidated affiliates[f]	2,919	2,400	1,743	32	225
Interest[g]	4,289	8,332	8,204	4,709	5,409
Sundries[g]	300	5,675	8,361	5,695	2,857
Total income	$505,778	$767,819	$523,043	$372,078	$416,612
Costs and expenses[g]					
Costs	403,335	574,253	460,781	306,656	340,656
General expenses	6,635	8,915	9,461	7,773	8,690
Depreciation	3,822	6,083	8,083	11,407	10,173
Total costs and expenses	$413,792	$589,251	$478,325	$325,836	$359,519
Net income before federal taxes	91,986	178,568	44,718	46,241	57,093
Federal income and excess profits taxes[g]	14,000	14,107	10,872	—	799
Net income after taxes	$ 77,986	$164,461	$ 33,846	$ 46,241	$ 56,294

---

[a] Extra dividend representing distribution of funds received back from disaffiliated companies.

[b] Common stock of $100 par changed in December, 1920, to $25 par, with four new shares substituted for one old share. Dividends for 1920 are reported on $100 par basis. In December, 1922, a stock dividend was declared of four new shares for one old share held. The dividend rate for 1922 is figured on the undivided stock; thereafter the dividend should be multiplied by five to get the rate per share held in 1922.

[c] Preferred stock of $100 par was issued in 1919, addi-

tional preferred was issued in 1920, and all preferred stock was retired in 1927.

[d] Earnings statements are nonconsolidated for 1919 through 1924 and consolidated thereafter. Specific differences between the two periods are noted below.

[e] For the period 1919 through 1924, this figure includes gross sales, marine earnings, and miscellaneous earnings of Jersey Standard only (marine earnings and miscellaneous earnings are recorded separately on Jersey Standard books for certain years, but were combined for consistency's sake in making up this table).

Table II *(cont.):* **DIVIDENDS AND INCOME STATEMENTS**
Standard Oil Company (New Jersey) and Affiliates

All dollar figures in thousands except dividends per common share

Cash dividends, Jersey Standard, 1912-1927

1920	1921	1922	1923	1924	1925	1926	1927	
$19,668	$19,702	$19,843	$20,014	$20,182	$20,396	$23,231	$35,066	Common stock, total
20.00	5.00	5.00	1.00	1.00	1.00	1.125	1.50	Common stock, per share[b]
10,036	13,767	13,855	13,998	13,998	13,998	13,998	3,500	Preferred stock, total[c]

Income statements, Jersey Standard and affiliates,[d] 1919-1927

1924	1925	1926	1927	
$409,996	$1,122,683	$1,283,555	$1,256,505	Gross earnings[e]
				Other income
				Jersey's portion
60,750				of consolidated affiliates' earnings
1,017	22,839	25,409	18,082	Dividends from nonconsolidated affiliates[f]
6,600				Interest[g]
2,168				Sundries[g]
$480,531	$1,145,522	$1,308,964	$1,274,587	Total income
				Costs and expenses[g]
377,437	972,694	1,119,236	1,135,147[h]	Costs
10,608				General expenses
10,293	48,407	55,968	74,899	Depreciation
$398,338	$1,021,101	$1,175,204	$1,210,046	Total costs and expenses
82,193	124,421	133,760	64,541	Net income before federal taxes
1,176	13,189	16,108	24,118	Federal income and excess profits taxes[g]
$ 81,017	$ 111,232	$ 117,652	$ 40,423	Net income after taxes

In 1925 and 1926 it includes Jersey Standard's proportionate share of gross sales of "affiliated" companies (those companies in which the parent company owned more than a 50 per cent interest and whose assets and liabilities were consolidated with those of the parent company in annual statements) and marine and miscellaneous earnings of Jersey Standard. In 1927 It Includes all sales of affiliated companies as well as marine and miscellaneous earnings of Jersey Standard.
f "Nonconsolidated affiliates" include those companies in which Jersey Standard owned a 50 per cent or smaller interest, as well as companies in developmental stages of operation. See Appendix 1, groups B and C.
g Includes Jersey Standard alone, 1918 through 1924; thereafter includes Jersey Standard and affiliated companies.
h Includes profits applicable to minority interests.
Sources: N. Y. Stock Exchange Listing Statement, March 1, 1920, for 1918 income statement, and SONJ, *Annual Reports*, 1918-1927. Tax figures for 1921, 1923-1924 from SONJ, Fin. Recs.

Table III: COMPARATIVE CONSOLIDATED BALANCE SHEETS
Standard Oil Company (New Jersey) and Affiliates[a], 1912-1927

ASSETS	Dollar figures in thousands						
Net real estate, plant, equipment, & marine facilities	1912	1913	1914	1915	1916	1917	1918
Jersey Standard	$ 28,514	$ 28,462	$ 33,528	$ 40,960	$ 53,869	$ 62,872	$ 67,766
Affiliates	109,845	121,624	121,147	141,187	156,397	159,840	182,062
Total	$138,359	$150,086	$154,675	$182,147	$210,266	$222,712	$249,828
Investments & marketable securities							
Jersey Standard	$ 41,172	$ 40,504	$ 42,762	$ 51,442	$ 56,748	$ 58,904	$ 91,515
Affiliates	10,489	13,655	20,534	18,999	19,995	17,878	24,947
Total	$ 51,661	$ 54,159	$ 63,296	$ 70,441	$ 76,743	$ 76,782	$116,462
Inventories							
Jersey Standard	$ 16,393	$ 26,193	$ 23,425	$ 26,801	$ 38,726	$ 55,688	$ 71,619
Affiliates	27,993	30,847	25,007	42,556	56,513	78,588	88,886
Total	$ 44,386	$ 57,040	$ 48,432	$ 69,357	$ 95,239	$134,276	$160,505
Accounts & notes receivable							
Jersey Standard	$112,933	$ 69,040	$ 65,063	$ 67,559	$ 76,797	$ 81,016	$ 90,400
Affiliates	17,625	21,879	24,961	29,243	38,090	44,760	60,920
Total	$130,559	$ 90,919	$ 90,024	$ 96,802	$114,887	$125,776	$151,320
Cash							
Jersey Standard	$ 465	$ 343	$ 413	$ 10,347	$ 1,354	$ 4,697	$ 1,646
Affiliates	3,835	4,500	6,802	8,846	6,854	9,906	11,556
Total	$ 4,300	$ 4,843	$ 7,215	$ 19,193	$ 8,208	$ 14,603	$ 13,202
Miscellaneous assets	—	—	—	—	—	—	—
Total assets							
Jersey Standard	$199,477	$164,542	$165,191	$197,111	$227,493	$263,177	$322,947
Affiliates	169,788	192,505	198,451	240,831	277,850	310,972	368,370
Total	$369,265	$357,047	$363,642	$437,942	$505,343	$574,149	$691,317
LIABILITIES & NET WORTH							
Accounts & notes payable							
Jersey Standard	$ 7,355	$ 8,996	$ 9,365	$ 20,335	$ 24,588	$ 33,027	$ 54,817
Affiliates	54,607	54,588	49,207	69,428	81,945	63,694	62,000
Total	$ 61,962	$ 63,584	$ 58,572	$ 89,763	$106,533	$ 96,721	$116,817
Tax reserves							
Jersey Standard	—	—	—	—	—	—	—
Affiliates	—	—	—	—	—	—	—
Total	—	—	—	—	—	—	—
Annuities & insurance reserves	—	—	—	—	—	—	$ 12,449
Deferred & accrued liabilities	—	—	—	—	—	—	—
Common stock	$ 98,338	$ 98,338	$ 98,338	$ 98,338	$ 98,338	$ 98,338	98,338
Preferred stock	—	—	—	—	—	—	—
Bonded indebtedness	—	—	—	—	—	—	—
Surplus	208,965	195,125	206,732	249,841	300,472	379,090	463,713
Capital & surplus of minority interests	—	—	—	—	—	—	—
Total liabilities & net worth	$369,265	$357,047	$363,642	$437,942	$505,343	$574,149	$691,317

[a] These balance sheets are the official published company statements, condensed and reclassified somewhat to facilitate presentation here. In 1927 extensive changes were made in the consolidated statements. The elimination of intercompany receivables and payables accounts for much of the pronounced change in the 1927 figures from the 1926 totals. At the same time, the 1927 statement reported assets and liabilities of affiliated companies in their entirety instead of just Jersey's share in them. This procedure required the re-

Table III (cont.): COMPARATIVE CONSOLIDATED BALANCE SHEETS
Standard Oil Company (New Jersey) and Affiliates[a], 1912-1927

Dollar figures in thousands

1919	1920	1921	1922	1923	1924	1925	1926	1927
$ 97,293	$ 133,795	$ 151,289	$ 145,114	$ 144,138	$ 142,296	$ 152,222	$ 165,519	b
214,980	250,788	280,280	296,868	320,628	332,664	362,090	385,271	b
$312,273	$ 384,583	$ 431,569	$ 441,982	$ 464,766	$ 474,960	$ 514,312	$ 550,790	$ 656,645
$ 72,034	$ 77,046	$ 77,500	$ 75,801	$ 92,617	$ 112,357	$ 101,726	$ 266,766	b
28,588	34,396	53,758	58,977	65,739	60,380	63,069	65,601	b
$100,622	$ 111,442	$ 131,258	$ 134,778	$ 158,356	$ 172,737	$ 164,795	$ 332,367	268,516
$ 69,165	$ 106,852	$ 101,561	$ 94,889	$ 80,075	$ 65,113	$ 89,069	$ 92,912	b
116,585	177,489	158,836	168,311	165,833	173,989	205,162	210,157	b
$185,750	$ 284,341	$ 260,397	$ 263,200	$ 245,908	$ 239,102	$ 294,231	$ 303,069	272,893
$146,715	$ 206,415	$ 186,498	$ 181,408	$ 184,844	$ 216,682	$ 233,419	$ 197,918	b
90,181	81,744	93,350	87,814	83,044	130,330	150,637	146,178	b
$236,896	$ 288,159	$ 279,848	$ 269,222	$ 267,888	$ 347,012	$ 384,056	$ 344,096	172,441
$ 1,220	$ 1,474	$ 3,790	$ 7,481	$ 4,144	$ 2,120	$ 2,126	$ 1,894	b
16,600	32,314	9,078	7,098	6,943	9,009	9,650	9,729	b
$ 17,820	$ 33,788	$ 12,868	$ 14,579	$ 11,087	$ 11,129	$ 11,776	$ 11,623	42,611
—	—	—	—	—	—	—	—	13,495
$386,427	$ 525,582	$ 520,638	$ 504,693	$ 505,818	$ 538,568	$ 578,562	$ 725,009	b
466,934	576,731	595,302	619,068	642,187	706,372	790,608	816,936	b
$853,361	$1,102,313	$1,115,940	$1,123,761	$1,148,005	$1,244,940	$1,369,170	$1,541,945	1,426,601
$ 40,514	$ 54,806	$ 73,231	$ 64,061	$ 57,182	$ 81,732	$ 93,933	$ 107,757	b
116,491	129,028	144,160	141,551	147,674	164,205	181,129	133,593	b
$157,005	$ 183,834	$ 217,391	$ 205,612	$ 204,856	$ 245,937	$ 275,062	$ 241,350	$ 82,267
—	$ 15,250	$ 4,378	$ 4,378	$ 3,579	$ 2,403	$ 4,127	$ 3,600	b
—	13,652	1,510	2,817	2,152	6,447	11,896	14,267	b
—	$ 28,902	$ 5,888	$ 7,195	$ 5,731	$ 8,850	$ 16,023	$ 17,867	8,486
$ 1,386	2,415	5,083	6,225	7,279	8,369	14,182	18,566	27,803
—	—	—	—	—	—	—	—	10,755
98,338	98,338	98,879	498,587	502,099	507,302	514,706	517,398	607,931
98,338	196,677	196,677	199,973	199,973	199,973	199,973	199,973	—
—	—	—	—	—	—	—	120,000	169,239
498,294	592,147	592,022	206,169	228,067	274,509	349,224	426,791	400,143
—	—	—	—	—	—	—	—	119,977
$853,361	$1,102,313	$1,115,940	$1,123,761	$1,148,005	$1,244,940	$1,369,170	$1,541,945	$1,426,601

cording of minority interests in the affiliates on the liability side of the balance sheet. The 1927 statement, therefore, is not comparable in many important respects to the earlier statements.

b Comparable breakdowns of account classifications not available because of changes in reporting procedures.

Source: SONJ, Fin. Recs.

Table IV: **ANALYSIS OF COMMON STOCK HOLDINGS AND PRICES**
Standard Oil Company (New Jersey) 1911-1927[a]

Common Stock Holdings

Year	Total Shares Outstanding	Total Number of Shareholders	Holders of Fewer Than 1,000 Shares		Holders of More Than 1,000 Shares	
			Number	Shares	Number	Shares
1912	983,383	5,832	5,727	245,556	105	737,827
1913	983,383	6,104	5,998	250,633	106	732,750
1914	983,383	6,617	6,512	258,471	105	724,912
1915	983,383	6,962	6,851	263,928	111	719,455
1916	983,383	7,158	7,044	267,801	114	715,582
1917	983,383	7,351	7,241	275,283	110	708,100
1918	983,383	7,898	7,785	292,815	113	690,568
1919	983,383	8,074	7,952	298,455	122	684,928
1920	983,383	8,190	8,063	299,481	127	683,902
1921	3,041,572	8,889	8,602	622,182	287	2,419,390
1922	3,705,272	9,407	9,039	728,833	368	2,976,439
1923	19,820,536	19,123	17,419	1,844,525	1,704	17,976,011
1924	20,083,407	25,982	24,282	2,135,187	1,700	17,948,220
1925	20,302,193	26,829	25,204	2,284,786	1,625	18,017,407
1926	20,585,516	44,914	43,235	3,233,532	1,679	17,351,984
1927	24,212,359	50,628	48,607	3,909,898	2,021	20,302,461

[a] 1912-1917 figures are as of September of each year; 1918-1927 as of December.
Source: SONJ, Analysis of Stock Ledger.

Table IV *(cont.):* **ANALYSIS OF COMMON STOCK HOLDINGS AND PRICES**
Standard Oil Company (New Jersey) 1911-1927

Common Stock Yearly High and Low Prices[a]

Year	Stock of $100 Par[b]		Stock of $25 Par[c]		New Stock of $25 Par[d]	
	High	Low	High	Low	High	Low
1911	$450	$300	—	—	—	—
1912	428	350	—	—	—	—
1913	439	328	—	—	—	—
1914[e]	434	356	—	—	—	—
1915	570	385	—	—	—	—
1916	702	495	—	—	—	—
1917	797	475	—	—	—	—
1918	706	490	—	—	—	—
1919	783	667	—	—	—	—
1920	880	570	$158	$146	—	—
1921	—	—	190½	125	—	—
1922	—	—	245½	170	$46½	$37⅛
1923	—	—	—	—	44¼	30⅞
1924	—	—	—	—	42¼	33
1925	—	—	—	—	47½	38⅜
1926	—	—	—	—	46⅜	37⅜
1927	—	—	—	—	41⅜	35⅛

[a] In these records, closing stock quotations were used through June 10, 1923, after which daily high and low sale prices were used. The stock was traded on the New York Curb until listed on the New York Stock Exchange on March 25, 1920.

[b] Prices exclude holdings in companies declared separated by the Supreme Court in 1911. Quotations for this stock of $100 par are given from September 1, 1911, through December 22, 1920.

[c] The old stock was called in and four new shares of $25 par were issued for each old share. Quotations for the $25 par stock started on December 23, 1920, and continued through December 22, 1922.

[d] A dividend of four shares of $25 par for each one held was distributed on December 23, 1922. Trading in the new stock "when issued" started on October 18, 1922.

[e] The New York Curb Market was closed from July 31 to November 12, 1914, owing to World War I.

Source: SONJ, Listing of Stock Prices.

Table V: **FINANCIAL COMPARISONS**
Standard Oil Company (New Jersey) and Selected Other Companies[a]
1918-1927

	Dollar figures in thousands			
	1918	**1919**	**1920**	**1921**
Standard Oil Company (New Jersey)				
Total assets	$ 691,317	$ 853,361	$1,102,313	$1,115,940
Net earnings	$ 58,110	$ 77,986	$ 164,461	$ 33,846
Per cent net earnings to net worth	10.3	11.2	18.5	3.8
Per cent common dividends to net earnings	33.8	25.2	12.0	58.2
United States Steel Corporation				
Total assets	$2,571,617	$2,365,882	$2,430,546	$2,339,105
Net earnings	$ 137,532	$ 76,795	$ 109,694	$ 36,617
Per cent net earnings to net worth	9.5	5.2	7.2	2.4
Per cent common dividends to net earnings	51.8	33.1	23.2	69.4
General Electric Corporation				
Total assets	$ 268,107	$ 276,471	$ 374,837	$ 339,275
Net earnings	$ 17,105	$ 25,078	$ 22,132	$ 21,652
Per cent net earnings to net worth	10.1	13.6	10.6	8.9
Per cent common dividends to net earnings	80.4	57.1	72.8	93.1
General Motors Corporation				
Total assets	$ 299,489	$ 446,653	$ 604,806	$ 515,123
Net earnings	$ 15,391	$ 60,518	$ 37,884	$ (38,680)[b]
Per cent net earnings to net worth	6.6	18.6	8.9	—
Per cent common dividends to net earnings	73.0	28.6	47.2	289.0
E. I. Du Pont de Nemours & Co., Inc.				
Total assets	$ 308,846	$ 240,983	$ 253,359	$ 252,208
Net earnings	$ 43,098	$ 17,683	$ 14,563	$ 5,762
Per cent net earnings to net worth	22.9	9.2	7.1	2.9
Per cent common dividends to net earnings	35.5	59.9	43.4	87.9

[a] Figures for all companies are on consolidated basis. Net earnings are after taxes. Net worth is capital stock plus surplus. Dividends include cash and stock. [b] Parentheses indicate net loss.

Table V *(cont.):* **FINANCIAL COMPARISONS**
Standard Oil Company (New Jersey) and Selected Other Companies[a]
1918-1927

			Dollar figures in thousands					
1922	1923	1924	1925	1926	1927	1918-1927		
$1,123,761	$1,148,005	$1,244,940	$1,369,170	$1,541,945	$1,426,601			
$ 46,241	$ 56,294	$ 81,017	$ 111,232	$ 117,652	$ 40,423	⟶ Total	$787,262
5.1	6.1	8.3	10.5	10.3	4.0	⟶ Average	8.8
42.9	35.6	24.9	18.3	19.7	86.7	⟶ Average	35.7
$2,340,653	$2,420,883	$2,414,195	$2,445,643	$2,454,139	$2,433,583		
$ 39,653	$ 108,707	$ 85,067	$ 90,603	$ 116,667	$ 87,897	⟶ Total	$889,232
2.6	7.1	5.3	5.6	6.9	5.2	⟶ Average	5.7
64.1	26.9	41.8	39.3	30.5	56.7	⟶ Average	43.7
$ 355,445	$ 373,566	$ 408,259	$ 397,248	$ 428,329	$ 428,149		
$ 26,231	$ 33,525	$ 39,235	$ 38,641	$ 46,673	$ 48,799	⟶ Total	$319,071
10.2	11.9	14.0	12.8	14.3	14.4	⟶ Average	12.1
87.0	69.6	59.4	60.6	57.9	70.3	⟶ Average	70.8
$ 522,335	$ 593,124	$ 592,571	$ 703,787	$ 920,894	$1,098,477		
$ 51,808	$ 62,386	$ 45,735	$ 107,070	$ 176,699	$ 239,265	⟶ Total	$758,056
12.8	14.1	10.2	21.0	27.9	31.5	⟶ Average	15.2
20.1	39.6	54.7	57.9	58.8	56.3	⟶ Average	56.4
$ 259,672	$ 279,744	$ 275,538	$ 395,731	$ 322,583	$ 251,440		
$ 9,991	$ 18,313	$ 17,031	$ 24,033	$ 41,969	$ 45,948	⟶ Total	$238,391
5.0	8.4	7.8	8.8	15.0	14.4	⟶ Average	10.2
51.0	33.9	44.7	47.5	79.1	78.0	⟶ Average	55.6

Source: Jersey Standard figures from SONJ, *Annual Reports* and stock listing statements; all other figures from Moody's *Manual of Investments.*

Table VI: **FINANCIAL COMPARISONS**
Standard Oil Company (New Jersey) and Other Oil Companies[a]
1912-1927

	Dollar figures in thousands			
	1918	**1919**	**1920**	**1921**
Standard Oil Company (New Jersey)				
Total assets	$691,317	$853,361	$1,102,313	$1,115,940
Net earnings	$ 58,110	$ 77,986	$ 164,461	$ 33,846
Per cent net earnings to net worth	10.3	11.2	18.5	3.8
Per cent common dividends to net earnings	33.8	25.2	12.0	58.2
The Texas Company				
Total assets	$191,152	$261,330	$ 333,434	$ 335,990
Net earnings	$ 20,641	$ 18,671	$ 31,089	$ 9,826
Per cent net earnings to net worth	16.5	11.5	13.7	3.9
Per cent common dividends to net earnings	30.3	41.2	82.0	183.8
Gulf Oil Corporation				
Total assets	$173,176	$218,477	$ 259,730	$ 272,774
Net earnings	$ 12,583	$ 11,461	$ 28,543	$ 9,069
Per cent net earnings to net worth	13.5	11.1	20.5	6.2
Per cent common dividends to net earnings	16.6	18.4	72.4	24.2
Standard Oil Company of Indiana				
Total assets	$145,428	$154,672	$ 237,635	$ 305,675
Net earnings	$ 23,263	$ 24,808	$ 40,973	$ 21,288
Per cent net earnings to net worth	19.8	18.4	20.1	8.5
Per cent common dividends to net earnings	31.0	29.0	22.3	73.7
Standard Oil Company of California				
Total assets	$145,231	$174,318	$ 245,755	$ 276,733
Net earnings	$ 14,953	$ 31,063	$ 41,655	$ 33,588
Per cent net earnings to net worth	12.8	19.6	18.6	14.3
Per cent common dividends to net earnings	83.2	43.1	33.3	46.1

	Per Cent				
	1912	**1913**	**1914**	**1915**	**1916**
Return on Investment[b]					
Standard Oil Company (New Jersey)	11.5	15.7	10.4	17.6	18.2
Representative Standard Oil refining companies	16.5	15.4	8.7	18.8	26.2
Representative independent refining companies	6.7	13.7	8.2	8.3	14.4

[a] Figures for all companies on consolidated basis. Net earnings are after taxes. Net worth is capital stock plus surplus. Dividends include cash and stock.

[b] This figure represents the ratio between net income and net worth, the net income figure being composed in this instance of earnings before taxes and interest.

Table VI (cont.): **FINANCIAL COMPARISONS**
Standard Oil Company (New Jersey) and Other Oil Companies[a]
1912-1927

	1922	1923	1924	1925	1926	1927	1918-1927	
	\$1,123,761	\$1,148,005	\$1,244,940	\$1,369,170	\$1,541,945	\$1,426,601		
	\$ 46,241	\$ 56,294	\$ 81,017	\$ 111,232	\$ 117,652	\$ 40,423	⟶ Total	\$787,262
	5.1	6.1	8.3	10.5	10.3	4.0	⟶ Average	8.8
	42.9	35.6	24.9	18.3	19.7	86.7	⟶ Average	35.7
	\$ 345,535	\$ 370,653	\$ 375,734	\$ 397,638	\$ 328,755	\$ 324,806		
	\$ 26,588	\$ 8,197	\$ 26,458	\$ 39,605	\$ 36,043	\$ 20,029	⟶ Total	\$237,147
	10.3	3.2	10.2	14.3	13.2	6.9	⟶ Average	10.4
	74.1	240.7	74.3	49.7	54.7	98.5	⟶ Average	92.9
	\$ 348,378	\$ 335,499	\$ 379,533	\$ 427,610	\$ 499,337	\$ 552,834		
	\$ 19,752	\$ 14,323	\$ 19,167	\$ 35,001	\$ 35,098	\$ 13,717	⟶ Total	\$198,714
	11.9	8.2	10.2	16.1	14.3	8.7	⟶ Average	12.1
	10.6	45.5	33.9	18.9	18.9	48.2	⟶ Average	30.8
	\$ 318,789	\$ 338,934	\$ 361,481	\$ 406,059	\$ 446,496	\$ 462,606		
	\$ 49,381	\$ 41,538	\$ 40,788	\$ 52,933	\$ 55,099	\$ 30,132	⟶ Total	\$381,194
	17.1	13.4	12.3	14.4	13.7	7.4	⟶ Average	14.5
	35.5	53.3	54.7	42.5	57.9	106.6	⟶ Average	50.7
	\$ 305,958	\$ 341,985	\$ 352,805	\$ 373,723	\$ 573,803	\$ 579,308		
	\$ 27,020	\$ 24,442	\$ 26,602	\$ 30,953	\$ 55,122	\$ 40,210	⟶ Total	\$378,602
	10.3	8.2	8.6	9.3	10.4	7.1	⟶ Average	11.9
	60.3	73.8	70.4	61.1	45.6	82.1	⟶ Average	59.9

Dollar figures in thousands

Per Cent										
1917	1918	1919	1920	1921	1922	1923	1924	1925	1926	1927
22.2	16.4	13.2	20.1	5.0	5.1	6.1	8.4	11.7	11.7	6.4
27.5	23.4	18.5	25.2	6.3	9.5	7.9	9.4	11.9	c	c
18.1	16.8	11.7	17.1	4.1	7.6	3.6	7.8	10.8	c	c

c No data.
Source: SONJ figures from company records, *Annual Reports* and stock listing statements. Texas, Gulf, Indiana, and California figures from Moody's *Manual of Investments*. Representative Standard Oil and independent refining companies' return on investment from FTC, *Prices, Profits and Competition, Petroleum Industry* (Washington, 1928), 303, 304.

Table VII: **NET CRUDE OIL PRODUCTION**
Standard Oil Company (New Jersey) and Affiliates
1912-1927

	Barrels per Day					
	1912	1913	1914	1915	1916	1917
Domestic						
Carter Oil	2,514	3,000	2,223	9,801	7,349	15,724
Louisiana Standard	4,781	8,109	6,306	6,629	5,243	3,531
Humble[a]	....	....	....	....	....	....
Gas companies	174	487	492	653	808	832
Total domestic	7,469	11,596	9,021	17,083	13,400	20,087
Canadian						
Imperial Oil[a]	....	....	....	....	....	....
European						
Româno-Americana	3,622	5,862	7,562	6,767	5,501	b
Standard-Nobel, Poland[a]	....	....	....	....	....	....
Società Italo-Americana	....	....	....	....	....	....
Total European	3,622	5,862	7,562	6,767	5,501	b
Latin American						
Tropical Oil Co., Colombia[a]	....	....	....	....	....	....
International Pet. Co., Peru[a]	....	....	....	4,988	5,143	4,951
Standard Oil Co. of Argentina	....	....	....	....	....	....
Standard Oil Co. of Bolivia	....	....	....	....	....	....
Transcontinental, Mexico	....	....	....	....	....	....
Standard Oil Co. of Venezuela	....	....	....	....	....	....
Total Latin American	....	....	....	4,988	5,143	4,951
Dutch East Indies						
Nederlandsche Koloniale Petroleum Maatschappij	....	....	10	15	22	75
Jersey's total world production	11,091	17,458	16,593	28,853	24,066	25,113

Percentage of Jersey Total World Production

	1912	1913	1914	1915	1916	1917
Domestic	67.3	66.4	54.3	59.2	55.7	80.0
Canadian	....	....	....	....	....	....
European	32.7	33.6	45.7	23.5	22.8	b
Latin American				17.3	21.4	19.7
Dutch East Indies	....	....	c	c	0.1	0.3
Total	100.0	100.0	100.0	100.0	100.0	100.0
Percentage Jersey's U. S. production to U. S. petroleum industry production	1.2	1.7	1.2	2.2	1.6	2.2
Percentage Jersey's world production to world industry production	1.1	1.6	1.5	2.4	1.9	1.8

[a] Entire production rather than Jersey's proportionate share of production.
[b] Comparable data not available.
[c] Too small to measure.

Table VII *(cont.):* **NET CRUDE OIL PRODUCTION**
Standard Oil Company (New Jersey) and Affiliates
1912-1927

Barrels per Day									
1918	**1919**	**1920**	**1921**	**1922**	**1923**	**1924**	**1925**	**1926**	**1927**
14,616	11,354	12,367	19,327	22,890	22,815	21,104	21,940	17,951	61,341
3,194	4,122	13,942	12,763	11,190	11,858	10,630	17,008	15,914	12,832
....	16,546	21,382	33,674	30,683	46,656	43,845	49,754	37,753	35,217
973	992	1,160	1,390	1,223	1,396	1,313	1,471	3,132	2,990
18,783	33,014	48,851	67,154	65,986	82,725	76,892	90,173	74,750	112,380
....	....	....	....	26	22	40	441	514	596
206	2,272	3,362	4,523	3,825	2,879	2,826	3,915	3,848	4,175
....	....	45	122	70	100	262	450	773	710
....	....	....	....	....	....	....	....	....	23
206	2,272	3,407	4,645	3,895	2,979	3,088	4,365	4,621	4,908
....	....	....	152	735	828	538	1,879	15,599	36,671
4,944	5,100	5,447	7,741	12,025	12,704	17,696	20,130	23,650	21,283
....	....	....	....	....	....	....	....	77	765
....	....	....	....	....	....	....	....	....	71
2,552	21,236	38,640	36,499	13,236	58,713	50,234	45,570	19,079	9,784
....	....	....	....	19	113	50	2	27	56
7,496	26,336	44,087	44,392	26,015	72,358	68,518	67,581	58,432	68,630
83	111	106	91	132	266	451	192	901	3,397
26,568	61,733	96,451	116,282	96,054	158,350	148,989	162,752	139,218	189,911

					Percentage of Jersey Total World Production				
1918	**1919**	**1920**	**1921**	**1922**	**1923**	**1924**	**1925**	**1926**	**1927**
70.7	53.5	50.7	57.7	68.7	51.6	51.6	55.4	53.7	59.2
....	....	....	....	e	e	e	0.3	0.3	0.3
0.8	3.7	3.5	4.0	1.9	2.1	2.1	2.7	3.3	2.6
28.2	42.6	45.7	38.2	45.7	46.0	46.0	41.5	42.0	36.1
0.3	0.2	0.1	0.1	0.2	0.3	0.3	0.1	0.7	1.8
100.0	100.0	100.0	100.0	100.0	100.0	100.0	100.0	100.0	100.0
1.9	3.2	4.0	5.2	4.3	4.1	3.9	4.3	3.5	4.6
1.9	4.0	5.1	5.5	4.1	5.7	5.4	5.6	4.6	5.5

Source: World and United States industry figures from   All other figures from SONJ, Stat.
N.I.C.B., *The Petroleum Almanac* (1946), 35 and 299.

Table VIII: **CRUDE OIL RUN**
in Jersey Standard and Affiliated Refineries[a], 1912-1927

	Thousands of Barrels per Day							
Jersey Company	1912	1913	1914	1915	1916	1917	1918	1919
Bayonne	35.1	33.7	31.4	36.7	34.8	36.5	42.7	51.5
Bayway	24.6	23.4	22.4	23.4	23.5	23.7	26.2	35.7
Eagle Works	13.8	13.6	11.2	12.9	12.1	11.5	10.5	10.3
Baltimore	5.6	5.3	5.7	6.2	6.6	7.3	6.7	11.7
Parkersburg	2.5	2.3	2.4	2.2	2.2	2.3	2.2	2.1
Charleston	......	......	......	......	......	......	......	......
Total	81.6	78.3	73.1	81.4	79.2	81.3	88.3	111.3
Louisiana Standard								
Baton Rouge	11.6	19.8	17.9	19.0	23.6	35.9	43.8	44.2
Haynesville	......	......	......	......	......	......	......	......
Total	11.6	19.8	17.9	19.0	23.6	35.9	43.8	44.2
Humble								
Baytown	......	......	......	......	......	......	......	......
McCamey	......	......	......	......	......	......	......	......
Burkburnett	......	......	......	......	......	......	......	......
San Antonio	......	......	......	......	......	......	......	......
Hearne	......	......	......	......	......	......	......	c
Total	......	......	......	......	......	......	......	1.5
Imperial Oil								
Ioco	......	......	......	1.1	1.5	1.6	1.7	2.0
Regina	......	......	......	......	0.5	1.8	2.0	2.3
Montreal	......	......	......	......	0.1	1.8	3.1	4.0
Sarnia	3.1	3.4	5.0	5.9	6.3	8.5	9.8	9.4
Calgary	......	......	......	......	......	......	......	......
Halifax	......	......	......	......	......	......	1.7	3.5
Total	3.1	3.4	5.0	7.0	8.4	13.7	18.3	21.2
Latin American								
Standard Oil Co. of Cuba, Havana	0.4	0.5	0.5	0.6	0.9	0.8	0.9	1.0
International Pet. Co., Talara, Peru	......	......	......	4.4	5.2	4.7	4.0	4.7
Tropical Oil Co., Barranca, Colombia	......	......	......	......	......	......	......	......
Nacional, Campana, Arg.	0.3	0.7	0.8	0.7	0.8	1.1	0.5	2.5
Transcontinental, Tampico, Mex.[d]	......	......	......	4.8	4.8	8.6	7.5	9.4
Total	0.7	1.2	1.3	10.5	11.7	15.2	12.9	17.6
Eastern Hemisphere								
Român̂o-Americana, Teleajen, Romania[e]	4.4	5.7	7.8	6.3	5.0	f	f	f
NKPM, Palembang, D.E.I.[g]	......	......	......	......	......	......	......	......
Other European[h]	......	......	......	......	......	......	......	......
Total	4.4	5.7	7.8	6.3	5.0	......	......	......
Total Jersey domestic refinery runs	93.2	98.1	91.0	100.4	102.8	117.2	132.1	157.0
Total Jersey foreign refinery runs	8.2	10.3	14.1	23.8	25.1	28.9	31.2	38.8
Total Jersey world-wide refinery runs	101.4	108.4	105.1	124.2	127.9	146.1	163.3	195.8

	1912	1913	1914	1915	1916	1917	1918	1919
Percentage Jersey domestic to Jersey total	91.9	90.5	86.6	80.9	80.4	80.2	80.9	80.2
Percentage Jersey foreign to Jersey total	8.1	9.5	13.4	19.1	19.6	19.8	19.1	19.8
	100.0	100.0	100.0	100.0	100.0	100.0	100.0	100.0
Pecentage total Jersey domestic to U. S. industry total	18.0	18.0	17.5	f	15.2	13.6	14.8	15.9

[a] Excludes refineries whose output in these years never went above 500 barrels per day.
[b] Reduced crude previously processed by other refineries; excluded from totals.
[c] Largely the throughput from San Antonio. A small refinery at Humble was sold in May, 1919, and the Baytown refinery was under construction.
[d] Refinery at Tampico owned directly by Jersey Standard through 1919.

Table VIII (cont.): CRUDE OIL RUN
in Jersey Standard and Affiliated Refineries[a], 1912-1927

			Thousands of Barrels per Day					
1920	1921	1922	1923	1924	1925	1926	1927	**Jersey Company**
72.8	59.2	64.3	64.4	76.2	57.3	57.1	49.3	Bayonne
30.1	30.1	41.1	53.1	72.7	73.2	58.3	73.9	Bayway
7.8	4.9	0.1	9.2[b]	11.8[b]	13.0[b]	13.4[b]	14.0[b]	Eagle Works
21.8	24.9	17.5	25.2	29.0	25.6	20.4	25.6	Baltimore
2.1	2.0	2.4	3.0	3.3	3.8	4.5	4.6	Parkersburg
0.2	7.0	6.7	8.0	9.3	13.8	11.7	9.6	Charleston
134.8	128.1	132.1	153.7	190.5	173.7	152.0	163.0	Total
								Louisiana Standard
43.3	52.2	61.5	63.7	78.5	92.5	94.9	98.7	Baton Rouge
......	......	5.3	4.0	......	......	......	......	Haynesville
43.3	52.2	66.8	67.7	78.5	92.5	94.9	98.7	Total
								Humble
2.5	5.8	11.8	21.7	36.8	42.6	57.0	77.6	Baytown
......	......	......	......	......	......	......	7.9	McCamey
......	0.1	1.1	1.2	1.8	2.8	2.0	2.1	Burkburnett
2.0	0.3	......	......	......	......	......	......	San Antonio
......	......	......	1.5	8.0	6.2	......	......	Hearne
4.5	6.2	12.9	24.4	46.6	51.6	59.0	87.6	Total
								Imperial Oil
1.8	2.7	2.8	3.4	3.7	3.7	4.1	8.2	Ioco
2.9	3.1	4.0	3.9	3.7	2.7	3.5	3.8	Regina
4.1	4.4	4.8	6.9	6.1	6.8	10.3	12.0	Montreal
9.9	9.9	10.0	9.0	9.8	10.4	10.7	12.2	Sarnia
......	......	......	0.3	4.6	3.1	4.8	4.0	Calgary
2.1	6.6	7.2	5.2	4.8	3.8	5.5	8.3	Halifax
20.8	26.7	28.8	28.7	32.7	30.5	38.9	48.5	Total
								Latin American
1.7	2.1	2.6	2.5	3.3	2.9	1.3	1.5	Standard Oil Co. of Cuba, Havana
5.1	7.1	8.5	9.9	8.9	11.5	12.0	13.0	International Pet. Co., Talara, Peru
......	......	0.6	0.9	0.8	1.6	2.0	3.3	Tropical Oil Co., Barranca, Colombia
3.3	3.2	2.5	3.3	3.6	2.0	2.8	4.7	Nacional, Campana, Arg.
d	d	d	0.5	7.4	9.1	10.9	0.5	Transcontinental, Tampico, Mex.[d]
10.1	12.4	14.2	17.1	24.0	27.1	29.0	23.0	Total
								Eastern Hemisphere
1.0	4.2	3.9	2.8	2.8	4.5	6.4	6.2	Romãno-Americana, Teleajen, Romania[e]
......	......	......	0.2	0.2	0.2	0.6	3.4	NKPM, Palembang, D.E.I.[g]
......	......	......	0.1	0.4	1.6	1.8	3.9	Other European[h]
1.0	4.2	3.9	3.1	3.4	6.3	8.8	13.5	Total
182.6	186.5	211.8	245.8	315.6	317.8	305.9	349.3	Total Jersey domestic refinery runs
31.9	43.3	46.9	48.9	60.1	63.9	76.7	85.0	Total Jersey foreign refinery runs
214.5	229.8	258.7	294.7	375.7	381.7	382.6	434.3	Total Jersey world-wide refinery runs
1920	1921	1922	1923	1924	1925	1926	1927	
85.1	81.2	81.9	83.4	84.0	83.3	80.0	80.4	Percentage Jersey domestic to Jersey total
14.9	18.8	18.1	16.6	16.0	16.7	20.0	19.6	Percentage Jersey foreign to Jersey total
100.0	100.0	100.0	100.0	100.0	100.0	100.0	100.0	
15.9	15.4	15.4	15.4	17.9	15.7	14.3	15.4	Percentage total Jersey domestic to U. S. industry total

[e] Includes output of about 500 barrels per day in 1927 of a small new refinery at Moreni.

[f] Comparable data not available.

[g] NKPM also had a small refinery at Kapoean which by 1927 was running about 300 barrels per day.

[h] Other European refiners include those in Libusza, Poland; Trieste, Italy; Vallö, Norway; Atlas, Belgium; and Fawley, England. All were small except the last, which in 1927 was running about 2,500 barrels per day.

Source: SONJ, Stat.

Table IX: **PRODUCTION OF CRACKED GASOLINE
1915-1927**

Amounts Produced

	Jersey Standard and Louisiana Standard Refineries			Total United States	
	Thousands of barrels per year	Per cent of their total gasoline production		Thousands of barrels per year	Per cent of total U. S. gasoline production
1915	2.3	a	1915	no data	no data
1916	849.9	10	1916	6,950	14
1917	1,746.6	16	1917	9,850	15
1918	2,599.5	21	1918	11,790	13
1919	3,488.0	23	1919	15,490	15
1920	3,900.4	22	1920	16,150	13
1921	4,505.7	25	1921	21,250	16
1922	5,122.4	22	1922	25,380	16
1923	5,937.9	22	1923	28,340	14
1924	8,034.0	26	1924	34,360	15
1925	10,870.8	34	1925	68,583	26
1926	13,588.4	40	1926	93,736	31
1927	10,731.0	32	1927	101,226	30

Methods of Production in Jersey Organization Refineries

Per Cent of Jersey's Total Cracked Gasoline

	Burton Process Stills	Tube-and-Tank Process
1920 and before	100.00	none
1921	98.71	1.29
1922	98.80	1.20
1923	94.28	5.72
1924	92.01	7.99
1925	76.73	23.27
1926	65.13	34.87
1927	20.71	79.29

a Less than 1 per cent.
Source: SONJ, charts and statistics from Manufacturing Department; Stat. U. S. industry figures computed from figures given in National Industrial Conference Board, *Petroleum Almanac*, 71.

Table X: **DELIVERIES OF REFINED PRODUCTS**
Foreign and Domestic Trade of Standard Oil Company (New Jersey)
and Affiliates, 1912-1927

	Thousands of barrels of 42 gallons					Exports as Percentage of Total U. S. Industry Exports[d]
Year	Total Domestic Deliveries[a]	Exports from U. S.[a]	Foreign Deliveries from Foreign Refineries[b]	Total Foreign Deliveries[c]	Total Domestic and Foreign Deliveries	
1912	18,569	20,924	3,011	23,935	42,504	51
1913	15,937	19,730	3,758	23,488	39,425	42
1914	15,392	18,533	5,147	23,680	39,072	36
1915	17,493	19,179	8,671	27,850	45,343	36
1916	19,157	19,323	9,217	28,540	47,697	33
1917	23,742	19,246	10,553	29,799	53,541	32
1918	28,376	22,328	11,372	33,700	62,076	36
1919	38,029	20,448	14,690	35,138	73,167	36
1920	49,194	17,428	16,095	33,523	82,717	25
1921	46,728	16,010	19,364	35,374	82,102	26
1922	48,651	22,807	17,018	39,825	88,476	36
1923	68,476	27,984	17,839	45,823	114,299	33
1924	85,503	37,406	22,028	59,434	144,937	38
1925	78,373	40,861	23,315	64,176	142,549	40
1926	81,138	48,307	27,838	76,145	157,283	41
1927	89,562	51,492	31,034	82,526	172,088	41

[a] Includes 100 per cent of Humble deliveries; excludes deliveries to domestic affiliated companies.
[b] These figures were computed by totaling foreign refinery runs, and must be taken as an approximation only of foreign refinery deliveries to the foreign trade.
[c] These figures must also be taken as approximations only. They do not include foreign purchases from non-affiliated companies of refined products for resale, net withdrawals from storage, and so forth. The series has since been superseded in company records by a more inclusive set of statistics covering foreign business.
[d] Industry figures are for total products exported from the United States.
Source: SONJ, Stat. National Industrial Conference Board, *Petroleum Almanac*, 113.

Table XI: **DELIVERIES OF REFINED PRODUCTS**
from Domestic Refineries, 1912, 1919, 1927

	Expressed as Percentages of Total								
	Home Trade			Export Trade			Combined Home and Export Trade		
	1912	1919	1927	1912	1919	1927	1912	1919	1927
Gasoline	19	34	39	12	23	44	15	30	41
Kerosene	21	15	5	65	47	20	44	26	11
Gas Oil	29	13	12	4	3	16	16	9	13
Fuel Oil	21	29	34	3	17	12	11	25	26
Lubricating Oil	5	3	4	12	7	6	9	5	5
Other Products	5	6	6	4	3	2	5	5	4
Total	100	100	100	100	100	100	100	100	100

[a] Includes 100 per cent of Humble refinery deliveries; excludes deliveries by Jersey Standard, Louisiana Standard, and Humble refineries to domestic affiliates.
Source: SONJ, Stat.

Table XII: **TREND OF DOMESTIC DELIVERIES OF REFINED PRODUCTS 1920-1927**
Standard Oil Company (New Jersey) and Affiliates
Compared with U. S. Petroleum Industry[a]

Percentage change from preceding year

1920	Gasoline	Kerosene	Gas Oil	Fuel Oil[b]	Lubricating Oil
Jersey Standard	+9	−5	−3	+90	+17
Industry	+24	0	c	+14	+8
1921					
Jersey Standard	+1	−19	−25	0	0
Industry	+6	−11	c	+5	−18
1922					
Jersey Standard	+17	+10	+79	−24	+29
Industry	+19	+15	c	+21	+29
1923					
Jersey Standard	+29	+3	+71	+67	+56
Industry	+21	+1	c	+10	+11
1924					
Jersey Standard	+22	+3	c	c	+11
Industry	+18	+5	c	+11	+5
1925					
Jersey Standard	+3	0	c	c	+7
Industry	+21	+9	c	+6	+14
1926					
Jersey Standard	+15	−2	+9	−6	+1
Industry	+17	−5	c	+11	+10
1927					
Jersey Standard	+13	−15	+23	+10	+16
Industry	+13	−2	c	0	−4
Percentage change, 1919-1927					
Jersey Standard	+181	−25	+118	+172	+200
Industry	+267	+13	c	+107	+59

[a] Jersey Standard figures include 100% of Humble deliveries. Deliveries to affiliated companies are not included.
[b] Industry figures include residual and distillate fuel oil.

[c] Comparable data not available.
Sources: National Industrial Conference Board, *The Petroleum Almanac* (1946), 146-147. SONJ, Stat.

Table XIII: **EXPORT DELIVERIES**
of Three Major Product Lines in 1924
Standard Oil Company (New Jersey) and Affiliates[a]

	Gasoline	Kerosene	Fuel Oil
Total export deliveries, in barrels	14,106,881	11,096,954	4,727,788

Percentage of total delivered to various markets

From United States to foreign affiliates	Per Cent Gasoline	Kerosene	Fuel Oil
EUROPEAN			
Germany: DAPG	5.7	9.1	2.7
Holland: American Pet. Co.	1.2	8.1	0
Belgium: American Pet. Co.	2.6	4.8	0
Holland: Pure Oil Co.	0	2.3	0
Italy: Italo-Americana	8.0	6.9	12.6
Denmark: Det Danske	5.6	7.8	6.1
Norwegian companies	1.1	2.2	0
French companies	13.6	3.3	1.1
Finnish companies	0.4	1.1	0
Spanish companies	3.5	0.7	0.1
Total	41.7	46.3	22.6
LATIN AMERICAN			
West India Oil Co.,			
Southern Division	3.6	2.5	1.5
Northern Division	1.0	1.2	1.6
West India Oil Refining Co.	0.4	0	0
Standard Oil of Brazil	3.0	3.3	0.5
Total	8.0	7.0	3.6
Grand Total to Affiliates	49.7	53.3	26.2

From United States to nonaffiliated companies	Gasoline	Kerosene	Fuel Oil
Britain: Anglo-American Oil	18.4	17.5	21.7
French companies	7.7	4.3	7.1
Vacuum Oil Co.	9.4	8.3	0
Italian Navy	0	0	12.2
Anglo-Persian Oil Co.	0.8	0	0
Asiatic Petroleum Co.	0	4.5	0
British Petroleum Co.	0	0	0.2
Anglo-Mex Petroleum Co.	1.6	1.0	0.5
Soc. Franco Egyptienne	0.1	2.1	0.3
Carson Petroleum Co.	0.4	0	0

From U. S. to nonaffiliated companies (cont.)	Per Cent Gasoline	Kerosene	Fuel Oil
United Fruit Co.	0	0	23.8
Atlantic Refining Co.	0.6	0.3	0
Spanish companies	0	0	1.8
Other	0.2	0.1	2.8
Total	39.2	38.1	70.4
Grand Total Exported from United States	88.9	91.4	96.6

Shipments from Româno-Americana refinery	Gasoline	Kerosene	Fuel Oil
DAPG	0.5	0	b
Italo-Americana	0.5	0.7	b
Anglo-American Oil Co.	0.4	0	b
Standard Oil of New York	0.3	0.1	b
Vacuum Oil Co.	0.5	2.2	b
French companies	0.2	0	b
Austrian companies	0.6	0.3	b
Yugoslavian companies	0.2	0.6	b
Czech companies	0.1	0.5	b
Total	3.3	4.4	1.8

Shipments from Talara (Peru) refinery	Gasoline	Kerosene	Fuel Oil
DAPG	1.2	0	b
West India Oil Co.	6.4	1.2	b
Standard Oil of Brazil	0.2	0	b
Total	7.8	1.2	1.6

Other exports for account of nonaffiliated companies	Gasoline	Kerosene	Fuel Oil
From Russia	0	2.8	0
From Poland	0	0.2	0
Total	0	3.0	0
Grand Total All Exports	100.0	100.0	100.0

a This table does not include shipments from Mexico or deliveries from Jersey's foreign refineries to the local markets of the countries in which domiciled.

b No data available.
Source: SONJ, Stat.

Table XIV: COMPARATIVE WAGES AND COST OF LIVING INDICES 1914-1918

Average annual earnings	1914	1915	1916	1917	1918
Jersey Standard refineries: Bayonne, Bayway, Eagle Works, Bergenport Chemical Co.	$708	$744	$864	$1,071	$1,407
Bayonne	783	818	940	1,162	1,542
Wage earners: all manufacturing industries	580	568	651	774	980
Steam railroads	795	815	867	989	1,424
Street railroads	737	748	798	872	1,111
Telephone	476	529	567	616	690
Gas and electricity	651	644	679	1,092	1,291
Coal mining	549	591	725	966	1,227

	Per Cent			
Change from preceding year	1915	1916	1917	1918
Jersey earnings: Bayonne, Bayway, Eagle Works, Bergenport Chemical Co.	+5.0	+16.1	+24.0	+31.3
Bayonne	+4.5	+14.9	+23.6	+32.7

Cost of living indices				
Hansen index	+2.0	+6.7	+18.0	+21.4
Burgess index	—1.4	+12.2	+30.3	+15.8
Douglas index	—2.2	+9.6	+20.1	+21.8

Sources: SONJ, Total Payrolls of the New Jersey refineries. U. S. Bureau of the Census, *Historical Statistics* of the U. S., 1795-1945: 68, Earnings: Average Earnings

Table XV: REPRESENTATIVE WAGE AND EARNINGS COMPARISONS 1915-1927

	Average Weekly Earnings				Average Hourly Earnings			
Year	Bayway Refinery[a]	All Mfg. Industry	Woolen and Worsted	Blast Furnaces, Steel Works, & Rolling Mills	Bayway Refinery	All Mfg. Industry	Textile Machinery	Textile Machine Foundry
1915	$18.25	—	—	$18.65	$0.291	$0.287	$0.21	$0.31
1916	17.74	—	$12.34	—	0.293	0.320	0.23	0.34
1917	22.12	—	—	—	0.461	0.364	0.30	0.37
1918	27.28	—	18.57	—	0.568	0.448	0.40	0.48
1919	36.45	$22.08	—	—	0.705	0.529	0.46	0.61
1920	41.00	—	30.33	45.65	0.801	0.663	0.54	0.77
1921	39.30	—	—	—	0.820	0.607	0.53	0.74
1922	35.91	—	23.13	31.67	0.748	0.574	0.48	0.62
1923	36.39	23.82	—	—	0.758	0.620	0.54	0.72
1924	36.56	23.93	26.17	35.22	0.762	0.636	0.65	0.72
1925	36.12	24.37	—	—	0.753	0.645	0.54	0.82
1926	36.15	24.65	24.21	34.41	0.753	0.647	0.57	0.85
1927	36.67	24.74	—	—	0.764	—	—	—

Year	Earnings Index Bayway Refinery 1926=100	Cost-of-Living Index (A) 1926=100	Wholesale Price Index (B) 1926=100
1915	50.48	56.65	69.5
1916	49.07	—	85.5
1917	61.19	64.31	117.5
1918	75.46	92.06	131.3
1919	100.83	—	138.6
1920	113.42	105.57	154.4
1921	108.71	—	97.6
1922	99.34	96.41	96.7
1923	100.66	93.93	100.6
1924	101.13	96.36	98.1
1925	99.92	96.14	103.5
1926	100.00	100.00	100.0
1927	101.44	98.35	95.4

[a] Hourly rates multiplied by scheduled hours of work. Sources: Bayway figures from SONJ, Stat. Textile machine industry figures from Gibb, *The Saco-Lowell Shops* (Cambridge, 1950), 498. All other figures from U. S. Dept. of Commerce, *Historical Statistics of the U. S., 1789-1945*, series D-119, 124, 166, and L-15. Cost-of-Living Index (A) is that used by Jersey executives at the time (U. S. Dept. of Labor Index). Index (B) is Bureau of Labor Statistics wholesale price index, all commodities.

Table XVI: **NUMBER OF EMPLOYEES**
Standard Oil Company (New Jersey) and Affiliates[a]
Various Years, 1911-1927

Totals by Geographic Areas

Dec. 31	United States	Canada	Latin America	Total Western Hemisphere	Other	Grand Total
1911	25,000[b]	c	c	c	c	c
1923	46,388	14,337	6,915	67,640	23,511	91,151
1924	49,271	14,320	7,611	71,202	24,520	95,722
1925	52,497	15,130	6,504	74,131	29,588	103,719
1926	51,736	16,883	7,299	75,918	32,742	108,660
1927	51,808	17,200	8,611	77,619	32,978	110,597

Jersey Standard and Certain Affiliates

Dec. 31	Jersey Company	Louisiana Standard and Louisiana Pipe Line Co.	Carter Oil Company	Gilbert & Barker	Natural Gas Companies
1921	15,906	8,143	2,227	1,451	5,508
1922	15,675	10,050	2,600	1,530	4,602
1923	16,916	7,063	2,130	1,496	4,394
1924	18,051	7,577	2,372	1,385	4,624
1925	20,708	9,066	2,393	1,648	4,783
1926	18,805	9,030	1,985	1,690	5,155
1927	17,526[d]	8,210	2,396	1,521	5,558

Jersey Standard—Various Divisions

Date	Staff Depts. 26 Broadway[e]	Bayonne Refinery	Bayway Refinery	Other Refineries	Total Manufacturing Dept.	Marketing Dept.
1912	328	c	c	c	c	c
1920	1,009	5,732	4,284	3,711	13,727	c
1921 (July)	1,054	4,059	2,369	3,328	9,756	c
1922 (Dec.)	1,135	5,191	3,333	3,128	11,652	3,802
1924 (Dec.)	1,301	5,215	3,730	3,496	12,592	3,893
1926 (Jan.)	c	3,354	4,806	c	c	c
1927 (Jan.)	c	3,018	3,551	c	c	c

European Affiliates—Year 1923

France	3,893		Germany	2,146
Italy	1,621		Switzerland	53
Sweden	555		Romania	5,330
Norway	423		Denmark	783
Holland	3,960		Poland	1,272
Belgium	1,437		Other	1,043
Total European Affiliates				22,517

[a] Includes companies in which Jersey Standard held 50 per cent or more interest.
[b] Estimate.
[c] Comparable data not available.
[d] Includes Standard Oil Company of New Jersey, Standard Shipping Company, and Standard Oil Development Company, all of which had previously been a part of the Standard Oil Company (New Jersey).
[e] Excludes directors and men on duty outside the United States.
Sources: SONJ, Annual Payroll Statistics, 1923-1927; Stat.; E. M. Clark correspondence files.

Appendix 3

Officers and Directors
Standard Oil Company (New Jersey)
1911-1927

Table I

OFFICERS OF THE STANDARD OIL COMPANY (NEW JERSEY)

1911-1927*

CHAIRMEN OF THE BOARD

Bedford, A. Cotton	Nov. 15, 1917-Sept. 21, 1925
Jones, George H.	Nov. 16, 1925-Nov. 22, 1928

PRESIDENTS

Archbold, John D.	Dec. 4, 1911-Dec. 5, 1916
Bedford, A. Cotton	Dec. 22, 1916-Nov. 15, 1917
Teagle, Walter C.	Nov. 15, 1917-June 1, 1937

VICE-PRESIDENTS

Moffett, James A.	June 23, 1909-Feb. 25, 1913
Bedford, A. Cotton	Dec. 4, 1911-Dec. 22, 1916
Teagle, Walter C.	Dec. 4, 1911-Jan. 27, 1914
Weller, Frederick W.	Jan. 27, 1914-Dec. 27, 1920
Bedford, Frederick H.	Jan. 27, 1914-Dec. 31, 1926
Asche, Frederic D.	Jan. 10, 1917-June 3, 1924
Hunt, Seth B.	Aug. 21, 1919-Apr. 5, 1933
Jones, George H.	Dec. 27, 1920-Nov. 16, 1925
Moffett, James A., Jr.	June 9, 1924-July 28, 1933
Reed, Frank A.	Feb. 25, 1927-June 4, 1931

* This appendix, while nominally applicable to the 1911-1927 period, necessarily lists many officers whose terms were not confined to these particular years.

Source: SONJ, Directors' records, 1911-1927.

TREASURERS

Bedford, A. Cotton	Jan. 20, 1910-Dec. 22, 1916
Hunt, Seth B.	Jan. 10, 1917-Aug. 21, 1919
	Nov. 16, 1925-Apr. 5, 1933
Jones, George H.	Aug. 21, 1919-Nov. 16, 1925

SECRETARY

White, Charles T.	Dec. 4, 1911-June 6, 1933

Table II

DIRECTORS OF THE STANDARD OIL COMPANY (NEW JERSEY)

1911-1927*

Archbold, John D.	May 5, 1892-Dec. 5, 1916
Pratt, Charles M.	June 19, 1899-May 15, 1913
Harkness, Charles W.	June 19, 1899-Jan. 14, 1913
Moffett, James A.	Jan. 8, 1901-Feb. 25, 1913
Jennings, Walter	Jan. 13, 1903-Jan. 9, 1933
Bedford, A. Cotton	Jan. 7, 1907-Sept. 21, 1925
Teagle, Walter C.	June 23, 1909-Jan. 27, 1914
	Nov. 15, 1917-Nov. 30, 1942
Tilford, Henry M.	June 23, 1909-Jan. 31, 1911
	Jan. 9, 1917-Nov. 15, 1917
Waring, Orville T.	Jan. 10, 1911-Dec. 27, 1920
Bedford, Frederick H.	Dec. 4, 1911-Dec. 31, 1926
Weller, Frederick W.	Jan. 14, 1913-Dec. 27, 1920
Asche, Frederic D.	Jan. 13, 1914-June 3, 1924
Hunt, Seth B.	Jan. 13, 1914-Apr. 5, 1933
Libby, William H.	Jan. 12, 1915-Jan. 25, 1917
Jones, George H.	Apr. 18, 1917-Nov. 22, 1928
Williams, Thomas J.	Aug. 21, 1919-Jan. 6, 1922
Moffett, James A., Jr.	Aug. 21, 1919-July 28, 1933
Black, Charles G.	Dec. 27, 1920-June 6, 1933
Sadler, Everit J.	Dec. 27, 1920-Nov. 30, 1942
Clark, Edgar M.	Dec. 27, 1920-June 6, 1933
Mayer, George W.	Jan. 6, 1922-Dec. 31, 1925
Weller, Daniel R.	Feb. 15, 1926-Dec. 31, 1931

New directors taking office in 1927:

Farish, William S.	(June 7)
Mowinckel, John A.	(June 7)
Payne, Christy	(June 7)
Riedemann, Heinrich	(June 7)
Senior, Joseph	(June 7)
Smith, G. Harrison	(June 7)
Swain, Chester O.	(June 7)
Bedford, Frederick H., Jr.	(Oct. 14)

* This appendix, while nominally applicable to the 1911-1927 period, necessarily lists many directors whose terms were not confined to these particular years.

Source: SONJ, Directors' records, 1911–1927.

Notes

SONJ: Standard Oil Company (N.J.) records. In many cases specific reference to location is meaningless or impossible, since a considerable number of records were found to have been moved from the departments to which they originally belonged. Many source documents, moreover, were not associated with a specific department or division, and present location is of no significance, particularly since this material is not available for public perusal. Where records of major importance are still identified with the department where they were compiled and preserved, and where such location reference is helpful in describing the nature of the source material, departmental identification of sources is supplied. The two departmental sources most frequently employed are listed and described briefly below; other references and abbreviations found in the footnotes either are self-explanatory or are identified when first employed.

Fin. Recs.: financial records. These records consist of the annual summary statistics for the Standard Oil Company (N.J.) and its affiliates as compiled at the time by the Jersey Company and recorded in master books of account—familiarly known as the "Red Books." Semiannual financial reports of affiliates are also included in this source classification.

Stat.: operational records and reports, both summary and detailed, the most frequently utilized being the "Annual Statistical Review." These figures, though constituting an irreplaceable source of valuable information, are by no means infallible or complete, since some compilations were made for special purposes and were not continued. Other series were adjusted and revised by the company to serve other than their original purposes. Such inconsistencies as have been detected, however, have not been numerous and are noted where they occur.

Corp. Recs.: records of ownership of stock of affiliated companies.

CHAPTER 1

1. Ralph and Muriel Hidy, *History of Standard Oil Company (New Jersey), Pioneering in Big Business, 1882-1911* (New York, Harper & Brothers, 1955), paraphrase of original quotation in chap. 1. Unless otherwise stated, all references to events before 1911 are taken from this source.

2. SONJ, J. I. C. Clarke to M. F. Elliott, Dec. 29, 1910.

3. Decision and Opinion of the Circuit Court of the U. S., for the Eastern Division of the Eastern Judicial District of Missouri, *U. S.* v. *Standard Oil Co. of N. J. et al.*, 173 Fed. 177 (Nov. 20, 1909).

4. *Ibid.*

5. Decision and Opinion of the Supreme Court of the U. S., *Standard Oil Co. of N. J. et al.* v. *U. S.*, 221 U. S. 1 (May 15, 1911).

6. SONJ, Fin. Recs.

7. *Ibid.*

8. *Ibid.*

9. *Ibid.*

10. SONJ, H. C. Folger, Jr., to J. G. Milburn, May 21, 1914.

11. SONJ, M. F. Elliott to F. E. Hurley, Jan. 4, 1912, commenting on a statement by Judge Schofield of the Marion County, Ohio, Court.

CHAPTER 2

1. SONJ, M. F. Elliott to J. O. Slonecker, July 12, 1911, to R. W. Stewart, May 4, 1911, and to F. E. Watrous, May 17, 1911; J. C. Milburn to C. O. Swain, Apr. 13, 1916.

2. SONJ, report by John G. Milburn to Hon. George W. Wickersham, Attorney General, on progress of dissolution proceedings, Nov. 13, 1911; Elliott to T. L. Eyre, Feb. 13, 1912.

3. *World* (New York), Sept. 7, 1912.

4. *Ibid.*

5. *Ibid.*

6. *New York Times,* Oct. 11, 1912.

7. *Ibid.,* Mar. 6, 1912; *Financial World* (New York), Mar. 16, 1912.

8. *Financial World* (New York), Mar. 16, 1912; *New York Times,* Mar. 6, 1912.

9. *Ibid.*

10. *Financial World* (New York), Mar. 16, 1912.

11. *New York Times,* Mar. 8, 1912; *Sun* (New York), Mar. 8, 1912.

12. *Financial World* (New York), Mar. 16, 1912; *Evening Post* (New York), Mar. 22, 1912.

13. *New York Times,* Feb. 15, May 25, May 28, Oct. 27, 1912; *New York Commercial,* Feb. 16, 1912; *New York American,* Apr. 12, Oct. 29, 1912; *St. Louis Globe-Democrat,* Mar. 1, Apr. 19, May 22, 1912; *Wall Street Journal,* Feb. 28, June 21, 1912; *World* (New York), Feb. 17, 1912.

14. SONJ, Judge W. I. McKie to Elliott, Jan. 5, 1912. Briefs and Testimony, *State of Texas* v. *Magnolia Petroleum Company et al.,* 1912-1913. Surrogate Court, County of N. Y., N. Y., Hall of Records, J. D. Archbold Estate, Hearing before Transfer Tax Appraiser, 1917. *New York Tribune,* Jan. 31, 1913.

15. R. E. Ferris, "Texas Corporation and Anti-Trust Laws, 1895-1917," Business History Foundation unpublished manuscript. *New York Times,* Aug. 30, Sept. 18, 1912; *New York Tribune,* July 22, 1913. N. Y. Surrogate Court hearing, 1917. SONJ, Fin. Recs. Humble records, certified copy of consent decree, *The State of Texas* v. *The Magnolia Petroleum Co. et al.,* No. 10232, July 19, 1913.

16. SONJ, J. C. Donnell to Elliott, Apr. 1, 1912.

17. *Financial American* (New York), Feb. 28, 1913.

18. *New York Herald,* Mar. 6, 1912.

19. The material concerning Jersey Company directors has been drawn from many sources. Facts concerning their careers have been taken from SONJ, Minutes of Directors' Meetings and Directors' Kardex Files. Information about the personalities of these men has been drawn from various correspondence files and from interviews with many persons now or formerly with the company. Other sources than these are specifically noted.

20. Allan Nevins, *John D. Rockefeller* (New York, 1940), II, 443-444.

21. *Ibid.,* 444.

22. *Ibid.*, 433–434, 505.

23. B. C. Forbes, *Men Who Are Making America* (New York, 1917), 25.

24. *The Lamp,* VII, No. 1 (June, 1924), 11-12.

25. *The Lamp,* XI, No. 4 (Dec., 1928), 11-12.

26. SONJ, Fin. Recs. Earnings figures are employed as a measure of comparison because adequate sales figures are not available for the 1912-1917 period. The figure quoted represents the Jersey Company's share of the earnings of companies more than 50 per cent owned (generally referred to as consolidated companies), together with actual dividends received from companies in which it held less than a 50 per cent interest (non-consolidated companies). Selected summaries of operating statistics are presented in Appendix 2.

27. SONJ, Fin. Recs.

28. This year was chosen in order to avoid the dislocations brought about by World War I, as well as certain operational incidents which abnormally affected The Carter Oil Co. and the Standard Oil Co. of Louisiana.

29. SONJ, analysis of stock ledger showing the different classes of holdings and the number of stockholders with the aggregate shares in each class, from 1901 to 1934.

30. SONJ, Elliott to Eddy, May 24, 1913.

31. National Industrial Conference Board, *The Petroleum Almanac* (New York, 1946), "Indicated U. S. and Foreign Consumption of Petroleum and Products, 1912-1945," 341. SONJ, Stat.

32. SONJ, Annual Reports. Earnings figure rounded off to nearest hundred thousand. The annual-report earnings figures for the years 1917, 1918, 1919, and 1920 differ from the book figures because of substantial tax adjustments, made retroactively. We have employed the adjusted earnings figures from the annual reports in order to give effect to these tax adjustments. Unless otherwise noted, all earnings figures are after taxes. Invested capital is taken in this case to mean net worth.

33. SONJ, Replies to 1916 Federal Trade Commission Charges; Stat.

34. SONJ, Fin. Recs.

35. *World* (New York), Sept. 7, 1912.

36. SONJ, Fin. Recs.

CHAPTER 3

1. Interview, N. S. B. Gras with E. J. Sadler, Aug. 8, 1944.

2. SONJ, Stat.; E. J. Sadler memo, Sept. 22, 1919. Total annual production and average barrels daily (42 gallons per barrel in each case) are two measures of production widely used for many years in the oil industry, and they will appear often in this volume. Net production, another common statistical yardstick which will be adopted, means total production less royalty oil. Royalty oil is the fraction (customarily one-eighth) of production turned over by the producer to the lessor of the producing property as a condition of the lease. Customarily, this oil was sold by the producer for the account of the lessor.

3. Interview, H. M. Larson, E. H. Knowlton, and G. S. Gibb with Walter C. Teagle, Oct. 4, 1949.

4. SONJ, Stat.

5. SONJ, account of A. F. Corwin trip to Mexico, with a report on Aguila Co., Sept., 1911. *Wall Street Journal,* June 3, 1914.

6. SONJ, undated memo on crude oil purchases, prepared in connection with the ICC (Gore-Chilton) pipeline investigation, 1914-1915.

7. SONJ, memo on FTC investigation of 1914, May 15, 1914; W. S. Fitzpatrick to Charles West, Sept. 5, 1914.

8. SONJ, memo on FTC investigation of 1914.

9. Ferris, "Texas Corporation and Anti-Trust Laws, 1895-1917."

10. SONJ, F. T. (Washington) Information Service Memorandum, Apr. 13, 1916.

11. SONJ, undated memo on crude oil purchases, ICC investigation of 1914-1915; Stat.

12. SONJ, Sadler memo, Mar. 5, 1917.

13. *Ibid.,* Sept. 22, 1919.

14. According to Sadler's memo of Sept. 22, 1919, production of these three com-

panies was virtually the same for 1919 as it had been in 1911 (69,359 barrels daily in 1919, as compared with 68,661 barrels daily in 1911). From 1912 to 1919 crude oil production in the United States had increased 72%, and crude runs in Jersey Standard's domestic refineries increased 68%.

15. Facts about the early Cushing development come from C. C. Rister, *Oil! Titan of the Southwest* (University of Oklahoma Press, Norman, Oklahoma, 1949), 119-124; from SONJ, Valuation Reports for U. S. Bureau of Internal Revenue, Field Summaries (hereafter referred to as Valuation Reports); and from talks with many men in the Tulsa offices of The Carter Oil Co.

16. SONJ, Valuation Reports; Stat.

17. Information on Carter eastern district properties comes from SONJ, Valuation Reports.

18. SONJ, A. C. Bedford to J. Edgar Pew, Nov. 1, 1915.

19. Unless otherwise noted, all subsequent information about Carter and Louisiana fields comes from SONJ, Valuation Reports.

20. National Industrial Conference Board, *The Petroleum Almanac* (1946), 15.

21. Interview, C. S. Popple, G. S. Gibb, and H. Kip with Walter Davison and Jack Conry, Tulsa, Oct. 26, 1949.

22. SONJ, Fin. Recs.

23. *Ibid.*

24. SONJ, Indian Leasing and Pipeline Regulations, 1917-1920; leases and royalty payments, The Carter Oil Co., 1915-1918.

25. Rister, *op. cit.*, 97-99.

26. Sam T. Mallison, *The Great Wildcatter* (Charleston, West Va., 1953), 207-209. SONJ, Valuation Reports.

27. Rister, *op. cit.*, 295, n. 24.

28. SONJ, Valuation Reports.

29. SONJ, Fin. Recs.

30. *Ibid.*

31. Interview, E. H. Knowlton with Christy Payne, Aug. 2, 1949.

32. SONJ, Christy Payne to Frank M. Surface, June 3, 1945.

33. SONJ, Valuation Reports; Stat.

34. SONJ, Stat. Figures are for net crude oil production.

35. See Hidy and Hidy, *Pioneering in Big Business.*

36. SONJ, Sadler memo, Sept. 22, 1919. Figures given are based on actual production in the United States and Mexico and refinery capacities as estimated by Sadler, with the exception of Jersey Standard refinery capacity, which comes from SONJ, Stat.

37. SONJ, Sadler memo, Sept. 22, 1919.

CHAPTER 4

1. SONJ, Stat.

2. SONJ, J. W. Flanagan to W. C. Teagle, Feb. 16, 1914. No evidence was found in available government documents to confirm or refute this story.

3. Memo of Nov. 17, 1952, from Teagle to G. S. Gibb and E. H. Knowlton.

4. Unless otherwise noted, all information about the Royal Dutch Co. is taken from C. Gerretson, *Geschiedenis der "Koninklijke"* (Utrecht, 1942), II and III, and Sir Henri Deterding, *An International Oilman* (London and New York, 1934), *passim.*

5. Admiralty Lord Fisher in a memorandum to the Royal Commission on Oil, Mar. 3, 1913, quoted in E. H. Davenport and S. R. Cooke, *The Oil Trusts and Anglo-American Relations* (New York, 1924), 15.

6. SONJ, letter and reports on producing operations in Romania, 1909-1917. Unless otherwise noted, all information in this section is taken from this source.

7. *The Lamp*, I, No. 6 (Apr., 1919), 14-20.

8. SONJ, Claim of Standard Oil Co. (N. J.) against Great Britain *et al.*, *in re* destruction of plant, etc., of its subsidiary, Româno-Americana, in November and December, 1916, I.

9. The authors are indebted to Henrietta M. Larson and Helen I. Cowan for their work in compiling the basic data on Latin American operations for Chapters 4 and 13, and to Professor Larson for her comprehensive summary of those data.

10. SONJ, Teagle to A. F. Corwin, Aug. 11, 1911; account of A. F. Corwin's trip to Mexico, Sept. 1911, report on the Aguila Co.; M. F. Elliott to A. C. Bedford, Mar. 26, 1912; Elliott to E. T. Wilson, Mar. 8, 1912. Interview, Teagle with H. M. Larson, G. S. Gibb, and E. H. Knowlton, Oct. 4, 1949.

11. SONJ, memo of Penn-Mex agreement dated Dec. 28, 1912; M. F. Elliott to Senator Thomas McManus, Mar. 12, 1913. See also Mallison, *The Great Wildcatter*, 239-240 and 248-259.

12. SONJ, Flanagan to Teagle, Dec. 4 and July 8, 1914; Skoien & Smith to Flanagan, Jan. 2, 1915; Flanagan memo relative to Moyutla Hacienda and letter to Teagle, July 6, 1916.

13. SONJ, list of leases protocolized in name of John Kee, Apr. 19, 1917.

14. SONJ, Sadler to S. B. Hunt, Feb. 18, 1918.

15. *Ibid.,* July 31, 1918.

16. *Ibid.*

17. SONJ, "Oil Possibilities of Alberta," M. N. Yost to John Worthington, Mar. 6, 1915. Material on Imperial operations was compiled by J. S. Ewing.

18. SONJ, "Report on Northern Canada," Harrington to Teagle, June 12, 1915.

19. Imperial Oil Co. records (hereafter designated by the abbreviation "Imperial Recs."), Bedford to Teagle, May 13, 1915; Teagle to Bedford, May 15, 1915.

20. Imperial Recs., Teagle to Hunt, Dec. 22, 1915, and to R. E. Sullivan, Dec. 2, 1915.

21. SONJ, William Warfield to Teagle, Apr. 8, 1924. Gerretson, *op. cit.,* III, 425.

22. SONJ, J. S. Sidwell report, 1918.

23. Federal Trade Commission, *Report on Foreign Ownership in the Petroleum Industry* (Washington, 1923), 132.

24. SONJ, S. A. Colter to A. F. Corwin, Feb. 22, 1917; J. C. Buchanan to J. S. Sidwell, Dec. 18, 1918.

25. Information about the London & Pacific and the early history of the La Brea y Pariñas Estate comes from manuscript of A. H. Clarke, "History of the La Brea y Pariñas Estate, Peru"; from *Bulletin of the Pan-American Union,* Vol. 28 (1929), 150; from minute books, agreements, memoranda, and sundry papers of the International Petroleum Co. (designated hereafter by the abbreviation "International Recs."); from SONJ, Balfour, Williamson & Co., Ltd., to F. H. Bedford, Apr. 2, 1913.

26. Interview, Teagle with Larson, Gibb, and Knowlton, Oct. 4, 1949.

27. SONJ, "Report on London & Pacific Properties and Lobitos," especially reports of Apr. 22 and July 15, 1913, by Colonel J. J. Carter and others.

28. Imperial Recs., Minute Book, June 12, 1913. International Recs., London & Pacific Minute Book, Aug. 7, 1913.

29. Imperial Recs., Carter to Teagle, Mar. 14, 1914.

30. Imperial Recs., Teagle to W. J. Hanna, Nov. 8, 1913.

31. Imperial Recs., Teagle correspondence, 1914, *passim;* Elliott to Teagle, Nov. 28, 1913.

32. Imperial Recs., Teagle to J. D. Archbold, A. C. Bedford, J. J. Carter, and others, 1913; O. O. Stillman to Teagle, Jan. 2, 5, 6, 1914, Feb. 26, 1915, and Jan. 25, 1916; Worthington and Hunt to Teagle, Jan. 2, 1914; Teagle correspondence, 1914-1916, *passim.*

33. SONJ, letter signed J. C. Donnell, Aug. 24, 1916. Imperial Recs., Teagle correspondence, 1915-1917, *passim.*

34. Imperial Recs., Teagle correspondence, 1915-1917, *passim.*

35. Imperial Recs., copy of letter of T. L. Scott (manager of Lobitos) to Milne & Co., Dec. 4, 1917.

36. Imperial Recs., R. V. LeSueur to Teagle, June 25 and 30, 1916; H. F. Revett to LeSueur, May 3, 1917; G. H. Smith to Teagle, Nov. 14 and 21, 1917; T. L. Scott to Milne & Co., Dec. 4, 1917; report of Negritos town manager, Dec. 13, 1917.

37. Imperial Recs., transcript of communication of Milne & Co. to President of Peru, May 8, 1911. U. S. National Archives, 323.415 In 8/6, dispatch No. 663, U. S. Consul General, Callao-Lima, to U. S. Secretary of State; 823.6363/7, Benton McMillin, U. S. Minister, Lima, to Secretary of State, Apr. 26, 1915, No. 123.

38. International Recs., W. H. Libby to Secretary of State, Apr. 12, 1915; certified

copy of report of Committee of the Privy Council, approved by His Royal Highness the Governor General, Sept. 1, 1916, and forwarded to the British Foreign Office.

39. U. S. National Archives, 323.415 In 8/1, U. S. Chargé, Lima, to U. S. Secretary of State, June 25, 1918, No. 217.

40. Imperial Recs., LeSueur to G. H. Smith, Mar. 6, 1917; LeSueur correspondence, 1916-1917, *passim*.

41. The first of the articles appeared in Lima papers on July 22, 1916. The booklet bore the title, "La Brea y Pariñas. Exposición que hace la London & Pacific Petroleum Company, Ltd. Impreso por Mimeographic Co. Casilla 2575. Lima-Peru."

42. Imperial Recs., LeSueur to Teagle, Sept. 10, 1916; memo, Nov. 8, 1916.

43. Imperial Recs., Teagle to LeSueur, July 6, 1916, to Sir Archibald Williamson, July 25, 1916, and to W. E. Edge, Oct. 12, 1916; LeSueur to Milne & Co., 1916; Flanagan to Teagle, June 5, 1916.

44. Imperial Recs., Teagle to M. Piesse, Aug. 22, 1917.

45. International Recs., certified copy of report of Committee of the Privy Council.

46. Imperial Recs., copy of opinion of Rt. Hon. Sir R. B. Finlay, K.C., M.P., dated Oct. 6, 1916, and attached to letter dated Oct. 10, 1916, from Montagu Piesse (addressee not indicated).

47. International Recs., memo of meeting in Lima, Wednesday afternoon, Nov. 8, 1916, between President Pardo of Peru, J. C. Donnell, R. V. LeSueur, C. E. Cooper, and W. C. Teagle.

48. International Recs., Teagle to W. E. Edge, Oct. 12, 1916.

49. International Recs., memos on Peruvian operations dated July, 1916, and Aug. 16, 1916; Flanagan to H. F. Miller, July 21 and 31, 1916, and to Teagle, July 11, 1916; Teagle to Flanagan, Sept. 11, 1916; expense accounts of Flanagan, various dates; LeSueur to Teagle, July 11, 1916; memo No. 11, Aug. 16, 1916, quoting Flanagan; Teagle to Flanagan, Sept. 11 and Oct. 2, 1916.

50. International Recs., *La Crónica*, Nov. 23, 1917, *El Tiempo*, Dec. 12, 1919.

51. International Recs., Teagle, LeSueur, and Smith correspondence, 1917, *passim*, particularly LeSueur to Teagle, July 11, 1916, G. H. Smith to Piesse, June 9 and 11, 1917, Teagle to Piesse, Aug. 22, 1917, and Teagle to LeSueur, Sept. 20, 1917. Memo, Teagle to Gibb and Knowlton, Nov. 17, 1952.

52. SONJ, copy of dictamen and letter of G. H. Smith to Teagle, Nov. 14, 1917, and Teagle to LeSueur, Nov. 27, 1917.

53. S. F. Bemis, *The Latin American Policy of the United States* (New York, 1943), 226-240, 276-294.

54. Imperial Recs., memo of W. J. Hanna to Government of Peru, Apr. 16, 1918; LeSueur to Smith, June 24, 1918. U. S., National Archives, 323.415 In 8/1, R. V. LeSueur to U. S. Chargé, Lima, June 24, 1918; 323.415 In 8/2, U. S. Chargé *ad interim*, W. Walker Smith, Lima, to Secretary of State, July 17, 1918, No. 221.

55. Imperial Recs., LeSueur to Teagle, June 5 and 10, 1918; Teagle to Smith, June 3, 12, and 17, 1918; Smith to Teagle, June 5 and 14, 1918.

56. Imperial Recs., copy of the Barreda Dictamen, Oct. 15, 1918.

57. *El Tiempo*, Sept. 24, 1918; *El Comercio*, Sept. 25, 1918; *La Prensa*, Sept. 26, 1918.

58. Imperial Recs., LeSueur to Piesse, Sept. 30, 1918. U. S. National Archives, 323.415 In 8/4, W. S. Penfield to Robert Lansing, Secretary of State, Oct. 11, 1918.

59. U. S. National Archives, 323.415 In 8/3, cable U. S. Minister, Lima, to Robert Lansing, Secretary of State, Oct. 11, 1918; 823.6363/12, M. de Freyre, Peruvian Minister to the U. S., to Robert Lansing, Secretary of State, Oct. 28, 1918; 323.415 In 8/6, American Consul General, Callao-Lima, Dec. 16, 1918, No. 663. Imperial Recs., Teagle correspondence, Oct. and Nov., 1918, *passim*; copy of letter of American Consul General, W. W. Handley, to Secretary of State, Dec. 16, 1918.

60. SONJ, Stat.

61. FTC, *Report on Foreign Ownership in the Petroleum Industry*, 132. SONJ, Stat. Nat. Ind. Conf. Bd., *Petroleum Almanac*, 295-298.

62. Howard F. Cline, *The United States and Mexico* (Cambridge, Mass., 1953), 149.

63. SONJ, Sadler memo, Sept. 22, 1919.

64. SONJ, Sadler memos, Sept. 22, 1919, and Mar. 5, 1917.

65. SONJ, Sadler memo, Mar. 5, 1917.

CHAPTER 5

1. SONJ, Stat. Unless otherwise noted, the figures in this section are taken from this source.

2. See Stuart Chase's description in *A Generation of Industrial Peace,* privately printed by Standard Oil Company (New Jersey), 1946.

3. Memo of Russell Wiles, Mar. 17, 1925, prepared in connection with the case *United States* v. *Standard Oil Company (Indiana) et al.,* In the District Court of the United States, for the Northern District of Illinois, Eastern Division, In Equity, No. 4131. [References to the Wiles memo are hereafter designated by the abbreviation "Wiles memo." References to other material from this case are designated hereafter by the abbreviation "*U. S.* v. *Standard Oil Co. (Indiana),*" followed by particular reference to the data.] Wiles was a member of the Chicago law firm of Dyrenforth, Lee, Chritton & Wiles, which handled Indiana Standard patent matters and, later, the patent affairs of Jersey Standard as well.

4. A. S. Dunstan, A. W. Nash, B. T. Brooks, and Sir Henry Tizard, editors, *Science of Petroleum* (London, 1938), III, 2078 ff., "A Brief History of Petroleum Cracking," by Benjamin T. Brooks. See also Eugene H. Leslie, *Motor Fuels, Their Production and Technology* (New York, 1923), chap. ix, and Wiles memo.

5. Wiles memo.

6. *Ibid.*

7. SONJ, G. W. McKnight to Teagle, Oct. 30, 1913; Teagle to Wm. Cowan, Nov. 6, 1913.

8. SONJ, Teagle to C. O. Stillman, Aug. 5, 1913. *U. S.* v. *Standard Oil Co. (Indiana),* I, Book of Exhibits, Agreement No. 1.

9. *U. S.* v. *Standard Oil Co. (Indiana),* Agreement No. 5.

10. *Ibid.,* Agreement No. 13.

11. SONJ, Teagle to McKnight, Oct. 31, 1913.

12. SONJ, Teagle to Standard Oil Co. (Indiana), Apr. 15, 1914.

13. Memo, Teagle to Gibb and Knowlton, Nov. 17, 1952.

14. *U. S.* v. *Standard Oil Co. (Indiana),* Agreements Nos. 4 and 15.

15. *Ibid.,* III, Exhibit No. 563.

16. See Edward J. Nichols, *Danger! Keep Out* (Boston, 1943), 25, for a graphic account of operating conditions on the pressure stills.

17. Leslie, *op. cit.,* chap. ix.

18. SONJ, Teagle correspondence files, 1915-1918, *passim.*

19. SONJ, F. A. Howard to Murphree, Sept. 20, 1949, containing notes on a speech delivered by Howard before a group of Standard Oil of Ohio executives at French Lick, Indiana, in 1948.

20. *The Lamp,* II, No. 1 (May, 1919), 22-25, "Engineering and Chemical Research Laboratories," by C. H. Haupt and C. I. Robinson. Howard speech at French Lick.

21. Interview, H. M. Larson with H. Vernon Smith, Mar. 12, 1945. *The Lamp,* II, No. 1 (May, 1919), 22-23, and VII, No. 3 (Oct., 1924), 8. Howard speech.

22. Information about the Bayonne, Bayway, and Baton Rouge refineries comes from SONJ, Stat., and manufacturing inventory cards; from *Bayonne Review,* Historical Edition, 1917; and from interviews by N. S. B. Gras, H. M. Larson, G. S. Gibb, and E. H. Knowlton with several men connected at one time or another with operations at the different refineries.

23. *U. S.* v. *Standard Oil Co. (Indiana),* Testimony of R. E. Wilson, IV, 1999-2000.

24. Information on the Imperial refineries was compiled by J. S. Ewing, whose sources included Imperial records, correspondence files, financial and manufacturing records, the *Imperial Oil Review,* and interviews with various persons connected with the company.

25. SONJ, Claim of Standard Oil Co. (N.J.) against Great Britain *et al., in re* Destruction of Plant, etc., of its subsidiary, Româno-Americana, in November and December, 1916, I.

26. SONJ, Fin. Recs.

27. *Ibid.*

CHAPTER 6

1. SONJ, M. F. Elliott to James K. Jones, Aug. 21, 1912.

2. C. J. Hicks, *My Life in Industrial Relations* (New York, 1941), 18.

3. See Nevins, *John D. Rockefeller,* II, 666-676, for a detailed description of the Ludlow Massacre, its background and its repercussions.

4. U. S. Commission on Industrial Relations, *Industrial Relations, Final Report and Testimony* (Washington, 1916), VIII, 7764.

5. Information on wage rates and working conditions has been taken from a great many sources. Information prior to 1921 is extremely fragmentary. One of the principal sources of material is the report of H. H. Anderson entitled "Historical Trend of Improvement in Working Conditions," Aug. 1, 1939 (*Petroleum-Industry Hearings before the Temporary National Economic Committee,* published by the American Petroleum Institute, New York, 1942, 443-509); this will be referred to hereafter as "Anderson Rept., TNEC investigation." Other material on hours and rates is found in SONJ, "Salary Wage Data," Feb., 1952. The material on process hours was substantiated by J. J. Slavin, Employee Relations Manager, Bayonne refinery.

6. *New York American,* Dec. 8, 1912; *New York Tribune,* May 5, 1913.

7. Iron and steel industry and all U. S. industry figures are from *Historical Statistics of the U. S., 1789-1945,* U. S. Bureau of the Census (Washington, 1949), 67 and 69, and from *Report on Conditions of Employment in the Iron and Steel Industry in the United States,* U. S. Dept. of Labor, Bureau of Labor Statistics (Washington, 1911), I, "Wages and Hours," xi-xv.

8. *Historical Statistics of the U. S., 1789-1945,* 67. Paul H. Douglas, *Real Wages in the United States, 1890-1926* (Boston, 1930), 296. SONJ, "Salary and Wage Data," Feb., 1952; total payrolls of the New Jersey refineries.

9. Speech by S. B. Hunt, reported in *The Lamp,* I, No. 1 (May, 1918), 12. Anderson Rept., TNEC investigation. Letter, J. J. Slavin to E. Y. Bricker, May 11, 1951.

10. Information about Louisiana labor practices was compiled by A. J. Fair from local company labor records and from many interviews with men who were employed by the company in the period described.

11. SONJ, G. B. Hennessey to G. B. Gifford, Oct. 16, 1915.

12. Chase, *A Generation of Industrial Peace,* 10.

13. Source material for the Bayonne strikes was compiled largely by Elizabeth Bricker Currier. Much information was obtained from talks with Bayonne employees. An exhaustive store of information, true and false, is found in the issues of New York and New Jersey newspapers, of which the following will be found to be of interest: *Jersey Observer* (Hoboken, New Jersey), July 15, 1915; *Bayonne Times,* July 20 and 21, 1915; *Globe and Commercial Advertiser* (New York), July 20, 1915; *World* (New York), July 27 and 28, 1915; *New York American,* July 22 and 24, and Aug. 20, 1915; *Financial American* (New York), July 22, 1915; *New York Times,* July 26-28, 31, and Aug. 18, 1915; *Wall Street Journal,* July 29, 1915; *New York Journal of Commerce,* July 22-24, 27, and 28, 1915; *New York Tribune,* July 25, 1915; *Evening Mail* (New York), July 27, 1915; *New York Press,* July 28, 1915; *New York Herald,* July 25 and 26, and Aug. 16, 1915. For a highly colored account of the strike see issues of the *New York Call* of this period. Other sources are as indicated in the text.

14. SONJ, F. D. Asche to Teagle, July 22, 1915; Teagle to Asche, July 23, 1915; Asche to Teagle, July 27, 1915.

15. SONJ, A. C. Bedford to Teagle, Aug. 9, 1915, with enclosed notes on telephone conversations of July 24, 1915.

16. *Ibid.*

17. SONJ, A. C. Bedford to Teagle, Aug. 9, 1915; Walter E. Edge to Teagle, Aug. 13, 1915.

18. SONJ, Edge to Teagle, Aug. 13,

1915; A. C. Bedford to Teagle, Aug. 9, 1915.

19. SONJ, A. C. Bedford to Teagle, Aug. 9, 1915. *New York Press,* July 28, 1915; *New York Times,* July 31 and Aug. 18, 1915; *New York Herald,* Aug. 16, 1915.

20. Interview, N. S. B. Gras with Teagle, Feb. 8, 1950.

21. SONJ, S. B. Hunt to Teagle, July 29, 1915.

22. SONJ, Teagle to R. V. LeSueur, July 24, 1916.

23. *The Lamp,* VIII, No. 2 (Aug., 1925), 3.

24. *Hudson Dispatch* (Union City, New Jersey), Oct. 7, 1916.

25. Information on the 1916 strike will be found in the *Hudson Dispatch,* Oct. 7, 9, and 10, 1916; the *New York Tribune,* Oct. 12, 17, and 19, 1916; *New York Times,* Oct. 13, 18, and 21, 1916; *New York Commercial,* Oct. 13, 1916; *Sun and New York Press,* Oct. 14 and 16, 1916; *Evening Mail* (New York), Oct. 19, 1916; *World* (New York), Oct. 20, 1916.

CHAPTER 7

1. SONJ, Register of Tankers, various years.

2. F. Bachof, History of DAPG (unpublished), chap. x.

3. SONJ, tanker charter files, 1911-1915.

4. *Ibid.*

5. SONJ, correspondence files of the Foreign Shipping Dept., 1911-1918.

6. SONJ, D. T. Warden memo of Dec. 22, 1914.

7. *The Lamp,* III, No. 6 (Apr., 1921), 5-6.

8. *The Statutes at Large of the United States of America* (Washington, 1915), Vol. 38, part I, 698-699.

9. Memo, W. C. Teagle to G. S. Gibb and E. H. Knowlton, Nov. 17, 1952.

10. *The Collected Papers of John Bassett Moore* (New Haven, 1944)—hereafter referred to as "Moore Papers"—Vol. V, 224-298, paper entitled "Beneficial Ownership of Property as Affecting Its Nationality." SONJ, correspondence of W. H. Libby, Sept., 1914, *passim;* penciled

and undated memo from J. B. Moore to A. C. Bedford, entitled "The Case of the DAPG Tankers"; M. Piesse to J. B. Moore, Dec. 27, 1919. *The Lamp,* II, No. 6, (Apr., 1920), 7.

11. Information about operations from 1911 to 1917, unless otherwise indicated, comes from SONJ, correspondence files of the Foreign Shipping Dept., 1911-1917, *passim.*

12. SONJ, D. T. Warden to International Petroleum Co. Ltd., Apr. 18 and May 4, 1917; R. Hand to F. D. Asche, May 1, 1917; memo of the Foreign Shipping Dept., Apr. 27, 1917.

13. SONJ, memo of the Foreign Shipping Dept., Apr. 27, 1917.

14. Information about the pipeline systems was compiled from SONJ, charts and miscellaneous transportation system data.

15. SONJ, Report of J. W. de Groot to Homer Eagles, July 20, 1949; R. W. Ostrander to C. O. Swain, Oct. 29 and Dec. 1, 1920.

16. Information about the common carrier cases comes from the following sources: SONJ, Elliott correspondence, 1912-1914, *passim; New York Tribune,* Jan. 25, 1912; *New York American,* Jan. 25, 1912; *New York Times,* Jan. 25, 1912; *Oil City Derrick,* Nov. 1, 1912; *New York Journal of Commerce,* May 11, 1912; *Wall Street Journal,* Mar. 20, 1913; *Oil, Paint & Drug Reporter,* Mar. 17, 1913.

17. SONJ, W. S. Fitzpatrick to M. F. Elliott, Nov. 27, 1912.

18. SONJ, Elliott correspondence, 1912-1914, *passim.*

19. See George S. Wolbert, Jr., *American Pipe Lines* (Norman, Oklahoma, 1952), *passim.*

20. SONJ, undated memo, C. O. Swain to Federal Trade Commission.

21. SONJ, Fin. Recs.

22. Interview, G. S. Gibb with S. R. Simmons, Interstate Oil and Pipe Line Co., Shreveport, Oct., 1949.

23. Dunstan, Nash, Brooks, & Tizard, *Science of Petroleum,* Vol. I, 758-768, article entitled "Modern Pipeline Practice," by W. G. Heltzel. Federal Trade Commission, *Report on Pipe Line Trans-*

portation of Petroleum (Washington, 1916), 75. SONJ, "Historical Sketch of Standard Oil Company of Louisiana, later Standard Pipe Line Company," by F. R. McGrew, Dec. 13, 1923, and supplement to McGrew's account by W. R. Fulton, Oct. 27, 1938.

24. Federal Trade Commission, *op. cit.*, 443-445.

25. *Ibid.*, 163-201, xxix, xxxi. Wolbert, *op. cit.*, 51.

26. Federal Trade Commission, *op. cit.*, 448-455. See Wolbert, *op. cit.*, 22-26, for a detailed discussion of the nature of and justification for minimum tenders.

27. See Wolbert, *op. cit.*, 10-48, 113-117.

CHAPTER 8

1. Descriptions of early Louisiana marketing conditions come from interviews of H. M. Larson in March, 1945, with a number of men who were employed in the Louisiana Company in the pre-World War I period.

2. Unless otherwise indicated, all statistical information on marketing comes from SONJ, Stat., and Fin. Recs. The statement about Jersey Standard attitudes toward the foreign market was made by W. C. Teagle in an interview with N. S. B. Gras, Oct. 16, 1945.

3. *The Lamp*, I, No. 3 (Sept., 1918), 20-26.

4. SONJ, undated memo, E. S. Hall to F. M. Surface.

5. *The Lamp*, I, No. 3 (Sept., 1918), 20-26. Unless otherwise indicated, all information in this and the following three paragraphs is taken from this source.

6. SONJ, Federal Trade Commission investigation, 1915-1916, "Replies to 1916 FTC Charges." See also *High Cost of Gasoline and Other Petroleum Products*, Hearings before a Subcommittee of the Committee on Manufactures, U. S. Senate, 67th Congress, 2nd and 4th sessions, pursuant to Senate Resolution 295 amending Senate Resolution 292 (Washington, 1923)—referred to hereafter as "La-Follette Report," Testimony of Walter Teagle, Vol. I, 161-162.

7. SONJ, copy of Socony-Vacuum Oil Co., Inc., statement entitled "Gasoline

Sales *vs.* Purchases from SOC(NJ), 1912-1931"; memo dated Feb. 28, 1925, entitled "Questionnaire and Answers, No. 10," prepared for *U. S. v. Standard Oil Co. (Indiana).*

8. SONJ, Teagle to A. P. Coombe, Nov. 13, 1912; list of fuel oil installations, May 22, 1919; *The Lamp*, II, No. 3 (Oct., 1919), 17-18.

9. SONJ, Stat. *U. S. v. Standard Oil Co. (Indiana)*, Vol. VIII, Book of Exhibits, p. 554.

10. *Loc. cit.*

11. SONJ, H. Leake to F. W. Weller, Dec. 29, 1914; "Replies to 1916 FTC Charges."

12. SONJ, J. H. Pou to R. W. Cull, Mar. 21, 1911.

13. SONJ, "Replies to 1916 FTC Charges."

14. SONJ, N & D Washington News Service to C. O. Swain, July 5, 1916; M. F. Elliott correspondence, 1913-1916, *passim.*

15. Information about the 1916 Federal Trade Commission investigation of gasoline prices comes from SONJ, correspondence and papers relating to the investigation, 1915-1916.

16. SONJ, undated memo, probably by A. C. Bedford, entitled "Complaint against the F. T. C. Investigation."

17. SONJ, "Replies to 1916 FTC Charges."

18. Information about marketing in Canada was compiled by J. S. Ewing and comes from SONJ, Imperial Recs., Teagle and Mayer correspondence; general marketing correspondence; various issues of the *Imperial Oil Review*; interviews, J. S. Ewing with various men connected with the marketing organization of the day; Stat.

19. SONJ, tanker charters, 1912-1917. *The Lamp*, II, No. 4 (Dec., 1919), 8-10.

20. SONJ, Teagle correspondence, 1911-1917, *passim.*

21. SONJ, foreign marketing correspondence, 1911-1915, *passim.*

22. SONJ, memo of June 20, 1910, on Deutsche Bank purchase.

23. SONJ, Teagle and A. C. Bedford to

J. A. Moffett, May 23, 1910. Gerretson, *Geschiedenis der "Koninklijke,"* Vol. III, chap. vi.

24. SONJ, legal contracts and marketing correspondence.

25. Information about the French Refiners comes from SONJ, Teagle correspondence, 1905-1915, *passim*. See also Francis Delaisi, *Oil, Its Influence on Politics* (London, 1922), 45-52, reprinted from original article published in *Le Producteur* in Paris in 1920.

26. SONJ, Fin. Recs.; translation of an article in a German trade paper sent by Charles E. Kern, Oct. 23, 1911; memo from president of Standard Oil Co. (New Jersey) to the Secretary of State, Apr. 20, 1914.

27. All information in the remaining paragraphs of this chapter not specifically referred to in footnotes comes from SONJ, Teagle correspondence with H. Riedemann, 1911-1914, *passim*. In most cases specific letters are cited, as a chronological check on the text.

28. SONJ, Teagle correspondence files, enclosure dated Feb. 26, 1914. *New York Times*, Feb. 20, 1912.

29. SONJ, A. C. Bedford to Teagle, Feb. 8, 1912.

30. SONJ, Riedemann to Teagle, July 17, 1911.

31. Teagle correspondence files, "Government Petroleum Monopoly," translation of a pamphlet issued by the German Petroleum Selling Co., Nov., 1912; Bedford to Teagle, Feb. 8, 1912; Asche to DAPG, Feb. 19, 1912; Elliott to Teagle, July 7, 1913. *Journal of Commerce*, Feb. 28, 1912; *Wall Street Journal*, Aug. 5, 1912; *World* (New York), May 28, 1913; *Oil, Paint & Drug Reporter*, Aug. 11, 1913. One phase of the attack was a lawsuit against DAPG, brought by the European Petroleum Union, seeking to dissolve the contract between the two companies. The suit was successful in the lower court, but DAPG won out on an appeal to the Supreme Court.

32. SONJ, H. C. Folger, Jr., to Teagle, Jan. 15, 1913; Teagle to A. C. Bedford, Feb. 27, 1914; confidential memo, Teagle to Hon. James W. Gerard, U. S. Ambassador, Berlin, Feb. 27, 1914.

33. SONJ, J. G. Lamont, general European manager of the Pure Oil Co., to Teagle, Aug. 26 and Oct. 19, 1912.

34. SONJ, Lamont to Teagle, Aug. 26, 1912, and Mar. 10, 1913; Riedemann to Teagle, Aug. 31, 1912.

35. SONJ, Teagle to A. C. Bedford, Feb. 6, 1912; W. H. Libby to Teagle, Feb. 7, 1912; Teagle to Bedford, Feb. 20, 1912; Libby to Senator Boise Penrose, Mar. 9, 1912; Libby to Secretary of State, Oct. 21, 1912; Libby to J. D. Archbold, Nov. 2, 1912; cable, Teagle to DAPG, Nov. 7, 1912.

36. SONJ, memo dated Oct. 25, 1912; copy of German Petroleum Selling Co. pamphlet of 1912.

37. SONJ, Riedemann to Teagle, Sept. 23, 1912.

38. SONJ, Teagle to Riedemann, Oct. 8, 1912.

39. *Ibid.*, Oct. 30, 1912.

40. SONJ, Teagle to A. C. Bedford, Nov. 28, 1912.

41. SONJ, Teagle to Riedemann, Sept. 19 and Oct. 8, 1912.

42. SONJ, Teagle to Directors of DAPG, Dec. 12, 1912.

43. SONJ, Teagle to Riedemann, Feb. 3, 1913.

44. SONJ, Teagle to A. C. Bedford, Nov. 26 and Dec. 5, 1912. *New York Times*, Dec. 15, 1912.

45. SONJ, Teagle to Riedemann, Jan. 6, 1913; Riedemann to Teagle, Oct. 11, 1912, and Feb. 18, 1913; Leishman to Hoff, Feb. 15, 1913.

46. SONJ, Riedemann to Teagle, Feb. 18, 1913; Hoff to Teagle, Mar. 4, 1913.

47. SONJ, Riedemann to Teagle, Feb. 18, 1913. Statement of Fritz von Friedlander-fuld, czar of German coal, quoted in *New York Times*, Dec. 15, 1912.

48. *Ibid.*

49. SONJ, Teagle to Riedemann, Feb. 7, Feb. 11, and Mar. 17, 1913; Lamont to Teagle, Mar. 10 and 20, 1913.

50. SONJ, Teagle to Riedemann, June 7, 1913; Teagle to Directors of DAPG, Dec. 31, 1912, and June 24, 1913; Teagle to Lamont, Aug. 25, 1913; Riedemann to Teagle, June 13, 1913.

51. SONJ, Riedemann to Teagle, Apr. 10, 1913; Teagle to Archbold, May 18, 1914. *National Petroleum News,* Vol. IV, No. 10 (Dec., 1912), 23.

52. SONJ, Teagle to Directors of DAPG, Mar. 27, 1914.

53. *Ibid.*

54. SONJ, Riedemann to Teagle, Apr. 10, 1913.

55. SONJ, memo, Standard Oil Co. (New Jersey) to State Department, Apr., 1914.

56. SONJ, Teagle to A. C. Bedford, Feb. 27, 1914; memo to State Department, Apr., 1914.

57. SONJ, Teagle to A. C. Bedford, Feb. 10, 1914, and to Riedemann, Feb. 17, 1914; cable, Teagle to 26 Broadway, Feb. 25, 1914.

58. SONJ, confidential letter, Teagle to A. C. Bedford, Feb. 27, 1914; confidential memo, Teagle to Hon. J. W. Gerard, Feb. 27, 1914.

59. SONJ, Teagle to Bedford, Jan. 26 and Feb. 10, 1914.

60. James W. Gerard, *My First Eighty-Three Years in America: The Memoirs of James W. Gerard* (New York, 1951), 187-188.

61. SONJ, Riedemann to Teagle, Mar. 5 and 11, 1913.

62. *Ibid.,* Apr. 10, 1913, and Mar. 16, 1914.

CHAPTER 9

1. SONJ, E. S. Scott, for British Ambassador, to J. P. Kirlin, Mar. 30, 1915. *Toronto Globe,* Oct. 27, 1915.

2. SONJ, J. B. Moore to W. H. Libby, Oct. 26, 1914.

3. SONJ, rough notes submitted by Professor Moore on prize court cases, Oct. 1, 1914.

4. SONJ, report on loss of S.S. *Palacine* (Dec. 2, 1916), Aug. 29, 1917. *The Lamp,* I, No. 2 (July, 1918), 9-11.

5. SONJ, report on loss of *Healdton* (Mar. 21, 1917), Aug. 29, 1917.

6. SONJ, reports on losses of vessels, July 31 to Oct. 31, 1917; F. D. Asche to E. J. Sadler, Feb. 19, 1917; Asche to D. T. Warden, Aug. 31, 1918; Warden to Secretary of the Navy, Mar. 12, 1917;

Warden correspondence, Feb.-Nov., 1917, *passim.*

7. *The Lamp,* II, No. 4 (Jan., 1920), 12-19; II, No. 2 (Aug., 1919), 6-8; III, No. 4 (Dec., 1920), 12–19. SONJ, report on tonnage losses during war; J. J. Hoff to W. C. Teagle, Feb. 12 and 19 and Mar. 31, 1915; Asche to Teagle, Mar. 16, 1916; French to Smith, May 7 and June 21, 1918. Victor Ross, *The Evolution of the Oil Industry* (New York, 1920), 134-143. Capt. Paul Foley, USN, *Petroleum Problems of the World War* (Proceedings of the U. S. Naval Institute, Vol. 50, Nov., 1924), 1802-1832, gives a concise appraisal of Allied war needs and how they were met.

8. *Statutes of the United States of America,* XXXIX, Pt. I, 728 ff. SONJ, Warden to Carry, Nov. 1, 1917; tanker charter files. *The Lamp,* II, No. 2 (Aug., 1919), 6-8, and II, No. 5 (Dec., 1920), 12-19.

9. *The Lamp,* II, No. 2 (Aug., 1919), 6-8, and II, No. 5 (Dec., 1920), 12-19. SONJ, Annual Reports of the Foreign Shipping Dept.; Stat.; Report of Deliveries, Standard Navy Specification Fuel Oil, Oct. 9, 1918.

10. SONJ, report of transport quartermaster of the *Yosemite,* Dec. 21, 1918; J. A. Moffett, Jr., to A. C. Bedford, Apr. 10, 1919. See also Foley, *op. cit.,* 1829-1830.

11. SONJ, M. Piesse to Warden, Apr. 30, 1917; Warden to Det Danske Petroleums-Aktieselskab, June 19, 1917; Warden to Asche, June 19, 1917; C. Holm to Warden, Aug. 3, 1917.

12. SONJ, Warden to Asche, Mar. 18, 1918; tanker charter files.

13. SONJ, Charles Piez, vice-president and general manager, U. S. Shipping Board, Emergency Fleet Corp., to Standard Oil Co. (New Jersey), Feb. 26, 1918; Asche to Warden, Mar. 1, 1918; Warden to Asche, Mar. 12, 1918; Piez to Warden, Apr. 5 and Sept. 5, 1918; Warden to Burling, Dec. 5, 1917; Hand to Zane, June 16, 1921; tanker charter files.

14. SONJ, W. B. Vanderhoff to R. L. Hague, Aug. 31, 1920; Warden to Asche, Mar. 28 and June 29, 1917.

15. SONJ, Fin. Recs.; Warden to Asche, July 27, 1918.

16. SONJ, Warden to Asche, Aug. 21,

1918; Vanderhoff to R. L. Hague, Aug. 31, 1920.

17. SONJ, Warden to Acting Secretary of State, Jan. 23, 1919.

18. *The Lamp*, II, No. 2 (Aug., 1919), 9-10.

19. SONJ, Stat.

20. SONJ, Holm to SONJ, Aug. 7, 1917; Warden correspondence, 1917, *passim*; exports, 1912-1917.

21. *The Lamp*, IV, No. 1 (June, 1921), 15.

22. SONJ, cables, W. Riedemann to A. C. Bedford, Feb. 5, 1917, and to National City Bank, Mar. 6, 1917.

23. SONJ, cable, A. C. Bedford to H. Riedemann, Feb. 5, 1917; SONJ to Dr. Paul Ritter, Swiss Legation, Washington, D. C., Feb. 28, 1917; Ritter to A. C. Bedford, Feb. 21, 24, and 26, 1917; "Summary of Stock Transfer Situation," Dec. 1, 1930.

24. SONJ, H. Riedemann to Teagle, Oct. 27, 1921.

25. SONJ, agreement between Hamburg-Amerikanische Packetfahrt-Aktien Gesellschaft (Hamburg-American Line), the Aktien Gesselschaft Hugo Stinnes für Seeschiffahrt und Uberseehandel (Hugo Stinnes Navigation and Overseas Trade Co.), and Deutsche Verwaltungs-und-Beteiligungs GmbH, May 2, 1918; Riedemann to Teagle, Oct. 27, 1921; Fin. Recs.; *New York Times*, July 21, 1918; *Hamburger Fremdenblatt*, June 18, 1918; *Daily Review of Foreign Press*, June 12, 1918.

26. SONJ, Sadler to S. B. Hunt, Oct. 31, 1916.

27. SONJ, V. Teremia to McKean, Jan. 9, 1917.

28. *Frankfurter Zeitung*, June 30, 1918. SONJ, H. G. Seidel to Sadler, Dec. 22, 1916, and Jan. 9, 1917.

29. SONJ, Seidel to Sadler, Jan. 9, 1917.

30. SONJ, report, Seidel to Sadler, Nov. 29, 1918.

31. SONJ, undated memo regarding employees of Româno-Americana; report, Seidel to Sadler, Nov. 29, 1918.

32. SONJ, report, Seidel to Sadler, Nov. 29, 1918.

33. *Ibid*.

34. SONJ, "Brief History of Româno-Americana Producing Activities," by C. Wiedenmayer, Dec. 17, 1942.

35. SONJ, memo on organization of the Oil Committee from A. C. Bedford to Teagle, Apr. 14, 1919; J. A. Moffett, Jr., to A. C. Bedford, Apr. 3, 1924. Bernard M. Baruch, *American Industry in the War: A Report of the War Industries Board*, Mar., 1921 (New York, 1941), 3, 17-28, 78-79, 81.

36. SONJ, manuscript history, "War Work of the Petroleum Industry," chap. 3.

37. SONJ, Bedford memo to Teagle, Apr. 14, 1919; Moffett to Bedford, Apr. 3, 1924; "War Work of the Petroleum Industry," *passim*.

38. Joseph E. Pogue, *Prices of Petroleum and Its Products during the War* (Washington, 1919), 7-8, 20-51. War Industries Board, *History of Prices during the War* (Washington, 1919), 42-49, 63, 83. U. S. Dept. of Labor, Bureau of Labor Statistics, *Indexes of Wholesale Prices of Petroleum and Products by Years, 1913-1945;* also, *Wholesale Price Indexes, All Commodities, 1801-1945*. U. S. Dept. of Interior, Bureau of Mines, *Production of Petroleum Products in U. S. Refineries, 1916-1945*.

39. SONJ, Moffett to A. C. Bedford, Apr. 3, 1924. *The Lamp*, VIII, No. 5 (Feb., 1926), 17-21, article by Mark L. Requa. Pogue, *op. cit., passim*.

40. Pogue, *op. cit., passim*. SONJ, "War Work of the Petroleum Industry," chap. 5. See also National Petroleum War Service Committee, *The Plan to Stabilize Prices and Maintain Uninterrupted Flow of Crude* (New York, Aug. 18, 1918).

41. SONJ, "War Work of the Petroleum Industry," chapter on taxation. For a detailed account see Paul Foraste, "Depletion in the Oil Industry," a thesis presented in 1943 to the faculty of the Graduate School of Business Administration, New York University, 30-31.

42. SONJ, copy of letters Standard Oil Co. of New York to War Trade Board, Sept. 16, 1918, and to U. S. Shipping Board, Sept. 18, 1917; Moffett to A. C. Bedford, Apr. 10, 1919. See also Foley, *op. cit.*, 1821-1822.

43. Interview, G. S. Gibb and E. H. Knowlton with Kenneth F. Beaton, historian of the Shell Oil Co. (American), Jan. 18, 1951.

44. SONJ, Moffett to A. C. Bedford, Apr. 10, 1919. Foley, *op. cit.*, 1824-1825.

45. For further information on the Petroleum Committee and on Bedford's wartime activities see Foley, *op. cit., passim; The Lamp,* VIII, No. 5 (Feb., 1926), 17-21, article by Requa; and SONJ, "War Work of the Petroleum Industry."

46. SONJ, Moffett to A. C. Bedford, Apr. 3, 1924; tanker charter files.

47. SONJ, A. C. Bedford to Teagle, Jan. 14, 1921, and to H. L. Doherty, May 3, 1921; checkbook of National Petroleum War Service Committee, 1918-1926.

48. SONJ, "War Work of the Petroleum Industry"; copy of Liebert speech in Petroleum War Service Committee files; *The Lamp,* II, No. 2 (Aug., 1919), 6-8.

49. The figure of $411,769,480.18 for sales, which was used in this computation, comes from *Standard Oil Company, Listing Statement,* Committee on Stock List, New York Stock Exchange, Mar. 1, 1920. Earnings figures are taken from Jersey Co. annual report of 1918 and include tax adjustments retroactively made at the close of the war.

CHAPTER 10

1. SONJ, M. F. Elliott to James K. Jones, Aug. 21, 1912.

2. SONJ, Jones to Elliott, July 23, 1912, and to Bedford, Sept. 29, 1914; Elliott correspondence, 1911-1914, *passim.*

3. SONJ, Elliott to F. W. Weller, June 24, 1914; Elliott correspondence, 1911-1914, *passim.*

4. SONJ, Jones to Elliott, Aug. 22, 1912.

5. *Congressional Record,* May 19, 1914, 9624.

6. Imperial Recs., C. O. Stillman to Teagle, Jan. 9, 1914; Teagle to Bedford, Feb. 12 and Aug. 2, 1915; Teagle to W. J. Hanna, June 10, 1916; J. J. Carrick, M.P., to J. F. Shatford, Feb. 24, 1916; J. E. Armstrong, M.P., to Hanna, Feb. 26, 1916; Hanna to F. F. Pardee, M.P., Feb. 12, 1917; Hanna to E. W. Nesbitt, M.P., Feb. 21, 1917; Charles Taylor to

G. H. Smith, Oct. 10, 1918; Stillman to Pouch and Co., Dec. 30, 1919; Teagle to Stillman, Dec. 29, 1921.

7. *Leslie's Weekly,* Jan. 4, 1912, article by John D. Archbold entitled "The Next Great Step."

8. Interview, N. S. B. Gras with Northrop Clarey, Oct. 16, 1945; *New York Journal of Commerce,* July 16, 1913.

9. Forbes, *Men Who Are Making America,* 20.

10. Nevins, *John D. Rockefeller,* vol. II, 675.

11. *Industrial Relations and Testimony Submitted to Congress,* Final Report by the U. S. Commission on Industrial Relations (Washington, 1916), vol. VIII, 7897-7916.

12. Information about Teagle comes from conversations with the men who worked with him and from a memorandum about Teagle compiled by Ed Lyman, about 1946.

13. Imperial Recs., Teagle to G. W. Mayer, June 21, 1915.

14. Interview, N. S. B. Gras with Clarey, Oct. 16, 1945.

15. Interview, N. S. B. Gras with Teagle, Sept. 27, 1945.

16. Federal Trade Commission, *Report on Foreign Ownership in the Petroleum Industry,* 39.

17. *The Annalist,* May 24, 1920. FTC *Report on Foreign Ownership,* xv-xx.

18. FTC *Report on Foreign Ownership,* 34. *The Annalist,* May 24, 1920.

19. *Forbes,* May 29, 1920, article by H. D. Frueauff, "U. S. Dominates World's Oil Industry." FTC *Report on Foreign Ownership,* Exhibit 13, 100-105, 132. *Literary Digest,* Apr. 16, 1921.

20. FTC *Report on Foreign Ownership,* 12-13.

21. Speech of Aristide Briand on June 24, 1920, reported in *Contemporary Review* (London), Aug., 1920.

22. "Memoirs of Calouste Sarkis Gulbenkian, with Particular Relation to the Origins and Foundation of the Iraq Petroleum Company, Limited" (privately distributed typewritten manuscript, dated

Sept. 16, 1944), hereinafter referred to as "Gulbenkian Memoirs."

23. SONJ, E. J. Sadler memo of Sept. 22, 1919; H. E. Bedford, Jr., to Sadler, Mar. 10, 1921; H. Riedemann to Sadler, Apr. 19, 1921.

24. *Forbes,* May 29, 1920, Frueauff article cited above. See also Davenport and Cooke, *The Oil Trusts and Anglo-American Relations,* 90-98, for a highly critical appraisal of the American attitude.

25. Addresses delivered at general sessions, annual meeting, American Petroleum Institute, Washington, D. C., Nov. 17-19, 1920, reported in American Petroleum Institute *Bulletin,* No. 132, Dec. 10, 1920.

26. *The Lamp,* III, No. 1 (June, 1920), 6, article entitled "Shall America Maintain Its Position in the World's Petroleum Production?"

27. *World's Work,* June, 1920, article by J. K. Barnes, "The British Lion Scratching for Oil," and Sept., 1920, issue, article by the same author, "Deterding—The Napoleon of the Oil World." See also FTC *Report on Foreign Ownership,* Table 6 (p. 131), for figures on Royal Dutch production in Mexico. SONJ, Powell to A. C. Bedford, Sept. 30, 1921.

28. SONJ, Meischke Smith to W. C. Teagle, May 5 and June 26, 1921, Feb. 6, 1922, Mar. 3, 1924. *World's Work,* Sept., 1920, Barnes article cited above. Edward Mead Earle, "The Turkish Petroleum Company: A Study in Oleaginous Diplomacy," *Political Science Quarterly,* Vol. 39 (1924), 265-279. Royal Dutch-Shell figures are taken from FTC *Report on Foreign Ownership,* Table 7 (p. 132). Jersey Standard figures come from SONJ, Stat. Since there is no indication as to whether the Royal Dutch-Shell figures represent gross or net production, Jersey figures for gross production are given in the interest of conservatism. Jersey Standard's net production in 1921 was equal to 5.5 per cent of total world production.

29. Information about the Royal Dutch-Shell in this paragraph comes from Gerretson, *Der Koninklijke,* Vol. III, part vi; FTC *Report on Foreign Ownership,* 21-32 and Table 6; and interview, Gibb and Knowlton with Kenneth F. Beaton, his-

torian of the Shell Oil Co. (American), Jan. 18, 1951.

30. See *The Annalist,* May 24, 1920; Leonard M. Fanning, *American Oil Operations Abroad* (New York, 1947), 3; and *Literary Digest,* June 12, 1920.

31. *The Annalist,* Oct. 25, 1920.

32. Fanning, *op. cit.,* 3.

33. Moore Papers, Vol. V, 224-298, article entitled, "Beneficial Ownership of Property as Affecting Its Nationality."

34. Moore Papers. SONJ, Guy Wellman to J. B. Moore, July 30, 1923; E. F. Anderson to F. D. Asche, May 12, 1919; Teagle to C. O. Swain, Jan. 27, 1919; Asche to Teagle, Mar. 24, 1919. *The Lamp,* II, No. 6 (Apr., 1920), 7-8.

35. SONJ, memo to State Department dated Aug. 19, 1920; Opinion and Brief of M. L. Gwyner, British solicitor and Member of Parliament, dated Mar. 10, 1921; Wellman to A. C. Bedford, Feb. 14, 1921, and to Swain, Mar. 15, 1921.

36. SONJ, Wellman to Teagle, May 13, 1921, and to Moore, July 30, 1923; telegrams, Riedemann to Teagle, Mar. 3, 1920, and Teagle to Riedemann, Mar. 4, 1920.

37. SONJ, Teagle to directors of the DAPG, Oct. 9, 1919; Capt. Z. H. Madison, American Unofficial Delegate to the Reparations Commission, to Capt. Paul Foley, Director of Operations, U. S. Shipping Board, Dec. 1, 1920; Teagle to Department of State, Mar. 30, 1920; Moore Papers.

38. SONJ, "Claims of Standard Oil Company (New Jersey) against Great Britain *et al.* re Destruction of Plant, etc. of Its Subsidiary, Romāno-Americana in November and December, 1916," signed by J. H. Hayes, attorney for claimant; J. P. Hughes to S. B. Hunt, June 8, 1921; Second Assistant Secretary of State to Standard Oil Co. (New Jersey), Feb. 1, 1919.

39. SONJ, undated memo of S. B. Hunt on Romanian war claims (the prewar conversion rate was approximately 5 lei to the dollar); Sadler memo of Aug. 15, 1918; Fin. Recs.; H. G. Seidel to J. H. Hayes, May 2, 1929.

40. SONJ, Hayes brief cited in note 38.

41. SONJ, memo of note from Lord Curzon to American Ambassador, July 2, 1920; unsigned confidential memo of conversation with Lampson of State Department, June 5, 1923. *New York Journal of Commerce,* Dec. 16, 1920.

42. See Fanning, *op. cit.,* 2, for a good summary of the transition.

43. U. S. Dept. of the Interior, Confidential Report No. 8, dated July 30, 1918, "Political and Commercial Control of the Mineral Resources of the World: Petroleum," by John D. Northrop, 5.

44. National Industrial Conference Board, *Public Regulation of Competitive Practices* (New York, 1929), 224-225, and *passim.*

45. SONJ, Sadler memo, Sept. 22, 1919.

46. Interview, E. H. Knowlton with W. P. Haynes, May 5, 1948. SONJ, memos on formation of European Committee.

47. SONJ, Sadler memo of July 23, 1920.

CHAPTER 11

1. Those interested in a wider study of the political topics treated in this chapter will find no difficulty in locating adequate and detailed published accounts. There are many works dealing with the general political, geological, geographical, and ethnical background of the Middle East. The articles that appeared in *The Lamp* are concise and accurate. These are: "Where Civilization Was Cradled," V, No. 4 (Dec., 1922), 9-19; and "Iraq, the Oldest Oilfield," VI, No. 4 (Dec., 1923), 10-17. An authoritative but quite condensed source of background material is E. A. Speiser, *The United States and the Near East* (Cambridge, Mass., 1950), 1-54. Edward Mead Earle's book, *Turkey, the Great Powers, and the Bagdad Railway* (New York, 1923), gives a wealth of detail leading up to the formation of the Turkish Petroleum Co. The reader is also referred particularly to Davenport and Cooke, *The Oil Trusts and Anglo-American Relations.* This book has a pro-British bias comparable to the pro-French bias in Delaisi, *Oil, Its Influence on Politics,* to which reference has also been made in earlier chapters. Both these works arose out of the intensely nationalistic atmosphere of the early 1920's and must,

therefore, be used with great care. *The Oil Trusts and Anglo-American Relations,* despite certain fallacies and an antagonistic attitude toward Standard Oil, contains information of interest and some shrewd interpretations of contemporary events. A detailed account of the negotiations leading to American entry into the Middle East is found in Federal Trade Commission, *The International Petroleum Cartel* (Washington, 1952), particularly 47-67. In addition to these, a great many periodical articles are worth perusing. The best and most pertinent of these that we have found dealing with the early years of the Turkish Petroleum Company is Earle's "The Turkish Petroleum Company: A Study in Oleaginous Diplomacy," 265-279. Jersey records indicate Earle was given access by the company to hitherto confidential information in preparing this article, which obviously favors the American side of the controversy but is valuable nonetheless.

2. SONJ, C. S. Morgan to T. D. Cree, Dec. 5, 1922. Gulbenkian Memoirs. A word of explanation is in order about our extensive recourse to Gulbenkian's memoirs in re-creating the story of the Turkish Petroleum Co. from its inception to about 1919, together with the sporadic references to those memoirs for the years after 1919. The fact is scarcely open to argument that C. S. Gulbenkian was one of the best qualified of all who were associated with this episode in petroleum history to know the details of what was going on. The contributions which his memoirs make are in some respects invaluable. The authors recognize the danger of utilizing the personal reminiscences of an individual around whom great controversy has swirled. Gulbenkian himself states, moreover, that the memoirs were compiled from memory and without recourse to substantiating documents. Nevertheless, the authors found that, while the memoirs occasionally were vague as to dates and the sequence of events, in a large number of instances they were borne out by evidence in the Jersey records or in authoritative secondary sources of information. Not all Gulbenkian's statements for the period preceding 1920 could be substantiated, and a relatively small part of the memoirs finds a place in this chapter, but the authors feel that the references that have been selected for inclusion are pertinent and accurate.

3. Gulbenkian Memoirs. Henry S. Fraser, *Diplomatic Protection of American Petroleum Interests in Mesopotamia, Netherlands East Indies, and Mexico* (Washington, 1945). Special Committee Investigating Petroleum Resources (Senator O'Mahoney, chairman), Senate Document 43, 79th Congress, 1st session, 15-16. Earle, *Turkey, the Great Powers, and the Bagdad Railway*, 15-93 and 218-219. SONJ, Guy Wellman to W. C. Teagle, June 14, 1922, with memo of conversation of June 13, 1922, with Allan Dulles, head of the Near East Bureau of the Department of State.

4. Gulbenkian Memoirs. Earle, "The Turkish Petroleum Company." For a detailed evaluation of political factors influencing the British and German positions in Turkey, see Earle, *Turkey, the Great Powers, and the Bagdad Railway*, 220-226.

5. Gulbenkian Memoirs. SONJ, U. S. State Department memorandum, "The Turkish Petroleum Company," undated but apparently written in 1920 or 1921. SONJ, "Confidential Memorandum of Negotiations with Turkish Petroleum Company, Limited," by W. C. Teagle, undated, but apparently written in 1922. This document makes no mention of Gulbenkian's part in the early negotiations and ascribes credit for the formation of the Turkish Petroleum Co. to Henri Deterding. Neither does this account mention Gulbenkian's claim of an interest in the company—a fact which was concealed from Teagle until late in 1922. In compiling his memorandum Teagle obviously relied for his information upon the major partners of the company, who were hostile toward Gulbenkian.

6. SONJ, report on visit to operations of Anglo-Persian Oil Co., in Persia and Mesopotamia, July 31, 1924, by A. F. Corwin, H. G. Seidel, and W. P. Haynes; memo of Oct. 11, 1922, from Assistant Secretary of State to Standard Oil Co. (New Jersey).

7. All material in this paragraph comes from SONJ, Corwin-Seidel-Haynes report; memo, "Oil in Persia and Asiatic Turkey," by Malcolm M. Thompson, Dec. 12, 1919; booklet, Wembly, "The Anglo-Persian Oil Co. Ltd.," prepared by the Anglo-Persian Co. for private distribution, undated.

8. SONJ, W. Warfield to Teagle, Feb. 10, 1921; John Worthington to A. C. Bedford, Oct. 4, 1911; undated report on trip to Persia by W. L. Morgan.

9. SONJ, W. Warfield to Teagle, Feb. 10, 1921; report on the Anglo-Persian Oil Co., by Maurice Wertheim, finance member of the American-Persian Relief Commission, Jan. 6, 1919.

10. Gulbenkian Memoirs. U. S. State Dept. memo on the Turkish Petroleum Co. British Foreign Office confidential memo on Turkish Petroleum Co., Mar. 19, 1914. Earle, "The Turkish Petroleum Company."

11. Gulbenkian Memoirs. U. S. State Dept. memo on the Turkish Petroleum Co.

12. Gulbenkian Memoirs.

13. Gulbenkian Memoirs. Speiser, *op. cit.*, 51. *Contemporary Review* (London), Aug., 1920. See Delaisi, *op. cit.*, 60-62, for a short but provocative account of the preliminary negotiations leading to the San Remo Agreement.

14. SONJ, copy of the San Remo oil pact. Speiser, *op. cit.*, 66-94, 114.

15. Sadler, in his memo on crude oil production dated September, 1922, indicates that the Jersey Company knew that an offer had been made to the French and had just learned of the negotiations in 1914 between the Turkish Petroleum Co. and the Sultan.

16. See *World's Work*, Aug., 1920, *Nation*, Sept. 18, 1920, and *Literary Digest*, Dec. 9, 1922, for a sampling of the more thoughtful American comments. See also Davenport and Cooke, *op. cit.*, 97-98.

17. SONJ, Teagle to S. B. Hunt, F. W. Weller, G. H. Jones, and A. C. Bedford, Feb. 24, 1919.

18. SONJ, Thompson memo of Dec. 12, 1919; Worthington to A. C. Bedford, Oct. 4, 1911.

19. John A. DeNovo, "Petroleum and American Diplomacy in the Near East,

1908-1928" (Doctoral thesis, Yale University, 1948), chap. ix.

20. *Ibid.*

21. SONJ, F. D. Asche to A. F. Corwin, Mar. 20, 1919; Corwin to Asche and Hunt, Mar. 21, 1919.

22. SONJ, unsigned memo of the Producing Dept., Mar. 21, 1919.

23. SONJ, Sadler to Hunt, Sept. 26, 1919, to Corwin, Oct. 30, 1919, and to J. A. Moffett, Jr., and H. E. Bedford, Jr., Dec. 12, 1919. DeNovo, *op. cit.*

24. SONJ, Memo on War and Postwar Oil Operations in Iraq, by C. Stuart Morgan, Aug. 3, 1922. Morgan was in charge of certain phases of Anglo-Persian field operations in Iraq until July of 1921 and was employed by Jersey Standard a year later.

25. SONJ, Van H. Manning, director, U. S. Dept. of Interior, Bureau of Mines, to Teagle, Nov. 21, 1919.

26. SONJ, Manning to Teagle, Nov. 21, 1919; confidential letter, Wellman to Teagle, June 14, 1922; Morgan to Wellman, Mar. 12, 1924; Heizer, American Consul at Bagdad, to U. S. Secretary of State, Jan. 10, 1920.

27. SONJ, confidential letter, Wellman to Teagle, June 14, 1922; Morgan to Wellman, Mar. 12, 1924; Sadler to Teagle, June 16, 1922.

28. SONJ, Sadler to Rear Admiral M. L. Bristol, USN, U. S. High Commissioner to Turkey, Jan. 8, 1920, and to J. A. Moffett, Jr., and H. E. Bedford, Jr., Dec. 11, 1919, containing report of conference with Admiral Bristol.

29. SONJ, Sadler to Hunt, Mar. 30, 1920; J. B. Moore to Teagle, Mar. 14, 1920; Admiral Bristol to Sadler, Apr. 22, 1920.

30. Fraser, *op. cit.*, 2-4. For British version of the diplomatic exchange see Davenport and Cooke, *op. cit.*, 99-102, and DeNovo, *op. cit.*; SONJ, Frank L. Polk for the Secretary of State to Standard Oil Co. of New Jersey, June 5, 1920; memo of conversation of Van S. Merle Smith, third assistant secretary, U. S. State Dept., and A. C. Millspaugh with Sadler, Aug. 9, 1920.

31. Fraser, *op. cit.*, 7-9. *London Times*, letter to the editor from A. Berriedale Keith, University of Edinburgh. (J. B.

Moore spoke highly of Keith's reputation in university and public service circles in Britain.)

32. Fraser, *op. cit.*, 9-14.

33. *Ibid.*, 18-19.

34. London *Sunday Pictorial*, Sept. 10, 1922. SONJ, Memo on the Turco-Greek Situation, by C. S. Morgan, Sept. 11, 1922; undated memo on political aspects of Mosul and the Turkish Petroleum Co., by Morgan; J. B. Moore to Guy Wellman, May 31, 1922; confidential memo from Wellman to Teagle on political situation in Iraq, June 10, 1922; C. S. Morgan to Teagle, Mar. 2, 1926.

35. John L. Offner, "Persian-American Relations in the Post-War Decade, 1918-1928" (Master's thesis, Pennsylvania State University, 1952), chap. vii.

36. SONJ, Sadler to Teagle, Sept. 27, 1921.

37. SONJ, Teagle to Sadler, Sept. 28, 1921; Sadler to Teagle, Oct. 29, 1921, and to C. F. Meyer, Nov. 1, 1921; joint letter of American group to Charles E. Hughes, U. S. Secretary of State, Nov. 3, 1921.

38. SONJ, Sadler to A. C. Bedford, Sept. 30, 1921, and to Teagle, Sept. 27, 1921; confidential memo, "Notes on the Near Eastern Oil Situation," by V. H. Manning, Aug. 9, 1921.

39. SONJ, memo of meeting of American group, Aug. 31, 1922.

40. Fraser, *op. cit.*, 20; SONJ, Charles Evans Hughes, Secretary of State, to A. C. Bedford, July 6, 1922.

41. Gulbenkian Memoirs; SONJ, cable, Teagle to A. C. Bedford, Aug. 1, 1922.

42. SONJ, Teagle to Bedford, July 31, 1922; H. E. Nichols to M. Piesse, Nov. 23, 1922; Teagle to Piesse, Aug. 25, 1922; Piesse to Teagle, Dec. 12, 1922.

43. SONJ, Teagle to Piesse, Aug. 25, 1922; Sadler to Piesse, Sept. 1, 1922; Van Dyke to Sadler, Aug. 29, 1922; Corwin to Warfield and Hunt, Dec. 13, 1922.

44. SONJ, H. E. Nichols to Piesse, Nov. 23, 1922.

45. *Literary Digest*, Dec. 9, 1922. Earle, "The Turkish Petroleum Company." SONJ, Robert S. Brewster to Hunt, July 7, 1920; Sadler to C. M. Chester, July 24,

1920; Chester to Sadler, Apr. 13, 1921; Henry Woodhouse to Hunt, Apr. 20, 1921; Sadler to Teagle, Aug. 31, 1920; Chester to Teagle, Oct. 16, 1922; T. W. Palmer, Jr., to Wellman, Apr. 25, 1923.

46. E. H. Keeling, general manager, Turkish Petroleum Co., to A. P. Hacobian, Aug. 7, 1946, quoted in Gulbenkian Memoirs. SONJ, Morgan to Teagle, Sept. 19, 1924; Warfield to Corwin, May 6, 1925; unsigned memo of American demands, Oct. 17, 1923, with letter of H. E. Nichols to American group dated Sept. 28, 1923.

47. SONJ, draft of 1925 convention between Iraq Government and Turkish Petroleum Co.; summary of convention in letters, Warfield to Corwin, May 6, 1925, and Davenport to E. Holman, Aug. 2, 1929; N. E. Baker to Armstrong, Sept. 24, 1926, containing opinion of American geologists then in Iraq; geological report of A. C. Trowbridge, Aug. 21, 1926, summarized by N. E. Baker, Sept. 16, 1926; Wellman to members of the American group, Aug. 31, 1926.

48. *The Lamp*, VII, No. 6 (Apr., 1925), 13; see also VIII, No. 6 (Apr., 1926), 4.

49. Gulbenkian Memoirs. SONJ, Wellman to Sadler, Jan. 27, 1925; Morgan to Teagle, Aug. 31, 1925.

50. *New York Times*, Dec. 16, 1925. SONJ, Morgan to Wellman, July 22, 1935.

51. SONJ, Gulbenkian to Riedemann, Oct. 19, 1923.

52. SONJ, Teagle to Bedford, Nov. 3, 1923.

53. *The Lamp*, VI, No. 5 (Feb., 1924), 6; VI, No. 2 (Aug., 1923), 3 and 5. SONJ, Stat.

54. SONJ, Morgan to Teagle, Sept. 19, 1924.

55. SONJ, H. E. Nichols to Teagle, Dec. 29, 1925.

56. Gulbenkian Memoirs. SONJ, Morgan to Teagle, Aug. 31, 1925.

57. SONJ, Teagle to Piesse, Oct. 9, 1925; Wellman to Sadler, Oct. 9, 1925; Sadler memo to Teagle on Iraq, Oct. 8, 1925.

58. Gulbenkian Memoirs. SONJ, Peter Hurll to Teagle, Dec. 3, 1925; Piesse to Teagle, Dec. 3, 7, and 17, 1925; Morgan

to Teagle, Mar. 2, 1926, Dec. 4, 1925, and Nov. 19, 1925; Riedemann to Teagle, Dec. 8, 1925; notes for meeting of American group, by C. S. Morgan, Jan. 11, 1926.

59. SONJ, Riedemann to Teagle, Dec. 8, 1925; Piesse to Teagle, Dec. 7, 1925.

60. SONJ, Sadler to A. C. Bedford, Apr. 12, 1925; G. S. Walden to H. G. Seidel, June 4, 1925; C. F. Bowen to Foreign Producing Dept., June 11 and 30, 1925, and to Walden, Sept. 17, 1925; Morgan to Teagle, Dec. 10, 1925.

61. SONJ, Shaw to Morgan, Nov. 12, 1925, and Jan. 15, 1926; Morgan to Shaw, June 22, 1926; memo of questions answered by S. L. Mason, undated.

62. SONJ, Morgan to Teagle, July 9, 1926; Shaw to Morgan, Jan. 15, 1926, and Aug. 13, 1926; Wellman to Teagle, Oct. 26, 1926; reports on geological prospects of Iraq, by A. C. Trowbridge, summarized by N. E. Baker, Sept. 16, 1926, and by S. L. Mason, Aug. 17, 1926.

63. SONJ, Morgan to Teagle, Jan. 15, 1926.

64. SONJ, summary of report on geological conference at Turkish Petroleum Co. offices, London, Sept. 2, 1926, by W. P. Haynes; Morgan to Teagle, June 10, 1926; Ben Cox to Morgan (undated but about middle of April, 1927), and another letter, Mar. 27, 1927.

65. SONJ, Cox letters mentioned in preceding footnote; also, G. S. Walden to Sadler, Oct. 18, 1927.

66. SONJ, Wellman to American group, Jan. 19, 1927; Teagle to Sadler, Jan. 20, 1927; Sadler to Teagle, Apr. 2, 1927; Teagle to H. E. Bedford, June 15, 1927.

67. SONJ, Wellman to members of American group, June 16, 1927; Piesse to Teagle and Wellman, May 18, 1927.

68. SONJ, Cox to Morgan, latter part of July, 1927.

69. SONJ, Piesse to Wellman and Teagle, May 18, 1927; Wellman to members of American group, June 16, 1927.

70. SONJ, cables, Piesse to Teagle, Oct. 17 and 19, 1927; letter, Walden to Sadler, Oct. 18, 1927.

71. SONJ, copy of an agreement between the D'Arcy Exploration Co., Ltd., the

Anglo-Persian Petroleum Co., Ltd., the Compagnie Française des Pétroles, S.A., the Near East Development Corp., the Participations and Investments Toronto and the Turkish Petroleum Co., dated July 31, 1928 (the Red Line Agreement); Wellman to Holman, Oct. 26, 1934, memo on group agreement.

72. SONJ, W. Worthington to A. C. Bedford, Oct. 4, 1911.

73. SONJ, Merza Ali Kuli Khan to J. D. Rockefeller, Jr., Dec. 1, 1921.

74. SONJ, copy of indenture of Mar. 25, 1920, between Akakie Khostaria, the Rupento Co., and the Anglo-Persian Oil Co.; Asche to Sadler, May 14, 1921.

75. SONJ, memo of June, 1921, by C. S. Morgan entitled, "Position of Anglo-Persian Oil Company in Northern Sphere and the Khostaria Concession"; F. D. Asche to Sadler, May 14, 1921.

76. Offner, *op. cit.*, chap. I.

77. SONJ, memo of June 5, 1925, about north Persian concession by Guy Wellman; Producing Dept. memos of Nov. 14 and Dec. 15, 1921; Ali Kuli Khan to Rockefeller, Dec. 1, 1921; Sir Charles Greenway to A. C. Bedford, Nov. 28, 1921; Sadler to Jones, Dec. 3, 1921; memos by Wellman, Dec. 3, 1921, and June 4, 1923.

78. SONJ, Morgan memo of June, 1921.

79. SONJ, Morgan memo of June, 1921; J. B. Moore to Wellman, Dec. 5, 1921; A. C. Bedford to Foreign Producing Dept., Nov. 18 and 25, 1921; Producing Dept. memo of Dec. 15, 1921.

80. Offner, *op. cit.*, chap. iii.

81. SONJ, memo of Feb. 6, 1922, concerning joint enterprise in northern Persia, signed by Sir John Cadman and A. C. Bedford.

82. SONJ, Morgan & Co. to Sadler, Feb. 4, 1922; Wellman to Sadler, Feb. 16, 1922; Sadler to Secretary of State, Feb. 4, 1922.

83. SONJ, Anglo-Persian Oil Co. to Wellman, Feb. 28, 1922; A. C. Bedford to Anglo-Persian, Mar. 3, 1922.

84. SONJ, Wellman to A. C. Bedford, May 4, 1922.

85. *New York Times,* Apr. 5, 1922. SONJ, Sadler to A. C. Bedford, Mar. 16, 1922;

Bedford to Sadler, Mar. 21, 1922; Anglo-Persian Oil Co. to A. C. Bedford, June 2, 1922; Wellman to Sadler, June 21, 1922; memo of conference between Secretary of State, A. C. Bedford, and Guy Wellman, June 23, 1922.

86. SONJ, Wellman memo of June 4, 1923; memo of conversation between Sadler, Wellman, and W. Morgan Shuster, June 30, 1922.

87. SONJ, Wellman memo of June 4, 1923; Wellman to Sir John Cadman, Aug. 3, 1922.

88. SONJ, H. E. Nichols to Wellman, Dec. 28, 1922; Wellman to A. C. Bedford and Sadler, Nov. 17, 1922.

89. SONJ, C. S. Morgan to Wellman, Mar. 5, 1923; Persian summary for week ending Mar. 9, 1923, by Morgan.

90. SONJ, Wellman to Bedford, Sept. 21, 1923.

91. SONJ, A. C. Bedford to Nichols, Sept. 28, 1923; Wellman to Bedford, Nov. 28, 1923.

92. *New York Tribune,* Dec. 27, 1923. SONJ, Charles Evans Hughes to Standard Oil Co. (New Jersey), Nov. 9, 1923; Morgan to Wellman, Feb. 7, 1924. *The Lamp,* VI, No. 5 (Feb., 1924), 4 and 9.

93. SONJ, Nichols to Wellman, Apr. 14, 1924; Morgan to Corwin, Mar. 13, 1934; Wellman to H. E. Bedford, Feb. 9, 1927.

CHAPTER 12

1. All information about the Paris office was obtained from the following sources: interview, E. H. Knowlton with W. P. Haynes, May 5, 1948; SONJ, Haynes correspondence with W. Warfield and others, 1922-1926, *passim*; letter, Sadler to Seidel, Mar. 16, 1926; annual reports of the Foreign Producing Dept., 1923-1927; C. Wiedenmayer report of July 11, 1946.

2. Unless otherwise noted, all information on Romanian producing operations has been taken from annual reports, operating summaries, and correspondence files of the Foreign Producing Dept., 1924-1927.

3. SONJ, Hunt to Sadler, Apr. 13, 1925; general memo of the Producing Dept. on Europe as of 1920, Sadler memo, Mar. 4, 1926, and Seidel report dated Feb. 10, 1926; Sadler to Seidel, Feb. 26, 1926.

4. SONJ, Teagle to Mowinckel, Oct. 4, 1924.

5. SONJ, analysis of Româno-Americana accounts by B. Bryan, Mar. 19, 1924; S. Schmeidler to Sadler, July 8, 1924. Romanian Mining Law as published in the *Moniteur Officiel*, July 4, 1924.

6. SONJ, Seidel to Teagle, Mar. 19, 1928.

7. SONJ, copies of letters from Austen Chamberlain to Ray Atherton, Chargé d'Affaires ad interim, July 5, 1928, and Atherton to Secretary of State, July 10, 1928.

8. SONJ, J. H. Hayes to Secretary of State, Sept. 28, 1928.

9. SONJ, confidential memo of the Producing Dept., Dec. 19, 1929; H. G. Seidel to Hayes, May 2, 1929.

10. SONJ, Hayes to Seidel, Sept. 27, 1928; Seidel to Hayes, May 2, 1929; Thring Commission to His Excellency, the Romanian Minister of Finance, June 12, 1929; Seidel to Hayes, Aug. 26, 1929; translation of summary of Româno-Americana award prepared for Romanian Minister of Finance, May 31, 1929; confidential memo on war-claims settlements, Dec. 19, 1929; memo of Sadler, Aug. 15, 1918.

11. SONJ, memo of meeting on May 10, 1919, between representatives of Jersey Standard and the Vega and Steaua refineries; Seidel to Hunt, June 18, 1919; Hughes to Hunt, Mar. 29 and Apr. 5, 1922, and Jan. 10, 1923; agreement between Româno-Americana and the Vega refinery, dated Jan. 24, 1922.

12. The general background of the Polish situation was reconstructed from several excellent letters written by H. E. Bedford, Jr., Sadler, Moffett, Teagle, and others in 1925, when the Polish situation was being examined and reviewed with great care by the Jersey directorate.

13. SONJ, memo from H. E. Bedford, Jr., to Moffett on Polish situation, Sept. 8, 1925; memo of conversation with Gustav Nobel, Apr. 5, 1920.

14. *Ibid.*; Sadler to Hunt, Apr. 7, 1925, and to Teagle, Sept. 11, 1925.

15. SONJ, Sadler to Teagle, Sept. 11, 1925.

16. SONJ, memo of the Producing Dept. on Poland, June 28, 1922.

17. SONJ, memo on Olej Skalny and Polnobel by H. G. Seidel, Sept. 22, 1925.

18. SONJ, "Summary of Search for Oil in Poland," by W. P. Haynes, Dec. 15, 1942; annual report of the Producing Dept. for 1925.

19. SONJ, G. S. Walden to Sadler, Sept. 23, 1927; annual report of the Producing Dept. for 1927.

20. SONJ, Sadler to Hunt, Apr. 7, 1925; Bedford memo to Moffett, Sept. 14, 1925; annual report of the Producing Dept. for 1927.

21. *Ibid.*; Sadler to Teagle, Sept. 11, 1925.

22. SONJ, Teagle to Riedemann, Apr. 20, 1925.

23. See *The Lamp*, IV, No. 5 (Feb., 1922), 9-14.

24. *Ibid.* SONJ, report by E. J. Sadler dated Jan. 23, 1920, and entitled "Data and General Information regarding Russian Oilfields Obtained on Trip to the Caucasus," hereafter referred to as "Sadler Report on Russia." In piecing together the story of Jersey's Russian adventure we have utilized more than 600 letters and reports from the Jersey files. Individual reference to each source of information, therefore, is next to impossible, and we have noted only the more important of the primary sources.

25. SONJ, memo, "General Data concerning Russia," by E. J. Sadler, Apr. 27, 1920; memo to Secretary of State, Aug. 19, 1920. *New York Times*, Dec. 12, 1920.

26. SONJ, Sadler Report on Russia.

27. *Ibid.*

28. SONJ, memo *in re* contract of Jan. 7, 1919, between Republic of Azerbaijan and Henry E. Bedford, Jr., Nov. 5, 1923.

29. SONJ, Sadler Report on Russia; copy of memo of Brigadier General E. Shuttleworth, commanding at Baku, July 5, 1919; General Shuttleworth to General Brough, July 15, 1919.

30. SONJ, memo by Sadler on meetings with Tchermoeff at Paris, May 20, 1919; Sadler to Teagle, Sept. 16, 1919.

31. SONJ, memo of conversation between Emanuel Nobel, Hans Olsen, Gustav Nobel, Hagelin, J. A. Moffett, Jr., and

Sadler, Paris, Nov. 5, 1919; Sadler to Teagle, Nov. 7, 1919; cable, Moffett to Teagle, Nov. 7, 1919.

32. SONJ, Sadler to Teagle, Nov. 7, 1919.

33. SONJ, cables, Moffett to Teagle, Nov. 7, 1919, and Asche to Moffett, Nov. 13, 1919; memo of meeting with Olsen, Nov. 11, 1919; memo of meeting between Olsen, Emanuel Nobel, Moffett, and Sadler, Nov. 13, 1919.

34. SONJ, memo of meeting with Olsen, Nov. 11, 1919.

35. SONJ, Sadler Report on Russia.

36. SONJ, A. C. Bedford to Româno-Americana, Mar. 13, 1920; Hunt to Sadler, Mar. 17, 1920; Sadler to Hunt, Mar. 30, 1920.

37. SONJ, memo of conversation between Sadler and representatives of the Mantashieff, Caspian, Neft, and Russe & Baku companies, Feb., 1920; cables, Sadler to Asche, Mar. 6 and 8, 1920.

38. SONJ, cable, Hunt to Sadler, Apr. 6, 1920; H. E. Bedford, Jr., to Gustav Nobel, Apr. 8, 1920.

39. SONJ, Teagle to A. C. Bedford, Apr. 27, 1920.

40. SONJ, Teagle to J. D. Rockefeller, Jr., May 1, 1920; J. D. Rockefeller, Jr., to Teagle, May 13, 1920.

41. SONJ, Riedemann to Teagle, Mar. 21, 1923; Teagle to A. C. Bedford, May 7, 1920.

42. SONJ, Teagle to Gustav Nobel, Oct. 24, 1920; memo of agreement of July 30, 1920, between SONJ and Gustav Nobel; memo of the Legal Dept. on Russia of Apr. 14, 1922.

43. SONJ, memo of the Legal Dept. on Russia.

44. *Ibid.*

45. SONJ, Teagle to Secretary of State, Aug. 19, 1920, and to Gustav Nobel, Sept. 8, 1920.

46. SONJ, Russian Socialist Federal Soviet Republic, Bureau of Representation in the USA to SONJ, Nov. 6, 1920; Gustav Nobel to Teagle, Aug. 31, 1920; Teagle to Hunt, Nov. 22, 1920; memo of Aug. 24, 1920, on visit from E. H. Shepherd, of the British Baku Trading & Shipping Co., Ltd.; memo of Dec. 1, 1920, on meeting of Russian petroleum firms in Paris.

47. SONJ, report by J. B. Moore on the Russian situation, Dec. 7, 1920; memo of Dec. 1, 1920, meeting of Russian firms in Paris; cable, Hunt to SONJ, Dec. 3, 1920.

48. SONJ, cable, A. C. Bedford to Hunt, Dec. 6, 1920; Moore report of Dec. 7, 1920; Hunt to A. C. Bedford, Dec. 7, 1920; Sadler to D. L. Harper, Aug. 11, 1920; Wellman to Sadler, Feb. 7, 1921.

49. SONJ, M. Piesse to Asche, Mar. 24, 1921.

50. SONJ, Teagle to M. Piesse, Apr. 26, 1921; Moore to Teagle, Apr. 24, 1921.

51. SONJ, Teagle to H. E. Bedford, Jr., Apr. 13, 1921, to Riedemann, May 3, 1921, and to A. C. Bedford, July 11, 1921.

52. SONJ, copy of statement of F. D. Asche, Apr. 8, 1922.

53. SONJ, cable, J. A. Mowinckel to Italo-Americana, Apr. 11, 1922; Mowinckel to A. C. Bedford, Apr. 24 and May 18, 1922.

54. SONJ, Mowinckel to Asche, May 31, 1922, and to Wellman, June 1, 1922.

55. SONJ, Teagle to A. C. Bedford, July 19 and 22, 1922.

56. SONJ, Riedemann to A. C. Bedford, May 24, 1922; Teagle to Riedemann, June 5, 1922; unsigned letter from England to A. C. Bedford, May 24, 1922.

57. SONJ, Teagle to Riedemann, June 5, 1922.

58. SONJ, Teagle to A. C. Bedford, July 22, 1922, and to Gustav Nobel, July 24, 1922; memo of agreement on Russia dated July 24, 1922.

59. SONJ, memo of Sept. 19, 1922, on Paris meeting; H. E. Bedford, Jr., to Teagle, Sept. 13, 1922; A. C. Bedford to H. E. Bedford, Jr., Sept. 15, 1922; Riedemann to A. C. Bedford, Sept. 17, 1922.

60. SONJ, Riedemann to Asche, Aug. 16, 1922; Asche to Mowinckel, Oct. 20, 1922; Peter Hurll to Asche, May 15, 1923. London *Financial News*, May 1, 1923.

61. SONJ, DAPG to SONJ, June 20 and Sept. 23, 1922.

62. SONJ, Speth to Teagle, Apr. 15, 1925; Wellman to Moffett, May 1, 1925; Riedemann to Wellman, May 5, 1925.

63. SONJ, Riedemann to Asche, Dec. 28, 1922; Asche to Mowinckel, Feb. 27, 1923; Riedemann to Asche, Jan. 10, 1923; H. E. Bedford, Jr., to Asche, Feb. 21, 1923.

64. SONJ, Teagle to Riedemann, Jan. 18, 1923.

65. SONJ, Riedemann to Teagle, Mar. 21, 1923.

66. *Ibid.*

67. SONJ, Teagle to Riedemann, May 6, 1925.

68. SONJ, Teagle to Riedemann, Apr. 22, May 6, and May 22, 1925; Riedemann to Wellman, May 5, 1925; Wellman to Teagle, Apr. 15, 1925, and to Moffett, May 1, 1925; Boris Said to Moffett, Dec. 30, 1925; memo of the Legal Dept., July 15, 1925, on Russian situation.

69. SONJ, Sadler to Teagle, Aug. 28, 1923; Teagle to Asche and Hunt, Feb. 15, 1924.

70. SONJ, F. E. Powell to Mowinckel, June 14, 1923; Riedemann to Asche, Oct. 9, 1923; Moffett to Hurll, Dec. 29, 1923; Riedemann to Teagle, Jan. 29 and June 15, 1923, and May 6, 1925; Wellman to Teagle, June 30, 1924; Teagle to Riedemann, Feb. 15 and June 21, 1924.

71. SONJ, Teagle to Riedemann, Feb. 21, 1924; Asche to Riedemann, Feb. 25, 1924.

72. SONJ, Riedemann to Asche, Mar. 13, 1924. See also Asche to Riedemann, Mar. 26, 1924; cable, F. H. Bedford, Sr., to 26 Broadway, Mar. 28, 1924; Sadler to Wellman, May 23, 1924; Teagle to Riedemann, Sept. 5, 1924.

73. SONJ, W. M. McGee to Teagle, Aug. 14, 1924; Teagle to Riedemann, Sept. 5, 1924, and to Deterding, Dec. 23, 1924.

74. SONJ, Riedemann to Teagle, Nov. 13, 1924.

75. Memo, Teagle to Gibb and Knowlton, Nov. 17, 1952. SONJ, Teagle to Riedemann, Nov. 28, 1924.

76. SONJ, Teagle to Riedemann, Nov. 26, 1924.

77. SONJ, Riedemann to Teagle, Apr. 18, 23, and 30, 1925.

78. SONJ, Sadler to A. C. Bedford, July 21, 1922; Teagle to Deterding, Apr. 24, 1925, and to Riedemann, May 6, 1925.

79. SONJ, Teagle to Riedemann, Aug. 21, 1925.

80. SONJ, Riedemann to Teagle, Sept. 2 and Oct. 6, 1925.

81. SONJ, memo of conference at 26 Broadway on Oct. 8, 1925, to discuss purchases of Russian oil; Teagle to Hurll, Oct. 9, 1925.

82. SONJ, Teagle to Riedemann, Oct. 9, 1925, and to Moffett, Oct. 12, 1925.

83. SONJ, Riedemann and Teagle to Hurll, Nov. 14, 1925; Hurll to Teagle, Nov. 17, 1925; C. F. Meyer to Teagle, Nov. 20, 1925; W. M. McGee to Teagle, Nov. 23, 1925.

84. SONJ, Riedemann to Teagle, Dec. 3, 1925; Deterding to Teagle, Dec. 4, 1925; Teagle to G. H. Jones, Dec. 27, 1925.

85. SONJ, Hurll to Teagle, Nov. 17, 1925.

86. SONJ, Teagle to Hurll, Nov. 27, 1925.

87. SONJ, Teagle to Riedemann, Dec. 8, 1925.

88. SONJ, Riedemann to Teagle, Dec. 24, 1925.

89. SONJ, Teagle to Moffett, Mar. 12, 1926, and to Jones, Apr. 2, 1926.

90. SONJ, memo of May 14, 1926, entitled "Fundamentals of Negotiations with Russians."

91. SONJ, Deterding to Teagle, May 15, 1926; Riedemann to Teagle, July 13, 1926; Teagle to Hurll and Riedemann, Aug. 12, 1926.

92. SONJ, Hurll to Teagle, July 9, 1926; Teagle to Riedemann, Aug. 17, 1926.

93. SONJ, Teagle to Hurll, Sept. 14, 1926; Hurll to Teagle, Sept. 16, 1926; Mowinckel to Hurll, Oct. 2, 1926, and to Deterding, Oct. 7, 1926; cable, Mowinckel to Hurll, Oct. 5, 1926.

94. SONJ, cables, Deterding to Teagle, Nov. 16 and 18, 1926; Teagle to Deterding, Nov. 17, 1926; Hurll to 26 Broadway, Dec. 29, 1926; letters, Teagle to Hurll, Nov. 26, 1926; Moffett to Teagle, Jan. 12 and 31, 1927.

95. SONJ, D. E. Ponrie to Teagle, Jan. 12, 1927.

96. SONJ, excerpt quoted in letter [Teagle] to Moffett, Feb. 10, 1927.

97. SONJ, Teagle to Jones, July 20, 1927; J. H. Hayes to Teagle, July 19, 1927.

98. SONJ, Teagle to Hayes, July 20, 1927.

99. *The Lamp,* X, No. 2 (Aug., 1927), 8.

100. SONJ, Teagle to Jones, Aug. 10, 1927. *New York Times,* July 21, 1927.

101. SONJ, Teagle to the Directors, Sept. 9, 1927, and to Jones, July 31, 1927.

102. *Ibid.,* Aug. 10, 1927.

103. SONJ, Teagle to Hurll, Sept. 27, 1927; Hurll to Teagle, Oct. 7, 1927.

104. SONJ, Hurll to Teagle, Oct. 7, 1927; Riedemann to Teagle, Oct. 11, 1927; Teagle to Riedemann, Oct. 24, 1927; Riedemann to Teagle, Nov. 7, 1927.

105. SONJ, Riedemann to Teagle, Oct. 25, 1927; Teagle to Riedemann, Nov. 18, 1927.

CHAPTER 13

1. See Dr. Alvin W. Schoenleber's book, *Doctors in Oil*—privately printed by the Standard Oil Company (N.J.) in 1950—for graphic descriptions of places which in the exciting years of the early 1920's even few company people were afforded the opportunity of visiting.

2. Cline, *The United States and Mexico,* 187.

3. SONJ, Fin. Recs.; Sadler memo of Oct. 1, 1925.

4. SONJ, Sadler memo on Compañía Transcontinental de Petróleo, S.A., Mar. 12, 1921; Teagle to E. J. Sadler, J. A. Moffett, and E. M. Clark, Mar. 2, 1920.

5. Senate Document 272, U. S. Senate, 66th Congress, 2nd session, 15. SONJ, C. O. Swain to Secretary of State, Oct. 25, 1919; Alvin Adee to Swain, Nov. 5, 1919; Swain to H. P. Fletcher, Dept. of State, Dec. 9, 1919; memo of the Legal Dept., Jan. 8, 1920. U. S. National Archives, 821.6363/641,645. *Foreign Relations of the United States, 1920* (Washington, 1936), Vol. III, 204.

6. *Foreign Relations of the United States, 1920,* Vol. III, 204. For an analysis of the background of American diplomatic attitudes at this time see Cline, *op. cit.,* 186-193.

7. SONJ, Sadler correspondence on Mexican strikes.

8. SONJ, J. B. O'Brien to A. F. Corwin, Sept. 23, 1924; S. B. Hunt to U. S. Secretary of State, July 25, 1922; Corwin to Sadler, Aug. 25, 1924.

9. SONJ, Sadler to P. E. Pierce, July 28, 1921; Teagle to Sadler, Aug. 8, 1921.

10. SONJ, Sadler to Pierce, Aug. 4, 1921. *Mexican Year Book,* 1920-1921, 319.

11. SONJ, Teagle to C. E. Hughes, Secretary of State, May 11, 1922.

12. Wendell C. Gordon, *The Expropriation of Foreign-Owned Property in Mexico* (Washington, 1941), 64-67. Cline, *op. cit.,* 206-208.

13. A translation of the 1925 mining law appears in *World Peace Foundation Pamphlets,* Vol. IX, No. 5, 1926, "The Mexican Revolution and the United States, 1910-1926," by Charles W. Hackett.

14. SONJ, C. H. Lieb to Pierce, Apr. 1, 1927, and to R. Pratt, Dec. 28, 1927. Bemis, *The Latin American Policy of the United States, An Historical Interpretation,* 217. Cline, *op. cit.,* 210.

15. SONJ, Fin. Recs.

16. *Ibid.*

17. SONJ, memo of C. O. Swain dated Apr. 4, 1927.

18. Imperial Recs., Peruvian title and tax papers, 1918-1919.

19. National Archives, 830.00/578, U. S. Ambassador to Secretary of State, Jan. 2, 1921.

20. International Recs., general correspondence files, 1920-1922. R. V. LeSueur to G. H. Smith, Mar. 3, 1922. R. A. Deustra, *Legislación del Petróleo en el Peru* (Lima, 1930). U. S. National Archives, 600.237/30, F. H. Sterling, Chargé, to U. S. Secretary of State, Mar. 13, 1922.

21. International Recs., general correspondence files, 1920-1922; cable, LeSueur to Smith, Mar. 3, 1922; letter, Robinson to Smith, Mar. 16, 1922. *British and Foreign State Papers,* 1922 (London, H. M. Stationery Office, 1925), 506-508.

22. International Recs., financial reports and statements. The 1927 figure includes approximately $1,500,000 of investments

in Colombia and Ecuador and an undetermined amount invested in marketing installations on the west coast.

23. *World Oil,* Jan., 1948, 197.

24. SONJ, memo by Sadler entitled "Early Development of the Oil Industry in Colombia, S.A."; memo on transfer of De Mares concession to The Tropical Oil Co. (including the contract executed Aug. 24, 1919); "Provisional Memorandum on the De Mares Concession"; Corwin to Sadler, June 22, 1918; *The Lamp,* VII, No. 2 (Aug., 1924), 9-15.

25. *The Lamp,* IX, No. 2 (Aug., 1926), 6-9. For a description of conditions prevailing in Colombia at this time, see Schoenleber, *op. cit.,* chap. iv. SONJ, Sadler memo, "Early Development of the Oil Industry in Colombia, S.A."

26. SONJ, T. R. Armstrong to Corwin, Apr. 20, 1920; memo, "Inquiry of Dr. V. H. Manning of State Dept., May 6, 1920," and reply.

27. SONJ, Corwin papers, reports on Colombia, 1919.

28. SONJ, Corwin to Teagle, Sept. 22, 1919; Swain to Corwin, Feb. 19, 1920; Teagle to Smith, Mar. 12, 1920.

29. SONJ, A. V. Hoenig to Corwin, May 22 and Sept. 29, 1919. Interview, G. S. Gibb with Hoenig, Oct. 25, 1949.

30. SONJ, A. McQueen to Corwin, Oct. 26, 1919.

31. SONJ, Teagle to Smith, Oct. 21, 1919.

32. SONJ, translation of De Mares concession contracts.

33. SONJ, Smith to G. W. Crawford, Jan. 20, 1920; telegrams, Crawford to Teagle, Aug. 5, 1920, and Teagle to Ross, Aug. 12, 1920; International Recs., minutes of directors' meetings, Aug. 20, 1920.

34. International Recs., W. S. Smullins to Smith, Jan. 18, 1921.

35. International Recs., General Letters of Progress; The Tropical Oil Co. annual report for 1928; memo, "Condition of Operations, Tropical Oil Company in Colombia, as of June 30, 1921."

36. International Recs., Tropical Oil Co. report for 1921.

37. International Recs., General Letters of Progress, 1920-1921. SONJ, Stat.;

"Conditions of Operations, Tropical Oil Company in Colombia, as of June 30, 1921."

38. International Recs., Sadler to McQueen, Mar. 20, 1924; "Tropical Oil Company Development during 1926"; Dept. of Economics statistical compilations.

39. SONJ, Corwin correspondence, notes of Apr. 2, 1924. International Recs., General Letters of Progress, 1925.

40. Except where otherwise indicated the information on labor relations comes from International Recs., files on general labor matters and labor legislation, 1921-1927, and General Letters of Progress, 1921-1927, and from annual reports of The Tropical Oil Co., 1921-1927.

41. International Recs., notes regarding visit of commission directed by the Minister of Labor, Mar.-Apr., 1924; Colombia Ministerio de Industrias, *Memoria Presentado al Congreso de 1924* (Bogotá, 1924), 25-27, and 1927, 60-61.

42. U. S. National Archives 821.6363/197, H. Phillips, U. S. Minister to Bogotá to U. S. Secretary of State, Dec. 15, 1921. *Oil & Gas Journal,* Oct. 14, 1926, article by Charles E. Kern entitled "Oil Possibilities of Colombia are Interesting Many Companies."

43. SONJ, Fin. Recs.

44. SONJ, "Memorandum referring to Oil Pipe Line, Cartagena, Colombia," Nov., 1919, by J. W. Flanagan. International Recs., correspondence with Flanagan, 1919; unsigned letter to Teagle, July 30, 1921.

45. See *The Lamp,* IX, No. 2 (Aug., 1926), 14-15, 17.

46. International Recs., Flanagan to W. F. Brock, Feb. 3, Apr. 27, May 10, and June 27, 1920.

47. International Recs., Flanagan correspondence, Aug., 1920–May, 1921; Flanagan memo regarding conferences with Urueta, Aug. 5-7, 1921; Flanagan memo to C. H. Smith, June 27, 1921.

48. International Recs., Flanagan to G. H. Smith, Oct. 4, 1922.

49. SONJ, Fin. Recs.

50. SONJ, G. S. Walden to Sadler and

Hunt, Jan. 26, 1916; Teagle to Heard, Mar. 23 and June 26, 1917.

51. SONJ, report by Flanagan on his Ecuadorian investigation, contained in two letters to M. M. Moore, of Cleveland, one covering progress from June 1 to Aug. 31, 1917, and the other dated July 24, 1917.

52. SONJ, copy of letter of Ernesto Morea to the Ecuadorian House of Representatives, Sept. 10, 1917.

53. *Foreign Relations of the U. S., 1920,* Vol. II, 213.

54. SONJ, McQueen to Sadler, Apr. 4, 1921.

55. SONJ, Asche to Corwin, June 8, 1917; report of T. R. Armstrong on Argentina, Apr. 19, 1926.

56. SONJ, memo on Argentina by Sadler, May 25, 1923, and "Summary of Oil Development in the Argentine and Government's Oil Policy, Aug. 15, 1933"; Stat.; Fin. Recs.

57. SONJ, memo on Y. P. F., Aug. 15, 1933; Armstrong report on Argentina.

58. *El Universal* (Mexico City), Feb. 8, 1928; SONJ, Armstrong to Stokely Morgan, U. S. Dept. of State, May 15, 1928.

59. SONJ, Corwin to Teagle, Sept. 23, 1918.

60. *Ibid.*

61. Schoenleber, *op. cit.,* 275-280. *The Lamp,* VI, No. 5 (Feb., 1924), 11-15.

62. SONJ, Report of Inspection Trip to Bolivia, by G. S. Walden, 1926, and annual reports on SOC Bolivia.

63. Schoenleber, *op. cit.,* 271.

64. U. S. *Consular Reports,* Mar., 1887, Vol. 75, 556-557; also report of Aug. 10, 1880. Deterding, *An International Oilman,* 97-98.

65. U. S. National Archives, 831.6 3/4, Minister McGoodwin to U. S. Dept. of State, Oct. 25, 1915.

66. *Leyes y decretos reglamentarios de los Estados de U. de V.,* Vol. 14, 194. U. S. National Archives, Caracas Post Records, 1919, Vol. 166, translation of code of 1918. H. J. Allen, *Venezuela, a Democracy* (New York, 1940), 222-227. *Gazete Oficial,* Oct. 9, 1918. SONJ, A. Moreno to J. H. Senior, Nov. 16, 1918.

67. SONJ, M. M. Thompson to Corwin, Jan. 16, 1919.

68. SONJ, report of M. M. Thompson. Apr. 18, 1919.

69. SONJ, preliminary report on Venezuela, undated but about June 1, 1919.

70. SONJ, A. V. Hoenig to Corwin, Sept. 4, 1919. Creole Petroleum Co. records, report of conference of Minister Preston McGoodwin, Hoenig, and T. R. Armstrong, May 19, 1920.

71. Creole Recs., J. H. Senior to Corwin, June 17, 1919.

72. Creole Recs., Armstrong memo of Dec. 9, 1919.

73. *Ibid.,* also memos of Dec. 12, 13, 15, and 16, 1919.

74. Creole Recs., Armstrong notes on conference with Julio Mendez, May 18, 1919, and with Preston McGoodwin, May 19, 1919; Armstrong to Corwin, Jan. 24, 1920, and May 24, 1920.

75. *Gazete Oficial,* June through December, 1920.

76. Creole Recs., Dawson to Sadler, Oct. 8, 1920.

77. Creole Recs., Armstrong to Sadler, Apr. 21, 1921; Dawson to Sadler, Apr. 9, 1921. Interview, H. M. Larson with Carter Pannill, June 26, 1951.

78. Creole Recs., Dalburg to Dawson, Oct. 5, 1921; Minute Book I of the SOC (Venezuela).

79. Deterding, *op. cit.,* 99.

80. *The Lamp,* IX, No. 1 (June, 1926), 15-16. Schoenleber, *op. cit.,* 265.

81. Creole Recs., H. A. Greenwood to A. W. Schoenleber, Oct. 20, 1922; reports on Venezuela, memo of A. L. Owens, Jan. 23, 1926.

82. Creole Recs., Sadler letters, 1924-1926, contain voluminous references to the Buchavacoa affair.

83. Creole Recs., Teagle to Sadler, Apr. 1, 1926. Deterding, *op. cit.,* 100-101.

84. Creole Recs., cable, Asche to Teagle, Apr. 25, 1921; Teagle to Wellman, May 7, 1921. *New York Tribune,* May 13, 1921. *Netherlands Orange Book,* 1921.

85. Creole Recs., Teagle to H. G. Seidel, June 30, 1926.

86. Creole Recs., cable, Emery to Producing Dept., Aug. 12, 1922; letter, Teagle to H. Riedemann, Feb. 7, 1923.

87. SONJ, Teagle memo to Asche, Hunt, and Sadler, Feb. 4, 1924.

88. SONJ, Teagle to Riedemann, Feb. 7, 1923; Warfield to Teagle, Apr. 8, 1924; Fin. Recs.

89. SONJ, Wellman to Asche, June 14, 1922; J. E. Horstmann, director of NKPM, to Teagle, Aug. 18, 1927.

90. SONJ, Klaare to Teagle, July 27, 1927; Horstmann to Teagle, Aug. 18 and 22, 1927.

91. SONJ, Seidel to Producing Dept., Oct. 28, 1927; Horstmann to Teagle, Nov. 2, 1927; translation of 1928 agreement with Dutch government; report on NKPM as of Jan. 10, 1928; review of NKPM operations for the year 1928; Brown memo of Jan. 10, 1928.

92. Schoenleber, *op. cit.,* 280. Unless otherwise noted, all information in this section comes from this volume.

93. SONJ, *Medical Bulletin,* June, 1948, *Thirtieth Anniversary Issue, 1918-1948,* foreword and p. 1; *The Lamp,* I, No. 1 (May, 1918), 15, and I, No. 3 (Sept., 1918), 28.

94. SONJ, report of A. V. Schoenleber to W. J. Denno, Jan. 1, 1921; see also Schoenleber, *op. cit.,* 71-75.

95. SONJ, International Recs., Schoenleber to G. H. Smith, Sept. 2, 1921.

96. Medical progress in Colombia is recorded in International Recs., "Medical Matters General" file and medical reports of the period.

97. Schoenleber, *op. cit.,* 264-269. Creole Recs., Venezuelan medical reports, 1924-1927.

CHAPTER 14

1. Unless otherwise noted, all statistical material in this chapter comes from SONJ, Stat.

2. SONJ, G. W. McKnight to W. C. Teagle, Dec. 30, 1920.

3. Interview, N. S. B. Gras with Teagle, Sept. 28, 1947. See also Rister, *Oil! Titan of the Southwest,* 144-147.

4. Material on Humble was compiled by Kenneth W. Porter. Sources of informa-

tion on the organization of the company included Humble Oil & Refining Co. records (designated hereafter as "Humble Recs."), principally correspondence of R. S. Sterling, W. S. Farish, W. W. Fondren, and H. C. Wiess; trade periodicals; and a large number of interviews by Porter with persons connected with the events described.

5. Teagle memo to Gibb and Knowlton, Nov. 17, 1952. Interview, Porter with W. N. Finnegan, July 13, 1945, and with G. Clint Wood, July 21, 1948. SONJ, memo by Guy Wellman, Sept. 26, 1918.

6. SONJ, telegram, C. O. Swain to Frank Andrews, Jan. 22, 1919; letter, Andrews, Streetman, Logue, and Mobley to Swain, Jan. 24, 1919; Humble Recs., Gay Carroll, "Financial Summary of the Transactions of Humble Co."; Directors' Minutes, I, 47-48. *Wall Street Journal,* Feb. 6, 20, 25, 1919; *Oil & Gas Journal,* Feb. 7, 14, Mar. 28, Apr. 11, Oct. 24, 1919; *Financial American* (New York), Mar. 12, 1919.

7. Humble Recs., R. L. Blaffer to R. S. Sterling and others, May 2, 1919. SONJ, Guy Wellman to W. C. Teagle, Mar. 11, 1919.

8. SONJ, The Carter Oil Co., Production, Purchases, and Sales of Crude Oil and Crude Held in Storage at the End of Each Year, 1914-1927, Western Division.

9. SONJ, E. M. Clark to F. H. Bedford, Feb. 25, 1921.

10. *The Lamp,* III, No. 5 (Feb., 1921), 21; III, No. 6 (Apr., 1921), 6; IV, No. 5 (Feb., 1922), 3, 17-18.

11. SONJ, Stat. *Humble Magazine,* 1921, May (p. 23), Aug. (p. 31), and Nov. (p. 39). Humble Recs., Finnegan to J. P. Moore, May 12, 1921, Arnold to Farish, Aug. 7, 1921; Corwin to Jersey Standard directors, Jan. 19, 1923.

12. Rister, *op. cit.,* 216. SONJ, Valuation Reports, Field Summaries; Fin. Recs.

13. SONJ, Valuation Reports, Field Summaries; memo dated Sept. 15, 1938, by R. G. Nusser, Louisiana Standard Land Dept., on history of Louisiana Standard producing operations; Teagle to K. R. Kingsbury, Dec. 1, 1922. Rister, *op. cit.,* 209-215.

14. SONJ, Louisiana Crude Oil Purchases by Areas, 1909-1948.

15. Information in this paragraph comes from interviews by G. S. Gibb with Carter men, Tulsa, Oct., 1949.

16. Rister, *op. cit.*, 195-197.

17. *Ibid.*, 196, 199.

18. *Ibid.*, 199. All figures on bonus payments by Carter are from SONJ, Valuation Reports, Field Summaries.

19. Rister, *op. cit.*, 197-198. SONJ, Background Data on Representative Oil Pools, The Carter Oil Co.

20. SONJ, Valuation Reports, Field Summaries.

21. Federal Trade Commission, *Prices, Profits, and Competition in the Petroleum Industry*, Report of Dec. 12, 1927, in response to Senate Resolution No. 31, 66th Congress, Senate Document No. 61, 70th Congress, 1st session (Washington, 1928), 118, 136-140.

22. SONJ, Christy Payne to George H. Jones. See also *The Lamp*, II, No. 6 (Apr., 1920), 9 and 25.

23. SONJ, Valuation Reports.

24. SONJ, A. F. Corwin to A. V. Hoenig, Apr. 27, 1925, and Apr. 8, 1926.

25. Material on Imperial producing operations was compiled by J. S. Ewing, utilizing the following sources: Imperial Recs., general correspondence; *Imperial Oil Review*, 1919-1927; *The Lamp*, 1919-1927.

26. SONJ, Background Data on Representative Oil Pools, The Carter Oil Co. Interviews, G. S. Gibb with E. O. Markham, Oct. 31, 1949, and with W. J. Rapson, Tulsa, Oct. 30, 1949.

27. SONJ, Valuation Reports; Stat.

28. SONJ, annual report of the Producing Dept. for 1925; note dated Apr. 15, 1926, addressed to W. S. Farish.

29. Interview, G. S. Gibb with Walter Davison and W. A. Watkins, Tulsa, Oct. 24, 1949.

30. Material on the Carter medical reorganization is taken from Schoenleber, *Doctors in Oil*, 23-39.

31. This and subsequent references to the Humble Oil Co. are taken from much more detailed accounts compiled by Henrietta M. Larson and Kenneth W. Porter.

32. SONJ, Corwin to R. M. Young, Dec. 19, 1923; "Brief History of Exploration and Exploration Technique," by C. Wiedenmayer. Dunstan, Nash, Brooks, & Tizard, *Science of Petroleum*, I, "Petroleum Geophysics," by Donald C. Barton, and "Historical Notes on the Development of the Techniques of Prospecting for Petroleum," by E. DeGolyer. Temporary National Economic Committee, *Hearings*, 1939, Statements of Witnesses, E. DeGolyer on production.

33. SONJ, annual report of the Producing Dept. for 1925.

34. SONJ, Wiedenmayer "History of Exploration"; annual report for Româno-Americana for 1925 and report of Standard Oil Co. of Venezuela for month of April, 1927.

35. Dunstan, Nash, Brooks, & Tizard, *op. cit.*, I, 274-275. SONJ, Notes on Petroleum Engineering by C. D. Watson, The Carter Oil Co. Interview, K. W. Porter with J. O. Lewis, Mar. 8, 1951. Letters to Porter from H. G. Botset, Mar. 27, 1951, L. C. Uren, Mar. 2, 1951, and H. W. Benischek, Mar. 9, 1951.

36. SONJ, General Statement of Production and Stocks of Crude Oil, Jan. 6, 1923. TNEC *Hearings*, Statements of Witnesses, Joseph E. Pogue on oil economics, Aug. 1, 1939.

37. Report to the Directors of the American Petroleum Institute, dated Sept. 22, 1923, and signed by H. C. Doherty, W. C. Teagle, E. C. Lufkin, and W. N. Davis; API Directors' Minutes, meeting of Sept. 24, 1923.

38. *Oil & Gas Journal*, Oct. 11, 1923, and Nov. 27, 1924.

39. *Oil & Gas Journal*, Dec. 13, 1923, 23 and 107; Nov. 20, 1924, 23; Feb. 19, 1925, 26 and 117; Feb. 26, 1925, 26 and 211. Report of Special Committee to the directors of the American Petroleum Institute, Sept. 23, 1923. H. L. Doherty, "Suggestions for Conservation of Petroleum by Control of Production," *Production of Petroleum in 1924* (American Institute of Mining and Metallurgical Engineers, New York, 1925). Leonard Marion Logan, *Stabilization of the Petroleum In-*

dustry (Norman, Oklahoma, 1930), 144-148. Robert E. Hardwicke, *Antitrust Laws, et al. vs. Unit Operations of Gas or Gas Pools* (AIMME, New York, 1948), 8-11, 23-26, 179-190. Humble Recs., Austin Hearing, Federal Oil Conservation Board Questionnaire, Jan. 10, 1925. SONJ, Teagle and Farish to A. C. Bedford, Jan. 5, 1925. API *Bulletin,* Jan. 24, 1925.

40. This section of the report of the Committee of Eleven was published under the title, *American Petroleum, Supply and Demand* (New York, 1925). API *Bulletin,* Jan. 6 and 20, 1926.

41. Humble Recs., Farish to Hubert Work, Mar. 31, 1925.

42. Humble Recs., W. E. Pratt to Isaac Marcosson, Nov. 3, 1927; H. C. Wiess to F. H. Farwell, July 9, 1930.

43. Hardwicke, *op. cit.,* 17-18 and 29-30, note 26. Logan, *op. cit.,* 149-150. Leonard M. Fanning, *The Rise of American Oil* (New York, 1936), 143. Humble Recs., copy of Report of Federal Oil Conservation Board, Sept., 1926; "Memorandum concerning Conservation and Production Policy," Feb. 7, 1930, by W. S. Farish, as amended by Hines Baker. Interviews, K. W. Porter with C. E. Reistle, Jr., Feb. 23, 1949. Letter, Reistle to Porter, Feb. 24, 1949. *The Lamp,* X, No. 1 (June, 1927), 6-7.

44. Humble Recs., copy of address by W. S. Farish before West Texas Chamber of Commerce, Amarillo, June 23, 1926; address by Farish entitled "The Oil Industries" before the third public conference on education and industry held under the auspices of the University of Chicago and the Institute of American Meat Packers, Oct. 27, 1926; Annual Address of the President, API, Tulsa, Dec., 1926.

45. James A. Veasey, "Legislative Control of the Business of Producing Oil and Gas," American Bar Association, *Report of the Fifteenth Annual Meeting,* 576-630.

46. SONJ, unsigned memo of June 30, 1921, from E. M. Clark files; General Statement of Production and Stocks of Crude Oil, Jan. 6, 1922.

47. SONJ, memo of agreement between SONJ and the Standard Oil Co. (Cali-

fornia) for purchases of crude, Sept. 28, 1922; Teagle to S. B. Hunt, Mar. 13, 1923.

48. SONJ, Teagle to Hunt, Mar. 13, 1923, and to A. C. Bedford, June 20, 1923.

49. SONJ, Teagle to E. M. Clark, Sept. 27, 1922, and to F. D. Asche, Oct. 26, 1922; R. L. Hague to Asche, Nov. 3, 1922; Teagle to Kingsbury, Dec. 1, 1922, and Feb. 6, 1923, and to Sheffield, Mar. 2, 1923; Clark to McKnight, Nov. 19, 1923.

50. FTC, *op. cit.,* 131.

51. SONJ, Clark to Teagle, Apr. 9, 1924.

52. See FTC, *op. cit.,* 99-136 and 196-201.

53. *Ibid.,* 117. *Oil & Gas Journal,* Nov. 23, 1922.

54. *Ibid.* SONJ, Teagle to Clark, Oct. 30, 1922; E. W. Dean to Clark, Nov. 19, 1923; Clark to Ewing, Jan. 29, 1923; Clark memo of Nov. 2, 1922; agreement between California Petroleum Co. and SONJ dated May 10, 1923.

55. SONJ, agreement between California Petroleum Co. and SONJ dated May 10, 1932. For statistical clarity, some figures were changed from fractions to decimals.

56. SONJ, Clark to Teagle, Nov. 21, 1923; Teagle to W. S. Farish, Feb. 23, 1924; Sadler to Teagle, Jan. 30, 1924; Clark memo of Jan. 2, 1924, on California Petroleum Co. contract.

57. Interview, H. M. Larson, G. S. Gibb, and E. H. Knowlton with W. C. Teagle, Oct. 4, 1949. SONJ, E. M. Clark to Teagle, Mar. 8, 1924.

58. SONJ, Clark to Teagle, Mar. 8, 1924; Sadler to Teagle, Jan. 30, 1924; Teagle to T. A. O'Donnell, Aug. 14, 1924; Clark memo to Teagle, undated but about middle of 1924; memo of proposed agreement between SONJ and California Petroleum Co., Apr. 16, 1924.

59. SONJ, memos of Mar. 20 and 21, 1923; contract of Jan. 23, 1924, between Marland and Carter; Corwin to E. W. Marland, Mar. 31, 1923; Marland Oil Co. to The Carter Oil Co., Mar. 22, 1923; Young to R. Pratt, Apr. 8, 1927.

60. SONJ, A. M. McQueen to Clark, Aug. 24, 1926; Teagle to G. H. Smith, Sept. 4, 1926.

61. SONJ, Clark to Teagle, Oct. 1, 1923; Sadler to Teagle, Aug. 29, 1923; Clark to Teagle, Nov. 2, 1926; Young to Corwin, Oct. 2, 1925.

62. *The Lamp*, VII, No. 4 (Dec., 1924), 5-9. Teagle's estimate of the situation was confirmed by the FTC investigation of 1927 (FTC, *op. cit.*, 2-3, 319, and *passim*).

63. FTC, *op. cit.*, 110, 118.

64. SONJ, Gross Crude Tankage of SONJ as of Nov. 1, 1925.

65. SONJ, Teagle to Clark, Mar. 5, 1926.

66. Rister, *op. cit.*, 233-237.

67. SONJ, Valuation Reports, Field Summaries.

68. Rister, *op. cit.*, 237-240, 247.

69. *The Lamp*, IX, No. 4 (Dec., 1926), 20, and IX, No. 6 (Feb., 1927), 7. FTC, *op. cit.*, 189, 193.

70. Interview, G. S. Gibb with E. O. Markham, Oct. 31, 1949.

71. *Ibid.* SONJ, F. B. Bimel to D. J. Vadermeer, Feb. 18, 1927. *The Lamp*, IX, No. 5 (Feb., 1927), 11.

72. Rister, *op. cit.*, 245. FTC, *op. cit.*, 193.

73. *The Lamp*, IX, No. 6 (Apr., 1927), 7.

74. SONJ, Valuation Reports, Field Summaries; Crude Oil Production Purchases and Sales; Production, Purchases and Sales of Crude Oil and Crude Held in Storage, The Carter Oil Co., 1914-1927; Maximum and Minimum Stocks of Crude Oil Held by SONJ Interests in the U. S., 1926-1927.

75. SONJ, Clark to Teagle, Feb. 16, 1927.

76. FTC, *op. cit.*, 327. *Oil & Gas Journal*, Feb. 24, 1927.

77. Interviews, Porter with W. E. Pratt (Jan. 4, 1949), H. H. Baker (Jan. 6 and Feb. 2, 1949), L. T. Barrow (Feb. 8, 1949), J. R. Suman (July 1, 1949), W. B. Calhoun (Apr. 29, 1949), R. L. Sloan (Apr. 29, 1949); H. M. Larson with C. E. Reistle, Jr. (May 20, 1952). Letter, L. T. Barrow to Porter, May 28, 1951. Humble Recs., R. W. Richmond to Farish, Apr. 10, 1926, H. L. Edwards to Wiess, June 8, 1926; unsigned letter of May 5, 1926, to Earl Sneed, Reiter-Foster Oil Corp., Tulsa; Farish to W. N. Davis, Feb. 23, 1929; reports, G. H. L. Kent to Bert

Broday, Oct. 26, 1926, and J. R. Suman to Farish, Mar. 9, 1927, covering inspection trip to Humble Northern Division. *Wall Street News*, Mar. 28, 1927. *Oil & Gas Journal*, 1927, Mar. 24-July 14, *passim*.

78. Humble Recs., Farish to W. N. Davis, Feb. 17, 1927, to T. L. Foster, Mar. 20, 1927, and to Teagle, June 20 and 21, 1927; Teagle to Farish, June 17, 20, 24 (2), 1927; F. C. Proctor to Farish, Aug., 1927.

79. Humble Recs., statement of W. S. Farish and W. C. Teagle to Hubert Work, chairman, Federal Oil Conservation Board, May 2, 1927. *The Lamp*, X, No. 1 (June, 1927), 6-7, and X, No. 3 (Oct., 1927), 16-24. FTC, *Prices, Profits and Competition in the Petroleum Industry*, 115, 191-193. *The Bache Review*, New York, May 21, 1927.

80. Humble Recs., R. L. Welsh to Farish, Dec. 13, 1926; telegram, E. W. Marland to Farish, Jan. 7, 1927; undated memo on Colorado Springs meeting by J. R. Suman. API *Bulletin*, Dec. 9, 15, 1926, Jan. 12, Oct. 31, Dec. 6, Dec. 9, 1927. Logan, *op. cit.*, 150. Hardwicke, *op. cit.*, 29, n. 26.

81. SONJ, Sadler to Teagle, Aug. 29, 1923.

82. SONJ, Stat.

83. SONJ, Stat. FTC, *op. cit.*, 76.

84. SONJ, Fin. Recs.

CHAPTER 15

1. Federal Trade Commission, *Prices, Profits and Competition in the Petroleum Industry*, 40-42 and 105-106.

2. William Beard, *Regulation of Pipe Lines as Common Carriers* (New York, 1941), *passim*.

3. SONJ, Sadler to Richardson Pratt, May 25, 1928. FTC, *op. cit.*, 36-38.

4. National Industrial Conference Board, *Petroleum Almanac* (1946), 58. FTC, *op. cit.*, 35.

5. SONJ, Teagle to A. C. Bedford, June 10, 1923.

6. SONJ, D. R. Weller to Teagle, Oct. 12, 1930.

7. SONJ, Standard Pipe Line Co. memo of 1935 to Guy Wellman on reasons for forming the Standard Pipe Line Co., Inc.

8. *Ibid.*; interview, H. Kip with Judge Thomas M. Milling, Feb., 1949.

9. FTC, *op. cit.*, 36-37. SONJ, Teagle to G. H. Jones, Apr. 21, 1923.

10. SONJ, E. M. Clark to Teagle, Mar. 18, 1922.

11. *Ibid.*

12. SONJ, Teagle to Sadler, Jan. 30, 1922.

13. FTC, *op. cit.*, 36-37.

14. SONJ, Teagle to Moffett, Mar. 8, 1923.

15. SONJ, Clark to Teagle, Nov. 12, 1923.

16. *Ibid.*, Apr. 17, 1922, and Nov. 13, 1923.

17. SONJ, Teagle to Clark, Nov. 12, 1923.

18. SONJ, Clark to Teagle, Nov. 13, 1923.

19. *Ibid.*, Sept. 28, 1923.

20. SONJ, Clark to Sadler, Oct. 21, 1926; Teagle to James Anderson, Aug. 6, 1926. FTC, *op. cit.*, 41.

21. FTC, *op. cit.*, Table 16, 352-353.

22. SONJ, memo, Sadler to Teagle, Clark, Weller and Harden, Aug. 26, 1926; memo concerning pipeline rates, gathering charges, and selling commissions, dated Jan. 28, 1927.

23. SONJ, memo of Dec. 13, 1926, from W. S. Farish; undated memo signed "Jim" (possibly Colonel J. H. Hayes, a Jersey legal consultant and a frequent Teagle correspondent); Teagle to Jones, Dec. 13, 1926.

24. SONJ, Register of Tank Vessels for year 1920.

25. SONJ, Agreement in Regard to Tankers of DAPG between the Reparations Commission and the U. S. Government, June 7, 1920; R. F. Hand to M. Piesse, Feb. 23, 1929.

26. SONJ, Piesse to Wellman, Apr. 29, 1921.

27. SONJ, copy of verdict of the arbitration court appointed by the covenant of June 7, 1920. Certain complications in the controversy are outlined in SONJ, Wellman to Moore, July 30, 1923, and Riedemann to Teagle, Oct. 16, 1923.

28. SONJ, Report of the Finance Section of the Reparations Commission: "Proceeds of Operation of Tankers," Oct. 1, 1929; R. L. Hague to C. G. Black, Jan. 5, 1927; Piesse to Hand, Feb. 23, 1929; Hand to Piesse & Sons, Jan. 8, 1927.

29. SONJ, annual reports of the Marine Department, 1921-1927. Unless otherwise stated, all information on tanker operations is taken from this source.

30. *The Lamp*, III, No. 6 (Apr., 1921), 21-22.

31. SONJ, annual report of the Marine Department for 1921. *The Lamp*, IV, No. 1 (June, 1921), 6-7.

CHAPTER 16

1. LaFollette Report.

2. *The Lamp*, V, No. 6 (May, 1923), 16.

3. *Oil & Gas Journal*, Mar. 8, 1923.

4. Federal Trade Commission, *Petroleum Industry, Prices, Profits and Competition.*

5. *Ibid.*, XIX, 136-181.

6. Nat. Ind. Conf. Bd., *Petroleum Almanac*, 146-147.

7. *Ibid.* SONJ, Stat.

8. *The Lamp*, IV, No. 5 (Feb., 1922), 6-7; V, No. 3 (Oct., 1922), 10; VIII, No. 5 (Feb., 1926), 12. SONJ, Kardex Files.

9. FTC, *op. cit.*, 54-55. *Hearings before the Temporary National Economic Commission*, statements of witnesses, S. A. Swensrud on marketing, Aug. 1, 1939. *Oil & Gas Journal*, Apr. 6, 1922.

10. FTC, *op. cit.*, 255-257. SONJ, memo (undated) from E. S. Hall to F. M. Surface on sale and distribution of finished products.

11. *U. S. v. SOC (Indiana) et al.*, VIII, Book of Exhibits, Exhibit 562, Growth of Competition in Gasoline since 1911; Questionnaire and Answers, No. 10, Jersey Standard and Standard Development Co. SONJ, Clark to Teagle, Nov. 18, 1926.

12. SONJ, memo, Hall to Surface.

13. SONJ, memo on 1924 marketing conference.

14. FTC, *op. cit.*, 56, gives table of gasoline service and bulk stations owned by all oil companies as of June 30, 1926.

SONJ, C. O. Swain to J. H. Senior, Oct. 14, 1925.

15. SONJ, memo, Hall to Surface, on dealer relationships; Legal Department memo of information supplied by Jersey Standard in response to questions by the Federal Trade Commission, 1926; various letters from field representatives to branch-office managers, compiled as evidence for the FTC investigation of 1926.

16. FTC, *op. cit.*, 228-240. SONJ, C. M. Byers to E. A. Holbein, Aug. 27, 1925.

17. SONJ, letter, Hall to Swain, July 27, 1925.

18. *Ibid.*

19. SONJ, memo, Hall to Surface, on dealer relationships; memo, Hall to domestic sales managers, Sept. 10, 1926.

20. LaFollette Report, testimony of A. L. Beaty, Jan. 26, 1923, 875.

21. SONJ, Byers to Holbein, Aug. 27, 1925.

22. SONJ, C. A. Straw to G. Wellman, Aug. 24, 1923; Wellman to F. A. Howard, Mar. 26, 1924.

23. SONJ, H. M. McLarin to Hall, Sept. 30, 1938. *SOC(Indiana)* v. *SONJ*, 1935, Defendants' Brief of Facts.

24. *SOC(Indiana)* v. *SONJ*, Defendants' Brief of Facts. SONJ, memo, marketing conference of Feb. 18, 1926.

25. SONJ, memo of marketing conference of Feb. 18, 1926; Barger to Teagle, Mar. 5, 1926.

26. FTC, *op. cit.*, 57, 225-226.

27. *Ibid.*, 263.

28. *Ibid.*, 262. *U. S.* v. *SOC(Indiana) et al.*, Questionnaire and Answers, No. 10, II, Book of Petitioners' Exhibits. SONJ, Secy. Dept., file of agreements.

29. FTC, *op. cit.*, 264-265, 331-335, and *passim*.

30. SONJ, confidential memo by G. Wellman on European affiliates, July 22, 1926.

31. SONJ, D. L. Harper files, 1921-1924, *passim*; Harper to Teagle, Nov. 10, 1924.

32. SONJ, Harper to Teagle, Nov. 10, 1924, and to Bedford, July 12, 1924.

33. SONJ, Harper to J. A. Mowinckel, Nov. 16, 1926, and July 29, 1927.

34. SONJ, Harper to Asche, Mar. 1, 1924; Asche to Teagle, Mar. 1, 1924; Harper to Teagle, Mar. 15, 1924.

35. SONJ, Harper to Mowinckel, July 29, 1927.

36. SONJ, Riedemann to Moffett, Apr. 29, 1925; Moffett to Riedemann, May 11, 1925; Teagle to Riedemann, May 28, 1925; Mowinckel to Harper, Aug. 31, 1927.

37. SONJ, Stat. API, *Petroleum Facts and Figures* (2d edition, 1929), 27-29.

38. SONJ, memo of Mar. 23, 1938. See also FTC, *The International Petroleum Cartel.*

39. Esso Export Co. Recs., World Sales Notebook.

40. Material on Canadian marketing was compiled by J. S. Ewing, whose sources included Imperial marketing files, general correspondence, and interviews with company executives.

41. U. S. National Archives 821.6363/-225, report of American consul at Bogotá, May 8, 1922.

42. International Recs., marketing files, 1921-1926; general letters of progress, 1922 and 1927. SONJ, G. H. Smith to E. Holman, Apr. 28, 1937.

43. International Recs., memo on competition on west coast of South America, Jan., 1920, to Jan., 1926; G. S. Laing to F. D. Asche, Mar. 23, 1923; W. S. Reid to E. Pombo, Aug. 8, 1924; W. W. Hall to J. H. Senior, Aug. 23, 1926; LeSueur to G. H. Smith, Dec. 4, 1923; International Petroleum Co. Ltd. to A. Fleming, Nov. 4, 1921, and to E. Pombo, Oct. 26, 1925; G. H. Smith to O. Harden, Aug. 27, 1934.

44. SONJ, G. S. Walden to Sadler, May 13, 1929; correspondence file on marketing arrangements for Palembang output, 1927-1929.

45. Copy of official text of law modifying the customs laws for petroleum products in France, June 12, 1919. *The Lamp*, III, No. 2 (Oct., 1920), 8.

46. SONJ, Corp. Recs., H. E. Bedford, Jr., to Asche, Aug. 13, 1920; agreement between Banque de Paris et des Pays-Bas and SONJ dated Aug. 5, 1920. H. E. Bedford, Jr., to Evelyn H. Knowlton, Feb. 17, 1954.

47. SONJ, memo of June 17, 1920, on French Refiners' contracts.

48. *Ibid.*

49. SONJ, letter (unsigned) to H. E. Bedford, Jr., May 11, 1922. *The Lamp,* IV, No. 3 (Oct., 1921), 8-9.

50. *The Lamp, loc. cit.* SONJ, memo of interview between Asche and Fenaille, July 31, 1922.

51. SONJ, agreement between Cie Générale des Pétroles and SONJ, Oct. 28, 1921; memo of H. E. Bedford, Jr., dated Aug. 16, 1922; Corp. Recs., World Sales Notebook.

52. SONJ, memo on socialization of petroleum industry in France, Nov. 20, 1933, by G. H. Michler; memo, H. E. Bedford, Jr., to Teagle, Apr. 8, 1926; G. H. Michler to O. Harden, May 10, 1935.

53. SONJ, Michler to Harden, May 10, 1935.

54. SONJ, American Petroleum Co. résumé of marketing conditions in Holland and Germany, July 15, 1924.

55. *The Lamp,* III, No. 6 (Apr., 1921), 10-15; IV, No. 3 (Oct., 1921), 11. SONJ, correspondence on Italian trade, 1920-1927, *passim.*

56. SONJ, Riedemann to Harper, Feb. 5, 1926; P. Hurll to Mowinckel, June 27, 1927; Petroleum Import Cie to Moffett, Feb. 23, 1927; memo of 1922 on Switzerland.

57. SONJ, Teagle to Asche, Sept. 16, 1919.

58. SONJ, Asche to Teagle, Aug. 17, 1919; copy of agreement between SONJ and Vallö Oljeraffineri, Ostlandske Petroleumscompagni, Aktieselskabet, and Vestlandske Petroleumscompagni, Aktieselskabet, Aug. 15, 1919.

59. SONJ, Teagle to Asche, Sept. 19, 1919; C. Holm to Asche, Apr. 24, 1920; agreement, Naphtha Production Co. Nobel Bros., Nobels Petroleumimport Aktiebolag in Finland, A. Parviainen & Co. Osakeyhtiö, and Director Leopold Lerche with Finska Petroleum & Benzin Co. Standard, Det Danske Petroleums-Aktieselskab, and SONJ, Apr. 22, 1920.

60. SONJ, Debell, of Nobel-Standard, to Asche, Apr. 3, 1924, and to Moffett, Mar. 11, 1925; Mowinckel to Moffett, Oct. 23, 1925; Harper to Holm, Mar. 30 and Apr. 13, 1927; Holm to Harper, Apr. 26, 1927; Mowinckel to Moffett, Jan. 19, 1926; cable, Harper to Hurll for Mowinckel, Sept. 1, 1926; Legal Dept. memo of Mar. 2, 1932, on anti-American agitation in Copenhagen.

61. SONJ, memo of July 11, 1923, by Holm on Iceland monopoly; Holm to Asche, June 30, Aug. 11, 16, 21, Sept. 2, Oct. 4, 1922, and Jan. 16, Mar. 6, May 7, and June 12, 1923.

62. SONJ, Wellman to Department of State, Aug. 18 and Nov. 15, 1922; Asche to Wellman, Dec. 19, 1922; Asche to Jones, Dec. 22, 1922; Department of State to SONJ, Feb. 5, 1923; Asche to Wellman, June 21, 1923; Wellman to Asche, June 26, 1923; Holm to Teagle, Dec. 4, 1924; Hughes to Jersey Standard, Dec. 31, 1925; memo of Mar. 30, 1925, on Polish markets.

63. SONJ, A. Weltman to Jersey Standard, Oct. 9 and Dec. 24, 1923.

64. SONJ, F. H. Bedford to Asche, Jan. 20, 1922; Asche to Harper, Aug. 16, 1922; Harper to F. H. Bedford, Jr., July 9, 1924; Harper to Jones, Sept. 2, 1926, and to Teagle, Feb. 7, 1925; copy of agreement between Jersey Standard, Industrias Babel y Nervión, and Société Espagnole d'Achats et d'Effrètements, 1923.

65. SONJ, H. E. Bedford, Jr., to Moffett, Sept. 12 and 20, 1927; Harper to H. E. Bedford, Jr., Sept. 28, 1927.

66. SONJ, general correspondence between 26 Broadway and the DAPG; Asche to Teagle, July 3 and 11, 1919; cable, Asche to Teagle, Aug. 4, 1919; memo of Dec. 1, 1930, on DAPG stock transfer. In 1922 Erwin and Dr. Tonio Riedemann were classified in a nonenemy status by virtue of their Danzig residency and received back their securities and cash. In 1929, following passage of the Settlement of War Claims Act of 1928, Heinrich Riedemann received back his confiscated securities.

67. SONJ, Riedemann to Teagle, Oct. 27, 1921.

68. SONJ, Asche to Teagle, Sept. 23, 1919; Harper to Teagle, Sept. 25, 1919; Riedemann to Harper, Feb. 5, 1926.

69. SONJ, Riedemann to Teagle, Dec. 5 and 10, 1924, May 8 and June 12, 1925, and to Moffett, Apr. 29 and May 19, 1925; résumé of marketing in Holland and Germany, July 15, 1924.

CHAPTER 17

1. SONJ, speech delivered by F. A. Howard before executives of The Standard Oil Co. (Ohio), French Lick, Indiana, 1948; O. Harden to E. M. Clark, June 20, 1928. Carleton Ellis, *The Chemistry of Petroleum Derivatives* (New York, 1934), section on commercial cracking processes. *The Lamp*, IX, No. 5 (Feb., 1927), 6. *U. S. v. SOC(Indiana) et al.*, No. 4131, 1924-1927, II, Petitioners' Book of Exhibits.

2. Interviews, N. S. B. Gras with F. A. Howard, Sept. 13, 1946, and with E. M. Clark, June 16, 1947. Howard speech at French Lick, 1948.

3. Interview, Gras with W. M. Burton, Nov. 8, 1946.

4. American Institute of Chemical Engineers, *Twenty Five Years of Chemical Engineering Progress*, 1908-1923 (New York, 1933), chap. v, "Twenty Five Years of Progress in Petroleum Refining," by H. W. Sheldon.

5. Howard speech at French Lick, 1948.

6. SONJ, F. A. Howard to Clark, May 12 and 15, 1918. *U. S. v. SOC(Indiana)*, 820.25 No. 1, correspondence, 1924, letter Russell Wiles to R. V. Lindabury, Mar. 17, 1925—hereafter referred to as *"U. S. v. SOC(Indiana)*, Wiles letter."

7. SONJ, Teagle to A. C. Bedford, June 5, 1919.

8. SONJ, Howard to Clark, June 9, 1919.

9. SONJ, notice of Sept. 27, 1919, to all heads of departments, by W. C. Teagle.

10. Howard speech at French Lick, 1948. SONJ, Howard to Teagle, Oct. 8, 1919.

11. SONJ, Howard to Teagle, Oct. 27, 1919, Feb. 10 and 17, 1920.

12. Information in this and the following four paragraphs comes from general correspondence files of the Standard Oil Development Co. and from the following interviews: E. H. Knowlton with F. A. Howard, Nov. 9, 1949, and with Charles Leaver, Aug., 1950; Gibb and Knowlton with G. A. Esty, Oct. 9, 1949, with W. J. Haley, Oct. 20, 1949, and with G. W. McKnight, Oct. 6, 1949; Knowlton and E. Y. Bricker with A. J. Ely, C. F. Pester, and E. W. Dean, Aug. 24, 1949; Gibb and Knowlton with N. E. Loomis, Aug. 30, 1949; N. S. B. Gras with Loomis, Aug. 27, 1946, and Aug. 8, 1944, with R. H. Dickson, June 18, 1945, with H. G. M. Fischer, June 20, 1945, with J. R. Carringer, Jan. 25, 1945, with R. P. Russell, Aug. 26, 1946, with F. A. Howard, Sept. 13, 1946, and with Clark, June 16, 1947.

13. SONJ, Howard to Teagle, Nov. 24, 1920; McKnight to Howard, Dec. 28, 1922.

14. SONJ, Howard to Teagle, Nov. 24, 1920; John E. Teeple to Teagle, Mar. 10, 1921; Howard to Teagle, Oct. 27, 1922; Clark to Straw, Nov. 23, 1922; notice to heads of departments, Jan. 4, 1922, signed by C. T. White, Secretary of the Corporation; Howard to Teagle, Aug. 18, 1922; assignment of patents held by SONJ to Standard Development Co., Dec. 6, 1922.

15. SONJ, report of G. W. McKnight to Board of Directors of activity of Manufacturing Dept. for year 1922; annual report of Development Department and Standard Development Co., 1924; Howard to McKnight, Jan. 14, 1924.

16. SONJ, Howard to Teagle, Feb. 17, 1927; memos, Sadler to the directors, June 27 and July 8, 1924. *The Lamp*, VIII, No. 4 (Dec., 1925), 18.

17. SONJ, Howard to Teagle, Feb. 17, 1927.

18. Leslie, *Motor Fuels, Their Production and Technology*, 31, and chap. ix, *passim*. SONJ, memo of Jan. 8, 1923, from N. E. Loomis to Clark on trend of refining processes.

19. SONJ, Howard to MacGinnis, Feb. 2, 1923.

20. *U. S. v. SOC(Indiana) et al.*, VI, Transcript of Testimony, testimony of F. A. Howard, Nov. 2, 1926, 3212-3213.

21. Leslie, *op. cit.*, 362-363. Ellis, *op. cit. U. S. v. SOC(Indiana)*, Wiles letter.

22. *U. S. v. SOC(Indiana) et al.*, VI, Transcript of Testimony, testimony of Howard, Nov. 2, 1926, 3214-3216.

23. *Ibid.*

24. *Ibid. American Chemical Industry*

(edited by William Haynes, New York, 1949), VI, 398-403.

25. SONJ, Howard to Teagle, Jan. 30 and Dec. 31, 1920. LaFollette Committee Report, testimony of E. M. Clark, Dec. 16, 1922, I, 204.

26. Interview, Knowlton with Howard, Nov. 21, 1949. SONJ, Howard to Teagle, Jan. 29, 1924. *U. S.* v. *SOC(Indiana) et al.*, VI, Howard testimony.

27. *U. S.* v. *SOC(Indiana) et al.*, II, Petitioners' Book of Exhibits, No. 84. SONJ, annual reports of Development Department and Standard Oil Development Co., 1925 and 1926.

28. Material in this and the following paragraph comes from general correspondence files of the Standard Oil Development Co., 1920-1927, and from the following interviews: Gibb and Knowlton with W. J. Haley, Oct. 20, 1949; with G. A. Esty, Oct. 5, 1949; with Loomis, Aug. 30, 1949; and with G. W. McKnight, Oct. 6, 1949; Knowlton with Howard, Nov. 9 and 21, 1949.

29. Material in this and the following two paragraphs comes from address by Bruce K. Brown before the American Chemical Society in Chicago, Sept., 1946; Leslie, *op. cit.*, section on the development and uses of cracking processes; interview, Knowlton with Howard, Nov. 9, 1949; SONJ, general correspondence files, 1920-1927; Standard Oil Development Co. records, Loomis to Clark, Jan. 8, 1923.

30. Interview, K. W. Porter with W. K. Lewis, July 14, 1950.

31. SONJ, report of G. W. McKnight to the Board of Directors, 1922; Loomis to Clark, Jan. 8, 1923.

32. Dunstan, Nash, Brooks, & Tizard, *Science of Petroleum*, III, 2271-2287, "Ferrous Metal Tubes for Refinery Service," by H. D. Newell. SONJ, Clark to Teagle, Feb. 1 and 8, 1927; Link to Fiero, Mar. 12, 1927; Clark to Harden, Oct. 7, 1929; memo on refining at Baton Rouge by H. J. Voorhies, Apr. 4, 1949.

33. *American Chemical Industry*, 398-403. F. A. Howard, *Buna Rubber* (New York, 1947), 51.

34. *American Chemical Industry*, 398-403. Interview, Knowlton with Howard,

Nov. 9, 1949. SONJ, Howard to Clark, May 12, 1918.

35. SONJ, Howard to Teagle, Mar. 29 and July 28, 1920.

36. *American Chemical Industry*, 398-403. SONJ, Howard to Teagle, Apr. 4, 1923.

37. Howard speech. SONJ, annual report of Development Department and Standard Development Co., 1924. *American Chemical Industry*, 398-403. Interview, Knowlton with Howard, Nov. 9, 1949.

38. *American Chemical Industry*, 398-403.

39. Material in this paragraph is taken from correspondence files of the Standard Oil Development Co. and from reports and correspondence of the Ethyl Gasoline Corp. contained in those files.

40. Standard Oil Development Co. records, general correspondence files, and synopsis of proceedings at Surgeon General's Conference, May 20, 1925. Report of Investigations, Department of the Interior, Bureau of Mines, "Exhaust Gases from Engines Using Ethyl Gasoline," Serial No. 2661, Dec., 1924. Report of Committee appointed by the Surgeon General of the U. S., "Health Hazards in Sale and Use of Ethyl Gasoline," Jan. 17, 1926.

41. SONJ, W. G. Thompson to Teagle, Apr. 27, 1925; Howard to Teagle and Clark, Jan. 25, 1927; Teagle to Clark, Dec. 23, 1925; annual report of the Development Department for 1926.

42. SONJ, Clark to Teagle, Nov. 18 and 22, 1926.

43. SONJ, Surgeon General of the U. S. to E. W. Webb, president, Ethyl Gasoline Corp., Mar. 6, 1926; Clark to J. A. Moffett, Feb. 25, 1926; Teagle to the Surgeon General, Feb. 11, 1927; Clark to Teagle, Nov. 9, 1927; E. W. Webb to Alfred Sloan, Jr., Mar. 8, 1926; memo on points of difference between the Ethyl Gasoline Corp. and Jersey Standard, June 18, 1927, by Howard.

44. SONJ, copy of minutes of Ethyl Gasoline Corp. directors' and executive committee meetings, 1926-1927; letter, A. E. Wittnacht to Teagle, Dec. 18, 1926; copy of memo of E. W. Webb to directors of Ethyl Gasoline Corp., Dec. 18, 1926.

45. Dunstan, Nash, Brooks, & Tizard, *op. cit.*, IV, 3080-3088, "Oil Shales, Cannel Coals, and Torbanites," by M. J. Gavin, and 3096-3106, "Scottish Shale Oils," by G. H. Smith, G. Grant, and S. Allen. SONJ, Teagle to Howard, Apr. 11, 1924; Howard to Teagle, Apr. 25, 1924; W. Warfield to Sadler, Oct. 16, 1920; miscellaneous letters and memoranda relating to oil-shale lands, 1917-1930. D. E. Winchester, *Factors Influencing the Value of Oil-Shale Lands*, Engineering and Mining Journal-Press, July 8, 1922.

46. Howard, *op. cit.*, 10-19. AICE, *Twenty Five Years of Chemical Engineering Progress*, chap. i. Dunstan, Nash, Brooks, & Tizard, *op. cit.*, III, 2130-2132, "The Historical Development of Hydrogenation," by Friedrich Bergius. Interview, Knowlton with Howard, Nov. 21, 1949. SONJ, Riedemann to Teagle, Mar. 4, 1922.

47. SONJ, Teagle to Riedemann, Oct. 14, 1920; Riedemann to Teagle, Dec. 9, 1920, and Mar. 4, 1922; Clark to Teagle, Mar. 23, 1922. Interview, Knowlton with Howard, Nov. 9, 1949.

48. SONJ, Teagle to Clark, Dec. 23, 1924; copy, I. Du Pont to T. Midgley, Dec. 30, 1924; Alfred Sloan, Jr., to Clark, Jan. 31, 1925; Howard to Teagle, Apr. 6, 1925; copy of report by E. W. Webb to directors of Ethyl Gasoline Corp., Dec. 28, 1925. Howard, *op. cit.*, 11-12.

49. SONJ, Teagle to Howard, Mar. 27, 1926. See Howard, *op. cit.*, 21-24, for a good account of the Jersey–I.G. Farben negotiations.

50. Howard, *op. cit.*, 21-22.

51. SONJ, Howard to Teagle, May 8, 1924, with memo on Dubbs process. *U. S. v. SOC(Indiana)*, Wiles letter.

52. *U. S. v. SOC(Indiana)*, Wiles letter; V, Transcript of Testimony, testimony of Richard J. Dearborn, Nov. 1, 1926, 3111-3114. Interview, Knowlton with Howard, Nov. 21, 1949. LaFollette Committee investigation, testimony of Amos L. Beaty, president of The Texas Company, II, 873.

53. *U. S. v. SOC(Indiana)*, Wiles letter.

54. *Ibid.*, I, Book of Petitioners' Exhibits, License Agreement No. 31, between SOC (Indiana) and The Texas Co., Aug. 26, 1921.

55. *Ibid.*, VI, Transcript of Testimony, testimony of Howard, Nov. 2, 1926, 3207-3208.

56. *Ibid.*, Wiles letter.

57. SONJ, R. Wiles to Howard, June 8, 1921; Howard to Wiles, May 18, 1921. LaFollette Report, testimony of E. M. Clark, I, 207. *The Lamp*, V, No. 3 (Oct., 1922), 8.

58. SONJ, Howard to Teagle, with memo on Dubbs process, May 8, 1924, and Jan. 29, 1924, with report on Development Department progress.

59. LaFollette Committee investigation, testimony of E. M. Clark, I, 207; testimony of Walter M. Cross, I, 719-724. SONJ, Howard to Teagle, May 31, 1924. *U. S. v. SOC(Indiana) et al.*, V, Transcript of Testimony, testimony of Fred Osborn, Oct. 29, 1926, 3029.

60. *U. S. v. SOC(Indiana) et al.*, V, Transcript of Testimony, testimony of Ralph O. Holmes, Oct. 28, 29, 1926, 2978; I, Book of Petitioners' Exhibits, Agreement No. 55 between The Texas Co. and the Gasoline Products Co., Jan. 26, 1923.

61. Interview, Knowlton with Howard, Nov. 21, 1949. *U. S. v. SOC(Indiana)*, Wiles letter. Standard Oil Development Co. records, copy of agreement between Joseph H. Adams and George T. Rogers, July 16, 1907.

62. SONJ, Teagle to Howard, June 14, 1920; Howard to Teagle, June 25, 1920. *U. S. v. SOC(Indiana)*, Wiles letter.

63. SONJ, Teagle to Howard, July 7, 1920; Howard to Teagle, July 9, 1920. *U. S. v. SOC(Indiana) et al.*, VI, Transcript of Testimony, testimony of Howard, Nov. 2, 1926, 3231; Wiles letter.

64. Wiles letter.

65. *Ibid.*

66. SONJ, report of Howard contained in letter, Teagle to Clark, Apr. 21, 1923.

67. SONJ, Teagle to Clark, Apr. 21, 1923. *U. S. v. SOC(Indiana) et al.*, I, Petitioners' Book of Exhibits, Agreements Nos. 73 and 74 between Jersey Standard, The Texas Co. and SOC(Indiana), Sept. 28, 1923; pamphlet, *Answer of the SOC(NJ) and Standard Development Company*, by C. O. Swain and Stuart Templeton, counsel for the defendant.

68. *U. S.* v. *SOC(Indiana)* et al., Brief for the U. S., Part 1, Memorandum of Facts. SONJ, Howard report in letter, Teagle to Clark, Apr. 21, 1923.

69. Howard, *op. cit.,* 189-190.

70. *U. S.* v. *SOC(Indiana)* et al., Brief for the U. S., Part 1, Memorandum of Facts.

71. *Sun* (New York), June 25, 1924. *Oil & Gas Journal,* July 10, 1923. See also *World* (New York), June 26, 1924; *Oil & Gas Journal,* July 17, 1924; *New York Tribune,* May 22, 1924.

72. *U. S.* v. *SOC(Indiana)* et al., I, Transcript of Testimony, testimony of R. H. McKee, 334-596, and, IV, of R. E. Wilson, Oct. 11, 1926, 1971-2413.

73. *Ibid.,* III, Brief before Master and District Court for the U. S. in support of its motion to recommit and its exceptions to the Master's Report, by George E. Z. Johnson; Brief for the U. S., 55-59.

74. *Ibid.,* IV, Transcript of Testimony, testimony of R. E. Wilson, Oct. 11, 1926, 2049.

75. *Ibid.,* Briefs before the Master, Brief of Defendants in support of Master's Report, Brief of SOC(Indiana); Wiles letter.

76. SONJ, Howard to Wiles, Nov. 6, 1925.

77. *U. S.* v. *SOC(Indiana)* et al., II, Transcript of Testimony, testimony of R. M. McKee, Nov. 4-5, 9-10, 12, 13, 16-19, 1925; 597-720, 725-874, 903-1155; III, Briefs before the Master, Brief of SOC(Indiana), Part XXXIII, Rules of Patent Construction.

78. *Ibid.,* III, Brief of Defendants in support of Master's Report; Johnson Brief for the U. S.

79. *Ibid.,* opinion and decree SOC(Indiana) et al., III, Transcript of Record, Supreme Court, No. 378. *New York Times,* Apr. 14 and 19, 1931; *New York Tribune,* Apr. 14, 1931; *Wall Street Journal,* Apr. 14 and 15, 1931. *Cases Argued and Decided in the Supreme Court of the U. S.,* October term, 1930, in 282-283 U. S. book 75, Lawyers' Edition (The Lawyers' Cooperative Publishing Co., Rochester, N. Y., 1931).

80. SONJ, Howard to Teagle, Aug. 3, 1925. Interview, Knowlton with Howard, Nov. 21, 1949.

81. SONJ, Stat. Unless otherwise stated, all crude throughput figures given hereafter are taken from this source.

82. This point is noted frequently in Jersey correspondence of the 1919-1924 period. A particularly succinct summary and illustration are presented in a letter from McKnight to C. G. Black and Clark, Dec. 3, 1924.

83. *Ibid.,* and interview, Gibb and Knowlton with G. A. Esty, Oct. 5, 1949.

84. SONJ, McKnight to Black and Clark, Dec. 3, 1924.

85. Material on the Humble Oil & Refining Co. was compiled by K. W. Porter from Humble records and correspondence.

86. SONJ, Seidel to Sadler, Jan. 4, 1924, and to Clark, Feb. 11, 1926, and Apr. 5, 1931; D. L. Harper to H. L. Shoemaker, Apr. 12, 1931; memo of S. B. Hunt on Romania, Oct. 28, 1922; reports of Romàno-Americana operations, 1922-1926.

87. SONJ, review of general European situation, by S. Schmeidler, July 8, 1924; Schmeidler report on Trieste refinery, June, 1924; Italo-Americana memo on Trieste refinery, July 27, 1925; "Notes on Refineries and Stations Visited by Graff and Husted on Their Recent Trip to Europe," Dec. 17, 1921; Teagle to Clark, June 7, 1925; T. R. Parker to Clark, Dec. 22, 1931; Clark to McKnight, July 21, 1925; Harper to McKnight, Dec. 8, 1925. F. Bachof, MS history of the DAPG.

88. Material on Canadian refining compiled by J. S. Ewing, principally from Imperial correspondence files of the period.

89. SONJ, Teagle to Clark, Mar. 11, 1925; Clark to Teagle, Mar. 12, 1925; NKPM report for 1926; memo on the Palembang refinery, Aug. 26, 1926.

90. International Recs., general letters of progress, 1922-1926. SONJ, general correspondence about Argentina, 1923-1926.

91. SONJ, confidential memo of Guy Wellman, July 22, 1926, on Jersey's European affiliations.

92. SONJ, Sadler to Clark, July 9, 1924, and to Teagle, Aug. 15, 1924; Clark to Teagle, July 19, 1925.

93. FTC, *op. cit.,* Table 30, 76. SONJ,

Stat. These figures include all refinery runs of partially owned affiliates. National Industrial Conference Board, *Petroleum Almanac* (1946), 334, gives foreign crude runs in 1927.

94. See LaFollette Report, *passim,* and FTC, *op. cit.,* 136, 301-306. *Petroleum Almanac,* 88, 146-147.

CHAPTER 18

1. Hicks himself, in the somewhat casual autobiographical account of his coming to Jersey, states that it was Bedford who saw the need and took the initiative. Hicks, *My Life in Industrial Relations,* 52-54.

2. See Nevins, *John D. Rockefeller,* II, Book IV, *passim.*

3. Nevins, *op. cit.,* 673. Letter, W. L. M. King to N. S. B. Gras, Jan. 19, 1950. Selekman and Van Kleek, *Employee Representation in the Coal Mines: A Study of the Industrial Representation Plan of the Colorado Fuel and Iron Co.,* 24 ff.

4. Hicks, *op. cit.,* 4-44.

5. Interview, Gras with J. D. Rockefeller, Jr., Feb. 8, 1950.

6. The account of setting up the Jersey Standard labor program is that of Hicks himself (Hicks, *op. cit.,* 53-58).

7. Account of the Apr. 1, 1918, gathering is taken from *The Lamp,* I, No. 1 (May, 1918), 5-12.

8. *Ibid.,* 2.

9. *Oil & Gas Journal,* Mar. 26, 1920.

10. Interview, Gras with T. H. A. Tiedemann, Nov. 20, 1949.

11. SONJ, Fin. Recs. United States Dept. of Commerce, *Historical Statistics of the United States, 1789-1945,* 186-187; *Statistical Abstract of the United States for 1941,* 215. J. F. Dewhurst and Associates, *America's Needs and Resources* (The Twentieth Century Fund, New York, 1947), 552.

12. *Historical Statistics,* 186-187. SONJ, Total Payrolls of the New Jersey Refineries.

13. *The Lamp,* III, No. 4 (Dec., 1920), 3 and 8; III, No. 5 (Feb., 1921), 3. SONJ, Minutes of Bayonne Industrial Representation meeting of Jan. 17, 1921.

14. Material on the Canadian experience was compiled by J. S. Ewing from Imperial Recs., general correspondence, and joint-conference minutes.

15. Report of A. J. Fair on history of employee relations at Baton Rouge, Business History Foundation MS.

16. *Ibid.*

17. Material on Humble was compiled by K. W. Porter from Humble records, joint-conference minutes, and from interviews with employees.

18. Interview, E. Y. Bricker with J. J. Slavin, June 19, 1950. Unless otherwise stated, all information in the following paragraphs is taken from the minutes of joint conferences at Bayonne and the Eagle Works.

19. *New York Tribune,* Apr. 23, 1919.

20. National Industrial Conference Board: *Works Councils in the United States* (Boston, 1919), *passim; Experience with Works Councils in the United States* (New York, 1922), *passim; The Growth of Works Councils in the United States* (New York, 1925), *passim; Industrial Relations: Administration of Policies and Programs* (New York, 1931), 8-11. C. E. French, *The Shop Committee in the United States* (Baltimore, 1933), chap. i.

21. SONJ, memo of Dec. 31, 1935, by J. W. Myers.

CHAPTER 19

1. Unless otherwise noted, all statistical information presented hereafter is taken from Jersey Standard ledgers and journals, from summary operating accounts, and from published financial statements. The instances when important discrepancies appear between book and published figures will be noted in the text or in statistical notes appended to text and appendix tables.

2. SONJ, Teagle to Riedemann, May 6, 1926.

3. Interview, N. S. B. Gras with Sadler, Aug. 26, 1946.

4. The information about staff departments has been compiled from many scattered sources, the most important among which are the SONJ payroll records; various issues of *The Lamp;* the survey of SONJ records prepared by N. S. B. Gras and H. M. Larson; and sundry correspondence and interviews.

5. Information concerning the Legal Dept. and on Jersey's legal retainers is taken from a very large collection of correspondence in company files.

6. SONJ, "Historical Notes Relative to the Accounting Organization and Its Responsibilities," by J. S. White, Apr. 11, 1949.

7. Information in this paragraph comes from correspondence files in the Legal Dept., particularly J. L. Darnell to C. O. Swain, Jan. 25, 1921; Corwin to Swain, Sept. 8, 1922; and Wellman to E. F. Rossmore, July 11, 1924.

8. Material on tax adjustments comes from the four-volume study prepared by SONJ, Valuation Division, on company depreciation policies for 1927 and subsequent years.

9. SONJ, Sadler memos dated Mar. 5, 1917, and July 22, 1919. Gras-Teagle interviews, Apr. 11, 12, and 13, Sept. 27, and Oct. 16, 1945.

10. *The Lamp,* V, No. 5 (Feb., 1923), 5.

11. SONJ, Clark to Teagle, Dec. 4, 1925. Gras-Teagle interview, Apr. 13, 1945.

12. The contents of this paragraph cannot be documented by specific references. It represents the authors' synthesis of all the research carried forward—of hundreds of letters in company files and of many talks with Teagle, Sadler, Clark, Howard, Riedemann, and many other men who were actively involved at a high level in company affairs of the day.

13. SONJ, Howard to Teagle, Feb. 17, 1927.

Index

Set in Linotype Caledonia
Format by Robert Cheney
Manufactured by The Haddon Craftsmen, Inc.
Published by HARPER & BROTHERS, *New York*